THE NEW YORK
PHILHARMONIC

THE NEW YORK PHILHARMONIC

FROM **BERNSTEIN** TO **MAAZEL**

JOHN CANARINA

af

AMADEUS
PRESS

An Imprint of Hal Leonard Corporation
New York

Published in 2010 by Amadeus Press
An Imprint of Hal Leonard Corporation
7777 West Bluemound Road
Milwaukee, WI 53213

Trade Book Division Editorial Offices
19 West 21ˢᵗ Street, New York, NY 10010

Printed in the United States of America

Book design by UB Communications

Library of Congress Cataloging-in-Publication Data

Canarina, John, 1934-
    The New York Philharmonic : from Bernstein to Maazel / John Canarina.
        p. cm.
    Includes bibliographical references and index.
    ISBN 978-1-57467-188-9 (hardcover)
    1. New York Philharmonic. I. Title.
    ML28.N5N384 2010
    784.206'07471—dc22

                                                    010026302

www.amadeuspress.com

To Audrey,
with love and gratitude

CONTENTS

ACKNOWLEDGMENTS

Mere words are inadequate to express my thanks for the great service and assistance provided by the New York Philharmonic Archives in the research for this book. The archivist, Barbara Haws, and associate archivist, Richard Wandel, were paragons of patience in helping me locate documents, clippings, and photographs, and in answering my many questions about one thing or another. When even I felt I was becoming a nuisance, they never betrayed any sign that they shared my perception.

Many thanks go to everyone who graciously agreed to be interviewed or speak with me: Edward Lee Alley, Deborah Borda, Walter Botti, John Carabella, Enrico Di Cecco, Stanley Drucker, Henry Fogel, Alan Gilbert, Paul B. Guenther, Robert Johnson, Roland Kohloff, Eric Latzky, Lorin Maazel, Newton Mansfield, Zarin Mehta, Frank Milburn, Carlos Moseley, Orin O'Brien, Elizabeth Ostrow, Maurice Peress, Carl Schiebler, Fiona Simon, Stephen Stamas, Laszlo Varga, Albert K. Webster, and Peter Wexler.

Additionally, I wish to thank the New York Philharmonic's personnel manager, Carl R. Schiebler, and his assistant, Nishi Badhwar, for their kind assistance in directing me to the right office or person; Bert Bial, contrabassoonist extraordinaire and former Philharmonic photographer, for his kindness in allowing the complimentary use of his photographs; Josh Marcum and Katie Klenn of the New York Philharmonic's Public Relations office for their help in obtaining recent photographs; and Norman Schweikert for providing his compilation of Philharmonic personnel for the years 1928—2001, which served as the basis for the personnel list in the appendix. His work is quite singular when one considers that he is a retired member of the Chicago Symphony. Richard Freed read a great portion of the manuscript and provided invaluable suggestions on improving it, for which I am most grateful. Some research was done in the Cowles Library of Drake University, whose staff I thank as well. Thanks are due, of course, to Amadeus Press and its publisher, John Cerullo, for accepting the idea of this book and providing encouragement from start to finish, to my indefatigable project editor, Marybeth Keating, and to my inimitable editor, Barbara Norton.

Finally, this volume would not have been completed in anything resembling a timely manner without the indispensable help of my dear wife, Audrey, who read the entire manuscript, assisted in the research in the Philharmonic Archives and in the Cowles Library, aided in assembling the photographs, and prodded me on numerous occasions to keep at it.

THE NEW YORK
PHILHARMONIC

INTRODUCTION

The most recent history of the New York Philharmonic (*Philharmonic: A History of New York's Orchestra*, by Howard Shanet) took the story to the beginning of Pierre Boulez's tenure as music director. Much has happened since. I have chosen to backtrack a bit, just as television programs often begin a new episode with a review of what occurred in the previous one. Thus my account begins a bit before the tenure of Leonard Bernstein.

I grew up with the Philharmonic, the first orchestra I ever heard in person and one for which I have maintained a keen interest and affection ever since. The highlight of my early professional life was the year spent as an assistant conductor during the amazing directorship of Leonard Bernstein.

As a student seated in the balcony of Carnegie Hall, I regularly heard the Philharmonic, the Philadelphia Orchestra, the Boston Symphony, and other visiting orchestras, not to mention the NBC Symphony. I remember likening the first three orchestras named to a grand piano. Philadelphia played with the lid down; Boston, with the lid up, but on the short stick. With the New York Philharmonic (and with NBC as well), the lid was all the way up. This does not mean that the Philharmonic played more loudly than other orchestras, but that its sound was—and still is—more open, more immediate, more thrilling.

A sub-theme of this book concerns the way the Philharmonic and its music directors have been treated by New York's critical press, the *New York Times* in particular. In the end, if I have concentrated on the *Times*, it is because the publications mentioned early in the book (the *Herald Tribune*, the *World-Telegram and the Sun*, the *Saturday Review*, and others) are, sadly, no longer with us. Of those that remain (the *New York Post*, the *Wall Street Journal*, the *New Yorker*, *New York* magazine, and others), only the *Times* reviews the Philharmonic week after week, year in and year out. In doing so, it is also the only one with a national presence.

A word about my choice of spelling for a particular composer's name: It is generally accepted practice today to spell his name Prokofiev. However, as his signature clearly shows, at least when he signed his name in the West, he spelled it Prokofieff. On the theory that he probably knew how to spell his own name, I have opted for the latter spelling.

CHAPTER 1

1956–60

TAUBMAN'S ATTACK

"The Philharmonic—What's Wrong with It and Why." That was the ominous headline over a lengthy Sunday article by Howard Taubman, chief music critic of the *New York Times*, that appeared in the paper on April 29, 1956. In that year, to be sure, the Philharmonic was in a rather precarious state artistically, and financially as well. Dimitri Mitropoulos was in his sixth season as musical director, and the brunt of negative criticism fell on his shoulders. The Greek-born Mitropoulos was one of the most supremely gifted conductors of the twentieth century, but his podium style was extremely idiosyncratic and physical, not in the balletic style of Leonard Bernstein, but less graceful. His batonless gestures were often rather difficult for the orchestra to decipher, even though they had worked with him for a number of years. Later, when at the orchestra's insistence he finally began using a baton, his gestures remained the same—the baton was no help. The result was that his performances, especially of the classical and early romantic repertoire, were not noted for precision. But in late romantic and twentieth-century repertoire he was capable of producing galvanically intense performances—Mahler's Sixth Symphony in particular comes to mind in this respect.

Mitropoulos's espousal of difficult modern works by Arnold Schoenberg, Alban Berg, Anton Webern, Roger Sessions, Ernst Krenek, Stefan Wolpe, and others, as well as some of the less well-known works of composers fixed more firmly in the repertorial canon, tended to have its effect on attendance at the orchestra's concerts; many empty seats were in evidence, affecting the orchestra financially. And yet the contemporary composer most favored by Mitropoulos was the extremely approachable Morton Gould, whom many critics regarded as a lightweight. All told, Mitropoulos performed eight of Gould's works with the Philharmonic.

Additionally, Mitropoulos was not a strict disciplinarian in the manner of his immediate predecessor as musical director, Artur Rodzinski, not to mention an earlier predecessor, Arturo Toscanini. The men of the orchestra (there were no women members at that time) genuinely liked Mitropoulos and appreciated his less-than-dictatorial approach, but at the same time they found it easy to take advantage of his good nature, with the result that some performances could border on the slipshod. In a famous 1954 broadcast of Beethoven's First Symphony there was some confusion as to whether or not the repeat in the finale should be observed, some players doing so for a few measures, most not. But just when one had grown accustomed to a lack of finesse in the classical repertoire, in 1956 along came a perfectly trim and buoyant reading of Haydn's Symphony No. 100 ("Military").

It was a combination of this inconsistency of approach, lack of discipline, and perceived faulty programming, resulting in a decline in attendance, that led Taubman to inveigh against the orchestra. No aspect of the Philharmonic's operation escaped his scrutiny. Although he commended the board of directors for its selflessness in serving the orchestra and the community, he also criticized it for lacking a forward-looking policy on the role the orchestra should play in the cultural life of the city and the nation. The fact that only two professional musicians (the composer Richard Rodgers and the musicologist Carleton Sprague Smith, head of the music division of the New York Public Library) served on the board was remarked upon, as was the lack of any representation from the orchestra's personnel. "The men who do the playing would be in a position to give the board invaluable guidance," said Taubman.

Severe criticism was leveled at the orchestra's co-managers, Arthur Judson and Bruno Zirato. At the time, Judson was "a powerful, if not the most powerful figure in America's concert business." Zirato, if not quite at that level, had been secretary to Enrico Caruso and had joined the Philharmonic's management during Toscanini's tenure. What opened them to criticism was the fact that they were both affiliated with Columbia Artists Management, Inc. (CAMI), the country's largest managerial organization, and were thus in charge of the careers of a multitude of conductors and soloists. Was it in the orchestra's best interest for them to be managing the Philharmonic and providing engagements for their own clients at the expense of those from other managements? It was a fact that the vast majority of artists engaged by the Philharmonic came from CAMI.

Judson and Zirato were especially involved in the management of conductors, and Taubman wondered if the Philharmonic's "unenterprising choice of conductors" was a result of their conflict of interest, though he offered no proof. Yet for several years, besides Mitropoulos, the Philharmonic was led by only three guest conductors who appeared each season: Bruno Walter, George Szell, and Guido Cantelli. Not a bad lineup, to be sure; but Taubman felt Philharmonic audiences were entitled to hear a greater variety of the world's leading conductors.

Taubman was also critical of the orchestra's programming, feeling that it was too haphazard and lacking in any particular theme or point of view. The programs were often not well balanced and were subject to the tastes and whims of the artists involved. It was his contention that the programs should be planned and announced first and the artists then engaged to perform them, not the other way around.

The orchestra itself came in for its share of criticism. When compared with the Boston Symphony and Philadelphia Orchestra, it was definitely below par. Standards had slipped in recent years, and the playing was often careless and undisciplined. But much of this could be blamed on Mitropoulos, and not just because of his somewhat imprecise conducting style. For all his considerable attributes, he did not have the personality of a martinet who could impose discipline by means of fear and intimidation, as was the case with a number of conductors of that era, such as Fritz Reiner and George Szell.

One may well ask why a great orchestra such as the New York Philharmonic needed to have discipline imposed on it. Were its gifted members so egregiously lacking in self-discipline? One can only attribute this situation to the circumstances in which such an iron-willed conductor as Toscanini, with his temper tantrums, was followed by the younger and more courteous John Barbirolli, and the disciplinarian Rodzinski was succeeded by the humble Mitropoulos—in other words, a conductor who produced a tense and stressful working atmosphere giving way to one whose methods were more civil.

Taubman did acknowledge Mitropoulos's sympathy and flair for a certain specialized repertoire, such as Richard Strauss, Gustav Mahler, Schoenberg, and Berg, but was critical of his work in the classical and early romantic music that constitutes a large portion of the standard repertoire. Taubman felt Mitropoulos would be "a valued guest conductor" in the works he did best; but he questioned his abilities as musical director and wondered why he continued to be reengaged every year.

Unwilling to give Taubman the last word on the subject, the critics of other New York papers, such as Paul Henry Lang of the *Herald Tribune* and Miles Kastendieck of the *Journal-American*, followed suit with similar articles of their own. The basic theme of them all was that Mitropoulos must go. An exception was Louis Biancolli of the *World-Telegram and The Sun*, who wrote that the season just concluded, which his colleagues had found so unsatisfactory, had ended on "a strong note of brilliance, the man largely responsible being its devoted and courageous music director, Dimitri Mitropoulos." In a later article he stated, "Both New York and the Philharmonic would be doing themselves a cruel service if, by failing to stand by this great man, they were to lose him. For what he can give, and has given, he is irreplaceable." Many letters to the editors appeared, both pro and con, and even Taubman conceded that it was too late to make any changes the following season,

1956–57; Mitropoulos had already been reengaged, and such drastic changes as were being proposed could not happen overnight. Nevertheless, some changes were already in place, or about to be.

On September 12, 1956, it was announced that the seventy-five-year-old Arthur Judson had resigned, leaving Bruno Zirato as the sole manager, now called managing director. Of the guest conductors announced for the next season, one was conspicuously absent, George Szell, and one was conspicuously present, Leonard Bernstein. Except for two seasons, 1948–49 and 1949–50, Szell had been an annual guest of the Philharmonic's subscription series since 1944. A strict disciplinarian, he had done as much as he could in that regard within the confines of his guest status and the time he spent with the orchestra, usually four weeks a season.

So much has been written about Bernstein's dramatic last-minute debut with the Philharmonic on November 14, 1943, substituting for Bruno Walter on a nationwide radio broadcast, that it is unnecessary to go into it in detail here. Bernstein was then the orchestra's assistant conductor, having been appointed by Rodzinski, and the next season, 1944–45, he appeared as a full-fledged guest conductor. He returned as a guest in two seasons, 1949–50 and 1950–51, in the latter season conducting the historic first complete performances of Charles Ives's Symphony No. 2—fifty years after it was written. (The broadcast performance is included in the Philharmonic's CD set devoted to Bernstein.)

Just as Leopold Stokowski before him had recognized the importance of audio recording, Bernstein embraced the emerging medium of television. Even before embarking on his celebrated series of Young People's Concerts with the Philharmonic, he began appearing in 1954 on CBS's *Omnibus*, a ninety-minute cultural program presented on late Sunday afternoons and hosted by Alistair Cooke. (Imagine CBS, or any commercial network, presenting such a program today.) Assisted by the Symphony of the Air (the former NBC Symphony), Bernstein gave a well-remembered and ingenious explanation of what a conductor does and why he is needed, an analysis of the first movement of Beethoven's Fifth Symphony that could be understood and appreciated by laymen and musicians alike, and many other presentations. So articulate and telegenic was he that he soon became a household name as America's leading spokesman for classical music.

Of the Philharmonic's guest-conducting triumvirate, Bruno Walter and Guido Cantelli were scheduled to return during 1956–57. But the season was marred by Cantelli's tragic death on November 25, 1956, in a plane crash in Paris; he had been on his way to the Philharmonic engagement. One of the most gifted conductors of his generation (born in 1920) and a protégé of Toscanini, who had introduced him as a guest with the NBC Symphony in 1949, he had been thought of in some quarters as a likely successor to Mitropoulos as musical director of the Philharmonic. It is fascinating to speculate what direction the Philharmonic would have taken had he lived. (Charles Munch, music director of the Boston Symphony at the time, had been so impressed with Cantelli that he hoped he would be the one to succeed Munch in that post.)

Cantelli's dates with the Philharmonic (eight weeks' worth) were taken over by Mitropoulos, Paul Paray (already one of the invited guests), Bernstein, Georg Solti, Heitor Villa-Lobos, and the orchestra's associate conductor, Franco Autori. In the meantime it was announced that Mitropoulos would cease to be musical director for the 1957–58 season, but he and Bernstein would share the season as principal conductors, along with more than the usual number of guests. Mitropoulos and Stokowski had shared the 1949–50 season in a similar manner, prior to Mitropoulos's promotion to the top job. There was little doubt in 1957 as to who would emerge triumphant this time.

Even so, in his season's-end summary on May 12, 1957, Taubman could not resist another opportunity to attack Mitropoulos, though he was obviously on the way out. Concerning the orchestra's forthcoming divided direction, Taubman wondered who would "be responsible for orchestral discipline and morale"—who would raise the playing standards to their former level and not allow them to deteriorate further. He answered his own question succinctly: "Certainly not Mr. Mitropoulos. He has had ample opportunity and failed." It must be mentioned that at the time, some also questioned Bernstein's ability to impose discipline on the group.

Even before Taubman's article appeared, the Philharmonic's board of directors had formed a Music Policy Committee to deal with some of these very issues. Among the topics discussed were thematic programming, with one program related in some way to another, and a greater variety of guest conductors. Thematic programming would become the norm during Bernstein's tenure, and he has been credited with the idea, yet the seed was planted long before he took over. Additionally, the committee reviewed the programs of the musical director and the guest conductors, as well as the works proposed for the guest soloists, and made suggestions for program changes and preferred works. Some of these were incorporated, others not.

In 1956–57 Paul Paray, then music director of the Detroit Symphony, made his debut in the orchestra's subscription series, as did Georg Solti, as a substitute for Cantelli. (It was Solti's New York debut.) Bernstein conducted two of Cantelli's weeks and then began his own four-week stint with nothing less than Handel's *Messiah*, the first time that work had been performed by the Philharmonic in forty years, though, of course, it had long been a New York holiday fixture with various choral societies and churches.

Bernstein did not perform the work in its original form, but rather in an edition by the English musician and critic Ebenezer Prout (1835–1909). Moreover, he rearranged Handel's three-part structure into two sections and made further reorderings of some of the numbers, in the process omitting others. Criticisms of Mitropoulos pale in comparison with what Bernstein could expect from the New York critics if he failed to please them. Paul Henry Lang of the *Herald Tribune*, author of *Music in Western Civilization* and of a future biography of Handel, vented his spleen in the paper's December 28 edition:

> I simply cannot understand how a literate, Harvard-educated musician can apparently be so ignorant of the nature and history of such a famous score. Surely, a person of his intellectual and musical capabilities should realize that this two-hundred-year-old masterpiece is encrusted with barnacles which should be scraped off. There is a five-foot shelf of literature to offer guidance.

And yet, here is the esteemed Irving Kolodin, writing of the same performance in *The Saturday Review* of January 12, 1957:

> There was neither self-seeking nor self-effacement in the presence of the masterpiece, rather a competence and a capability that made this one of the finest things yet to his credit in New York.... As an artistic endeavor this "Messiah" has a high place among recently valuable services of the Philharmonic to its public, which, through the Sunday broadcasts, takes in the whole country.

The 1957–58 season brought more first-time guest conductors: André Cluytens, Fernando Previtali, Rafael Kubelík, Ernest Ansermet, Robert Shaw, and Aaron Copland (in half a program of his own music). Thomas Schippers, who in previous seasons had conducted two Saturday night concerts, was allotted two subscription weeks. Of these guests, Ansermet and Cluytens were among those mentioned by Taubman as meriting engagement. Since several of Taubman's ideas were already being discussed prior to the appearance of his article, at least one member of the Philharmonic family suspects that someone on the board leaked this information to Taubman so he could use it as ammunition and then take credit for the results. (It is worth noting that just the year before, Taubman's long-tenured predecessor, Olin Downes, in summing up the season just concluded, voiced no concerns over the Philharmonic's condition. Downes died on August 22, 1955.)

As the 1957–58 season approached there was much concern over the fact that the Philharmonic and Local 802 of the American Federation of Musicians could not agree on a new contract, the old one having expired on May 12. At issue were salaries and the length of the season. The minimum weekly wage for a Philharmonic musician was then $145 for a twenty-nine-week season, which included one week of vacation. The musicians were seeking a raise of $33 over the weekly minimum and a season of thirty-six weeks, while the Philharmonic-Symphony Society had offered a $5 weekly raise, later increased to $7.50, and sixty-four weeks over two seasons, an offer the union rejected. Local 802's president, Al Manuti, compared the Philharmonic's situation with that of the Boston Symphony, which had a minimum wage of $135, but spread over a forty-eight-week season, which included the Pops and Tanglewood. Thus a Boston Symphony musician earned at least $6,480 annually, as against a Philharmonic man's $4,205. Of the two alternatives, a longer season was more important than a salary increase. A Philharmonic spokesman warned that the union's demands might lead to the cancellation of the 1957–58 season—and that would cause the orchestra's pension plan to be terminated.

While it did not come to that, the negotiations dragged on long enough to force the cancellation of the opening two concerts of the season, only the second cancellation in the 115-year history of the Philharmonic. The death of President Franklin D. Roosevelt had been the reason for the first, on April 12, 1945. (Eighty years earlier the death of another president, Abraham Lincoln, had caused the postponement of a concert scheduled for April 22, 1865.) What the Philharmonic's musicians finally accepted was a two-year contract, each season to be thirty-two weeks; the minimum weekly wage was to be $155 the first year, $157.50 the second. (As always, the salary was higher for principal players, who negotiated their own contracts.)

In the *Herald Tribune* of October 13, Lang lamented that the Philharmonic's master musicians earned roughly $5,000 less in a year than master plumbers, carpenters, and electricians. "Surely something is radically wrong in our cultural life if this is all we can provide for a world-famous group of American artists." That they had to go on strike for an additional $12.50 a week demonstrated that "we have no musical culture, only its equivalent in Potemkin villages."

For the first time in its history, the Philharmonic had announced its entire season's programs in advance, but already the opening Thursday-Friday pair had been canceled. Thus the season uncharacteristically began with a Saturday night concert on October 12, with Mitropoulos on the podium and the young American pianist Lilian Kallir as the soloist in her Philharmonic debut, playing Mozart's Piano Concerto No. 17 in G Major, K. 453.

So as to leave no doubt, if there ever had been, as to who would be in charge the following season, on November 19, 1957, the Philharmonic held a press conference at the Century Club, where it was announced that Leonard Bernstein would be the orchestra's musical director for the next three years. The move would make him the first American to hold that post (actually the second, if we count Ureli Corelli Hill, the very first in 1842), and at age thirty-nine, the second youngest. (John Barbirolli was thirty-eight when, in 1937, he had the unenviable task of succeeding Toscanini.)

It was Mitropoulos who made the announcement. Rather than resigning, he was "abdicating with joy," and Bernstein was his choice to succeed him. He then spoke a few cautionary words to the New York music critics. It was all right for them to write their opinions, but they should realize that writing something disagreeable hurt not only the conductor, but also the Philharmonic. The Philharmonic needed more support and less criticism. Too much adverse criticism would cause the public to lose faith. It cannot be said that the critics took his advice to heart. Bernstein, for his part, said, "Mr. Mitropoulos is a great genius and I hope I'll be worthy to follow him."

Although Bernstein's appointment was generally well received in the press, the enthusiasm was more muted than celebratory. No one took issue with his musical and communicative gifts. What was questioned was his readiness for the job. Taubman, in the November 24 *Times*, also wondered if Bernstein was "wise to take [the post] in view of the suspicion that New York and his job in particular are supposed to be death on conductors." It is ironic that Taubman should have expressed any such suspicion, since he had helped bring the executioner's ax down on Mitropoulos. The diversity of Bernstein's musical interests was a cause for some concern, but Taubman felt that if he concentrated his efforts on the Philharmonic he had an excellent chance of succeeding, in spite of the fact that "his weaknesses resemble those of Dimitri Mitropoulos."

The composer Lester Trimble, writing in the *Nation* of December 21, 1957, was glad that Bernstein had been appointed, yet sorry that Mitropoulos had to go. He felt the latter had not deserved the severe criticism he had received, and that the Philharmonic's basic problem was that it was in New York, where the conductor and musicians were not esteemed and supported to the degree their counterparts in Boston were. Rather, they were subjected to intense criticism and not well supported by their union or by the city, this scrutiny exaggerated by the orchestra's nationwide radio broadcasts. Reiterating that he was pleased with Bernstein's appointment and expected him to give authentic performances of American music, he feared that he had been selected because he was a "personality boy" who could bring glamour to the organization and benefit its box office. If so, "that would have been a wrong reason and an insulting one. But it would not necessarily be a handicap."

A mini-controversy erupted on the evening of December 12, 1957. Fernando Previtali, principal conductor of the Orchestra of Santa Cecilia in Rome, was the guest conductor and Yehudi Menuhin the violin soloist. Menuhin had been one of the Philharmonic's most popular soloists over the years, dating back to his debut with the orchestra (the New York Symphony, before it merged with the Philharmonic) in 1927 at the age of eleven. He had since established himself as a masterly performer not only of the standard repertoire, but of contemporary works, such as the Bartók Concerto No. 2. On this occasion he presented the Violin Concerto by Ernest Bloch, composed in 1938, in its first, and to date only, Philharmonic performances.

Menuhin's interpretation of the imposing Bloch work received much praise from the critics, as did the concerto itself. People wondered why it had taken two decades for such a notable score to be performed by the Philharmonic. What incurred the critics', and the Philharmonic's, wrath was that Menuhin had the temerity to play an encore, the Preludio from J. S. Bach's unaccompanied Partita in E Major, without consulting anyone, though it was later reported that Previtali had given his blessing. At that time encores were just not given in the regular season, though they were common enough in the summer Lewisohn Stadium concerts. The objection to encores was that they upset the balance of the program and delayed its conclusion, thus playing havoc with the travel schedules of those subscribers who were commuters (and at that time the evening concerts began at 8:45). And if one soloist was permitted an encore, the flood gates would be opened to all of them. And "worst of all," according to Taubman, "Mr. Menuhin played the encore badly."

Menuhin was strongly requested by the Philharmonic's management not to repeat the incident at the Friday matinee performance, whereupon he proceeded to play a different encore, this time the Gavotte from the same Bach partita. At that point the Philharmonic contacted Menuhin's manager, urgently asking him to order his client to cease and desist. Saturday night brought a change of program, with Menuhin playing Paganini's Concerto No. 1 in D Major instead of the Bloch work. The Paganini, with its violinistic fireworks, is a piece guaranteed to bring down the house, and all those present could not help but ask themselves, "Will he or won't he?"

After much applause Menuhin raised his hand for silence. Smiling, he said, "I am not allowed." More applause. "I am not at all sure you are allowed to applaud either. I am sure that if Bach could realize what damage even two or three minutes of his music could do to the traditions and budget of this great orchestra, he would be very sorry." The assistant manager, George E. Judd, later stated that the Philharmonic had no feud with Menuhin. Perhaps not, but it would be seven years before he was invited to play with the Philharmonic again.

The evening of January 2, 1958, brought the highly anticipated return of Leonard Bernstein to the Philharmonic's podium, his first appearance since the announcement of his appointment as musical director. One might have thought he had already taken over the job, so enthusiastic and lengthy was the ovation on his entrance. No doubt for his own sentimental reasons, his program included two works from his unscheduled debut performance in 1943, Schumann's *Manfred* Overture and Richard Strauss's *Don Quixote*, with the cellist Laszlo Varga and the violist William Lincer in the solo parts. To add further excitement to the evening, there was the American premiere of the Piano Concerto No. 2 by Dmitri Shostakovich, with Bernstein himself the soloist, conducting from the keyboard. This the critics found trivial and even sentimental, hardly up to the standard of the First Concerto, let alone that of some of the symphonies. But Bernstein played it, as expected, with such panache as to merit an ovation after the very first movement. Although the concerto is certainly not profound, nor even overly virtuosic (it was written for the composer's young son to play), it is certainly an attractive and exuberant work and is frequently performed by young pianists. Maurice Ravel's *La valse* concluded the program brilliantly. If the public's excitement that evening was typical of what could be expected in the future, then the Philharmonic's troubles were over.

A harbinger of things to come occurred at noon on January 18, 1958, when Bernstein presided over and conducted his first televised Young People's Concert with the Philharmonic. Until then most of the Young People's Concerts had been under the direction of someone specifically engaged for that purpose, most recently Wilfrid Pelletier, with occasional appearances by the associate conductor, Franco Autori (and those earlier concerts were not televised, though they were heard locally on the radio). With Bernstein all that changed. He felt it was his job to educate young people in music, and he was certainly supremely qualified to do so, plus he already had significant television experience with his Omnibus programs.

Nothing less than "What Does Music Mean?" was the title of his first program, which developed the idea that even program music—music that is supposed to be about something—is really not about anything other than the notes themselves and how they make one feel. Already apparent was Bernstein's wise and witty way of not talking down to the children and of holding their attention. In so doing, he also held the attention and interest of their parents.

At the conclusion of the 1957–58 season the Philharmonic left on its first-ever tour of Latin America: thirty-nine concerts in Venezuela, Colombia, Ecuador, Peru, Bolivia, Paraguay, Chile, Uruguay, Brazil, Argentina, Panama, and Mexico. Of these, twenty-eight were conducted by Bernstein, eleven by Mitropoulos.

Upon returning to New York, conductors and orchestra were feted in a ceremony at City Hall.

Soviet Triumph

The 1958–59 season was Leonard Bernstein's first as music director of the New York Philharmonic. Note the change in his title, made at Bernstein's request—music director, the usual designation for such positions today, rather than musical director, the title bestowed on Rodzinski and Mitropoulos. He felt the new title signified authority in all aspects of the organization having to do with music. (However, in a radio interview with George Szell, whose title with the Cleveland Orchestra was musical director, he was asked to explain the difference between the two titles. His reply was to the effect that anyone can direct *music*, but to be *musical....*)

Several innovations in the Philharmonic's way of doing things were announced well in advance of the season. The most controversial was the change in format of the Thursday night concerts. These would now be considered "previews," in which the conductor would speak to the audience about some aspect of the program, even with musical examples before the actual performance. (Some cynics felt that Bernstein would now be giving children's concerts for adults.) There could even be some rehearsing if necessary. The critics would not review the previews, but rather the Friday afternoon concerts, though they did, for a time, report on the previews. In effect, the previews served the purpose of an extra rehearsal before the first official performance.

The second innovation was the orchestra's attire for the previews, not the customary white tie and tails, but a specially designed off-black outfit with stand-up collars on the jackets and cuffs with white piping. This idea, received with some jocularity, was eventually thought better of, and the costumes were discarded before the season was over.

Yet another change in the Philharmonic's routine involved the radio broadcasts. Since 1930 the Sunday afternoon CBS broadcasts had been a national institution, but their ninety-minute duration frequently resulted in some reshuffling of the week's program, with an additional work often performed after the broadcast. With Bernstein's arrival the broadcasts were moved to prime time, 8:30–10:30 p.m., on Saturday nights, with the entire concert being broadcast.

Speaking of Saturdays, in previous years the orchestra did not perform every Saturday, but only fourteen to sixteen times during the twenty-eight week season. And usually the Saturday program was different from the Thursday–Friday series, as was, often, the Sunday concert. It was not unusual for the orchestra to play three different programs over a four-day span. Again, all that changed with Bernstein. Not only would there be a concert every Saturday night, but the program for the entire week would be the same (though occasionally there were still some changes for Sunday afternoon, at least initially). And the subscription season was now increased to thirty weeks.

But the most important innovation was the idea of thematic programming, which had already been discussed in meetings of the Music Policy Committee. This did not mean thematic for individual concerts—the theme now applied to the entire season. For his part, Bernstein's eighteen weeks of concerts encompassed a survey of American music from the earliest years of the twentieth century to what was then the present day. Almost all his programs included a representative American work, opening with William Schuman's *American Festival Overture*, appropriately followed by Ives's Second Symphony. Obviously, Bernstein was uniquely qualified to perform American music in an authoritative way, and his performances of works by Samuel Barber, George W. Chadwick, Copland, Lukas Foss, George Gershwin, Roy Harris, Edward MacDowell, Walter Piston, Ned Rorem, Carl Ruggles, Schuman, Sessions, Virgil Thomson, and others served to emphasize, if emphasis was needed (and it probably was), the extremely rich and varied repertoire of our country's music. (A composer conspicuously absent from the survey was Bernstein himself.) Besides all the Americana, Bernstein laced his second series of concerts with works by Vivaldi and his final series with the music of Handel, commemorating in 1959 the two hundredth anniversary of the latter composer's death. Included in that series were Handel's seldom-performed *Passion According to St. John* and his *Ode for Saint Cecilia's Day*.

Four guest conductors were announced for the season: Thomas Schippers, Herbert von Karajan, Sir John Barbirolli, and Dimitri Mitropoulos. Each was to emphasize a specific national school in his programs, respectively Italian, German and Austrian, English, and French. Obviously, Schippers was not Italian, but he had conducted frequently in Italy and was quite conversant with that country's music. Nor, of course, was Mitropoulos French, but his sympathies were wide ranging and, as he liked to say, because he was Greek, he was "good for everything." For Barbirolli, the engagement would be his first with the Philharmonic since 1943, and he would be returning as a highly regarded world-class conductor, not as someone who had been, in his relative youth, the Philharmonic's less-than-successful musical director.

It was the engagement of Karajan that provoked some controversy. One might wonder why Bernstein, with his emphatic identification with his Jewish heritage and his support of Jewish causes and of Israel, would have engaged for his first season Karajan, who at the time was suspected of having had Nazi affiliations, which were in fact later documented. When Karajan and the Berlin Philharmonic made their first New York appearances in 1955, there had been long picket lines of protesters outside Carnegie Hall. But as the minutes of the Music Policy Committee show, the Philharmonic had been trying to engage Karajan for quite some time, long before Bernstein's appointment. So this was just a matter of rather odd timing—Karajan's availability and acceptance simply happened to coincide with Bernstein's first season.

Although there were no picket lines for Karajan's New York Philharmonic concerts, there was some unrest in the orchestra prior to his arrival. At the time it was customary for the orchestra to rise when the conductor came on stage to begin a concert. But the Philharmonic had quite a few Jewish musicians, some of whom had lost family members at the hands of the Nazis. There was no way they were going to stand up for Karajan, and they made this known in no uncertain terms. Eventually the orchestra's manager, Bruno Zirato, made the announcement in his inimitable Italian-inflected English: "If one man no stand, everybody no stand."

The main work on Karajan's first program, November 13–16, was Richard Strauss's tone poem *Ein Heldenleben* (A Hero's Life), and its extensive violin solos would normally have been played by the Philharmonic's concertmaster, John Corigliano. However, Corigliano was ill, so the solos were played in the first two performances by Michael Rosenker, the assistant concertmaster, with Corigliano returning for the final two. For his second week, November 20–23, Karajan led performances of Beethoven's First and Ninth Symphonies, the latter with the Westminster Choir and Leontyne Price, Maureen Forrester, Ernst Haefliger, and Norman Scott as soloists.

The four weeks of Barbirolli's engagement were crowned by the first Philharmonic performances, beginning January 23, of Edward Elgar's great oratorio *The Dream of Gerontius*. Appreciation of this fine work is largely limited to England, where it has become a staple of the country's many choral societies. Performances in other countries are extremely rare, and then only when an English conductor is at the helm. Inspired by a poem by Cardinal John Newman, it has been described as a sort of English *Parsifal*. Barbirolli's belief in the work is evidenced not only by his fervent Philharmonic performances, but also by his superb EMI recording with his own Hallé Orchestra in Manchester. In New York his affecting soloists were the contralto Maureen Forrester, the tenor Richard Lewis singing the title role in his Philharmonic (and New York) debut, and the baritone Moreley Meredith, all joined by the Westminster Choir, of which Warren Martin was then the director. Howard Taubman praised the performance, yet acknowledged that the work did not touch American listeners as it did their English counterparts.

Decades after the fact, the impact of Leonard Bernstein's first season with the Philharmonic is still fresh in the memory. So great was the excitement he generated that not only were his concerts sold out, but those of the guest conductors as well. Not since the time of Toscanini had the Philharmonic made its presence felt so strongly in New York City. But all did not go according to plan. Several weeks before his scheduled appearances, Dimitri Mitropoulos suffered a heart attack. It was his second. The first, in December 1952, had caused him to miss half the season; now he had to cancel his four-week engagement. Because the Philharmonic still wished to feature French music in that time period, it fell to Zirato to cast about for suitable replacements, of which none were more suitable than the actual French conductors he came up with: Pierre Monteux for two weeks, and Jean Morel and Paul Paray for one week each. Monteux, one of the great conductors of the era, had been a very intermittent guest with the Philharmonic, though he was a regular visitor to the summer Lewisohn Stadium concerts. He did not retain Mitropoulos's programs, which were not entirely French anyway, but did treat New York audiences to his magnificent interpretation of Berlioz's *Symphonie fantastique*. The pianist Rudolf Serkin, who performed Beethoven's "Emperor" Concerto on the same program, paid Monteux the compliment of sitting in the audience to hear his Berlioz.

Jean Morel was then in his heyday as director of the orchestral and conducting program at the Juilliard School of Music and as a regular conductor at the Metropolitan Opera. His many Juilliard conducting pupils included James Levine, Leonard Slatkin, and James Conlon. Morel was brought in to take over Mitropoulos's scheduled concert performances of Debussy's masterpiece *Pelléas et Mélisande*, with Phyllis Curtin, Nicolai Gedda, and Martial Singher in the principal roles. Although Monteux would have been a good choice for that week (he had played viola in the orchestra at the work's world premiere in Paris in 1902 and had conducted it at the Met only a few years before), Morel was certainly an authoritative substitute, having also conducted the opera many times, including a televised production by the NBC Opera Theatre. (Imagine a commercial TV network today presenting live, or even taped, operatic performances.)

The only problem with this, Morel's Philharmonic debut, was that he did not get along well with the orchestra. A rather peppery, often caustic individual, he had the curious habit of treating the members of student orchestras like professionals and those of professional orchestras like students. Because a number of the Philharmonic's members were his colleagues at Juilliard, this created a certain level of antagonism, most notably with the master timpanist, Saul Goodman; Morel thought Goodman had missed an entrance at one point in the first performance and registered his displeasure with angry gestures at the player. A former percussionist in Paris (he had played on the first recording of Stravinsky's *L'histoire du soldat* [The Soldier's Tale], with the composer conducting), Morel was particularly sensitive to errors by percussionists. A backstage confrontation between Goodman and Morel during the intermission revealed that Goodman's printed part did not contain the disputed entrance, something Morel had strangely failed to notice during the rehearsals. Angry words were exchanged between the two, and after two days, during which Morel repeatedly but unsuccessfully attempted to apologize to Goodman, the two finally met at the personnel manager's insistence, before the final performance. Goodman then gave Morel a playful elbow nudge in the ribs and told him to be more careful in future.

On May 31 Bruno Zirato retired as the Philharmonic's managing director, thus concluding the period of the "old guard" that had begun with Arthur Judson and had continued with the two as co-managers until Judson's retirement. Appointed to succeed Zirato was thirty-four-year-old George E. Judd Jr., who had for several years been the assistant and then the associate manager under Zirato. Judd had managed the Oklahoma City Symphony and had also managed the Philharmonic's tour of Central and South America in 1958. He had good genes for the job: his father, George E. Judd, had managed the Boston Symphony for many years. Taking over as associate managing director was the forty-four-year-old Carlos Moseley, the orchestra's press director, a job that in turn fell to Frank Milburn.

In the summer and early fall of 1959, the Philharmonic undertook one of its most extensive tours ever, to Europe and the Near East, beginning August 5 in Athens and ending October 10 in London—forty-nine concerts in nine weeks. Bernstein conducted most of them, with Thomas Schippers in charge of thirteen and Seymour Lipkin one. Lipkin had recently been appointed one of the Philharmonic's assistant conductors (of which more later). The tour was arranged by President Dwight D. Eisenhower's International Program for Cultural Presentations and administered by the American National Theatre and Academy (ANTA).

Two concerts in Athens were given in the historic open-air Odeon of Herod Atticus, famous for its fabulous acoustics. As one reads the various newspaper reviews of the tour, one is struck by the fact that, in city after city, critics and the public alike report that never had they experienced such enthusiasm or such a magnificent orchestra. In Austria, contemporary American music was performed for the first time by an American orchestra at the prestigious Salzburg Festival. It is significant that each program on the tour included at least one work by an American composer, something that cannot always be taken for granted today when American orchestras tour abroad.

It was during the visit to Moscow, where the orchestra played five concerts August 22–26 and three more September 9–11, that Bernstein had his much-publicized meeting with the Soviet novelist Boris Pasternak, who was persona non grata in his homeland, after the "crime" of winning the Nobel Prize for Literature with *Dr. Zhivago*. Shostakovich's Fifth Symphony was a Bernstein specialty throughout his career, and its rendition in Moscow was a particular triumph, in spite of the fact that Bernstein's tempo for the finale's coda was much faster than the composer and Soviet audiences were accustomed to. When Columbia records issued Bernstein's New York Philharmonic recording of the work, the cover photograph showed the almost-smiling composer onstage congratulating the conductor after the performance and the orchestra members joining in the applause.

At the Moscow concert of August 25, the Philharmonic was augmented by nine Soviet musicians for a performance of Stravinsky's *Rite of Spring*, the first time that great work had been played in Moscow in thirty years. The reaction of the Moscow audience, according to the *Times* correspondent Osgood Carruthers, was "overwhelming." Also included was Stravinsky's Concerto for Piano and Wind Orchestra, with Seymour Lipkin as soloist—the work's first performance in the Soviet Union. (Stravinsky, too, was persona non grata there because of his "formalistic" and "bourgeois" creations.) This work, too, was enthusiastically received, as was *The Unanswered Question* by Charles Ives, the latter so much so that it had to be immediately repeated. Bernstein had spoken a few words to the audience before the Ives, explaining the Transcendentalist philosophy behind it, and also spoke to them about Stravinsky and his life and works after he left Russia. For this he was roundly criticized by one of the Moscow critics, who objected not only to the unprecedented (in Moscow) practice of addressing the audience, but to the repetition of the Ives piece. He was firmly in the minority. (Bernstein had told the audience that it would be the first performance of the *Rite* in the Soviet Union in thirty years, but the authorities claimed that it had been played in Tallinn, Estonia, the year before.)

The tour actually ended not in Europe but in Washington, D.C., on October 12, with a concert before a packed house in Constitution Hall. The orchestra immediately launched into its 1959–60 season on October 15 in Carnegie Hall. It was agreed by all concerned that the most enthusiastic of all audiences on the tour had been those in the Soviet Union, even at the height of the cold war. The *New York Times* of October 13, 1959, quoted Bernstein as saying, "The Russians are a race apart, the most demonstrative of all, and almost pathological in their relationship to music. [They have] a kind of fanatic quality. They're almost wild in their enthusiasm for music." He added, "You can't go to jail for liking Beethoven's Fifth."

On its return to New York the orchestra was feted with a ceremony at City Hall, where Mayor Robert F. Wagner presented Bernstein with a gold key to the city and proclaimed the week "Philharmonic Week." Fifty-seventh Street, where Carnegie Hall is located, became "Philharmonic Street." At the time, it was feared the coming season would be the orchestra's last in Carnegie Hall.

MAHLER'S TIME

For many years the Philharmonic had, in addition to a music (or musical) director, an assistant conductor. During Rodzinski's tenure the assistant had been, of course, Bernstein himself for one season, then Ignatz Strasfogel for another, followed by Walter Hendl, who would hold the post for four years, encompassing Rodzinski's final years and the two seasons of guest conductors when Bruno Walter had the title of musical adviser.

For the 1949–50 season, with Dimitri Mitropoulos and Leopold Stokowski as co-conductors, the post went to Franco Autori, whose title was advanced to associate conductor, most likely because he was older than his predecessors and was also more experienced than they had been at the time of their appointments. Autori was to hold the job for ten years, during which time he was assigned two or three Saturday night concerts each season and occasionally conducted a complete week of concerts when the scheduled maestro was indisposed. From time to time he also conducted a children's concert. Otherwise, in the tradition of such posts, he sat around and observed.

Autori continued as associate conductor for Bernstein's first season, 1958–59, during which time he conducted no concerts. Neither did he accompany the orchestra on its European tour. On October 4, 1959, the *New York Times* announced that, for the coming season, the Philharmonic would have not one, not two, but three assistant conductors. It was Bernstein's plan to have three each season—young men at the outset of their careers who would benefit from close association with a great orchestra, attending all its rehearsals and concerts, observing Bernstein and the guest conductors, and gaining firsthand knowledge of the ensemble's inner workings. Additionally, they would be expected to know the complete repertoire of the season so as to be able to take over a concert in an emergency, and would also be given the opportunity to conduct their own sched-uled performances, usually a single work on a concert otherwise conducted by Bernstein.

The first three assistant conductors to be selected were Seymour Lipkin, Stefan Mengelberg, and Kenneth Schermerhorn. Lipkin at the time was better known as a pianist; he had played the solo parts in Bernstein's *Age of Anxiety* and Stravinsky's Concerto for Piano and Wind Orchestra on the recent tour. He had also conducted a concert in Baalbek, Lebanon, on August 9. Mengelberg (later known as Stefan Bauer-Mengelberg) was a nephew of Willem Mengelberg, former conductor of Amsterdam's Concertgebouw Orchestra, and had studied with Bernstein at Tanglewood, as had Schermerhorn, who had conducted the American Ballet Theatre Orchestra and the Seventh Army Symphony. So all three were obviously known to Bernstein prior to their appointments. (Toward the end of the season Schermerhorn left to conduct a tour of the Ballet Theatre and was replaced by Arnold Gamson, conductor of the American Opera Society in New York.)

Bernstein continued the idea of thematic programming during his second season. One series of concerts featured different varieties of concertos; another, music written for the theater. The concerto series included an all-Bach program on which was performed the Concerto in C Major for three pianos (the harpsichord not yet considered de rigueur in this music)—a bit of a family affair, for the three solo parts were taken by the president of the Philharmonic's board of directors, David M. Keiser; the associate managing director, Carlos Mosley; and Bernstein himself. But the primary focus, in the middle of the season, was the observance of the centennial of the birth of Gustav Mahler, who had been the orchestra's music director during 1909–11, the last two years of his life.

Even in 1960 Mahler's music could hardly have been called central to the symphonic repertoire; he was very much a peripheral cult figure. True, he had his champions, most conspicuously Bruno Walter and Dimitri Mitropoulos, and the First and Fourth Symphonies were often played by other conductors, most likely because they are the only two lasting under an hour. Still, the performance of any Mahler symphony took on the character of a special event, much as Beethoven's Ninth Symphony did in those days, before it became an almost everyday occurrence.

Bernstein did not begin the Mahler Festival but gave that honor to Mitropoulos in his first Philharmonic concerts since his heart attack the year before. Those who had not seen him in some time were shocked at his appearance, his fringe of hair now totally white. Mahler's Fifth Symphony began the cycle on December 31, 1959, and the Ninth concluded Mitropoulos's engagement on January 22, 1960. In between came the First Symphony and the Adagio movement from the unfinished Tenth. To give an idea of how infrequent Mahler performances were at that time, it is worth mentioning that the Philharmonic had not played the Fifth since 1947, and the Ninth had not been heard there since 1945 (the orchestra's very first presentation of it), both under Bruno Walter.

Bernstein followed Mitropoulos, performing the Fourth Symphony and the Second ("Resurrection") between January 28 and February 21, with the *Kindertoten-lieder* (Songs on the Death of Children) and a selection of other lieder in between, sung by Jennie Tourel. Even here, the Fourth had not been played by the Philharmonic since 1953, though the Second had been given in 1957, both with Bruno Walter conducting. Walter, who had effectively retired from conducting two years before, except for recordings, returned in April for four performances of *Das Lied von der Erde*, with Maureen Forrester and Richard Lewis as the soloists.

If any event can be said to have put Mahler into the standard repertoire, this festival was it. First of all, the nationwide CBS broadcasts brought the concerts to millions of people, and the ensuing recordings by Bernstein and Walter, with more to come from Bernstein in the following years (when he was then at the height of his popularity), were greatly responsible for the Mahler renaissance. "My time will come," the composer had said, and so it did, with a vengeance not even he could have foreseen.

But the Mahler celebration was not limited to the subscription series. On February 13, Bernstein's Young People's Concert bore the title "Who Is Gustav Mahler?" This may have been the only Young People's Concert anywhere ever, before or since, to conclude with the heartbreaking final ten minutes of *Das Lied von der Erde*. As seen on the video of the concert, Bernstein told his young listeners that if they did not feel like applauding at the end, he would understand. To his surprise, the applause began while the last chord was still fading away.

A guest conductor new to the Philharmonic appeared that season, though not in the Mahler Festival: the Brazilian Eleazar de Carvalho. Like Bernstein, he was a Tanglewood alumnus, a pupil of Serge Koussevitzky. Returning after absences of many years were Fritz Reiner and Leopold Stokowski. Reiner, who had taught Bernstein at Philadelphia's Curtis Institute, collaborated with Rudolf Serkin in a staggering performance of the then rarely heard First Piano Concerto of Bartók. At the start of his first rehearsal Reiner noted that he was pleased to be conducting his pupil's orchestra. Writing in the *Saturday Review* of March 19, Irving Kolodin wrote of Reiner's March 10 performance of the Brahms Second Symphony that it "was of an order of excellence that would command attention at any time," and that such excellence was "increasingly a rarity today."

Another guest new to the Philharmonic was Paul Hindemith. Unlike Stravinsky, he did not often conduct programs devoted to his own music; the Cello Concerto with Aldo Parisot as soloist was the sole example of his work. Pride of place on his concerts of February 25–28 went to Bruckner's Seventh Symphony, which, coming immediately after the Mahler series, treated subscribers to yet another massive work.

In his season-ending retrospective column in the *Times* of May 15, Howard Taubman wrote that the Philharmonic had "had another good season." He was laudatory toward Bernstein and commended the orchestra on its "esprit de corps, which had sunk abysmally low in recent years" but now had "had an infusion of pride." The Mahler Festival came in for special praise, "whatever one thinks of the composer." (Another factor in the relative paucity of Mahler performances before 1960 may have been general critical hostility to the music. Taubman, in his past writings, had not appeared to be much of a Mahler fan, and Olin Downes certainly was not.)

Taubman did feel that although Bernstein had commendably devoted the bulk of his time to the Philharmonic, certain aspects of the season did not live up to expectations, such as the two series featuring, respectively, concertos and music for the theater, as well as one dealing with twentieth-century problems in music. He disliked the fact that it was thought necessary to provide special labels for these series, felt that the choice of concertos was not terribly inspired (the Beethoven Violin Concerto and Third Piano Concerto, the Berg Violin Concerto—in its first Philharmonic performance in ten years—and the Brahms Double Concerto were included, as well as most of the Bach Brandenburg Concertos and Bartók's *Concerto for Orchestra*). The idea of attaching labels to series, which Taubman thought smacked of gimmickry, was unusual at the time, but it is now a frequent marketing ploy, even for individual concerts.

At one time it was thought that the 1959–60 season would be the orchestra's last in Carnegie Hall, which was threatened with the wrecker's ball when the creation of the Lincoln Center for the Performing Arts was announced. In the spring of 1959 President Eisenhower had raised the first shovelful of dirt for that project. Carnegie Hall was to be demolished and a large office building erected on the site.

Construction of the new Philharmonic Hall at Lincoln Center had begun soon afterward, and it was hoped that it would be ready in time for the 1959–60 season, after which hopes were held out for 1960–61, to no avail. A *New York Times* article on January 6, 1960, reported that Carnegie Hall was set to close in May of that year and that it would be the autumn of 1961 before Philharmonic Hall was ready. As a stopgap measure, New York's Hunter College had agreed to make its Assembly Hall available for that season to accommodate not only the Philharmonic, but also the Philadelphia Orchestra and Boston Symphony for their regular New York series, as well as other visiting orchestras and soloists. Hunter College, located on Sixty-ninth Street near Park Avenue, would be unselfishly relocating most of its own activities.

Robert E. Simon Jr., president of the corporation that operated Carnegie Hall, was quoted in the article as saying, "There is no excuse for this situation to have arisen. With reasonable foresight and a coordinated planning effort there was plenty of time to have a new concert hall completed for next season's opening— that is, if this had been made a matter of priority. It wasn't."

But "Save Carnegie Hall" had been a rallying cry for various civic-minded groups and music lovers ever since the hall's demolition was announced. Finally, on March 31, 1960, the *Times* carried the news that a Citizens Committee for Carnegie Hall, headed by Isaac Stern, had the day before visited Mayor Wagner, who assured them of his "full cooperation" in attempting to save the historic hall. A few weeks later Governor Nelson A. Rockefeller signed a bill designed "to save Carnegie Hall for posterity," thus creating the nonprofit Carnegie Hall Corporation, which would own and operate the hall after the city purchased, improved, and modernized it. Bonds would be issued for this work and the hall leased to the corporation, which would own the building once the bonds had been retired. At an organizational meeting Stern was elected president of the corporation, a post he was to hold until his death.

When the news broke that Carnegie Hall had been saved, Leopold Stokowski, who was conducting a children's concert there with the Symphony of the Air, interrupted the program and announced it from the stage, whereupon the large audience of children and parents cheered and applauded for three minutes.

Once the future of Carnegie Hall was guaranteed, Hunter College released the Philharmonic from its commitment there, and it was further announced that the opening of Lincoln Center would now take place in the spring of 1961 (more wishful thinking). Meanwhile, on June 1, 1960, the Philharmonic announced the appointment of its second batch of assistant conductors: Gregory Millar, Elyakum Shapira, and Russell Stanger. Millar, a Canadian, had conducted various orchestras in Vancouver, San Francisco, St. Louis, and other cities, while the Israeli-born Shapira (later Shapirra) had studied conducting at Tanglewood with Serge Koussevitzky and at Juilliard with Jean Morel. Stanger had been a guest conductor of the Philadelphia Orchestra, the Buffalo Philharmonic, and the Paris Conservatory Orchestra, among others. The next day it was announced that a new contract for the 1960–61 season assured the orchestra members of a thirty-eight-week season at a minimum of $180 a week.

On August 10 the orchestra embarked on a seven-week tour of the continental United States, Hawaii, and Canada, with two concerts in West Berlin thrown in at the end for good measure. These last were financed by the Ford Motor Company Fund. The five-day trip was the first time an American orchestra had traveled to

Europe for so short a visit and also the first time an American industrial company had sponsored a foreign visit by a major orchestra. The purpose of the trip was to participate in the West Berlin Festival. Ford had been sponsoring the Philharmonic's television appearances for two years, and, in the words of Henry Ford II, president of the company, this was "a fine opportunity to aid the courageous people of West Berlin in their ideological battle with Communist East Germany."

As for the pre-Berlin bulk of the tour, the two concerts in an outdoor bowl in Honolulu were the orchestra's first ever in Hawaii, while that in the Hollywood Bowl was the first ever by a non–Los Angeles orchestra. A tour-ending concert in Washington, D.C., on September 25, immediately after a flight from West Berlin, gave the orchestra just two days' respite before the start of the new season.

On September 1 Howard Taubman switched desks at the *New York Times*, succeeding the long-serving Brooks Atkinson as chief drama critic. Moving up in the music department to the post of senior music critic was Harold C. Schonberg. If Mitropoulos had his Taubman, then Bernstein would soon have his Schonberg.

CHAPTER 2

1960–63

Upset Plans

What a season opener it was! For the first time in its history the Philharmonic began a season with a non-subscription concert, this one for the benefit of the orchestra's pension fund. The evening of September 27, 1960, was gala in more ways than one. Firstly, it was the orchestra's first concert in Carnegie Hall since the dramatic announcement that it had been saved. The hall had been newly redecorated, the walls now off-white and trimmed in gold, the carpeting ruby red, the upholstery velvet, the lobby white and adorned with two chandeliers.

Secondly, the concert's guest soloist was the man responsible for saving the hall, Isaac Stern, who had interrupted a European concert tour to fly home for the event. When he made his entrance to perform the Beethoven Violin Concerto, he was greeted with a standing ovation. Appropriately brilliant works by Bernstein, Roy Harris, and Ravel had begun the evening, with Bernstein, of course, on the podium.

In one respect the orchestra's 1960–61 season was rather curious. In 1958–59 Bernstein had conducted eighteen weeks of the thirty-week season, his concerts divided into four blocks of time, with guest conductors filling in the gaps. The following year followed the same schedule. Now, for 1960–61 it was announced that he would conduct only twelve weeks, six at either end of the season, with a huge gap in the middle for guests. No explanation was given for the change.

The idea of thematic programming continued, the first six weeks of the season bearing the designation Schumann and the Romantic Movement in observance of the 150th anniversary of the composer's birth. The four symphonies, the Cello Concerto, and the *Manfred* Overture were programmed, with the Piano Concerto following a few weeks later. Harold Schonberg had already complained about this lineup, pointing out that these works were frequently heard anyway during the normal course of a season, and that if the Philharmonic really wished to honor Schumann it should offer one of his less well-known works, such as the oratorio *Das Paradies und die Peri*.

However well planned, the season suffered more than the usual number of unplanned occurrences, and the wisdom of having three assistant conductors was almost immediately put to the test. The subscription concerts began on September 30 with a rather conventional program: Beethoven's *Leonore* Overture No. 3 and Piano Concerto No. 1, and Schumann's Fourth Symphony. Bernstein was himself the soloist in the concerto, conducting from the keyboard, as he had done in several performances on the recent tour. While praising much of the concert, Schonberg felt it was time to retire the idea of simultaneous pianist-conductors: "While a man can learn to ride two horses at once, such a feat really belongs in the circus."

In the course of the Saturday evening broadcast Bernstein became ill during the performance of the concerto and, though he completed it, felt too unwell to continue the concert, so Gregory Millar conducted the Schumann symphony. Bernstein's ailment persisted and the Sunday program was revised, with Elyakum Shapira conducting the Beethoven overture, Millar repeating the symphony, and, since none of the trio was equipped to play and conduct the Beethoven concerto, Russell Stanger conducting two works that had been performed on the recent tour, Debussy's *Prelude to the Afternoon of a Faun* and Stravinsky's *Firebird* Suite. It was the first time in memory that three conductors had led the Philharmonic in a regular concert, at least as far as anyone could recall, though in the orchestra's early years such an arrangement was not uncommon.

The most serious, and most tragic, of the unplanned occurrences was the death of Dimitri Mitropoulos on November 2, at age sixty-four. He was in Milan rehearsing the orchestra of La Scala in Mahler's gigantic Third Symphony when he suffered a heart attack, collapsed, and fell from the podium. He died on the way to the hospital. In his younger years Mitropoulos had been an inveterate mountain climber and had said that when he died, he hoped it would be by falling off a mountain. One could say that his wish had been granted. The retired Philharmonic double bassist Walter Botti described Mitropoulos as "a great conductor, a gentleman, a prince among men."

Mitropoulos had been scheduled to conduct the Philharmonic for four weeks later in the season, but as a memorial tribute Bernstein opened the week's concerts with the serene fourth movement, "Urlicht" (Primal Light), from Mahler's Second Symphony, with Jennie Tourel as the mezzo-soprano soloist. Mitropoulos had, of course, been in the forefront of what was to become the Mahler boom.

The next two weeks did not go as planned either. Fritz Reiner canceled his two-week engagement due to illness. No assistant conductors took over this time, but rather two composers, one leading some of his own music (Aaron Copland), the other not (Carlos Chávez). Copland, in fact, was heard uncharacteristically conducting Antonín Dvořák's Violin Concerto with the concertmaster, John Corigliano, as soloist.

Two great Austrian conductors made their Philharmonic debuts in the following weeks. Hans Rosbaud was highly regarded as a specialist in difficult twentieth-century music, and he did not disappoint in his second week, leading from memory such daunting works as Schoenberg's *Five Pieces for Orchestra*, Webern's *Six Pieces for Orchestra*, and Hindemith's *Concerto for Orchestra*. It was a rare sight in those days to see the Philharmonic's musicians unanimously applauding the conductor after each piece. The retired Philharmonic horn player John Carabella has said that during Rosbaud's first rehearsal the associate principal horn, Joseph Singer, told him, "Enjoy this while you can. You'll never play under such a conductor again." Carabella himself said that Rosbaud was "head and shoulders over any other conductor I ever played under."

Karl Böhm (like Rosbaud, born in Graz) was also engaged for two weeks, only one of which was fulfilled. After the final rehearsal of his second week, for an all–Richard Strauss program, Böhm, who had been feeling ill, consulted an ophthalmologist, who recommended immediate surgery for a detached retina. Since Böhm preferred to have the surgery done in Vienna, off he went. Once again, two of the valiant assistant conductors stepped in, with Stanger conducting *Don Juan* and Millar taking over for the closing scene of *Capriccio*, in which Lisa della Casa was the soprano soloist, and the *Sinfonia Domestica*. The *Capriccio* excerpt had never been performed by the Philharmonic, though they had played the symphony several times with Mitropoulos, who had made a specialty of it.

The last-minute illnesses of Bernstein and Böhm and the cancellation by Reiner with a couple of weeks' notice (not to mention the death of Mitropoulos) illustrate a fact of life for assistant conductors. If there has been a cancellation a week or more ahead of time, usually an available conductor of repute is engaged to substitute, and with normal rehearsal time. If, on the other hand, the cancellation occurs so close to the concert (or during the concert) that there is absolutely no possibility of engaging anyone else, then the assistants get their chance, and with no rehearsal whatsoever. This was, of course, what had happened to Bernstein in 1943.

The four weeks that had been scheduled for Mitropoulos were filled by Stanisław Skrowaczewski and Paul Paray, each for two weeks. Skrowaczewski, then in his first season as music director of the Minneapolis Symphony (now the Minnesota Orchestra) and making his New York debut, included on his first program the New York premiere of Witold Lutosławski's *Concerto for Orchestra*. In an interesting coincidence Mitropoulos, for whom Skrowaczewski was substituting, had also originally come to the Philharmonic from the Minneapolis Symphony.

Alfred Wallenstein also made his Philharmonic debut that season. Formerly music director of the Los Angeles Philharmonic and one of the few American conductors active at that time with major orchestras, he was already quite well-known in New York. In fact, he had been the Philharmonic's principal cellist in the Toscanini era prior to embarking on a conducting career. For this engagement he conducted the Philharmonic's first complete performance since 1942 of Berlioz's dramatic symphony *Roméo et Juliette*.

Any hopes that the season would continue without further incident were dashed when yet another conductor canceled. This time it was Igor Markevitch, who also was to have made his Philharmonic debut. His first week was taken over by Vladimir Golschmann, the second by Bernstein, who returned a week early from his long absence to begin his concluding series, entitled Keys to the Twentieth Century. Major works by Berg, Ives, Hindemith, Stravinsky, Ravel, Bartók, Pierre Boulez, Ben Weber (the world premiere of his Piano Concerto, with William Masselos as the soloist), Jean Sibelius, Aram Khachaturian, and Sergei Prokofieff were featured, along with a sprinkling of more standard fare. In memory of Mitropoulos, Bernstein performed Mahler's Third Symphony, which the Greek maestro had scheduled for his engagement, and which he had been rehearsing at the time of his death. Following a stupendous performance of *The Rite of Spring* on April 16, the orchestra left for a tour of Japan.

On the same date, in his first column as senior music critic, Harold Schonberg summed up the season that had just ended. While taking note of the various conductor cancellations, he took Bernstein to task for his absence of four months in the middle of the season, a situation that was to continue in the recently announced coming season. No orchestra, he said, could maintain its quality under a constant stream of guest conductors. David M. Keiser, president of the Philharmonic-Symphony Society, was quoted as saying that it was hoped Bernstein would be able to conduct for longer periods in the future. If not, the idea of an additional principal conductor might be explored. And yet, for Bernstein's concerts, at least, the orchestral playing was truly stunning, not only in the Mahler and Stravinsky works already mentioned, but in Ravel's complete score for *Daphnis et Chloé*, the first Philharmonic performances of the entire work, and in Bartók's Music for Strings, Percussion, and Celesta.

Schonberg also felt that, brilliant musician though Bernstein was, he had not developed an identification with the bulk of the standard repertoire—meaning that of the eighteenth and nineteenth centuries. He could be "the equal of any living conductor. But when will he settle down to it?" His activities in television, radio, education, touring, and recording were all very well, but were they "more important than the actual season itself?" In reviewing Glenn Gould's performance of the Beethoven Piano Concerto No. 4 on March 17, Schonberg, perhaps as a warm-up for one of his most famous reviews ever in the following season, had noted that Gould had sipped from a glass of water from time to time. "What next? Can we look forward to Mr. Gould's playing Beethoven next year with a seidel of beer and a ham sandwich to occupy himself during orchestral tuttis?"

Tragedy struck again on July 1 with the death at age thirty-six of the Philharmonic's managing director, George E. Judd, Jr., who in a very short time had proven himself to be an outstanding administrator. He was succeeded by his associate, Carlos Moseley, a native of Spartanburg, South Carolina, who had studied music at Duke University and piano with Olga Samaroff and had been for five years director of the University of Oklahoma School of Music. He had also held several government music administration posts and may well have been the first trained musician to hold this position with the Philharmonic, at least in modern times.

And the opening of Lincoln Center was further postponed to September 1962.

FAREWELL TO CARNEGIE

On April 12, 1961, the new crop of assistant conductors (often referred to as "The Three Musketeers") was announced: Seiji Ozawa, Maurice Peress, and me. Ozawa surely needs no introduction today. Suffice it to say that, having studied at Tanglewood, he had been recommended to Bernstein by Olga Koussevitzky (the wife of the conductor) and Charles Munch. Peress had been active in New York as a trumpet player and was then on the faculty of New York University, whose orchestra he conducted, as well as the Washington Square Orchestra. I had studied with Jean Morel at Juilliard and with Pierre Monteux at his summer school in Hancock, Maine, and, like Schermerhorn, had conducted the Seventh Army Symphony.

How were assistant conductors, at least these three, selected? After receiving a hundred or more applications, Bernstein narrowed the field down to twelve and then divided them into two groups of six, each of which was to meet with him in his studio in the Osborne apartment building, located on Fifty-seventh Street diagonally across from Carnegie Hall, after one of the Friday afternoon Philharmonic concerts. The choice of Ozawa had already been made. With only two slots open, he explained to those assembled that although it would be logical to have auditions for assistant conductors, it would mean setting aside a week with the Philharmonic while a parade of young maestros appeared before it, and that would be rather expensive. Also, he astutely pointed out that not everyone does his best at an audition. Therefore, we would engage in a general conversation about music, ourselves, the Philharmonic, and whatever else might develop, and he would see whether or not he could "smell a conductor." After an hour or so of rather animated discussion, his olfactory sense sniffed out Peress and the author.

A brief tour to Philadelphia, Baltimore, Richmond, and Washington led to the opening of the 1961–62 season on September 26, a pension-fund benefit concert on which the soprano Eileen Farrell sang Wagner's *Wesendonck-Lieder* and Immolation Scene from *Götterdämmerung*, as she had done on the tour (though not on the same program). In his opening remarks to the audience, Bernstein announced that the concert would be dedicated to the memory of "two saintly men," George E. Judd Jr. and Dag Hammarskjöld, secretary-general of the United Nations, who had died in a plane crash in Africa on September 18. He had been there trying to resolve a crisis in the Congo.

The first six weeks of the season were designated The Gallic Approach, a survey of French music interspersed with works by American composers who had studied in France with the great Nadia Boulanger, such men as Copland, Thomson, Harris, and David Diamond, whose Symphony No. 8 received its world premiere on October 26. But again not everything went as planned, for labor unrest returned. The contract between the Philharmonic and the musicians had expired on May 31, and the orchestra had agreed to play its tour and the first week of the season without a new contract while negotiations continued. However, matters came to a head when the musicians rejected management's "last and best offer," even though the executive board of Local 802 had recommended acceptance. At issue were salaries, length of season, overtime, per diem allowances during tours, vacations, and the length of the contract. The musicians wanted a one-year contract, under which they had played for many years, but one with year-round employment and an increase of $32.50 over their then current minimum weekly salary of $180, while management, for the first time ever, had offered a three-year contract with a gradually increased season, reaching forty-two weeks by 1963–64.

For the first time in the orchestra's history, the musicians went on strike and an entire week of concerts was canceled. In the end, the players voted to accept the contract originally offered, though at 57 to 41 the vote was hardly unanimous. In his article of Sunday, October 15, Schonberg wrote that the musicians felt they had not been granted an adequate say in the Philharmonic's policies. He cited the fact that a few weeks previously, the management had invited members of the press and various concert managers to visit the unfinished Philharmonic Hall at Lincoln Center to show them how the construction was progressing. "Why weren't we invited?" asked one of the orchestral musicians. "After all, we're the men who are going to make music there. Aren't we entitled to look, too?" Schonberg hoped that management would realize they were dealing not with workmen, but with artists, and that those artists would be a bit less emotionally hysterical when the new contract expired in three years.

As the Mahler theme had done, the Gallic Approach series carried over to the Young People's concerts. For a program entitled "What Is Impressionism?" on October 14, the young audience was treated to a complete performance, with explanations, of Debussy's *La mer*, another rarity for such concerts. Following this series an actual Gallic conductor took over as guest for two weeks: Paul Paray of the Detroit Symphony, who had come to be a fairly regular visitor since his first appearances in 1956. Perhaps in deference to the series just concluded, he offered no French music except for Ravel's *Bolero*. His programs were mostly Germanic, save for the closing work in his first week, Ottorino Respighi's *Pines of Rome*.

Most music lovers assume that concerts by major symphony orchestras are played without serious mishaps, and usually that is the case. An exception was the Friday matinee concert of November 12. *The Pines of Rome* is noted (or notorious) for a particularly delicate moment that occurs at the end of its third section, "The Pines of the Janiculum." Here a lovely moonlit scene has been evoked: a beautiful soft unaccompanied clarinet solo gives way to some quietly trilling violins, after which a nightingale is heard singing in the distance. Respighi felt that no musical instrument could do justice to the sound of a nightingale and specified that a recording of a nightingale should be played at that point. In fact, when one receives the orchestral material from the publisher, the recording is included.

All had gone well at the Thursday preview. On Friday afternoon, one heard the solo clarinet, beautifully played by Stanley Drucker, then the hushed trilling violins, wonderfully atmospheric, followed by some rather loud scratchy surface noise and then what sounded for an instant like the screaming of an eagle, which suddenly ceased. After a few seconds the nightingale emerged in proper perspective, but the effect had been ruined. It seems that someone had, most likely inadvertently, increased the volume level on the phonograph. Paray was furious, and for the remaining performances the recording was taped and kept under lock and key in the office of the personnel manager, Joseph De Angelis. (Today, of course, a CD is used.) Alan Rich was the *Times* critic for this concert, which also included Beethoven's Symphony No. 6 ("Pastoral"), in which a nightingale is impersonated by a flute. Rich concluded that "Beethoven's imagined nightingale, however hurried, is a far more musical bird than Respighi's canned concoction."

The respected Viennese maestro Josef Krips, then conductor of the Buffalo Philharmonic, had made his New York City debut in 1957 with the Symphony of the Air and was further known to New York audiences and members of the Philharmonic through his conducting at the Lewisohn Stadium summer concerts, where he presided over Beethoven festivals. On November 23, 1961, began a four-week guest engagement, his first with the Philharmonic in Carnegie Hall. His first program was a typical one for him: Mozart's "Haffner" Symphony, Prokofieff's Piano Concerto No. 2, and Brahms's Symphony No. 1. The soloist in the concerto was the Russian-born American pianist Shura Cherkassky, also making his debut with the Philharmonic. He had been absent from the United States for many years prior to returning in the previous season.

Krips made an initial great impression on the orchestra in works they already knew extremely well. The Friday matinee performance of the Brahms symphony, for example, was regarded by many as the finest they had ever played. Harold Gomberg, the veteran principal oboist and not one to praise conductors unduly, was heard to exclaim later, "I've played hundreds of performances of the Brahms First, but I never played one as good as that!"

But again the week's concerts were not without incident. When Cherkassky sat down to begin the concerto on Thursday evening, he had to turn the knobs on the side of the piano bench several times to adjust it to the proper height. Afterward he expressed great displeasure to the management, for the bench had been left at the correct height when he finished his rehearsal. Strict instructions were then issued that no one was to tamper with Cherkassky's bench. On Friday there was no problem.

Before the Saturday night CBS broadcast, Jim Fassett, the urbane radio commentator, asked the stagehands if they could move the piano into place as quickly as possible, for the program was running a bit longer than usual. After the "Haffner" Symphony, out came the piano in record time, followed very soon by Cherkassky and Krips. Seating himself, Cherkassky began turning the knobs, or at least he tried to. They were stuck and the bench could not be raised. He looked helplessly at Krips and at nearby orchestra musicians, some of whom tried to assist in turning the knobs, to no avail.

Meanwhile the audience began chattering and tittering a bit, wondering if the performance would ever begin. The third-chair second violinist Armand Neveux left the stage, then reappeared moments later holding aloft a very large bright red cushion, causing the audience to burst into laughter and applause (Fassett dutifully describing the scene to the radio audience). When Cherkassky, a rather diminutive person, sat upon the cushion, it was much too high for him—his feet did not touch the floor. More laughter. But the bench could be lowered from that point, and the concerto was finally performed. On Sunday afternoon the cushion was already in place. Later Neveux explained, in his distinctive French accent, "You know, there were two cushions backstage, a brown one and a red one. Naturally I chose the red one, for the effect!"

The Philharmonic's Saturday night performances, broadcast nationwide, were often the least satisfactory of the week, while the best were usually the Friday matinees. The explanation for this odd situation lies in the rest of the schedule. The Thursday night concerts, coming on the heels of that morning's dress rehearsal, were invariably well performed. Between Thursday night and Friday afternoon—about eighteen hours—nothing else was scheduled, so with Thursday's fine concert under its belt, the orchestra would always surpass itself on Friday with a truly magnificent performance—Krips's Brahms First is a case in point. However, in the thirty hours or so between Friday afternoon and Saturday night the orchestra may have had a Young People's Concert on Saturday morning, or some other activity collectively or for the musicians individually, such as teaching. Thus, by the time the Saturday night broadcast came around, the musicians were often tired or distracted, which in turn led to such mishaps as missed entrances and other mistakes. Krips's Brahms First on Saturday was not the equal of what it had been on Friday. Sunday afternoon was almost comparable to Friday afternoon: in the few hours between Saturday night and Sunday afternoon, no extra concerts, lessons, or other activities were scheduled.

In December the first Dimitri Mitropoulos International Music Competition was held under the sponsorship of the Federation for Jewish Philanthropies. This initial competition was for pianists and resulted in four finalists performing with the New York Philharmonic at the Metropolitan Opera House on December 17. Josef Krips, who had told the Philharmonic assistants without explanation, "I never conduct one note by Lehár or Rachmaninoff," had been scheduled to conduct, only to learn that one of the finalists, Agustin Anievas, was to play the dreaded Rachmaninoff's *Rhapsody on a Theme of Paganini*. Krips remained true to his principles and withdrew, and Theodore Bloomfield, music director of the Rochester Philharmonic, arrived virtually at the last minute to conduct the rehearsal on Saturday and the concert on Sunday. The New York–born Anievas, a Juilliard graduate, emerged the winner. (The assistant conductors were a bit miffed that they were not asked to take over, but the concert was not under Philharmonic auspices.)

Other guest conductors that season were Thomas Schippers, Georg Solti, William Steinberg (in his first Philharmonic appearances since 1944), Leopold Stokowski (substituting for Fritz Reiner, who again canceled), Alfred Wallenstein, and, the most special of all, Nadia Boulanger. In an engagement honoring her seventy-fifth birthday, the great French teacher of composition and theory to more than two generations of American composers became the first woman to conduct the Philharmonic in a complete concert.

The first half of her program was devoted to the Fauré Requiem, of which she was a noted interpreter, and which received an absolutely glowing performance under her hands (the last two performances were dedicated to the memory of Bruno Walter, who had just died). Unfortunately, Columbia Records did not seize the opportunity to record the work with her, but it is included in the Philharmonic's CD set of historic broadcast performances. On the second half were a short orchestral work by one of her pupils, Virgil Thomson, and three psalm settings by her sister, Lili Boulanger, who had died tragically young. Nadia Boulanger always claimed that her sister was the great musician in the family, and dressed in black for the rest of her life in perpetual mourning for her.

Boulanger charmed the orchestra at the beginning of her first rehearsal by announcing, in decidedly unconductorly fashion, "Gentlemen, I realize that I need you more than you need me," a remark that brought forth a round of applause from the men (at the time the Philharmonic was still an all-male orchestra). By the end of her rehearsal period, however, she had outstayed her welcome a bit by her fastidious insistence on proper rhythmic values, such as the fact that a dotted quarter note followed by a sixteenth note should be the equivalent of four sixteenth notes, and not be rushed. One often felt she was just a step away from having the orchestra clap out the rhythms as if it were a student ensemble. It was the good fortune of the assistant conductors to be asked by the management to take her to lunch at the Russian Tea Room on rehearsal days. At one point the conversation concerned some of her gifted pupils who had become well-known conductors, such as Igor Markevitch and Stanisław Skrowaczewski. "Yes," she commented, "I wish they would all break their arms!"

Stokowski had not met the assistant conductors before his first rehearsal but, once he had begun, noticed them seated at the rear of the stage, their scores in their laps. He stopped the rehearsal and asked loudly, "Who are those young men sitting over there?" A chorus from the orchestra replied, "Assistant conductors, assistant conductors," whereupon Stokowski said, "I thought they looked strange." As was his custom, Stokowski completely reseated the orchestra, with all the violins and violas massed to his left and in front of him and the woodwinds to his right, where the violas and cellos normally sat. The cellos were lined up on a platform at the rear of the stage, the double basses on the stage floor to their left as one faces the stage. The brass and percussion were in the center and to the right, behind the strings and woodwinds. The idea behind the string seating was to have all the instruments' f holes, the curved cutouts on the top, facing out toward the audience. The positioning of the woodwinds meant they did not have to force to be heard through the strings. Whatever his reasoning, there is no denying that, with a minimum of rehearsal for a program that included music from the third act of Wagner's *Parsifal* and the Shostakovich Fifth Symphony, Stokowski produced an absolutely glorious sound from the orchestra. (During his week he had mildly belittled the idea of three assistant conductors. Why not five or seven? he wanted to know; seven was a better number than three! In the fall of 1962 Stokowski began the first season of his newly formed American Symphony Orchestra, for which he appointed three assistant conductors.)

One of Bernstein's most interesting television programs was not a Young People's Concert, but one of several intended for adult viewers, of the type he had presented on *Omnibus* before taking over the Philharmonic. Entitled "The Drama of Carmen" and focusing on the characters of Carmen and Don José, this presentation went back to Bizet's original version with spoken dialogue, rather than the version normally heard at that time, for which Bizet's friend Ernest Guiraud had composed musical recitatives. By alternating the sung *Carmen*, performed in French, with the spoken version in English delivered by actors, Bernstein was able to cast a new light on a familiar score, especially because the spoken dialogue provided insights into the characters of the two main protagonists. Jane Rhodes and William Olvis were the principal singers, Zohra Lampert and James Congdon the actors, with subsidiary vocal roles taken by William Chapman, Reri Grist, and Janis Martin. As Harold Schonberg put it, "A few million people yesterday ended up knowing much more about *Carmen* than when they had turned the dial ninety minutes previously." Today Bizet's original is no longer a rarity, but the preferred version.

Bernstein returned for the final portion of the season, which bore the label "The Middle-European Approach" (originally announced as "The Teutonic Approach"). The repertoire was largely Austro-Germanic, and before the first program of the series Bernstein spoke apologetically to the audience concerning his long absences in the middle of the current season and the preceding one and announced, "I will never do it again," for which he received much applause.

No performances aroused greater controversy than those of the Brahms Piano Concerto No. 1 on April 5, 6, and 8, 1962, with Glenn Gould returning as the soloist. The event has now passed into the realm of legend. Before Gould's arrival in New York, Bernstein told his assistants and others of having received a phone call from Gould the previous week in which the pianist spoke of his ideas about tempos in the piece and then began singing themes from the concerto as Bernstein, who was in the midst of a dinner party, passed the phone around among the guests. When the phone was returned to Bernstein, Gould was still singing. The upshot was that Gould's proposed tempos were markedly slower than what was considered the norm in those days.

When Gould arrived for rehearsals he was adamant about observing the slower tempos, with which Bernstein did not agree. In the end, Bernstein felt he had to make a disclaimer to the audience to the effect that while he did not agree with Gould's concept of the concerto, he felt the opinions of a great artist deserved to be heard. It is not clear which was more controversial, Bernstein's remarks to the audience (given with Gould's approval), or the performance itself, which indeed was slower than usual, with some changes of dynamics as well. Columbia Records canceled its plans to record the work with Gould and Bernstein, but the complete performance of April 6 (taped for the CBS broadcast), along with Bernstein's speech, can be heard on compact disc (Sony CD SK 60675).

It was by no means certain, even after the final rehearsal, that the performances would take place. The orchestra had the Brahms First Symphony in its folders, just in case. (The symphony had been programmed for the Saturday night concert, for which Gould was not scheduled.) The principal oboist, Harold Gomberg, who was not to play the concerto but would play the symphony, was standing by backstage before the performance. Only when the portentous opening of the concerto burst forth did he leave the hall.

Many reviews, articles, and books have been written about this performance, none of which mention its most unusual visual aspect—that Gould played the Brahms concerto from the orchestral score. He had two large pieces of stiff cardboard, on each of which were pasted four pages of the score, two above two. The cardboards, arranged as a normal score or book would be, stretched across the music rack and beyond (in fact, the music rack had to be extended), enabling him to have eight pages of the score in front of him. In this way he did not have to turn pages very often, but when he *did*—fortunately, during orchestral passages—his laborious efforts were something to behold.

Gould appeared to thoroughly enjoy the whole event, including the loud boos from some audience members at the end. He was pleased that his interpretation had provoked some controversy, which he preferred to complacent acceptance. Before the Sunday afternoon concert, Bernstein suggested to Gould that, since the work had been played twice according to his wishes, they could at least meet halfway for the final performance. Gould agreed, with the result that Bernstein did not make his speech on Sunday, and the performance, if not a halfway meeting, was a shade or two brisker.

Preceding the Brahms concerto were the Overture to *Maskarade* and the Symphony No. 5 by Carl Nielsen, the first works by the great Danish composer ever played by the New York Philharmonic. Just as controversial as Bernstein's speech and Gould's interpretation was Harold Schonberg's review in the *Times* of

April 7. It was written in the form of an imaginary conversation with someone named Ossip (as in Ossip Gabrilowitsch, a pianist of an earlier generation who had also been conductor of the Detroit Symphony).

"Such goings-on at the New York Philharmonic concert yesterday afternoon! I tell you, Ossip, like you never saw." Schonberg continued by speculating that the reason "the Gould boy" played the Brahms concerto so slowly was that his technique was "not so good." He further criticized Gould for the relative softness of the performance and for his invention of inner voices that were so prominent. But Bernstein did not escape criticism—not only for the speech, but for engaging "the Gould boy" in the first place. "Who is the musical director? Somebody has to be responsible." The other New York critics were equally negative, though they expressed their opinions in a more traditional format. It is thought the whole episode played a part in Gould's decision, a year later, to retire from the concert stage and devote himself to recording.

On May 10, 1962, the announcement was made that three new assistant conductors had been selected for the following season: Serge Fournier, Yuri Krasnopolsky, and Zoltán Rozsnyai, all of whom had been chosen not through group meetings with Bernstein, but as a result of auditions with the Juilliard Orchestra. Fournier, a graduate of the Paris Conservatory, had won the 1961 Koussevitzky Conducting Prize at Tanglewood and had appeared with various orchestras in France. The American-born Krasnopolsky, a pupil of Bernstein's at Tanglewood, had conducted operatic performances in St. Louis and Los Angeles and had been associate conductor of the American Ballet Theatre. Rozsnyai, born in Budapest, had been conductor of the Philharmonia Hungarica, an orchestra of Hungarian refugees with which he toured the United States in 1959.

In his summation of the season on May 20, Schonberg took Bernstein to task in often rather scathing terms, chastising his decision to conduct for only twelve weeks with a long absence in the middle (the fact that he would conduct two additional weeks in the following season was "not exactly a big deal"), for attaching "synthetic labels" to his concert series, and for abdicating the music director's responsibility in the Glenn Gould incident. He felt the Philharmonic was not playing up to its full potential and concluded by dubbing Bernstein "the Peter Pan of Music."

Since the 1958–59 season CBS had been broadcasting the Saturday evening concerts over its nationwide radio network. But not all the local stations liked that arrangement, and some began carrying the programs on a tape-delay basis at what was for them a more convenient time. New York's WCBS was one of these. And what was a more appropriate time than three o'clock on Sunday afternoons, for so many years before 1958 the traditional time for the Philharmonic's broadcasts?

This format began during the 1961–62 season, but did not survive it, for WCBS also carried the Yankees games, and when April arrived a conflict arose between New York's orchestra and its baseball team when the latter played on Sunday afternoon, as they usually did, especially when there was a doubleheader. The Yankees won this particular contest, and the Philharmonic's broadcasts were shifted to Sunday evenings, often at rather odd times, such as 7:11, 9:45, 8:17, and 8:31— whenever the games were over.

To make up for a week of concerts lost because of the musicians' strike, an extra week was added at the end of the season, May 16–20, during which the eightieth birthday of Igor Stravinsky was observed with his *Greeting Prelude* (based on "Happy Birthday" and composed to honor Pierre Monteux's eightieth in 1955), *Fireworks*, and the Capriccio for Piano and Orchestra, with Seymour Lipkin as the soloist. (On the Young People's Concert of March 24, entitled "Happy Birthday, Igor Stravinsky," the complete *Petrushka* had been performed.) Joseph Fuchs gave the New York premiere of Walter Piston's Violin Concerto No. 2. The program, and the season, ended with Brahms's Second Symphony. It had already been announced that Lincoln Center would finally open on September 23, so these concerts were the Philharmonic's farewell to Carnegie Hall, where it had performed for seventy-one years. On Sunday afternoon, as an emotion-laden ten-minute standing ovation following the Brahms symphony was drawing to a close, Bernstein impulsively threw his baton into the audience.

Following a short tour to Baltimore, Washington, and suburban Philadelphia— all-Tchaikovsky concerts conducted by André Kostelanetz—the orchestra assembled on the morning of June 4 on the stage of the as yet unfinished Philharmonic Hall to begin the all-important "tuning week." Under the supervision of the acoustician Leo Beranek, of the firm of Bolt, Beranek, and Newman, extensive and elaborate procedures were carried out to test the new performing space's acoustics. Rifle and pistol shots were fired to determine the hall's degree of reverberation, dummies were placed in the seats to simulate the presence of an audience, and a musical composition written expressly for the occasion, Daniel Pinkham's *Catacoustical Measures*, was played many times under differing acoustical circumstances.

Besides Bernstein, such esteemed conductors as Leopold Stokowski and Erich Leinsdorf were in attendance, not to mention the three assistant conductors, who led the orchestra in a wide range of pieces of differing styles and instrumentation, from Mozart to Rachmaninoff. Stokowski himself took the podium, his sole conducting consisting of the two opening chords of Beethoven's "Eroica" Symphony, played at different dynamics, from *fortissimo* to *pianissimo*, sometimes with the addition of a bass drum, after which he remarked, "I wasn't called soon enough."

Lincoln Center at Last

September 23, 1962, was a historic date in the annals of New York City: the grand opening of Lincoln Center for the Performing Arts, so many years in the planning. Not that Philharmonic Hall was completely ready for the occasion, but at least it was usable. Bernstein had assembled an unusual program for the event: the Gloria from Beethoven's *Missa solemnis*, the world premiere of Aaron Copland's *Connotations* (one of ten works commissioned by the Philharmonic for its first season at Lincoln Center), Ralph Vaughan Williams's enchanting *Serenade to Music*, and the first movement of Mahler's Eighth Symphony. There was some press criticism over this program, consisting as it did of excerpts from two larger works, but Bernstein defended it, declaring that a special event deserved a special kind of program, not an ordinary symphony concert. Participating in the program were the Schola Cantorum of New York, the Juilliard Chorus, the Columbus Boychoir, and the vocal soloists Adele Addison, Lucine Amara, Donald Bell, Charles Bressler, Lili Chookasian, Eileen Farrell, Ezio Flagello, George London, Jennie Tourel, Richard Tucker, Shirley Verrett (then Verrett-Carter), and Jon Vickers.

President and Mrs. John F. Kennedy had been invited to the opening night, and there was much consternation when it was learned that neither would be attending, especially because they had expressed their support of American culture. Finally, at the eleventh hour, Mrs. Kennedy changed her mind. Among the endearing visual memories of the evening was Bernstein kissing Mrs. Kennedy during the intermission, on national television, and apologizing for being "all sweaty." Another was Governor Nelson Rockefeller starting to applaud after "The Star Spangled Banner," the sole person to do so. (In those days one was taught not to applaud the national anthem, something apparently no longer true today.)

The Copland work was not in the composer's folksy Americana style, but rather a dissonant, severe piece in the twelve-tone idiom. In its own way it probably set back the cause of American music at least ten years, for millions of television viewers across the country, people who in their everyday lives had little or no exposure to modern symphonic music, reacted to it with such negativity that the composer of *Appalachian Spring* and *Rodeo* became the symbol for extreme dissonance in music. A conductor of a mid- to lower-echelon orchestra could be accused of playing "too much Copland" when he had not played any Copland at all.

What drew the attention of those in the hall at least as much as the musical program, if not more, was the acoustics. What did the new hall sound like? Depending on where one sat, excellent or not very good, with the latter opinion more in evidence. The main criticism had to do with weakness of the bass frequencies and a general muddiness of texture, though concerts later in the week by other orchestras led to a reassessment of that view. But if the bass was more pronounced in the program by Eugene Ormandy and the Philadelphia Orchestra, a powerful bass sonority was one of that orchestra's normal characteristics. If greater clarity was evident when George Szell and the Cleveland Orchestra occupied the stage, was that not one of their prime attributes anyway?

The first orchestra to perform in Philharmonic Hall after the New York Philharmonic was the Boston Symphony Orchestra on September 24. This concert was notable for being the orchestra's first in New York with its new music director, Erich Leinsdorf, and for presenting the world premiere of Samuel Barber's Piano Concerto, performed by John Browning, for whom it was written. As the season progressed there was ample opportunity to tinker with the acoustics (the many overhead "clouds" allowed for this), but George Szell, never at a loss for a caustic remark, said they should simply tear the place down and start over. Orchestra musicians complained they could not hear each other well on the stage, but, incredible as it may seem, the same complaint was heard when the Philharmonic was at Carnegie Hall.

Other works commissioned by the Philharmonic and performed in the opening season were by Barber (*Andromache's Farewell*), Hans Werner Henze (Symphony No. 5), Hindemith (Organ Concerto), Darius Milhaud (*Ouverture philharmonique*), Francis Poulenc (*Sept répons des ténèbres* [Six Responses for the Tenebrae]), and William Schuman (Symphony No. 8). None of these works have yet entered the active repertoire. Three more were to follow in later seasons. The Schuman symphony was premiered in the Philharmonic's first subscription week, causing Winthrop Sargeant, music critic of the *New Yorker*, to complain about what he considered to be the politics of having a major work by the president of Lincoln Center performed in such a high-profile situation.

A change in format marked this gala season: the elimination of the Thursday night previews. These would now be normal concerts as before, with the critics in attendance then rather than on Fridays. Also gone, at least for this season, was thematic programming. Along with the commissioned works, the new hall was the main attraction. Guest conductors were Karl Böhm, Sir John Barbirolli, Lorin Maazel (in his Philharmonic debut), George Szell (after an absence from the Philharmonic of six years), Paul Hindemith, and Thomas Schippers. As he had been doing for several years, André Kostelanetz led several programs of lighter classics, although one could hardly place the pension-fund concert of January 22 in that category, when he conducted the final scene from Richard Strauss's *Salome* with Birgit Nilsson as soloist, definitely uncharacteristic repertoire for "Kosty."

A serendipitous occasion became one of the season's high points. Glenn Gould had been reengaged for the concerts of January 31 and February 1, to play a Bach concerto and the Richard Strauss *Burleske*, but on January 29 he informed the Philharmonic management that he was ill and could not appear. In his place Bernstein selected a sixteen-year old pianist who had made a great impression in the Liszt Concerto No. 1 on a Young People's Concert a few weeks before. His name was André Watts, and he made a sensational formal debut with the orchestra playing the same concerto. Watts has since gone on to a stellar solo career.

In the middle of the season the orchestra made a quick trip to London, where, with Bernstein conducting, it performed at the Royal Festival Hall on February 13, 1963, as part of the celebrations honoring the 150th anniversary of the Royal Philharmonic Society. An additional London concert and one in Manchester, as well as a Young People's Concert in London, completed the visit, after which the Philharmonic flew directly to Florida for a week of concerts in Miami, Miami Beach, and Ft. Lauderdale—the orchestra's first appearances in the Sunshine State.

It was decided that although the first Dimitri Mitropoulos Competition had been for pianists, the second would be for conductors. There would be three winners, and as part of their prize, they would become the Philharmonic's assistant conductors for the 1963–64 season. After the usual preliminary and final rounds, the winning trio shared a special Philharmonic concert on April 7: Claudio Abbado, Pedro Calderón, and Zdeněk Koslĕr. Like Seiji Ozawa and André Watts, Claudio Abbado, who studied at Tanglewood in 1958 and had conducted in his native Italy, requires no introduction today. The Argentine Calderón had conducted regularly in Buenos Aires, and the Czech Koslĕr was a regular guest conductor in Prague with the Czech Philharmonic. For the first time since the inception of the program, there were no Americans among the Philharmonic assistant conductors.

A significant damper on the 1962–63 season, and not just for the Philharmonic, was a New York newspaper strike lasting 114 days. Young musicians who depended on New York reviews to further their careers were the most severely affected, and the lack of advance publicity took its toll on attendance at concerts not subscribed or already sold out. Many solo recitals were canceled or postponed by various managements.

Through it all, the music critics continued to attend, in the hope that, once the strike ended, they could publish a summary of events. Some of them appeared on television and radio newscasts, such as the *New York Times* critics on WQXR, the classical music station owned by the *Times*; and some reports did see the light of day in other newspapers, as the critics filed their reviews with the wire services. While the Philharmonic and the Metropolitan Opera were not seriously affected, many in New York's musical community, those organizations included, felt as though they were operating in a vacuum. At the time, concerts were regularly reviewed in several New York papers besides the *Times*, including the *Herald Tribune*, the *Journal-American*, the *World-Telegram and the Sun* (one paper), and the *Post*. Very occasionally the *Daily News* also reviewed a classical concert. Also important in the reviewing of New York concerts were three magazines: the *New Yorker*, the *Saturday Review*, and *Musical America*, though this last was soon to cease publication.

A potentially more serious vacuum for the Philharmonic was threatened by the announcement on May 27, 1963, that, after thirty-three years, the Columbia Broadcasting System was discontinuing the orchestra's radio broadcasts. A national institution when they had been heard on Sunday afternoons, the broadcasts had lost impact with the move to Saturday night, a time when many people are out and about, and with the decision by some local stations to carry them on a tape-delay basis. CBS felt the radio audience had been "constantly diminishing." The Philharmonic disagreed, citing the millions of listeners and radio members throughout the country. For the 1963–64 season the Philharmonic followed the lead of the Metropolitan Opera in forming its own radio network of participating stations throughout the country. In New York the Sunday afternoon concerts were carried live over WOR, with the Met's venerable Milton Cross delivering the commentary. CBS did, however, continue to televise the Young People's Concerts.

Also announced as the 1962–63 season drew to a close was Leonard Bernstein's plan for a sabbatical during the 1964–65 season, something his contract allowed. The announced reason for the leave was to allow Bernstein to compose another Broadway musical. The Society's president, David Keiser, reiterated that Bernstein's contract called for his conducting a minimum of twelve weeks per season in New York, along with myriad other activities in education, television, radio, touring, and recording. He added that it was hoped that in the future Bernstein could conduct a longer portion of the season, but if not, an additional principal conductor could be found to fill in. To this end, the same announcement stated that William Steinberg, music director of the Pittsburgh Symphony, would conduct a significant number of concerts during the sabbatical year.

In an effort to extend the orchestra's season—and to take advantage of Philharmonic Hall's air conditioning—a spring concert series was planned, to take place immediately following the subscription season. The Promenade Concerts would be patterned somewhat after the famous Boston Pops concerts. Seats were removed, and the young Peter Wexler was engaged to design the Promenades: scenery, lighting, interior and exterior of the hall, graphics, and costumes. The downstairs section of the hall was converted into what amounted to a large restaurant, with many tables at which light refreshments could be served, while the seats of the loge and terraces remained in place. Decor appropriate to the theme of the concert graced the stage. Wexler was also responsible for the outside banners calling attention to the concerts.

André Kostelanetz became the principal conductor of the Proms, as they were soon called, in the manner of the BBC's Promenade Concerts in London, although those were (and still are) serious symphonic concerts. The Philharmonic's Proms consisted mostly of the lighter fare associated with Kostelanetz, though a bit more sophisticated than Arthur Fiedler's Boston Pops programs, which tended to include, besides more standard fare, such novelty numbers as *Classical Juke Box*, *Jingles all the Way*, and arrangements of popular songs of the day. The opening program was devoted to American music and included Copland's *Lincoln Portrait*, with Carl Sandburg as narrator; William Schuman's *New England Triptych*; and the New York premiere of *Catfish Row*, Gershwin's own suite from *Porgy and Bess*. The hall was gaily decorated for the occasion, and a good time was had by all, including Harold Schonberg. Other programs were to include vocal and instrumental soloists and dancers. Appearing as guest conductors in the first season of Proms, which were given five times a week, were Morton Gould and, in his debut as a Philharmonic conductor, André Previn. The Proms developed into a New York springtime institution and continued until shortly before Kostelanetz's death in 1980.

Summing up the Philharmonic's subscription season on May 26, Schonberg felt that, in spite of the glittering opening of Lincoln Center and the commissioning of new works, "the entire season was somewhat grey and lacking in adventure." The choice of commissioned composers, Henze excepted, was unenterprising, consisting as it did of well-established figures; some younger, talented, more adventuresome composers should also have been invited to contribute. Mostly the season was made up of fairly safe standard repertoire, with a few exceptions, such as Leoš Janáček's *Glagolitic Mass*, Roberto Gerhard's First Symphony, Berg's Violin Concerto, and Hindemith's Requiem.

Since Bernstein had conducted less than half the season, the orchestra had had to accustom itself to a series of guest conductors. Bernstein's interpretation of classical and romantic repertoire also came in for criticism. Though Schonberg acknowledged "the genius that makes Bernstein Bernstein," he felt that, with his various other activities, he was spreading himself too thin, and that neither he nor the Philharmonic was living up to its potential.

CHAPTER 3

1963–67

THE AVANT-GARDE AND "KADDISH"

When Josef Krips and George Szell were announced as the sole guest conductors for the 1963–64 season, each for eight weeks, some members of the orchestra cringed a bit, fearing an inundation of Bruckner symphonies. Bruckner lovers may not realize how strongly disliked the master is by orchestral musicians on account of the great length and general massiveness of his symphonies. Strangely enough, Mahler does not provoke the same reaction, perhaps because his works are more varied in their textures and orchestration.

In the event, only two Bruckner symphonies appeared that year, No. 4 (under Krips) and No. 7 (under Szell). The engagement of these two conductors, steeped in the central European tradition, was the Philharmonic's solution to filling the gaps left by Bernstein's absences. They would bring stability to the season and present audiences with works from the core repertoire, in contrast with Bernstein's more adventuresome programming.

Nothing was more core repertoire than the all-Beethoven program with which Szell began his engagement on November 21, 1963: *Leonore* Overture No. 3, the Piano Concerto No. 4 with Robert Casadesus as soloist, and the Fifth Symphony. At the Friday matinee, as the orchestra was concluding the overture, the news was received that President John F. Kennedy had been assassinated in Dallas. The remainder of the concert was canceled, and on Saturday and Sunday the Funeral March from Beethoven's "Eroica" Symphony substituted for the overture. It was the third time in the orchestra's history that a concert had been affected by a presidential death, the second by an assassination.

Bernstein's adventuresome programming had already been illustrated by the concerts of October 17–20, an all-Stravinsky program unusual in two respects: it was the first such program the Philharmonic had ever given that was not conducted by the composer, and it included none of the expected ballet music. It was devoted instead to the three mature symphonies, *Symphony of Psalms*, Symphony in C, and *Symphony in Three Movements*, perhaps the first time anywhere that the three were given on the same program. The last had been commissioned by the Philharmonic and first performed by them in 1946, with the composer conducting. Word had it that Stravinsky was annoyed the work had not been played by the Philharmonic since, so possibly this program was a way of making amends. Bernstein had planned to conduct the entire program, but a slight eye injury made it difficult for him to prepare all three works, so he handed over the Symphony in C to one of the assistant conductors, Zdeněk Koslěr.

The season had opened on September 24 with a pension-fund benefit that included scenes from Richard Strauss's *Der Rosenkavalier*, with Phyllis Curtin, Judith Raskin, and Regina Sarfaty as the soloists. The benefit was followed by the opening of the subscription season on September 26, the first of four performances of Mahler's Symphony No. 2 ("Resurrection"), in which the soloists were Jennie Tourel and Lee Venora, with the Collegiate Chorale. The next week brought the world premiere of one of the Philharmonic's commissioned works for the opening season of Lincoln Center, the Violin Concerto by the Argentine Alberto Ginastera, for which Ruggiero Ricci was the soloist.

Krips and Szell were, in fact, not the only guest conductors that season, though the other two were of a special nature. In 1962 the American Conductors Project, a three-year program sponsored by the Ford Foundation, had begun at Baltimore's Peabody Conservatory, whose president, Peter Mennin, had been the project's instigator. By the time it actually began, Mennin had moved to the presidency of the Juilliard School, where he succeeded William Schuman, who had taken the reins at Lincoln Center. Under the terms of the project, four young conductors were selected each year to spend ten weeks in Baltimore taking part in daily conducting workshop sessions with the Baltimore Symphony under the supervision of Alfred Wallenstein and such distinguished guests conductors as Szell, Max Rudolf, and Fausto Cleva. Beginning with the 1963–64 season, the New York Philharmonic and other major orchestras set aside a week in which graduates of the project would appear as guest conductors.

The Philharmonic chose Robert La Marchina and Amerigo Marino, the former directing the concerts of December 19 and 20, 1963, the latter those of December 21 and 22. Both were well received by the critical press, and La Marchina soon became the music director of the Metropolitan Opera National Company, a touring arm of the parent company, and then of the Honolulu Symphony, while Marino took over the Birmingham (now Alabama) Symphony.

No series embodied Bernstein's adventuresome programming better than that centered around the avant-garde (January 2–February 9), when works by Larry Austin, Earle Brown, John Cage, Morton Feldman, György Ligeti, Edgard Varèse (a classicist compared with the others), Yannis Xenakis, and Stefan Wolpe were interspersed with symphonies of Beethoven, Mendelssohn, and Tchaikovsky, along with three of the concertos of Vivaldi's *The Four Seasons*, with John Corigliano as the violin soloist. Additionally, Zino Francescatti performed French violin showpieces, Rudolf Serkin played Beethoven's Piano Concerto No. 3, and Aaron Copland was heard in his own Piano Concerto, once considered an avant-garde piece because of its integration of jazz elements.

Several factors combined to ignite the controversy the series provoked. The first was, of course, the conservative Philharmonic audience's general antipathy to modern music. The second was the extensive verbal comments Bernstein delivered before each piece, comments that in some instances were longer than the piece itself. Of course, Bernstein was known for these kinds of explications, but in this case many felt he was attempting to sugarcoat the music for the audience. For Harold Schonberg, this was "bad: bad psychology, bad music making, bad show business, bad everything." And the third was the feeling that Bernstein had programmed this music out of a sense of duty—that his heart was not really in it.

One of the works, the extremely complex Symphony No. 1 by the German-born Wolpe, was to receive its world premiere on January 16, to which Bernstein had assigned one of his former assistant conductors, Stefan Bauer-Mengelberg, on the grounds that he was a mathematician as well as a conductor and could thus somehow solve the score's complexities. Once rehearsals began, the work proved to be of even greater difficulty than first realized, and in the end only two movements could be given. While Schonberg did not care for what was heard of the Wolpe symphony, he was extremely complimentary toward Bernstein's performance of Beethoven's First Symphony ("one of the best and most convincing performances heard hereabouts in some time"), as he had been toward the Second Symphony two weeks earlier.

Originally scheduled for a six-week period, the avant-garde series lost a week when Bernstein absented himself from the concerts of January 30 to February 2 so he could attend the rehearsals and American premiere of his Third Symphony ("Kaddish") by the Boston Symphony, with Charles Munch conducting. The work had been one of those commissioned for the orchestra's seventy-fifth-anniversary season (1955–56), a deadline unmet by Bernstein, who had, in fact, conducted the world premiere in Israel a few months prior to the U.S. premiere. The lost avant-garde week, however, gave an opportunity to two of the Philharmonic's assistant conductors, Claudio Abbado, who directed the concerts of January 30 and 31, and Pedro Calderón, who led those of February 1 and 2. For both conductors the soloist was the American violinist Charles Treger, winner of the 1962 Wieniawski Competition in Poland, who impressed the audience in Mozart's Concerto No. 3 under Abbado and Szymanowski's Concerto No. 2 under Calderón.

Bernstein extended his adventuresome programming to the Young People's Concerts, for on January 25 he presented his young listeners with a program devoted to music of Paul Hindemith, who had died on December 28. Even for adults an all-Hindemith program is extremely rare, if not unheard of. A complete performance of the *Mathis der Maler* Symphony was the highlight of the program, which was reviewed in the *Times* by Howard Klein, who wrote that even though Bernstein talked over the heads of most of his audience, the "intensity of the experience" was what counted: "He could as well address the youngsters in Urdu, and they would get the point of the music, for the music is what is always uppermost."

An interview with George Szell appeared in the *New York Times* of Sunday, April 5, 1964, the last day of his subscription engagement. When the interviewer complimented him on his recent performances with the Philharmonic, he replied: "It takes about three weeks to pull the men out of improper playing habits, to sound like the great orchestra they can be. Once they're playing well they take a real pride in what they're doing and they enjoy it."

But one concert remained in Szell's engagement, a pension-fund benefit on April 7, on which the seventy-five-year-old Arthur Rubinstein would play both Brahms piano concertos. According to Schonberg in the *Times*, between Sunday and Tuesday Szell "came down with one of those virus things," and his place was taken by Alfred Wallenstein. Some people questioned the veracity of Szell's virus story. Had he withdrawn to avoid facing the Philharmonic after his comments on "improper playing habits"? On the other hand, Szell was not someone easily intimidated. As for Rubinstein, Schonberg found his playing full of "the kind of joie de vivre [that] is his and his alone, and the likes of it is [*sic*] not to be found in the music world today."

Bernstein returned to the podium for the concerts of April 9–12 and 14, concerts that featured the New York premiere of his "Kaddish" Symphony. Scored for narrator, mezzo-soprano, adult and children's choruses, and orchestra, it remains one of Bernstein's most controversial works, not only because it was based on the Jewish Kaddish (the prayer offered at synagogue services for the dead), but because it addresses God in a confrontational manner. Reviewed in the *Times* by Ross Parmenter, who had also attended the American premiere in Boston, the strictly musical portion of the work was now found to be less interesting and more derivative than before. The *New Yorker*'s Winthrop Sargeant wrote in the April 18 issue that during much of the narration and the solo singing "the listener is not quite sure whether God created Mr. Bernstein or Mr. Bernstein created God." The performers, however, received much praise from Parmenter: Bernstein's wife, Felicia Montealegre, as narrator, Jennie Tourel, the Camerata Singers, and the Columbus Boychoir.

Another commissioned work was given its world premiere on May 7: the Symphony No. 6 by Carlos Chávez. Perhaps to compensate for his having conducted only Stravinsky's Symphony in C in the early part of the season, while his two colleagues had each conducted entire subscription programs, Zdeněk Košler conducted the final work on the program, the lovely and lushly romantic Symphony in B-flat by Ernest Chausson. It had been a favorite of Mitropoulos, who programmed it several times with the Philharmonic; but so unfashionable has it now become that after the performance under Košler it was thirty-six years before the work appeared again on one of the orchestra's programs.

Beethoven's Ninth Symphony closed the season impressively on May 14–17, a season that was extended to thirty-two subscription weeks, two more than had been the norm since Bernstein's arrival. Beethoven symphonies predominated during the season because the orchestra was in the process of recording all of them with Bernstein for Columbia Records.

The most significant news of the season, announced on May 1, was that the Philharmonic would become the first orchestra in the nation to be employed on a fifty-two-week basis, effective with the beginning of the 1964–65 season. The new three-year contract provided for four weeks of paid vacation and a minimum weekly salary of $200 for the first two years and $210 for the third, along with other benefits related to scheduling, touring, the pension plan, and insurance. For the first time, a committee of orchestra members participated in the negotiations. Amyas Ames, president of the Philharmonic's board of directors, expressed great pride that an important goal had been reached, one of which orchestral associations and their musicians throughout the country had long dreamed. Al Manuti, president of Local 802, said, "I am sure that this year-round employment will enhance the cultural life of our city." That it did, but first the Philharmonic management had somehow to fill forty-eight of those fifty-two weeks.

SUMMER IN THE PARKS

On July 1, 1964, the great conductor Pierre Monteux died at the age of eighty-nine. He had been an intermittent guest of the Philharmonic during the winter seasons, but an annual one for the summer Lewisohn Stadium concerts. His place in music history is secure, for he conducted the world premieres of *The Rite of Spring*, *Petrushka*, *Daphnis et Chloé*, and other twentieth-century classics.

The 1964–65 season was Bernstein's sabbatical year, during which he planned to work on a musical adaptation of Thornton Wilder's *The Skin of our Teeth*. He was not giving up conducting altogether, however; his devotion to the Young People's

Concerts, and the importance he attached to them, were confirmed by his continuing to lead these events, still televised by CBS even though the network had discontinued the radio broadcasts.

Two maestros of the Germanic tradition were engaged to conduct the bulk of the season: William Steinberg for twelve weeks, Josef Krips for ten. The remainder would be divided between Thomas Schippers (six weeks) and Lorin Maazel (four weeks), plus one week for Seiji Ozawa, who was appointed the sole assistant conductor for the season, and one week to be shared by two graduates of the Peabody/Ford Foundation American Conductors Project. Those who are counting will note that the season would consist of thirty-four subscription weeks, the most ever.

The musicians' earlier fears were realized this season with the announcement of a cycle of Bruckner symphonies. Nos. 4 and 7 having been played the previous season, Steinberg would conduct Nos. 5, 6, and 8, while Krips would offer Nos. 3 and 9, as well as the Mass in F Minor. At the time, Nos. 3, 5, and 6 were rarely heard and had not been given by the Philharmonic in many years; the same was true of the F minor Mass. (The absence of Nos. 1 and 2 indicates they had almost disappeared from the repertoire, a situation that has improved a bit today. Also virtually nonexistent is the early symphony that Bruckner designated No. 0 ("Die Nulte"), and its predecessor, the "Study Symphony," sometimes listed as No. 00 but which, by this numbering system, really should be labeled No. -1.)

Philharmonic Hall had been closed from August 17 to September 12 so that changes in the acoustics could be implemented. The solutions proposed by the German acoustician Heinrich Keilholz, brought in by Lincoln Center and the Philharmonic, included a new design for the stage and a repositioning of the overhead clouds. Everything was put to the test on the evening of September 29, when Krips led the opening-night pension-fund benefit, a Viennese program of Schubert, Richard Strauss, and Johann Strauss.

Schonberg commented on the increase in reverberation time, from about 2 seconds to 2.2 seconds, and on the hall's "smoother and mellower sound," with "virtually no relation to that heard last season." The musicians were happy now they could hear themselves better onstage; they no longer felt as if they were playing in a vacuum. But there was still some echo in the hall, and the bass sonorities were still too weak. With no further alterations planned in the immediate or distant future, it became apparent that the hall would remain imperfect, a condition everyone would just have to live with.

An important personnel change within the orchestra occurred this season: the appointment of Lorne Munroe as principal cellist. Laszlo Varga, who had filled the post since 1951, had departed in 1962, and the associate principal, Carl Stern, had filled in until his retirement in 1964. Munroe came to the Philharmonic from a similar post with the Philadelphia Orchestra, his appointment setting off a chain reaction in other orchestras as Samuel Mayes went from Boston to Philadelphia and Jules Eskin left Cleveland for Boston. Munroe's Philharmonic debut took place on October 22–25 in the Dvořák Cello Concerto, with Krips conducting.

After an absence of seven years, Yehudi Menuhin returned as soloist for the concerts of October 15–18, finally forgiven for his audacity in playing an encore in 1957. This time he played the Bach Concertos in A Minor and E Major, and no encore. Krips, who had made a good impression conducting the Philharmonic in 1961 and again in 1963–64, was less fortunate this time. Many of his performances were found to be lacking in variety of pacing, such as the Bruckner Third on the program with Menuhin; stiff and literal in a contemporary work such as William Schuman's *Credendum*; and so flabby that he turned portions of Mahler's Fourth Symphony into "a blob of molasses," to quote Schonberg, who nevertheless found much to admire in the conductor's rendition of the Bruckner Ninth. In fact, Irving Kolodin in the *Saturday Review* of February 27, 1965, thought Krips gave this last work the best Philharmonic performance since Bruno Walter's in 1957. (There had been only one other presentation of the work since then, Bernstein's in 1962.)

Steinberg, on the other hand, made a predominantly good impression in virtually everything he conducted, especially in concert performances of Richard Strauss's *Elektra* on December 10–12. This work had been a specialty of Mitropoulos, who gave it in two of his seasons with the Philharmonic, the last time in 1958. According to Howard Klein in the *Times*, Steinberg's conducting was authoritative, producing shattering climaxes from the orchestra, yet allowing the music to breathe and not overpowering the singers, all of whom were highly praised: Astrid Varnay in the title role, Regina Resnik as Klytemnestra, and Phyllis Curtin as Chrysosthemis.

It came as no surprise, therefore, when the announcement was made on February 25, 1965, that Steinberg had been given the title of principal guest conductor of the Philharmonic and would direct twelve weeks per season during 1966–67 and 1967–68, preceded by four weeks during 1965–66. He was then in the midst of a year's leave of absence (one could hardly call it a sabbatical, given his workload at the time) from his regular post as music director of the Pittsburgh Symphony Orchestra, conducting twelve weeks (forty-eight concerts) with the Philharmonic and twenty-four performances at the Metropolitan Opera, where his repertoire consisted of *Aida*, *Die Walküre*, and Barber's *Vanessa*.

As far as can be determined, Steinberg, born in Cologne, Germany, in 1899, was the first conductor with any orchestra to be given the title principal guest conductor, one commonly in use today. From 1958 to 1962, in the midst of his tenure in Pittsburgh, he was also principal conductor of the London Philharmonic Orchestra, making him one of the first conductors of an American orchestra to be in charge of two orchestras simultaneously, a situation also common today, when some conductors even hold three or more posts at a time. Later (1969–72) he would direct both the Pittsburgh and Boston Symphony Orchestras. (Earlier, however, Willem Mengelberg was principal conductor of the Concertgebouw Orchestra of Amsterdam and the New York Philharmonic from 1921 to 1929.) These multiple music directorships today demonstrate a certain amount of greed on the part of conductors and their managements and are often cited to support the generally held but erroneous belief that there are not enough qualified conductors to go around. As Sir Colin Davis once remarked to the author, "It's hard enough to do one job properly."

Schippers and Maazel leavened the season with non-Germanic repertoire (works by Bizet, Stravinsky, Mussorgsky, Tchaikovsky, and Bartók, among others). Schippers was especially praised for his performances on January 14, 15, and 17 of Rossini's seldom-heard *Stabat Mater*, preceded by an even more rarely performed work, Beethoven's youthful *Cantata on the Death of Emperor Joseph II*, both of which he recorded with the Philharmonic.

The two Ford Foundation conductors appeared in March, Elyakum Shapira on the 11th and 14th, George Cleve on the 12th and 13th. Shapira, it will be recalled, had been a Philharmonic assistant conductor during 1960–61, and there was an unusual aspect to his engagement, worthy of being publicized, but curiously not mentioned in the New York press. The reason for the gap in his Philharmonic dates was that on March 12 and 13, he was conducting a similar engagement with the Philadelphia Orchestra. As far as is known, Shapira was the first and only conductor to appear with both great orchestras not only in the same week, but on successive days. Presumably he rehearsed in Philadelphia while Cleve was rehearsing the Philharmonic. Cleve, who was born in Vienna but grew up and was trained in the United States, had been a pupil of Pierre Monteux. No doubt his performances of Berlioz's *Symphonie fantastique* reflected his teacher's classic interpretation.

The Philharmonic has long presented several major choral works each season, and two of them received, incredibly, their first performances by the orchestra when, on April 15–18, Maazel conducted Haydn's genial oratorio *The Seasons* and, on May 27–30, Steinberg closed the season with Bach's Mass in B minor. It may have been the end of the season, but the orchestra's work was far from over. The five-week season of Promenade Concerts had become an annual fixture, and a popular one, with André Kostelanetz continuing to be in charge of the bulk of the series. The English maestro Sir Malcolm Sargent was a Promenade guest conductor for three years, 1964–66—chosen no doubt because of his involvement with the BBC's Proms in London. He proved to have just the right touch.

Since 1918 summer music in New York had been dominated by the Stadium Concerts, given in the Greco-Roman-style amphitheater known as Lewisohn Stadium, on the campus of the City College of New York (CCNY) in Manhattan between 136th and 138th Streets on Amsterdam Avenue. For many years the New York Philharmonic gave popularly priced concerts there, the cheapest seats, on the stone steps that extended in a semicircle at the rear of the amphitheater, selling for as little as 25 cents. Although the orchestra was nominally the Philharmonic, a number of substitute musicians could be found in the ranks, and the six-to-eight-week Stadium season was not managed by the Philharmonic, but contracted independently. In 1955 the summer orchestra was officially designated the Stadium Symphony Orchestra, under which name it had already made some recordings, including Leonard Bernstein's first of major symphonic repertoire. The orchestra continued to be manned largely by Philharmonic musicians.

Now that the fifty-two-week contract had taken effect, the responsibility for full-time employment rested with the Philharmonic management, not outside employers, which meant the 1964 summer season was the last at Lewisohn Stadium for the Philharmonic's members. (In 1965 the Metropolitan Opera Orchestra took over the series.) But two new and exciting ventures began in 1965. Starting on July 14 (Bastille Day) and continuing through July 31, the Philharmonic offered, at Lincoln Center, a French-American festival. Six orchestral programs were offered under the artistic direction of Lukas Foss (some in double performances) and four of chamber music. Charles Munch, who had not conducted the Philharmonic since 1949, opened the festival with music of Debussy, Poulenc, and Ravel, with Adele Addison as the soprano soloist in Poulenc's *Gloria*, as she had been in 1961 when Munch conducted the world premiere of that wonderful piece with the Boston Symphony, and Robert Casadesus as the piano soloist in Ravel's Concerto for the Left Hand. Debussy's Prelude to *Le martyre de Saint Sébastien* opened the program and the two suites from Ravel's *Daphnis et Chloé* closed it, the Camerata Singers also participating, as they had in the Poulenc work.

July 15 and 16 brought the much-anticipated return of Leonard Bernstein from his sabbatical, in a program of his own music. Unfortunately, *The Skin of Our Teeth* did not materialize for him; but those dates saw the premiere of one significant composition resulting from his conducting hiatus, a work of such rhythmic verve and endearing beauty as to more than compensate for any others that might have been. The *Chichester Psalms*, one of Bernstein's most enduring scores, has since been performed by orchestras and choral societies the world over. Also on the program,

Zino Francescatti was the soloist in the Serenade for Violin, Strings, and Percussion, inspired by Plato's *Symposium*, and Philippe Entremont was heard in the piano part of the Symphony No. 2, "The Age of Anxiety," after the poem by W. H. Auden. All three works have become part of the symphonic repertoire, the *Psalms* most firmly.

Munch also led two performances of Berlioz's great dramatic legend *The Damnation of Faust*, a work that is still not often encountered in its entirety. On a July 24 program otherwise conducted by Lukas Foss, Darius Milhaud appeared, to a standing welcome from the audience, to conduct the New York premieres of his Tenth Symphony and an elegy composed in memory of President Kennedy, entitled *Murder of a Great Chief of State*. Other highlights of the festival included the premiere of the specially commissioned Concerto for Three Pianos by Casadesus, with Robert, his wife, Gaby, and their son Jean as the soloists; Duke Ellington conducting the premieres of his *New World a-Coming* and *The Golden Broom and the Green Apple*; and Copland conducting a concert performance of his opera *The Tender Land*.

The excitement of this largely sold-out festival was nothing compared with what came next: the beginning of the Parks Concerts. On the night of August 10, 1965, William Steinberg conducted the Philharmonic, the specially formed Manhattan Chorus, and the soloists Ella Lee, Joanna Simon, Richard Cassilly, and John West in Beethoven's Ninth Symphony in Central Park's Sheep Meadow before an audience conservatively estimated at seventy thousand. According to the orchestra's managing director, Carlos Moseley, this was the largest audience for which the Philharmonic had ever played in person in its 123 years of existence.

The Parks Concerts had been in the planning stage for quite some time, but even up to a few days before opening night Philharmonic officials were not sure many people would attend such a program. It was, after all, free, and prospective audiences are often suspicious of events that are offered for nothing. Not this time, though. The Joseph Schlitz Brewing Company contributed heavily to the series, inspired by the success of an outdoor concert the Philharmonic had given in Milwaukee a couple of years before, which they had also sponsored. (Despite the brewery's generosity, though, few of the countless beer cans found in the post-concert debris bore the name Schlitz.)

The opening program also included a specially composed *Philharmonic Fanfare* by William Schuman and Wagner's Prelude to *Die Meistersinger*. Maurice Peress, a former Philharmonic assistant conductor, had been engaged as the understudy, or cover conductor, for the concerts. He has told of examining Steinberg's score for the Beethoven Ninth and finding in it various and sundry strange markings and emendations, about which Steinberg was curiously unforthcoming. It developed that Steinberg was performing the work with revised orchestration by Gustav Mahler. In light of Steinberg's circumspection, it is amusing that in later years some conductors have made a point of publicly proclaiming their use of Mahler's edition. And at the late-afternoon performance at New York's Botanical Gardens, the audience was treated to the sight of Steinberg, with the sun beating down upon him, suddenly whipping out a beret and placing it on his extremely bald head.

For the Parks Concerts a special movable stage was constructed and named for Minnie (Mrs. Charles S.) Guggenheimer, who had been the indefatigable and irrepressible guiding spirit of the Lewisohn Stadium concerts. Other conductors for these concerts, which took place in all the boroughs of the city, were Seiji Ozawa and Alfred Wallenstein. The former's program featured Benny Goodman, no less, in Mozart's Clarinet Concerto, and the latter's presented Aaron Copland performing his own Piano Concerto. Attendance for the Ozawa-Goodman program in Central Park was announced as 73,500, for Wallenstein-Copland again 70,000. Total attendance for the entire series was estimated at 462,500, about 100,000 more than the audiences for the regular season, the Promenades, and the French-American Festival combined. It goes without saying that the Parks Concerts brought the Philharmonic to many people who would not ordinarily have heard it.

Two Surprise Decisions

In October 1964 it was announced that, beginning with the 1965–66 season, the Philharmonic's traditional Sunday afternoon concerts would be moved to Monday nights. This came as a blow not only to the Sunday afternoon subscribers, but also to many other music lovers who attended those concerts from time to time, students who had more or less graduated from the Young People's Concerts, and all those who had grown up with the Sunday afternoon broadcasts. The change gave the orchestra members a guaranteed day off each week. There was a nominal day off, Monday, on the existing schedule, but during weeks when Bernstein was conducting, that day was invariably used for recording. Now they, like most other people, would have Sunday off. Of course, if recordings were scheduled on a Monday, they would still have to play a concert that night, making for a rather full day, but having Sunday off compensated for that. But the Sunday matinees had long been a valued New York tradition, and any orchestra that does not take into account the needs and wishes of the community it serves runs the risk of becoming irrelevant to that community.

As for those broadcasts, they would now be carried live by WOR in New York on Saturday evenings, as they had been by CBS when Bernstein's tenure began.

The radio network now consisted of about sixty stations throughout the country, some of which aired the concerts on a tape-delay basis.

From the standpoint of orchestra personnel, 1965–66 was notable for two significant reasons. The previous season, 1964–65, had been the last for the long-time principal flutist, John Wummer, whose place was taken in the fall of 1965 by Julius Baker, an eminent New York performer known especially for his membership in the Bach Aria Group. The new season would also see the farewell of John Corigliano, the orchestra's distinguished concertmaster, who had occupied that chair since 1943, having first been engaged as the Philharmonic's assistant concertmaster by Toscanini in 1935. Corigliano, the father of the composer of the same name, would make his final solo appearances on January 20–22 and 24, 1966, in Édouard Lalo's *Symphonie espagnole*, conducted by William Steinberg, who had also programmed for the occasion Richard Strauss's *Ein Heldenleben*, with its extensive solos for the concertmaster.

Both Corigliano and Wummer had reached the then (but no longer) mandatory retirement age of sixty-five. Demonstrating that sixty-five was not an age of infirmity, Corigliano went on to become concertmaster of the San Antonio Symphony, while Wummer continued to play chamber music and teach in New York. For some reason, that retirement age did not apply to conductors, many of whom were (and are) active in their seventies and eighties. Leopold Stokowski conducted, at least for recordings, almost until his death in 1977 at age ninety-five.

Although Bernstein's first two seasons at Lincoln Center had dispensed with thematic programming, that concept returned in 1965–66 and was carried over to 1966–67, a two-year survey entitled Symphonic Form in the Twentieth Century. At a press conference on April 27, 1965, Bernstein made a statement that has since been often quoted or referred to:

> The symphony is not really in the mainstream of what is being written now in the world. . . . If this is true, it means that symphony orchestras have a museum function. A conductor is a kind of curator. He hangs symphonies up in the best possible lighting.

He went on to say that it was "better to expose the problem and provoke the question in the minds of the thinking public." When asked whether the Philharmonic would be able to continue if it were out of the mainstream, he replied, "I give the Philharmonic forever. It is a great curatorial institution."

The composers whose symphonies were curated by Bernstein, including some led by William Steinberg, were Marc Blitzstein, Copland, Diamond, Elgar, Irving Fine, Harris, Hindemith, Arthur Honegger, Ives, Janáček (his Sinfonietta), Mahler,

Carl Nielsen, Prokofieff, Schoenberg, Schuman, Shostakovich, Sibelius, Leo Smit, Vaughan Williams, and Webern. Special attention was paid to Sibelius's music in the centennial year of his birth: all the symphonies were performed and recorded during 1965–67, as well as some of the tone poems. For his service to the composer, Bernstein received a bronze plaque from the New York Metropolitan Chapter of the Finlandia Foundation.

Besides Steinberg, guest conductors for the season were Szell, Schippers, and Foss, each for four weeks. Philharmonic Hall underwent further renovations from August 1 to September 2, 1965, and the results were unveiled at the opening concert on October 1. Schonberg reported on "the new acoustic setup in the Hall—wooden free form attached to the side walls, a new color scheme (light blue), and more seats. Philharmonic Hall, which started with 2,680 seats, now has 2, 840," giving it the largest seating capacity of any New York concert hall. The sound was now found to be brighter, with more presence and improved bass. All of this was "a decided plus." Unfortunately, there were minuses: a persistent echo in the side locations, uneven sound throughout the hall, and an uneven sound-decay rate. Another newspaper strike clouded the opening of the season, but this one was relatively brief, barely two weeks long.

On February 11, 1966, it was announced that David Nadien, a forty-year-old violinist from Brooklyn, had been appointed the Philharmonic's new concertmaster. While the *Times* article pointed out that he had almost no major symphonic experience, it mentioned that he was "almost a legend" among New York freelance musicians because of his work in just about every aspect of commercial music, from TV background music to rock and roll. Bernstein hailed him as "an extraordinary musician" who would "become a worthy successor to John Corigliano." Nadien had, in fact, already appeared with the Philharmonic as the winner of the prestigious Leventritt Competition, playing the Glazunov Violin Concerto with George Szell conducting on December 22, 1946.

Again the Philharmonic had three assistant conductors, all winners of the Mitropoulos Competition: the American James DePreist, the Dutchman Edo de Waart, and the Frenchman Jacques Houtmann. Unlike Abbado and Calderón in 1964, they were not given entire programs to conduct but, like most assistants, conducted single works on concerts otherwise conducted by Bernstein. The reason Bernstein gave for the relative paucity of assistants' appearances was that the subscribers tended to object if they were not getting the experienced, certified maestros—unless of course, there had been a conducting emergency.

Meanwhile, on January 19, 1966, three new Mitropoulos winners were announced as assistant conductors for the following season: Sylvia Caduff of

Switzerland, Juan Pablo Izquierdo of Chile, and Alain Lombard of France. Much attention was given Caduff in the press, Schonberg devoting an entire Sunday article to her and the fact that women conductors were a great rarity at that time. At the end of the 1965–66 season, Schonberg wrote that he had found the programs largely uninteresting, in spite of the twentieth-century theme. Szell was acknowledged as "one of the greatest of living conductors," and Steinberg's "level-headed, clear, well-proportioned approach" was much appreciated, but not by everyone, according to Schonberg. Others found him unimaginative. Schippers and Foss did not receive kind words, but a new maturity was found in Bernstein's work following his sabbatical, to the point that, if continued, "musicians will no longer be calling him 'Lenny.' They will be saying 'Maestro.'"

The success of the previous year's French-American Festival brought about a second festival in 1966, this one featuring the music of Igor Stravinsky, in combination with that of composers whom he influenced and who influenced him. Orchestral concerts were conducted by Bernstein, Foss (the festival's artistic director), Ernest Ansermet, Kiril Kondrashin, Robert Craft, and Stravinsky himself. As before, there were several programs of chamber music. The opening concert, conducted by Bernstein on June 30, began with related works by Barber, Copland, and Silvestre Revueltas and culminated with what was by then Bernstein's celebrated interpretation of *The Rite of Spring*. Stravinsky was paid $1,000 merely to attend the concert.

Ansermet conducted the concerts of July 9 and 12, which featured *Perséphone*, a work from 1934 for speaker, tenor soloist, chorus, and orchestra, the recitation performed by the actress Yvette Mimieux, with Leopold Simoneau as the tenor and the Camerata Singers. In a Sunday *New York Times* interview on July 3 the eighty-two-year-old Ansermet, who had been closely associated with the eighty-four-year-old Stravinsky's early to middle-period works, told of his eventual falling-out with the composer because of his disapproval of the twelve-tone system, in which most of the later works were written. He had therefore been surprised to be invited to conduct *Perséphone*, not one of those later works but one he had never conducted, and accepted only when told Stravinsky had asked for him specifically for that work. Ansermet concluded they were now friends again, and were "too old to be bothered by differences."

In a concert otherwise conducted by Robert Craft, Stravinsky concluded the festival on July 23 by conducting the *Symphony of Psalms*. As the composer appeared onstage, his frailty was evident, though it disappeared once he ascended the podium and began to conduct. A more moving and more authoritative performance of this great work could not be imagined.

The Philharmonic had long been the last outpost of male supremacy in the American musical world. All the major orchestras had several women members in their ranks (Doriot Anthony Dwyer had been the principal flutist of the Boston Symphony since 1952), and the lower-echelon orchestras had many. Thus it was a historic occasion (though not treated as such) when, at the beginning of the 1966–67 season, it was announced that among the seven new members of the Philharmonic was Orin O'Brien, a double bassist and the first woman other than a harpist to become a member of the orchestra. A year later she was joined by a new cellist, Evangeline Benedetti.

No sooner did Bernstein conclude his first four-week series than he shocked the musical world by announcing he would be leaving his post as music director of the Philharmonic at the end of the 1968–69 season. He was quoted in the *New York Times* of November 3, 1966: "A time is arriving in my life when I must concentrate maximally on composing, and this cannot be done while retaining the great responsibilities inherent in the Philharmonic post, which is a full-time commitment, and indeed, more than that."

It was announced that he would still conduct for several weeks during the regular season, as well as make recordings with the orchestra and, significantly, continue with the Young People's Concerts, so dear to his heart. Amyas Ames announced that a special post and title had been created for Bernstein, laureate conductor; the title is often seen today in other orchestras, but Bernstein was the first ever to be so designated. In an article published on Sunday, November 13, 1966, entitled "Bernstein: Wrong Time to Leave?," Harold Schonberg, in commenting on the maturity of interpretation Bernstein had begun to achieve since his sabbatical, "threatening to turn into the kind of conductor that his talent originally had indicated," called his action "a typically Bernsteinian gesture." Bernstein said that the reason he had made his announcement so far in advance was to give the Philharmonic sufficient time to find a successor.

The announcement had the effect of transforming every guest conductor who appeared with the Philharmonic into a potential candidate for the job, or at least so the press speculated. The first to appear, less than a week after the announcement, was, significantly, Lorin Maazel, whose performances over a three-week span of Beethoven's Ninth and Brahms's Second Symphonies, as well as works by Bartók and Ravel, were highly praised by Schonberg.

For the first time in its history the Philharmonic had a composer-in-residence when David Amram was appointed to the position for the 1966–67 season. Best known in New York for his incidental music for theatrical productions, including some for the New York Shakespeare Festival, his *King Lear Variations* were performed on March 23, 24, and 27, conducted by Sylvia Caduff on a program she shared with her fellow assistants.

Caduff and Izquierdo got their big break when Steinberg suddenly canceled his appearance on February 13 in order to be with his seriously ill wife in Pittsburgh. As luck would have it, the scheduled program was devoted to two works that were extreme rarities in concert programs of the time and are only barely less so today: Max Reger's *Variations and Fugue on a Theme of Mozart*, which Izquierdo conducted, and Tchaikovsky's "Manfred" Symphony, led by Caduff. Steinberg was not noted for popular programming; he once told an interviewer that he delighted in presenting works nobody wanted to conduct and nobody wanted to listen to. In the event, the two substitutes acquitted themselves handsomely. Curiously, their appearance on that date is not listed in the Philharmonic's traditional season-ending tabulation of concerts.

On March 25, 1967, the musical world celebrated the centennial of the birth of Arturo Toscanini. To mark the occasion, Bernstein and the Philharmonic performed a pension-fund benefit concert devoted to Verdi's Requiem, a work with which Toscanini had been particularly associated and of which he made an iconic recording. Bernstein had a stellar lineup of soloists: Galina Vishnevskaya, Marilyn Horne, Richard Tucker, and Justino Díaz, along with the Camerata Singers. Writing in the *Times* of March 27, Schonberg found it to be "one of the most brilliant, and most convincing performances [Bernstein] has ever conducted."

The number of New York City newspapers diminished in 1966 with the merger of the *Journal-American*, the *World-Telegram and the Sun*, and the *Herald Tribune*, all of them, as their names imply, products of previous mergers. (A cartoon by Frank Modell in the April 16 *New Yorker* showed a newspaper delivery truck about a block long, its side emblazoned with "Read the World Herald Telegram Tribune American Journal Sun.") But before the merger, scheduled for the spring of 1966, could take effect, the *Herald Tribune* ceased publication. It was only after an acrimonious 140-day strike against the three papers by the various unions involved that the *World Journal Tribune* finally published its first edition on September 12, 1966; eight months later the new paper breathed its last, on May 5, 1967. Among the many employees who lost their jobs were, of course, those who reported on the fine arts in New York City. That left only the *New York Times* as the city's major source of arts coverage.

CHAPTER 4

1967–72

LAUREATE CONDUCTOR

The Philharmonic did not present its own summer festival in 1967. Instead, it was one of several participants in the first Lincoln Center Festival, with Lukas Foss, Ned Rorem, and Gunther Schuller commissioned to write special works for the orchestra in honor of its coming 125th-anniversary season in 1967–68. Rorem's song cycle *Sun* received its premiere on July 1, with Jane Marsh as soprano soloist and Karel Ančerl as guest conductor; Bernstein conducted Schuller's *Triplum* on June 28. Major works presented by the Philharmonic during the festival were Mahler's "Resurrection" Symphony under Bernstein and Honegger's dramatic oratorio *Joan of Arc at the Stake*, with Seiji Ozawa conducting and Vera Zorina and Michael Wager in the principal speaking roles. Foss's *Baroque Variations* was to have preceded the Honegger work but was not performed because the orchestral materials were not ready.

The evening of June 28 was a busy one for Schuller, who conducted the American premiere of his opera *The Visitation* at the Metropolitan Opera House with the visiting Hamburg State Opera. During the intermission after the first act, he rushed across the plaza to Philharmonic Hall so he could hear the premiere of *Triplum*. He just had time for a few bows before hurrying back to the opera house to conduct the second act.

On October 5, just before the 1967–68 season began, it was announced that the Philharmonic-Symphony Society and the musicians had agreed on a new three-year contract, by the end of which the basic weekly salary would be $270. That made the Philharmonic the highest-paid symphony orchestra in the country. Less happy news, especially given the significance of the anniversary season, was that the organization canceled its radio broadcasts, which had been heard throughout the nation since 1922. Originally aired on Sunday afternoons and later in various time slots, the broadcasts had long been without commercial sponsorship, and the musicians had been playing them without extra compensation. Now they decided they would no longer do so without pay, and the Society, which had never financed the broadcasts, was not willing to pay the approximately $140,000 a year required.

Twenty-one composers were commissioned to write music for the anniversary celebration, the most ever commissioned by the Philharmonic for a specific project. Milton Babbitt, Richard Rodney Bennett, Luciano Berio, Elliott Carter, Aaron Copland, Roberto Gerhard, Howard Hanson, Roy Harris, Leon Kirchner, Frederic Myrow, Nicholas Nabokov, Walter Piston, Rodion Shchedrin, William Schuman, Roger Sessions, Karlheinz Stockhausen, Toru Takemitsu, and Virgil Thomson were to provide works for the subscription series, while Alan Hovhaness, Dimitri Kabalevsky, and Ezra Laderman would write pieces for the Promenade Concerts, the last commissioned by André Kostelanetz himself.

Besides the commissioned works, the season's repertoire would consist largely of works of which the Philharmonic had given the world or American premieres. These ran the gamut from Beethoven's Fifth Symphony to Karl Goldmark's *Rustic Wedding Symphony*, Mahler's Fourth Symphony, Ives's Second Symphony, and Copland's *Appalachian Spring*. A nice touch was the inclusion on the program of March 14, and its repetitions, of a concerto grosso by Dimitri Mitropoulos, which received its American premiere with Bernstein conducting.

In addition to Steinberg, the guest conductors engaged by the orchestra, each for one week, had long and continuing relationships with the Philharmonic: Sir John Barbirolli, Thomas Schippers, Leopold Stokowski, and George Szell, along with two former assistant conductors who had made good internationally, Claudio Abbado and Seiji Ozawa. There were again three assistant conductors, Paul Capolongo of France, Helen Quach of China, and Alois Springer of Germany. Lester Trimble was named composer-in-residence for the season.

Also celebrating its 125th anniversary in 1967 was the Vienna Philharmonic, which, while on tour in the United States, was invited to play a pension-fund benefit concert for the New York Philharmonic on October 4. Most of the program was conducted by Karl Böhm, who led Schubert's "Unfinished" Symphony and Strauss's *Ein Heldenleben*. In between, Bernstein conducted Beethoven's *Leonore* Overture No. 3. At an intermission ceremony in the green room, Bernstein was presented with the Vienna Philharmonic Ring of Honor. Accepting it for the New York Philharmonic, he said it was "one of the greatest honors ever bestowed on us." There was also some amusement as Bernstein wondered aloud whether the two ensembles were "Bruder" or "Schwester" orchestras—brother or sister. Böhm returned the favor by conducting Mozart's "Haffner" Symphony on the New Yorker's concert of October 12.

On the evening of December 7, the exact date of the orchestra's first concert in 1842, the Philharmonic performed a gala concert duplicating (mostly) the original program, with Leonard Bernstein conducting (again mostly):

Beethoven: Symphony No. 5 in C Minor
Weber: Aria from *Oberon* (Eileen Farrell, soprano)
Hummel: Quintet in D Minor (first movement)
    (Leonard Bernstein, piano; David Nadien, violin; William Lincer, viola;
    Lorne Munroe, cello; Robert Brennand, double bass)
Weber: Overtore to *Oberon*
Rossini: Duet from *Armida* (Reri Grist, soprano; Nicolai Gedda, tenor)
Beethoven: Aria from *Fidelio* (Nicolai Gedda, tenor)
Mozart: Aria from *The Abduction from the Seraglio* (Reri Grist, soprano)
Kalliwoda: Overture No. 1 in D Minor

In 1842 the complete Hummel Quintet had been performed. In those days it was standard practice to include chamber works on orchestral programs. Johann Nepomuk Hummel (1778–1837) was a highly respected Austrian composer of the generation after Mozart who has virtually disappeared from symphonic concerts today, with the possible exception of his sprightly and engaging Trumpet Concerto. Johann Wenzel Kalliwoda (1801–1866), a distinguished Czech composer, has almost completely disappeared from the repertoire; his Overture was performed in 1951 on the Philharmonic's five thousandth concert and not again until the 125th-anniversary program. As a gesture toward the orchestra, Bernstein gave the down-beat for it and immediately walked offstage, leaving the musicians to perform it on their own. The audience was as gala as the concert and included many luminaries from the worlds of music, entertainment, and high society, all visible in a famous panoramic photograph taken that night.

Shortly thereafter the Philharmonic announced its guest conductors for 1968–69, Bernstein's last season as music director: Pierre Boulez, Colin Davis, Carlo Maria Giulini, Zubin Mehta, Seiji Ozawa, and Stanisław Skrowaczewski. Of these apparent candidates to succeed Bernstein, only Ozawa and Skrowaczewski had conducted the orchestra before. Conspicuously absent was Steinberg, who, at age seventy, was probably considered too old for the music directorship (although a year later the Boston Symphony appointed him to succeed Erich Leinsdorf).

In the December 12 *New York Times*, Mehta was quoted as saying that his orchestra (the Los Angeles Philharmonic) was better than the New York Philharmonic and that it would not be a step up for him to go to New York. He did not want the job, for he was very happy in Los Angeles. A week later he was quoted in *Newsweek* as saying that the Philharmonic should be led by an American, who should be able to deal both with the orchestra and with New York City. The Philharmonic stepped over conductors, he said, concluding, "A lot of us think why not send our worst enemy to the New York Philharmonic and finish him off, once and for all."

It should be mentioned that at one time the Philharmonic did indeed have a reputation as an unruly orchestra for conductors to deal with. Guido Cantelli certainly had his difficulties with them and even tried to cancel his 1956–57 engagement as a result, the engagement to which he was traveling when he was killed in a plane crash. Mitropoulos, in spite of his benevolence, was not treated well. Josef Krips, in his 1961 engagement, was treated with great respect for two weeks, but by the end of his fourth week many of the musicians were so disruptive during rehearsals that he found himself screaming at the orchestra for silence. But all of that was in the past. By the time of Mehta's remark the Philharmonic had evolved into a more cooperative group (as it has remained since).

Neither the Philharmonic nor Local 802 of the American Federation of Musicians took kindly to Mehta's remarks, with the result that he was called to appear before the union's executive board. Max Arons, Local 802's president, presided over the meeting, in which Mehta said his claim that his orchestra was better than the New York Philharmonic was meant as a statement of pride in the Los Angeles Philharmonic, not as a disparagement of the New Yorkers. He complained that his remarks in *Newsweek* were "distorted out of all proportion" (though *Newsweek* stood by them). Arons described the meeting as "strict and stern, but friendly," and even advised Mehta "to study what he says before he talks, like studying a score. Like a bad note, you can't take it back once it's played." On April 27, 1968, it was announced that Mehta's engagement with the Philharmonic had been postponed to an unspecified date. His place on the roster was taken by the Polish maestro Jerzy Semkow.

Before the 1968–69 season began, the Philharmonic undertook a five-week tour of Europe and Israel. It was the first time the orchestra had toured Europe since 1959, and there were only two concerts in Israel, August 29 in Jerusalem and August 31 in Caesarea. Bernstein characteristically included two major American works in the tour repertoire, the third symphonies of Roy Harris and William Schuman. There was some concern in Venice on September 7 when the assistant conductor Alain Lombard replaced Bernstein for the performance of the Schuman symphony, which he also did in Montreux on September 13. No specific reason was given for the substitution, but rumors circulated in the European press that Bernstein was ill. So rife did these rumors become that Bernstein began a September 23 press conference in Berlin by saying, "I am here to prove I am not dead." After referring to newspaper articles that reported he had a "heart attack," had "collapsed," and was in "delicate health," he complained, "I don't understand the press anymore.

It used to be that if you were asked a simple question and gave a simple answer it came out that way. But now you are asked if you have had a heart attack. You answer 'no' and it comes out 'yes.'"

Bernstein's last season as music director began on October 3, 1968, with two works by William Schuman, followed by his celebrated and exciting interpretation of the *Symphonie fantastique*. The first Schuman work, which was given its world premiere, was *To Thee Old Cause*, subtitled *Evocation for Oboe, Brass, Timpani, Piano and Strings* and composed in the aftermath of the assassinations of Martin Luther King and Robert F. Kennedy. The title comes from Walt Whitman. The composer's exuberant Third Symphony followed.

On October 10 a significant world premiere was given: that of Luciano Berio's *Sinfonia*, commissioned for the 125th-anniversary season and, as it turned out, one of the most influential works of its era. The composer himself conducted this score, which included the popular vocal group the Swingle Singers. The work's most striking section is the third movement, in which the scherzo of Mahler's Second Symphony weaves in and out of the sound picture while music of other composers is heard simultaneously and the singers intone fragments of vocal miscellany. The effect is that of a stream of consciousness, and the work can be said to have begun the trend of composers extensively quoting other composers' compositions, as can be found in the Third Symphonies of George Rochberg and Sir Michael Tippett.

To commemorate the centennial of the death of Berlioz, Colin Davis made his Philharmonic debut on October 31 with a program of that composer's works. The highlight of the observance occurred on February 13, 1969, when Seiji Ozawa led the Philharmonic's first performance of the Berlioz Requiem. Leopold Simoneau was the tenor soloist, the Collegiate Chorale the chorus. In addition to commemorating Berlioz, the work was performed in memory of Charles Munch, one of its greatest interpreters, who had died the previous fall. Irving Kolodin, in the March 1 *Saturday Review*, felt that Ozawa, although he clearly had the score in his head since he conducted from memory, did not have it completely under his belt, meaning that the work's full potential was not realized. He did write of the Sanctus, the only movement in which the tenor soloist is heard, as "not merely beautiful, but beatified, by Simoneau's artistry."

Acoustical problems still plagued the concerts, especially those on which large choral works were programmed. An example was Beethoven's *Missa solemnis*, performed under Bernstein's direction the week before the Berlioz Requiem. Schonberg wrote on January 31 of the hall's lack of bass and warmth: "What should sound noble instead sounds shrill; what should sound massive sounds jagged." Yet he had nothing but praise for Bernstein's "powerful and fervent presentation of the score."

On the concerts beginning on January 23, Bernstein had conducted Bruckner's Ninth Symphony. The *New Yorker*'s Winthrop Sargeant, well-known for his admiration of and advocacy for Bruckner, wrote in the February 1 issue that Bernstein had led "a great performance ... a masterly reading." Lamenting that Bernstein was retiring from the Philharmonic having programmed only one Bruckner symphony, he hoped the conductor would one day do for Bruckner what he had done for Mahler, that is, record all the symphonies (alas, it was not to be). Finding Bernstein's interpretation comparable to those of the great Bruckner conductors of the past, he concluded, "There are few great Bruckner conductors alive today, and Mr. Bernstein is one of them."

A February 26 pension-fund benefit performance of scenes from Wagner's *Tristan und Isolde* under Bernstein's direction was the composer's sole representation in the season. Eileen Farrell and Jess Thomas performed the title roles, with Joanna Simon as Brangäne. Although all the performers were acclaimed, the evening was a special triumph for Bernstein and Farrell. Irving Kolodin wrote in the *Saturday Review* of March 13 that the conductor's affinity for and mastery of the score deserved to be heard in theatrical circumstances, preferably at the Met (where he never did conduct the work), and that Farrell was magnificent in the role, to the point of evoking memories of Kirsten Flagstad.

The most significant of the season's guest conductors was undoubtedly Pierre Boulez. Except for two seldom-played Haydn symphonies (Nos. 89 and 91) and five Fantasias for strings by Henry Purcell, his four weeks of programs, beginning March 13, were devoted to music of the twentieth century, from Debussy and Ravel to Stravinsky and Ives, from Bartók and Varèse to Schoenberg, Berg and Webern. Not since Bernstein's avant-garde series had Philharmonic subscribers been treated to such a massive dose of the music of their own century, though many found it rather difficult to swallow. For the orchestra most of this repertoire was not standard; for Boulez it all was, and in his unflashy way he succeeded in getting the Philharmonic to sound as if they had been playing this music all their lives.

Bernstein was to have conducted the last four weeks of the season, but the death of his father caused him to miss the second week, leaving two of his assistant conductors, the Belgian François Huybrechts and the Iranian Farhad Mechkat (the third assistant was the Canadian Boris Brott), to take over an all-Stravinsky program on extremely short notice. Both were praised by Schonberg for their professionalism and their talent.

And so May 15–17, 1969, arrived—Bernstein's final concerts as music director of the New York Philharmonic. For the occasion he chose Mahler's Third Symphony, a work he had conducted in 1961 in memory of Mitropoulos. Lasting well over an hour and a half, it is the longest symphony in the standard repertoire, though even then it could not be considered standard. Betty Allen was the mezzo-soprano soloist, with a women's chorus from the Schola Cantorum and boys' choruses from the Little Church around the Corner and the Browning School.

Bernstein was an ideal interpreter of this piece, able to convey superbly the conflicting elements of the first movement, its dynamic upward ending virtually lifting the audience out of their seats as no other performance had; and then there were the folklike qualities of the second movement, the innocence of the children's chorus, the nostalgia of the posthorn solo, the deep humanity of the finale. A five-minute standing ovation followed the third and final performance, which culminated in the appearance onstage of Amyas Ames, who announced Bernstein's appointment as laureate conductor (the first to be so honored) and also presented him with a laurel wreath. It was further announced that Bernstein would receive from the board of directors a nineteen-foot Chris-Craft motor boat christened *The Laureate*. For once, Bernstein was speechless. Later, at a party given in his honor, he said, "I just couldn't find a word. I was too moved. But I could have said something—should have said something—about that magnificent, that truly great orchestra." Probably the gift that meant most to him had been presented earlier by the members of the orchestra: a mezuzah, the small symbol of faith attached to the doorposts of Jewish homes.

Schonberg, who praised the performance of the Mahler symphony, concluded his Sunday article of May 11:

> What Bernstein did at the beginning by animal magnetism and a driving necessity to be loved, he now does through craft—without having surrendered any of the magnetism. . . . He still has an amazing quality of youth about him, but he is no longer the Peter Pan of music. In the last five years he has proved himself.

On June 11, 1969, came the announcement that Pierre Boulez had been named music director of the New York Philharmonic beginning with the 1971–72 season.

TRANSITION

It was a bold move on the part of Carlos Moseley and the Philharmonic's board of directors to select Pierre Boulez as the next music director, for in so doing they had awarded the post to the anti-Bernstein. Undemonstrative, musically straightforward, Boulez was everything Bernstein was not. In addition, Boulez had made his reputation as a, if not the, leading interpreter of twentieth-century music, especially that of the so-called Second Viennese School (Schoenberg, Berg, and Webern), a predilection not likely to endear him to the hearts of the conservative Philharmonic subscribers. More traditional maestros who had been mentioned as possible candidates for the job included Colin Davis, Zubin Mehta (in spite of his past remarks), Lorin Maazel, Seiji Ozawa, and Daniel Barenboim.

Born in 1925 in Montbrison, France, Boulez had first made his mark as a composer of extremely difficult and rigorous music such as *Le marteau sans maître*; still his best-known work, it is often compared to Schoenberg's *Pierrot lunaire*. He began conducting primarily in order to direct his own compositions, for he was not happy with other conductors' performances of them. Before long he was conducting more traditional repertoire as engagements with European orchestras materialized; an American broadcast of Schubert's Sixth Symphony with Amsterdam's Concertgebouw Orchestra was especially memorable. At the time of his Philharmonic appointment, Boulez was already principal guest conductor of the Cleveland Orchestra and was scheduled to be chief conductor of the BBC Symphony Orchestra in London, an organization noted for presenting the latest in contemporary music. Even as a composer-conductor, Boulez was the antithesis of Bernstein, whose music was rooted in tonality and accessible to a wide public. There is no *Left Bank Story* in Boulez's output.

But Boulez's appointment was not to take effect until the 1971–72 season, leaving the Philharmonic with two seasons to fill following Bernstein's departure. In 1947–49 Bruno Walter had held the title of musical adviser between the musical directorships of Artur Rodzinski and Dimitri Mitropoulos. Now, for the 1969–70 season, the Philharmonic turned to its old friend George Szell, on whom was bestowed the titles of music advisor and senior guest conductor. Still musical director of the Cleveland Orchestra, he would be in charge of eight weeks of concerts, the remainder of the season to be divided among the laureate conductor, Bernstein, and the guest conductors, Claudio Abbado, Rafael Frühbeck de Burgos, Istvan Kertész, Lorin Maazel, and Seiji Ozawa. André Kostelanetz would continue to conduct special Saturday evening concerts, and the new crop of assistant conductors, Mitropoulos winners all, were Alfredo Bonavera, Mesru Mehmedov, and Uri Segal. Irving Kolodin, writing of the finals of the Mitropoulos Compeition in the February 15 *Saturday Review*, had singled out Mehmedov for special praise: his fellow finalists were primarily "conducting the orchestra," while Mehmedov was "conducting the music." Even before learning of the results, Kolodin felt it would not be the last time Mehmedov would appear at Philharmonic Hall. Sadly, this promising young conductor died in a plane crash two years later while on his way to an engagement in his native Bulgaria.

On September 7, 1969, Harold Schonberg opined that there was very little that was new in the Philharmonic's coming season. Kertész, who had recorded all nine Dvořák symphonies, would be conducting the ever-popular "New World"; the French pianist Jeanne-Marie Darré, known as a Saint-Saëns specialist, would play that composer's well-known Concerto No. 4 instead of the less familiar and charming No. 3; and George Szell, with over a hundred Haydn symphonies from which to choose, had selected No. 88, which he had often performed in New York. Wrote Schonberg, "Doesn't he know any other Haydn symphony?" For this critic, "the one really adventurous touch of the entire season" would be Lorin Maazel's performances in the final week of Schumann's virtually unknown oratorio *Das Paradies und die Peri.*

Before Szell even began his first four-week series, following the five weeks of Ozawa, the Philharmonic, in deference to Szell's authority and no doubt at his insistence, scheduled a full week devoted entirely to rehearsals, with no concerts. This period was undoubtedly designed as a means of purging the orchestra's "improper playing habits," referred to by Szell some years earlier. Szell's actual concerts began with two programs in his first week, starting with a November 13 pension-fund benefit in which Rudolf Serkin played two concertos, Mozart's No. 21 in C Major, K. 467, and Beethoven's No. 4 in G Major. Extremely enthusiastic about the entire concert, Schonberg hailed the performance of the latter as "one of the criteria against which all performances are measured." Beethoven's Ninth Symphony was featured on Szell's first subscription program. In this, and in the preceding *Leonore* Overture No. 2, Szell conducted, according to Schonberg, "the kind of organized, balanced, meaningful Beethoven that is all but in a class by itself." Mahler's Sixth Symphony was still something of a rarity in 1969, but Szell devoted his second week's concerts to that formidable work. Donal Henahan, who was fairly new at the *Times,* thought it a "gleaming performance," but an objective one that did not engage his mind and heart.

Bernstein's series, from January 15 to February 16, 1970, was uncommonly interesting, even for him. First, to lead off the Beethoven bicentennial year, there were concert performances of *Fidelio* featuring not world-renowned singers, but members of Juilliard's newly formed American Opera Center. Bernstein had written in the program booklet that he believed the Juilliard School's inclusion in Lincoln Center was the ultimate justification for the center's existence and hoped these performances would be symbolic of that purpose. Nevertheless, for Schonberg "it was unfair and even unprofessional to put such inexperienced singers into so difficult an opera." He also questioned whether the Philharmonic should be performing concert versions of operas and employing soloists "not of top level."

More opera occupied Bernstein's second week—not a complete work, but extended excerpts from Wagner's *Götterdämmerung*. Eileen Farrell and Jess Thomas were the soloists. The great soprano had been heard in Bernstein's two previous Wagner presentations, the first act of *Die Walküre* in 1968 and scenes from *Tristan und Isolde* in 1969. (The *Götterdämmerung* excerpts can be heard in the Philharmonic's CD collection devoted to Bernstein.)

Two world premieres highlighted Bernstein's remaining two weeks, William Schuman's *In Praise of Shahn: Canticle for Orchestra* (composed in memory of the artist Ben Shahn) on January 29, and Elliott Carter's *Concerto for Orchestra* on February 5. Schuman's score, reviewed in the *Times* by Raymond Ericson, was well received, but Schonberg found Carter's piece "essentially uncommunicative, dry, and a triumph of technique over spirit," though he did acknowledge that it "received a surprisingly warm welcome" from the audience.

Bernstein's last two programs featured two Haydn symphonies (Nos. 101 and 103) and were also notable for the inclusion of the unfamiliar and neglected (even today) Third Symphony ("Polish") of Tchaikovsky and for the Philharmonic's first performances of Nielsen's Fourth Symphony ("Inextinguishable"). Bernstein had given Nielsen's Fifth its Philharmonic premiere in 1962 and was in the process of recording all the Tchaikovsky symphonies. The performance of the lovely Third caused Schonberg to wonder, "What kind of snobbery has kept it away for so long?" The Philharmonic had in fact performed the work in February 1879, a little more than three years after its Russian premiere—apparently the first American performance of any Tchaikovsky symphony. Prior to Bernstein's performances, the Philharmonic had most recently played it thirty years before, when Igor Stravinsky conducted it.

But it was not Bernstein's conducting or programming that attracted the most attention in the press. On January 14 the Bernsteins hosted a cocktail party in their Park Avenue apartment in order to raise funds for the legal defense of the Black Panthers, members of which were present. The Panthers had been indicted on April 2, 1969, for plotting to kill policemen and conspiring to blow up various locations in New York City. The case was scheduled for trial on February 2, 1970.

Bernstein adamantly denied that the occasion had been a "party," stating in no uncertain terms that it was "a meeting, a very serious meeting, involving civil liberties," and that whether we agreed with the aims of a particular group or not, they were entitled to the same means of defense as anyone else. Nevertheless, the controversy surrounding the Black Panthers, and the meeting itself, aroused divided opinion throughout the city. Most vocal was the Jewish Defense League, which accused Bernstein of remaining "silent about Jewish civil rights" and began picketing his apartment building.

For the first time ever, Bernstein was greeted by some boos from the audience when he made his entrance to conduct the Philharmonic. Meanwhile, the idea of the Black Panthers and their allies mixing with New York's "beautiful people" over cocktails and canapés brought forth a new phrase in the language, for in the June 8, 1970, issue of *New York* magazine, the author Tom Wolfe entitled a lengthy article "Radical Chic: That Party at Lenny's." A total of $10,000 was raised for the Panthers.

• • •

Some changes in the Philharmonic's administrative structure took effect on April 1, 1970. Carlos Moseley became the first full-time paid president of the board of directors of an American orchestra, such positions always having been unsalaried, and Amyas Ames moved from the presidency to the chairmanship of the board of directors. Simultaneously, Helen M. Thompson became the orchestra's managing director, the first woman ever to manage a major American orchestra. Thompson was well-known in the orchestra field as the executive vice president and secretary of the American Symphony Orchestra League, which she had helped found in 1943. It sponsors workshops for conductors and training sessions for managers, publishes the highly regarded *Symphony* magazine, and is in general a clearinghouse for American orchestras of all categories, although initially it served smaller community orchestras. As head of the ASOL (now the League of American Orchestras), Thompson had a great deal of experience in dealing with government agencies, not to mention Congress, when it came to the kinds of problems American symphony orchestras faced, and it was thought that the Philharmonic could benefit from her experience. Although she was manager of the Charleston Symphony Orchestra in West Virginia for ten years, she had never managed a major orchestra.

The season ended with Maazel's May 21–23 performances of Schumann's *Das Paradies und die Peri*, so eagerly anticipated by Schonberg. His anticipation proved to be justified: although he found flaws in the work itself, its good points outnumbered the bad, and the piece contained many sections of poignant beauty elegantly performed. He remarked that "it is safe to say that this city has not heard a performance for generations," apparently forgetting that, only six years previously, he had reviewed a performance of the work given by forces of City College.

The world of music received a double shock in the summer of 1970 with the deaths, on successive days (July 29 and 30) of Sir John Barbirolli and George Szell. Barbirolli, of course, had been the Philharmonic's music director from, unfortunately for him, 1937 to 1942—Toscanini's successor. Although his recently reissued Philharmonic recordings certainly show some fine work, at the time he was judged a failure in that position. After his return to England and his rebuilding of

Manchester's Hallé Orchestra, he gradually emerged as one of the world's great conductors, and particularly in the works of Mahler, Elgar, and Sibelius. He had returned to the Philharmonic several times as a beloved guest conductor. Szell, who had a long history at the Philharmonic, was about to begin his second season as its musical advisor and senior guest conductor.

Bernstein opened the 1970–71 season on September 24 with Mahler's Ninth Symphony, dedicating the performances to the memories of Barbirolli and Szell. While Schonberg had nothing but praise for Bernstein's conception of this "monumental" work—"and one does not have to like it to understand and respect its importance"—he was scathing in his condemnation the next week of the use of amplification for the vocal soloists in Stravinsky's *Les noces*. Schonberg was not alone in decrying this practice on that and subsequent occasions, wherever it occurred: "It is a precedent that should be fought by everybody interested in live music—or soon there will be no live music."

Only five weeks had been scheduled for Szell this time, three of which in the end provided opportunities for the American conductors Robert Shaw, Milton Katims, and Dean Dixon. Dixon, then music director of the Hessische Rundfunk Orchestra in Frankfurt, had conducted the Philharmonic during the 1970 Parks Concerts and now became the first African American to direct it in a subscription concert. Shortly after the start of the season, the concertmaster, David Nadien, resigned, returning to the world of a New York freelancer. His chair was temporarily filled by the associate concertmaster, Frank Gullino (the first to be given that title), until a replacement could be found—Rafael Druian, who had been Szell's concert-master in Cleveland for many years.

In the summer of 1969 two African American musicians, the cellist Earl Madison and the double bassist J. Arthur Davis, had filed charges against the Philharmonic, claiming that after auditioning for the orchestra several times, they had been rejected each time because they were black. Hearings were held by the City Commission on Human Rights, at which Moseley testified, denying the allegations. Bernstein had also been called to appear but was never questioned. As reported in the *Times* of November 17, 1970, the longest such deliberation in the commission's history ended fifteen months after it had begun, with the Philharmonic found not guilty of racial discrimination insofar as the claims of the two musicians were concerned. However, it was found guilty of such discrimination when it came to the hiring of extra and substitute musicians. It was found that over a ten-year period, the Philharmonic had hired 277 different substitutes or extra musicians, who played for a total of 1,773 weeks. Of these, only one was African American, and he played for just one week. At that time the Philharmonic did have one

African American member, the violinist W. Sanford Allen, who had joined the orchestra in 1962—the only black member in its 128-year history—but none in its management structure or office staff. Moseley expressed gratification that the hearings had confirmed that the Philharmonic was not discriminatory in its hiring practices and claimed that the organization had already begun reviewing its procedures related to the extras and substitutes "well before this decision was rendered."

After the decision had been handed down, the two musicians issued a challenge to the Philharmonic's cellists and double bassists: they would play against any of them, with everyone behind a screen. Said Madison, "We have everything to lose. They have nothing. They say they are the greatest, so let them prove it." The challenge was not accepted.

The 1970–71 season was the last for which three winners of the Mitropoulos Competition were appointed assistant conductors of the Philharmonic: the Frenchman Philippe Bender, the Argentine Mario Benzecry, and the American David Gilbert. Although the season included guest appearances by such conductors as Daniel Barenboim, Karl Böhm, Aldo Ceccato, Seiji Ozawa, and Stanisław Skrowaczewski, as well as Aaron Copland conducting a program of his own compositions in honor of his seventieth birthday (during which he was made an honorary member of the Philharmonic-Symphony Society), it was the last five weeks to which many people looked forward, if not necessarily the subscribers: the arrival of Pierre Boulez in a sort of preview of what his music directorship would be like. In fact, his first program (April 15–17 and 19) was labeled by Alan Rich in *New York* magazine as "a shot across the bow." He presented early works by the second Viennese triumvirate: Webern's *Passacaglia*, Schoenberg's *Verklärte Nacht*, and Berg's *Seven Early Songs*, *Altenberglieder*, and *Three Pieces for Orchestra*. After describing the works as examples of late romanticism and early expressionism, Schonberg commented on April 17, "Nevertheless, a good part of the audience fled the last half of the program as though sirens warning of an atomic attack had been set off." The English soprano Heather Harper was the soloist in the vocal works, and her performances were hailed as "beautiful. She is a fine artist, one with imagination and a big, rich-sounding voice." Concerning Berg's *Three Pieces*, Schonberg concluded, "Is any living conductor superior in this repertory? One doubts it."

The death of Igor Stravinsky on April 6, 1971, moved Boulez to perform a memorial tribute on April 29–30 and May 1 and 3: the complete ballet scores for *Pulcinella* and *Petrushka*, separated by the *Requiem Canticles* (in its first New York performance by a major ensemble). Schonberg found Boulez "in a surgical minded way" as far as *Petrushka* was concerned: "He dissected the score, exposing nerve and sinew. . . . The result was brilliant in its way, but also curiously cold and dispassionate."

Kolodin, however, in the May 15 *Saturday Review*, wrote that *Petrushka* was "magnificently re-created under the Boulez baton" (metaphorically speaking—Boulez never used a baton) and, though the rendition was "cool [and] objective," it was "an elegy both searching and heartfelt."

The Philharmonic's subscribers were apprehensive as to what Boulez would offer them, but New York's intellectual community greatly looked forward to his tenure. There was some concern, however, as to how much Boulez knew, or cared, about contemporary American music.

THE FRENCH CORRECTION

Just as Bernstein had developed his seasons around particular themes, such as featuring different composers or surveying twentieth-century symphonies, so did Boulez have his themes. His first season, 1971–72, included a retrospective of two composers, Franz Liszt and Alban Berg. The latter came as no surprise, for Boulez is a master interpreter of his music. Liszt, however, was a surprise, for no one even suspected that Boulez had any interest in his music. Liszt has always been popular—the piano concertos, *Les préludes*, the Second Hungarian Rhapsody, perhaps the *Mephisto Waltz*. Pianists like to tackle the great Sonata in B Minor. But at the time, those works constituted the public's entire knowledge of Liszt and contributed to the attitude of sophisticated musicians and musicologists that Liszt's music was cheap, shallow, and vulgar.

But there is much more to Liszt than that, as Schonberg pointed out—music that is more introspective, more harmonically advanced for its time, that points the way to Wagner and beyond. On September 30, 1971, Boulez gave a rare hearing of the oratorio *The Legend of St. Elizabeth*, a work completely devoid of the Lisztian stereotypes. Schonberg deplored the fact that Boulez cut the work heavily, omitting about half an hour's worth of music, though the performance still took about ninety-five minutes. What was heard possessed moments of great beauty and dignity and was conducted by Boulez in a very direct manner, as is his wont, emphasizing rhythm and clarity of expression.

Several innovations marked Boulez's first weeks. The most unusual was the beginning of a four-concert chamber series entitled Prospective Encounters: 7–12. These were given initially at the Shakespeare Festival Public Theater in Greenwich Village, and were devoted to new music, which would be performed between 8:00 and 10:00 p.m. The time before and after would be given over to discussions involving the conductors, performers, composers, and audience members, who were free to ask questions.

The first concert in the Encounter series, on October 1, presented works by Mario Davidovsky and Charles Wuorinen, neither of which Schonberg found terribly interesting. As for the discussions, which promulgated the idea that there was a culture gap between the new music and the audience and that something should be done about it, Schonberg suggested that "in the future, Mr. Boulez might well think of getting a dissenter into these sessions, someone who can stand up to the pious generalities heard Friday night." Yet, in the October 16 *Saturday Review* Kolodin wrote quite positively about Davidovsky's *Synchronism* No. 6, which blends live musical sounds with electronics, and Wuorinen's *Politics of Harmony*, a work whose artistry produced "obvious attributes of enjoyment and communication."

As a supplement to the Encounters, there would be two concerts in a series called Informal Evenings in the Juilliard Theater. These, too, would feature twentieth-century music, but classics of the genre rather than new works. The first such evening, on February 8, was devoted to Berg, with discussion and audience participation. The full orchestra performed excerpts from *Wozzeck*, with Christa Ludwig as the soloist. Schonberg, ever the expert on acoustics, wrote that this was the first time he had heard an orchestra concert in the Juilliard Theater and declared the sound "absolutely gorgeous."

Another Boulez innovation was the introduction of half-hour recitals before ten of the orchestra's subscription concerts, each of which would include music by either Liszt or Berg. Still another was the change in the orchestra's attire, from white tie and tails to black tie and tuxedos, the preferred uniform of Boulez himself.

Because of prior commitments, Boulez was able to conduct only seven weeks with the Philharmonic, which left room for more than the usual number of guest conductors. The most interesting (Bernstein excepted, and he was technically not a guest conductor) was undoubtedly the very first, Michael Gielen, at that time music director of the National Orchestra of Belgium. Like Boulez, the German-born, Argentine-raised-and-trained Gielen had made his reputation in Europe as a composer and conductor of advanced modern music, a relatively small amount of which he programmed on his Philharmonic concerts. In general, Gielen gave the impression of a man bending over backward to avoid popular success, for not one standard repertoire work was included in his four weeks of concerts. The closest he came to such a piece was Mozart's great Serenade for thirteen wind instruments, K. 361, which opened his first program. It was paired with Schoenberg's seldom-played early symphonic poem *Pelleas und Melisande*. Raymond Ericson in the *Times* found Gielen to be "a first-rate conductor," his reading of the Mozart serenade "both sensitive and expressive," that of the complex Schoenberg score "completely assured."

Other works performed by Gielen were Richard Strauss's *Metamorphosen*, Luigi Nono's *On the Bridge of Hiroshima* (in its American premiere), Berg's *Lulu* Suite, Liszt's *From the Cradle to the Grave*, Ligeti's Cello Concerto (with Siegfried Palm as the soloist), and Bruckner's Second Symphony (in its first Philharmonic performances). Gielen's most unusual program was that of October 21, when he paired two little-known works, Liszt's *Dante Symphony* and Mozart's cantata *Davidde penitente*. The latter, with the vocal soloists Sheila Armstrong, Margaret Price, and George Shirley, along with the Schola Cantorum, is the composer's reworking of material from his unfinished Mass in C Minor. Schonberg found it "a masterpiece," and even he had to admit that the Liszt work was "not one of the composer's major scores," though he praised its harmonic freedom.

In summing up Michael Gielen's time with the Philharmonic, Schonberg noted that he was "one of the most nourishing conductors we have had for some time. His ideas make sense, and his projection of them is that of a dedicated conductor in the Hans Rosbaud tradition." He felt the Philharmonic should reengage him as soon as possible, and not merely "as a specialist in the arcane." Gielen did not return to the Philharmonic until November 1978, however, and then only for a single week. He has not been back since.

Bernstein's four weeks at the end of 1971 began with a vengeance as far as the Liszt retrospective was concerned—an all-Liszt program, probably the first and only such in the Philharmonic's history. The featured work was *A Faust Symphony*, which he had performed and recorded with the orchestra in 1960. Comparable in length to a Mahler symphony, it was preceded by a rarity, *Psalm 13* ("Lord, How Long?"), once recorded by Sir Thomas Beecham. This seemed a strange program for Schonberg to miss, but his colleague Raymond Ericson found much to praise in it, especially the psalm setting. William Cochran was the fine tenor soloist in both works, which also featured the Westminster Choir.

Given the popularity today of Gustav Holst's suite *The Planets*—having been given a boost by the development of the space program—it is surprising that on November 24, 1971, Bernstein and the Philharmonic gave the orchestra's first complete performance of the work in fifty years. Also of interest on his programs was the concert premiere on December 9 of two scenes from Samuel Barber's originally ill-fated opera *Antony and Cleopatra*. Barber had revised the scenes for concert performances, and with Martina Arroyo as the affecting soprano soloist, the opera was deemed worthy of a second chance.

The high point of Bernstein's engagement was the special non-subscription performance of December 15, his one thousandth concert with the Phillharmonic— a total to which no other conductor in the orchestra's history even came close. For this event he chose one of his specialties, Mahler's Symphony No. 2 ("Resurrection"), in which Shirley Verrett, Martina Arroyo, and the Camerata Singers participated. A ten-minute ovation followed; Schonberg averred that "every bit of applause he earned was fully deserved."

Boulez's programming influence was felt not only in his own concerts, but in those of the guest conductors, who had also included Michael Tilson Thomas. In his Sunday article on December 12, Schonberg wrote about the number of letters he and the Philharmonic management had received, most of them complaining about the programming. According to Schonberg, "some of the complaints approached hate mail." The Philharmonic was no longer a "fun" place to go. There was too much modern music, too much unfamiliar music, too much vocal music. Boulez's conducting was described as "uninteresting," his approach to music cold and mathematical—all of this on the basis of his having conducted only two weeks of the season. (Perhaps his five weeks at the end of the previous season played a part in this assessment, not to mention his four weeks as a guest two years before.) Even the critics came in for their share of vitriol, for they were perceived as "meekly falling in line and giving Boulez a blank check." Many writers threatened to cancel their subscriptions. And the season not even half over.

To all these harangues, Schonberg responded that the Philharmonic, and all other major orchestras as well, had "been in a rut, playing much the same things over and over again, year after year." The repertoire had stagnated: "There is so much that can be played, and so little that is." The Philharmonic's programs were now "of absorbing interest," and the emphasis on Liszt and Berg should certainly not drive listeners away, and for the most romantic of the twentieth-century avant-garde composers, Alban Berg, to arouse such dissent demonstrated "an appalling lack of sophistication or intellectual curiosity" on the part of the Philharmonic's subscribers.

On December 13 the Mitropoulos Competition concluded with the first prize of $5,000 being won by the twenty-nine-year-old Frenchman Jacques Delacote. Second prize went to the thirty-year-old German Wolfgang Balzer, and third to the twenty-nine-year-old Englishman Timothy Reynish. In a change of format, the three winners were not appointed assistant conductors of the Philharmonic. Rather, Delacote was awarded an engagement as guest conductor for three subscription concerts in January. It was odd that his program included no French music, but was devoted to Mozart and Bruckner.

As a conductor of advanced twentieth-century music, especially that of the Second Viennese School, Boulez was judged to be without peer. He had grown up with this music and had lived with it to the point that it was in his blood. It was second nature to him. Thus he conducted such works in a thoroughly romantic manner, with much freedom of tempo allied to his basic clarity of approach. In short, he interpreted this repertoire, rather than playing it straight, in the manner of most conductors. On the other hand, when he conducted romantic repertoire, such as Schumann symphonies, which could benefit from the same approach, he was stricter and more dispassionate. It was a curious paradox, one often remarked upon by the critics. Meanwhile, so fastidious was Boulez in his rehearsals, correcting intonation and balancing chords to an unprecedented degree, that the musicians began referring to him as "The French Correction," an appellation he reportedly enjoyed.

At the concert of February 24, 1972, the Philharmonic honored four of its members who would be retiring at the end of the season. Boulez introduced them in order of their length of service, beginning with Saul Goodman, who had been the orchestra's timpanist for forty-six years. He had obtained that position in 1926 at the age of nineteen (Boulez was one year old at the time) and had played over six thousand concerts. Next was Engelbert Brenner, the solo English horn player, who had been a member for forty-one years, followed by William Lincer, the principal violist, who had appeared as a soloist fifty-seven times in his twenty-nine years. Frank Ruggieri, the orchestra's second bassoonist, had never in his twenty-three years missed a rehearsal or even been late for one, and he had missed only one concert, because of a death in his family.

On March 9, in his one hundredth appearance with the orchestra, Rudolf Serkin, "after playing the life out of the Brahms D minor Concerto,", this "'titan among pianists'" was made an honorary member of the Philharmonic-Symphony Society of New York. Aaron Copland, Igor Stravinsky, and Paul Hindemith had been the most recent musicians to be so honored.

The Liszt festivities came to an end with the concerts of May 9, 10, and 11, when Lorin Maazel directed a rarity, the "Gran" Mass, or, to give it its official title, the *Missa Solemnis for the Consecration of the Basilica of Gran*. Schonberg found the work "frankly sensuous, passionate and theatrical,.... a lush, dramatic work with many beauties." Liszt's influence on Wagner, Strauss, and other future composers was duly noted.

Other guest conductors for the season were Karel Ančerl, Dean Dixon, Istvan Kertész, James Levine, and Bruno Maderna (like Boulez and Gielen, an avant-garde composer—his Violin Concerto received its American premiere with Paul Zukovsky as the soloist). Although subscribers' complaints about the programming continued throughout the season, many wrote in toward the end saying they had changed their minds. They now appreciated the new and unfamiliar music they had heard. An interesting statistical aspect is that two composers who had long dominated past programming had been reduced to cameo roles, for the season included only three works by Beethoven (excerpts from the *Creatures of Prometheus* ballet music, *Leonore* Overture No. 1, and Symphony No. 4) and two by Brahms (the *Variations on a Theme by Haydn* and Symphony No. 2).

CHAPTER 5

1972–75

NOT EVERYONE IS HAPPY

"Ha! That's better than the Rolling Stones." That was Pierre Boulez's comment when told that his Philharmonic concert in Central Park had drawn an audience of between sixty thousand and seventy thousand. The date of Boulez's first appearance in the Parks Concerts series was July 25, 1972, and although he appeared to be an unlikely participant in these vast outdoor events, he was an extremely successful one. One of the works performed, Haydn's intimate Symphony No. 31 in D Major ("Hornsignal"), seemed similarly unsuited to the surroundings; yet its charm and vigor carried well in the al fresco setting, as did the subtleties and brilliance of Ravel's *Daphnis et Chloé* Suite No. 2. Another success in the series was achieved by Jean Martinon, former music director of the Chicago Symphony and, at the time, head of the Orchestre National de France in Paris. His concerts, begun on August 1, featured Berlioz's *Symphonie fantastique*, and constituted his one and only engagement with the Philharmonic.

Boulez's Haydn symphony was, in fact, a prelude to the thematic programming of 1972–73, when the featured composers were Haydn and Stravinsky. At a time when Haydn was still primarily known for about half a dozen symphonies, most of them with nicknames, the season was notable for presenting an array of less familiar works, some of which had never before been played by the Philharmonic: Nos. 31, 49, 57, 60, 75, 86, and 95 (of which Nos. 31, 49, 86, and 95 were already in the orchestra's repertoire). Of even greater significance was the inclusion of two of the composer's great masses, works seldom encountered in symphonic concerts: the *Theresienmesse* and the *Harmoniemesse*. For good measure there were scenes from Haydn's comic opera *L'incontro improvviso*.

Stravinsky, too, was represented mostly by seldom-heard works, beginning with his Op. 1, the decidedly un-Stravinskian Symphony in E-flat. Also included were the opera *The Nightingale* and a host of shorter works: *Symphonies of Wind Instruments*; *Four Etudes for Orchestra*; *A Sermon, a Narrative, and a Prayer*; *Ragtime for Thirteen Instruments*; *Rénard*; the *Capriccio for Piano and Orchestra* (with William Masselos as the soloist); *Scherzo à la Russe*; and *Fireworks*. More-familiar Stravinsky was given in the form of the *Firebird* Suite (in its original 1910 version), the *Pulcinella* Suite, and the *Symphony of Psalms*.

It was Bernstein who conducted this last work on February 10, 1973, preceding it with Stravinsky's less familiar Mass, and preceding them both with the Haydn *Harmoniemesse* (also known as the "Wind Band" Mass, so called because of the prominence given the wind instruments). In concluding his laudatory review of the concert, Schonberg proclaimed that Bernstein had "arrived at the stage where he no longer has to prove anything to anybody." His conducting that season was "that of a mature master," his musical confidence enabling him to achieve whatever results he wanted from both orchestra and chorus. In reviewing Bernstein's earlier performance of Haydn's Symphony No. 95 in C Minor, Schonberg had referred to Boulez's "rather aseptic ideas about the composer. His approach is analytical. Mr. Bernstein's, as always, was warm and rich."

Boulez conducted fourteen subscription weeks, Bernstein four. Guest conductors for the season were Daniel Barenboim, Aldo Ceccato, James De Preist, Lorin Maazel, Max Rudolf, Stanislaw Skrowaczewski, and Rafael Kubelík in his first Philharmonic engagement since the 1957–58 season. Kubelík was to become a regular and beloved guest.

And still there were complaints about Boulez, not only from subscribers, but from members of the orchestra. In the March 25, 1973, issue of the *New York Times Magazine* a lengthy article by Stephen E. Rubin appeared entitled "The Iceberg Conducteth." While the article acknowledged Boulez's effectiveness as a music director, his mastery of difficult modern music, and the much-improved playing of the orchestra, considerable space was devoted to what were perceived as his defects in performing the standard repertoire—detached and passionless, causing many listeners to leave the concerts early and noisily. Audiences were rude, or perhaps bored, and audience reaction was often tepid.

One orchestra member was quoted anonymously: "I'm going crazy. When he first came here, the idea of playing all that modern stuff made me sick. Now that I've seen and heard the way he conducts the classics, I'd rather he'd program nothing but contemporary music." Such comments were typical of Philharmonic musicians who did not wish to be identified. Others, who did, were more complimentary. The timpanist Roland Kohloff, who had succeeded his teacher, Saul Goodman, exclaimed, "He's one of the finest musicians on this planet." According to the contra-bassoonist, Bert Bial, "he has everything—an acute and discriminating ear, and he always understands the soul of the music."

It was the same with soloists who had performed with Boulez: the negative comments came from those who wished to remain anonymous because they wanted to work with the Philharmonic again, and positive assessments from those who allowed their names to be used. Among the latter was the mezzo-soprano Christa Ludwig: "He is not a star conductor. He shows us only the clear, pure music. He doesn't project Boulez into Beethoven."

Boulez himself was quoted extensively throughout the article. Aware of his reputation for nontraditional interpretations of traditional repertoire, he said that he did not enjoy Schumann, for instance, played in the style that was usually considered "romantic." To him it was not romantic—it was just flabby. Musical interpretation today, he felt, was often exaggerated, comparable to the film-acting style of the 1920s. Distorted musical gestures that "make the music overblown and fat" shocked him. He thought the words "tradition" and "style" were usually mis-understood: "The right tradition is to give a new face to each generation. A work, finally, is interesting because you change the approach."

As someone who has attended many of his concerts in New York, Chicago, and London, I can say that the lack of visual interest on the podium causes one to concentrate ever more on the music. That cannot be a bad thing.

Of all Boulez's programming innovations—the Prospective Encounters, the Informal Evenings at Juilliard, the pre-concert recitals, the change in the orchestra's attire—none enjoyed the popularity of the Rug Concerts, begun the week of June 14, 1973. The impetus for these events came from conversations between the Philharmonic's president, Carlos Moseley, and the scenic designer Peter Wexler, whose concept and design for the Promenade Concerts had been so successful. Commenting on how good the auditorium looked after the Promenades, with the tables and chairs cleared away, Moseley mentioned that the Parks Concerts had attracted large audiences from a broad spectrum of the city, and the Promenades had brought in suburbanites from New Jersey, Long Island, and Westchester, often in group bookings. He then asked Wexler what he felt might be done to attract a different audience. What did he feel was missing?

Wexler replied that there were no concerts that appealed directly to people of his age group, late twenties to early thirties—a group that would later become known as yuppies—and that at home he liked to listen to music while lying on the floor. Thus were born the Rug Concerts. Wexler was put in charge of the spatial conception and design of the project. And at his suggestion the orchestra was moved farther into Philharmonic Hall, and rugs and cushions were placed on the floor on which listeners could recline or sit while enjoying the concert. The main stage also served as a listening area behind the orchestra, which was divided into two groups of seventy and thirty-five players, respectively, alternating in different programs at popular prices. The remainder of the hall had seating as usual. Dmitri

Shostakovich, then on a visit to the United States to receive an honorary doctorate from Northwestern University, tried his best to be inconspicuous but was unmistakable in the first terrace on opening night.

In no way could the programming be considered light fare. Boulez's first concert offered Weber's Overture to *Der Freischütz*, Brahms's Serenade No. 2 in A Major, Ives's *Three Places in New England*, and Stravinsky's *Firebird* Suite (1919 version). According to Donal Henahan in the June 16 *Times*, those sitting downstairs on the rugs and cushions were "the audience Mr. Boulez has been looking for ever since he became music director of the Philharmonic: young and enthusiastic, quietly attentive. . . . The music itself could not have been more happily received." The Rug Concerts would continue for the remainder of Boulez's tenure and even a bit beyond.

The following week the Philharmonic began a series, called Neighborhood Concerts, of performances in various areas of New York City. For these the orchestra was divided into two fifty-member ensembles. The first program, at Brooklyn College, was conducted by James De Preist; the second, at Pace University in Lower Manhattan, was under the direction of David Zinman, who was making his Philharmonic debut. The concerts, for which extremely low admission fees or in some cases none at all were charged, were designed to attract audiences that would normally not venture to Lincoln Center.

On May 11, 1973, it was announced that Harold Lawrence, manager of the London Symphony Orchestra, was to become manager of the New York Philharmonic, succeeding Helen M. Thompson. He had held the London post since 1967 and was the first American to manage a British orchestra. His Philharmonic duties were to begin with the 1973–74 season, and he would have his work cut out for him.

AN UNUSUAL TOUR

Two big news events occurred in the fall of 1973. The first was announced on the date of the equinox: Avery Fisher, founder of Fisher Radio in 1937 and a leading manufacturer of high-fidelity equipment, had made a "major gift" to Lincoln Center. Although details of the gift were not revealed, those in the know estimated it to be between $8 million and $10 million, at that time one of the largest and most important gifts to the arts made by a private individual. Unlike most such gifts, it was not to be used for construction (though Fisher said he had originally considered financing a new hall), but for the maintenance of Philharmonic Hall and for meeting the operating expenses, which, according to Amyas Ames, chairman of the board of both Lincoln Center and the Philharmonic, were about $500,000 a year. In recognition of the gift, Philharmonic Hall was immediately renamed Avery Fisher Hall. A report circulated that Fisher had not planned to have his name on the hall, but he certainly accepted the honor. As he told the *Times* on September 21: "Someday it will be Avery Fisher Hall. They'll say, 'Who the hell was Avery Fisher?' It doesn't bother me.... It doesn't mean as much to me as I suspect it to mean to my family."

Furthermore, 20 percent of the grant money, of which only the interest would be spent, was to be used to award grants to further the careers of young American musicians. "We intend to scour the country for talent," said Fisher, "but we will not subject the young artists to contests. I have been totally opposed to competitions, which a worthy runner-up may be 'scarred for life' by losing." Later, in an interview in the October 6 *New York Post*, he said, "I'll be honest with you. I did not want the name. The idea was theirs. I did want my name on the scholarship."

Fisher's gift was certainly an important one. Yet, when Philharmonic Hall became Avery Fisher Hall, the New York Philharmonic lost its identification with its home.

The second news event initially had less of an impact, but its significance grew, taking on more and more frustration and bitterness as it did so. The Philharmonic had begun the season with a pension-fund benefit concert on September 18 and played the first week of subscription concerts under Boulez's direction beginning September 20, even though the musicians' contract expired that very night. Negotiations for a new contract had been under way for some time, and the new manager, Harold Lawrence, was now thrust into the middle of them. The possibility of a musicians' strike had loomed over the start of the season, and on September 25 that possibility became a reality. The following day orchestra members began picketing Avery Fisher Hall.

The previous contract had provided for a basic weekly salary of $330. The musicians, through their union, were now asking for an additional $70 a week, while the management was offering a $35 increase spread over three years, a figure Max Arons, president of Local 802, described as "ridiculous." Also at issue were improved pensions, welfare and health benefits, and higher seniority pay.

As it happened, two other local musical organizations had also been going through similar negotiations. The New York City Opera Orchestra had been on strike for three weeks, but it was resolved just as the Philharmonic's strike was beginning; and an agreement preventing a threatened strike at Radio City Music Hall was reached at the same time. The Philharmonic's strike led to the cancellation of the Philadelphia Orchestra's first New York concert of the season when its members refused to cross the picket lines outside Avery Fisher Hall.

The previous strike in 1961 had lasted one week, so no one was prepared for the length of the current one: it dragged on for nine weeks. Tempers flared often on both sides, the management accusing the musicians of trying to capitalize on the size of Avery Fisher's gift, which was made to Lincoln Center, not to the Philharmonic, and the musicians adamantly denying the accusation, claiming that their proposals had been made long before there was any indication the Fisher gift would be made. The Society agreed to accept arbitration, but the musicians union refused.

There was also talk by the musicians of a conspiracy among the managements of the top major orchestras, who, according to one member, had "contracted in blood to each other to show the union that they must fight for every nickel." The violist Ralph Mendelson, part of the Philharmonic's negotiating team, said, "We're absolutely convinced the management wanted a strike here... to demonstrate the orchestra's failure to get Government funds." The aim, it was said, was to humiliate the Philharmonic, as had been done to the Cleveland Orchestra four years before. It was felt that Amyas Ames would have a feather in his cap in the eyes of other orchestra board chairmen. Harold Lawrence pointed out, however, that the National Endowment for the Arts was withholding a grant to the Philharmonic until the strike was settled. Although Amyas Ames admitted he and other symphony officials discussed their mutual problems, there was no conspiracy among them.

The root of the problem was that the musicians of the Chicago Symphony Orchestra, after a four-week work stoppage, had very recently won a $60-a-week increase over a three-year period, a settlement the Philharmonic management said it could not match. Before the Chicago agreement the Philharmonic's $330 weekly minimum exceeded Chicago's by $10. Now Chicago had jumped $50 ahead. It was deemed important for the Philharmonic to lead Chicago because of New York City's higher cost of living. The Philharmonic's management maintained that the size of the Chicago settlement, which had surprised them, should disprove any claims of conspiracy among managements.

Meanwhile, the musicians prepared for an undertaking the likes of which had never been attempted by an orchestra—a foreign tour not under the management of the parent organization. Arranged through Ibermusica of Madrid, seven concerts were planned during a nine-day period in Spain, Portugal, and the Canary Islands, with the first concert on November 12 in Lisbon. Before that, though, New Yorkers got an opportunity to hear what they had been missing when the orchestra played a concert in Carnegie Hall on October 29 to benefit its emergency strike fund. The musicians had asked Pierre Boulez to conduct. He initially agreed but had to withdraw when the board denied him permission, though Ames said that Boulez "was right to accept." Originally scheduled for October 16, the concert had to be postponed as the orchestra cast about for a conductor. About forty well-known conductors and soloists had been approached, but all declined. Some felt they had been pressured by the management to refuse for fear of never appearing with the Philharmonic again—assuming there ever would be a Philharmonic again, which at that point was very much in doubt.

In the end, a very adept conductor agreed to participate: Léon Barzin, conductor of the New York City Ballet and founding music director of the National Orchestral Association, a premier training orchestra in New York City in which many Philharmonic members had played as students. The Belgian-born Barzin had been principal violist of the Philharmonic many years before and had played under such conductors as Willem Mengelberg, Wilhelm Furtwängler, and Toscanini. This concert became a sort of homecoming for him. Performing as soloists were the principal flutist, Julius Baker; the principal horn, John Cerminaro; and the principal cellist, Lorne Munroe.

Eugene Becker, for many years a violist in the Philharmonic, told of the excitement of that concert, first of all because it marked the orchestra's return to Carnegie Hall and what that meant both historically and acoustically. Secondly, the musicians did not straggle onto the stage in the time-honored manner. Having tuned up backstage, they appeared in single file, walking smartly to their seats, followed immediately by Barzin, who, after a quick bow to the audience, turned and gave a decisive downbeat for the explosive opening of the Overture to Berlioz's *Benvenuto Cellini*. Said Becker, "It was electrifying."

The musicians rejected what the management said was its final offer of a $50 raise over three years, with other increased benefits. With nothing settled, they took off for Portugal. For their tour they had engaged the Russian-born, Israeli-based conductor Yuri Ahronovitch. Some members remained in New York to continue the negotiations, while substitute pickets appeared in the form of wives and children, as well as additional reinforcements provided by Local 802.

Most of the arrangements and logistics for the tour were in the capable hands of John Schaeffer, the orchestra's principal double bassist and assistant personnel manager, who earned much praise from his colleagues for his yeoman efforts. The expedition turned out to be a triumph for all concerned, orchestra and conductor alike, with enthusiastic capacity audiences and rave reviews all along the way. The only difficulty arose over the manner in which the ninety-five-member orchestra was listed on posters and programs, ranging from "members of" or "professors of" the New York Philharmonic to simply the New York Philharmonic. This last billing raised objections from the orchestra's management and board, and a lawsuit over use of the name was threatened.

Upon returning, the musicians were greeted by a six-page letter from Amyas Ames offering the same package they had rejected before leaving. On November 29 the *New York Times*, under the headline "Agreement Reached in Orchestra Strike," told of the tentative agreement on a new contract, soon ratified, under which the members would receive an increase of $50, prorated over three years, bringing the base salary at the end of that time to $380 (the same as for the Chicago Symphony), along with increases in pension, medical and dental benefits, and life insurance. Additionally, a rotating seating arrangement, later adopted by many other orchestras, was established for string players. Thus, what the musicians accepted was the package they had rejected earlier, and they still lacked superiority to Chicago. The board president, Carlos Moseley, missed the whole episode. He had suffered two heart attacks prior to the beginning of negotiations and was unable to participate. The musicians felt that, had he been involved, matters would have been settled quickly and amicably.

Ames's letter of November 19 concluded with some personal comments on allegations he had heard during the negotiations. According to the letter, he had been most distressed over the allegation that management had wanted the strike and hoped no one had actually believed that. He went on to cite management's willingness to have the dispute submitted to binding arbitration, with the concerts resumed immediately, even though he was concerned about the financial risks of doing so. "It was important to end the strike," he said.

After the loss of nine weeks of concerts, the season resumed without fanfare on December 6, 1973, with the program originally scheduled for that date. However, the scheduled conductor, Daniel Barenboim, had withdrawn to be in England with his wife, the cellist Jacqueline du Pré, who had been stricken with multiple sclerosis. Filling in was the Polish conductor Jerzy (then Georg) Semkow, who had made his Philharmonic debut in 1969. Vladimir Ashkenazy was the soloist in the seldom-heard Scriabin Piano Concerto, and Tchaikovsky's Fifth Symphony, the main orchestral work, was a work Semkow had conducted during his previous engagement. (One critic, apparently not realizing that the originally scheduled program had been retained, took him to task for repeating himself.)

Boulez returned the following week to devote the entire program to a real rarity, Schumann's Scenes from Goethe's *Faust*. Calling for a chorus and multiple vocal soloists, it is not a *Faust* piece that turns up often, as do certain works by Berlioz, Gounod, and others, though it is very lovely ("a bit *too* lovely," in the words of the conductor Michael Gielen). As expected, Schonberg found Boulez's presentation of Schumann's romanticism to be very objective and not very romantic at all, though certainly well organized.

For the concerts beginning December 20, Boulez revived Copland's *Connotations*, the work that had aroused such a storm of protest when premiered on the opening night of Lincoln Center in 1962. This time there was no storm at all, merely very warm applause, with a few cheers, as the composer took a bow. Time marches on.

A Season of Substitutes

In his autobiography, *Cadenza: A Musical Career*, Erich Leinsdorf wrote, "If I am asked to pinpoint the most confused, maddening, and puzzling day of my professional career I must select without any close second December 31, 1973." The day had begun with a phone call from the Philharmonic president, Carlos Moseley, who informed Leinsdorf that the orchestra's first rehearsal for the next Thursday's concert had begun with an assistant conductor in charge because the scheduled guest conductor had not arrived, was not in his hotel, and, as far as anyone knew, was not even in New York. Even his agent could not locate him.

Leinsdorf was asked if he could take over the week's concerts, to which he "agreed lightheartedly," feeling there was some sort of misunderstanding between the absent conductor and the Philharmonic that would soon be cleared up: "I could not conceive in my wildest dreams that a thirty-two-year-old man, making his Philharmonic debut, would simply not show up." The statute of limitations having presumably run out, it can now be revealed that the conductor in question was Riccardo Muti.

Muti was ill with the flu and bronchitis in Italy. Apparently his efforts to contact the Philharmonic had been thwarted by an Italian postal strike as well as difficulties with both the telegraph and the telephone systems there, exacerbated by the Christmas and New Year holidays. In short, he did not appear and Leinsdorf did, thus making his debut with the Philharmonic in its subscription series. Nor did Muti appear for his second week, thus clearing the way for Leonard Slatkin to make *his* debut with the orchestra. For both Leinsdorf and Slatkin, it was the beginning of long associations with the Philharmonic.

For the concerts beginning January 17, Leinsdorf was again at the helm, this time replacing Thomas Schippers, who was recovering from major surgery. (Owing to his commitments at the Metropolitan Opera, Leinsdorf was not available for the Saturday night concert, so his place was taken by Morton Gould, who was not generally known for conducting the scheduled Mozart and Brahms symphonies.)

On January 31, Pierre Boulez denied a report that he would be leaving the Philharmonic when his second three-year contract expired in 1977. "No, I have not closed the door to the Philharmonic. I could not, because it has not been opened yet," he told the *New York Times*, adding that his first contract had just ended and he had not discussed any future plans after 1977 with the Philharmonic. The confusion was apparently caused by his decision to return to Paris in 1975 as founding director of the Institute for Research and Coordination of Acoustics and Music (IRCAM) and by the announcement that he would be giving up the directorship of the BBC Symphony the same year.

Boulez had planned the season to include an exploration of the *Faust* theme. Schumann's Scenes from Goethe's *Faust* had already been given, and the week beginning with the concert of February 14 was devoted to Mahler's Eighth Symphony, the second and final movement of which is a setting of the last scene from Goethe's masterpiece. The work is infrequently performed—previous Philharmonic presentations had been given by Leopold Stokowski in 1950 and Leonard Bernstein in 1965—because of the extremely large orchestral and choral forces required, not to mention the eight vocal soloists. Although it has been dubbed the "Symphony of a Thousand," performances generally do not involve a thousand participants; it just seems that way, what with the stage packed and, often, an extension built out into the hall. A performance of the Mahler Eighth is not merely a concert, it is an event. And this was for the most part a very successful event, even though at times the hall's acoustics mitigated against a favorable balance of the performing forces. Especially in the second movement, according to Schonberg, Boulez seemed close to the spirit of the music, employing tempo changes appropriate for the score though unusual for the normally straightforward Boulez.

During his tenure Boulez conducted only one Brahms symphony; that composer apparently did not appeal to his intellect. But that one, of course, was the most intellectually conceived of the Brahms symphonies: the Fourth, with its magnificent concluding chaconne. His reading, according to the *Times*'s Raymond Ericson, "lightened the string texture and put more emphasis on the winds.... It was a fat-free performance, healthy nourishment for ears afflicted with musical cholesterol."

At the concert of April 25 four musicians were honored upon their retirement: the violinist William Dembinsky, who had joined the orchestra in 1934; the associate principal horn player, Joseph Singer, who had held that position since 1943; the cellist George Feher, who had become a member in 1948; and the second flutist, Robert Morris, who had been with the orchestra since 1955. On April 27 it was announced that Eliot Chapo, age twenty-eight, would be the new concertmaster, succeeding Rafael Druian. A graduate of the Curtis Institute, Chapo had been associate concertmaster of the Pittsburgh Symphony. On hearing him play Mozart's Concerto No. 3 in G Major, K. 216, on April 26, Raymond Ericson noted that his "articulation was among the cleanest this listener has ever heard from a violinist."

What with nine weeks lost due to the orchestra's strike and several conductor substitutions, including a substitute for a substitute, the 1973–74 season was a difficult one. Again Barenboim canceled his remaining two scheduled weeks, which gave opportunities to two young conductors, the Italian Aldo Ceccato and the German Bernhard Klee. But the most highly anticipated guest conductor appeared for the last two weeks, Zubin Mehta. Mehta's originally scheduled engagement had been canceled after his insulting remarks about the Philharmonic years earlier, and now here he was in his debut with the orchestra (not counting his Lewisohn Stadium concerts in 1960, technically with the Stadium Symphony Orchestra). Apparently the hatchet was buried during his rehearsals, when he apologized for his earlier statements and told the musicians how much he respected them. Bygones were thus allowed to be bygones.

His first week of concerts began on May 9 with a most unusual program. As a subtheme for the season, Boulez had selected the music of Weber, and since Weber is best known for the overtures to his various operas, a sprinkling of them were heard during the latter part of the season. There was no sprinkling for Mehta, however, who began his concert with a succession of three of the least familiar overtures, followed by Messiaen's sonically imposing work for winds and percussion, *Et exspecto resurrectionem mortuorum*. The program concluded with Saint-Saëns's Third Symphony ("Organ").

The season did end on a note of concern, for there was an unusually large operating deficit of $2.2 million, and a huge net deficit was anticipated. A fund-raising campaign was organized by the Friends of the Philharmonic, which brought in over $800,000, with another $160,000 projected, but $200,000 remained to be raised. There was also a campaign to raise $12 million in endowment funds, and an existing endowment of equal amount produced interest income of $600,000. Inflation and increased costs were creating hard financial times for many arts organizations. The Philharmonic had done well with income from ticket sales and recordings, but this is never enough to completely cover the operating budget, and the management had refused to raise admission above the astronomical top price of $10.

The second season of Rug Concerts occupied the week of June 11 and proved to be as successful as the first, if not even more so. Offered at reduced prices and attracting a largely youthful audience, the concerts played to full and appreciative houses. Never before in the history of Philharmonic concerts had there been such enthusiastic responses to the music of Berg, Webern, Varèse, Ligeti, and Boulez himself, not to mention such canonic composers as Bartók and Stravinsky, whose

Rite of Spring closed the series in triumph. Boulez had found the audience for which he had been searching ever since the beginning of his tenure. So successful were the concerts—in the *Times* of June 30, Donal Henahan wondered "how the same kind of wild acclaim could greet both a drab performance of the Brahms Fourth Symphony and a totally gripping one of Stravinsky's *Le Sacre*"—that two weeks were planned for the following year. Only the evening on which Schoenberg was the featured composer (in honor of his centennial) failed to attract many listeners. The very presence of his name on a program has always been anathema to regular concertgoers, and apparently the same was true of the young and adventurous.

On June 26 was announced the death of Helen M. Thompson, the Philharmonic's manager from 1970 to 1973. As executive secretary of the American Symphony Orchestra League, she had overseen a remarkable expansion and improvement of orchestras of every caliber throughout the country and had been a tireless advocate for the arts, especially music.

Leonard Bernstein, who had taken a sabbatical during 1973–74, returned for a concert in Central Park on August 6, drawing an audience estimated by the police at 130,000. Soon afterward the orchestra left on a tour of Australia, New Zealand, and Japan, with conducting duties shared between Bernstein and Boulez.

The *Times* of October 14, 1974, carried news of the death of the conductor Josef Krips at the age of seventy-two. Best known for his interpretations of the Viennese classics, his music directorships in the United States were of the Buffalo Philharmonic (1954–63) and the San Francisco Symphony (1963–70), and he was, of course, a frequent guest with the New York Philharmonic. Of all the guest conductors during the 1961–62 season, he was the only one who showed an understanding of why the three assistant conductors were there, that it was a learning experience for us. Accordingly, he discussed his repertoire with us, explaining his interpretive decisions. Well remembered is a limousine trip with him to Princeton, New Jersey, where he rehearsed the Westminster Choir in the finale of Beethoven's Ninth Symphony prior to their performing it with the Philharmonic.

The 1974–75 season was marked by two mini-festivals jointly presented by the Philharmonic and the Chamber Music Society of Lincoln Center. The first, on October 8–12, in honor of the composer's centennial, was titled Mini-Festival around Ives. The great American iconoclast's works were played alongside those of other composers of his time, allowing them all to be heard in their chronological and musical context. The joint sponsorship resulted in programs resembling concerts of the nineteenth century, in which orchestral works were interspersed with chamber and solo instrumental pieces. Thus, the opening concert on October 8, over which Boulez presided, consisted of orchestral works by Ives, Copland, Webern, and

Stravinsky, along with a string quartet by Ives and piano pieces by Ruth Crawford Seeger. For this performance the stage of Avery Fisher Hall was extended, with the orchestra further into the hall than usual, much in the manner of the Rug Concerts. There were no rugs, but seating space was now available behind the orchestra so listeners could face the conductor. The arrangement was, in fact, an acoustic experiment, for there was still much dissatisfaction with Fisher Hall's acoustics. Performances of a more intimate nature were given in the Juilliard Theater, which had proven so hospitable in the past, and the mini-festival concluded on October 12, back in Fisher Hall, with the full Philharmonic holding forth in Ives's extremely complex and cacophonous Symphony No. 4, though the third-movement fugue is a model of simplicity. Some conductors have since devised a way in which the score can be led by a single maestro, but at the time the work's complexities, with more than one tempo occurring simultaneously, required at least two conductors. Second in command here was David Gilbert, a former pupil of Boulez, who had recently appointed him the Philharmonic's assistant conductor. The *Times*'s Allen Hughes praised the "eloquent performance" of the symphony, with the mainly youthful audience remaining to applaud for several minutes (in contrast to the normal subscription audience, which would immediately begin heading for the exits the moment the last chord sounded).

A mini-festival around Schubert occupied the dates March 4–8, again with the featured composer heard in combination with others, and not necessarily of his time. Ravel's *Valses nobles et sentimentales* and Hugo Wolf's *Italian Serenade* certainly stretched the time frame, although the former was at least nominally inspired by Schubert. The great novelty of the series, and it would have been so in any context, was Schubert's one-act opera-cantata *Lazarus*, which Boulez offered on March 7. The designation "one-act" is deceptive, for Schubert began a second act but soon abandoned it. Boulez presented the complete score as left by Schubert, which Raymond Ericson found to be "sublime... with an angelic glow hovering over all." In fact, the entire program, which included Schumann's Andante and Variations and Mozart's String Quartet in F Major, K. 590, was proclaimed "an extraordinary concert!"

Administrative news appeared on March 1 with the announcement that Albert K. Webster, general manager of the Cincinnati Symphony, had been appointed managing director of the Philharmonic, effective in July. Known in the profession as Nick Webster (the "K." stands for Knickerbocker), he had joined the Philharmonic in 1962 as an assistant to the manager, Carlos Moseley, and had been assistant manager from 1966 to 1971. Harold Lawrence was leaving to become an independent arts consultant.

On March 26 came the announcement that because of long-standing frustration with its acoustics, Avery Fisher Hall would be gutted the following year and a completely new interior built, supervised by the acoustician Cyril M. Harris and the architect Philip Johnson. Work would begin in May 1976, the hall would be closed for five months, and the estimated cost would be between $2 million and $3 million. The Boston Symphony and the Philadelphia Orchestra had already announced their plans to return to Carnegie Hall for their New York concerts, mainly on account of Fisher Hall's poor acoustics. The Philharmonic was not about to follow suit. Amyas Ames said that it was clear that something needed to be done and that the reputation of Lincoln Center was at stake. A responsibility to the musicians who play there was also a factor: "We have great confidence in Dr. Harris and Mr. Johnson, and we look forward to a hall equal to any in the world."

Shortly after this announcement, Leonard Bernstein returned to the podium for three weeks after a year's absence from the subscription season. His programs included two suites from his recently completed ballet score, *Dybbuk*. But what really made news was a statement he made to the audience on April 24 after a typically impassioned performance of Tchaikovsky's Fourth Symphony, the concluding work on his final program: "I've just made a decision. I don't know how, I don't know when, but I'm going to come back to this orchestra." Philharmonic officials, and no doubt everyone else, were caught by surprise at this announcement, delivered in an emotional tone. Harold Lawrence described it as "an impulsive thing" and said that "there had been no discussion about any announcement." Carlos Moseley declared that everyone was "delighted that Mr. Bernstein had been so pleased. We have wanted him for more weeks than he has been able to give us, and there will be great joy if he will give us more time." Friends of Bernstein spoke of how much he had enjoyed himself during this engagement, and that the orchestra had reciprocated: "It was like the resumption of an old love affair."

In a dramatic sequel to Bernstein's remark, Pierre Boulez announced on May 15 that he would indeed be closing the door on the Philharmonic; he would not return as music director after the expiration of his contract in 1977. Now speculation increased as to Bernstein's plans. "All I meant," he said, "was that when the other guy's contract was up, I'd like to talk the situation over with the Philharmonic." Referring to Boulez as "the other guy" does denote a certain lack of respect on Bernstein's part. Of course, they were worlds apart both in conducting and compositional styles, and were not professionally or personally close. A Philharmonic musician has said that on the return flight from Japan the year before, Bernstein and Boulez sat far apart from each other and did not exchange a word for the entire flight. In any case, it was reported that Boulez was leaving voluntarily. Everyone knew that Bernstein had no interest in returning to the administrative duties required of a music director, so what the future held in store was anybody's guess. What was not a guess was that another Great Conductor Search was about to begin.

CHAPTER 6

1975–78

LOSING MONEY WISELY

Before the start of the 1975 Rug Concerts, Boulez joked that the Philharmonic should play thirty weeks of Rug Concerts and two weeks of subscription concerts. Many a truth is spoken in jest. The audiences at the Rug Concerts had shown themselves to be deeply attentive and attuned to the music, as well as extremely enthusiastic toward advanced repertoire that would drive the Philharmonic's regular audiences out of the hall, with much banging of seats. It was this devoted and largely youthful audience that prompted the decision to extend the 1975 series to two weeks, this time with sponsorship from Exxon, the National Endowment for the Arts, and the New York State Council on the Arts.

Boulez's previous innovations had mostly fallen by the wayside. Gone were the composer retrospectives, pre-concert recitals, and informal evenings at Juilliard. Even the Prospective Encounters had been reduced to two each season, while the mini-festivals had failed to attract the type of audience for which they were apparently intended (with certain exceptions, such as the performance of the Ives Fourth Symphony). Only the Rug Concerts endured and, indeed, flourished. To open the 1975 series on June 18, Boulez conducted three orchestral excerpts from Berlioz's *Romeo and Juliet*, Stravinsky's *Song of the Nightingale*, Ives's *Robert Browning Overture*, and three dances from Manuel de Falla's *Three-Cornered Hat*. David Hamilton noted in the *Times* that there was "a greater warmth and urgency in [Boulez's] music making in June" than in the regular season, and Raymond Ericson commented, apropos of the program just described, that Boulez conducted "with clarity and elegance" and that the concert "was a splendid opening to one of New York's best musical experiences."

The orchestra did have some help during the series, for the Tashi Quartet performed Messiaen's *Quartet for the End of Time*, and members of the chamber ensemble Speculum Musicae offered Bartók's Sonata for Two Pianos and Percussion and Luciano Berio's *Circles*. The problem facing the Philharmonic was how to transfer the immediacy and excitement of the Rug Concerts to the regular subscription season. (A subscription audience buys a series of concerts and attends all or most of them more or less dutifully, while others attend individual concerts because they want to hear a particular program, or even a particular piece on a program.)

Knowing that Avery Fisher Hall would not be available in the summer of 1976, and possibly not even in the fall, because of its interior reconstruction, on August 11 the Philharmonic held a day of rehearsals at the Beacon Theater, located on Broadway between Seventy-fourth and Seventy-fifth Streets. In preparation for the forthcoming European tour, Mahler's Ninth Symphony, which had been performed the previous fall and at the recent Rug Concerts, was the order of the day. Carlos Moseley found the acoustics fine but stressed that this rehearsal was entirely provisional, and that other possible venues were under consideration.

The tour, which would be Boulez's only foreign excursion with the orchestra, began with concerts at the Edinburgh Festival and then continued to London, Ghent, Brussels, Lucerne, Berlin, Bonn, Frankfurt, Stuttgart, Mannheim, Munich, Paris, and Chartres, where the orchestra performed in the great cathedral. In London two concerts were played in the large, circular Royal Albert Hall as part of the BBC's Proms, for which the seats in the central area of the hall are removed, the space then occupied by standees and others seated on the floor, perhaps on cushions. The members of this largely youthful group were the real "Promenaders," and they were the same type of audience Boulez was attracting with the Rug Concerts.

One of the Promenaders' traditions is to indulge in unison chants directed at the performers before the start of the concert. In this instance the Philharmonic was greeted by "Welcome to our friends in the Colonies" and "What's a nice orchestra like you doing in a place like this?" Bert Bial, the orchestra's contrabassoonist and official photographer, on being observed snapping pictures, was asked if he was from the CIA.

Such high jinks aside, the sold-out concerts were extremely successful wherever the orchestra played, with audiences and critics equally enthusiastic. The critic for Paris's *Le Monde*, as reported in the *New York Times* of September 21, enthused that "the Philharmonic was one of the finest orchestras in the world, that Mr. Boulez's conducting was beyond praise and that he had never in his life heard a more unbelievably beautiful *Petrushka*, making it sound 'like brand new music.'" (Boulez had not conducted in Paris for twelve years, having left France because he did not feel it was musically progressive enough.) Only some British critics dissented, disapproving of Boulez's sequencing of the excerpts from Berlioz's *Roméo et Juliette*. On the other hand, there was unanimous acclaim for the program of Elliott Carter's *Concerto for Orchestra* and Mahler's Ninth Symphony.

A sad note intruded with the announcement on September 2 of the death, at age seventy-four, of John Corigliano, the Philharmonic's concertmaster for twenty-three years, who had retired from the orchestra, but not from music, in 1966. (Upon leaving the Philharmonic he headed for San Antonio, where the music director, Victor Alessandro, had engaged him as concertmaster.) He had been appointed assistant concertmaster by Toscanini in 1935 and was heard as a soloist in a wide variety of repertoire in practically every season thereafter.

A happier note was sounded less than two weeks later with the announcement that, after a hiatus of eight years, the Philharmonic was returning to the airwaves. Carried live by CBS for many years, from 1963 the broadcasts were heard on tape on the Philharmonic Radio Network until 1967, when the musicians decided they were not being compensated sufficiently for them. Now, sponsored by the Exxon Corporation, they would be heard via tape for a thirty-nine-week broadcast season, with commentary by Martin Bookspan. In the New York City area the concerts would be carried by WQXR in the traditional Sunday afternoon time slot. The opening concerts of the 1975–76 season concluded with Boulez's celebrated rendition of *The Rite of Spring*. Donal Henahan noted on September 27 that Stravinsky himself preferred a steady pulse and clarity over the normally heard theatrical violence presented by most conductors, and that Boulez was, as expected, true to the composer's wishes. The following week Beethoven's Ninth Symphony was heard "in an honest performance" such as "can not only increase the pulse rate but also creep into the imagination, where it may stay for days." Boulez had previously been found wanting in the classic repertoire, so this was encouraging news. However, Irving Kolodin, in the November 15 *Saturday Review*, wrote of the performance as having been "brittle, swift, high-strung rather than emotionally taut." He felt that Boulez's "time-beating" did not produce the best results from the soloists Johanna Meier, Betty Allen, Jerry Jennings, and Simon Estes, or from the Westminster Choir, which has a long history of fine performances of the Ninth. The complete score for Bartók's early ballet *The Wooden Prince*, a Boulez favorite heard on October 10, was found by Henahan to be "interminable," making for "tedious concert listening."

The *Times* of November 27 announced the death of David M. Keiser, long active in the life of the Philharmonic as its president (1956–63), board chairman (1963–70), and honorary chairman since 1970. He had been involved in the selection of Leonard Bernstein as music director, as well as that of Pierre Boulez. A retired executive in the sugar industry, he also had musical training and in December 1959, along with Bernstein and Carlos Moseley, had participated in performances of Bach's Concerto in C Major for three pianos. On November 26 Boulez and the orchestra played, in Keiser's memory, Mozart's Adagio and Fugue in C Minor before proceeding with the scheduled program, which ended with Edgard Varèse's formidable *Amériques*, the first score he wrote in the United States. Schonberg concluded his largely favorable review by noting that "there was no move toward the exits, as there has been with unfamiliar music in recent years. Perhaps the proselytizing of Mr. Boulez has converted the pagans."

Today the *Live from Lincoln Center* telecasts are a regular, if intermittent, feature on the Public Broadcasting System, so it is of interest to note that the first such event, with support from Exxon and several foundations, took place on January 30, 1976, with a New York Philharmonic concert conducted by André Previn. Van Cliburn was the soloist in Grieg's Piano Concerto (supposedly a popular piece, but one the Philharmonic had not programmed since 1957), and Strauss's *Ein Heldenleben* was the major orchestral work. Writing of the performance given two days before the telecast, Henahan found it "a rather tedious preview," though, as one who viewed the program at home, the author cannot agree.

It is unusual for an orchestra to present Beethoven's Ninth Symphony twice in the same season under two different conductors. Boulez had opened the season with it, and here it was again on February 4, 1976, for a pension-fund benefit concert conducted by Sir Georg Solti, who had last appeared with the Philharmonic in January 1962. In the meantime, of course, he had become music director of the Chicago Symphony Orchestra, a post that undoubtedly prevented him from accepting American guest-conducting engagements. However, he was available for special occasions such as this one. His chorus was the Camerata Singers, of which Abraham Kaplan was director; and his soloists were Heather Harper, Mignon Dunn, Stuart Burrows, and John Macurdy. Raymond Ericson wrote in the *Times* that Solti's typically propulsive style was detrimental to the majesty of the first movement, which was too heavily accented and harshly driven, but that matters improved as the work progressed, leading to "an electrifying finale." In general, orchestra members did not feel the same chemistry between them and Solti as he had found in Chicago.

The Great Conductor Search was not unusually protracted, for on February 26, 1976, it was announced that the new music director of the Philharmonic, to take effect with the 1978–79 season, would be Zubin Mehta. Although the newspapers could not help but recall the remarks Mehta had made about the Philharmonic in 1967, nor refrain from commenting on the obvious differences between him and Boulez (the latter "cool, austere and rigorous," Mehta "more in the Leonard Bernstein mold—dashing, vigorous, glamorous"), he was given credit for being a hard worker, "a musician of integrity and courage, as well as of dash and passion." And he had spent fourteen years with one orchestra, the Los Angeles Philharmonic, which had improved markedly under his direction.

Born in Bombay (now Mumbai) in 1936, Mehta was also music director of the Israel Philharmonic Orchestra, a position he holds for life. The press mention of courage may refer to his directing that orchestra in concerts during the Six-Day War in 1967, when at least one other noted conductor canceled his Israeli engagements. That bravery would also come in handy in New York, as far as the *New York Times* was concerned: an editorial on February 28 concluded that "the young man from Bombay is entering a musical lion's den. It is fortunate that he knows it."

Because Mehta's appointment would not take effect for two years, it was announced that the 1977–78 season would be led entirely by guest conductors. This was not unprecedented, as witness the 1969–70 and 1970–71 seasons following Bernstein's departure and preceding Boulez's arrival. Meanwhile, however, Boulez had still to complete the current season and prepare for 1976–77, his own farewell season. One of the major works he presented, shortly after the Mehta announcement, was the Third Symphony of Roger Sessions on March 4. The program book, and thus the newspapers, erroneously stated that it was the New York premiere of the 1957 work. In fact, the Sessions Third, composed for the seventy-fifth anniversary of the Boston Symphony Orchestra, had been played in New York by that ensemble, Charles Munch conducting, on December 11, 1957. The "new" work was found by Schonberg to be "impressive" but "academic." Writing of a later performance on March 6, his colleague Raymond Ericson thought it "an eloquent and rich work." That later hearing was part of the opening concert of a Celebration of Contemporary Music given jointly by the Philharmonic, Juilliard, and the Fromm Music Foundation. Other composers included on that program were Jacob Druckman and Bruno Maderna; works by Gunther Schuller, Easley Blackwood, and Peter Maxwell Davies were heard on March 13. Sessions's Second Symphony had been given its New York premiere in 1950 by Mitropoulos and the Philharmonic, who recorded it for Columbia Records, but that splendid score has not been heard again by Philharmonic audiences, nor has the Third. The music of Sessions continues to be difficult for audiences to assimilate.

When Leonard Bernstein returned on March 25 to conduct Bruckner's rather infrequently heard Sixth Symphony, it was hoped he would do for that Austrian master what he had done for Mahler—that is, popularize him. In spite of his "superb performance," it never happened, for all that Bruckner is nevertheless recognized as one of the greats.

Within fifteen minutes after Boulez gave the downbeat for the last chord of Mahler's Seventh Symphony on May 16, thus concluding the 1975–76 season, Avery Fisher Hall was inundated by stagehands and other workmen, who began removing the seats. This was the beginning of a complete dismantling of the hall for the purpose of overhauling the acoustics. The process was expected to take five months, at a cost of more than $5 million, and all concerned began to hold their collective breath in the hope that everything would indeed be ready in time for the opening of the 1976–77 season on October 21.

Of course, there were other places for the Phillharmonic to play in the meantime—and no place better than Carnegie Hall, where Bernstein, on May 20, conducted an all-American program in honor of the U.S. bicentennial. The orchestra, audience, and critics reveled in the warmth and mellowness of the sound, something that had been sorely lacking in fourteen years at Lincoln Center.

Bernstein and the orchestra took the bicentennial program to Europe, the first time an American orchestra had toured Europe with an all-American program. Appropriately, the tour ended in Paris on June 18 with a performance of Gershwin's *An American in Paris*, the concluding work on a concert given in the Tuileries Garden. It was another first—the first time the Philharmonic had played in a circus tent—and all part of a summer festival, complete with shooting galleries and merry-go-rounds. An unusual aspect of the program was William Warfield's French narration of Copland's *Lincoln Portrait*. About the program, Bernstein commented: "It went differently in different places. In London, they thought Roy Harris was the greatest [thing] going, and in Germany they thought it was banal. But they all loved Gershwin, and my music too." Bernstein also remarked on "how much of a risk it is to bring an all-American program on tour." Indeed, though artistically successful, the tour resulted in a deficit of $300,000. As Nick Webster put it, "We are in the business of losing money wisely."

BOULEZ BIDS ADIEU

The Philharmonic embarked on its second overseas tour in less than a year (less than three months, in fact), when it paid a visit to Scandinavia and its first to the Soviet Union since its historic tour of 1959. No Bernstein this time, not even Boulez, who was still, after all, the orchestra's music director. Instead, Erich Leinsdorf and Thomas Schippers shared the conducting duties that began on August 31 in Malmö, Sweden, and ended on September 17 in Moscow. Leinsdorf came in for special praise for the concert in Leningrad on September 7. As reported the next day in the *New York Times*, the Soviet news agency Tass found Leinsdorf to be "a conductor with great knowledge and creativity. The concert of the New York Philharmonic orchestra became a veritable fête... [with] the performance of extra-class musicians." Leinsdorf's program included the first performance in the Soviet Union of Roy Harris's Third Symphony.

But concerts were not the only thing that occupied the musicians on that tour. Conscious of a wide gap separating Soviet and American musical life in terms of knowledge and economic and working conditions, orchestra members gave lectures, clinics, and workshops for music students at the Leningrad and Moscow Conservatories. Webster bought tickets for the last two concerts in each city to distribute free to interested Russians who could not afford or obtain tickets and brought along scores of significant American works for Soviet musicians unfamiliar with them. Additionally, reeds and mouthpieces were given to young Soviet musicians who could not otherwise obtain good ones.

Back on home ground, the orchestra embarked on a series unique in its history. As mentioned earlier, in 1960 the Philharmonic performed a series of concerts featuring Mahler symphonies and lieder to commemorate the centennial of the composer's birth, and the event was credited as beginning the Mahler boom. But it was several years before all the symphonies were given. Now, in the space of one month, and in Carnegie Hall no less (the reconstruction of Avery Fisher Hall not yet completed), the Philharmonic would play all the Mahler symphonies, something that had not been done even in Mahler's brief tenure as the orchestra's conductor.

Leinsdorf opened the series on September 26 with the Fifth Symphony, preceded by the *Songs of a Wayfarer*, sung by Frederica von Stade, who was praised by Schonberg for "the combination of ravishing lyricism with the kind of simplicity that conceals high art." This was Leinsdorf's only appearance in the Mahler Festival. The remaining concerts would be shared between Boulez and James Levine. As Schonberg put it, "They will have the memory of this brilliant concert to shoot at." All the symphonies were given, including the Adagio from the unfinished Tenth, though not Deryck Cooke's (or anyone else's) performing version of the complete work, and not *Das Lied von der Erde*. Of the song cycles, only *Kindertotenlieder* was not heard. A Philharmonic musician has told of encountering Bernstein at a later time and asking him why he had not appeared in the Mahler cycle, to conduct some, if not all, of the concerts. His reply: "I wasn't asked."

Before the 1976–77 season could begin, storm clouds began brewing in the form of yet another musicians' strike. The last contract having expired on September 20, the orchestra had been playing the Mahler Festival under an extension of it. Now Max Arons, president of Local 802, recommended that the players vote to go on strike on October 19, which just happened to be the date scheduled for the reopening of Avery Fisher Hall. Again the musicians wanted a contract comparable to that of the Chicago Symphony, which gave them a minimum salary of $500 within three years. The current minimum for the Philharmonic was $380 a week, as it had been in Chicago before their new contract. A settlement was reached at the proverbial eleventh hour on October 19 as the assembling audience wondered whether there would actually be a concert. Perhaps the memory of the nine-week strike of three years before was a bit too fresh, for the musicians voted sixty-seven to thirty-six to accept a new three-year contract guaranteeing a minimum of $480 in its final year. It was reported that they had settled for $20 less than Chicago because of the Philharmonic's "tenuous financial condition."

And so the season opened on schedule, with a pension-fund benefit concert, Boulez conducting. Nathan Milstein, the soloist in the Brahms Violin Concerto, was making his first appearance with the orchestra since 1965. He had performed annually with the Philharmonic for many years up until 1958, after which he declined to do so as long as Bernstein was in charge. The nature of his antipathy to Bernstein is not known, but it is interesting to note that his 1965 engagement was during Bernstein's sabbatical year.

But the music on this occasion, including Stravinsky's complete *Firebird* score, took second place to the acoustics of the new Avery Fisher Hall, which was judged by Schonberg to be "infinitely superior to the old." The renovation allowed instruments to be heard in greater detail, the Philharmonic sounding like "a large chamber group." Everyone was happy, especially the musicians, who could now hear one another without difficulty, and what they could hear was of high quality. Boulez found the sound to be "very clean, precise—but not clinical. That's a kind of blend." What had been problematic before—the balance between the wood-winds and the strings—was now very good. Carnegie Hall was still held up as the standard, but according to Boulez, Carnegie's sound was darker, Avery Fisher's lighter, yet with greater bass projection than Carnegie. That view was seconded by the Philharmonic bassist James V. Candido, who said that the bass section had "a tremendous response now that we never had before," though without the warmth of Carnegie Hall.

The subscription season opened on October 21 with Boulez leading Mahler's Third Symphony, a holdover from the just-completed Mahler Festival. Again acoustics were the first point of interest. Despite the immense orchestra Mahler requires, plus a chorus and alto soloist, the acoustics were found to be "even more impressive than on opening night." Yvonne Minton was the soloist, "a marvelous vocalist to begin with, and the hall perfectly reproduced her big, warm, luscious singing."

Schonberg, an inveterate timer of performances, noted that in 1961 Bernstein (no speed demon where Mahler was concerned) had finished the symphony in 98 minutes, whereas Boulez took 113. The great difference in timing was the result of the latter's extremely slow tempo for the last movement, which he somehow managed to hold together. Schonberg found Boulez to be at his best, stressing coherence and shaping the music "with well paced tempos and with a canny use of ritards and other devices to lend variety." Overall the concert was "a magnificent evening in all respects."

Even in his last season Boulez was not afraid to offer his audience works that might upset them. The program of October 28 concluded with Olivier Messiaen's *Et exspecto resurrectionem mortuorum*, scored for woodwinds, brass, and percussion, without strings. After the third movement, according to Schonberg, "a group of subscribers fled the hall as though angry hornets were on their trail." Among the work's sonorities must be counted several massive solo strokes on an enormous gong, probably the loudest such sound ever called for by a composer (though the gong in Respighi's *Church Windows* might offer some competition).

The following week, on November 4, the subscribers were treated to John Cage's *Renga with Apartment House 1776*, a bicentennial commission that the Philharmonic shared with several other orchestras. Allen Hughes's *Times* review the next day bore the headline "Hundreds Walk Out of Premiere of John Cage Work at Fisher Hall." He wrote of "the mass exodus, the like of which this reporter has never witnessed in 25 years of professional concert-going." Although Boulez had been an early supporter of Cage, the two had had a falling out, so it was a reconciliation of sorts for Boulez to conduct this example of avant-garde cacophony.

On the same day the *Times* announced the death in Italy of Joseph De Angelis, a former bass player and the longtime personnel manager of the Philharmonic, at the age of seventy-two. He had always been an imposing presence onstage before rehearsals and concerts.

Bernstein conducted three weeks of concerts beginning November 25, when he offered the premieres of four of his own songs "from a work in progress." Poems by Conrad Aiken, Gregory Corso, Edna St. Vincent Millay, and Julia de Burgos supplied the texts, and Elaine Bonazzi, Victoria Canale, John Reardon, and Florence Quivar were the soloists. The work in progress, heard complete the following year, turned out to be *Songfest*. Allen Hughes thought the songs featured "admirable vocal writing that was both sensitive to the texts and affecting for the listener."

A songfest of a different sort was led by Bernstein on December 4 in the Philharmonic's first performance of Shostakovich's Symphony No. 14. This work is actually a setting of eleven poems about death by Federico García Lorca, Guillaume Apollinaire, Rainer Maria Rilke, and Wilhelm Küchelbecker, a nineteenth-century Russian writer. The verses were set in Russian translation and were sung idiomatically by the soprano Teresa Kubiak and the bass Isser Bushkin. Bernstein, who was selective in performing Shostakovich symphonies, proclaimed No. 14 a "towering masterpiece." Raymond Ericson found it to be "very striking and special" and expressed gratitude to Bernstein for programming it. Following the work on the program was the Third Symphony of Saint-Saëns, the "Organ" Symphony. Unfortunately, this programming choice emphasized the fact that Avery Fisher Hall had lost its pipe organ during the reconstruction, and that works calling for an organ had now to be given with an electronic instrument that produced an "ugly tone and snapping attacks." As of this writing, there is still no organ in Fisher Hall.

Every so often an article appears in the *Times* indicating that all is not well with the Philharmonic, as witness the Taubman article with which this book began. On December 19, 1976, a piece appeared by Helen Epstein, an assistant professor of journalism at New York University, with the headline "The Philharmonic—A Troubled Giant Facing Change." Epstein began by quoting a statement from a recent Philharmonic program book, published by Stagebill: "Between now and next May, the orchestra in well over 100 subscription and non-subscription concerts, will resent [*sic*] an imposing array of conductors, not to mention music covering a chronological span of three centuries." According to Epstein, "the typographical error inadvertently spoke much truth," and that issue of Stagebill was quickly snapped up by the musicians.

The gist of Epstein's extensive article was that the orchestra members, many of whom were quoted by name, did in fact resent what they regarded as a constant parade of conductors who "suck the blood" of the orchestra and a management that gives the musicians little or no say in artistic decisions. Said one member, "We are the lifeblood of the orchestra; the conductors are the vampires." She pointed out that although it was still one of the world's great orchestras, the Philharmonic had no distinctive personality of its own—unlike the Philadelphia Orchestra, known for the sheen of its string section, or the Cleveland Orchestra, for its perfection of ensemble playing. Those orchestras tend to retain their own personalities regardless of who is on the podium, while the Philharmonic plays very well or less well, depending on who is conducting. The co-principal trumpet, Gerard Schwarz, now an established conductor himself, was quoted as saying, "We perform a conductor's concert: if he doesn't conduct well, we won't play well. If he's great, we're great."

Also mentioned was the "schizophrenic" aspect of playing for both Bernstein and Boulez, the one conducting with great emotion, putting his very lifeblood into the music, but with poor rehearsal organization, and the other cool and dispassionate, as though "performing an autopsy." but with excellent use of rehearsal time. In general, the orchestra was looking forward to the arrival of Mehta, although one brass player said, "We're reserving judgment [about him]. We're a skeptical orchestra."

Of Boulez's remaining programs, interest centered particularly on the one scheduled for January 13, 1977, which opened with the New York premiere of his own *Rituel*. It was written in memory of Bruno Maderna, like Boulez a composer and conductor of avant-garde scores. Before this Boulez had programmed very little of his own music with the Philharmonic—only the *Improvisations on Mallarmé* in 1975. Schonberg found *Rituel* to be "a formidable score," though "a triumph of theory over substance," with "so little charm, so little variety." On the same program Boulez conducted Debussy's Symphonic Fragments from *Le martyre de Saint Sébastien* and Stravinsky's complete *Firebird*, both sensuous scores that he led "diligently" but with scant regard for their sensuousness.

An unusual soloist appeared on January 29 when Roland Kohloff was heard in the New York premiere of Franco Donatoni's *Concertino for Strings, Brass, and Solo Timpani*. Kohloff had succeeded his teacher, Saul Goodman, as the Philharmonic's timpanist in 1972 and, according to Raymond Ericson in the *Times* the next day, performed the "lively and attractive" Bartók-influenced work "with all the great skill and control at his command."

"One of Mr. Boulez's great evenings" was Schonberg's verdict on the concert of February 4. It might be called an "all-Boulez concert" from the standpoint of repertoire, for the program included Debussy's *Nocturnes* and Bartók's Piano Concerto No. 2 (with Maurizio Pollini as the soloist) and *Village Scenes*, concluding with Stravinsky's *Symphony of Psalms*. The Camerata Singers took part in all but the piano concerto, of which Schonberg had "not heard a stronger account" from either soloist or conductor. In this demanding program Boulez conducted everything "according to the spirit as well as the letter of the score."

February 18 brought the world premiere of Elliott Carter's *Symphony of Three Orchestras*. The composer, one hundred years old and still active at the time of this writing, had produced one of his typically complex pieces, with the orchestra, as the title implies, divided into three groups spread across the stage. The Philharmonic audience, normally resistant to dissonant compositions, received Carter and his work most cordially. Irving Kolodin, writing in the *Saturday Review* of April 2, 1977, found the symphony "a work of stunning authority and imposing imagination."

The orchestra's revolving concertmaster chair continued its spin with the appearance on March 11 of its new occupant, Rodney Friend. An Englishman, he had held the same position with the London Philharmonic before coming to New York. His solo vehicle on this occasion was the seldom heard Concerto No. 1 by Karol Szymanowski, an atmospheric piece that had not been programmed by the Philharmonic since 1951, when it was also performed by the concertmaster, John Corigliano. Friend's playing was highly praised by Donal Henahan, who commented on his flawlessness in the high positions, his full tone without heavy vibrato, and his "temperamental fire beneath [an] elegant surface." Erich Leinsdorf, the guest conductor, paid particular attention to the work's imposing sonorities without drowning out the soloist, which could easily happen in this piece.

Another world premiere was given by Boulez on May 6: *Star Child* by George Crumb. This is an immense score for large orchestra (including eight percussionists), children's chorus, and soprano soloist. Four conductors were needed to keep it all together, with the orchestra again divided into several groups and instrumentalists scattered throughout the hall. Schonberg found the work to be "sensitive, powerful, full of personality,...a significant step in Mr. Crumb's development." Irene Gubrud, the soprano soloist in her Philharmonic debut, possessed "a most impressive voice—strong, secure, always on pitch...and with perfect musicianship."

Following the intermission two members were honored on their retirement, to take effect at the end of the season: James Smith, trumpet, who had joined the orchestra in 1942, and the great principal oboist, Harold Gomberg, who had joined in 1943 and become a legend in his own time. Boulez presented Smith with a watch, but Gomberg was not onstage. Boulez explained that he was too shy, though this was not an adjective one would normally apply to Gomberg.

The Boulez era ended with the concerts beginning May 12, performances of Berlioz's great "dramatic legend" *The Damnation of Faust*, last given by the Philharmonic in 1966 with William Steinberg conducting. Thirty American composers were guests of the Philharmonic for Boulez's performance, composers who had works performed during the six years of Boulez's tenure, either by the full orchestra or in the Prospective Encounters series. Speeches were made by Amyas Ames and Aaron Copland, who said that American composers owed Boulez "a special debt of gratitude. His mere presence has brought our musical scene into the 1970s....We hate to see you go." This encomium is all the more striking when one remembers that when Boulez's appointment was announced in 1970, many American composers protested, feeling that he had very little sympathy for American music and that their music would not be performed by the Philharmonic (perhaps true in certain cases).

As for the performance of the Berlioz masterpiece, Schonberg on May 13 wrote that Boulez "did not give the feeling that the score was in his blood." Having conducted Berlioz "beautifully in the past...he was restrained, matter-of-fact and relatively colorless." Schonberg had more to say in his summing up of the Boulez era on May 15. While praising his performances of contemporary music, both the classics of the genre and the latest complex works, of which he was a supreme master, Schonberg reiterated his list of Boulez's shortcomings in the standard repertoire and mentioned his failure to win over the public (in spite of the fact that the concerts of the last season were 99 percent sold out) and, more seriously, the musicians, many of whom complained he did not appear to be very touched by music. Others felt that the Philharmonic was a better orchestra for having been exposed to so much modern music. Schonberg's feelings can be boiled down to one observation: "Going to one of his concerts was like taking a pill. It was good for you, but not an event you looked forward to with great anticipation."

But Schonberg did not have the last word. On June 19 the *Times* printed letters from four readers defending Boulez. Three of them objected to Schonberg's characterizing the audiences at the Rug Concerts as "kids," and all chastised him for allowing his own prejudices against modern music to cloud his perception of Boulez.

SEVERAL PREMIERES

After the yearlong hiatus brought about by the reconstruction of Avery Fisher Hall, the Rug Concerts returned for June 17–27, 1977. With Boulez gone, the principal conductor for the series was Erich Leinsdorf, with appearances also by Sergiu Comissiona (then music director of the Baltimore Symphony), Dennis Russell Davies, and Pinchas Zukerman. But the revisions to the hall did not permit the orchestra to be seated, as before, on the main floor in front of the stage. Rather, they were installed on the stage itself, as for a normal concert. Although a certain intimacy was thus lost, it was compensated for by a temporary floor installed over the main floor seats, which reduced the total area of the hall and aided the acoustics. And the "ruggers" could still recline, in which position they heard Leinsdorf conclude the final concert with as exhilarating and exciting a performance of Beethoven's First Symphony, a work often taken for granted, as one could possibly wish for.

It will be recalled that in 1969–70 the Philharmonic underwent a protracted period of legal procedures brought about by charges of racial discrimination for its failure to hire two African American musicians. So it was ironic that on the eve of the orchestra's pre-season Celebration of Black Composers, its sole African American member, the violinist Sanford Allen, resigned. Allen, who had joined in 1962, had been the only black member in the Philharmonic's history, which stretched back to 1842. As quoted in the *Times* of August 29. 1977, he was "simply tired of being a symbol" and felt he could do as well financially pursuing a free-lance and solo career as at the Philharmonic. Concerning the orchestra's almost all-white makeup, he said, "This is not a Philharmonic problem. And it's not a Boston Symphony or Chicago Symphony problem. It's part of a national social problem...a failure in selling—blacks are simply not plugged into this system."

Allen was, in fact, one of the soloists in the Celebration of Black Composers, a five-concert series that included three orchestral programs and two of chamber music. His vehicle was a concerto by the Panamanian-born Roque Cordero. Writing in the *Times* of September 3, Schonberg found the work strongly romantic in feeling, though basically academic and uninteresting. Allen, however, "played the difficult concerto very well indeed." He was praised for his great technical ability, his secure intonation, and his assured projection of the score. Schonberg pointed out that Allen was playing the Kneisel Stradivarius, over which the critic felt that violinists in the audience were lusting. He concluded, "It was a beautiful fiddle, but it takes a good violinist to bring out the best in it, and Mr. Allen did."

Other composers whose works were performed in the series included, from the eighteenth and nineteenth centuries, the Frenchman Joseph Boulogne (known as the Chevalier de Saint-Georges), the Cuban José White, and the Brazilian José Nuñes-Garcia; from the turn of the twentieth century, the Englishman Samuel Coleridge-Taylor; and from the later twentieth century, the Americans David Baker, Adolphus Hailstork, Ulysses Kay, Hale Smith, William Grant Still, and George Walker. Two of the three orchestral concerts were led by Paul Freeman, conductor-in-residence of the Detroit Symphony, who had made a series of recordings of music by black composers for Columbia Records, while the third was conducted by Leon Thompson, the Philharmonic's director of educational activities, who had organized the Celebration.

In earlier years, when there was an interregnum between music directors, the Philharmonic appointed a senior conductor as "musical adviser." Bruno Walter held that title from 1947 to 1949, between the directorships of Artur Rodzinski and Dimitri Mitropoulos. Likewise, between the tenures of Leonard Bernstein and Pierre Boulez, George Szell served as musical advisor and senior guest conductor during 1969–70, his unfortunate death in 1970 precluding a second year, though undoubtedly he was involved in the planning for the 1970–71 season. Yet following the departure of Boulez, no such appointment was made before Zubin Mehta's arrival, perhaps because only one year was involved. The logical choice would have been Erich Leinsdorf, who had been making annual appearances with the Philharmonic since 1973. As it was, he was allotted six weeks during 1977–78, including the opening week and the pension-fund benefit preceding it. For many years the Philharmonic had been opening the season with this gala benefit concert. This time, on September 14, 1977, Leinsdorf presided over an all-Wagner program consisting of the Overture and Venusberg Music from *Tannhäuser* and the complete second act of *Parsifal*, with Jon Vickers in the title role.

On the same day came the news of the death, at age ninety-five, of Leopold Stokowski. If anyone deserved the designation "a legend in his own time," it was certainly he. He had been a frequent guest conductor of the Philharmonic and had made quite a few recordings with it, as well as, during 1949–50, having been the orchestra's co-conductor with Dimitri Mitropoulos, prior to the latter's being named musical director. In tribute to his older colleague, Leinsdorf opened the first week's subscription concerts on September 15 with Stokowski's orchestral transcription of Bach's *Come, Sweet Death.*

A preview of things to come occurred on September 22, the beginning of a week's engagement by Zubin Mehta. The programs, televised by PBS, included the Prelude and "Liebestod" from Wagner's *Tristan und Isolde*, with Shirley Verrett as the soprano soloist in the "Liebestod"; and a Mehta specialty, Stravinsky's *Rite of Spring.* Writing in the *Times* of September 24, Donal Henahan admired the virtuosity and excitement of the *Rite* while lamenting a failure to discover "the proportion and the moods that give this mighty score its connective tissue."

A strike by the American Guild of Musical Artists, which represented professional chorus members, forced the Philharmonic to drop Schubert's Mass in G Major from the concerts beginning October 13. The Camerata Singers were to have participated, but the point at issue concerned the Philharmonic's insistence on engaging amateur choruses from time to time, as it had long done with the Westminster Choir and other college choral groups. It is ironic that several professional singers have told the author how much they had loved singing with the Philharmonic when they were students at Westminster Choir College and other academic institutions. Now that they were professionals, they apparently did not want other students to enjoy the same experience.

Notable in the season was the inclusion of world premiere performances of several works—concertos featuring first-desk players of the orchestra and commissioned with funds provided by Francis Goelet of the board of directors, who was chair of the Music Policy Committee. Audiences heard Andrew Imbrie's Flute Concerto, with Julius Baker as soloist, on October 13; Michael Colgrass's *Déja vu* for percussion quartet, performed by Roland Kohloff, Walter Rosenberger, Elden ("Buster") Bailey, and Morris ("Arnie") Lang, on October 20; Vincent Persichetti's Concerto for English Horn and String Orchestra, played by Thomas Stacy, on November 17; and John Corigliano's Clarinet Concerto, with Stanley Drucker, on December 8. Erich Leinsdorf conducted the first three works, Leonard Bernstein the last. The Goelet commissions would continue for several seasons.

Bernstein returned for three weeks in December 1977, each of his programs featuring a first performance: *American Cantata* by Lukas Foss on December 1 (New York premiere); the Clarinet Concerto by John Corigliano on December 8 (world premiere); and Bernstein's *Songfest* on December 15 (New York premiere). Written to celebrate the American bicentennial in 1976, it was first given in our nation's capital on October 11, 1977, with Bernstein conducting the National Symphony Orchestra and the soloists for the New York premiere: Clamma Dale, Rosalind Elias, Nancy Williams, Neil Rosenshein, Donald Gramm, and John Reardon.

Of all the concertos commissioned by Francis Goelet, none attracted more attention than Corigliano's for clarinet. It is in some ways a sonic blockbuster of a score, with instrumentalists from the orchestra making their contributions from various locations in the hall. A touching moment occurs in the second movement, a violin solo in tribute to the composer's father, who had been the Philharmonic's concertmaster for many years.

Not all conductors live into their seventies, eighties, or nineties. December 16, 1977, saw the death of Thomas Schippers, of cancer at the age of forty-seven. He had been a frequent guest of the New York Philharmonic since his debut in 1955 and first came to national attention as the conductor for the world premiere of Gian Carlo Menotti's television opera, *Amahl and the Night Visitor*, which he led on Christmas Eve, 1951, at the age of twenty-one. At the time of his death he was music director of the Cincinnati Symphony.

The real high point of the season took place on Sunday, January 8, 1978, at 4:00 p.m. in Carnegie Hall—a pension-fund benefit concert on which Vladimir Horowitz made his first appearance with an orchestra in twenty-five years. The occasion commemorated the fiftieth anniversary of Horowitz's American debut on January 12, 1928, also with the Philharmonic. At that time he had played Tchaikovsky's Concerto No. 1, with Thomas Beecham conducting. This time it was Rachmaninoff's Concerto No. 3, with Eugene Ormandy on the podium. The event brought in a record $168,000 to the pension fund. It was a rare Philharmonic appearance for Ormandy as well, for he had not conducted the orchestra since the summer broadcast series of 1945. The performance was recorded by RCA and issued almost immediately. As of this writing, it is still available.

Erich Leinsdorf was in charge of six weeks of the season, and so was Rafael Kubelík. The great Czech maestro had become a fairly regular guest since 1972–73. His six consecutive weeks (an unusually concentrated engagement for one conductor at this time, in the final third of the twentieth century) began on January 5, 1978, with the Sixth Symphony of Vaughan Williams, not a work in his normal repertoire. This great score had been given its New York premiere by the Philharmonic in 1949 with Leopold Stokowski conducting, and a Columbia recording quickly followed. It had not appeared on a Philharmonic program since then. It is a curious fact of musical life that, with a few exceptions, such as Elgar's *Enigma Variations* and Vaughan Williams's *Fantasia on a Theme by Thomas Tallis*, there is little or no interest in English music by most non-British conductors. According to Schonberg, a Vaughan Williams admirer, Kubelík delivered a "sensitive and often powerful" performance. His engagement also included such major works as Beethoven's *Missa solemnis* and the Ninth Symphonies of Bruckner and Mahler.

Fund-raising is, of course, an important activity for any orchestra, and on February 23 the Philharmonic tried something new—its first Phone Festival, or, as it would later be called, radiothon, with the cooperation of WQXR, which carried the radio broadcasts in New York. The idea for the event originated with Henry Fogel, the Philharmonic's new orchestra manager, who had been doing them in Syracuse, New York, over station WONO for the benefit of the Syracuse Symphony. In fact, his success with the radiothons was a factor in his gaining the Philharmonic position. For four days, beginning at 7:00 p.m. on Thursday, volunteers manned thirty telephones in Avery Fisher Hall's chorus room, taking pledges for monetary contributions, promises for donated premiums, and even bids for a chance to conduct the Philharmonic. The first night alone raised $25,000, with $1,500 for a private violin recital in the donor's home by the concertmaster, Rodney Friend, who immediately offered a second recital. Over $285,000 was raised from six thousand donors.

Guest conductors for the season included, besides those already mentioned, Andrew Davis, Bernard Haitink, Eugen Jochum, James Levine, Lorin Maazel, and Klaus Tennstedt. The assistant conductor, David Gilbert, also appeared, as a substitute for an indisposed Levine. Of these, only the venerable Jochum was making his Philharmonic debut. He had actually been suggested to the management by several of the musicians as an example of a respected European conductor under whom they would like to play. In the event, however, his three-week engagement was not particularly successful. On March 31 Henahan wrote of a sturdy and vigorous reading of Hindemith's *Mathis der Maler* Symphony, but Beethoven's "Eroica" was given a routine performance, the orchestra less than its best in the opening movement, in which a "glaringly early entry... threw things out of kilter at a climactic moment." During his three weeks with them, Jochum and the orchestra never did achieve rapport.

Yet another conductor death occurred on May 16, 1978—that of William Steinberg at age seventy-eight. He is remembered as the Philharmonic's first principal guest conductor, and in fact he was the first conductor to hold that title with any orchestra. His major music directorships were of the Pittsburgh Symphony and the

Boston Symphony, and he was especially known for his performances and recordings of the great German and Austrian classics.

In spite of the success of the Rug Concerts, the absence of Boulez, their originator and guiding spirit, and the physical changes in the hall led the Philharmonic to abandon both the Rugs and the equally successful Promenade Concerts in favor of two series called Music in May and June Favorites. For the former the orchestra was split into two approximately fifty-member groups, with alternating programs conducted by Neville Marriner and Alexander Schneider, the latter in his Philharmonic debut. The June Favorites were led by Leinsdorf and consisted of staples of the repertoire that would be performed on the forthcoming tour of Japan and South Korea. A rendition of the Beethoven Violin Concerto with Pinchas Zukerman on June 1 was highly praised by Henahan.

Meanwhile, on June 1 came the announcement of the retirement of Carlos Moseley at the age of sixty-three, after twenty-three years with the Philharmonic in various capacities, from director of press and public relations to associate managing director, then managing director, and finally president. He would continue on a volunteer basis as a vice chairman of the board of directors. Moseley's accomplishments with the Philharmonic were significant. He had helped bring about the orchestra's fifty-two-week employment, and he was responsible for the establishment of the Promenades under André Kostelanetz and the free summer Parks Concerts. Throughout his tenure he maintained his skills as a pianist and had appeared as a soloist with the Philharmonic in triple concertos by Bach and Mozart. Said Moseley, "I intend to give some real time to the Philharmonic. I wouldn't dream of turning my back on an organization that has meant so much to me."

In its previous tours to Japan in 1961, 1970, and 1974, the Philharmonic had been conducted by Bernstein, who had become a hero to the Japanese, as seemed to happen wherever he conducted. He was to have led the 1978 tour as well but had to withdraw because of what proved to be the final illness of his wife, Felicia Montealegre. In his place was engaged the more conservative Leinsdorf, whom the Japanese accepted with some hesitancy at first, but who soon won them over with his fastidious musicianship. Leinsdorf, in turn, had nothing but praise for the extremely enthusiastic audiences, whether in Tokyo, Osaka, or Kyoto. "They are like our nonsubscription audiences in New York," he said. "That's a great compliment. They are the music lovers who sacrifice to hear us. Not the subscription people who often come only to be seen."

At a rehearsal before the tour, Leinsdorf, unhappy with the results he was getting from the violins, shouted at them, "You should all go to your teachers and demand a refund!" Indignant, the entire orchestra got up and proceeded to walk out.

Because it was time for a rehearsal break anyway, one was called. The orchestra committee then informed Henry Fogel that an apology from Leinsdorf would be needed before the musicians would return. They would play that night's concert, but would not resume the rehearsal. Fogel told them that the terms of their contract left them with no legal recourse: "People are yelled at by bosses all the time—that's the way life works sometimes." If they did not resume the rehearsal, their pay would be docked. They said they knew that, and that was all right. They wanted an apology.

Fogel, new at the job, went with some trepidation to the conductor's room. Before he had a chance to speak, the cigar-smoking Leinsdorf said, "You need an apology, don't you? Tell everyone I'll have one for them." When they all returned, Leinsdorf said to the orchestra, "All my life I have lived according to a certain civility. I have not lived up to my ideals. I apologize. Let's make music." Fogel's stature rose considerably, for the orchestra members thought he had somehow cajoled or browbeaten the irascible Leinsdorf into an apology. In reality, he had not said a word to the conductor.

CHAPTER 7

1978–82

ARRIVAL OF MEHTA

Zubin Mehta's first appearances as music director of the New York Philharmonic were in the Parks Concerts during the summer of 1978, after which he led the orchestra on a tour to Brazil and Santo Domingo. A former Philharmonic violinist, Carlos Piantini, who also became a conductor, was from the Dominican Republic and was now its minister of culture. He had extended the invitation to the Philharmonic, which was at first reluctant to accept it. A high fee was asked and was agreed to on the condition (insisted upon by the manager, Nick Webster) that the orchestra would play, in addition to two formal indoor concerts, two free outdoor concerts in a park, stadium, or other appropriate venue. These concerts would be for the general working-class population who could not afford to attend the formal concerts, a condition to which the sponsor of the tour, Gulf and Western, agreed.

The orchestra had rooms in Santo Domingo in a gorgeous resort hotel. On an off day, Henry Fogel and Webster's assistant, Mary DeCamp, were driven to the site of the outdoor concerts. Supposedly a forty-five-minute drive from Santo Domingo, it was actually close to two hours, even at the dizzying pace adopted by their driver. What greeted their eyes was a baseball field, with seating for about three hundred, covered with garbage and other debris and surrounded by a rusty fence. Fogel protested that this site, in its present condition, was thoroughly inadequate. It had to be cleaned up and more seating provided, or there would be no concert. On being told that the presenters planned to charge $1.00 for tickets, so as to keep out the sugarcane workers, Fogel flatly stated that unless the concert were free, as had been agreed, there would be no concert.

After all this had been sorted out, when the orchestra arrived for the concert everything had been cleared and cleaned up, but there was still a relatively small audience in attendance, while outside the gates was a rather large crowd. While Mehta conducted Wagner's Overture to *Rienzi*, Fogel and Webster insisted that the crowd be allowed in, or *Rienzi* would be the end of the concert. The presenters feared they would not behave properly and would create disturbances if admitted. In the end, Fogel and Webster prevailed, informing Mehta of the situation. He agreed to wait until everyone had entered before continuing. The large audience was extremely quiet, respectful, and enthusiastic.

Mehta's official tenure began with the subscription concerts beginning September 14. His program then consisted of Beethoven's *Leonore* Overture No. 3, the world premiere of Samuel Barber's *Third Essay*, specially composed for the occasion, and Mahler's First Symphony. As luck would have it, his first weeks occurred in the midst of another newspaper strike.

A point of interest throughout the season was a commemoration of the 150th anniversary of the death of Franz Schubert, with the Philharmonic performing all his symphonies and a few other works. This was the first time the Philharmonic had ever programmed the complete Schubert symphonies in a single season, something few other orchestras have done. And the youthful First Symphony is almost never given.

Once the newspapers again saw the light of day, Schonberg opined that Mehta's performance of the Schubert Fourth Symphony ("Tragic") had been the finest he had ever heard. In fact, he had nothing but praise for Mehta's Schubert conducting in general, as well as for the impression he had made on the orchestra and on the public. Mehta had hitherto been perceived as a glamour-boy conductor because of his good looks, his Hollywood connections, and his exotic Indian heritage. But in his first few weeks in New York he impressed everyone as a serious, straightforward, no-nonsense conductor and musician. His reputation had been built on conducting the great romantic classics, so his affinity for Schubert was all the more striking. In contrast to his immediate predecessor, he drew a warm, rich sound from the orchestra, certainly appropriate for the late-romantic repertoire and not at all out of place for the late classical and early romantic.

As a sort of homage to Boulez, Mehta's second week's programs included two of the former's specialties, Webern's *Six Pieces for Orchestra* and Varèse's *Intégrales*. Even the Webern, normally so austere, was performed in a personal, colorful, romantic manner, yet one that clarified its textures and its rhythmic complexities. Only his Beethoven performances were judged to be a bit cautious and somewhat pedantic, as though he had too much respect for the composer and was afraid to let himself go. As an accompanist, Mehta earned high marks for his hand-in-glove support of Vladimir Horowitz, who returned for another airing of the Rachmaninoff Third Concerto, this one televised nationally by CBS. Schonberg, who had praised Horowitz's dramatic return to the concerto repertoire early in the year, now objected to the pianist's willful and self-indulgent distortions, which Mehta somehow managed to coordinate with the orchestra.

Like any music director worthy of the name, Mehta programmed contemporary music as well. Early in his first season he presented the New York premiere of the

Symphony No. 1 by Peter Maxwell Davies, a composer of formidably difficult music, and honored the seventieth birthday of Olivier Messiaen with half a program of his music, including *Et exspecto resurrectionem mortuorum*, that extremely sonorous work for winds and percussion, with its tremendous tam-tam crashes. Another seventieth birthday was honored on November 30, that of Elliott Carter. The work chosen for the occasion was his Piano Concerto (1965), performed by Ursula Oppens. Carter's music is nothing if not dauntingly complex, but Donal Henahan, writing in the *Times* the next day, referred to the concerto as "a faceless work." He concluded that "there are ways to make audiences like good music, but Mr. Carter seems happy to ignore them."

In his year-end summary on December 31, Schonberg again praised Mehta for his conducting of early nineteenth-century and contemporary scores, not to mention those of the romantic and postromantic periods. He acknowledged that some of his colleagues disagreed, finding Mehta's interpretations insensitive and superficial, but Schonberg felt that they might have been influenced by the conductor's reputation as a "musical showman and playboy" rather than restricting themselves to the great versatility he displayed. "Mr. Mehta is off to a most impressive start," he concluded.

But it was not only Schonberg who praised Mehta. On February 2 his *Times* colleague Donal Henahan, not an easy person to please, wrote of a concert the night before "that could serve as a model and a standard. This is what the Philharmonic should sound like, always, and this is what orchestral concerts should sound like." Schubert's exhilarating Second Symphony was heard in a precise and breathtaking performance that marked it as the high point of Mehta's work to date in New York. On the same program Daniel Barenboim was the soloist in the Brahms Piano Concerto No. 1, a difficult score in which "one's attention was concentrated on the power and beauty of this familiar music in a way that rarely happens."

Barenboim was also the guest conductor for the two weeks following, in such varied repertoire as Haydn's Symphony No. 48 ("Maria Theresia"), Bruckner's Seventh, Schumann's First ("Spring") and Ravel's *Daphnis et Chloé* Suite No. 2, along with *Mi-parti* by Witold Lutosławski. Henahan reviewed both weeks glowingly and concluded, "If the Philharmonic has not already nailed Mr. Barenboim down to a lifetime contract as a guest, it ought to have its administrative head examined."

Claudio Abbado, Michael Gielen, Erich Leinsdorf, James Levine, Raymond Leppard, and, in his Philharmonic conducting debut, Mstislav Rostropovich were also among the guest conductors, but it was another debuting Russian who attracted the most attention of the guests: Gennady Rozhdestvensky, who led for three weeks from February 22 to March 13. He pulled no punches with his first program, presenting the Philharmonic's first performances of the then seldom heard Fourth Symphony of Shostakovich. Even today it stands on the fringe of twentieth-century repertoire. Over an hour in duration, with echoes of Mahler not only in its length, but in its scoring for an immense orchestra, it is a fascinating and riveting work, one that, according to the *Times*'s Raymond Ericson, Rozhdestvensky and the orchestra delivered stunningly. He also received high marks for his stylish rendition of Mozart's Symphony No. 34 in C Major, K. 338, another work not frequently encountered.

The program for his second week could only be described as eccentric. Another seldom-heard Russian symphony was offered, this time Prokofieff's raucous Symphony No. 2. Surrounding it was such a quantity of what Henahan described as "cotton candy" that he wondered if Rozhdestvensky "might be auditioning to become our next pop-concert maestro." Among the fluff were the Overture to Paisiellos's *Barber of Seville* (not to be confused with Rossini's opera), several obscure pieces by Johann Strauss Jr. (*Homage to the Russian Public*, *Nothing Polka*, and *Train of Joy Polka*, also known as *Excursion Train Polka*), Shostakovich's Overture to Dressel's opera *Der arme Columbus*, and, of all things, his orchestration of Vincent Youmans's "Tea for Two," known as *Tahiti Trot*, which concluded the program. According to Henahan on March 2, "Mr. Rozhdestvensky led all these trifles and the Prokofiev as well with prissy, schoolmasterish mannerisms that added to the supposedly humorous effect."

The season's final program, on May 2, featured Vladimir Ashkenazy as the soloist in a stupendous performance of Bartók's Second Piano Concerto. According to Schonberg the next day, he played the piano as Bartók himself had done, lyrically, in spite of the temptation to treat the piano as a percussion instrument. In other words, whatever harshness or percussiveness one hears is that written into the music—it does not need further reinforcement from the pianist. (The conductor Jean Morel, in a rehearsal of Bartók's *Miraculous Mandarin* with the Juilliard Orchestra, told the orchestra upon hearing the ugly sounds it was producing, "If you put mustard and pepper in your coffee, it will taste terrible. You don't have to use dirty mustard and bad pepper.") Schonberg felt that Ashkenazy and Mehta gave "a performance that will set a standard, and the audience knew it."

On May 3 came the announcement that Zubin Mehta's contract as music director of the New York Philharmonic had been extended through 1986. In the *Times* article Mehta expressed his displeasure with the subscription format employed by major orchestras. "Four rehearsals and four concerts September to May for how many subscribers—30,000? We play to our own little club. When are we going to break out? I wish the whole season would be nonsubscription. When a person buys a ticket for a particular concert, he wants to go to *that* concert. But when you have to buy them all in July...."

Leonard Bernstein returned for two special concerts on June 6 and 9 prior to leading the orchestra on another tour to Japan, His programs included such Bernstein staples as the First Symphonies of Schumann and Mahler and the Fifth Symphony of Shostakovich, as well as the world premiere of a work dedicated to him, Jacob Druckman's *Aureole*, which includes references to a theme from Bernstein's "Kaddish" Symphony. For both concerts the orchestra played magnificently. No matter how many times Bernstein conducted the programmed symphonies (including Haydn's No. 104), he never failed to give his utmost in feeling and intensity. A video of the Tokyo performance of the Shostakovich work clearly shows how passionately he threw himself into everything he conducted, each score led by him as though for the first time.

On its return the orchestra again appeared in the Parks Concerts. On the night of August 8, in Central Park's Sheep Meadow, a concert conducted by André Kostelanetz of Rimsky-Korsakoff's *Scheherazade*, Stravinsky's *Firebird* Suite, and four Sousa marches followed by fireworks, drew a crowd estimated by the police at more than 200,000. It was the largest attendance ever for any kind of musical event in New York City, perhaps anywhere.

Because of prior commitments, Mehta was not on hand to open the 1979–80 season. That honor fell instead to Rafael Kubelík, who had become a frequent and popular guest of the Philharmonic, conducting on this occasion his countryman Bohuslav Martinů's Double Concerto and Beethoven's "Eroica" Symphony. Concerning his performance of the latter, Schonberg wrote on September 14, "Mr. Kubelík leaves flamboyance to others, interested only in an honest interpretation of the composer's wishes. One will not hear many performances of equal integrity this season."

This concert illustrates how orchestral programs have evolved. The Martinů and Beethoven works made up the entire program, but when Kubelík conducted the Chicago Symphony Orchestra in New York in 1953, the program included not only those works but Wagner's Prelude to *Die Meistersinger* and Ravel's transcription of Mussorgsky's *Pictures at an Exhibition*. Many other examples could be given of the length of programs decreasing as ticket prices continue to increase. The absence of overtures and other short pieces on many programs today is particularly regrettable.

Good news arrived shortly after the season's opening, for on September 22 it was announced that the Philharmonic's members had voted to approve a three-year labor contract, one that would give them an increase of $50 a week each year, so that by the third year the minimum weekly salary would be $630. The negotiations had been fairly amicable—no threats of work stoppages or concert cancellations. The contract provided some increases in pension benefits and, beginning in the third year, the introduction of seniority pay.

Kubelík's engagement was cut short by an attack of gout that caused him to miss the fourth performance of his second week and all of the third. Filling in on September 25, in a program of Britten, Dvořák, and Schumann, was Larry Newland, a violist in the orchestra who became a standby conductor after the resignation of assistant conductor David Gilbert. A member of the Philharmonic since 1960, Newland had studied conducting with Pierre Monteux at his school in Hancock, Maine, and had recently been appointed music director of the Harrisburg Symphony in Pennsylvania. Conducting without a rehearsal, Newland was able to make a good impression in Kubelík's program. Taking over Kubelík's third week was Sir Charles Mackerras, then in the midst of an engagement at the Metropolitan Opera. He retained Kubelík's program featuring Janáček's *Taras Bulba*, which just happened to be a Mackerras specialty.

When Mehta returned on October 18, he began a seven-week series with a program of two large-scale works, the Brahms Piano Concerto No. 1, with André Watts as the soloist, and the Berlioz *Symphonie fantastique*. Of the Brahms, Schonberg said "there was never a dull moment," though he did suggest that a moratorium on the Berlioz work might be appropriate, "say for the next 10 seasons."

On November 29 it was announced that Rodney Friend, the concertmaster since September 1976, would be leaving the Philharmonic on December 22 to become the concertmaster (or leader, as the position is called in England) of the BBC Symphony Orchestra in London. Though auditions were being held for a new concertmaster, the post of guest concertmaster would temporarily be held by Sidney Harth. Harth had been the associate conductor and concertmaster of the Los Angeles Philharmonic and really wished to pursue a conducting career, but he agreed to the short-term position in New York "to help Zubin out."

The next day brought the news that gifts and pledges totaling $10.4 million had been made to the Philharmonic as part of an $18 million endowment campaign. Endowment funds of $12 million already existed, so the new campaign would increase the endowment to $30 million, of which an annual income of about $2 million would result.

Mendelssohn's oratorio *Elijah* is not a work one encounters often in the United States, though it has always been fairly popular in England. The Philharmonic performed it under Dimitri Mitropoulos in 1952 and Thomas Schippers in 1966. It returned more or less on schedule when Mehta presented it on November 29, 1979, with the participation of the Westminster Choir and the soloists Leona

Mitchell, Carol Wyatt, Seth McCoy, and Sherrill Milnes, who sang the title role. Though he found the score "emotionally empty stuff, all rhetoric and pious attitudes," Henahan praised Mehta's "forthright approach," which "worked extremely well." He thought thirteen years to be "just about the proper interval" for *Elijah* performances.

Another vocal work was heard on December 13 when James Levine led the first New York performance of the *Lyric Symphony* by Alexander Zemlinsky. At the time Zemlinsky (1871–1942) barely registered in the consciousness of most music lovers; he was known primarily, if at all, as the teacher and brother-in-law of Schoenberg. Recent years have seen an interest in his music, notably the operas, through the efforts of the conductor James Conlon. The *Lyric Symphony* (1923) is a setting of seven poems by Rabindranath Tagore for soprano and baritone soloists and an extremely large orchestra. Mahler's *Das Lied von der Erde* is often cited as an influence on this work. Johanna Meier and Dale Duesing were the soloists in Levine's performance, conducted "with love and affection," according to Schonberg, though the work itself was thought to be "a relic, a period piece written long after its period." (Be that as it may, the score does have its champions today.) The following week Levine combined two great choral works, Stravinsky's *Symphony of Psalms* and Mozart's Mass in C Minor, marking the debut of the newly formed New York Choral Artists, a professional group that was to become the Philharmonic's official chorus.

HAPPY BIRTHDAY, AARON AND ISAAC

The year 1980 began on a youthful note with the American debut, on January 3, of the sixteen-year-old Anne-Sophie Mutter in the Mendelssohn Violin Concerto. Mehta has always been a champion of young performers, and it is to his credit that Mutter proved to be no flash in the pan, but the genuine article. Her distinguished career includes many subsequent visits to the Philharmonic. According to Henahan the next day, it was a Mendelssohn of "delicate shadings and sweet tone rather than emotional fire," which was all to the good in this exquisite concerto.

On January 9 NBC presented a televised program entitled "Live from Studio 8H," a tribute to Arturo Toscanini and the NBC Symphony Orchestra, who performed live concerts from that venue in Radio City from 1937 to 1950. With the advent of television, the concerts were moved to Carnegie Hall, where they continued until 1954, 8H having been converted to a TV studio. The network disbanded its orchestra upon Toscanini's retirement. The program presented Zubin Mehta and the New York Philharmonic with the soprano Leontyne Price and the violinist

Itzhak Perlman. It was estimated that an audience of 900,000 watched the program in the New York area, and about 10–12 million nationally. As the *Times* television critic, John J. O'Connor, wrote on January 11, "Only in television could that figure possibly be considered a failure."

A rare all-Elgar program ensued the following night, with Mehta conducting a suite from *The Crown of India*, the *Sea Pictures* with Marilyn Horne as the mezzo-soprano, and the popular *Enigma Variations*. It was a canny mixture of Elgar's better- and lesser-known works, and Mehta was praised by Schonberg for his "energetic, eloquent, well-shaped performance" of the *Variations*. Horne, "a sensitive musician as well as a virtuoso singer," sang the introspective *Pictures* "with due simplicity."

There was sadness in the Philharmonic community, and no doubt elsewhere, with the death of André Kostelanetz on January 14, at the age of seventy-eight. He had long been associated with the Philharmonic, not only for the Promenade Concerts, which he had introduced in 1963, but for his occasional Saturday night performances during the regular seasons, programs that adroitly mixed popular standard symphonic repertoire with lighter pieces. He was also responsible for commissioning patriotic scores from American composers, of which Copland's *Lincoln Portrait* and William Schuman's *New England Triptych* have become classics.

On the televised pension-fund benefit concert of January 15, the tenor Luciano Pavarotti, the featured soloist, opened the program with the Ingemisco from Verdi's Requiem in tribute to Kostelanetz. After a few spoken words from Mehta, a telegram in praise of Kostelanetz was read from President Jimmy Carter. The event netted over $100,000 for the orchestra's pension fund. A surprise appearance was made by Itzhak Perlman toward the end of the program when, during the introduction to the third act of *Tosca*, he sang the part of the jailer in a sonorous baritone, just before the great tenor aria "E lucevan le stelle."

As had happened a number of times in the past, conductor cancellations played havoc with the season's plans. First the Soviet maestro Yuri Temirkanov bowed out of his scheduled week, coming down with, according to Henahan, "a sudden inability to travel." His absence created an opportunity for the American Henry Lewis to take over the concerts beginning February 6. At the same time it was announced that Bernard Haitink was ill in Holland and had canceled his three-week engagement, which was to have begun February 14. His replacements were Christoph Eschenbach, Walter Weller, and Neeme Järvi, all in their debuts with the Philharmonic (though Eschenbach had previously appeared as a piano soloist).

While Sidney Harth was performing his duties as acting concertmaster and had played the Sibelius Violin Concerto in the subscription concert series beginning February 28, on March 1 it was announced that Glenn Dicterow would be the new concertmaster as of September 25, 1980. A graduate of the Juilliard School, he had been associate concertmaster of the Los Angeles Philharmonic from 1972 to 1976, then concertmaster from 1976 to 1979—all during Mehta's tenure in Los Angeles, so it was evident they would make a good team. Of special interest is that, as of this writing, Dicterow is still the Philharmonic's concertmaster, his tenure the longest since John Corigliano's and, in fact, in the orchestra's history.

Handel's *Messiah* has long been associated with the Christmas season. But this masterpiece has more to do with the Resurrection than with the Nativity and was, in fact, premiered shortly after Easter, on April 13, 1742, in Dublin. Mehta recognized this by presenting the work in four nonsubscription performances beginning April 3, 1980. Participating were seventy members of the New York Choral Artists and the soloists Margaret Marshall, soprano; Florence Quivar, mezzo-soprano; Henry Price, tenor; and Benjamin Luxon, baritone. Mehta was praised for respecting the performance practices of Handel's day by using a harpsichord and a portable organ, having the soloists and the chorus insert many appoggiaturas and other embellishments into the vocal line, and by eschewing the solemnity and ponderous religiosity that had afflicted *Messiah* performances for many years—Handel had, after all, described his score as "an entertainment." Tempos were on the swift side, textures were light, and orchestral forces were reduced. While it may not have been the last word in baroque performance practice, it was a joyful experience, which is surely what Handel wanted.

Over the years the Philharmonic had sought to increase its community involvement through its radio and television broadcasts, recordings, and Parks Concerts. A further step was taken on April 21 when the orchestra paid its first visit to Harlem, performing in the Abyssinian Baptist Church on West 138th Street, the home church both of Adam Clayton Powell Sr. and of his son, Adam Jr. "When I heard that the Philharmonic had not been to Harlem, I thought it was a scandal," said Mehta, who had performed many times in Watts with the Los Angeles Philharmonic.

At this sold-out concert, for which the $5 tickets were obtained through the church because the Philharmonic was unable to obtain corporate funding, excerpts from Handel's *Messiah* were performed, as well as the finale from the "Organ" Symphony of Saint-Saëns, Wagner's *Meistersinger* Prelude (conducted by Leon Thompson, the Philharmonic's education director and music director of Abyssinian Baptist), and two arias and a spiritual sung by Leontyne Price ("There's *no* way you're going to keep me out of it," she had told Mehta when she heard of the concert). Two thousand additional persons were admitted free to the dress rehearsal. "We haven't seen anything like this since Adam [Clayton] Powell's funeral," said the church's pastor, Samuel DeWitt Proctor. "The whole community is lit up like they haven't been for years."

Following the subscription season the orchestra presented a Beethoven festival, during which all the symphonies and concertos were performed, beginning on May 14 with Nos. 1 and 9 conducted by Leinsdorf, who in a later program led a rare presentation of the complete incidental music to Goethe's *Egmont*. Other conductors for the festival were Mehta and Klaus Tennstedt. On June 18 a special concert was given for the delegates to the American Symphony Orchestra League Conference, which included, as a preview of his eightieth-birthday celebrations, Aaron Copland conducting his *Symphonic Ode*. The performance was a preamble to the evening's final work, Mahler's Fifth Symphony, with Tennstedt conducting.

During the summer the orchestra traveled once again to Europe, this time with Mehta on the podium in his first such tour with the Philharmonic. A grant of $300,000 from Citicorp partially underwrote the tour, which began on August 24 and 25 with concerts in the Edinburgh Festival, then continued with performances in Malmö, Stockholm, Oslo, Berlin, Hanover, Bonn, Vienna, Salzburg, Brussels, Ghent, Paris, and London. The tour was announced as a celebration of the fiftieth anniversary of the Philharmonic's first European visit, in 1930, with Arturo Toscanini conducting, a tour that astounded all who heard the orchestra at that time.

The 1980–81 season began with the announcement that Harold C. Schonberg was retiring as chief music critic of the *New York Times*. He would be succeeded in that post by Donal Henahan, who had come to the *Times* in 1967 from the *Chicago Daily News* and had been taking on increasing critical duties at the *Times*. Schonberg would continue as an occasional music (and chess) columnist.

To open the season on September 24 there was, as had become customary, the gala pension-fund benefit concert. Isaac Stern was on hand for the Philharmonic's celebration of his sixtieth birthday. Though his first appearance with the orchestra in 1944 has always been mentioned as having been on December 7—in the Tchaikovsky Violin Concerto, conducted by Artur Rodzinski—that was his subscription concert debut. The actual debut had been on August 6 of that year, in the Sibelius Concerto under Dimitri Mitropoulos, for the Philharmonic's summer series of Sunday broadcast concerts. Now here he was, some eighty appearances later, the orchestra's most frequent violin soloist, becoming the first violinist in Philharmonic history to perform four concertos in a single concert. For the televised occasion he was joined by Mehta, of course, and two younger violinists whose careers he had helped establish, Itzhak Perlman and Pinchas Zukerman. The program opened with Perlman joining his mentor in the Bach Double Concerto, followed by Mozart's *Sinfonia concertante*, in which Zukerman was heard as the violist, then Vivaldi's Concerto in F Major for Three Violins. After intermission Stern had the stage to himself in the Brahms Concerto. For Henahan the next day, though he was extremely laudatory toward the entire program, the high point of the evening came with the Mozart work.

The regular season opened on October 2 with Mehta conducting Mahler's colossal Third Symphony, which Henahan felt "represented both Mr. Mehta and the orchestra at their best." Also participating were the contralto Maureen Forrester, women of the New York Choral Artists, and the Brooklyn Boys Chorus. A tribute to André Kostelanetz was given on October 11, one of the special Saturday concerts for which he had been scheduled. Mehta conducted, and the program began with the premiere of *A Musical Toast* by Leonard Bernstein, a boisterous two-minute piece with a theme based on the rhythm of Kostelanetz's name. It is part of a musical tradition in which a name of six syllables, such as André Kostelanetz or Zino Francescatti, is sung to the tune of Gershwin's *Fascinatin' Rhythm*. Toward the end of Bernstein's tribute, the orchestra sings the name itself. The composer came onstage for a bow and then proceeded to repeat the work for an encore. According to Raymond Ericson in the *Times* of October 13, "It was just as much fun to hear a second time." It was also the first time two conductors had led the same piece on a Philharmonic program.

On November 20 the Philharmonic officially celebrated Aaron Copland's eightieth birthday (the actual date was November 14) with the first of four performances of his Third Symphony, Mehta conducting. It is a major work by this composer, grand, majestic, folksy, acerbic, in fact combining all the characteristics one associates with Copland in the same piece. Although the Third Symphony has never attained the popularity of Copland's ballet scores, such as *Appalachian Spring*, neither has it suffered the neglect of his more abstruse pieces, such as *Inscape*. Nevertheless, it is one of the great American symphonies and deserves to be performed at least as often as some of the symphonies of Shostakovich (than which it is actually more difficult). According to John Rockwell in the *Times*, Mehta "addressed this score with his characteristic energy and flair."

A week later it was announced that the Philharmonic would begin having open rehearsals on twelve Thursday mornings, for which a $3 admission fee would be charged to benefit the orchestra's pension fund. These rehearsals, in increased numbers, continue to the present day.

Perhaps because of his student days in Vienna, where the music of Bruckner is as omnipresent as that of Johann Strauss, Mehta has always had a special affinity for the great Austrian symphonist. Of all the Bruckner symphonies, the Eighth is the most monumental in scope and in depth, and on November 27 Mehta addressed himself to that monolith. Rockwell wrote the next day that the performance "cleansed Bruckner without scrubbing him clean of mystery, and it confirmed that when Mr. Mehta is at his best, he is a major conductor."

END OF THE HONEYMOON?

Guest conductors for 1980–81 included Erich Leinsdorf, Rafael Kubelík, James Levine, John Nelson, and James Conlon. On January 29, 1981, Leonard Bernstein returned after a sabbatical year during which he had concentrated on composition. His two weeks, fewer than in any previous engagement as laureate conductor, were devoted to American music, of which he was a supreme interpreter. Continuing the Copland eightieth-birthday celebrations, he led five of the composer's works: on January 29, *Appalachian Spring*, the Clarinet Concerto with Stanley Drucker as the soloist, and the *Dance Symphony*; on February 5, *Quiet City* with Philip Smith on trumpet and Thomas Stacy on English horn, and seven of the *Old American Songs* performed by Marilyn Horne.

His first program also included the New York premiere of *Quintets* by Lukas Foss; the second presented the New York premiere of Ned Rorem's *Sunday Morning* and the magnificent Third Symphony of William Schuman, a work of which Bernstein had been a major champion over the years. The latter was played in honor of the composer's seventieth birthday (orchestras do like anniversaries) the previous August. Of Schuman's symphony, Henahan wrote on February 6 that the score seemed more important with each passing year, at least when led by Bernstein: "Has any American orchestral piece in the last 40 years worn so well as this one? Perhaps, but it does not come immediately to mind."

The orchestra returned to the Abyssinian Baptist Church in Harlem on February 16, this time with Leona Mitchell as the soprano soloist and Mehta again conducting. "To be invited back is the real test," said Mehta to the audience. "After five minutes of playing for you last year, we knew we had to come back." The church's acoustics were judged to be excellent. According to Peter G. Davis in the *Times* the next day, "Hearing Verdi's mighty 'Libera me' thundering out in this ambience was a thrilling musical experience."

Another anniversary was celebrated with the concert series beginning March 25: the centennial of the birth of Béla Bartók, for which Kubelík led the *Music for Strings, Percussion, and Celesta* and a concert performance of the one-act opera *Bluebeard's Castle*. By coincidence, Antal Doráti and the Detroit Symphony had presented *Bluebeard* only two nights before in Carnegie Hall, giving critics an opportunity to compare the performances. Considering that the Detroit rendition had a Hungarian conductor noted for his Bartók interpretations and two Hungarian soloists, while the Philharmonic's featured a Czech conductor, an American mezzo-soprano, Tatiana Troyanos, and a German baritone, Siegmund Nimsgern, it may come as a surprise to learn that Henahan preferred the Philharmonic performance, in which Kubelík and the orchestra, in this basically gloomy score, "managed to find enough variety of timbre and dynamics to carry the listener along."

The next week, beginning April 2, Kubelík was heard as both conductor and composer when he gave the world premiere of his *Orphikon*, subtitled *Music for Orchestra in Three Movements*. According to Henahan the next day, it "held the attention throughout and won far more than the polite applause usually granted new music." The orchestra, which had played the score with great virtuosity and authority from the composer-conductor, joined the audience in applauding Kubelík affectionately.

On May 7 came the announcement that Constance (Mrs. Robert L.) Hoguet had been elected president of the Philharmonic-Society of New York, the first woman to hold that office. She succeeded Sampson R. Field, who had been president since Carlos Moseley's retirement in 1978. A graduate of Smith College, where she majored in music, Mrs. Hoguet had been a member of the Philharmonic's board of directors since 1951 and vice chairman of the board since 1960.

Yet another anniversary was celebrated on May 5, the ninetieth birthday of Carnegie Hall. The program, conducted by Mehta, was a replica of the one presented on that exact date in 1891: Beethoven's *Leonore* Overture No. 3, Tchaikovsky's *Marche solennelle* (the world premiere of which Tchaikovsky himself had conducted on that night), and the *Te Deum* by Berlioz, in which the tenor John Garrison, the Westminster Choir, the Oratorio Society of New York, and the Brooklyn Boys Chorus participated. Berlioz asks for a "grand noise," mitigated on this occasion by the use of an electric organ, the hall's original pipe organ having been removed some years before (one thing Carnegie has in common with Avery Fisher Hall).

On May 30 it was announced that Henry Fogel, the Philharmonic's orchestra manager, would become the executive director of Washington's National Symphony Orchestra in mid-July. Fogel is today best-known for his long tenure as president of the Chicago Symphony Orchestra and for his presidency of the American Symphony Orchestra League (now the League of American Orchestras). Since 2009 he has been the dean of Roosevelt University's Chicago College of Performing Arts and distinguished professor of the arts. Fogel was succeeded at the Philharmonic by Edward Lee Alley.

Having devoted a spring festival to the music of Beethoven in 1980, the Philharmonic now presented a festival entitled The Romantic Era, which presented eight concerts from May 27 to June 18. In his debut with the orchestra, Christoph von Dohnányi led a program containing Schubert's Symphony No. 9 ("Great C Major") and Mendelssohn's Violin Concerto, with Itzhak Perlman as soloist. Henahan felt the conductor "made a splendid impression . . . particularly in the Schubert."

Also conducting in the series were James Conlon, Andrew Davis, James Levine, and, as a harbinger of events to come, Kurt Masur in his Philharmonic debut. Masur's program on June 16 was devoted to Wagner and Richard Strauss, and he was judged by Henahan on June 17 to be "a superior example of the good Kapellmeister type that a generation or so ago was not hard to find in central Europe." He thought Masur was someone who might be easier to take over the long haul than many flashier conductors, and that he obviously had much talent and authority, not to mention the ability to impart his ideas to an orchestra in a short time. Henahan also felt it would be interesting to discover what he could achieve with more rehearsal time. "No doubt," the critic wrote, "he will be given an opportunity to show us at some point."

The spring festival closed on June 19 with James Levine leading the Berlioz Requiem. It is rarely heard (at least in the concert hall) because of its large choral and instrumental requirements, the latter involving four brass ensembles at the north, east, south, and west sides of the hall, as well as multiple timpani—all for the Requiem's astounding Dies irae. For this event Levine had the services of the two-hundred-voice Singing City Choir of Philadelphia and the tenor Philip Creech. After expressing some reservations, inevitable in a work such as this, Rockwell wrote on June 21 of "a passionate, personal and altogether convincing vision of this sometimes problematic score."

The summer also saw the ripening of the talents of a figure associated with the Philharmonic, though not actually a member. After his retirement, Carlos Moseley, the orchestra's former general manager and president, decided to brush up his piano playing. On Saturday, July 4, he performed Mozart's Concerto No. 19 in F Major, K. 459, in Tarrytown, New York, with the County Symphony of Westchester under Stephen Simon's direction. The concert was part of the Summer of Music on the Hudson Festival at the historic Lyndhurst estate.

Some indication that the honeymoon might be in jeopardy between Mehta and the critics, especially now that Schonberg had retired, could be found in some of the *Times* reviews early in the fall of 1981. On September 10, writing of a performance of Mahler's Second Symphony, Rockwell felt that Mehta "just didn't sound at home in the music; it didn't speak through him." September 28 brought the further comment from Rockwell that "Mr. Mehta's Brahms Third was a flaccid affair"; and on October 6 Henahan, writing about excerpts from *Tristan und Isolde* with the soprano Montserrat Caballé as soloist, spoke of "a somewhat meandering and pedestrian reading of the Prelude by Mr. Mehta." Caballé herself earned nothing but praise for her bel canto and Wagner offerings. After the New Year, on January 8, Henahan wrote of "an absent-minded quality" that pervaded the Brahms *Haydn Variations*, "a faceless, somewhat chilly reading that had no peaks or valleys of expression, and by no means enough variety in color and tempo." On January 15 he described "a rough and inelegant performance of Mozart's Symphony No. 25."

No negative comments greeted the pension-fund benefit concert of September 23, 1981, however, when the orchestra was conducted by the great entertainer Danny Kaye in his third Philharmonic appearance. Schonberg emerged from retirement to review the event. It was not only the audience that was reduced to gales of laughter, but the orchestra itself, which at times could barely hold it together enough to play, so convulsed were they. Schonberg stressed that while Kaye's antics were funny, there was nothing funny about the actual music, and the musicians respected his knowledge and feeling for the music. A record $335,000 was raised for the pension fund.

Henahan had high words of praise for Klaus Tennstedt for his breathtaking account of Schubert's "Great C Major" Symphony on February 12 and his engrossing one of Mahler's Ninth Symphony on February 20. Tennstedt's performance of the Schubert "dared the orchestra to follow him into those fearsome regions that lie beyond instrumental and ensemble excellence." The Philharmonic responded readily to the conductor's inspirational leadership, for they believed in what he had to offer. Henahan continued, "It is remarkable how few conductors really suspect what a fine orchestra is capable of, simply because their own level of mediocrity and routine satisfies them." (Henahan was not one to suffer conductors gladly.) The Mahler performance, which was dedicated to the memory of Bruno Walter on the twentieth anniversary of his death, was "direct, intense and passionate," one "to remember—and one that did ample honor to Walter's memory."

A Philharmonic milestone was reached on March 7, 1982, the orchestra's ten thousandth concert. It had racked up more performances than any other orchestra in the world, including the Vienna Philharmonic, which was also founded in 1842. For this occasion, on which Mehta conducted, Mahler's Second Symphony was again brought out. That day Bernard Holland wrote in the *Times* about the Philharmonic's recording activity, concentrating on selected recordings by Toscanini, Mitropoulos, Walter, Bernstein, Boulez, and Mehta, though mentioning in passing the work of Stokowski, Rodzinski, Beecham, Barbirolli, Munch, and others.

What impressed Holland was the Philharmonic's ability to adapt its tone and playing style to the demands and personality of whoever was on the podium. This was in marked contrast to the Vienna Philharmonic, which, in its native repertoire, "has a way of making conductors play as it wants them to." In our own country, the Philadelphia Orchestra, at least during the tenures of Leopold Stokowski and Eugene Ormandy, had its own opulent sound that no guest conductor could alter. The New York Philharmonic, by contrast, was a musical chameleon, able "to adapt its sound and its technique to any conductor with a personality strong enough to command its attention." Mehta redeemed himself in Henahan's eyes on April 29 with "a marvelous atmospheric performance of Beethoven's 'Pastoral' Symphony," one that found the conductor "at his musicianly best."

The 1982 Spring Festival (though it was designated a Spring Series) paired Mozart with Stravinsky, in honor of the centennial of the great Russian master's birth. Opening on May 26, the series was immediately hampered by a conductor cancellation, that of Rafael Kubelík because of illness. He was to have led an unusual combination of works, Mozart's Serenade No. 10 in B-flat Major, K. 361, for thirteen wind instruments, and Stravinsky's ballet score *Les noces*, for the unusual combination of four pianos, percussion, four vocal soloists, and chorus.

With musicians of the caliber of the Philharmonic's, it was deemed possible to perform the Mozart work without a conductor, which the players did elegantly. The Stravinsky was another matter, however. For this work the Philharmonic obtained the services of the noted British ballet conductor John Lanchbery, whose "expertise served him and the music admirably," according to Rockwell the next day. The four pianists were Paul Jacobs, Ken Noda, Yefim Bronfman, and Stephanie Brown, while the vocal soloists were the soprano Phyllis Bryn-Julson, the mezzo-soprano Janice Meyerson, the tenor John Gilbert (filling in for another canceller, John Garrison), and the bass John Paul Bogart. The New York Choral Artists completed the ensemble.

Further plans went awry when the scheduled guest conductor Klaus Tennstedt suffered a concussion in a fall. His place was taken on June 2 by the ever-reliable Leinsdorf, whose "baton technique in *Petrushka* was a textbook illustration," said Rockwell. "Mr. Leinsdorf proved himself far more valuable than a mere substitute could ever be."

Meanwhile, in the midst of this festival, on June 3, the Philharmonic and the Israel Philharmonic played a combined benefit concert for both orchestras, raising over $500,000 in the process. Mehta, who has a knack for conducting such extravaganzas (viz. "The Three Tenors" and the *Turandot* performed in China), directed a program that opened with the New York Philharmonic playing Tchaikovsky's *Romeo and Juliet*, continued with the Israel Philharmonic in Bartók's Suite from *The Miraculous Mandarin*, and climaxed with both Philharmonics raising the roof in Berlioz's *Symphonie fantastique*. Televised from Avery Fisher Hall in the *Live from Lincoln Center* series, the event was also a visual extravaganza, with the two orchestras changing places with military precision and the television cameras moving in and out of the action.

CHAPTER 8

1982–84

FAILED POTENTIAL AGAIN

From August 21 to September 9, 1982, the Philharmonic was once more in South America, this time visiting Venezuela, Brazil, Argentina, Uruguay, Chile, and Ecuador. Special interest attached to the concerts in Argentina, for at the time relations between that country and the United States were strained in the aftermath of the war between Great Britain and Argentina over control of the Falkland Islands, with the British emerging victorious. The United States sided with Great Britain in that conflict, and some wags in the orchestra opined that the Philharmonic should play a festival of British music in Buenos Aires. Of course, no such program was given, and the six concerts in the Argentine capital did much to assuage any hostile feelings the residents may have had.

One of those events was a free Sunday afternoon concert in a large gymnasium, with an audience of more than ten thousand, many of them young, handicapped, or elderly. The other concerts, all sold out, were given in the famous Teatro Colón, which Philharmonic musicians judged to be one of the finest halls they had ever played in. They had not been enthusiastic about coming to Argentina, having been pickpocketed in Rio de Janeiro and witnessed a murder in São Paulo; but the Argentines won the musicians over with the tremendous enthusiasm with which they greeted both the orchestra and its performances. The entire visit was seen as a triumph for American artistry. The U.S. government contributed $50,000 to the tour, and the remainder of the $1.5 million cost was borne by Citibank, Diners Club, and the Philharmonic itself.

Every so often an article appears that is critical of the Philharmonic, comparing it with other orchestras in its category and complaining that the orchestra has failed to reach its potential. This was the gist of a lengthy piece by John Rockwell that appeared in the magazine section of the Sunday *Times* of September 19, 1982. After describing the Philharmonic as "among the top orchestras of the world" and citing its recent success in South America, its New York performances before near-capacity audiences, and its 1981 budget exceeding $13 million, with the lowest-paid of its musicians earning over $40,000 a year, Rockwell went on to claim that "there is a dark undercurrent to all this success, and that is the orchestra's half-century tradition of failing to fulfill its potential."

He spoke about the other American orchestras of the Big Five, those of Philadelphia, Boston, Chicago, and Cleveland, and how there seemed to be a rotation among them as to which one was considered the best, although, according to some critics, the Philharmonic was rarely granted that designation. This half-century tradition has dogged the orchestra since the departure of Toscanini in 1936. Barbirolli, Mitropoulos, and even Bernstein and Boulez all had to endure the specter of unfulfilled potential.

Like just about everyone else, Rockwell cited New York City's complex urban personality as having shaped the orchestra's personality, as opposed to the more genteel and elegant qualities of the rival cities (though Chicago can certainly give New York a run for its money in the complex-urban-personality department). The orchestras of Philadelphia, Boston, Cleveland, and Chicago are really the center of the musical life in those cities, whereas in New York the Philharmonic must compete with the Metropolitan Opera, the New York City Opera, recitals and chamber music, and a heavy influx of visiting orchestras, both domestic and foreign. To make matters worse, the visiting orchestras come in with programs that have been polished to perfection through much repetition, while the Philharmonic must prepare a different program each week. As Rockwell put it, "The Philharmonic is the only orchestra that cannot tour to New York." And he also cited the acoustical failure of the original Philharmonic Hall as contributing to poor orchestra morale.

One might think the lengthy parade of guest conductors appearing with the Philharmonic had been detrimental to the orchestra, but the Philharmonic was severely criticized even when it had only three regular guests each season (and one of them, George Szell, a strict disciplinarian). Zubin Mehta was perceived by the public and musicians alike as an orchestra builder, on the basis of his lengthy stay in Los Angeles; as a result of retirements and deaths, at the time of Rockwell's article Mehta had engaged one-fifth of the Philharmonic's musicians and was beginning to put his stamp on the orchestra.

Rockwell concluded that was all well and good but that Mehta "may have come along too late." The Philharmonic was just beginning to develop special characteristics at a time when other orchestras were losing theirs because of the changing face of the music world, what with jet-setting conductors and a more collegial relationship between orchestras and their maestros. No more the tyrannical leadership of a Toscanini or a Koussevitzky; now, instead, the benevolence of a Bernstein or a Mehta.

Samuel Lipman, publisher of the magazine *New Criterion*, in the April 1983 issue echoed much of what Rockwell had to say. Referring to what he termed "absentee landlords," he cited Mehta, Riccardo Muti in Philadelphia, and Seiji Ozawa in Boston as music directors who spent less than half the season with their orchestras, not to mention Georg Solti in Chicago and Carlo Maria Giulini in Los Angeles, both of whom conducted all of eight weeks a season. The result of their divided attentions was an increase in the power of an orchestra's management in the decision-making process, even in artistic matters, and it led to the advent of a new member of the administrative team: the artistic administrator. Szell, Ormandy, Koussevitzky, and other music directors of an earlier age did not need an artistic administrator. Today's maestros apparently do.

Labor troubles loomed again with the announcement on September 30 that the musicians had rejected a management contract offer by a vote of ninety-seven to seven. The previous contract had expired on September 20, but the season had begun while bargaining continued. Management was offering a three-year contract with a raise of $70 the first year, $60 the second, and $50 the third, which would have brought the minimum weekly scale to $810 by 1984–85. Negotiations continued until October 19, when the musicians voted to strike, although on October 23 a new three-year contract was ratified by a vote of eighty-three to eighteen, accepting the salary scale and increased health, welfare, insurance, and pension benefits. Ironically, a strike had forced the Chicago Symphony to cancel the first three weeks of its season. They settled on October 26 for the same figures as the Philharmonic, except that at the end of three years, their minimum salary would be $830.

On October 4, 1982, Glenn Gould died unexpectedly at age fifty, two days after suffering a stroke. Especially known for his performances and recordings of Bach, he is remembered by Philharmonic followers for his 1962 renditions of the Brahms Concerto No. 1, when Leonard Bernstein disagreed so strongly with his interpretation that he made a speech stating as much. A year later Gould retired from the concert stage and devoted his life to recordings and television documentaries in his native Canada.

On December 20 Arthur Rubinstein died at the age of ninety-five. Of all the great pianists of the twentieth century, he was probably the most loved by the public at large, a notable exponent not only of his countryman Chopin, but also of an immense repertoire from Mozart to Rachmaninoff, and even a bit beyond. Others may have been his superior in specific repertoire, but in totality he fully deserved the label bestowed on him by Harold C. Schonberg, "the complete pianist."

Maxim Shostakovich made his Philharmonic debut on October 7, conducting two of his father's major works, the wartime Eighth Symphony of 1943 and the postwar Violin Concerto No. 1. Both works had been given their American premieres by the Philharmonic, the symphony on April 2, 1944, with Artur Rodzinski conducting, the concerto on December 29, 1955, with David Oistrakh as the soloist and Dimitri Mitropoulos conducting. (Though the Philharmonic recorded the concerto shortly after performing it, the live Sunday afternoon account is available in the CD set of historic Philharmonic broadcasts.) Rodzinski repeated the symphony on October 12, 13, and 15, 1944, after which it lay dormant as far as the Philharmonic was concerned until the composer's son directed it in a performance that, according to Rockwell, "was shaped as it only can be by someone who knows it intimately and has a deep need to communicate it to a broader audience," an audience that cheered both conductor and the work itself at its conclusion. Glenn Dicterow, the Philharmonic's concertmaster, was splendid in the concerto, its first Philharmonic performance since Oistrakh's.

Another composer was represented by a program devoted to his music: the Pole Witold Lutosławski, whose seventieth birthday was celebrated with the concerts beginning January 7, 1983. Mehta conducted the *Concerto for Orchestra*, dating from 1954, and the composer himself was on hand to lead performances of two more recent works, the *Novelette* from 1979 and the Cello Concerto of 1970, the latter with Roman Jablonski as soloist.

The *Concerto for Orchestra* is probably Lutosławski's most popular piece, second only to Bartók's classic score in the number of performances for a work of that title. And, in truth, it is greatly influenced by Bartók, though Lutosławski rejected the Hungarian's style not long after finishing the concerto. His later works are in a more advanced idiom, with much use of aleatory passages (music of chance, with unmetered measures and unsynchronized passages), yet they are the work of a master composer in full command of his materials. Writing in the *Times* of January 9, Bernard Holland commended Lutosławski for his imagination and originality: "He has nearly everything any composer could want—taste and originality to be sure, but also the steely technical grasp that transforms both into music that works." *New York* magazine's Peter G. Davis wrote, in the January 24 issue, of the way the composer's music "urgently communicates to civilized, open-minded listeners," who were apparently in a minority on Friday afternoons, for many early departures greatly depleted the audience.

An example of generosity on Mehta's part was his allocating a week of subscription concerts to his assistant conductor, Larry Newland, who was therefore not dependent on a scheduled conductor's illness for his opportunity. Newland continued in his capacity as a Philharmonic violist even during his tenure as assistant, while at the same time serving as music director of the Harrisburg Symphony in

Pennsylvania. On the concerts beginning January 14 he presided over a difficult program that included Elliott Carter's *Variations for Orchestra*, Bernstein's Symphony No. 1 ("Jeremiah," with Janice Meyerson as the mezzo-soprano soloist in the last movement), and the Fifth Symphony of Sibelius.

On January 27, with Mehta conducting, Yehudi Menuhin appeared as soloist in one of his signature pieces, the Elgar Violin Concerto, which he had recorded in 1932 at the age of sixteen, with the composer conducting. Now sixty-six, he had been a frequent Philharmonic soloist, in spite of that seven-year gap after he impertinently played an encore in 1957. Age had brought about some inconsistency in his playing, though it had not detracted from his great musicianship and humanity, both of which qualities were evident on this occasion. During the season Mehta was presenting a survey of works by Arnold Schoenberg, never an audience favorite, whose early Chamber Symphony No. 1 was also heard on this concert.

A high point of the season was Rafael Kubelík's conducting, on March 24, of the American premiere of a concert version of Janáček's opera *From the House of the Dead*, based on the novel by Dostoyevsky. It was the composer's last opera, completed three months before his death in 1928. The Czech-born Kubelík had an obvious sympathy for this grim work by his countryman, which describes life in a Russian gulag in the mid-nineteenth century. Twenty vocal soloists participated, along with a male chorus, all on a raised platform behind the orchestra. As part of the dramatic context, the lights in Avery Fisher Hall were extinguished at the very end. Janáček's compositional style is based on the speech rhythms of the Czech language, a point not readily apparent because of the English translation used and printed in the program booklet. However, the music is so powerful that the work could not fail to make its intended effect. As Donal Henahan wrote the next day, it is "a timely and timeless work that sounds in many ways as if it were written last week."

Bruckner's Seventh Symphony was the featured work on the concerts beginning March 31, with Mehta in charge. These performances "did the orchestra and its conductor honor," according to Henahan on April 1. The centennial of Wagner's death was commemorated on the same program with the playing of the Prelude and "Good Friday Spell" from *Parsifal*; the latter score was also appropriate for the Easter season then in progress. It should be mentioned that the great Adagio movement of the Bruckner symphony is also a commemoration of Wagner's death, news of which Bruckner had received while working on it.

On April 13 it was announced that Amyas Ames, after an almost thirty-year association with the Philharmonic, would be retiring as the chairman of the society's board of directors, of which he had been a member since 1955 and president from 1963 to 1977. "I will be 77 years old," he said, "and it is a good policy of management that changes occur." Referring to Mehta's tenure, he continued, "The important thing about this period is that there has been a rising interest in symphonic music. We are moving in to a period when the orchestra will be at its greatest." It was anticipated that Carlos Moseley, only recently retired himself, would replace Ames as chairman of the board.

Of all the seldom-performed large-scale works, none makes a greater impression when it is actually given than Schoenberg's *Gurre-Lieder*. The large number of performers required undoubtedly mitigates against frequent hearings. Mehta concluded his Schoenberg survey by assembling 280 chorus members (the combined Westminster Choir and New York Choral Society), 130 instrumentalists, and six vocal soloists for the Philharmonic's April 21 presentation of this two-hour score—another reason for its rare appearances in the concert hall. Yet another factor in its neglect is possibly Schoenberg himself, whose name is anathema to the majority of concertgoers because they associate him with the dissonant works of his expressionist period and with his later espousal of the twelve-tone system. But the early *Gurre-Lieder* is nothing if not lushly romantic—the last gasp of late romanticism.

Apart from the orchestra and choral groups, those who distinguished themselves in the work were the mezzo-soprano Florence Quivar in the "Song of the Wood Dove," the tenor Robert Tear as Klaus the Fool, and the great lieder singer Hans Hotter in the Speaker's monologue, of which he had made a specialty in his later years. As Henahan put it on April 22, Tear and Hotter "showed what intelligent artists can do with parts that in this score are sometimes tossed away." Peter G. Davis, generally not a great admirer of Mehta, wrote in *New York* on May 9 that this performance may well have been "Mehta's finest achievement with the orchestra."

Another visit to the Abyssinian Baptist Church, another Radiothon, the expected assumption of the chairmanship of the board by Carlos Moseley—these were some of the events marking the closing weeks of the season. New Yorkers also saw the retirement of six orchestra members, the most prominent of them the principal flutist, Julius Baker, who performed the Nielsen Concerto with Mehta conducting on May 5. Also honored were the violist William Carboni, the associate principal bassoonist Harold Goltzer, the violinist Bernard Robbins, the violist Raymond Sabinsky, and the violist Robert Weinrebe.

On May 7 the orchestra celebrated the 150th anniversary of the birth of Johannes Brahms. For this pension-fund benefit concert under Mehta's direction, the violinist Gidon Kremer and the cellist Yo-Yo Ma were on hand for an impassioned and riveting performance of the Double Concerto, with Mehta also offering the Fourth Symphony. The Philharmonic would soon embark on a series that would focus on the present, one devoted to music written since 1968.

HORIZONS '83

For a brief time during Leonard Bernstein's tenure as music director, the Philharmonic had two composers-in-residence, David Amram and Lester Trimble, though their duties appear to have been rather minimal. For the 1982–83 season the orchestra appointed Jacob Druckman to that post, now sponsored by the organization called Meet the Composer, with support from the Exxon Corporation, the National Endowment for the Arts, and the Rockefeller Foundation.

Druckman's duties were more far-reaching than those of his predecessors. They included not only advising the music director on contemporary music and composing a work for the orchestra, but actually organizing a festival of new music. Thus was presented, on June 2–15, 1983, Horizons '83—The New Romanticism? The festival was to highlight music of the past fifteen years. Music had begun to break away from the rigor and dissonance of many of the post–World War II scores, which had failed to find a general audience, and much of the music composed since 1968 was more accessible to listeners. Assisting the Philharmonic would be three groups specializing in new music: the Group for Contemporary Music, the New York New Music Ensemble, and Speculum Musicae. The conductors would be Zubin Mehta, Larry Newland, Lukas Foss, Gunther Schuller, and Arthur Weisberg, while the works to be performed were by John Adams, Sandor Balassa, Luciano Berio, Marc-Antonio Consoli, George Crumb, Peter Maxwell Davies, David Del Tredici, Lukas Foss, John Harbison, Aaron Jay Kernis, Barbara Kolb, Fred Lerdahl, Donald Martino, Bernard Rands, George Rochberg, Leonard Rosenman, Frederic Rzewski, Gunther Schuller, William Schuman, Joseph Schwantner, Tison Street, Morton Subotnick, Toru Takemitsu, Nicholas Thorne, Charles Wuorinen, and Druckman himself.

There was much discussion among the various critics who reviewed the series as to just how "romantic" much of the music was, if at all, or, for that matter, what was "new" about it. One of the works performed was already a classic of sorts, Berio's *Sinfonia*, dating from 1968 and the reason for that starting date of the festival. The work was commissioned by the Philharmonic for its 125th anniversary and had received its world premiere on October 10, 1968, conducted by the composer, who also led the Columbia recording made a few days later. In those performances the popular Swingle Singers sang or recited texts by Claude Lévi-Strauss, the syllables in the name Martin Luther King, words by Samuel Beckett, and revolutionary slogans that had been inscribed on the walls of the Sorbonne in 1968. A striking feature of the work, and one that had a great influence on other composers, was the third movement, in which the entire scherzo of Mahler's Second Symphony served as the backdrop, and sometimes the foreground, to the texts mentioned as well as to Berio's own music, weaving in and out of the sonic tapestry.

It was the New Swingle Singers who were heard in the 1983 rendition, which Mehta conducted. The work was seen, as described by Edward Rothstein on June 9, as "a Romantic look backward at what was lost, a rather tendentious call for music to become a part of the restorative revolution." Whether one agreed with the choice of music or not, whether one thought the festival's theme was appropriate to the music heard, it was generally agreed that the event had been a success. It had immersed listeners in new music and led them to ponder the question of where music was heading.

Shortly after the end of the festival, on June 30, an article by Rothstein appeared in the *Times* reporting on the results of a survey by the orchestra's artistic committee that had been taken among the musicians, who were asked to comment anonymously on several subjects, including the music director, the management, and the work schedule. At the time of the article's appearance, half the players had responded, with more expected.

What distressed the members of the board of directors was that the vast majority of the musicians expressed dissatisfaction with Zubin Mehta, citing his failings in artistic and administrative skills. The nature of these failings was not disclosed, though the several board members who were quoted were of the opinion that dissatisfaction with the conductor was nothing unusual and could be found in all orchestras. Constance Hoguet, the president of the Philharmonic, acknowledged that there was discontent but felt it should not be magnified. One of the board members, Sampson R. Field, felt musicians were occasionally unwilling to blame themselves for musical problems and preferred to blame the music director.

Other concerns expressed by the musicians were the acoustics of Avery Fisher Hall, still poor in spite of the renovation in 1976, and, most important, the expiration in 1982 of their recording contract with CBS (formerly Columbia Records). During the tenures of Bernstein and Boulez the musicians received between $2,000 and $3,000 a year in recording fees, as well as about $800 in royalties. CBS, however, claimed that the cost of recording in New York was too high. In addition, representatives of two of New York's leading record stores claimed that the recordings that the Philharmonic made under Mehta simply did not sell as well as those made with Solti, Karajan, Bernstein, and even Boulez. In fact, however, recording activity was beginning to decline for many American orchestras in the early 1980s. According to Field, the Philharmonic no longer wished to have a contract, but preferred to have "freedom of action."

Hoguet felt that some of the players' discontent with Mehta had to do with orchestra personnel changes and his efforts to enforce artistic discipline. She also said the orchestra was upset because of negative criticism in the press, of which there had been much more recently than even two years before. She thought this situation "seems to happen with any conductor. When he comes in, he's the golden boy. Then a certain ennui sets in on the part of the press."

When Mehta left the Los Angeles Philharmonic in 1978, he was succeeded as music director by the great Carlo Maria Giulini. Now, when Giulini announced he would be leaving the post in 1984, rumors circulated that *his* successor might be none other than Mehta himself. These rumors were strongly denied. In the end, Mehta did not return to Los Angeles, even though some members of the Philharmonic fervently hoped he would.

"The world's most exciting orchestra" is how the Philharmonic was proudly described in its publicity material for the 1983–84 season, which set Donal Henahan to wondering if it could live up to its advertising. Published on September 11, this was yet another article detailing the orchestra's problems. Chief among them, according to Henahan, was morale, not only because of the loss of income from the cancellation of the recording contract, but also because of dissatisfaction with Mehta. Henahan cited the occasional memorable results achieved, such as with Schoenberg's *Gurre-Lieder*, but lamented the more frequently encountered "mediocre playing and humdrum interpretations." Again the Philharmonic was compared to other orchestra-and-conductor pairings, such as "Berlin/Karajan or Chicago/Solti or Vienna/Anybody," and found wanting in its failure to achieve prestige in international music circles. The Philharmonic, it was felt, lacked sufficient pride and esprit de corps to maintain high standards, no matter who was at the helm artistically or financially.

Mehta did not open the season. That honor went instead to Rafael Kubelík, by now an annual and highly esteemed guest conductor. His program consisted of just two symphonies, William Schuman's Tenth and Beethoven's "Eroica." The Schuman work, subtitled "American Muse," was written for Washington's National Symphony to honor the American bicentennial. While there were a few problems in its execution, none of these cropped up in the "Eroica," in which, according to Holland on September 16, "conductor and orchestra seemed to understand one another perfectly at every step along the way.... This was not a slashing or an explosive 'Eroica,' but in its unhurried way, a very satisfying one."

On September 26 the *Times* reported the death, at age fifty-three, of Paul Jacobs, who had been the Philharmonic's official pianist since 1961. A brilliant performer and musician who was comfortable in all periods of music, he concentrated on the twentieth century, becoming known as a formidable exponent of the works of Elliott Carter, Aaron Copland, Pierre Boulez, Arnold Schoenberg, and many, many others. In the fall of 1961 he gave a Saturday afternoon recital in New York's Town Hall that included major works of Ferruccio Busoni, after which he strolled over to Carnegie Hall to play the modest celesta part in Ravel's *Bolero* with the Philharmonic.

Mehta did not return until October 11, when he led "a muscular, frequently gripping performance of Mahler's massive Symphony No. 5." Henahan, who had been critical of Mehta's absence in the first weeks of the season, acknowledged that he had been leading a tour of the Israel Philharmonic, of which he is music director for life, and had directed that orchestra's season-opening concerts. "It seems there simply are not enough music directors to go around nowadays. Even if you are the New York Philharmonic, time-sharing is called for." He concluded, "If Mr. Mehta can keep the Philharmonic playing at this kind of alert and committed level, this season may develop interestingly."

A nationally televised pension-fund benefit concert on October 19 brought a rave review the next day from Allen Hughes, who cited the performance of Stravinsky's *Petrushka* as demonstrating that "the Philharmonic was a virtuoso ensemble playing at the height of its power," with the various solo passages "knit by Mr. Mehta into an overall musical fabric of extraordinary color and design." Mstislav Rostropovich's rendition of the Dvořák Cello Concerto "was so compelling that one's attention was riveted to it," while Mehta and the orchestra were praised for their collaboration.

On November 4 it was announced that Zubin Mehta's contract had been extended for four more years, which guaranteed his presence in New York until 1990, by which time his tenure of twelve years as music director would have been the longest in Philharmonic history. The orchestra's managing director, Nick Webster, denied that the extension had anything to do with reports of dissatisfaction by the musicians or complaints by the critics: "It was certainly a vote of confidence, but not in response to anything." Said Carlos Moseley, "Zubin Mehta's commitment to us, and ours to him, is a strong and happy one, and will be greeted with enthusiasm by a wide and devoted audience." It was pointed out that Mehta's responsibilities with the Israel Philharmonic would continue and that the final agreement on the contract came about when Webster, Moseley, and Hoguet flew to Israel to meet with him.

The news of the contract extension was greeted by Henahan on November 13 with the observation that Mehta now had a mandate to change the Philharmonic. For years the orchestra had the reputation, deserved or not, of a really difficult orchestra for conductors to work with, with inconsistent results in performances. (My own experience as a young assistant conductor, in the few opportunities I had to actually conduct the orchestra, was just the opposite. They could not have been kinder or easier to work with.) Henahan concluded that, player for player, the Philharmonic's musicians ranked with the world's best, but that their attitude needed improvement. Some players were conscientious in their preparation, others were not. Some cooperated with whomever was on the podium, others delighted in conductor baiting. No wonder, said Henahan, that from one night to the next, from one maestro to the next, "the Philharmonic can sound like half a dozen different orchestras. Zubin Mehta's mandate is to change all that, and good luck to him."

MORE CANCELLATIONS AND NOT JUST ANOTHER TOUR

The noted and venerable East German conductor Kurt Sanderling made his Philharmonic debut in the two weeks that spanned the end of 1983 and the beginning of 1984. His second week, which began on January 5, was devoted to Mahler's Tenth Symphony, in the performing version by Deryck Cooke. Mahler had left the score unfinished at the time of his death, save for the opening Adagio movement and a brief scherzo called "Purgatorio." The remaining three movements were left in sketch form, from which Cooke and several others devised performing versions. Working independently of each other, the various arrangers came up with results sufficiently similar as to confirm the validity of the completed Tenth Symphony as a Mahlerian work. (Some well-known Mahler conductors have balked at performing any of the versions of the Tenth Symphony, on the grounds that it is not authentic. Yet the same conductors have had no qualms about performing Mozart's Requiem in any of its completed versions.)

Although Henahan found Sanderling's rendition "straightforward and often pedestrian," he expressed no such reservations the following week when Leonard Bernstein returned on January 12 to conduct Mahler's "Resurrection" Symphony, a work with which he had been closely associated since the beginning of his career: "This was easily the most thrilling 'Resurrection' I have heard since—well, since the last one I heard Mr. Bernstein lead." Jessye Norman and Barbara Hendricks were the soloists, while the choristers were the Choir of St. Patrick's Cathedral and the New Amsterdam Singers.

Zubin Mehta reappeared on January 26 with a program celebrating the centennial of the birth of Anton Webern, normally a difficult composer for audiences to embrace, not to mention for orchestras to play. However, Mehta began with the early and lushly attractive *Im Sommerwind*, following it with Webern's official Op. 1, the *Passacaglia*. Two more works were given, both in his spare and somewhat austere later style, the *Six Pieces for Orchestra* and the *Concerto for Nine Instruments*. To leaven the menu for the audience, Murray Perahia was the soloist in the two Mendelssohn Piano Concertos, No. 2 on the first half of the program and No. 1 on the second half. The attraction for the audience of Perahia and Mendelssohn caused Henahan to comment, "I have never seen so few mid-program dropouts at a Philharmonic concert containing this much difficult music."

As has been noted, the best-laid plans of a Philharmonic season can be disrupted by conductor cancellations. So it was with a vengeance this season. On February 29 it was announced that Rafael Kubelík had suffered a broken elbow and would be unable to fulfill his engagement on March 8–27, during which time he was scheduled to perform Czech music, including Bedřich Smetana's symphonic cycle *Má vlast* (My Country) in its complete form. Kubelík's absence brought an opportunity for the young Russian-born conductor Semyon Bychkov, at the time music director of the Grand Rapids Symphony in Michigan. It was, and still is, quite unusual for the conductor of a second-tier orchestra to appear with a major ensemble such as the New York Philharmonic. Bychkov was, however, known in New York, having attended Mannes College and conducted the New York premiere of Tchaikovsky's *Yolanta*. He has since established an international career, including appearances at the Metropolitan Opera. Kubelík's Czech programming was a casualty of his cancellation: the major work on Bychkov's program was the Second Symphony of Rachmaninoff, and the Russian pianist Alexander Toradze was the soloist in Liszt's First Concerto.

The year 1984 marked the sixtieth anniversary of the Philharmonic's Young People's Concerts. Although these concerts, founded by Ernest Schelling, had been presented in a rather low-key manner in their early years, they had usually been conducted by someone engaged specifically for that purpose. Igor Buketoff and Wilfrid Pelletier were in charge of them during the 1940s and 1950s, when the concerts were broadcast locally on radio station WNYC. Occasionally a guest conductor, such as Leopold Stokowski, would lead one of them. (In 1949 he conducted George Kleinsinger's *Tubby the Tuba*, with the Philharmonic's William Bell as the soloist. For an encore Bell sang and played *When Yuba Plays the Rhumba on the Tuba down in Cuba*—pronounced "Cooba" by Stokowski. After much applause Stokowski announced that Bell would sing *When Veronica Plays the Harmonica on the Pier in Santa Monica*, then added apologetically, "Oh, we don't have the music for that one.") All that changed with the arrival of Bernstein, the first music director to conduct the Young People's Concerts, which then became a national institution seen on television across the country.

Sharing the anniversary was the Portland (Oregon) Youth Philharmonic, the oldest youth orchestra in the country, which, on the way to a European tour, was invited to New York for a joint concert with the Philharmonic on March 14, 1984. Under its regular conductor, Jacob Avshalomov, the Portlanders performed three pieces, after which Bernstein led them in the second movement of Mahler's "Resurrection" Symphony. Then an excerpt from Bernstein's 1960 telecast "Who Is Gustav Mahler?" was shown, followed by his conducting the combined Philharmonics, 210 musicians in all, in Tchaikovsky's *Romeo and Juliet*.

Kubelík's cancellation had the happy result of bringing Bernstein back for an additional week beginning with the concert of March 22. With the season in mind, he programmed three works appropriate for the vernal equinox: Copland's *Appalachian Spring*, Schumann's "Spring" Symphony, and Stravinsky's *Rite of Spring*. The last, of course, had been a specialty of his since early in his career, and although his tempos had slowed a bit over the years, there was no denying the visceral dynamism of his performance.

No sooner had Bernstein given his concerts than the announcement appeared, on March 28, that Zubin Mehta was canceling his final six weeks of subscription concerts as the result of surgery "to correct a severe chronic inflammation of the muscles in his right elbow," a condition similar to tennis elbow. (The cancellations of Kubelík and Mehta bring to mind the 1951 mishap that befell Paul Paray during his guest conducting engagement with the Philadelphia Orchestra. He had slipped on the ice in Philadelphia and sprained his right wrist. Undaunted, he conducted the concerts in Philadelphia and New York entirely with his left arm and hand, his right arm in a sling.) Filling in for Mehta were two conductors new to the Philharmonic, Václav Neumann and Günther Herbig, and three returning figures, Michael Tilson Thomas, Andrew Davis, and Robert Shaw. Shaw led performances of the Brahms *German Requiem*; David Zinman, who had conducted the orchestra in summer concerts in the city's housing projects, made his subscription debut.

The 1983–84 season actually did end with three weeks under the direction of a scheduled maestro—the reliable Erich Leinsdorf, whose programs included the seldom-heard First Symphony of Bruckner and the more frequently scheduled Third Symphony of Mahler. In his senior years Leinsdorf had evolved into an extremely undemonstrative conductor. Like Boulez, he was not very interesting to watch, but, also like Boulez, his straightforward and functional gestures caused one to concentrate on the music rather than podium pyrotechnics, of which there were none.

On May 20 a Sunday article by Henahan discussed the never-ending acoustical problems of Avery Fisher Hall. In the view of the Philharmonic players—those in the string and woodwind sections, at least—the brass and percussion sections were entirely too dominant. It was not clear whether that could be blamed on the hall or on conductors who did little or nothing to correct the balance. According to one player, "Every guest conductor who comes complains that the brass plays too loud and the brass players say that's the way they're used to playing, take it or leave it." The strings resented being asked to compensate by bearing down harder with the bows, thus producing an ugly and, in the end, a more feeble sound. No solution was offered other than that conductors should be more insistent. "The old-time conductors would not have put up with such things," said a veteran player.

As it had done in 1983, the Philharmonic presented a festival of new music, this time called Horizons '84, with the additional title The New Romanticism—A Broader View, implying the inclusion of a wider range of music than in the year before. Jacob Druckman was again in charge of the festival, which opened on May 30 with two major composers leading their own works: Hans Werner Henze with his *Tristan* ("Preludes for Piano, Tape and Orchestra") in its American premiere, and Krzysztof Penderecki with his First Symphony, which was given its New York premiere.

The pianist in the Henze work was the admirable Emanuel Ax, one of the few prominent soloists who take an interest in contemporary music. A mixture of Wagner, Brahms, various orchestral effects, and, of course, the piano and tape-recorded sounds, *Tristan* was acclaimed by Rockwell on June 1 as "a real modern masterpiece." Penderecki's symphony did not fare so well in critical estimation, having been found neither musically convincing nor dramatically coherent.

The inclusion of the tape recorder went hand in hand with the "broader view" aspect of the festival, for there were also programs devoted to computer-generated and theatrically motivated music by such composers as Milton Babbitt, John Chowning, Stuart Dempster, Charles Dodge, Kenneth Gaburo, Diamanda Galas, York Hoeller, Paul Lansky, George Lewis, Michael McNabb, Roger Reynolds, Jean-Claude Risset, Laurie Spiegel, Charles Wuorinen, Iannis Xenakis, Joji Yuasa, and the Philharmonic's own Jon Deak. Other composers heard were Gilbert Amy, Irwin Bazelon, Robert Beaser, Harrison Birtwistle, Pierre Boulez, Martin Bresnick, Elliott Carter, George Crumb, Anthony Davis, Robert Dick, Dean Drummond, Donald Erb, Betsy Jolas, Oliver Knussen, Joan La Barbara, Salvatore Martirano, Thea Musgrave, Christopher Rouse, Peter Sculthorpe, and George Walker.

As before, the programs alternated a seventy-five-piece Philharmonic with a thirty-five-piece one, as well as offering performances by the American Composers Orchestra, the American Brass Quintet, Speculum Musicae, and assorted chamber music combinations and solo instrumentalists and singers. Some composers led their own pieces—not only Henze and Penderecki, but also Amy and Wuorinen. The other conductors were Zubin Mehta (in his first appearance following his elbow surgery), Larry Newland (in his last appearance as assistant conductor), Leonard Slatkin, and Arthur Weisberg.

Mehta and Weisberg shared the program of June 7. Weisberg, a specialist in contemporary music, led the world premiere of Crumb's tone poem *A Haunted Landscape*; Mehta presided over the American premiere, in concert form, of Knussen's one-act opera *Where the Wild Things Are*. For Henahan, on June 8, "both proved to be works worth paying attention to," the Crumb "exquisite" in detail, the Knussen displaying "charm and magical atmosphere." *Wild Things*, with a libretto by Maurice Sendak, was surely the hit of the festival; the soprano Karen Beardsley was splendid in the difficult role of the child Max, an operatic cousin of the bad boy in Ravel's *L'enfant et les sortilèges*.

There was sadness in the Philharmonic family with the death on July 22, at age sixty-five, of Constance Hoguet, president of the Philharmonic Society. The first woman to hold that office, she was in fact one of the very few women of that time who were in charge of a major New York cultural institution.

Another major tour was on the agenda from August 15 to September 19. Although a tour to Japan and other Far Eastern countries was no longer unusual for the Philharmonic, this one would conclude with five concerts in India, Mehta's homeland. Although he had toured there with the Los Angeles Philharmonic in 1967, this visit would be the first time the New Yorkers had played in India, with concerts in New Delhi, Calcutta, and Bombay. As Mehta pointed out, he had never conducted in Calcutta. He had left India at the age of eighteen to study in Vienna, and it was many years before he returned. He considered himself "still a foreigner" there, though an Indian "culturally and spiritually" nevertheless.

One of the tour stops was to be Kuala Lumpur, Malaysia, where concerts were scheduled for September 2 and 3. The program for the latter date was to include Ernest Bloch's *Schelomo: Hebrew Rhapsody for Cello and Orchestra*. But officials in Malaysia, a largely Muslim country, objected on the grounds that a government policy prohibited the "screening, portrayal or musical presentation of works of Jewish origin." After discussing the matter with the Malaysian prime minister's office, officials of Citibank (which was partially underwriting the tour), and the American Embassy in Kuala Lumpur, it was decided to replace the Bloch work with Tchaikovsky's Violin Concerto, much to the displeasure of American Jewish leaders and some orchestra members. Nick Webster pointed out that it was the orchestra's policy to make program changes if so requested by a host, and that the concert program of September 2 listed works by Gershwin, Copland, and Bernstein, all composers of Jewish origin, to which no objection had been made. Apparently it was the word "Hebrew" that was found offensive.

Orchestra members, Jewish leaders, and Philharmonic subscribers made a number of passionate appeals urging cancellation of the concerts "if the Malaysians seek to tell the orchestra what music to play." And after a few anxious hours, the Malaysian concerts were indeed canceled, causing the Malaysian information officer to comment that the cancellation "won't hurt anybody." But it was good for the residents of Bangkok, Thailand, where the orchestra played instead on September 3.

To perform in Bangkok on short notice involved a major logistic effort in that city. An acoustic shell had to be quickly assembled for the university auditorium where the concert would take place, the hall had to be cleaned after a rock concert, posters advertising the concert had to be printed—in fact everything that would normally be done in preparation for a concert, but in a very condensed time period. The orchestra played a program of music rooted in America, yet deemed suitable for an audience unaccustomed to Western music: Bernstein's Overture to *Candide*, Copland's *Quiet City*, Gershwin's *American in Paris*, and Dvořák's "New World" Symphony; among several encores was John Philip Sousa's "Stars and Stripes Forever." According to Webster, in his twenty-two years of involvement with symphony orchestras, he did not know of any other situation, at any time, where such a concert had been organized in such a short time: "This is unprecedented and unique." The concert was a great success, even though one Thai musician commented that he wished the Philharmonic had brought something "more meaty."

Although the entire tour was very successful musically, once the orchestra arrived in India there were complaints from the musicians about the hotel accommodations. In fact, at least forty members angrily departed a government-owned hotel in New Delhi when cockroaches were discovered in the not-very-well-cleaned rooms and moved into a more expensive, privately owned hotel. The incident as reported in the Indian press created quite a stir, though Mehta attempted to quell local indignation by pointing out that the musicians were, after all, New Yorkers, and thus apt to be opinionated and vocal.

Everyone commented on how excited Mehta was to be in his homeland with his orchestra. "I've never seen him this excited, ever," said one orchestra member. "He's like a little boy bringing home a new toy." Mehta countered, "But if I get too excited, the orchestra won't play well." Play well they did, as always. Bombay (as it was then called), where Mehta's father, Mehli, had founded the Bombay Symphony in 1935, was more westernized than many on the tour, so there were many people there who appreciated Western classical music—enough to fill the 3,000-seat hall for three concerts. Mehta said there were "not more than three good halls on the entire tour," and some were actually "lousy." But, he pointed out, "acoustics are secondary at such a time." The important thing was "the interaction between the orchestra and the people."

CHAPTER 9

1984–86

HAPPY BIRTHDAY, JOHANN AND GEORGE

After the retirement of the principal violist Sol Greitzer, Paul Neubauer was appointed to the chair, becoming, at age twenty-one, the youngest principal player in the orchestra's history. One of the results of his appointment was that he would be leading a section of very experienced musicians, even though he would be playing many of the staples of the repertoire for the first time. After only three weeks in the job he said that everyone had been very nice to him, and he felt no resentment from his colleagues.

Making his Philharmonic debut on October 10, 1984, was the Korean-born conductor Myung-whun Chung, whose sisters are the violinist Kyung-wha Chung, who was his soloist in his second week of concerts, and the cellist Myung-wha Chung. He made a very good impression on the critics, Rockwell finding him "a sure, practiced and occasionally eloquent young conductor." It is always wise for a young conductor to program works that are not in an orchestra's standard repertoire so as to avoid comparisons of his interpretations with those of past masters, so Chung's programs included Mozart's rarely played Symphony No. 28 in C Major, K. 200, last given by the Philharmonic in 1971; Dvořák's even more rarely performed Symphony No. 3 in E-flat Major, which the orchestra had never played; and Prokofieff's Symphony No. 6, the American premiere of which the Philharmonic had given under Stokowski in 1949 and which had not been offered since. Although the Prokofieff work has never achieved the popularity of its immediate predecessor, perhaps because of its relative austerity (save for its bouncy finale), many consider it to be equally great.

In 1964 Arthur Rubinstein had performed both Brahms piano concertos in a single concert to benefit the orchestra's pension fund. Twenty years later, on November 26, Daniel Barenboim did the same, with Mehta conducting. Barenboim's heroic interpretations put Henahan in mind of none other than his illustrious predecessor: "Praise for a pianist does not go much further than to mention his name in the same sentence [as Rubinstein's]." The occasion was "a grand one on almost every count."

The Philharmonic gave two world premieres in the fall of 1984, works that were part of the series commissioned by Francis Goelet to feature the orchestra's principal players. On November 21 was heard the *Concerto Quaternio* by Gunther Schuller, in which the soloists were Charles Rex, violin; Paige Brook, flute; Joseph Robinson, oboe; and Philip Smith, trumpet. It was no doubt by design that the solo instruments were the same as in Bach's Brandenburg Concerto No. 2, and Henahan felt the work could be "the best thing Mr. Schuller has produced in a long time." On December 13 came the premiere of the Oboe Concerto by George Rochberg, with Robinson as soloist. This score Henahan found to be "heartfelt, but oddly vaporous and diffuse," though it received a warm reception from the audience.

On December 6 the Philharmonic-Symphony Society announced that Stephen Stamas would succeed the late Constance Hoguet in the position of president. He held a Ph.D. from Harvard University, had been a Rhodes scholar at Oxford, and was at the time a vice president of Exxon. Known for his love of the arts and his fund-raising ability, he had helped bring into being the *Live from Lincoln Center* series, sponsored by Exxon on public television, and was involved with several other artistic endeavors such as the Exxon/Arts Endowment Conductor Program, the Meet the Composer Orchestra Residency Project, and the American Symphony Orchestra League Management Fellowship Program. He was thus, at age fifty-three, a natural to lead the Philharmonic.

The Philharmonic began the new year by presenting, on January 3, 1985, the American premiere of *Offertorium*, a work for violin and orchestra by the Soviet composer Sofia Gubaidulina. The Latvian violinist Gidon Kremer, for whom the piece was written, was the soloist, with Mehta conducting, as he had done for the Schuller and Rochberg world premieres. Gubaidulina had begun her career just after the death of Stalin, which meant she did not suffer the indignities to which Shostakovich, Prokofieff, and other Soviet composers were subjected under the Soviet dictator's regime. She was thus able to be more free in her musical expression and explore the techniques employed by composers in the West. Rockwell found *Offertorium* to be "an open, accessible yet unmistakably personal statement," with Kremer's playing "a real act of commitment," supported "with uncommon care" by Mehta and the Philharmonic.

Another world premiere occurred on January 10 when the New Zealand soprano Kiri Te Kanawa, in her Philharmonic debut, sang the lovely *Four Last Songs* by Richard Strauss. As it happened, these were not actually his very last songs, for there was one more to come. In late 1948 he composed a single song, "Malven" (Mallows), which he dedicated to the soprano Maria Jeritza, who had performed so many of his operatic roles. The dedication reads, "To beloved Maria, this last rose!" Composed with piano accompaniment, the song was performed by Te Kanawa and the pianist Martin Katz as a sort of appendage to the *Four Last Songs*. Rockwell found "Malven" to be "not insignificant" and deserving of "an afterlife in the song repertory." Te Kanawa was praised for her performances of the entire Strauss group, and Mehta concluded the program with a "grandly done" rendition of Elgar's First Symphony, normally the province of English conductors but occasionally effective, as here, when done by others.

As it progressed, the 1984–85 season saw the Philharmonic receiving higher-than-usual accolades from the press. Take, for instance, the reaction to the concert of January 18, on paper a very unadventurous program of Beethoven's Fifth Symphony and Richard Strauss's *Don Quixote*. But under Klaus Tennstedt, a conductor noted for revivifying the standard repertoire with his intense personality, the works emerged as if freshly minted. According to Holland, the Fifth "sounded nothing like the music world's most drained and overworked composition," while in *Don Quixote* the musicians "created theater…without a touch of artifice." Lorne Monroe and Paul Neubauer were, respectively, the expert cello and viola soloists.

On February 1 Mehta and the Philharmonic presented a concert performance of the first act of Wagner's *Die Walküre*, with the roles of Sieglinde, Siegmund, and Hunding taken respectively by Eva Martón, Peter Hofmann, and Martti Talvela. In previous Philharmonic performances of this work, it had been preceded by other music. For example, on October 7 and 8, 1954, Dimitri Mitropoulos had begun with Weber's Overture to *Der Freischütz* and his own orchestral transcription of Bach's Fantasia and Fugue in G Minor. In 1968 Leonard Bernstein's concerts on May 23, 24, and 25 had opened rather incongruously with the Third Symphony of Roy Harris. But on February 1, 1985, and for the ensuing performances, there was no opening work: the hourlong Wagner act stood alone. In effect, Avery Fisher Hall served as a recording studio, for CBS issued a CD made up of takes from these concerts. Henahan felt that Mehta "kept the action flowing inexorably, and the orchestra played with unusual verve and alertness" (the adjective unhappily planting in the reader's mind the notion that verve and alertness were not the norm in Philharmonic performances).

The programming of the single act without any other music, perhaps so all efforts could be concentrated on the recording, was nevertheless emblematic of many of Mehta's programs, which tended to be on the short side. Beethoven's Ninth Symphony, running to around sixty-five minutes on average, is often the sole work on a program today. Gone are the days when Pierre Monteux in San Francisco could precede the Ninth with the same composer's *Leonore* Overture No. 3 and Violin Concerto (admittedly an extreme example).

In 1985 the Philharmonic, in common with many other musical organizations, observed the three hundredth anniversary of the births of Johann Sebastian Bach and George Frideric Handel (though not that of Domenico Scarlatti). Handel was the first to be honored when, on February 22, Kurt Masur led an all-Handel program (the Philharmonic's first since Bernstein's Handel celebration of 1959 commemorating the two hundredth anniversary of the composer's death). Performed were the Second Coronation Anthem ("The King Shall Rejoice"), the Second Suite from the *Water Music*, and the *Ode for St. Cecilia's Day*, with the soprano Arleen Augér, the tenor Philip Creech, and the Westminster Choir, directed by Joseph Flummerfelt.

The Los Angeles–born Augér had built a substantial reputation in Europe as a baroque stylist before the concert, her Philharmonic debut. Her many recordings of this and other repertoire had whetted the appetite for these appearances, as had her New York recital debut the year before. She did not disappoint; Henahan wrote that "for vocal purity and exquisite musical taste she has few peers, especially in Bach and Handel." As for Masur, he was "a man worth paying attention to." Prophetic words, indeed.

A month later, on March 22, Bach had his day, this time with Rafael Kubelík in charge. Not known as a baroque specialist, but a warmly romantic interpreter, he led a program consisting of the Third Orchestral Suite, the Cantata No. 50 ("Nun ist das Heil und die Kraft"), the Concerto in D Minor for two violins, and the *Magnificat*. Although Kubelík's approach ignored the basic elements of baroque performance practice that even then had become de rigueur in performances of this music, his personal style of conducting and interpretation were convincing in their own right (except, perhaps, to die-hard early music purists). What one could take exception to, as Henahan did, was that the program was made up of works that are normally heard anyway. He felt a three-hundredth-anniversary program should feature something special.

Two Philharmonic members, Charles Rex and Kenneth Gordon, were the soloists in the Double Violin Concerto, and the singers were Benita Valente, soprano; Claudia Catania, mezzo-soprano; Birgit Finnilä, contralto; Philip Creech, tenor; and Wolfgang Schoene, baritone, again with the Westminster Choir. The last numbered two hundred voices, causing Henahan to wonder why Kubelík chose to reduce the orchestra by half rather than go all out with the full orchestra, as Thomas Beecham was prone to do.

Research into performance styles of the baroque era has led some orchestra conductors to agonize over choices involving ornamentation, tempo, and performing forces, to name just a few. In 1985 Kurt Masur was scheduled to conduct Bach's

Saint Matthew Passion in Leipzig on Bach's three hundredth birthday, March 21. It would be, remarkably, Masur's first *Saint Matthew*, and the event would be attended by critics and musicologists from all over the world. Somewhat reflectively, Masur remarked, "I know that, whatever I do, it will be wrong."

By 1985 Mahler's Fifth Symphony had become a standard repertoire item. Though routine performances are a danger for well-known fare, Mehta's rendition on April 4 was played for the maximum in visceral excitement, with brilliant results. Henahan proclaimed, "One never had any doubt that a fine Mahler orchestra was in full cry. . . . I am sure I will hear from some ancient citizen who heard Mahler himself do it better, but that can't be helped. Mahler was then, Mehta is now."

In spite of Henahan's approval of this concert, and of a Russian evening that paired Prokofieff's *Alexander Nevsky* with scenes from Mussorgsky's *Boris Godunov* (with Matti Salminen as Boris) on May 9, he was not happy with the season as a whole. In his May 19 Sunday column he bemoaned the virtual omnipresence of competence rather than inspiration and faulted Mehta as a program builder: "In spite of his abilities as a leader and a musician, he somehow does not regularly produce concerts that are exciting to experience or, failing that, stimulating to think about." He was pleased, however, with the prospect of the 1985–86 season, which would celebrate the eighty-fifth birthday of Aaron Copland with a season-long presentation of many of his works, would include the world and American premieres of a number of interesting compositions, and would open with the Philharmonic's participation in a Festival of India.

HAPPY BIRTHDAY, AARON (AGAIN)

Another tour of Europe opened in London on May 30, 1985, and continued to Frankfurt, Munich, West Berlin, Dresden, Leipzig, Amsterdam, Stuttgart, Budapest, Vienna, Paris, Bonn, Zurich, Florence, Milan, Rome, Madrid, and Istanbul. The tour concluded in Tel Aviv with a joint concert with the Israel Philharmonic. Originally included in the tour was Athens, where the orchestra was to perform as part of the Athens Festival, itself incorporated into a six-month international cultural celebration. However, on June 14 a TWA airliner was hijacked at the Athens airport, after which the U.S. State Department issued a warning to American travelers of the potential for terrorist activity at that airport. At a news conference, President Ronald Reagan stated that this advisory would be rescinded only when security had been improved there by the Greek government.

Initially, while in Rome, the Philharmonic had planned to continue its tour to Greece, where two sold-out concerts were to be given at the foot of the Acropolis, but in Madrid they decided to cancel the visit after many of the musicians and staff members expressed fears for their safety. Zubin Mehta said he would go as an individual but could not take responsibility for others. With American-Greek relations somewhat strained to begin with, the orchestra's decision angered Greek officials, none more than Melina Mercouri, the actress and Greek minister of culture. Because Athens had been designated that year's cultural capital of Europe by the European Community, she said that she considered the Philharmonic's "unfriendly act" an affront to the entire European community. But the Philharmonic's concerns for the safety of their musicians were paramount.

The Philharmonic triumphed as usual in the cities in which it did play. One of the tour's high points was the concert on June 20 at La Scala in Milan, where the wildly applauding audience was treated to three encores, the last of which, the Overture to Verdi's *La forza del destino*, was described by the Philharmonic official Francis Little as being "like carrying coals to Newcastle." But the discerning Scala audience roared its approval.

In Tel Aviv on June 30 the Philharmonic participated in one of those spectacular concerts that Zubin Mehta relishes. The New York and Israel Philharmonics joined forces, as they had in New York in 1982 to benefit the New Yorkers' pension fund, for the benefit of the Israel Philharmonic's endowment fund. First Mehta led the Israel orchestra in Beethoven's *Leonore* Overture No. 3 and Mendelssohn's Violin Concerto, with Itzhak Perlman as the soloist. Then it was the New York Philharmonic's turn, playing Dvořák's *Carnival Overture* and Bruch's Violin Concerto No. 1, again with Perlman, who later commented that he had previously played two or three concertos in one evening, but never with two different orchestras. For the grand finale, as in New York, the two orchestras combined for Berlioz's *Symphonie fantastique*, played by all 220 musicians. The audience definitely got its money's worth that night.

At tour's end, many members of the New York Philharmonic were quoted as saying they found the European and Israeli audiences more attentive and enthusiastic than those in New York: "There's no program rustling, coughing or extraneous noises from the audience." The applause was much longer, "not like in New York where people rush to the limos to get home." On the other hand, they felt that playing repeatedly in New York for the same audiences caused their listeners to become more demanding: "Our subscribers judge us by our own best standards."

Before the 1985–86 subscription season got under way, the Philharmonic took part, on September 6 and 7, in an unusual event, a concert presentation of Stephen Sondheim's *Follies*—unusual in that the Philharmonic is not normally in the business of performing Broadway shows. Assembled by the RCA record producer Thomas

Z. Shepard to be recorded live, the cast was composed of such Broadway veterans as Barbara Cook, Mandy Patinkin, Elaine Stritch, Betty Comden, Adolph Green, Carol Burnett, and Phyllis Newman, not to mention Licia Albanese and Erie Mills from the classical world, with Paul Gemignani conducting.

Who better to review this production than the *Times*'s theater critic, Frank Rich? He described it as a "thrilling—and possibly historic" event, "as complete, gorgeously sung and sumptuously played as Mr. Sondheim or his fans could wish." He went even further to proclaim that, on the basis of these performances, *Follies*, along with "such other initial commercial failures as *Porgy and Bess* and *Candide*, can take its place among our musical theater's very finest achievements."

The Philharmonic's next order of business was the season-opening gala concert on September 11, dubbed a "Salute to the Festival of India," which was attracting much attention in New York City. With the possible exception of Zubin Mehta, who conducted, the most world-renowned Indian musician of that time was Ravi Shankar, master performer on the sitar, who appeared in the New York premiere of his Sitar Concerto No. 1, a 1971 work commissioned by the London Symphony Orchestra. (His second sitar concerto had been commissioned by the Philharmonic and premiered by them with Shankar in 1981.) Additionally, with the tabla player Alla Rakha and two droning string players, he performed a raga lasting about forty minutes.

By Western standards, ragas seem completely devoid of harmony and counterpoint, but they are notable for their rhythmic complexity and melodic content, which is based on non-Western scale structures. Almost entirely improvised, they can and often do go on for hours; in the hands of the right musicians, they can be thoroughly mesmerizing experiences. So, too, with the concerto, whose orchestral parts are basically in unison, though complex nonetheless.

The Festival of India theme carried over to the first week's subscription concerts, which began the next night, on September 12. The program included the world premieres of two works by Indian composers: the *Fantasy on Vedic Chants for Indian Violin and Orchestra*, by Lakshminarayana Subramanian, with the composer as soloist along with three assisting musicians; and a song cycle by Naresh Sohul based on Rabindranath Tagore's *Gitanjali*, performed by the American bass John Cheek. For Henahan the *Fantasy* was a meandering "hodge-podge in which the familiar pitfalls and weaknesses of third-stream music were all too evident." The Tagore songs, however, were found to be composed "with considerable skill and sophistication in an acceptably advanced . . . international style."

Also of interest was the beginning of a season-long retrospective of the music of Aaron Copland in celebration of his eighty-fifth birthday. Heard on this occasion were two little-known works and one popular score: the *Inaugural Fanfare*, the "Cortège Macabre," and the Suite from *Billy the Kid*. The 1925 "Cortège" is an excerpt from *Grohg*, a grotesque ballet that was Copland's first purely orchestral work, portions of which were recycled into his *Dance Symphony*.

An American premiere was given at the concerts beginning September 19, that of the Piano Concerto for the Left Hand by Erich Wolfgang Korngold. Born in 1897, the onetime *wunderkind* Viennese composer was at the time (and perhaps even now) renowned for his music for Hollywood films of the 1930s, '40s, and '50s, many of the swashbuckling variety, though his romantically oriented concert pieces continue the tradition of Mahler and Richard Strauss. Probably the best-known of these is the Violin Concerto, introduced and recorded by Jascha Heifetz, though there is a splendid symphony deserving of further exposure.

The Concerto for the Left Hand, dating from 1924, is one of several such works commissioned by Paul Wittgenstein, an Austrian pianist who lost his right arm in World War I; of them, the Ravel concerto is the most famous. For the Philharmonic premiere the soloist was Gary Graffman, who had lost the use of the fourth and fifth fingers of his right hand, at least for piano-playing purposes. Unfortunately, while praising Graffman's performance, Henahan was rather unkind to the concerto, finding it "disjointed, diffuse, without a strong profile melodically, harmonically or rhythmically," and averring that "the piece is impossible to pay attention to." He had friendlier words for Mehta's reading of the Schubert Ninth Symphony on the same program, calling it "a noble, sonorous performance."

On the next day, September 20, it was announced that the Philharmonic's members had ratified, by a vote of fifty-six to thirty-four, a new three-year contract, under the terms of which the weekly base pay of $810 would rise by $50 for each of the first two years and $70 for the third, bringing the total to $980 for the 1987–88 season. Pension, health, welfare, and insurance benefits were also increased, as well as payments for extra rehearsals, overtime, and longevity. The only drawback in the agreement, for which the negotiations had been amicable, was a failure to alleviate what the musicians deemed an excessive workload.

Among the Soviet composers who followed Shostakovich, the most prominent at that time was Alfred Schnittke, whose *In Memoriam* received its New York premiere on September 26 under Mehta. Thanks to a thawing of the musical atmosphere in the Soviet Union, Schnittke was able to pursue his own avant-garde style without interference from the government, a luxury that had been denied Prokofieff, Shostakovich, and their contemporaries. And yet, there is nothing particularly advanced about *In Memoriam*, written in memory of the composer's mother. His style, or rather styles, tended to range widely, from works employing the latest compositional techniques to neoclassical and neobaroque pastiches. In this work the mood is appropriately solemn, but with extremely varied sonorities and textures. Henahan called it "a piece worth hearing again" (although the Philharmonic rejected his assessment and has never programmed it since).

On the same program the seventy-three-year old Russian-born pianist Nikita Magaloff gave an extraordinary, finely nuanced performance of Rachmaninoff's Concerto No. 1. His only previous Philharmonic appearance had been in 1950, which caused Henahan to comment, "A shorter interval between his New York visits would seem only just, particularly in view of the scarcity of master pianists with his special qualities." Yet, again, the orchestra ignored Henahan's recommendation; there were no further appearances, and Magaloff died in 1992.

One conductor who had an ongoing relationship with the Philharmonic for several years was Giuseppe Sinopoli, with whom the orchestra made a series of recordings for Deutsche Grammophon. Also a composer, on October 9 he led the world premiere of the Suite No. 2 from his opera *Lou Salomé*. The title character was a formidable woman who had been the lover and/or muse of several intellectuals and artists of her day, including Friedrich Nietzsche and Rainer Maria Rilke, as well as a follower of Sigmund Freud. Sinopoli's style in this work is in the lineage of Schoenberg, Berg, and Webern, Berg especially. It sounds something like Berg, but without the tunes.

The *Times* of November 7 published an article by Rockwell about that consummate gentleman, Carlos Moseley, who was to be honored that day at a luncheon of the Friends of the Philharmonic in the Grand Ballroom of the Waldorf-Astoria Hotel. The occasion marked Moseley's retirement as chairman of the orchestra's board of directors. Described by Rockwell as "the man who may have been the New York Philharmonic's greatest friend of all, at least over the last 30 years," since 1955 Moseley had been director of press and public relations, then associate managing director, then managing director, then president, then vice chairman of the board, and finally chairman, reflecting the organization's admirable policy of promoting from within. On his watch the musicians' contracts expanded from thirty-six to fifty-two weeks, Lincoln Center became the orchestra's home, Philharmonic Hall was redesigned and became Avery Fisher Hall, audiences tripled in size, tours and festivals increased, the annual free summer Parks Concerts were begun, the Philharmonic radio network was formed, telecasts increased, the Leonard Bernstein era reached fruition, and Pierre Boulez and Zubin Mehta were engaged as music directors.

Yet Moseley had concerns for the orchestra as well—audiences' decreasing musical knowledge, the pitfall of year-round contracts ("it's a terrible strain—two hundred concerts a year is a lot of concerts"), the short amounts of time most music directors were spending with their orchestras, and the disadvantages of trying to balance the large number of mini–subscription series that had arisen, which he found "artistically more and more difficult to justify."

"A birthday party disguised as a concert" is how Henahan described the program of November 14, the eighty-fifth birthday of Aaron Copland, devoted entirely to his music. Zubin Mehta conducted all but one of the seven pieces, for it was Leonard Bernstein who opened the program with the popular *Fanfare for the Common Man*. The date was also the forty-second anniversary of Bernstein's dramatic Philharmonic debut. The concert featured mostly seldom-heard short works of a folksy nature, but also included were the equally seldom heard jazzy Piano Concerto of 1926, played by Bennett Lerner, and the Symphony No. 1, which began life in 1924 as the Symphony for Organ and Orchestra and became the First Symphony in 1928, with the organ part arranged for orchestra. The concert was televised as part of the *Live from Lincoln Center* series.

Bernstein returned on November 27 to begin his own two-week engagement, which, as was typical for him, included programs of more than passing interest. The first was devoted to that wonderful mixture of angst, ghostly doings, amorous feeling, and sheer joy that is Mahler's Symphony No. 7. Even then recognized as a supreme interpreter of that composer, he could not but deliver the goods handsomely and excitingly on this occasion. In Henahan's words, the Mahler Seventh is "an hour and twenty minutes of emotional extravagance and instrumental exuberance that only a master conductor can hold together and that only a virtuoso orchestra can hope to keep from dissolving into episodic chaos. That conductor and that orchestra came together on this night."

On December 5 Bernstein conducted a historic program of American music bound together by the number 3. It is a curious fact that three of the most celebrated American composers of their generation wrote significant Third Symphonies. The series of symphonies by Roy Harris and William Schuman, in fact, would appear to begin with No. 3. The first two by Harris were little known until recently, while Schuman's first two were withdrawn by the composer, who was dissatisfied with them. Harris is still principally known for his Third Symphony, even though his total eventually reached fourteen, though there is apparently no No. 13, perhaps for reasons of Harris's interest in numerology. Schuman, too, is perhaps best-known for his Third, though his total of ten includes several others that are encountered from time to time.

The third member of this symphonic triumvirate is, of course, Copland, whose magnificent Third Symphony is a canny amalgam of his popular and his more severe and angular styles. It was a masterful gesture for Bernstein to perform all three on one program, and who better to do so? He came of age with this music, felt it in his blood and bones, and was supremely qualified to deliver impassioned performances of music deserving them. Henahan concluded his laudatory review by observing that the concert "was another of those Bernstein concerts that make one wish the Philharmonic's former music director could spare a few more weeks of his time for New York each season."

BOULEZ RETURNS

In lieu of yet another article on the problems of the Philharmonic, the *Times* of December 22, 1985 published a piece by Will Crutchfield dealing with the problems facing all orchestras—"Why Today's Orchestras Are Adrift." One area discussed had already been cited by Carlos Moseley in the interview of November 7: the splintering of the main subscription series into smaller units of four, five, or even three, concerts. Over the years fewer and fewer people had been willing to commit to a full series of twelve or fourteen concerts, opting instead for the lesser (and cheaper) number. The problems thus created in balancing the programs, so that each audience would hear a representative cross-section of the repertoire, became the musical and artistic equivalent of trying to solve Rubik's cube. A program containing a difficult modern work or some other bit of esoterica would be easier to assimilate in the context of a twelve- or fourteen-concert series (to say nothing of the twenty-four once provided by the Boston Symphony) than in one of four or five, where each concert has to be an "event," preferably with familiar masterworks.

Also mentioned by Crutchfield were the problems caused by the year-round contracts in effect for most major orchestras. The conductor Michael Tilson Thomas was quoted in the article to the effect that there is no longer an off-season. Although the musicians obviously deserve economic security, it is impossible "to achieve an apocalyptic level of performance on a 52-week basis."

Other problems centered on the increasingly large settlements for orchestras, which exceeded the abilities of the organizations to pay for them, and the proliferation of concerts beyond what a given community could absorb. Even in 1985 there were many options for spending the entertainment dollar besides going to the symphony, and marketing began to take on an important role in promoting concerts, with every concert having a catchy title or theme of some sort, however tenuous. An interesting program could be rejected by the management or marketing department as not being "saleable." The tail seemed to be wagging the dog.

The Philharmonic began 1986 with Klaus Tennstedt's canceling his engagement because of illness. The managing director, Nick Webster, knowing of Tennstedt's precarious health, had anticipated this development and in November had contacted the Soviet minister of culture to ascertain the availability of either Yuri Temirkanov or Gennady Rozhdestvensky to fill Tennstedt's second week. (The first, at the end of December, had been taken by the Dutch conductor and former Philharmonic assistant conductor Edo de Waart.) In the end it was Temirkanov who thus made his Philharmonic debut, along with his countryman, the pianist Nikolai Petrov, on January 9, 1986. They were the first Soviet musicians to perform in the United States since the cultural agreement between the two countries was signed in Geneva the previous November, and also the first to appear with the Philharmonic since 1979.

At the time the artistic director and chief conductor of the Kirov Opera in Leningrad, as well as the principal guest conductor of the Royal Philharmonic in London, Temirkanov made an excellent impression in his program of Prokofieff and Sibelius, as did Petrov, who had won the silver medal in the first Van Cliburn Competition in 1962. The program was Prokofieff's *Classical Symphony* and Piano Concerto No. 2 and Sibelius's Symphony No. 2. Temirkanov returned to the Philharmonic several times and recorded with them as well. Later he was better-known in the United States as music director of the Baltimore Symphony.

Of the Philharmonic's regular guest conductors, none was more dependable at turning out a thoroughly professional performance than Erich Leinsdorf, who was praised by Henahan on January 17 for being "one of the best in the business at making an orchestra sound like an orchestra rather than a random collection of talents, and that is a gift not to be undervalued ... rarely does one hear this orchestra so carefully blended and so judiciously registered as it was throughout this all-German, beer-and-sausages program" (Weber's Overture to *Preziosa*, Hindemith's *Symphonic Metamorphosis of Themes by Weber*, and Bruckner's Symphony No. 6). Henahan did acknowledge, however, a certain workmanlike objectivity on the conductor's part.

The *Times* of February 12 ran a feature article by Bernard Holland on the Philharmonic's newest, as of May 19, and youngest member, the twenty-year-old violist Rebecca Young. At that time she was still a student at Juilliard, where she was a member of the Juilliard Orchestra, scheduled to perform that very evening in a joint concert with the Philharmonic. In the article she said that she was used to playing first chair at Juilliard, so it would be a challenge to play on the last stand at the Philharmonic (which she didn't do for long—she soon became assistant principal of her section.) As for the joint concert, the concluding excerpts from Wagner's

Götterdämmerung seemed made for an ensemble of two hundred, which included eighteen double basses and seven harps. At one point during the evening Zubin Mehta introduced the fifty-six Philharmonic musicians who were Juilliard graduates, Young included.

A pianist who was one of the Philharmonic's most frequent and esteemed guest soloists was Rudolf Serkin, who performed on the February 20 pension-fund benefit concert that celebrated the fiftieth anniversary of his debut with the orchestra. On this occasion he was heard in Beethoven's Concerto No. 4, which he had played with Toscanini conducting in 1936 (when he also offered Mozart's Concerto No. 27). This time Mehta was on the podium for what Henahan described as "a remarkable performance... Beethoven pianism on Mr. Serkin's highest level." The pianist was eighty-three years old.

Nine years after leaving the Philharmonic, Pierre Boulez returned for a two-week visit, only one week of which involved actually conducting the Philharmonic. Why such a long gap between appearances? Boulez said that he had been invited back for the 1977–78 season but wanted a break to concentrate on composition and his work at the Institute for Research and Coordination of Acoustics and Music (IRCAM), which he had founded in Paris in 1977. He had told the Philharmonic management he would return when he had something to present. Now he did.

His visit consisted of three concerts by his Paris-based Ensemble Intercontemporain, four Philharmonic performances of his *Rituel*, conducted by Mehta, and four Philharmonic concerts conducted by Boulez himself. The first concert by the Ensemble Intercontemporain took place in the unlikely location of the Columbia University Gymnasium, the only venue that could accommodate the spatial complexities of Boulez's *Répons*, a work for six soloists, chamber orchestra, and computer technology. Henahan on March 7 felt that Boulez was experimenting with acoustical effects for their own sake, describing the work as "a static, shimmering piece of intermittent beauty," but, in the end, "Boulez's homage to catatonia."

In his week with the Philharmonic, beginning with the concert of March 13, Boulez presented Stravinsky's *Song of the Nightingale*, Debussy's *Jeux*, and his own *Improvisations on Mallarmé* Nos. 1–3. He had long been a distinguished interpreter of the first two scores, which Rockwell felt pointed directly to the Boulez of the *Improvisations*. The program was thus all of a piece. It had long been Boulez's philosophy to familiarize audiences with the classics of the early twentieth century as a means of gaining their acceptance of more modern works—"if they're still in the hall, that is," added Rockwell, for in truth the audience diminished as the evening progressed, leaving a small group to cheer lustily at the end. Boulez's intricate vocal lines were sung stupendously by the soprano Phyllis Bryn-Julson.

For Rockwell, the performance of this "colorful" yet "enigmatic" score was "near-definitive."

Boulez ended his visit by conducting seven members of the Philharmonic in Stravinsky's Suite from *L'histoire du soldat* on March 17 at the Church of the Holy Trinity on East Eighty-eighth Street. The performance was part of a chamber music series called Philharmonic Ensembles. As reviewed by Will Crutchfield on March 19, "the music snapped like a whip and danced like the devil (indeed, that's part of the histoire)."

The Copland celebration continued on March 27 when Raymond Leppard led performances of *Inscape* and the Clarinet Concerto, with Stanley Drucker as soloist. The former was an example of the composer's austere side, the latter of his popular style. Although the concerto was commissioned by Benny Goodman and first performed by him in 1950, it can be said that Drucker, the Philharmonic's principal clarinetist, owns the work, having given many inimitable performances of it. In this instance, according to Henahan, it "provided Mr. Drucker with a wonderful weapon with which to blow this audience away."

On April 18 it was announced that Zubin Mehta would take a year-long sabbatical beginning in January 1987. His contract included a provision for a sabbatical between 1986 and 1990, with the time away to be made up during the 1990–91 season. He planned to spend several months entirely away from conducting. The rest of the time he would spend with the Israel Philharmonic and guest conducting.

A Sunday article by Holland in the *Times* of April 13 discussed the recent infusion of younger players into symphony orchestras, the Philharmonic in particular, as the older players gradually retired. Many of the newcomers were arriving straight out of the conservatories, with no intermediate assignments. They were described as being better educated and more inquisitive than their older counterparts, more open to new ideas and techniques. More often than before they were women, changing the orchestra's social dynamic. Several young musicians were quoted in the article, as were the Philharmonic's concertmaster, Glenn Dicterow, and the conductor Erich Leinsdorf, who felt that the young players show "a wider freedom of interest.... [They are] more liberal, more versatile and therefore more impersonal. It is impossible to be as intimate when your interests are so wide. Like anything else in the world, there are pluses and minuses." On May 18, however, the *Times* published a letter of protest from a longtime Philharmonic violinist, Martin Eshelman, which concluded, "If, as it is said, youth must be served, surely it can be done without maligning the mainstay of any major symphony orchestra, its veteran players."

The season's final program, beginning on May 16, ended with Carl Orff's *Carmina Burana*. At the beginning of the concert the retirement of two members was announced: the violinist Eugene Berman, after twenty-four years of service; and James Chambers, after forty years, during which he was the stellar principal horn and, for the last seventeen years, the personnel manager.

CHAPTER 10

1986–88

THE ARCHIVES

After a year's hiatus when the orchestra was on tour, the Philharmonic resumed its post-season festivals of new music with Horizons '86—Music as Theater. Again under the artistic supervision of the composer-in-residence, Jacob Druckman, the 1986 festival included music by Louis Andriessen, Luciano Berio, John Corigliano, Paul Dresher, Morton Feldman, Morton Gould, Mauricio Kagel, György Ligeti, Witold Lutosławski, Conlon Nancarrow, Betty Olivero, Arvo Pärt, Bernard Rands, Steve Reich, Poul Ruders, Hale Smith, Karlheinz Stockhausen, Toru Takemitsu, and Druckman himself. Because of commitments elsewhere, Zubin Mehta did not participate. The conducting was shared by such new-music experts as Oliver Knussen, Zoltan Pesko, Gunther Schuller, and Leonard Slatkin, with Luciano Berio leading a program devoted to his own music. Besides the Philharmonic, the performing groups were Electric Phoenix, Speculum Musicae, and Reich's and Dresher's own ensembles.

The festival opened on the night of May 21 with a program devoted to the music of the Hungarian Ligeti. Pesko conducted scenes from two of the composer's theater pieces, *Le grande macabre* and *Aventures/Nouvelles aventures*. Henahan had kinder words to say about the latter than the former, finding the 1962–65 works "a pair of phantasmagorical theater pieces…which continue to hold fascination today, when most music of the period is as outdated as the Nehru jacket." In Ian Strasfogel's witty production, *Aventures* was "a rarity in contemporary music, a fondly remembered work that in revival did not disappoint." By contrast, *Le grande macabre* was "depressing."

Although the inclusion of Morton Gould on the list of new-music composers might occasion some confusion, because he is perhaps best-known as the creator of lighter works such as the *Latin-American Symphonette* and *American Salute*, rhythmic vitality is an important element in his music, and nowhere more so than in the Tap Dance Concerto performed on May 22. Fred Strickler was the solo dancer in this engaging work, which undoubtedly makes its best effect when heard (and seen) in person. On a recording it sounds like a concerto for wood block and orchestra.

Attendance having gradually dwindled during the three Horizons festivals, it was decided that the 1986 offering would be the last devoted to new music, especially because it also marked the expiration of Druckman's contract as composer-in-residence. Whether another would be appointed was not known. At the time, plans for the corresponding time period in 1987 were uncertain. There were many who objected to ghettoizing new music into a concentrated period such as a festival. George Szell had, in fact, once described the all-contemporary concert as the "common grave" of new music. The problem, then, was how to introduce the newest music into the subscription series without antagonizing the subscribers. As far as Henahan was concerned, on June 15, it was up to Zubin Mehta as music director to lead the way: "That is what the great conductors of the past spent much of their time doing, and that is what the best of conductors still should be trying to do."

The 1986 Parks Concerts concluded on August 4 in Central Park with Leonard Bernstein's first appearance in the series since 1974. On this occasion he conducted his Overture to *Candide* and Serenade for Violin, Strings, and Percussion, with the Philharmonic's concertmaster, Glenn Dicterow, as the soloist, and Tchaikovsky's "Pathétique" Symphony (which he had also programmed in 1974). An audience estimated at 200,000 turned out, many of whom had undoubtedly been reared on Bernstein's televised Young People's Concerts of two decades before. According to Tim Page in the *Times* the next day, Bernstein mesmerized both the orchestra and the audience, as much the educator as the conductor and composer. There was still no denying the fact that even though the Philharmonic could play more or less well for a given conductor, they gave of their very best for Bernstein.

On September 19 was announced the death of Engelbert Brenner at the age of eighty-two. He had been a Philharmonic member since 1932, first as oboist and then for many years as its English horn player. A native of Vienna, his artistry in the latter capacity can be heard in Bernstein's recordings of Dvořák's "New World" Symphony and the César Franck Symphony, among many others.

The 1986–87 season brought another visit from Klaus Tennstedt, whose two successive weeks beginning October 16 featured, respectively, Bruckner's Seventh and Mahler's Sixth Symphonies. Tennstedt had been on the international scene only since 1974, when he made his highly acclaimed American debut with the Boston Symphony in Bruckner's Eighth Symphony. An East German who traveled to the West in 1971 and remained there thanks to an administrative fluke, since then he had appeared with all the major American orchestras and had also been principal conductor of the London Philharmonic. Always at his best in the Bruckner and Mahler repertoire, Tennstedt, according to Holland on October 18, "seems one of the few guest conductors who truly catch the Philharmonic's attention."

The Mahler Sixth was the last of the composer's symphonies to be given a performance in the United States. Not until 1947 did it receive its American premiere by the New York Philharmonic under the guest conductor Dimitri Mitropoulos. When Mitropoulos, by then musical director, revived the work on April 7, 8, and 10, 1955, it was only the score's second American presentation. Since then it has been given fairly frequently by the Philharmonic and other orchestras. Henahan wrote on October 24 that "all in all, it was a draining experience, as any acceptable performance of this work must be.... [Tennstedt] is one of those rare conductors who, when he is in good form, can pick up an orchestra and its audience and take it somewhere else entirely."

The year 1986 marked the centennial of the Statue of Liberty, and New York City celebrated in style. For a gala concert on October 28, the date of the statue's dedication in 1886, William Schuman was commissioned to write a commemorative work, which became the cantata *On Freedom's Ground*, with a text by Richard Wilbur. Scored for a baritone soloist, chorus, and orchestra, the work brought together Sherrill Milnes, the Crane Centennial Chorus (from the Crane School of Music in Potsdam, New York), and, of course, the Philharmonic with Mehta conducting. The premiere was part of a program featuring participants from the classical and pop worlds, after which the piece was heard in the week's subscription concerts beginning on October 31. Schuman, after Copland probably the most frequently performed American composer in the Philharmonic's repertoire, produced a handsome work suitable for the occasion, though Rockwell on November 2 found it "more noble in its patriotic intentions than in its esthetic realization."

On November 23 the *Times* published an article by Tim Page on the New York Philharmonic Archives and its first official archivist, Barbara Haws, who had been hired only two years before. A trained musician, though not a professional one, she had convinced the Philharmonic management that what they needed for the job was not a musician or musicologist, but a historian, an institutional archivist. Her archival experience was not musical: she had "established the archives of the Bowery Savings Bank as well as the Jackie Robinson Archives—both wonderful jobs. The Bowery is 150 years old, even older than the Philharmonic." Haws described some of the contents of the Philharmonic's archives: "thousands of hours of Philharmonic recordings, scores marked by Gustav Mahler, the minutes of a meeting held to plan the first post-Toscanini season, and some 1500 cubic feet of different papers." At that time, through a computer software program, work was under way to collate and automate performance data from 1842 onward, information concerning composers, repertoire, artists, instrumentation, Philharmonic programs, and orchestral scores and parts, many with conductors' markings, as well as broadcast tapes and disks going back to the 1930s. All this material and more, still under Haws's super-vision, is now housed in the archives' quarters on the fourth floor of the Rose Building in Lincoln Center, where it is available to musicians and researchers.

On November 26 the Philharmonic took a trip back to late nineteenth-century America when Zubin Mehta unearthed the Second Symphony of John Knowles Paine (1839–1906). A Harvard professor whose music was much performed in his time and whose teaching produced a host of New England composers seldom heard today, Paine wrote music of great skill and craftsmanship that was redolent of Mendelssohn, Schumann, Brahms, and other German composers. Henahan described the 1880 symphony as "derivative and second-rate stuff," but "good second-rate stuff." Mehta and the orchestra soon recorded the work for New World Records.

After several years of annual visits to the Abyssinian Baptist Church in Harlem, visits that abounded in goodwill between the Philharmonic and the local community, a harsh note was struck in connection with the performance on December 9, when over a third of the musicians refused to play the concert. Because these concerts had always been an extra service for the orchestra, not part of the regular season, the musicians could opt out of them if they wished. However, the absence of forty-one members did put a damper on the event, and substitute musicians had to be hired. What provoked the boycott was the failure of the church's pastor, the Reverend Calvin O. Butts III, to denounce the Black Muslim leader Louis Farrakhan for the extremely derogatory remarks he had made against Judaism the year before. At the time Butts had maintained that he did not feel Farrakhan's statements were injurious to any special group.

Most of the protesting musicians were Jewish, but so was the soloist for the concert, Isaac Stern, who did perform, and who had been quoted as saying that Jews had also made mistakes regarding blacks. The Philharmonic's president, Stephen Stamas, said that the management "had nothing but respect" for the musicians' decision. "What we have tried to make clear," he continued, "is that we can understand why some of them felt the way they did. We came to a different conclusion, but all of us share the same common values."

On December 11 Zubin Mehta began his final week of concerts before his sabbatical. Verdi's magnificent Requiem was his chosen work, with the New York Choral Artists and the soloists Susan Dunn, Shirley Verrett, Luciano Pavarotti, and Matti Salminen. Henahan wrote the next day, "This may not have been the perfect Verdi Requiem in all respects, but it certainly must rank as the finest Mehta performance of this half season."

Only five days later the Philharmonic was back in Carnegie Hall, which had been closed for seven months for a $50 million renovation project. This was a gala re-opening night, and although Mehta conducted most of the Philharmonic's portion of the program (Frank Sinatra also appeared with Peter Duchin and his orchestra), Leonard Bernstein led the first performance of his *Opening Prayer*, composed especially for the occasion. The piece was not listed on the program, nor was the surprise performer who opened the evening, Vladimir Horowitz, who played a Chopin waltz and polonaise. Also taking part were Isaac Stern, Marilyn Horne, Yo-Yo Ma, Benita Valente, Kurt Öllmann, and Joseph Flummerfelt's New York Choral Artists, the program ending with the finale of Mahler's "Resurrection" Symphony. Carnegie's acoustics were always its pride and joy, of course, and they were judged to have survived the process relatively unscathed, though some thought that a bit of the hall's resonance had been sacrificed and that there was less impact to the sound.

On December 19 the *Times* reported the death, at the age of eighty-two, of Jim Fassett, who had long been the urbane commentator and intermission host on the Philharmonic's CBS radio broadcasts, as well as the director of the network's music department from 1942 until his retirement in 1963. He preferred to be known as Jim, never James.

MORE MAHLER

As the first guest conductor during Mehta's sabbatical, Erich Leinsdorf continued to demonstrate his reliability in a program of Richard Strauss and Beethoven on January 22, 1987, with Kathleen Battle as the soprano soloist in a group of Strauss songs. A heavy snowstorm reduced the audience to half a house, and there was some doubt that enough musicians would arrive to perform the "Pastoral" Symphony (Mozart's "Jupiter" Symphony was held in reserve, just in case). Arrive they did, and, according to Henahan the next day, the hardy concertgoers were "rewarded with what surely will rank as one of this season's premiere musical events." Battle sang "exquisitely" and, in contrast to Menuhin's performance thirty years before, sang three encores without incident, Leinsdorf accompanying two of them at the piano. And Leinsdorf's leisurely tempos and expansive phrasing in the "Pastoral" allowed the musicians to produce their most beautiful sound, with the result that Beethoven was played "in a ruminative, relentlessly genial manner…balm for the ear and the soul on this occasion."

Following Leinsdorf on the podium on January 29 was Kurt Masur, who had begun to make his mark on the Philharmonic and in New York. His program of Hindemith's Concert Music for Strings and Brass, Chopin's Piano Concerto No. 2 with Horacio Gutiérrez as soloist, and Mendelssohn's Symphony No. 3 ("Scottish") clearly demonstrated his strengths. As conductor of the Gewandhaus Orchestra of Leipzig he was certainly steeped in the tradition of Mendelssohn, for whom Henahan found him to be "a splendid conductor."

In celebrating his sixtieth birthday, Mstislav Rostropovich was not content to rest on his laurels or simply to be feted by others. Rather, he involved himself in a two-month series of concerts in New York, Boston, and Washington, a marathon of concertos. In New York on February 19 he performed three works with the Philharmonic, opening with the Cello Concerto No. 2 by Krzysztof Penderecki. The Polish composer himself conducted the work he had written for Rostropovich in 1982. For the remainder of the program Maxim Shostakovich was the conductor for Haydn's Concerto in C Major and Tchaikovsky's *Variations on a Rococo Theme*. Rostropovich was described by Henahan as "the complete musician, or as near to one as we are likely to encounter on the concert stage nowadays." Two days later he performed three works composed especially for him, Britten's Symphony for Cello and Orchestra, Bernstein's Three Meditations from *Mass*, and the Shostakovich Concerto No. 1, the composer's son again collaborating, this time for the entire concert.

On March 5 Leonard Slatkin conducted a performance of the John Adams work *Harmonielehre*, so named after Schoenberg's 1910 treatise on traditional harmony. Adams, whose style has evolved in the ensuing decades, was in the forefront of the so-called minimalist school of composition. Although Henahan acknowledged "his great economy and no little craft...the musical effect is ultimately to make little out of little." The soloist for the concert was Shura Cherkassky, he of the 1961 recalcitrant piano bench, who performed brilliantly a piece decidedly out of the mainstream, the Concerto No. 4 in D minor by Anton Rubinstein. It had not been given on a Philharmonic program since Oscar Levant played and recorded it in 1952.

Rostropovich returned on March 19 to conduct Britten's *War Requiem*, a massive score from 1962, first performed in England's restored Coventry Cathedral, which Nazi bombs had destroyed in World War II. The work alternates the Latin text of the Requiem Mass with words by the English poet Wilfred Owen, who lost his life in World War I. Participating in the Philharmonic's performance were Rostropovich's wife, the soprano Galina Vishnevskaya, who had sung in the world premiere; the tenor Anthony Rolfe Johnson; the baritone John Shirley-Quirk; and the Westminster Choir and the Brooklyn Boys Chorus. The score calls for a chamber orchestra separated from the main orchestra; it was directed by the Philharmonic's new assistant conductor, Felix Kruglikov.

Leonard Bernstein's appearances were always special events. Two works made up his program for the concerts beginning on April 9, the Second Symphony of

Charles Ives and the Ninth of Schubert, also known as the "Great C Major" (to distinguish it from the "Little" one in the same key, No. 6). Originally an all-Ives program had been planned that was to include the complex posthumous Fourth Symphony, which Stokowski had premiered in 1965 with his American Symphony Orchestra. Bernstein had given the world premiere of the Second Symphony in 1951, and he returned to it from time to time, in this case to make a "live" recording of the piece for Deutsche Grammophon (his favorite method of recording in his later years). On April 10 Henahan wrote, "Perhaps it takes a great Mahler conductor such as Mr. Bernstein to adjust the voices in an Ives sonority as beautifully as this." Unfortunately, the resulting recording does not measure up to Bernstein's 1958 version, especially because the trombones' final blaring quotation of "Columbia, the Gem of the Ocean" is barely audible.

The "great Mahler conductor" returned the following week on April 16 for that composer's "Resurrection" Symphony, which he had performed with the Philharmonic only three years before. This was one of Bernstein's signature pieces, one that he had been conducting since early in his career, both with the Boston Symphony and with the short-lived New York City Symphony. For this occasion the vocal soloists were the soprano Barbara Hendricks and the mezzo-soprano Christa Ludwig, while the chorus was Joseph Flummerfelt's Westminster Symphonic Choir, which, with or without the word "Symphonic" in its name, had a long history of collaborations with the Philharmonic. As Bernstein advanced in years his tempos began gradually to get slower in much of his repertoire. For Henahan, writing the next day, it was "a singular but heart-piercing performance by a composer who has long been Mahler's most devoted secular prophet." Perhaps Henahan meant to use the word "conductor" instead of "composer," but, of course, Bernstein was both. He identified with the composer in everything he conducted, and once even claimed that when he conducted Mahler's music, "I am Gustav Mahler."

More Mahler was heard on May 28, this time the Third Symphony conducted by Giuseppe Sinopoli, with the mezzo-soprano Florence Quivar, women of the New York Choral Artists, and the Brooklyn Boys Chorus. Though Sinopoli was also a composer, he did not achieve Bernstein's level of identification with the score, even if his deliberate tempo for the Adagio finale managed to correspond to Bernstein's timing of twenty-five minutes. Henahan compared the interpretation with that of Boulez, who "polished off this Adagio in just twenty minutes. Five minutes may not seem a lot, but in a Mahler slow movement a minute can be an eternity."

The programming of the Second and Third Symphonies a few weeks apart, not to mention the Mahler Festival of 1976 and other seasons in which multiple

Mahler symphonies were performed, brings to mind the occasion in 1956 when Mitropoulos conducted the (in those days) rarely played Third Symphony. He had already given the equally rarely played Sixth the year before. After the performance of the Third, a backstage visitor asked Mitropoulos which Mahler symphony he would play the following year. He replied that he would not do any because Bruno Walter would be conducting the Second Symphony, then added apologetically, "You know, we cannot do two."

An article by Michael Kimmelman in the *Times* of May 31 told of the gradual shrinking of the repertoire performed by major symphony orchestras. Contemporary music had never occupied a major space in concert programming, but also fewer and fewer baroque works were appearing, mainly because of the proliferation of period-instrument groups that had appropriated this music for themselves in "historically informed" performances. Traditional orchestras were now afraid to play baroque repertoire, and when they did, were criticized for ignoring the niceties of baroque performance practice.

To make matters worse, the period-instrument ensembles had begun appropriating the classical repertoire of Haydn, Mozart, and Beethoven, playing it on "original instruments" with little or no vibrato and little or no tempo variation, all in the name of "historically aware" practices. It was pointed out that modern audiences tended to prefer big sounds anyway, which is why the bulk of the orchestral repertoire was heavily weighted toward the late romantics—Mahler, Bruckner, Richard Strauss, Tchaikovsky, and others. Now even those composers, as well as Brahms, are often encountered in "historically correct" interpretations.

The period-instrument movement has spawned a younger generation of conductors who are applying historical performance practices to orchestras with modern instruments, so perhaps a compromise has been reached. As for the baroque repertoire, no act of Congress has forbidden symphony orchestras to play it. In fact, Lorin Maazel and the Philharmonic programmed all the Bach Brandenburg Concertos in the 2008–9 season. The Philharmonic even went several steps further in 2007 when Alan Gilbert led it in Bach's Toccata and Fugue in D Minor in the now thoroughly unfashionable and once-reviled (by the authenticists) orchestral transcription by Leopold Stokowski.

EVEN MORE MAHLER

Zubin Mehta interrupted his sabbatical on June 9 to conduct a special concert for the delegates to the annual conference of the American Symphony Orchestra League (now the League of American Orchestras). The main item on the program was Bruckner's Eighth Symphony, a work for which Mehta has always had an affinity. This was especially evident in the lengthy Adagio movement, which was allowed to progress according to its own unhurried time scale. Preceding the Bruckner was the New York premiere of a brief piece by Elliott Carter entitled *A Celebration of 100 × 150 Notes*, signifying the number of notes in the score. After the concert Mehta, who had grown a beard during his sabbatical, flew immediately to Vienna, whence he had come, to conduct the first performance at the Staatsoper of a new production of Verdi's *Otello*.

Mehta's sabbatical from the Philharmonic applied only to the New York subscription season, for he led the orchestra in the final Parks Concert of the summer, in Central Park on July 20, the program a preparation for the Philharmonic's approaching tour of Latin America. Although no American work was selected for the tour, the repertoire did include a major work from Brazil, *Bachianas Brasileiras No. 7* by Heitor Villa-Lobos, which was played that night. Occupying a place in Brazil comparable to that of Sibelius in Finland, Villa-Lobos is probably best-known for the sequence of suites in which he strove to meld his admiration for the music of Bach with characteristics of Brazilian folk music. Except for the *Bachianas Brasileiras* No. 5, with its lovely soprano line over a rich accompaniment of eight cellos, the sad fact is that the music of Villa-Lobos is today little known outside his native country. A highlight of the tour was an outdoor concert on August 9 in Buenos Aires before an enthusiastic audience of 240,000.

Not necessarily a lowlight, but an upsetting incident nonetheless, had occurred two days before. A chamber group from the Philharmonic was to play a concert in Iguassu, Brazil, the site of famous and spectacular waterfalls. When Mehta and the members of the ensemble arrived, it was discovered that the cello and double bass were missing. They had been unloaded by mistake in São Paulo when the plane had made a stop there. Mehta commented that it was uncommon for the orchestra to lose instruments on its many travels around the world, but here they had brought only eight people on a little excursion and two instruments were lost! The instruments never did turn up, so the one work requiring the cello and bass, the Beethoven Septet that was to have closed the program, had to be dropped. Instead, the clarinetist Stanley Drucker played some solo Stravinsky pieces that he happened to have in his instrument case.

The 1987–88 season began excitingly with Sir Colin Davis on the podium. That adverb may surprise those who find his more recent work to be a bit restrained. After an opening nationally televised pension-fund benefit on September 15, on which Murray Perahia was heard in Beethoven's Piano Concerto No. 4, the subscription season commenced two nights later with a performance of the complete

Damnation of Faust by Berlioz. The tenor Thomas Moser sang the title role, with the mezzo-soprano Anne Sofie von Otter as Marguerite, the bass Paul Plishka as Méphistophélès, and the bass-baritone Terry Cook as Brander. The New York Choral Artists held forth as assorted students, soldiers, demons, and angels.

Davis had not conducted the Philharmonic since 1968, his debut appearances, when he programmed quite a bit of Berlioz. He has since become recognized as one of the composer's greatest interpreters, having recorded all his major works and some minor ones as well. It had been ten years since the Philharmonic had performed the *Damnation*, on Boulez's final concerts as music director. At the end of his positive review of September 19, Henahan noted that, even though it was the season's first subscription concert and a great Berlioz interpreter was conducting "one of the grandest works of the French repertory," the hall was not filled. "Is the famously unadventurous Philharmonic audience now drawing the line at Berlioz?" he wondered. Perhaps not. More likely they were drawing the line at a lengthy work featuring solo voices and choruses. Surveys have shown that such compositions are the least popular with audiences.

For his second week, beginning September 24, Davis programmed two masterpieces from the first half of the twentieth century, the Sixth Symphony of Vaughan Williams and the Fifth of Sibelius. By a coincidence of programming, the Sibelius had been given the night before in Carnegie Hall by Leonard Bernstein and the Vienna Philharmonic. The *Times*'s Will Crutchfield had good things to say about both performances, different though they were. He concluded that "duplication is only dull when the performances themselves are."

Mahler's Third was performed again on November 25, this time with Bernstein in charge. It was unusual, if not unprecedented, for that work to be presented in two consecutive seasons, but Bernstein was in the process of rerecording all the Mahler symphonies for Deutsche Grammophon with different orchestras, so apparently the time was right for No. 3. (He had already given No. 1 with the Philharmonic the week before, though his new recording was with the Concertgebouw Orchestra.) For this Mahler Third the soloist was one of his favorites, Christa Ludwig, who had sung in his Mahler Second the previous season, and the choral groups were the same ones Sinopoli had used, the women of the New York Choral Artists and the Brooklyn Boys Chorus. Holland reviewed the performance and felt that Bernstein's success with the score came from his self-control rather than any overt emotionalism. All the details of this hugely scored and extremely lengthy work emerged with the greatest clarity, all the subtle tempo shifts with great finesse.

Philharmonic officials were caught off guard when, on December 15, Zubin Mehta said he would leave the Philharmonic at the end of the 1990–91 season.

Then, in almost the next breath, he conjectured it was possible that he might change his mind. Later he said he had never told the Philharmonic for certain that he was leaving. At the moment, he was leaving. But his contract did not expire for four years. If an offer was made to him in two years' time, he would think about it then. He continued that he had "no plans to take another position. I have never liked being a guest conductor, but I've also been a music director since I was twenty-four years old. I think by 1991 I should stop being a music director." The whole episode was reminiscent of Boulez in 1974.

In any case, Mehta returned from his sabbatical, sans beard, in January 1988. During his time off he had conducted *Otello* in Vienna and *Tristan und Isolde* in Los Angeles, and he had led the Israel Philharmonic on a tour of Eastern Europe and the New York Philharmonic on a tour of South America. For relaxation he and his wife, Nancy, had taken a cruise to Antarctica. There Nancy took a photograph that was seen around the world—Mehta in white tie and tails, baton in hand, surrounded by thousands of penguins.

More serious matters occupied him on the night of January 7—the Philharmonic's first performance of the sprawling ten-movement *Turangalîla Symphony* by Olivier Messiaen. The work's title is a Sanskrit word, which the composer translated and interpreted as follows: "*Lîla* literally means 'play,' but play in the sense of divine action on the cosmos, the play of creation, of destruction and reconstruction, the play of life and death. *Lîla* is also Love. *Turanga* is Time, the time which runs like a galloping horse, time which slips like sand through the hourglass. *Turanga* is movement and rhythm. *Turangalîla* thus signifies, at one and the same time, a love song, a hymn to joy, time, movement, rhythm, life and death."

Premiered in 1949 by Leonard Bernstein and the Boston Symphony, for a long while the work had relatively few performances (Bernstein never played it again), but recent years have seen a gradual awakening of interest on the part of conductors and record companies. As with so many of the composer's works, it is an amalgam of lush harmonies, austere unisons, themes taken from birdsong, sections that bring Hollywood to mind, and a panorama of religious rapture and mysticism. The scoring is for an immense orchestra, with lots of percussion, much of it delicate, and important parts for the piano and the ondes Martenot, an electronic keyboard instrument. These last two were played, respectively, by the composer's wife, Yvonne Loriod, and her sister, Jeanne Loriod. Mehta programmed the work in honor of the composer's eightieth birthday. Messiaen was present, and it was touching to watch him, seated in the audience, totally absorbed in following the score on his lap, oblivious to the many audience members who were leaving. This can only be ascribed to the public's unwillingness, at least on that night, to embrace the new and unfamiliar, for *Turangalîla* is not a difficult work to listen to—far from it.

On January 13, 1988, the Philharmonic celebrated the twenty-fifth anniversary of the pianist André Watts's spectacular debut by inviting him to perform three concertos with Mehta conducting: Liszt's No. 1, the vehicle of his debut, and the Second Concertos of Beethoven and Rachmaninoff. In the words of Henahan, it was "a pleasure to hear the piano played so beautifully, with so much poise and so little apparent struggle."

Although Mehta had originally been scheduled to conduct the concerts beginning January 21, he graciously relinquished the week upon learning that Erich Leinsdorf was celebrating the fiftieth anniversary of his American debut. For his celebration Leinsdorf conducted Haydn's oratorio *The Seasons*, one of the most genial works by this genial composer, with Benita Valente, soprano; John Aler, tenor; Benjamin Luxon, baritone; and the New York Choral Artists. Holland, in the *Times* of January 23 (the paper was no longer reviewing concerts the day after), missed the lightness and clarity that would have resulted from the original instruments of Haydn's day but concluded that "Mr. Leinsdorf conducted the way we expect him to." Haydn's overall effects obviously delighted him, as did the details that produced them: "If we had to decide where the progress of his long career fits into the seasonal scheme of things being celebrated here, it would certainly be no later than midsummer."

Giuseppe Sinopoli returned on January 28 to lead a program most assuredly dictated by the needs of the recording industry. If it is planned to record Scriabin's Third Symphony ("The Divine Poem") and his *Poem of Ecstasy* (often referred to as his Symphony No. 4, though it is more a symphonic poem than a symphony), it might make sense, for the sake of convenience, to place them on the same program, as was done here. But the tonal extravagance of both works, replete with orgiastic climaxes and expressions of sexual ecstasy, make for an indigestible program. And to separate the two with Mozart's delightful Horn Concerto No. 3, no matter how expertly performed by principal horn Philip Myers, only served to dwarf Mozart's unassuming composition.

On February 4 Charles Dutoit made an excellent impression conducting Rachmaninoff's *Symphonic Dances*, and Mehta returned on February 11 with one of his specialties, *The Rite of Spring*, in a performance "of irresistible momentum and visceral excitement," according to Henahan. Mehta also conducted a pension-fund benefit concert on February 15, for which the soloist was the Soviet émigré pianist Vladimir Feltsman, who had attracted international attention because of his government's refusal to allow him to emigrate and the attendant cancellation of his concert dates in the Soviet Union. It was only through the intervention of the U. S. secretary of state, George P. Schultz, with Soviet Premier Mikhail Gorbachev that Feltsman was allowed to leave his homeland. In his Philharmonic debut he played the Brahms Second Concerto, and Henahan described a "solid and musicianly performance [that] had enough flashes of individuality to encourage one to want to hear him again." He also felt that Mehta had "bulldozed his way" through the opening work, Hindemith's *Mathis der Maler* Symphony, in a way that emphasized the fact that the sixteenth-century painter Matthias Grünewald had led a peasant revolt but accomplished little else.

The Philharmonic returned to Harlem on April 25, but not to the Abyssinian Baptist Church. This time the venue was the historic Apollo Theater on 125th Street. James DePreist conducted a mixed program that featured the Boys Choir of Harlem in Bernstein's *Chichester Psalms*, and the Modern Jazz Quartet in some of their own inimitable numbers. Music by Duke Ellington and Billy Strayhorn (what else but "Take the 'A' Train") was also included in this benefit concert for the Boys Choir of Harlem, the Harlem School for the Arts, and the Philharmonic's Orchestral Fellowship Program.

DePreist, a Philharmonic assistant conductor in 1965–66, was at the time music director of the Oregon Symphony. One of the few African American conductors pursuing a major career (the way had been paved by Dean Dixon), his program on April 22 included the amiable Fourth Symphony by Vincent Persichetti, who had taught at Juilliard and at the Philadelphia Conservatory, where DePreist had been one of his students. As of this writing DePreist is the director of orchestral studies at Juilliard.

Zubin Mehta offered a debut on May 19—not of a performer or of a new piece of music, but of his own first performance of Mahler's Ninth Symphony. The Philharmonic, of course, is a great Mahler orchestra and had played the Ninth under Walter, Mitropoulos, Bernstein, Barbirolli, and others. Mehta, in turn, had conducted his share of Mahler symphonies, but never the Ninth, probably the most difficult to pull off. As Henahan heard it, Mehta "on the whole fashioned a Mahler Ninth that as sheer sound could stand comparison with the best." He did feel that Mehta was "on automatic pilot" at times, merely trying to get the notes played correctly. As for the great final Adagio movement, he felt that "there seems to be a tortoise race among conductors" as to who could take the movement "at the most ponderous pace without letting it fall apart. Mr. Mehta certainly put himself in the forefront of contenders."

Next on the agenda was another tour of the Soviet Union.

Dimitri Mitropoulos, *left*, and CBS radio commentator Jim Fassett outside Carnegie Hall, 1952. (Courtesy of Philharmonic Archives)

Bruno Zirato signs the contract naming Dimitri Mitropoulos, *left*, and Leonard Bernstein, *right*, principal conductors of the Philharmonic for the 1957–58 season as the two maestros look on. (Courtesy of Philharmonic Archives)

Left to right: Principal cellist Laszlo Varga, Leonard Bernstein, and concertmaster John Corigliano review Beethoven's Triple Concerto prior to the 1959 European tour. (Photo by Bakalar-Cosmo. Courtesy of Philharmonic Archives)

Sir John Barbirolli, *left*, and concertmaster John Corigliano, 1959. (Photo by Bert Bial. Courtesy of Philharmonic Archives)

Left to right: Leonard Bernstein signs the contract extending his tenure as music director to May 1968 as Philharmonic president David M. Keiser and managing director George E. Judd Jr. look on. (Photo by Bakalar-Cosmo. Courtesy of Philharmonic Archives)

Leonard Bernstein, *left*, and Isaac Stern listen to a playback during a recording session, c. 1960. (Courtesy of Philharmonic Archives)

The Three Musketeers: Philharmonic assistant conductors for the 1961–62 season. *Left to right*: Maurice Peress, the author, and Seiji Ozawa. (Photo by Bakalar-Cosmo. Author's collection)

Nadia Boulanger, the first woman to conduct a complete Philharmonic concert, 1962. (Photo by Bert Bial. Courtesy of Philharmonic Archives)

Igor Stravinsky rehearsing at Lewisohn Stadium, 1962. (Photo by Bert Bial. Courtesy of Philharmonic Archives)

Leonard Bernstein, *right*, confers with Aaron Copland, 1962. (Photo by Bert Bial. Courtesy of Philharmonic Archives)

Leonard Bernstein, *left*, and William Schuman, 1970. (Photo by Bert Bial. Courtesy of Philharmonic Archives)

Managing director Carlos Moseley, *left*, and Leonard Bernstein, *right*, wave upon arrival in Japan for the 1970 tour. To Bernstein's left is music administrator Frank Milburn. (Photo by Bert Bial. Courtesy of Philharmonic Archives)

Josef Krips, c. 1963. (Courtesy of Philharmonic Archives)

William Steinberg, c. 1964. (Courtesy of Philharmonic Archives)

George Szell, c. 1964. (Courtesy of Philharmonic Archives)

Leonard Bernstein, *left*, and Pierre Boulez, c. 1974. (Photo by Christian Steiner. Courtesy of Philharmonic Archives)

André Kostelanetz recording, c. 1966. (Photo by C. J. Zumwalt. Courtesy of Philharmonic Archives)

Pierre Boulez in concert, Avery Fisher Hall, c. 1976. (Courtesy of Philharmonic Archives)

Erich Leinsdorf in concert, Avery Fisher Hall, c. 1977. (Courtesy of Philharmonic Archives)

Left to right: Erich Leinsdorf, Rudolf Firkušny, and Carlos Moseley rehearse Mozart's Concerto for Three Pianos, 1975. (Photo by Bert Bial. Courtesy of Philharmonic Archives)

Thomas Schippers conducting in Leningrad, 1976. (Photo by Bert Bial. Courtesy of Philharmonic Archives)

Left to right: Philharmonic president Carlos Moseley, Pierre Boulez, and managing director Albert K. Webster, c. 1976. (Photo by Mary Hilliard. Courtesy of Philharmonic Archives)

The audience at a Rug Concert, 1974. (Courtesy of Philharmonic Archives)

Rudolf Serkin at the keyboard, with Zubin Mehta, c. 1982. (Photo by Marianne Barcellona. Courtesy of Philharmonic Archives)

Zubin Mehta, *left*, and benefactor Avery Fisher. (Photo by Suzanne Faulkner Stevens. Courtesy of Philharmonic Archives)

CHAPTER 11

1988–89

BERNSTEIN AT SEVENTY

The orchestra's third tour of the Soviet Union, from May 28 to June 9, 1988, encompassed six concerts within a ten-day period, three each in Leningrad (now called, as it was when it was founded, St. Petersburg) and Moscow. At the same time, President Ronald Reagan and Premier Mikhail Gorbachev were having a summit meeting in Moscow. Underwritten by Coca-Cola, Combustion Engineering, and RJR Nabisco, the trip was the result of months of negotiations between Nick Webster, the Philharmonic's managing director, and Gosconcert, the Soviet state concert agency.

The musical high point of the tour was Mahler's Ninth Symphony, played on June 5 in Moscow's Tchaikovsky Hall. Afterward the euphoric Mehta exclaimed, "This is the most wonderful performance this orchestra has ever given me." After the bleakly resigned closing measures the audience remained silent for about a minute, then began a fifteen-minute ovation, replete with cheers and demands for an encore. None was forthcoming—no other music is appropriate to follow Mahler's farewell to the world.

Included in the tour repertoire was a work by the American composer Ellen Taaffe Zwilich. The first woman to win a Pulitzer Prize for music, with her First Symphony in 1983, she was commissioned to write a piece specifically for the tour. Entitled *Symbolon*—after an ancient Greek custom in which two people break a pot and each keeps half of it as a token of friendship—it is believed to be the first American score to receive its world premiere in the Soviet Union.

Mehta conducted all the concerts save one, which was led by the Soviet maestro Genaddy Rozhdestvensky (known as "Noddy" in England). To conclude the Moscow visit and the tour, an outdoor concert was given on June 9 in Gorky Park, a joint performance by the Philharmonic and the Soviet State Symphony Orchestra—two hundred musicians altogether. Inclement weather threatened the event, with wind and intermittent rain testing the patience and devotion of a hardy audience. Rozhdestvensky opened the program with Shostakovich's Fifth Symphony, and Mehta closed it with his staple for these kinds of collaborative concerts, the Berlioz

Symphonie fantastique, during which the sky cleared in time for the rousing finale and an encore, Sousa's *Stars and Stripes Forever*, and, of course, fireworks. Rozhdestvensky stated that it had been almost thirty years since an outdoor classical concert had been held in Moscow and the first time in his memory that an American and a Soviet orchestra had played there together.

On returning to New York, the orchestra plunged immediately into the First New York International Festival of the Arts. The idea was to focus on important works of the twentieth century, with special emphasis on the indisputable master-works. The Philharmonic opened the festival on June 13 with Mehta conducting the American premiere of Zwilich's *Symbolon*, Bartók's Violin Concerto No. 2 with Itzhak Perlman as the soloist, and *The Rite of Spring*. Henahan liked *Symbalon*, finding it "a forceful, listenable piece" with brief suggestions of Bartók, Stravinsky, Messiaen, and others. He wrote of Perlman's "flabbergastingly proficient" rendition of the Bartók, and felt that in the Stravinsky Mehta "demonstrated a grasp of theatrical pacing that sometimes eludes conductors of what is, after all, a ballet score."

The Philharmonic was not the only participant in the festival, which also presented Yuri Temirkanov conducting the Philadelphia Orchestra and Leonard Bernstein leading the Chicago Symphony in the Shostakovich Seventh Symphony. Great interest attached to the Philharmonic's concert of June 18, only the second time Pierre Boulez had appeared with his former orchestra since leaving in 1977. His program was made to order for his special qualities: Berio's *Sinfonia*, with the New Swingle Singers; his own *Notations*; and Debussy's *La mer*, of which he is a prime exponent now that the days of Toscanini, Monteux, and Munch are long past. Bernard Holland on June 20 enthused over the concert: "What an exceptional—almost unique—orchestra this can be under someone who knows how to push its buttons!"

Rozhdestvensky was scheduled to conduct the concert of June 16, with his wife, Viktoria Postnikova, as the piano soloist. However, the couple canceled their visit because of a dispute with Gosconcert, which insisted on scheduling their concerts, whereas the Rozhdestvenskys wanted the right to make their own concert arrangements. The cancellation provided an opportunity for two Soviet émigrés, one of whom was the Philharmonic's assistant conductor, Felix Kruglikov, who took over the program planned by Rozhdestvensky: a piece by the Soviet composer Alfred Schnittke entitled *(K)ein Sommernachtstraum*, Prokofieff's Piano Concerto No. 2 with Alexander Toradze as the soloist, and the Shostakovich Fifth Symphony.

Once again the orchestra crossed the Atlantic, this time on August 18 for a European tour sponsored by Citicorp/Citibank. The concerts began on August 20 in Athens's Odeon of Herod Atticus and continued to London, Frankfurt, Hamburg,

Berlin, Stockholm, Helsinki, Amsterdam, Brussels, Lucerne, Madrid, and Paris—sixteen concerts in all, with a return on September 10, again just in time to begin a new season.

Meanwhile, on August 21 the *Times* featured an article by Donal Henahan entitled "America's Musician at 70." The musician was, of course, Leonard Bernstein. It was hard to believe, as Henahan put it, that "the perennial wonder boy of American music" was now "a white-maned eminence in the tradition of" Stokowski, Toscanini, Monteux, and Walter. He went on to delineate the several dichotomies of Bernstein's career, first of all as both conductor and composer, then as the composer of Broadway musicals and serious concert works, of music for a jazz ensemble, and of works on biblical themes. Also covered were his proficient pianism, his lectures on linguistic themes, and his Young People's Concerts.

Henahan also pointed out that Bernstein had his detractors, who were critical of his branching out in so many directions rather than concentrating on a single endeavor. He concluded, "It is a career with more heads than Hydra, who had nine of them, but no less fascinating for that. A one-headed Leonard Bernstein would not be Leonard Bernstein, and American music would be markedly poorer than it is today. Certainly more boring." To that his many admirers can only add "amen."

The 1988–89 season opened on September 14, Mehta conducting with Isaac Stern the soloist in Beethoven's Violin Concerto. It was Stern's one hundredth Philharmonic appearance. Orchestral fireworks and majesty were provided by excerpts from Wagner's *Götterdämmerung*, which had been part of the tour repertoire. The subscription season commenced on the 16th, opening with Webern's *Six Pieces for Orchestra*, an odd choice for a season opener and one practically guaranteed to keep subscribers away, great though it is. The hall was far from full. Perhaps the presence of Schoenberg on the program also played a part, though the Chamber Symphony No. 1 is a tonal piece. Those who attended reserved their greatest applause for the concluding Ninth Symphony of Schubert, the performance of which the *Times*'s Will Crutchfield found "businesslike."

On September 19 came the announcement that the American composer David Del Tredici would be the Philharmonic's composer-in-residence for the next two years. His appointment was made as part of a nationwide residency program administered by Meet the Composer, an advocacy group for new music.

To honor Bernstein on his special anniversary, the Philharmonic scheduled a number of his major works throughout the season. On September 23 Mehta conducted the *Chichester Psalms* and the "Kaddish" Symphony. The latter originally called for a woman's voice in the role of the speaker, first taken by Bernstein's wife, Felicia Montealegre. In 1977 he revised the score to allow either a male or female speaker, and the role in this instance taken by the actor Sam Waterston (of *Law and Order* fame). Wendy White was the mezzo-soprano soloist, with the New York Choral Artists. While acknowledging the work's controversial theological aspects, Henahan was kinder to it than his predecessor and others in 1964, calling it "a work that invariably seizes and holds an audience's attention" and observing that "it works well as theater." As for the *Chichester Psalms*, "it sings and dances irresistibly in the recognizable Bernstein style."

Henahan, who had lately written more and more approvingly of Mehta's work, reverted to form in his description of the all-Bruckner concert on October 6. An all-Bruckner program is quite a rarity, unless one counts such a work as the Eighth Symphony, which is sufficient to fill a program all by itself (though in days of yore, and more leisurely evenings, another work usually preceded it). On this occasion the unfinished Ninth was followed by the *Te Deum*, which, on realizing he would not live to finish the symphony, the composer had suggested might make a suitable finale, in the manner of Beethoven's Ninth. A few conductors have followed Bruckner's suggestion, though Mehta took the sensible expedient of placing an intermission between the two works.

Mehta had become recognized as a fine Bruckner interpreter, so it came as a surprise to read Henahan's comments about a "ponderous and hard driven" performance of the symphony, one that "fell roughly on the ear." It was "an unfeeling performance" that made Bruckner "seem gross and almost repellent." The *Te Deum*, on the other hand, received "a magnificently buoyant performance," with the participation of Marvis Martin, soprano; Gail Dubinbaum, mezzo-soprano; Vinson Cole, tenor; Paul Plishka, bass; and the Westminster Symphonic Choir.

Writing of the Philharmonic's adaptability to different conductors in his review of the October 13 Shostakovich-Bernstein concert, Bernard Holland spoke of how "this virtuoso orchestra, which can so often sound garish and explosive," became "eloquently reasonable in its music-making" when led by "the good-sense musicality of men like Andrew Davis," the young English conductor who was then music director of the Toronto Symphony. Shostakovich's Violin Concerto No. 1 was "splendidly played" by Vladimir Sitkovetsky. The Bernstein pieces were part of the seventieth-birthday celebration: the *Prelude, Fugue and Riffs* for clarinet and jazz ensemble, with Stanley Drucker the idiomatic soloist in a piece written for Benny Goodman, and the Symphonic Dances from *West Side Story*. As Holland put it, Bernstein took "everything about American popular culture that is excessive, loud, sentimental and in questionable taste [and] somehow converted it into precious materials."

Having played without a contract since September 21, the musicians, by a vote of seventy-three to twenty-four, reached a new agreement with the Philharmonic

Society on November 1, 1988. The contract provided for an increase of 14.5 percent in the minimum weekly salary over a three-year period, bringing the minimum to $1,120 in the 1990–91 season. Also addressed were pensions, working conditions, and touring issues. By the third year the maximum annual pension benefit of $30,000 would be the highest orchestra pension in the country.

Zubin Mehta definitely announced his resignation on November 2. It was to take effect at the end of the 1990–91 season, by which time he would be the longest-tenured music director in the orchestra's history. One associates the Philharmonic with the celebrated tenures of Toscanini and Bernstein, but neither of those gentlemen achieved Mehta's thirteen years. When Mehta announced his resignation to the musicians at a rehearsal, he said that he believed them to be "the greatest orchestra in the world." In a statement, he said that he had been a music director with several North American organizations since 1964 and felt it was time to pursue other endeavors that would involve fewer administrative duties than are normally required of a music-director position.

Stephen Stamas, the Philharmonic's president, issued a statement to the effect that Zubin Mehta "has provided outstanding artistic leadership to the orchestra, and our musical life has been enriched by his contributions." Although Mehta did enjoy the support of the board, the management, and the public, the musicians' opinions of his work were decidedly mixed. And although the critics were very positive about the orchestra's playing, with some exceptions their reviews of his concerts were rather lukewarm, often complaining of what appeared to be indifference and perfunctoriness when it came to the bulk of the standard repertoire. Musicians often say they do not read reviews, yet one wonders if continued critical negativism played a part in Mehta's decision. If so, matters did not improve with Henahan's comment about Mehta's tempos in Beethoven's "Pastoral" Symphony on November 3: "At Mr. Mehta's pace, Beethoven's day in the country began to seem like a month." (Only a few years previously, Henahan had praised Mehta's performance of the same piece, and in January 1987 he wrote favorably about Leinsdorf's leisurely tempos in this symphony.)

In any case, it was now open season for the Great Conductor Search.

Many Candidates

"Please do not say 'the cemetery.' Frivolity is out of order here." That was Donal Henahan's view on November 13 when musing over where the Philharmonic should look for its next music director. The days of the great maestros of the past were long gone, and it was no use waxing nostalgic over them. Whoever the Philharmonic selected would have to be a living entity. Henahan named several who might fill the bill: Claudio Abbado, whom the Chicago Symphony had courted as a possible successor to Solti, but who seemed content with the London Symphony; Klaus Tennstedt, "one of the most stimulating conductors around," but one who was plagued with health problems; Charles Dutoit of the Montreal Symphony, whose flair had garnered him some success in New York; Giuseppe Sinopoli, whose New York concerts had been erratic, but who could be a "sleeper"; Kurt Masur, "a solid Middle European Kapellmeister type"; Leonard Slatkin, "a solid Middle American Kapellmeister type"; and André Previn, "a solid West Coast Kapellmeister type." Everyone, whether critic, musician, or interested observer, had a list of candidates, including some of those named by Henahan and quite a few others.

Meanwhile, the Bernstein celebration continued, and who better to continue it than the man himself. On November 14, forty-five years to the day after his dramatic debut, he conducted a special pension-fund concert in Carnegie Hall devoted to his music. To enhance the occasion, nine members of the 1943 Philharmonic were present and were hugged and kissed by Bernstein onstage after the intermission, when the conductor was presented with an engraved silver box commemorating the anniversary. The works performed were the *Chichester Psalms*, sung by the Westminster Symphonic Choir; the Serenade for Violin, Strings, and Percussion (after Plato's *Symposium*), with Gidon Kremer as soloist; and the Symphony No. 2 (*The Age of Anxiety*—after the poem by W. H. Auden), in which Krystian Zimerman was the piano soloist. Though Henahan had some reservations about the music, except for the *Chichester Psalms*, he praised Bernstein's heartfelt and obviously authoritative conducting.

Bernstein then conducted the next two weeks of subscription concerts, the first an all-American program that also included *The Age of Anxiety*. Preceding it on the program were a suite of six short pieces by Charles Ives and the American premiere of a work entitled *Tattoo* by David Del Tredici. Bernstein's outsize personality was such a draw that even the normally conservative Friday afternoon audience filled the hall on November 18 for this program of twentieth-century music. He had them in the palm of his hand when he turned to them before one of the Ives pieces, the *Tone Roads* No. 1, and declared, "You'll hate this one." According to Rockwell in his review of November 20, "everyone chuckled and gave the piece a chance." Del Tredici's score struck the critic as "good-natured and occasionally ingenious," but also "terribly undisciplined."

The following week, on November 23, before leading the Philharmonic in Tchaikovsky's Fifth Symphony, Bernstein offered the American premiere of the revised version of his latest work, *Jubilee Games*, which had been composed two years previously for the Israel Philharmonic. Whatever reservations Henahan had about the piece were dispelled by Bernstein's sense of rhythm, which could "transform clumps of unpromising notes into irresistible music." In another new American piece on the program, Ned Rorem's Violin Concerto, Gidon Kremer was the intense and sympathetic soloist. Henahan found the work "immediately digestible and pleasant enough" in a genial sort of way, at times remindful of Sibelius and Barber.

On November 29 it was announced that the Philharmonic's radio broadcasts, which had resumed in 1975, would be suspended after December 25. They had been sponsored by Exxon, which was discontinuing its support, and Nick Webster said that a new sponsor was being sought.

One of the most admired composers of the late twentieth century was Witold Lutosławski, whose Piano Concerto the Philharmonic presented in its American premiere on November 30. The composer's compatriot Krystian Zimerman was the soloist, with Mehta conducting. Henahan praised Lutosławski for at least simulating "the sound and feel of music, rather than of a publish-or-perish dissertation." (Earlier he had railed against "the formally ingenious, arrogantly ugly music that has been mediocrity's passport to academic respectability since World War II.")

The eightieth birthday of Elliott Carter was still being celebrated, and the concert of December 9 offered two of his works, the recently heard *Celebration of 100 × 150 Notes* and the by now almost classic *Variations for Orchestra*, dating from 1955, the performance of which Rockwell found "very impressive." Also heard were two piano works for the left hand, Britten's *Diversions* and Ravel's Concerto, with Leon Fleisher as the commanding soloist. Although in recent years Fleisher has regained the use of his right hand, allowing him to play concertos by Brahms and Mozart, at that time he was still in the throes of the focal dystonia that restricted his playing.

A Philharmonic concert entirely without strings (except for Orin O'Brien's lone double bass) was given on December 16 when Mehta conducted one of his specialties, also in honor of a composer's eightieth birthday: Messiaen's awesome *Et exspecto resurrectionem mortuorem* for brass, woodwinds, and percussion, and Mozart's great Serenade No. 10 in B-flat Major for thirteen wind instruments (the double bass alternating with the contrabassoon). The contract had long allowed for some "optional" weeks in which works for smaller ensembles were scheduled. Rockwell referred to the "rich and brilliant sonic onslaught" of the Messiaen piece, which the Philharmonic musicians delivered with great assuredness. The Mozart Serenade, which they had played without a conductor only a few years before, was "beautifully shaped by the orchestra's top-line wind and horn players."

The year 1989 began on a sad note with the death of James Chambers at age sixty-eight. Chambers had been the Philharmonic's stellar principal horn for twenty-three years and its personnel manager from 1969 until his retirement in 1986. He was also a highly regarded horn teacher, having been on the faculty of the Juilliard School for forty years up until the time of his death. As reported in the *Times* of January 3, Leonard Bernstein, on learning the news, said, "I can't believe my Jimmy is gone. When first I knew him well he was arguably the finest horn player in the world. He played solo horn on all my early Mahler recordings—to say nothing of Beethoven, Brahms and the rest—and always magnificently." Zubin Mehta said that "working with him on a daily basis for nearly a decade enriched my life enormously."

Having given the strings a week off in December, Mehta gave almost everyone else a free week with the concerts beginning January 5, a program for the strings. Handel's Oboe Concerto No. 3 in G Minor was the opening work, in which Sherry Sylar, the orchestra's new associate principal oboe, was the engaging soloist. Honegger's formidable Symphony No. 2 followed, a work for strings to which a single trumpet is added at a climactic moment in the finale, to very moving effect. Finally there was Mendelssohn's Octet for Strings, a wonderful and delightful work the composer wrote at, incredibly, the grand old age of sixteen. The Philharmonic performed the piece with its full string section, a more or less common practice among conductors (Toscanini and Munch played it so), and Rockwell found it not only interesting, but "downright satisfying" to hear the piece in this manner. Mehta was "deeply involved in the music . . . and the Philharmonic string players responded superlatively."

Another opportunity was given to the assistant conductor, Felix Kruglikov—this time a scheduled one in the concerts beginning January 12. His program included the great Sixth Symphony of Prokofieff, less often presented than the popular Fifth and heard here in "a taut, well-played, surely considered performance," according to Rockwell. Primary interest, however, centered on the extremely belated Philharmonic debut of the highly regarded Czech pianist Ivan Moravec, who played the Schumann Concerto. Modest in demeanor, Moravec did not call attention to himself, but, in Rockwell's words, "simply played the music, beautifully." It is odd that so fine an artist has not been heard since with the Philharmonic.

On January 19 Mehta surrounded Strauss's *Four Last Songs* with music by John Knowles Paine, the late nineteenth-century American composer whose Second Symphony had been given and recorded two seasons previously. This time it was the *As You Like It* Overture and the Symphony No. 1 in C Minor. The symphony evoked Beethoven and Berlioz at times, with Henahan finding both works "not at all like neglected masterpieces," but rather like "respectable academic efforts" befitting a composer who was the first professor of music at Harvard. As for the

Strauss songs, these were sung superlatively by the American soprano Susan Dunn, who was substituting on short notice for the Hungarian Júlia Várady.

A well-received debut was made on February 1, that of the young American conductor Hugh Wolff, who was then music director of the New Jersey Symphony. A former assistant conductor to Rostropovich in Washington, D.C., he offered Bernstein's jazzy ballet score *Fancy Free*, Ravel's almost equally jazzy Piano Concerto in G Major with Peter Serkin as the soloist, and orchestral excerpts from Berlioz's dramatic symphony *Roméo et Juliette*. For Henahan, Wolff was "a natural conductor for whom a musician might actually enjoy playing."

It is generally acknowledged that of Shostakovich's wartime symphonies, Nos. 7, 8, and 9, the greatest is the Eighth, whose American premiere was given by the Philharmonic in 1944 under Artur Rodzinski's direction. Since then performances of the work in the United States have been few and far between. The Philharmonic did not return to it until 1982, when the composer's son Maxim led it. Now here was Leonard Slatkin conducting the score on the concerts beginning February 9. Henahan wrote that the Eighth is "a masterly score whose nerve-exposing intensity can be felt keenly in a performance such as Leonard Slatkin conducted." He later praised the orchestra for its magnificent playing of "a tortured but gripping and oddly neglected work."

Preceding the Shostakovich on the program was the Violin Concerto by the American composer Stanley Wolfe, in which Mark Peskanov made his American debut as the soloist. Wolfe, a longtime member of the Juilliard faculty, had been a teacher of both Slatkin and Peskanov (and of the author as well), and his concerto's basically conservative tonal idiom, tinged with elements of the blues, was easy to assimilate, a point that brought no complaints from Henahan.

Once again we must return to Erich Leinsdorf, who had become, in effect, the Philharmonic's principal guest conductor, but without the title. He was especially known for assembling interesting programs that strayed from the beaten path. An example was the concert heard on March 10. Opening with a Stravinsky rarity, the wartime *Four Norwegian Moods*, it continued with the Piano Concerto No. 2 by the then little-known late nineteenth–early twentieth century Swedish composer Wilhelm Stenhammar, for which the soloist was the Brazilian pianist Cristina Ortiz, in her Philharmonic debut. After intermission came Stravinsky's *Jeu de cartes* (The Card Game) and Ravel's *La valse*.

A week later Leinsdorf continued in similar vein, when, in Henahan's opinion, he "took a prize for imaginative programming." Three of the works performed involved the participation of a women's chorus: Debussy's early cantata *La damoiselle élue* (The Blessed Damozel); Brahms's *Four Songs for Women's Voices, Horns, and*

Harp; and Debussy's *Three Nocturnes* (women's chorus in the third), in all of which the women of the New York Choral Artists participated. To complete the program the soprano Maria Ewing was heard in Berlioz's early cantata *La morte de Cléopatre* (The Death of Cleopatra).

The Great Conductor Search continued. A *Times* article by Rockwell on March 13 mentioned several possible replacements for Mehta, beginning with a few unlikely picks: Herbert von Karajan, Georg Solti, Carlos Kleiber, and Klaus Tennstedt—men who were too advanced in their careers, too entrenched in a current position, too eccentric, or not in good health. Rockwell went on to say that Sir Colin Davis, Claudio Abbado, and Charles Dutoit had been approached, and all, for various reasons, had declined. Others mentioned were Giuseppe Sinopoli, Simon Rattle, James Levine, Leonard Slatkin, Dennis Russell Davies, Roger Norrington, Gerard Schwarz, and Hugh Wolff. Some were deemed more suitable than others, and these were certainly not the only possibilities. Nick Webster hoped the successor to Mehta would be chosen by late summer; he doubted it would be any sooner than that.

On March 22 it was announced that Tennstedt had canceled his forthcoming three-week engagement in order to undergo hip surgery, and that the first replacement conductor for the concerts beginning March 23 would be the Romanian-born Israeli Yoel Levi, then in his first season as music director of the Atlanta Symphony. He retained Tennstedt's program, Schubert's "Unfinished" Symphony and Mahler's Fourth, giving what Henahan termed "confident, technically well-knit performances" of both works. Benita Valente was the soprano soloist in Mahler's Finale.

Taking over Tennstedt's second week was none other than Leonard Bernstein, who turned to one of his special favorites, Mahler's "Resurrection" Symphony, which he presented for the third time in five years, with Benita Valente and Wendy White as the soloists and the New York Choral Artists. Henahan, who had praised Bernstein's two previous renditions, felt that "this 'Resurrection' seemed not so much a symphony as a vast acoustical and mystical environment. This listener, helpless to resist, was borne along as by a great flood."

The great choral maestro Robert Shaw was in charge of the third week, conducting one of his favorites, Haydn's oratorio *The Creation*. Again the New York Choral Artists participated, with the soprano soloists Sylvia McNair and Edith Wiens, the tenor Jon Humphrey, and the baritones Benjamin Luxon and James Michael McGuire. It was a performance that, according to Henahan, did not plumb the work's dramatic possibilities, but rather gave it "a reflective, melancholy tinge."

In a *Times* article of April 9 entitled "Tea Leaves at the Philharmonic," Henahan wrote about the orchestra's approaching 1989–90 season, in which close to half of the concerts would be conducted by Mehta, with the rest shared among eight guests, two of whom, Bernstein and Tennstedt, were not candidates for the permanent position. A third was the German Helmuth Rilling, basically a choral conductor, who was obviously engaged as a specialist in his favored repertoire. Four others could be considered candidates to succeed Mehta: Dutoit, Sinopoli, Slatkin, and Temirkanov. None of those mentioned would conduct more than two weeks, totaling eight concerts. But one maestro was allotted twenty-one concerts. Surely he would have the inside track on the job. Apparently not, for the favored one turned out to be Leinsdorf, whom Henahan felt was in a caretaker's role. "Mr. Leinsdorf, an impeccable technician," said he, "is good at cleaning up the debris left by other guests."

JILTED

On April 24, 1989, Herbert von Karajan resigned as chief conductor and artistic director of the Berlin Philharmonic. In fragile health, the eighty-one-year-old Karajan had held the post for thirty-four years, the last several of which had been marked by fractious relations between the maestro and the members of the orchestra. His resignation came somewhat as a surprise, since his appointment had been "for life."

The impact of this development on the New York Philharmonic was that several supposedly leading candidates for their position were now automatically mentioned as candidates for the Berlin job, one of the most prestigious in the world. Lorin Maazel and James Levine seemed to be at the top of the list.

Another almost entirely unhackneyed program was offered by Leinsdorf on May 4, one that caused Henahan to comment that although Leinsdorf "has access to the same music libraries as everyone else," few other conductors seemed able to match him in devising interesting programs that also sounded good: "These days, what with good conductors at a premium, he is beginning to look like a giant." This particular program opened with Dvořák's sweetly rustic Serenade for Winds, Cello, and Double Bass and continued with *Music for Prague 1968* by the twentieth-century Czech American composer Karel Husa. Composed at the time of the Soviet invasion of Czechoslovakia and originally written for concert band, it has become Husa's most frequently played composition. It is one of the great works of the twentieth century, and one of very few to employ aleatory (chance music) passages in a meaningful and convincing manner. Next came Busoni's Sarabande and Cortège (Two Studies for *Doktor Faust*), and the program concluded with its one standard-repertoire piece, the orchestral excerpts from Wagner's *Die Meistersinger* (Prelude to Act III, Dance of the Apprentices, and Prelude to Act I). With no permanent post to worry about, Leinsdorf, at age seventy-seven, was obviously in the enviable position of being able to play anything he wished.

Shortly after his resignation from Berlin, Karajan died of a heart attack on July 16. Owing to his associations with the Berlin Philharmonic, La Scala, London's Philharmonia Orchestra, the Vienna State Opera, and the Salzburg Festival, he had been dubbed the "general music director of Europe." Long a controversial figure, his death threw into sharper relief the vacancy in Berlin, for which there was now an even longer list of candidates.

Certainly Leinsdorf was not among them. On July 24 he helped the New York Philharmonic celebrate the silver anniversary of its Parks Concerts by leading a program on the Great Lawn in Central Park consisting of Smetana's *Moldau*, the Brahms Second Symphony, excerpts from Bizet's *L'Arlésienne*, and excerpts from Stravinsky's *Firebird*. Because printed programs had failed to arrive, he spoke entertainingly about each piece to the estimated 120,000 people present. Introducing the Bizet piece, he spoke of the folk tunes of Provence included in the piece, adding, "For those of you who haven't been there, it's where they cook with garlic." Earlier in the day he had spoken of the stuffy attitude of musicians who disapprove of applause between movements, an opinion he shared with Pierre Monteux. That evening, not only did he acknowledge the applause between movements of the Brahms symphony, but he also asked solo instrumentalists to take bows. The performances themselves were relaxed when necessary, yet full of rhythmic life and vitality when called for. Leinsdorf had always been the most technically adept of conductors, and one of the wittiest of his profession. Now, in his autumnal years, he was displaying the latter aspect in public, as well as a greater expansiveness of musical interpretation.

The *Times* of September 1 reported the death of the Philharmonic's former principal violist, Sol Greitzer, at age sixty-three. He had played in the NBC Symphony under Toscanini prior to joining the Philharmonic in 1954. It was Boulez who appointed him to the first chair in 1972, a position he held until his resignation in 1985. He had been an active teacher and served on the faculties of Mannes College and the State University of New York at Purchase.

In September the orchestra returned to the Far East for a fifteen-concert tour, partially underwritten by Citibank/Citicorp, that encompassed visits to Singapore, Hong Kong, Taipei, Seoul, Tokyo, Osaka, Nagoya, and Bangkok. Performing as the soloist in Japan was the seventeen-year-old Japanese-born violinist Midori, who had made her debut with Mehta and the Philharmonic at the age of ten. As usual, the musicians played to extremely enthusiastic audiences, including one of 60,000 in Singapore, cheering performances of such works as Beethoven's "Pastoral"

Symphony and Richard Strauss's *Heldenleben*. Everyone was happy to perform in new and excellent concert halls in several of the cities. Said Stephen Stamas, "I think it was the biggest discovery of the tour. We were pleased to find new halls with very good acoustics in Taiwan, Thailand and Korea and played Suntory Hall (in Tokyo) for the first time."

The 1989–90 season began on September 20 with what had become the traditional season-opening pension-fund benefit. For this occasion Jessye Norman was the soprano soloist in Wagner's "Liebestod" from *Tristan und Isolde* and Mahler's *Rückert-Lieder*. Henahan had nothing but praise for Norman, but he was less than kind to Mehta's treatment of Wagner's Overture to *Tannhäuser* and Mozart's Symphony No. 40 in G Minor.

Helmuth Rilling made his Philharmonic debut on October 5, the beginning of a two-week engagement for which he brought along his own chorus, the Gächinger Kantorei. His first week was devoted to an undisputed masterpiece, Bach's Mass in B Minor, a work not often heard in the context of a symphony season. With the soloists Sylvia McNair, soprano; Marjana Lipovsek, mezzo-soprano; Howard Crook, tenor; and Mark Pedrotti, bass, Rilling offered, according to Henahan, a "view of the mass as an essentially devotional rather than a quasi-operatic event."

His second week presented an extreme rarity. The *Times* titled the review "The American Premiere of an 1869 Musical Camel." In that year Giuseppe Verdi recruited twelve other Italian composers to collaborate on a mass in memory of Rossini, who had died the year before. Verdi himself composed the "Libera me," which he later revised for inclusion in his own Requiem in memory of Manzoni. It was this hybrid *Messa per Rossini* that Rilling conducted with the Philharmonic, again with the Gächinger Kantorei. The soloists were Gabriela Benackova, soprano; Florence Quivar, mezzo-soprano; James Wagner, tenor; Jacob Will, bass-baritone; and Brian Mathews, bass. Verdi is the only one of the thirteen composers who is known today outside Italy, the others worthy gentlemen whose names have lapsed into obscurity. It came as no surprise that Verdi's contribution stood head and shoulders above the rest.

Meanwhile, on October 9 came the announcement that Claudio Abbado had been elected to succeed Herbert von Karajan as chief conductor of the Berlin Philharmonic. "Elected" is the proper word: the Berliners are a self-governing orchestra that chooses its own conductors. Abbado's selection came as something of a surprise, for Maazel and Levine were thought to head the list of finalists, of which there were eight. At the time Abbado was music director of the Vienna State Opera and frequently appeared with the Vienna Philharmonic. He had also been principal conductor of the London Symphony Orchestra. Of course, as mentioned earlier, he was also one of the three winners of the first Dimitri Mitropoulos Conducting Competition.

A month after this announcement, on November 8, an article by Rockwell appeared in the *Times* asserting that, according to unidentified music executives in New York, Abbado had all but signed a contract to succeed Mehta. "All but" is the operative phrase here, because apparently Abbado and the Philharmonic had reached a verbal agreement with the understanding that he would retain his Viennese post, which he would now do in tandem with Berlin. Holding the two positions would make him comparable to Karajan, who did not stay long in Vienna. New York Philharmonic officials declined to comment on this state of affairs, but it was obvious that the Great Conductor Search was not over. Negotiations would have to be resumed with some of the conductors who had reportedly turned down the position previously—Bernard Haitink was mentioned.

On October 18 Bernstein returned to lead an all-Copland program a year in advance of the composer's ninetieth birthday. Stanley Drucker was his inimitable self as the soloist in the Clarinet Concerto, which was preceded by *Music for the Theater* (1925) and *Connotations* (1962), which had upset so many listeners at the opening night of Lincoln Center. Closing the program was the ever-popular *El salón México*. Bernstein's second week, beginning October 26, was devoted to Tchaikovsky: *Romeo and Juliet*, *Francesca da Rimini*, and the Fourth Symphony. Rockwell noted that, given the overt emotionality of the music, it was perhaps just as well that Bernstein was in a rather subdued mood that night. As with most of his concerts in recent years, the Copland and Tchaikovsky programs were recorded "live" by Deutsche Grammophon.

On October 26 it was announced that Stephen Stamas, a former Exxon executive, had been named chairman of the Philharmonic-Symphony Society, the post having been vacant since the retirement of Carlos Moseley. The Society's new president would be H. Frederick Krimendahl II, a partner with Goldman, Sachs.

November 6 brought the news of the death of Vladimir Horowitz the day before, of a heart attack at age eighty-six. Technically the most prodigiously gifted of all twentieth-century pianists, he had made his American debut with the New York Philharmonic in 1928 and, after not appearing with any orchestra for twenty-five years, returned to the Philharmonic in 1978. In his later years, his preferred performing time was four o'clock on Sunday afternoons—which was also the day and approximate time of his death.

Of contemporary pianists, the one most comparable to the great Artur Schnabel is the American Richard Goode. His repertoire is similar (Mozart, Beethoven,

Schubert, et al.), as is his approach to it. Like Schnabel, Goode is not a glamorous figure. He merely plays the piano with unerring musicality and integrity. On November 2 he played the Schumann Concerto with the Philharmonic, Mehta conducting, after which Rockwell declared that "this was the most enjoyable performance of this score that I can recall." Mehta and the orchestra were also praised for their sympathetic contribution.

Mehta liked to experiment with program combinations. The first half of the concert on December 14 consisted of Beethoven's Overture to *Fidelio* and Fourth Symphony, while the second half featured the Jerry Mulligan Quartet playing jazz compositions by Mulligan himself. The connection between Beethoven and Mulligan was not clear, though Mulligan's first piece, called *Entente*, was for solo saxophone and orchestra, with the orchestra having clearly composed passages to play. As for the Beethoven symphony, which Rockwell thought the orchestra could play in its sleep, it was given with all its repeats and was "very deftly played."

Mehta's performance of Beethoven's Ninth Symphony on December 21 was not well received by the *Times*'s James R. Oestreich, who faulted it for its lack of sufficient dynamic contrasts, finding it "a bullied account [that] did not encourage fine distinctions." At the same time he called attention to the fact that eight members of the orchestra were missing, having gone to West Germany to perform in an international orchestra under Leonard Bernstein's direction. To celebrate the fall of the Berlin Wall, two Freedom Concerts would be given that very week in West and East Berlin. These were the performances of Beethoven's Ninth in which Bernstein famously changed the word *Freude* (joy) to *Freiheit* (freedom).

The Ninth was preceded on Mehta's program by William Schuman's *To Thee Old Cause*, an oboe concerto in all but name, in which the orchestra's principal player, Joseph Robinson, "gave an exquisite solo performance," according to Oestreich. The work had been commissioned to open the Philharmonic's 1968–69 season and was written in response to the assassinations of Robert F. Kennedy and Martin Luther King Jr. The title is from Walt Whitman's *Leaves of Grass*.

In his year-end summary on December 24, Henahan cited the orchestra's performance under Bernstein of Mahler's "Resurrection" Symphony as one of the outstanding musical events of 1989. "It was one of those dangerously personal, eccentric readings that leave one grateful that there is a Leonard Bernstein and grateful, too, that there is only one."

CHAPTER 12

1990–91

THE CHOICE IS MADE

Still smarting from having been rebuffed by Claudio Abbado, and a bit embarrassed by their failure to engage any of several leading candidates, the Philharmonic's board and management turned to Leonard Bernstein in the hope that he would consider a second term as music director. After all, he had once declared publicly, "I will come back to this orchestra." But the *Times* of February 5, 1990, reported that he had declined the engagement. However, he was willing to increase the time he spent with the orchestra, from two weeks a season to six, beginning with the 1991–92 season.

Ten days later, on February 15, another article by Rockwell appeared. In this one he claimed that the Philharmonic was considering an arrangement whereby three conductors would share the direction of the orchestra: Bernstein, Colin Davis, and Kurt Masur. Because Bernstein had already agreed to six weeks, it remained for the others to agree or not. Davis, in his recent engagements, had proven himself to be a fastidious yet agreeable leader. At the time head of the Bavarian Radio Symphony in Munich, he confirmed the Philharmonic's invitation and said he would decide by the following week whether he would, or could, accept. The article mentioned that he had already been offered the music director-ship the year before and had declined, citing the need to keep his family together. His young family—he had school-age children living in London—was also the reason for his indecision in accepting the more limited offer. He was quoted as saying that he could not be the music director, though he had not refused the offer outright. He also thought he was too old for the job (he was sixty-two). And working in the United States would take time away from his special commitments in London, Vienna, Dresden, and Munich. But, he said, he enjoyed conducting the Philharmonic—"they're not the bunch of wild men that everybody makes out." Kurt Masur was based in Leipzig, where for twenty years he had been conductor of that city's celebrated Gewandhaus Orchestra, once directed by Mendelssohn. At the time Masur was deeply involved in the politics of East Germany—an under-standable distraction. Leinsdorf, who was committed to four weeks with the orchestra in each of the next two seasons, was quoted as saying that the era of the music director, in the time-honored sense, was long gone: "The music director today is the orchestra manager. The music director has to be constant. No conductor today who is in the international class can be one. They are all absent."

Undoubtedly the most powerful manager of conductors since the early 1970s has been Ronald Wilford, president of Columbia Artists Management, whose clients include many of the world's most prominent maestri. In a *Times* article of February 25, Donal Henahan wrote of having received a letter from Wilford in which he blamed the New York critical press for the predicament in which the Philharmonic found itself. The "disrespectful" tone of the music criticism did not make the Philharmonic post appealing to prospective music directors. He also complained that "referring to currently active conductors as inferior is a sign of disrespect."

Henahan countered that "it is a fact of life . . . that some artists will be judged as superior to others," and that Wilford himself had regularly to decide which conductors were worthy to be under his management: "No doubt many aspirants to glory whom he passes over would regard his rejection of them as disrespect." The year-round seasons of most major orchestras do make it difficult for any one person to be the single music director today, hence the proliferation of such titles as resident conductor, principal guest conductor, and the like, in addition to the music director.

Meanwhile, the season progressed with concerts by Mehta and guest appearances by Charles Dutoit and the reliable Leinsdorf. Finally, on April 12, came the surprise announcement that Kurt Masur had been selected to succeed Zubin Mehta as music director of the New York Philharmonic, beginning in the 1992–93 season. The surprise was that although Masur had been approached about being one of a conductorial triumvirate, he had never been on anyone's short list of candidates for the top job, at least not publicly. It is safe to say that not since the appointment of Bernstein had the announcement of a director of a major arts organization engendered so much comment in the press.

Masur was by no means a glamorous figure on the podium. He was perceived, however, as a serious musician of integrity, a faithful interpreter of the great German classics and other nineteenth-century repertoire, with particular sympathy for the Russians. He did have the reputation in some circles as a Kapellmeister— that is, a good authoritative conductor but not a greatly inspiring one. But perhaps a Kapellmeister is what the Philharmonic needed at that point. Masur had, after all, brought the Gewandhaus Orchestra to the highest level it had enjoyed since before World War II. He was also known as a strict disciplinarian, a trait that had been crucial to his success in Leipzig. How the disciplinary methods that worked in Leipzig would transfer to New York remained to be seen. However, said Masur,

"I believe that most musicians who know me know that in rehearsal I am quite tough. But I am still a friend."

In earlier times, and not necessarily at the Philharmonic, the selection of a music director was often made by a powerful manager, a major patron, or a committee from the board of directors. Rarely if ever did the musicians have any say in the matter. It is, therefore, striking to read that six orchestra members were on the search committee, and that three of them accompanied the orchestra's general manager, Nick Webster, and president, Frederick Krimendahl II, on a trip to Paris, where Masur was offered and accepted the position.

A potential obstacle to Masur's acceptance was his commitment to the democracy movement in East Germany. The previous year had seen demonstrations in Leipzig, where Masur was a leader of the New Forum, an opposition group to the East German government. He had advised against violence and was thought of as a possible candidate for president. As he said, "I came into politics unwillingly. But I had to, because I have some influence in the city, and I thought it very important that we avoid bloodshed." Once Germany was reunified, he gave up politics and returned to music.

On accepting the appointment, Masur was quoted in the *Times* as saying he was very surprised by the Philharmonic's offer. He felt a friendship had been established since he first conducted the orchestra, one that had continued to grow, but he had often expressed his concern that the orchestra's full capacity was not always utilized. He hoped that together ways could be found to improve its quality, and "to provide a steadier musical life for its audience." It was also announced that Masur would continue his association with the Gewandhaus Orchestra, at least until the 1993–94 season, when it would celebrate its 250th anniversary. When asked if he felt troubled that he was not the Philharmonic's first choice, or even its second or third, he replied, "I was not running for the job; I was not waiting for the job. I was surprised but pleased when I was asked."

In his Sunday column of April 22, Henahan wrote cautiously about Masur's appointment. Citing the conductor's predilection for the standard conservative Germanic repertoire of the eighteenth and nineteenth centuries, with occasional forays into the twentieth century with the works of such composers as Richard Strauss or Prokofieff, Henahan speculated that "unless he has a few surprising ideas up his sleeve, Leipzig-on-the-Hudson could be a duller town than Mehtaville." About the inclusion of six orchestra members on the search team, along with important board members and administrators, he concluded, "Purely from a tactical standpoint, of course, it was sensible to involve all concerned parties: If Mr. Masur is a success, everyone can take credit; if not, nobody in particular will be to blame."

As the season continued, the Philharmonic's audiences heard several fine programs. On April 12 Leonard Slatkin conducted Haydn's rarely played Symphony No. 68 in B-flat Major, Paul Creston's Fantasy for Trombone and Orchestra with principal player Joseph Alessi as soloist, and Elgar's *Enigma Variations*. The inclusion of that particular Haydn symphony is notable because most conductors seem content to select from the composer's London symphonies, occasionally from the Paris symphonies, with one or two others thrown in. Haydn wrote 104 symphonies, and the relative neglect of most of them displays a shocking lack of curiosity or interest, or both, on the part of most conductors. And they are not difficult to learn.

Creston was an American composer whose music was frequently performed by all the major orchestras in the 1940s and 1950s, only to gradually recede into semiobscurity in later years. The Philharmonic gave the premiere of his Second Symphony in 1945, a marvelous work that would be well worth reviving today. His music is characterized by great rhythmic energy along with an attractive songfulness. Fortunately, he wrote some music for solo instruments, such as the marimba, saxophone, and trombone, that manages to keep his name alive (though barely) today. Had not Alessi wished to perform the Fantasy, Creston would not have made his first appearance in many years on a Philharmonic program.

Yuri Temirkanov conducted Shostakovich's Seventh Symphony ("Leningrad") on April 26, and Mehta led an all-Brahms program of the First Symphony and First Piano Concerto on May 10, with Alfred Brendel as the soloist. It is rare for the Philharmonic to engage an instrumental soloist for two consecutive weeks, but Brendel did return on May 17 to play the Brahms Second Concerto. He was well received in both instances by Oestreich and Holland, respectively. The second program included Bartók's Suite from *The Miraculous Mandarin*, which, according to Holland, "gave Mr. Mehta the chance to luxuriate in the brilliant loudness he seems to enjoy."

Collective alarms went off on May 21 with a *Times* story headlined "Chest Pains Send Masur to Hospital." The symptoms had appeared while the conductor was on a flight from Tel Aviv to Frankfurt, and he had been hospitalized at a heart clinic in West Germany. According to his wife, Tomoko Sakurai, Masur had high blood pressure and a circulatory problem, but his doctors said that he had not had a heart attack. On June 5 came the news that he had been released from the clinic in Bad Nauheim, and two days later he conducted the Gewandhaus Orchestra in Bruckner's Third Symphony. After visiting Masur both at the clinic and after his release, Nick Webster said, "He did not strike me as a man who is ill."

Leinsdorf's program of May 24 concluded with the music from the *Carmen Ballet*, arranged and recomposed by the Soviet composer Rodion Shchedrin. This score, for strings and a large percussion section, takes the music of Bizet's great opera and subjects it to all manner of tweakings and take-offs, yet it retains the essence of the original. If one is in the mood, it can be quite amusing, but it is not the sort of thing one expects to find on a serious symphony program. The work had been recorded by none other than Arthur Fiedler and the Boston Pops. In a program note, Leinsdorf justified his choice: "Concert music can be greater than any other spiritual uplift, but it does not have to be that forty times a year."

As if to atone for this frivolity, Leinsdorf concluded the season on May 31 with Mahler's Seventh Symphony, perhaps the most infrequently performed of his symphonies except for the Eighth (though that is because of the enormous forces required). Again in a program note, Leinsdorf confessed that he was making a few cuts in the work. Rockwell took him only slightly to task for these transgressions. After all, the work is eighty minutes long, and Mahler himself was known to cut the works of other composers. While giving Leinsdorf credit for "'fessing up," Rockwell did find the performance a bit wanting in charm—rather clinical, in fact. But, he concluded, Leinsdorf "is an honorable conductor. . . . [who] plays the music as he sees it, frankly and forthrightly. Better that than empty posturing."

THE MUSICIAN

The two-week Horizons festivals of contemporary music had been discontinued several years before. Now the Philharmonic resumed them with a shorter event during the week of July 24, 1990, Horizons 90: New Music for Orchestra. Two days of public rehearsals and symposiums preceded a single concert on the 28th, all held not in Avery Fisher Hall, which was occupied by the Mostly Mozart Festival, but in Davis Hall at City College on Convent Avenue and 133rd Street in Manhattan, near the site of the old Lewisohn Stadium concerts. Lawrence Leighton Smith, in his Philharmonic debut, was the conductor. Then the music director of the Louisville Orchestra, he had ample experience with contemporary music and was assisted in the symposiums by David Del Tredici, the Philharmonic's composer-in-residence. Works by Deborah Drattell, Edward Knight, and Augusta Read Thomas received their world premieres and one by Daron Hagen its New York City premiere; other pieces presented were by Michael Daugherty and Olly Wilson. All were received well in the *Times* by Allan Kozinn.

To conclude the 1990 season of summer Parks Concerts, on August 20 in Central Park the Philharmonic formally dedicated its new movable outdoor stage, fittingly named the Carlos Moseley Music Pavilion, which would be shared with the Metropolitan Opera. With Peter Wexler as the project leader for design and planning, the pavilion, designed by F.T.L Architects and Jaffe Acoustics, was a high-tech facility capable of being completely assembled and ready for sound check in two hours.

Isaac Stern was the soloist for the occasion, with Mehta conducting. The program was a celebration of Stern's seventieth birthday, William Schuman's eightieth, and Carnegie Hall's approaching one-hundredth-anniversary season. Unfortunately, the weather did not cooperate; the evening turned cold and quite windy and was punctuated with rainshowers. As a result, attendance was a relatively paltry twenty thousand, all huddling under nearby trees to keep warm and dry during the abbreviated program, which was to have included Schuman's *American Festival Overture* and the Second Symphony of Sibelius. Only Stern's portion was performed, the Violin Concerto No. 1 by Max Bruch and two short Fritz Kreisler pieces, *Liebesleid* and *Schön Rosmarin*. To conclude the orchestra played "Happy Birthday" for all three honorees. Stern was adjudged to be in good form, and the new sound system far superior to the old. Immediately after the parks season the orchestra left on a ten-day tour to Wolf Trap Farm Park in Vienna, Virginia; Tanglewood in Lenox, Massachusetts; the Ravinia Festival in Highland Park, Illinois; the Midland Center for the Arts in Midland, Michigan; Roy Thomson Hall in Toronto; Hancher Auditorium in Iowa City; and Meyerson Symphony Center in Dallas.

On August 26 Rockwell wrote in the *Times* of the relatively sudden influx of German conductors in American musical life. Prompted, no doubt, by the imminent arrival of Kurt Masur in New York, Rockwell cited the likelihood, soon confirmed, that Wolfgang Sawallisch of Munich's Bavarian State Opera would succeed Riccardo Muti as music director of the Philadelphia Orchestra. Also active at that time were Christoph von Dohnányi in Cleveland, Christoph Eschenbach in Houston, Gunther Herbig, late of Detroit but then in Toronto, and Herbert Blomstedt in San Francisco (Blomstedt, though American born, grew up in Sweden and had spent some years in Dresden). It was felt the time had come when audiences and musicians favored "solid German musicians playing solid German music," which makes up a large portion of the standard repertoire. Rockwell concluded with a reminiscence of a Masur performance of Beethoven's Fifth Symphony (that most standard of standards) which he had found "utterly engrossing." He opined, "If that's what German music-making in German masterpieces can mean for New York and Philadelphia, then both cities should have many satisfying concerts in store."

The next month Mehta began his final season as music director of the New York Philharmonic. At a tenure of thirteen seasons, he had held the post longer than any of the orchestra's previous music directors (under any of their various titles). The annual opening-night pension-fund benefit on September 12 brought Mstislav Rostropovich as soloist in Ernest Bloch's *Schelomo* and Tchaikovsky's *Variations on a Rococo Theme*. Henahan observed that conductor and soloist "made an incendiary combination." Significantly, the event marked Mehta's one thousandth appearance with the Philharmonic.

The eightieth birthday of Samuel Barber was posthumously celebrated on the concerts beginning September 26. Two of his works were presented by Mehta, the exciting *Medea's Dance of Vengeance* and the eloquent *Knoxville: Summer of 1915*, to a text by James Agee, in which the soprano soloist was Marvis Martin. Toward the end of his life (he died in 1981), Barber had a hard time maintaining his proper place in the repertoire, except for the moving *Adagio for Strings*. His basically conservative idiom did not sit well with those who espoused the music of the avant-garde, but since his death Barber has been making a steady comeback, and not only the *Dance*, *Knoxville*, and the *Adagio*, but also works such as the Violin Concerto, turn up with fair frequency on concert programs.

A surprise announcement came on October 6 of the resignation of Nick Webster, effective December 31. During his fifteen-year tenure as the Philharmonic's managing director and executive vice president, the musicians' annual salary increased from $19,760 to $59,280, fifty new players were hired, the Philharmonic chamber ensemble was founded, and orchestra members increasingly performed as soloists. There was also an increase in the orchestra's touring. The board chairman, Stephen Stamas, had only praise for Webster: "The New York Philharmonic has grown artistically and financially under his leadership. His tireless devotion to the organization and his insistence on high artistic and business standards are responsible for much of the Philharmonic's success." Webster's plans included becoming an arts consultant and possibly finding another position; at age fifty-two, he was still a viable candidate in the profession. It was thought, however, that the Philharmonic board wished to engage a new managing director to work in tandem with the new music director.

Plans to have Leonard Bernstein conduct three weeks of the season received a jolt with the announcement on October 10 that Bernstein was retiring from the concert stage for health reasons, effective immediately. His health had been poor for quite some time, though in spite of this he had conducted the Boston Symphony at Tanglewood on August 19 in the annual Serge and Olga Koussevitzky Memorial Concert. But he did not look well at all and had coughed into a handkerchief during the Beethoven Seventh Symphony. Tired and in poor health he may have been, but there was nothing tired about the Beethoven performance, nor that of Britten's Four Sea Interludes from *Peter Grimes*, which opened the program. To conserve his energy, Bernstein had turned over the conducting of his own piece, *Arias and Barcarolles*, to Boston's assistant conductor, Carl St. Clair. But the afternoon's activities had taken their toll, and on his doctor's advice Bernstein withdrew from a European tour by the Tanglewood Music Center Orchestra that was to begin a few days later. He planned to take a few months off to rest, recuperate, and compose prior to returning to the Philharmonic in December, so his announced retirement was not a complete surprise.

But it was with profound sadness that the world of music, and perhaps the world in general, learned of Bernstein's death on October 14, from a heart attack brought on by progressive lung failure. He was seventy-two. A heavy smoker, he was also plagued by emphysema, pulmonary infections, and a pleural tumor. His contribution to American music as a composer, conductor, pianist, and educator is immeasurable. Tributes from all over the world flowed in to his family, the Philharmonic, and the newspapers, which printed many of their own. The *Times* obituary of October 15 by Donal Henahan referred to him as "Music's Monarch."

On October 16 Rockwell wrote an article entitled "The Last Days of Leonard Bernstein." The article mentioned his emphysema and told of Bernstein's attending a memorial service for Alan Jay Lerner in 1986, when a group of his admirers held up a sign that read, "We love you—stop smoking." Said an orchestra manager, "Lenny is the only conductor I have ever seen who simultaneously gasps into a respirator and lights up a cigarette the minute he comes off stage." Bernstein himself had said, "The great thing about conducting is you don't smoke and you breathe in great gobs of oxygen."

In the same issue Holland wrote an article entitled "Remembering a Musician's Musician," in which several Philharmonic musicians reminisced about their former music director. The violinist Newton Mansfield told of the difference between Bernstein and his era and conductors of today, who strive above all for technical competence. What they prepare in rehearsal is exactly how it will be in the concert. Bernstein was very talkative in rehearsal, discussing the meaning of the piece, but he was unpredictable when it came to the performance. "He might get a little faster than planned. The audience might get him excited. It was the unexpected that drew us all in." Mansfield said that too many conductors concentrated on getting absolute precision from the ensemble. Bernstein was more concerned with the meaning and direction of a phrase, and his personality was such that it overrode technical imperfections. "We had a relationship with Bernstein like that with no other conductor I have ever known."

The violist Leonard Davis, a Philharmonic veteran who had succeeded Sol Greitzer in the first chair, spoke of how Bernstein came to every rehearsal fully prepared, with specific reasons for why he phrased and interpreted a piece of music in a certain way, all based on his study of various editions. Tchaikovsky's Sixth was a case in point. He erased all his old markings because he wanted to start fresh and learn something new. The same with Mahler's Second, in which he found many small details that few orchestra members had noticed before. "We were surprised they were there. And really, he had the modesty of all truly talented people. He did all his work in private. No one ever knew how long it took him to learn a piece or compose something."

A *Times* editorial on October 16 bore the simple headline "The Musician." After giving a few biographical details, the writer spoke of Bernstein's seventy-two years of life, noting that they were insufficient for all he wanted to do, could have done, should have done. Bernstein had said that he did not want to devote his life to fifty pieces of music, as Toscanini had done. It would bore him to death. He wanted to conduct, to play the piano, to write for Hollywood, to write symphonic music. "I want to keep on trying to be, in the full sense of that wonderful word, a musician." The editorial concluded that for forty-seven years, "Leonard Bernstein was an important part of America's culture, and its conscience. Forty-seven years: not long enough."

At Lincoln Center the flags flew at half-staff, while orchestras across the nation and the world paid tribute. The Philharmonic itself, with Leonard Slatkin conducting, added the poignant Adagietto from Mahler's Fifth Symphony to its Tuesday night program and changed the following week's concerts to an all-Bernstein program. Seiji Ozawa and the Boston Symphony and Sir Georg Solti and the Chicago Symphony added the Mahler Adagietto to their programs. In Philadelphia, David Zinman and the Philadelphia Orchestra performed Barber's *Adagio for Strings* in Bernstein's memory. The city of Vienna, whose Philharmonic Orchestra Bernstein frequently conducted, declared a period of mourning.

Although Bernstein had been the first American-born conductor in the Philharmonic's modern history, there was hope in the conducting profession that the road was being paved for more Americans to be seriously considered for important positions. Yet for many years Bernstein's appointment was an anomaly. With the subsequent emergence of such conductors as James Levine, Leonard Slatkin, David Zinman, and Michael Tilson Thomas, perhaps the road is a bit less rocky today, but much paving still remains to be done.

Slatkin's all-Bernstein program, beginning on October 20, included the Overture to *Candide*, the "Jeremiah" Symphony with Wendy White as the mezzo-soprano soloist; the *Serenade for Violin, Strings, and Percussion*, with the concertmaster,

Glenn Dicterow as the soloist; and the *Chichester Psalms*, in which the New York Choral Artists participated. On the morning of November 14 a special memorial concert was given in Carnegie Hall. The date had special significance for Bernstein: it was the anniversary of his dramatic debut with the New York Philharmonic forty-seven years before, the ninetieth birthday of his friend and mentor Aaron Copland, the thirty-sixth anniversary of his first television appearance on the CBS *Omnibus* series, one month after his death, and one year after the birth of his grandson. The concert was a joint presentation by Bernstein's family and staff, the New York Philharmonic, and Carnegie Hall. An extremely crowded stage was the result of the presence, in addition to the Philharmonic, of representatives of other orchestras with which Bernstein had close ties: the Boston Symphony, the Israel Philharmonic, the London Symphony, the Orchestre National of France, the Orchestra of the Academy of Santa Cecilia in Rome, and the Vienna Philharmonic, as well as the Westminster Choir.

The music performed was mostly by Bernstein but also included selections by Copland, Mahler, Schumann, Haydn, and Bach, the last in a performance by Mstislav Rostropovich of the Sarabande from the Suite No. 5 for solo cello. The conductors were Michael Tilson Thomas, Michael Barrett, Christoph Eschenbach, and James Levine, while the soloists were Thomas Stacy and Philip Smith, the Philharmonic's English horn player and principal trumpet, respectively; the soprano Clamma Dale; the mezzo-sopranos Marilyn Horne and Christa Ludwig; the tenor Jerry Hadley; and the baritone Chester Ludgin. The musical selections were interspersed with remarks by Bernstein's children—Jamie, Nina, and Alexander—and by Lauren Bacall, Michael Wager, and Schuyler Chapin. Although the occasion was very moving, it was also a celebration, as Jamie Bernstein Thomas proclaimed: "What fun we all had while it lasted."

The musical highlight was the concluding number: the Overture to *Candide*, played by the full orchestra with no one on the podium, and a more ebullient rendition cannot be imagined. In fact, it was this performance that started the tradition of the Philharmonic's playing it as a "solo" encore on many occasions.

A second death soon saddened the world of music, that of Aaron Copland on December 2 at the age of ninety, of respiratory failure following the onset of pneumonia. In discussing American composers, Bernstein said at least once of his friend and colleague, "He's the best we have." Copland, who managed to divide his works into a popular style tinged with folk music and a more acerbic, declarative one that was once described as his "laying down of the law" style, has much in common with Stravinsky. Both are probably best-known for three great ballet scores; the later pieces of both employ the twelve-tone system in their own idiosyncratic manners; and despite many imitators, when each is heard there is no difficulty recognizing the real thing.

On December 6 Leonard Slatkin led a program in memory of both Bernstein and Copland, opening with the latter's reflective *Quiet City*, in which the soloists were the Philharmonic principals Philip Smith on trumpet, and Thomas Stacy on English horn. Bernstein was represented by his recent *Arias and Barcarolles* in the orchestration by Bright Sheng, with soloists Judy Kaye, soprano, and Kurt Öllmann, baritone. The program concluded with Shostakovich's Fifth Symphony, one of the staples of Bernstein's repertoire. Shortly thereafter, on December 13, the Philharmonic's new assistant conductor, Samuel Wong, made his debut with the same Shostakovich symphony and Alfred Schnittke's *(K)ein Sommernachtstraum*. The evening's soloist was the Russian émigré pianist Vladimir Feltsman, who was heard in Rachmaninoff's *Rhapsody on a Theme of Paganini*.

Meanwhile, on December 8 it was announced that the Philharmonic's orchestra manager, Allison Vulgamore, had been named acting managing director as of January 1. She would be in charge until a successor to Nick Webster was formally chosen. And on December 18 came the announcement that Kurt Masur, scheduled to begin his tenure as music director with the 1992–93 season, would in fact start a year earlier. He was to have conducted two weeks during 1991–92, but the death of Bernstein left six vacant weeks, of which Masur, after rearranging his schedule, would now conduct five. Four additional weeks were mutually agreed upon by Masur and the Philharmonic, which meant he would be present for eleven weeks of the season (Boulez, in his first season, led only seven weeks). Said Stephen Stamas, "When Mr. Masur agreed to take on Mr. Bernstein's concerts we felt that the next logical step was to invite him to take up the music directorship next year, so that he and the orchestra could begin their partnership a year early."

Bernstein had been scheduled to conduct Mendelssohn's *Elijah*, a work that would have been new to his repertoire, on December 18. Appropriately, it was Masur, an old hand with the score, who took over. Bernstein's performances were to have had an all-star cast of soloists, along with Joseph Flummerfelt's Westminster Symphonic Choir, and were to have been taped by Deutsche Grammophon. With Bernstein's death most of the soloists withdrew from the project, as did Deutsche Grammophon. The Canadian baritone Kevin McMillan was the substitute Elijah, who, according to Rockwell, created "a tirelessly demanding impression." The audience's cheers at the end led Rockwell to speculate that they might "signify the onset of Mr. Masur's honeymoon with the New York public." He concluded with the observation that the conductor was "giving first-rate performances. May the honeymoon continue."

MUCH MOZART AND MEHTA'S FAREWELL

Overshadowed by the deaths of Leonard Bernstein and Aaron Copland was the passing of Franco Autori at age eighty-seven, as reported in the *Times* of October 19. He had been the Philharmonic's associate conductor from 1949 to 1959, then music director of the Tulsa Philharmonic from 1961 to 1971. Although his podium personality could be volatile (presumably not with his New York colleagues), he was a good-hearted man who worked especially well directing student and amateur ensembles.

Whatever problems the Philharmonic may have had in the past with conductor cancellations and substitute conductors were nothing compared with the happenings during the 1990–91 season. First was the three-week gap in the schedule in December left by Bernstein's death, eventually filled by Slatkin, Wong, and Masur. Then, in the early weeks of January, the outbreak of war in the Persian Gulf caused Zubin Mehta to leave abruptly for Israel, where he is music director for life of the Israel Philharmonic. In a program insert he declared, "I know my place is in Israel," to show solidarity with its citizens, especially its musicians. Wong replaced him for the concerts beginning January 17, at least for two of the three works on the program, Haydn's Symphony No. 96 in D Major and Lalo's *Symphonie Espagnole*, the latter with Mark Peskanov as the violin soloist. Peskanov was himself a substitute for Shlomo Mintz, who was ill. The third work, in its New York premiere, was Jacob Druckman's *Brangle*, conducted by the composer.

Wong, then twenty-eight, had been the Philharmonic's assistant conductor only since the Parks Concerts in August, at which time he was almost immediately pressed into service to conduct Mendelssohn's "Italian" Symphony on three minutes' notice because Edo de Waart was stuck in traffic. Trained as a physician before taking up conducting, he was later quoted as saying, "Now, when I hear the personnel manager say 'Five minutes' backstage before a concert, I get a feeling of terror." Since 1987 that personnel manager has been Carl Schiebler, who came to the Philharmonic from the St. Louis Symphony, where he held the same position and was also a member of the horn section. (The demands of the Philharmonic's schedule put an end to his horn playing.)

For the second week of Mehta's absence, the Czech conductor Zdeněk Macál, music director of the Milwaukee Symphony (and later of the New Jersey Symphony), was the substitute. His performance of Mendelssohn's Symphony No. 5 ("Reformation") "emphasized the graceful, feminine side of the composer's artistic personality," according to Henahan on January 26—an approach that might not have been the most appropriate to the "Reformation," one of Mendelssohn's more turbulent scores.

Anyone reading these lines today should be reminded that the year 1991 marked the 200th anniversary of the death of Mozart. One could argue that every year is a Mozart year, for his music is always with us. But that argument would not have flown in the light of what was planned for Lincoln Center. There, from January 27, the composer's birthday, through August 1992, every note of Mozart's music would be performed: symphonies, concertos, operas, masses, chamber music, sonatas, everything—626 works in the Köchel catalog and 200 more besides. Participating in this marathon would be the Philharmonic, the Metropolitan Opera, the New York City Opera, the Chamber Music Society of Lincoln Center, the Juilliard School, the Mostly Mozart Festival, and many assorted guests.

For the concert scheduled on the composer's 235th birthday, Raymond Leppard led the Philharmonic and members of the Juilliard Orchestra in a three-hour program that duplicated a concert Mozart himself gave in Vienna on March 23, 1783: the "Haffner" Symphony, the Piano Concertos Nos. 5 and 13, excerpts from the "Posthorn" Serenade, and various piano and vocal works. Honoring historical precedent, the first three movements of the symphony opened the program and the finale closed it.

Mehta returned from Israel in time for the Philharmonic's subscription concerts beginning January 31, when he had the happy idea of presenting Mozart's first and last symphonies, No. 1 in E-flat Major, K. 16, and the mighty No. 41 in C Major ("Jupiter"), K. 551. In between was the rarely heard cantata *Davidde Penitente*, a reworking of sections from the Mass in C Minor with two additional arias. The soprano Ruth Ann Swenson, the mezzo-soprano Suzanne Mentzer, and the tenor Vinson Cole were the soloists, with the Westminster Symphonic Choir. Rockwell complimented the "brisk, sprightly performances" of both symphonies and Mehta for conducting the cantata "with his familiar propulsion." Rockwell also praised Mehta's performance of Mozart's Symphony No. 34 in C Major, K. 338, given on February 8, as "about the best Mozart conducting that Zubin Mehta has given us in New York—warm, graceful, refined and affectionate," though he felt the rendition of the Brahms Third Symphony on the same program "lacked distinction."

The Philharmonic family suffered another loss on February 10, when Sampson R. Field, a former president and board member, died at the age of eighty-eight. He had also been chairman of the Marlboro School of Music and the Marlboro Festival in Vermont.

The Gulf War had a dire effect on foreign travel by symphony orchestras. As of February 25, fears of terrorism and international travel difficulties had caused the Saint Louis Symphony to cancel a European tour, the Minnesota Orchestra a tour of Japan, and the Juilliard Orchestra a tour of France. The Philharmonic was still scheduled to inaugurate an Easter festival in Lucerne and to perform in Holland and Belgium. On February 16 a considerable minority of the orchestra voted against the tour. Those who felt their lives would be in danger were to inform the personnel manager of their intention to stay home.

On February 21 the young Austrian conductor Franz Welser-Möst made his Philharmonic debut in a program including Mozart's Symphony No. 28 in C Major, K. 200; Tchaikovsky's Violin Concerto, in which the soloist was the sixteen-year-old Russian virtuoso Maxim Vengerov; and Mendelssohn's Third Symphony ("Scottish"). Rockwell found the conductor rather understated in his approach, even introverted—unusual for a conductor on the international scene. (At the time principal conductor of the London Philharmonic, he is now music director of the Cleveland Orchestra.) In spite of his reticence, he did manage to throw his back out and was forced to cancel the last two performances of his first week and the entire second week. More work for Samuel Wong. The young assistant retained Welser-Möst's program for the remainder of the first week and, for the second week, substituted Copland's Third Symphony for the scheduled Fourth by the Austrian composer Franz Schmidt. Meanwhile, the Philharmonic canceled the European trip.

The conductor cancellations continued apace. The ongoing illness of Klaus Tennstedt brought about another two-week gap in the schedule, the first week of which was filled by the young American Christopher Keene, the general director of the New York City Opera. He led a most interesting program on March 9, opening with Mozart's little-known Symphony No. 19 in E-flat Major, K. 132, and closing with the Fourth Symphony by the esteemed American Walter Piston. (In the over-all scheme of things, one could say that the Piston symphony is, unfortunately, also little known.) In between, the much-admired American soprano Arleen Augér was heard in Mozart's concert aria "Ch'io mi scordi di te?," K. 505, Ravel's *Shéhérazade*, and his *Pièce en forme de habañera*.

Tennstedt's second week was filled by the Finnish conductor Paavo Berglund in his Philharmonic debut, an engagement that was extended for a second week when the Austrian maestro Christoph Perick abruptly withdrew because of a family emergency. An all-Mozart program had been scheduled for March 23, which Berglund retained, except for substituting the Symphony No. 33 in B-flat Major for the Symphony No. 25 in G Minor. Jeffrey Kahane was the soloist in the Piano Concerto No. 22 in E-flat Major, and the evening concluded with Symphony No. 38 in D Major ("Prague"). An interesting aspect of Berglund's work is that he is one of the very few established conductors who hold the baton in their left hand. From the players' perspective, of course, his second and fourth beats are the reverse of the usual pattern (for beat 2, for instance, his baton moves to the right instead of the left), but since his beat is very clear, it is quite easy for them to adjust to it.

The cancellation of the European tour meant that the Philharmonic had to fill a gap in its schedule domestically. Six concerts were arranged at short notice, one of which, conducted by Leonard Slatkin on April 4, was devoted to American music, mostly of a celebratory nature. Opening with Copland's popular *Fanfare for the Common Man*, the program continued with its natural counterpart, Joan Tower's *First Fanfare for the Uncommon Woman*. Also performed were William Schuman's *American Festival Overture*, Morton Gould's *American Salute*, Bernstein's Three Dances from *Fancy Free*, and works by Barber, Ives, and Virgil Thomson, as well as Copland's *Lincoln Portrait*, with E. G. Marshall as a restrained narrator rather than the oratorical type often encountered in this piece.

In his April 13 review of an April 11 concert, Henahan expressed mild surprise that a Philharmonic program "went off exactly as scheduled," with no cancellation of either conductor or soloist. The latter was Stanley Drucker, who performed the Mozart Clarinet Concerto most elegantly. On the podium was the Estonian-born Neemi Järvi, returning to the Philharmonic after an eleven-year absence, who brought with him an attractive work by his countryman Jaan Rääts, the Concerto for String Orchestra. An early work by Brahms concluded the program, the bucolic Serenade No. 1 in D Major, one of the composer's first attempts at producing a symphony.

The "exactly as scheduled" situation did not last long, however, for Giuseppe Sinopoli withdrew from the following week's concerts beginning April 18. His place was taken by the Israeli-born Yoel Levi, music director of the Atlanta Symphony. Sinopoli had programmed Mahler's imposing Ninth Symphony, which Levi retained. According to Rockwell on April 20, Levi's performance was even slower than Bernstein's, clocking in at over ninety minutes, but it was a calmer and more contemplative interpretation.

Sinopoli did appear the following week for the concerts beginning April 25. For these he led a program that might have been given by Toscanini: Mendelssohn's Symphony No. 4 in A Major ("Italian") and two of Respighi's Roman tributes, *The Fountains of Rome* and *The Pines of Rome* (though Toscanini probably never programmed the last two pieces together). Henahan gave the Respighi performances a good review, though he felt that more poetry and dramatic excitement would have benefited the *Pines*. As for the Mendelssohn symphony, played by too large an orchestra, it was at times heavy and lacking buoyancy, even a bit dragged in the lively finale. "Rest easy, Toscanini," was his final comment.

The major musical event of the season, at least from a celebratory standpoint, was the series of concerts marking the centennial of Carnegie Hall, which had opened on May 5, 1891. One hundred years later, concerts by the New York Philharmonic, the Philadelphia Orchestra, the Cleveland Orchestra, and the Metropolitan Opera Orchestra; a chamber music recital by Emanuel Ax, Isaac Stern, and Yo-Yo Ma; and jazz and folk evenings all paved the way for the gala celebration on Sunday May 5, two concerts, in fact, one at 4:00 p.m., the other at 9:00 p.m., separated by a cocktail party and banquet at the Waldorf-Astoria Hotel.

For both concerts the orchestra was the New York Philharmonic, with the conducting shared by Zubin Mehta and James Levine. The solo artists included Alfred Brendel, Plácido Domingo, Marilyn Horne, Yo-Yo Ma, Midori (at nineteen the youngest performer), Jessye Norman, Leontyne Price, Samuel Ramey, Mstislav Rostropovich, Philip Smith (the Philharmonic's principal trumpet), Isaac Stern, and Pinchas Zukerman. Also taking part were the Empire Brass and the New York Choral Artists. The afternoon concert began with a specially commissioned piece, Joan Tower's *Third Fanfare for the Uncommon Woman*, and the evening concert ended with Mehta conducting the final movement of Mahler's Third Symphony in memory of Leonard Bernstein, who had been scheduled to lead that very work. PBS televised the entire event nationally, the afternoon concert on tape, the evening one live—a four-hour program in prime time.

Rostropovich performed Tchaikovsky's *Rococo Variations*, an appropriate choice given that Tchaikovsky had participated in the inaugural concerts in 1891. Isaac Stern gave the opening remarks: "This is a consecrated house. It's not consecrated because *we* say so, but because of the musicians who play there. The name 'Carnegie Hall' is synonymous with the United States for musicians and performers from around the world."

As a prelude to its 150th anniversary, to take place in the 1992–93 season, the Philharmonic launched the most ambitious fund-raising campaign in its history. The goal was $75 million over five years, of which over $26 million had already been pledged. At the time the Philharmonic's endowment was $72 million. Annual operating expenses were $23 million, of which 4 percent came from city, state, and national support—and that percentage was expected to decrease.

Sad but expected news was announced on May 10, the death of the revered pianist Rudolf Serkin, at the age of eighty-eight, after a long illness. He had been one of the most frequent soloists with the Philharmonic, performing almost every season since his debut with the orchestra in 1936 with Toscanini conducting, and in 1972 he had been made an honorary member of the Philharmonic Society. Especially prized are his recordings of Beethoven concertos and sonatas. As a tribute to Serkin, Mehta began the all-Mozart concert of May 16 with the composer's *Masonic Funeral Music*, for which there was no applause, after which the Overture to *Don Giovanni* was played. While the latter was not necessarily appropriate, except in its somber moments, the two works together replaced *A Musical Joke*. For the rest, Mehta continued his policy of featuring the orchestra's principal players as soloists, on this occasion the hornist Philip Myers in Mozart's Concerto No. 1 in D Major, K. 412, and two shorter pieces, and the flutist Jeanne Baxtresser and harpist Sarah Bullen in the Concerto for Flute and Harp in C Major, K. 299. The program closed with the Symphony No. 29 in A Major, K. 201, in a performance that Allan Kozinn found to be "as spirited and attentively accented as any Mozartean could want."

With the concerts beginning May 23, Zubin Mehta conducted his final performances as music director of the New York Philharmonic. He chose to depart not with an ordinary program, but with nothing less than Schoenberg's massive *Gurre-Lieder*, the composer's farewell to romanticism, which Mehta and the Philharmonic had last given in 1983. Scored for a huge orchestra, five vocal soloists, a speaker, a large male chorus, and a mixed chorus, the work's spatial demands meant that several rows of seats had to be removed from the front of the hall so that the stage could be enlarged to accommodate the more than four hundred performers required.

The soloists were the soprano Susan Dunn, the mezzo-soprano Florence Quivar, the tenors Gary Lakes and Jon Garrison, and the bass Jon Cheek. In the part of the speaker, who narrates the penultimate scene, "The Wild Hunt of the Summer Wind," was the incomparable Hans Hotter. The great German bass-baritone was renowned for his Wagner performances, particularly in the role of Wotan, and for his lieder singing, in which he was a prime interpreter of Schubert's *Winterreise*. In the final years of his long career, he had a virtual monopoly on the role of the *Gurre-Lieder* speaker (not that the work is performed very often). Joseph Flummerfelt's ever dependable New York Choral Artists also participated. The performances were recorded live by Sony and released as a tribute to Mehta. Although Henahan wrote positively about the event in general, his highest praise went to Hotter, "who lifted the evening to another artistic level entirely."

After the intermission of the final performance, on May 28, several speakers lauded Mehta and his accomplishments. New York's mayor, David Dinkins, said, "I speak for eight million New Yorkers and millions of visitors to this city when I say that at your departure we will feel a great loss." The Philharmonic's chairman, Stephen Stamas, read a telegram from President George H. W. Bush, who called Mehta "a man of the people" who had "helped reinvigorate and broaden the appeal of classical music." During the week Mehta had been presented with two gifts from the Philharmonic's board of directors: a page from the original score of

Mahler's Ninth Symphony, written while the composer was music director of the Philharmonic; and a replica of the baton used at the orchestra's first concert in 1842. After the intermission ceremonies, Mehta himself spoke: "I cannot tell you what this means to me. Now I really want to continue this concert." Several gala dinners were held in the music director's honor, and on May 29 he and his wife, Nancy, left for Florence, Italy, where he was the director of the spring Maggio Musicale Fiorentino. He was scheduled to conduct two operas there.

Mehta's tenure in New York was not a great success from the standpoint of critical reception. He had been welcomed warmly by Harold Schonberg in the *Times*, who continued to write appreciatively of him until his retirement. But Schonberg's was virtually the lone voice in his favor. Although he came out with the occasional favorable review, Donal Henahan became to Mehta what Schonberg had been to Bernstein throughout most of his Philharmonic tenure. Other Mehta antagonists included Henahan's colleagues at the *Times*, as well as Peter G. Davis of *New York* magazine. In his autobiography, *Zubin Mehta: The Score of My Life*, the conductor spoke of "malicious attacks in the New York press" and complained that Harold Schonberg's successor "constantly wrote really vicious things about me."

Mention has been made of the dissatisfaction of some of the orchestra musicians about midway through his tenure. And yet, Mehta must have done something right. An inept music director does not last in his position for thirteen years—especially not in New York. Many musicians have spoken of his gentlemanly demeanor during rehearsals. Said one, "If he has a fault in rehearsal, it's that he might be a little too gentle. New York is not a gentle city." The noted actor Werner Klemperer, son of the great conductor Otto Klemperer, observed, "Most of the time, orchestras—and I don't mean the New York Philharmonic specifically—need a benevolent dictator. But dictator is a big word here. Zubin is benevolent, but he's not a dictator."

He remained popular with the public, and if his records did not sell well, as was claimed, and the Philharmonic lost its CBS/Sony recording contract, so did other major orchestras. It was the beginning of a gradual decline of the classical recording industry in the United States.

CHAPTER 13

1991–92

ENTER MASUR

A new managing director was appointed on May 22, Deborah Borda, the general manager of the Minnesota Orchestra. A former violist, she had held the Minnesota job for only a year, having gone there from the Detroit Symphony, where she had the title of executive director. At the Philharmonic she replaced Allison Vulgamore, who would soon be appointed to the newly created position of general manager.

On May 31, 1991, a major step was taken in further consolidating the orchestra's historic material in the recently created archive. Several steps, in fact—for on that day a number of musicians, board members, and others affiliated with the Philharmonic, with Zubin Mehta in the lead on his last official day as music director, walked across the bridge from Avery Fisher Hall to the Samuel B. and David Rose Building, Lincoln Center's newest addition, each carrying books and other items for deposit in the archive's new location on the fourth floor. Spacious and boasting an impressive view, the site was a welcome change from the cramped quarters in the Hall's basement. For this symbolic transfer, each participant carried a single volume of season programs. Mehta bore the earliest volume. The principal clarinetist, Stanley Drucker, chose the programs from the 1948–49 season, his first with the orchestra. Jamie Thomas, daughter of Leonard Bernstein, carried the volume for 1967–68, one of the seasons of her father's tenure as music director. The archivist, Barbara Haws, commented on how, down through the years, "everything" was saved, all of it unorganized and uncatalogued when she arrived in 1984.

Another death in the world of music was reported on June 10: that of the great Chilean-born pianist Claudio Arrau, at the age of eighty-eight. He had been a frequent guest soloist with the Philharmonic and was especially noted for his performances of the Beethoven and Brahms concertos. And on July 10 The *New York Times* announced the retirement of Donal Henahan, its chief music critic since 1980 and a member of its music staff since 1967. His successor would be Edward Rothstein, who had been music critic for *The New Republic* since 1984 and had also been a member of the *Times*'s music department from 1980 to 1984.

Although not due to take over officially until September, Kurt Masur made a preview appearance on July 14 as part of the orchestra's three-week residency at the Tilles Center of C. W. Post College in Brookville, Long Island. He led a program of all Mendelssohn, a composer who had long been one of his specialties. The "Italian" Symphony and substantial portions of the Incidental Music to *A Midsummer Night's Dream* made up the bill, the latter with B. D. Wong speaking excerpts from the play in order to place the musical numbers in the proper context. Women of the New York Choral Artists took part, as well as the soprano Margaret Brooks and the mezzo-soprano Mary Ann Hart. For the *Times's* Oestreich, "This was a fine, invigorating way to whet the appetite for Mr. Masur's tenure."

Masur's official debut as music director took place on the evening of September 10, 1991. The concert was televised nationally as part of PBS's *Live from Lincoln Center* series. The conductor explained in an intermission chat that his choice of program was designed to illustrate his newfound entry into American musical life in combination with the huge Germanic tradition from whence he came. Thus, the first half was devoted to American music, opening with two brief pieces by John Adams, *Tromba lontana* and *Short Ride in a Fast Machine* (Masur had earlier said he hoped the latter title would not symbolize his tenure with the Philharmonic). Next came the second set of Aaron Copland's *Old American Songs*, in which the much-admired baritone Thomas Hampson was the soloist. The Seventh Symphony of Anton Bruckner occupied the second half.

A standing ovation greeted Masur as he made his entrance. As seen and heard on television, he impressed as a conductor of great strength and purposefulness. There was absolutely nothing glamorous about him. A tall (six foot three) man with a trim beard, he conducted without a baton (an early accident to his right hand prevented his holding one—then again, Boulez had also been batonless) but with strong, mostly vertical and choppy gestures. There was no question, however, but that he was all business. Projection of the music, not of Kurt Masur, was the most important thing.

The critics were generally positive but guarded, in their response. Rothstein wrote that Masur showed "himself thoroughly comfortable and unpretentious about his musical goals," which included "a steadier musical life" and a "warm, human sound." The Bruckner symphony was given "an ambitious but common-sensical reading," which meant that he did not plumb all of the work's depths but also did not exaggerate sections to almost interminable lengths. It was a very musical performance in which everything proceeded naturally. There were still challenges to be faced, some edginess of orchestral tone to be overcome (the hall itself could be held partially responsible for the strident, rather than grand, fortissimos). Overall, however, it was a successful evening.

Masur altered the orchestra's seating arrangement, no doubt for acoustical reasons. The cellos exchanged seats with the violas, which were now on the edge of the stage, to the right of the podium as seen from the audience. The move brought out more clearly this inner voice in the orchestral texture. The double basses were arrayed in a straight line on a platform across the rear wall of the stage, with the brass instruments moved away from the wall, in the hope of increasing the hall's notoriously weak bass sound and subduing the brass somewhat, whose sound had bounced off the wall, amplifying it in the hall.

In an article on September 22, Rothstein noted that the brilliant and charismatic Bernstein had been a corrective to the annual appearances of the traditionalists Guido Cantelli, George Szell, and Bruno Walter; that the severe and analytic Boulez had been a corrective contrast to Bernstein's flamboyance; that Mehta, in turn, was a corrective designed to return the orchestra to the glamour of the Bernstein era. And now, here was the solid Central European Masur, yet another corrective, one who, it was hoped, would restore the Germanic tradition out of which the Philharmonic had originally emerged. It was felt that once the excitement of the opening week had faded, there was much work to be done.

The Masur influence carried over into the work of the guest conductors, just as the Bernstein influence had done over thirty years before. Leonard Slatkin was the first guest, his program of September 19 consisting of the rarely heard Haydn Symphony No. 60 ("Il distratto") and the first symphonies of Samuel Barber and Sir William Walton, both of which Slatkin has ardently championed. For Rothstein on September 21, Slatkin and the orchestra "exhibited refined ideas, coherent execution and the virtues of articulate expression."

For many years, in spite of the composer's supposed popularity, the music of Edvard Grieg has occupied a minuscule place on the programs of major symphony orchestras. His once-popular Piano Concerto and the two *Peer Gynt* Suites have been relegated mostly to pops concerts or, pops concerts being what they are today—that is, virtually devoid of classical music—family concerts on which lighter music is the predominant fare (although there is very little that is really light about this music).

It must have come as quite a shock, therefore, to the New York intelligentsia when Masur returned for his second program on September 26, bringing with him his own concert version of substantial portions of Grieg's complete incidental music to the Norwegian playwright Henrik Ibsen's *Peer Gynt*. It involved a narrator, the actor Len Cariou, who also spoke some of Gynt's lines, as well as the soprano Edith Wiens and the New York Choral Artists. What Masur offered was a dramatic context in which the familiar, thematically linked music could make its maximum impact. What stood out most of all was the playing of the orchestra, warm, supple, and descriptively dramatic. Rothstein even described it as "sweet," a word he claimed had never before been used to describe a Philharmonic concert. In fact, the author knows of some hard-bitten concertgoers who were actually moved to tears by the performance.

Another rarity on a symphony concert was the program's opening work, Bach's *Wedding Cantata* (No. 202), a rarity because baroque works have virtually disappeared from mainstream orchestra concerts. Edith Wiens participated in this performance as well, in which a reduced orchestra played with refinement, the whole consisting, according to Rothstein, of "moments of pleasure taken and pleasure provided."

Like Bernstein before him, Masur was an educator and wished to be involved in the presentation of the Young People's Concerts. Accordingly, he led the first one of the season on September 28, offering a slightly condensed version of the *Peer Gynt* music, preceded by instrument demonstrations in which themes from Grieg's work were heard. He also spoke with warmth and humor, with only occasional stumbles of language. Holland wondered if the program might have been heavy going for young ears but felt that Grieg's melodies, already having been introduced, "did their work."

Masur also conducted the Young People's Concert on October 20, and this time Rothstein attended, taking with him his eight-year-old daughter and two young friends. Nothing less than Dvořák's complete "New World" Symphony was performed, again preceded by instrument demonstrations and thematic and programmatic introductions. One of Rothstein's young colleagues pronounced the event "great," another said he was ready to forget about New Kids on the Block, and his daughter "liked the loud exciting sections, was reminded at one point of the *Nutcracker* Suite, was bored by the talk, and liked one advantage of compact discs: 'you can fast forward some parts.'" But again, Rothstein felt there was much work to be done before these concerts approached the level of Bernstein's televised programs.

The "New World" Symphony was also part of that week's subscription concerts, which began on October 19 and included as well Alfred Schnittke's Cello Concerto No. 1, with the work's dedicatee, Natalia Gutman, as soloist. In describing the concert, Rothstein observed that "Mr. Masur is making it clear how beneficial an Old World Kapellmeister can be to the oldest New World symphony orchestra. . . . The concert was another demonstration of how Mr. Masur's disciplined but relaxed approach is proving effective with the orchestra."

Also on October 19 came the announcement that Masur planned "to have a series of open discussions with the public at Avery Fisher Hall," beginning on November 19. He wished to be able to contact his subscribers and other New

Yorkers personally and directly in an informal question-and-answer session and said that he was "very interested in the thoughts and wishes of the New York subscribers." Such a forum would be similar to the meetings the conductor held each year in Leipzig prior to the opening of the Gewandhaus Orchestra's season. The only differences were that the New York meetings would not be limited to subscribers and that they would be held more frequently.

A guest conductor for two weeks, making his Philharmonic debut on October 25, was the young German Klaus Peter Flor, who had been mentored by Masur. His first program paired Mozart's youthful Piano Concerto No. 14 in E-flat Major, K. 449, in which the soloist was Rudolf Firkušny, then approaching his eightieth birthday, with the Shostakovich Symphony No. 10, considered by many to be his greatest work in that genre. Flor made a good impression in that program, though he was greeted somewhat less favorably the next week by Oestreich, who found the readings of Mozart's Symphony No. 34 and Mendelssohn's "Reformation" Symphony a bit heavy-handed. However, the American premiere of a timpani concerto, *Der Wald* (The Forest), by the contemporary German composer Siegfried Matthus, riveted the audience's attention thanks to the playing of the Philharmonic's brilliant timpanist, Roland Kohloff, whose sense of showmanship contributed to the effect.

Ominous news was announced on October 31 that the Philharmonic's musicians, who had been playing without a contract since the previous one had expired in September, voted unanimously to strike if a settlement was not reached by November 13, the day before Kurt Masur's next scheduled performance (a deadline that was later extended). The minimum salary was now $1,120 a week, and the announcement noted that the Chicago Symphony had recently struck for seventeen days before winning a new contract that would reach $1,300 in 1993. The higher cost of living in New York was deemed crucial to obtaining salaries that would exceed Chicago's.

On November 16 it was announced that Avery Fisher Hall would undergo yet another attempt to improve its much-maligned acoustics (though each previous effort resulted in claims of improvement). This time the eminent acoustician Russell Johnson was engaged for the job. Preliminary measurements were to begin the following Monday, although the actual work would not be done until late summer 1992. Masur had already been experimenting with the orchestra's seating arrangement to compensate for sonic deficiencies and had been responsible for the placement of sound-absorbing baffles on each side of the stage, as well as a wooden baffle over the orchestra. He said he hoped Johnson would take these measures into account. Also mentioned was Masur's wish to have a pipe organ installed in the hall (the original Philharmonic Hall had one), but to date money had not been found for this project. However, said Masur, "I am a dreamer."

Also announced was the signing of a contract between the Philharmonic and Masur with Teldec Records, a German company owned by Time Warner. The contract specified thirty-two live recordings over a six-year period. The Philharmonic, once a prolific recording orchestra for CBS Masterworks (originally Columbia Records), had been without such a contract since 1980. Since then it had recorded only sporadically for CBS and other labels. Teldec had been Masur's label since 1979 and now would have exclusive rights to his recordings with the Philharmonic, though the orchestra could still record for other labels with other conductors. The opening-night Bruckner Seventh would be the first release, with the "New World" Symphony soon to follow.

Also to be issued was a disc containing three works from the week of concerts beginning November 15, a program of variations: Charles Ives's *Variations on America*, in the orchestration by William Schuman; Brahms's *Variations on a Theme by Haydn*; and a rarity on Philharmonic programs, Max Reger's *Variations and Fugue on a Theme of Mozart*. (Not included on the disc was Rachmaninoff's *Rhapsody on a Theme of Paganini*, in which the Soviet pianist Viktoria Postnikova was the soloist.) Rothstein had nothing but praise for the entire concert, citing Masur's skill in softening the edges of the orchestra's tone, making the sound more expressive and focused. Although listening to so many works in variation form could produce an episodic effect, "by gradually varying the elements in each performance, [he was] highlighting nuance and clarifying intention. So far he is leaving us with something very familiar, yet also something quite different."

Masur met members of his audience on November 19 when about six hundred of them attended the first Philharmonic Forum at Avery Fisher Hall, the first such meeting in the Philharmonic's history. One member was critical of Masur's choice of the Bruckner Seventh for his opening concert. Another said he disliked programs that included works calling for a reduced orchestra, such as Mozart symphonies— apparently, if a man paid full price for a ticket, he expected to hear a full orchestra, and otherwise he wasn't getting his money's worth. Masur patiently replied that the Bruckner had been chosen to symbolize a bridge between his Leipzig orchestra and its New York counterpart. And if a Mozart work had been selected, say, to precede a Mahler symphony, the refinement of Mozart would make Mahler sound even more grand than if another romantic work had been played first. Another member wondered if the Philharmonic would consider installing a giant mirror at the rear of the stage so the audience could see the conductor's facial expressions rather than just his back. Masur responded, "When I conduct Beethoven, I wouldn't like to replace Beethoven. He should be in your mind, not me." Another asked about the tuning before concerts. Was this really necessary? It was, said Masur, but he was trying to dissuade the musicians from playing themes from the concert while warming up, so they would sound fresh in their proper context. There were complaints about the ticket prices, about program notes that were too technical, and even about audience decorum. Deborah Borda, the managing director, said nothing could be done about the ticket prices, and Masur said they were seeking a new approach for the program notes. They both admitted there was not much that could be done about decorum, but that they were trying to do something about excessive coughing, particularly since the concerts were being recorded for release by Teldec Records, and it cost $100,000 every time a recording session had to be held to remake sections that had been spoiled by coughing. When asked to compare the Gewandhaus Orchestra with the Philharmonic, Masur responded, "I will answer you honestly. I like them both."

December 7 was the two hundredth anniversary of the death of Mozart, a date on which many musical organizations performed the master's Requiem. The Philharmonic was no exception. Mozart did not live to complete the Requiem; at his death he left behind some completed sections and quite a few fragments. For many years the work has been performed in the version by the composer's pupil Franz Xaver Süssmayr, assembled at the request of Mozart's wife, Constanze, who had first asked Joseph Eybler to work on it. Under Erich Leinsdorf, the Philharmonic presented a version that was part Süssmayr, part Eybler, and part Richard Maunder, an English musicologist who had composed his own version in 1987. Yet what Rothstein, following along in the Süssmayr score, found remarkable was how little the different arrangers altered the work's character and dramatic effect. Joining the Philharmonic were Roberta Alexander, soprano; Florence Quivar, mezzo-soprano; John Aler, tenor; Paul Plishka, bass; and the New York Choral Artists. Also on the all-Mozart program were the *Masonic Funeral Music*, K. 477, and the last piano concerto, No. 27 in B-flat Major, K. 595, in which Alicia de Larrocha was the soloist. Rothstein felt that Leinsdorf "made the Requiem seem to be both an invocation of the Baroque and an anticipation of the Romantic oratorio." He concluded by speculating how critics, "weary of devout worship, vainly try to see how a man could write such music, why it sometimes fails, and why it so often seems beyond human judgment altogether."

The dependable Leonard Slatkin ended 1991 with a New Year's Eve gala and began 1992 with two weeks of subscription concerts. The former featured the pianists Emanuel Ax and Jeffrey Siegel in Saint-Saëns's grand zoological fantasy known as *Carnival of the Animals*. This work is today often performed accompanied by humorous verses by Ogden Nash, written many years after Saint-Saëns's death in 1921. However, for this occasion the Philharmonic invited the composer Peter

Schickele (alias P. D. Q. Bach) to devise and deliver some verses of his own. Whether or not the punning Schickele outdid the urbane Nash in displays of drollery is a matter of taste. Music by Johann Strauss and family made up the second half of the program.

Slatkin's first subscription week, beginning on January 3, included the premiere of a clarinet concerto by William Bolcom, whose music can be described as eclectic with a capital "E." It includes whatever style he deems appropriate for the moment—neoclassicism, jazz, Broadway, marching band, serious lyricism, and much more besides. In this respect, his scores are not unlike those of Charles Ives, though without the latter's simultaneity of idioms. Bolcom, a pupil of Darius Milhaud, writes extremely attractive and approachable music, and this concerto was no exception, especially with Stanley Drucker as the most persuasive soloist.

On a marked contrast, the program closed with the dynamic and gritty Fourth Symphony of Vaughan Williams. Once a staple on Philharmonic programs during the tenure of Mitropoulos, it was revived by Bernstein in 1965 but had not been heard since on the orchestra's programs. One of the great symphonies of the twentieth century, it deserves more frequent exposure, and Slatkin did it justice.

Another premiere was heard during Slatkin's second week: the first New York performance of the Symphony No. 1 by John Corigliano, the son of the Philharmonic's onetime long-term concertmaster. Premiered in 1990 by the Chicago Symphony under Daniel Barenboim, the score was written in response to the AIDS crisis and memorializes several of the composer's friends. Even if one does not know what the piece is about, it conveys an impression of the composer's anger, so violent is much of the work. Yet there are also sections that are extremely touching. Halfway through the first movement an offstage piano is heard playing the famous *Tango* by Isaac Albéniz, a favorite of one of Corigliano's departed friends, accompanied by sustained string lines. There is a dreamlike quality to the music at this point. Corigliano has said that his symphony was inspired by the AIDS quilt, sections of which were on display in the lobby of Avery Fisher Hall during the concert.

After six months of negotiations reaching back to the summer of 1991 and several deadline extensions, a new labor agreement was finally achieved between the Philharmonic's musicians and its management on January 20, 1992. Retroactive to September 21, 1991, the new contract was unusual in that it was for four years rather than the usual three. By the fourth year, base pay would have risen $280 a week to a total salary of $72,800, which would then be equal to that paid the members of the Chicago Symphony. However, the New York contract also called for a "New York differential," a cost-of-living adjustment, as well as a weekly bonus of $20, all of which would put the Philharmonic musicians ahead of their Chicago colleagues by 1993. A significant feature of the contract provided for the creation of an experimental Cooperative Committee composed of Kurt Masur, Deborah Borda, two other management representatives, and four members of the orchestra. This would be the first time the musicians ever had a say in planning and artistic matters, such as programming. The committee would operate for a trial period of eighteen months, after which either side, management or musical, could withdraw. The contract, which also addressed issues of health benefits and pensions, was described by the musicians' lawyer, I. Philip Sipser, as the best settlement he had seen in twenty-four years of representing symphony musicians. Borda said it was the kind of agreement that allowed both sides to claim victory.

On February 1 the death of William L. Weissel was reported. He had joined the Philharmonic as its assistant manager in 1962, after three years as manager of New York's Little Orchestra Society. A native of Vienna, he had earned a law degree there and worked as a lawyer for firms in Vienna, London, and Paris before coming to the United States in 1938. Weissel became executive secretary of the Philharmonic's board in 1970, a position he held until his retirement in 1977.

Oestreich wondered on February 9 at the Philharmonic audience's resistance, not to new music, which was expected, but to more or less traditional music that is slightly off the beaten path. This time, the work that sent subscribers fleeing up the aisles, not only between but within movements, was Elgar's eloquent and relatively conservative First Symphony. Andrew Davis was the conductorial victim of this retreat, and Oestreich placed much of the blame on the Philharmonic's program notes, which were negative rather than supportive of the work.

Yet another death was reported on February 16, that of the composer William Schuman at the age of eighty-one. President of the Juilliard School for many years and then the first president of Lincoln Center, this recipient of the first Pulitzer Prize for music had more works of his performed by the Philharmonic over the years than any American composer except Aaron Copland. His career was a combination of composing and administration, but he carefully kept a log of his composing time, which came to a minimum of six hundred hours a year. As a memorial tribute, Kurt Masur began the following week's Philharmonic programs with the poignant second movement, "When Jesus Wept," from Schuman's *New England Triptych*. (The three-movement work was inspired by music of William Billings, an American composer of the Revolutionary War period. "When Jesus Wept" is one of his many choral pieces.)

A review by Rothstein on March 1 compared the New York Philharmonic with the Vienna Philharmonic. The two orchestras had performed in New York on successive days, and each had offered something by Richard Strauss. For some time the New Yorkers had been playing occasional Friday concerts at 11:00 a.m. rather than at the traditional 2:30 time, and it was on such a Friday, February 28, that Masur conducted the composer's *Metamorphosen*, for twenty-three solo string instruments. The night before, the Viennese, with Lorin Maazel conducting, had played *Till Eulenspiegel's Merry Pranks*. Although Rothstein had found the Vienna performance "extremely entertaining," he thought our Philharmonic's "just as well executed." It is difficult to compare the two pieces; *Metamorphosen*, a lament for the collapse of Munich and German culture at the end of World War II, is hardly an entertaining work. Masur's program also featured Beethoven's "Eroica" Symphony, from which the theme of its funeral march is heard at the end of *Metamorphosen*. Rothstein found the "Eroica" in Masur's hands to be "not particularly heroic," but "full of good sense" nonetheless. In the same review, he also wrote approvingly of Masur's rendition of César Franck's Symphony in D Minor on the previous week's program and concluded that his "quiet, earthy sensitivity" might be just what the Philharmonic needed at that point.

Conductor cancellations continued, with Giuseppe Sinopoli the victim this time. In his stead on March 6, André Previn took over the originally scheduled program, which included Mahler's Fourth Symphony. Holland wrote that "it was beautifully tailored and full of grace and sweep," and that June Anderson, though slightly indisposed, sang the concluding soprano solo "with more than usual tenderness."

Two substantial articles in the *Times* of April 5 were devoted to the legacy of Leonard Bernstein—not only his compositions, but his recordings and videos. In one, Oestreich mentioned how the sales of a performer's recordings usually decrease after his death, and cited Vladimir Horowitz and Herbert von Karajan as examples. Just the opposite was true of Bernstein, however, according to representatives of the labels for which he recorded, Sony Classical and Deutsche Grammophon (DG). (Additionally, he had made some recordings for EMI and, in his early years, for RCA and American Decca.) Almost all of Bernstein's more than five hundred recordings were still in print at that time, and Sony was planning to issue what it called a Royal Edition of his CBS recordings, to encompass 119 compact discs. The appellation "Royal" related to the fact that watercolors by Prince Charles would grace the covers. DG was also planning its own series, which would include performances not yet released, such as a Mahler Ninth with the Berlin Philharmonic and a Bruckner Ninth with the Vienna Philharmonic, not to mention two pieces from his very last concert, with the Boston Symphony at Tanglewood: the Four Sea Interludes from Britten's *Peter Grimes* and Beethoven's Seventh Symphony.

Oestreich also mentioned that while Bernstein was alive, other conductors rarely played his music. Now that he was no longer with us, his colleagues were beginning to take up his cause, most notably Michael Tilson Thomas, who was soon to record the Broadway show *On the Town* for DG. He would also give the premiere of a newly created suite from Bernstein's opera, *A Quiet Place*. The music publisher Boosey and Hawkes was planning to issue a definitive edition of all of Bernstein's works.

The second *Times* article, by Joseph Horowitz, dealt with Bernstein's television programs—not only the Young People's Concerts, but the *Omnibus* series and the Philharmonic specials. These were beginning to be shown in Europe, but as yet no market had been found for televising them again in the United States. The headline for the article summed up the situation: "Is Bernstein Passé on Television? Only in America." The failure to find a place for them even on noncommercial television only served to emphasize the degree to which classical music had become marginalized in America. Sony Classical has since issued twenty-five of the fifty-three Young People's Concerts on DVD (so far only available as a boxed set), but they have yet to reappear on television. Allowing for some out-of-date topical references and the fact that many of them are in black and white, they still hold up extremely well and are as informative as ever.

His ill health having forced the cancellation of several Philharmonic engagements, it was encouraging to find Klaus Tennstedt returning to conduct one of his signature pieces, Bruckner's Eighth Symphony, on April 10. So massive is this work, however, requiring such intense concentration (and Tennstedt was normally an intense conductor to begin with), that the effort may have contributed to Tennstedt's canceling his second week. Kurt Masur himself filled in, keeping the original program: Sibelius's Violin Concerto and Brahms's First Symphony. The soloist in the Sibelius was the English violinist Nigel Kennedy, who subsequently billed himself simply as Kennedy, just as Jascha Heifetz billed himself as Heifetz in his late years. But Kennedy was only thirty-six years old at the time of his Philharmonic debut on April 17 and was already known for his rather eccentric persona and interpretations. Holland described the impression he made when he walked onstage: "With his coonskin-cap haircut, patched jacket, flowing scarf, running shoes and amazing parti-colored socks, Mr. Kennedy moved among the tail-coated members of the New York Philharmonic like a myna bird among penguins." What Masur thought of all this was not recorded, but he did respond to what can only be described as Kennedy's assault on the Sibelius Concerto with an accompaniment that was with the soloist every step of the way (the work is difficult enough to accompany even in a traditional performance). When all was said and done, Holland felt that Kennedy's "musical sins somehow end up being endearing." As for Masur and the Brahms First, the performance was "beautifully calculated, deeply felt, luxurious sounding in every respect. . . . Mr. Masur is making a difference."

The *Times* of April 29 reported the death of the great French composer Olivier Messiaen at the age of eighty-three. His music is some of the most singular of the twentieth century, with its densely packed chords, its massive climaxes, its moments of religious and sensual ecstasy, and its paeans to nature, including the incorporation of over 250 varieties of birdsong. The Philharmonic had performed his *Et exspecto resurrectionem mortuorum* several times, as well as his grand *Turangalîla Symphony*, and had recorded *L'ascension* under Stokowski.

Sir Georg Solti made one of his rare appearances with the Philharmonic on May 2, again for a pension-fund concert. The program was tailored to his strengths: the Prelude and *Liebestod* from Wagner's *Tristan und Isolde*, Liszt's symphonic poem *Les préludes*, and Berlioz's *Symphonie fantastique*. Known for his fiercely energetic conducting style, he did not disappoint on this occasion; Holland described the Wagner excerpts as "not so much performed as stalked, pounced upon and eaten alive." The rest of the program brought forth the comment that Solti had "turned Kurt Masur's shiny romantic instrument, the New York Philharmonic, into an assault weapon of devastating effectiveness." These comments were meant as compliments, for Holland concluded that one reason we like Solti's conducting so much "is that it makes us uneasy," as though we were confronting "a slightly maniacal and potentially devouring life force."

As part of the ongoing Mozart celebration, Masur presented the composer's last three symphonies, Nos. 39, 40, and 41, in the concerts beginning May 8. Having previously written so positively about Masur and his work with the Philharmonic, Rothstein was disappointed with this program, finding the performances perfunctory, with occasional wiry string tone, and generally underwhelming in effect. Mozart is a very difficult composer to perform, and on this occasion the notes were played, but the inner, darker Mozart was not revealed.

The subscription season closed with Masur conducting the concerts of May 21, 22, and 23 in performances of Benjamin Britten's *War Requiem*. Composed in 1962 for the consecration of the new Coventry Cathedral in England, the original having been destroyed by Nazi bombs in 1940, the work combines sections of the Latin Mass for the dead with antiwar poetry by Wilfred Owen, who lost his life in World War I. Large performing forces are called for: a full orchestra, a separate chamber orchestra (conducted by Samuel Wong on this occasion), a large chorus, a boys' choir, and three vocal soloists. Participating were the New York Choral Artists, the American Boychoir (singing from the top balcony), the soprano Yvonne Kenny, the tenor Jerry Hadley, and the baritone David Wilson-Johnson. Rothstein praised the performance but had little good to say about the piece itself, though many, Masur included, regard it as one of the great choral works of the twentieth century. For Rothstein, there was "a fallacy at the heart of this work," a cleverness that failed to get at the heart of its sentiment, its effects remaining no more than just effects. The performance was repeated on Memorial Day at the Cathedral of St. John the Divine.

On May 24 Rothstein summed up Masur's first season with the Philharmonic as "impressive," citing among its highlights a gracious and convincing performance of Tchaikovsky's Fifth Symphony; a Beethoven "Eroica" that, while not entirely heroic in tone, "made good sense"; the lovely *Peer Gynt*; and an "organic, fluid" version of Strauss's *Metamorphosen*. Many people thought of Masur as a solid, methodical workman, yet Rothstein felt that was exactly what the Philharmonic needed: someone to whip it into shape, bring vitality to its playing, and restore the traditions related to its great repertoire. Whether or not Masur's intrepid groundwork would eventually lead to greatness in interpretation remained to be seen.

CHAPTER 14

1992–93

150 Years

A tour of South America had to be delayed because one of the corporate sponsors withdrew, leaving the Philharmonic with some time to fill in New York. On relatively short notice four concerts were scheduled in Carnegie Hall, beginning July 8 and billed as a mini-festival of music by Tchaikovsky. This was just the thing to raise critical eyebrows. Tchaikovsky's music has never been highly regarded in upper intellectual circles, where the sun rises and sets on the late Beethoven quartets. But Masur's idea was to demonstrate that Tchaikovsky was no philosophical lightweight, nor was he wanting in musical flexibility.

Whether or not Masur's aim succeeded is open to question, for, with one exception, he chose from among the composer's most popular works: the Symphonies Nos. 2 (the exception), 4, and 6; the Piano Concerto No. 1 (with Shura Cherkassky); the Violin Concerto (with Midori); *Romeo and Juliet*; the *Capriccio italien*; and the Serenade for Strings. But Masur's care for balances, phrasing, and dynamics, coupled with his relatively straightforward readings, made everything sound fresh. The "Pathétique" Symphony, for one, with its disciplined playing, brought back memories of Artur Rodzinski's Philharmonic, and Masur proved himself a master accompanist to the eighty-year-old Cherkassky's rather capricious way with the Piano Concerto. Then, of course, there was Carnegie Hall itself, revealing the orchestra with greater impact, clarity, and warmth than could be achieved in its regular home. In the end, the critics were pleased with what they heard, as was the public.

The South American tour brought the orchestra once again to Brazil and Argentina, where, predictably, they were rapturously received. As always, the highlight in Argentina was playing in the historic Teatro Colón in Buenos Aires. The Colón is considered one of the great halls in the world, comparable to the best in Europe and the United States both acoustically and visually.

On August 3 Masur made his debut in the Parks Concerts before an audience estimated at seventy thousand on the great lawn of Central Park. His program did not pander to the crowd: it included three of Dvořák's *Slavonic Dances*, Ravel's *La valse*, and Beethoven's Seventh Symphony, with all the repeats, followed by the customary fireworks display.

Meanwhile, plans were announced for the coming renovation of Avery Fisher Hall, which would take place from August 23 to September 12. The changes would be to the stage, not to the hall itself, and would consist of large adjustable reflectors over the stage floor and smaller curved reflectors on each of the side walls. There would also be new stage lighting and individual risers for string players. Masur said that when the work was completed the double basses, which had been lined along the back wall, would return to their usual position behind the cellos. It was his contention that the improved stage acoustics would result in better ensemble playing, which would in turn give the impression of better sound in the hall.

On August 20 it was announced that Leonard Bernstein's personal music library would be given to the New York Philharmonic, to become part of the orchestra's archives. The collection included his marked orchestral scores, operas, piano music, and vocal works—more than three thousand scores in all. Among the items were a score of Debussy's *La mer* with alterations by Toscanini, a first edition of Beethoven's Ninth Symphony that had been given to Bernstein by the orchestra in 1962 to celebrate his five hundredth Philharmonic concert, and a score of Stravinsky's *Rite of Spring* given to Bernstein by his mentor Serge Koussevitzky, in which the work's complex rhythmic passages had been rebarred by Nicholas Slonimsky to make them easier to deal with. Many of Bernstein's scores were annotated with his own personal markings. The Bernstein collection would prove a treasure trove for scholars wishing to avail themselves of his working methods and interpretive ideas.

The big musical news in New York was the Philharmonic's 150th anniversary, to be celebrated throughout the 1992–93 season. The programs would include works of which the orchestra had given the world or American premieres, as well as the premieres of pieces commissioned for the occasion. The commissioning project would actually continue for ten years, with new works by thirty-five composers expected.

The season-opening gala, conducted by Masur on September 16 and televised by PBS in its *Live from Lincoln Center* series, offered two pieces with the same subject matter: excerpts from Prokofieff's ballet *Romeo and Juliet* in a sequence designed by Masur, and the Symphonic Dances from Bernstein's *West Side Story* (an update of Shakespeare's story). In between, the soprano Kathleen Battle sang songs by Bernstein and Richard Strauss. It was delightfully fascinating to hear and watch the jazzy *West Side Story* dances, which the Philharmonic has in its blood and bones, as conducted by the German-born Masur, to whom the idioms of the piece must have been a bit foreign. And yet, how he threw himself into it! It was reported he once dismissed the orchestra early from a rehearsal of the Bernstein, saying that this was their music and admitting that he had to go home and learn it better. Learn it he did, though not with the most idiomatic results, according to some critics.

As for the results of the acoustical changes, it was generally felt that it would take many more concerts before they could be judged properly. Rothstein felt that visually the stage, with its new clouds and baffles, was not aesthetically pleasing, and although the sound at times was less distant, at others it seemed nondirectional. Apparently Masur was not satisfied, for the old panels still stood at the rear of the stage.

The subscription season began the next night, on September 17, with a program that would have been fairly adventurous for a Philharmonic audience in 1842, opening with Schubert's Symphony No. 8 ("Unfinished") and closing with Beethoven's Fifth Symphony, which had begun the orchestra's very first concert. Between the two Masur programmed the little-known (in 1992) Symphony No. 1 in G Minor by the late eighteenth–early nineteenth-century French composer Étienne-Nicolas Méhul, a work that was quite popular in Beethoven's time. In fact, the two composers admired each other's music, and Méhul wrote his First Symphony in Paris at the same time that Beethoven was writing his Fifth in Vienna. It is doubtful that either composer knew of the other's work in progress; strikingly, however, Méhul's work includes themes that resemble Beethoven's, most significantly in the finale, which contains the same rhythmic figure as the "dit-dit-dit-dah" motto of Beethoven's first movement. Masur and the Philharmonic gave superlative performances of the entire program, and it is regrettable that they did not record the Méhul.

An article by Allan Kozinn in the *Times* of September 20 outlined the plans for the anniversary season and also described Masur's programming philosophy, which strove for connections between works and composers, as exemplified by the pairing of Beethoven and Méhul. Additionally, old and new scores would be juxtaposed in ways that would complement and illuminate both. Although Masur had the last word when it came to programming, he held regular meetings to exchange ideas with three members of the managerial staff: the managing director, Deborah Borda; the music administrator, Elizabeth Ostrow; and the general manager, Allison Vulgamore. Borda's remark that "Mr. Masur calls us his amazons" suggested that difficulties were on the horizon, although the article spoke of nothing but a spirit of cooperation.

Masur's reputation as a master conductor of Bruckner was strengthened on September 24 by a performance of the Ninth Symphony that Oestreich felt produced, at the end of the first movement, "the most thrilling sound this critic has heard from the Philharmonic in years." He found a soft timpani solo by Roland Kohloff "positively breathtaking" and concluded that Masur had provided "a wonderful outing that left parts of the score riveted in the listener's ear long after the performance."

A new member of the *Times*'s critical staff, Alex Ross, reviewed the concert of October 2. (Ross later became the music critic of the *New Yorker* and also wrote the highly acclaimed *The Rest Is Noise: Listening to the Twentieth Century*.) Masur conducted Mussorgsky's *Pictures at an Exhibition*, but with a difference. Instead of the usually heard orchestral transcription by Ravel, Masur offered his preferred version, that by the Russian composer and conductor Sergei Gorchakov, whose textures are darker and more string oriented than Ravel's. Said Ross, "These 'Pictures' glowed and glared; the orchestra played as if the ink were not yet dry on the page."

On October 5, at Borda's instigation, the Philharmonic began a new series designed to attract young professionals who might wish to sample a concert without devoting an entire evening to it. Called Rush Hour Concerts, they lasted about an hour, beginning at 6:45 p.m., with programs taken from the regular subscription concerts. The first such program contained Kodály's *Háry János* Suite and the aforementioned *Pictures at an Exhibition*. Masur introduced each piece with informal comments, and following the concert audience members attended a reception at which they mingled with the players and Masur. With a full house and reduced ticket prices, the concert was decidedly a success. Similar programs, called Casual Saturdays, would be offered beginning on November 28 at 2:00 p.m.

An all-Stravinsky program was heard on October 8, with Erich Leinsdorf conducting the *Song of the Nightingale*, the Symphony in Three Movements, and the *Firebird* Suite (in Leinsdorf's own arrangement). As he had often done in the past, Holland wrote approvingly of Leinsdorf's minimal gestures, which "invite us to listen rather than watch." He also wrote of the conductor's "moving from orchestra to orchestra reminding everybody within earshot how little they know about music."

Once again an engagement was canceled by Klaus Tennstedt, his ill health unfortunately continuing. This time Mahler's Sixth Symphony had been scheduled for the concert sequence beginning October 29, and it was to the credit of Zdeněk Macál, the replacement conductor, that the formidable work was retained. On October 31 Oestreich wrote admiringly of Tennstedt's 1990 performance of the score with the Philadelphia Orchestra and of Pierre Boulez's with the Philharmonic in 1972. In the face of such memories Macál may have been at a disadvantage; although his account had its impressive moments, it did not always allow certain key climactic moments to make their full impact, and faulty brass playing did not help. Such errors may have been the result of the common practice of holding a program's final rehearsal on the morning of the concert day. Asking any orchestra to play Mahler's Sixth twice in one day is unreasonable.

Zubin Mehta returned on November 5 to conduct the world premiere of a work commissioned by the Philharmonic for its 150th anniversary, Messiaen's *Éclairs sur l'au-delà…* (Illuminations on the Beyond…). Again the composer wove the representation of bird calls into the musical fabric, and the score could be considered a summation of his entire life's work. For Rothstein, however, it was more a collection of episodes, some of them very beautiful, than a unified whole; the sense of mystery that Messiaen was searching for was suggested, rather than evoked. Some of the blame fell on Mehta, whose somewhat imprecise performance was lacking in lyricism, the playing often having "a hard, glassy quality."

Another major new work was premiered on the concerts beginning December 3 when Kurt Masur led David Diamond's Symphony No. 11. A respected American composer, Diamond had a long history with the Philharmonic, which gave the world premieres of his First Symphony in 1940, his Fifth in 1966, and his Eighth in 1961, as well as the New York premiere of his Fourth in 1958. The Eleventh proved to be a large-scale, forty-five-minute work that would have been even longer had not Masur cut part of the finale, no doubt with the composer's approval. (Composers are often amenable to such truncations if the alternative is not having the work performed at all.) Alex Ross wrote glowingly of the symphony and its performance, concluding that it "should stand as a highlight of the current celebratory season."

And so the actual anniversary date arrived, December 7. As on the 125th anniversary in 1967, a special concert was given, this one televised nationally by PBS in the *Live from Lincoln Center* series. Pierre Boulez returned to conduct Debussy's *La mer*, Zubin Mehta led Strauss's *Till Eulenspiegel*, and Kurt Masur did the honors for Dvořák's "New World" Symphony, of which the Philharmonic had given the world premiere in 1893. As an added fillip to honor Leonard Bernstein, the orchestra played a conductorless Overture to *Candide*. After his performance Boulez was made an honorary member of the Philharmonic Society. Before the concert there were activities on the Lincoln Center Plaza: a free concert by the Juilliard Chorus, the New York Philharmonic Brass, the Lincoln Center Jazz Orchestra, and the New York City Opera Orchestra, and even an appearance by a performing elephant and a clown from the Big Apple Circus. Then came a gala buffet inside the hall, with post-concert champagne concluding the event. Rothstein felt that only Masur's performance merited the ten-minute ovation that followed his rendition of the "New World' Symphony, which had been one of the triumphs of his first season. For the rest, *Till Eulenspiegel* seemed more episodic than necessary, and *La mer* was rather perfunctory and lacking in forward motion.

A special concert on December 10 honored Isaac Stern not only for his great career, but for his long association with the Philharmonic. On this occasion he was joined by five of the orchestra's string players for a performance of Brahms's Sextet in G Major, after which, with the full Philharmonic, he played Bartók's early Violin Concerto No. 1, of which he had given the American premiere in 1961, and Dvořák's Romance in F Minor. He was then awarded honorary membership in the Philharmonic Society.

Another occasion of note was the tenth anniversary of the founding of the New York Philharmonic Ensembles, the chamber-music group in which most of the orchestra's members participate at one time or another. Their celebratory concert took place on December 13 at the Ninety-second Street Y on Lexington Avenue, and included the chamber versions of Wagner's *Siegfried Idyll*, Schoenberg's *Verklärte Nacht* (Transfigured Night), Copland's *Appalachian Spring*, and Strauss's *Till Eulenspiegel*, in an arrangement by Franz Hasenhorl entitled *Till Eulenspiegel einmal anders* (Till Eulenspiegel Once Again).

A step forward in the presentation of the Young People's Concerts was noted by Rothstein, who attended the program of December 12 with his "young colleagues." Preceding the regular concert was a Children's Promenade designed for younger listeners. Each of these promenades focused on a particular group of instruments, and in this case it was the percussion section, with Morris Lang and Daniel Druckman as the demonstrators. During this event the children had the opportunity to mingle with the players and to try out various instruments themselves. The actual concert featured two young performers who had been selected at auditions from among 130 applicants: the fourteen-year-old violinist Colin Jacobsen, who was an "impressively accomplished soloist" in Max Bruch's *Scottish Fantasy*, and the nine-year-old pianist Helen Huang, who played the first movement of Beethoven's Concerto No. 1 "with the energy, accuracy and taste of someone three times her age." As she matured into her teens, Huang went on to record several concertos with Masur and the Philharmonic.

The program ended with the premiere of a commissioned piece by Jon Deak of the Philharmonic's double bass section. Entitled *New York, 1842: A City on Fire*, it was one of the composer's dramatic works. It involved the participation of Masur in an amusing description of the state of culture in New York City in 1842, the year of the Philharmonic's birth, and a narration by Deak himself about the orchestra's early years, finishing with a tale about a heroic firefighter protecting a baby in his stovepipe hat.

The *Times* of December 22 reported the death of the great violinist Nathan Milstein at the age of eighty-eight. He had been an annual guest soloist with the

Philharmonic throughout the 1940s and '50s. His appearances were less frequent later on, but they were always welcomed. Harold Schonberg's lengthy obituary gave a quite detailed account of his long career. In it the Philharmonic's concertmaster, Glenn Dicterow, spoke of Milstein as "the complete violinist.... He set a standard that nobody today can touch." Also noted was the fact that, unlike many of his colleagues, Milstein maintained his technique and continued to perform almost to the end of his days.

No Coughing, Please

Another anniversary commission had its world premiere on December 30, 1992: the Trombone Concerto by Christopher Rouse, already well-known for such brief orchestral works as *The Infernal Machine* and *Bump*. The Philharmonic's principal trombonist, Joseph Alessi, was the masterful soloist in a work that was by turns lyrically introspective and furiously fortissimo. So loud were portions of the Scherzo movement that some of the string players were observed placing their fingers in their ears. Leonard Slatkin, ever faithful to American music, conducted. There is not exactly a plethora of trombone concertos, so Rouse's piece was a major addition to the repertoire.

One of the most significant of the later works of Shostakovich is his Symphony No. 13 ("Babi Yar"). Composed in 1962, the work commemorates the murder in 1941 of 33,000 Jews, as well as a lesser number of Russians and Ukrainians, at the hands of German occupation forces in a ravine called Babi Yar outside of Kiev. The symphony is a setting of five poems by Yevgeny Yevtushenko, the first of which, entitled *Babi Yar*, describes and laments the massacre. Because the poem is a scathing denunciation of Russian anti-Semitism, its inclusion caused great consternation in the Soviet Union, with no less a figure than Nikita Khrushchev exerting pressure to have the work withdrawn. Only after some cosmetic changes were made in the text was the symphony allowed to be performed. The score, with the original text, reached the West in January 1970, when Eugene Ormandy gave the American premiere with the Philadelphia Orchestra, the Mendelssohn Club of Philadelphia, and Tom Krause, baritone.

Masur has always been sympathetic to the music of Shostakovich. He conducted the German premiere of "Babi Yar" in Leipzig in 1974 and now programmed it on January 14, 1993, in its first performance by the New York Philharmonic. Sergei Leiferkus was the baritone soloist, along with the men of the New York Choral Artists. Immediately before the performance Yevtushenko himself read three of his poems, including *Babi Yar* in Russian; the other two were given in English.

Opening the program was a work by the Chinese-born composer Bright Sheng, entitled *H'un* (Lacerations), a searing piece dealing with China's Cultural Revolution, which the composer had lived through—he was eleven years old when it began. Juxtaposing the Sheng and Shostakovich works, along with Yevtushenko's readings, made for a somewhat grim evening, though both end with the hope that better times will arrive soon. The other poems set by Shostakovich deal with different aspects of Soviet life, less dire than *Babi Yar*. The two works together, and their performances, made up one of the great concerts of Masur's tenure.

Aside from the Philharmonic, a significant aspect of Masur's time in New York was his involvement with the city's three major music conservatories: the Juilliard School, the Manhattan School of Music, and Mannes College (now Mannes College The New School for Music). At each he gave master classes for student conductors and, in a yearly rotation, conducted a concert with the school's orchestra. On January 28 Masur led the Mannes Orchestra in a free concert at Riverside Church, a tribute to the Reverend Martin Luther King Jr. At first glance one might not associate Masur with the music of Duke Ellington, but he is, in fact, an admirer of the composer's jazz and symphonic works, as he is of Gershwin's. For this program he conducted Ellington's *Les Trois Rois Noirs* (The Three Black Kings), the three movements of which describe the kings of the Magi, King Solomon, and Martin Luther King Jr. As Allan Kozinn wrote on January 20, "One did not have the sense that Mr. Masur was out of his element, even in the full-tilt jazz writing in the finale." Also programmed for the occasion were Bach's Suite No. 3 and Mendelssohn's "Reformation" Symphony.

Erich Leinsdorf, who had been such a reliable guest conductor for over twenty years, both in his own scheduled concerts and as a substitute for others, was forced to cancel his engagement for the week beginning February 4 because of a back injury. It was just one day before the first performance when Leinsdorf notified the Philharmonic that he would be unable to appear. The young American Richard Westerfield, who had been the cover (that is, understudy) conductor for Leinsdorf's rehearsals and concerts, took over the Wednesday morning rehearsal as a matter of course, with no idea that he would actually conduct the concert. However, after the rehearsal the principal players met with the management, and the decision was made that Westerfield would indeed be given his opportunity.

Westerfield inherited a rather daunting program: Weber's seldom-given Overture to *Preziosa*, Britten's Nocturne for Tenor and Orchestra (with John Aler as the soloist) and Richard Strauss's autobiographical tone poem, *Ein Heldenleben*. He was rewarded with Holland's review of his "splendid debut," in which he described how the young conductor "seemed to enjoy the confidence of the Philharmonic players."

A related article in the *Times* on February 9 revealed that although Westerfield's passion had always been music, the thirty-five-year-old had a day job as a banker with J. P. Morgan.

Kurt Masur returned to the Philharmonic on February 18 to conduct a great work with which he had become closely associated since performing it for the first time only in 1985, Bach's *Passion According to St. Matthew*. In earlier years, when Bruno Walter presented it annually with the Philharmonic, the work was given in two sections, with a substantial interval for dinner in between. In 1962 Bernstein made several cuts in order to accommodate a normal concert time. Masur presented a complete performance, starting early and ending more than three hours later. Rothstein wrote on February 20 of a performance "that spoke of a deep love for this music and its powers." The soloists were the baritone Andreas Schmidt in the role of Jesus, the tenor Peter Schreier as the Evangelist, the soprano Edith Wiens, the mezzo-soprano Carolyn Watkinson, and the bass Alastair Miles, along with Joseph Flummerfelt's Westminster Symphonic Choir, the American Boychoir, and boys from Trinity Church in Princeton, New Jersey. Bernstein and Walter had performed the work in English, while Masur offered it in German (the original language, of course; "but," Ralph Vaughan Williams is reputed to have said when asked why he presented it in English, "the Bible is in English," implying that the work should be given in the language of the audience).

It was Masur's turn to cancel a concert series when a case of the flu forced him to withdraw from the concerts beginning February 25. Replacing him was the Indonesian-born Chinese conductor Jahja Ling, who was then on the staff of the Cleveland Orchestra with the title of resident conductor. It fell to Ling to conduct the world premiere of the Third Symphony of Ellen Taafe Zwilich, who in 1983 was the first woman to win the Pulitzer Prize in music for her First Symphony. (The first person to win that prize was William Schuman in 1943 for his secular cantata *A Free Song*. Zwilich, who was often asked how it felt to be the first woman to win the prize, once asked Schuman how it felt to be the first man to win it.) Zwilich is one of the most successful of contemporary American composers, writing in a style that, while it may possess echoes of Bartók, Prokofieff, and Shostakovich, is definitely her own. The Third Symphony was even judged by Holland to be a "big post-Mahlerian statement." The remainder of Masur's substantial program, which Ling retained, included the Piano Concerto No. 2 by Saint-Saëns, in which the French pianist Cécile Ousset made her Philharmonic debut, and Schubert's Ninth Symphony ("Great C Major"). Holland opined that Ling had "a good effect on the Philharmonic and should be asked back."

The subscription week beginning March 4 was the first designated Composer Week, in which a composer would conduct his own works and those of others as well. In this instance the Englishman Oliver Knussen was the honoree. He was already known to New York audiences as the composer-in-residence for the Chamber Music Society of Lincoln Center. In 1968, at the age of sixteen, he had conducted the American premiere of his Symphony No. 1 with the London Symphony Orchestra in Carnegie Hall. For the Philharmonic program he was scheduled to conduct his Fourth Symphony, but he is a notoriously slow worker (perhaps his conducting duties interfere), and the piece was not ready in time. Another, slighter work was then to be substituted, but this was not ready either. In the end Knussen, one of the most inventive of contemporary composers, offered his three-minute *Flourish with Fireworks* and more substantial *Whitman Settings* for soprano and orchestra, in its American premiere, with Lucy Shelton as the soloist. Although the first piece had some echoes of Stravinsky's equally brief *Fireworks*, Rothstein felt that in the second "the composer's voice was precise, elegiac and exuberant." Knussen also conducted Ferruccio Busoni's *Berceuse elegiaque* and excerpts from Stravinsky's *The Fairy's Kiss*.

Most orchestras, when they tour, do so before the beginning or after the end of their regular season, so it was unusual for the Philharmonic to travel to Europe in the midst of its New York season, leaving a gap in the schedule for its New York audience. (Such mid-season absences have lately become more common.) The tour began in Frankfurt on March 25 and continued on to Berlin, Paris, Vienna, Madrid, Brussels, Leipzig, Warsaw, Budapest, and London. Both the Philharmonic and Kurt Masur, as conductor of Leipzig's Gewandhaus Orchestra, had performed in all those cities before, but not together. So it was a special occasion for him to appear in Leipzig with his "other orchestra" on April 7, when the Philharmonic played its twelve thousandth concert. As usual, the orchestra was almost unanimously well received by audiences and the press, and the German and Austrian critics in particular felt that Masur had transcended his onetime reputation. There was "no trace of the Kapellmeister," said the critic of the *Vienna Kurrier*, while the reviewer for the *Berlin Tagesspiegel* felt his interpretations were comparable to those of Bruno Walter.

On April 9 was reported the death of the great contralto Marian Anderson at the age of ninety-six. Although not a frequent soloist with the Philharmonic (she sang with them in 1946 under Artur Rodzinski and in 1956 with Pierre Monteux at the Lewisohn Stadium), her significance in American musical history is unquestionable, from her historic 1939 concert at the Lincoln Memorial before an audience of 75,000 to her equally memorable 1955 debut as the first African American singer to perform at the Metropolitan Opera.

Occasionally symphony orchestra conductors like to present concert or, sometimes, semistaged versions of operas. This is an especially valuable endeavor if the opera in question is a rarity in the opera house. Another attraction is a brilliant orchestral score. Richard Strauss's *Elektra*, for example, has often been given in concert. The Philharmonic returned to the concert opera lists on May 13 when Sir Colin Davis offered Weber's *Der Freischütz*. This work has often been celebrated as the foundation of German romantic opera and the forerunner of the great music dramas of Wagner. Yet for all that, it is rarely encountered on the stage. True, both the Metropolitan Opera and the New York City Opera have mounted productions of it at one time or another. But the failure of the stage directors to take the work seriously, especially its supernatural elements, resulted in resounding flops.

It was Davis's intention, therefore, to demonstrate what a truly great score *Der Freischütz* is. In this aim he largely succeeded, with the collaboration of Sharon Sweet as Agathe, Thomas Moser as Max, Ekkehard Wlaschiha as Kaspar, and Barbara Kilduff as Ännchen, with the other roles taken by Nathaniel Watson and John Connell and all backed up by the New York Choral Artists. Because *Der Freischütz* is technically a singspiel (that is, an opera with spoken dialogue), a narration was devised by Amanda Holden and delivered by Werner Klemperer. In spite of Davis's fervent belief in the score, Rothstein found the work dramatically hopeless, "partly a soap opera of its era, using elements that were already pop clichés."

In an article entitled "Speak Loudly, Carry No Stick" in the May 23 *Times*, Oestreich wrote of how the Philharmonic's collective blood pressure shot up on the return of Masur for his final weeks of the season. The gist of the article was that an orchestra is always under a bit more tension when the music director is present, and that was especially true with the Philharmonic because of what was described as Masur's "volatile temperament." Mention was made of the fact that when he was hired, he promised the players involved in the search that he would be tough. And tough he turned out to be indeed, to a degree unimaginable from his previous engagements as a guest conductor.

The fact is that Masur was (and is) an uncompromising taskmaster to a degree not experienced by the Philharmonic since the many appearances of George Szell. Oestreich wrote that after two seasons of Masur "there is still talk of a honeymoon. There is also talk of a reign of terror." Whatever Masur's methods, they got results that the musicians were proud of and that the public and the critics recognized. Although some conductors tend to end rehearsals early, Masur was just the opposite. The violinist Newton Mansfield was quoted as saying that none of his colleagues complained about rehearsals as they had in the past, even though Masur would work "up to the last second." With another conductor there would be complaints about such doggedness, but not with Masur, "simply because people feel they are producing."

For the concerts beginning May 20 Masur conducted Beethoven's Ninth Symphony with the participation of the soprano Benita Valente, the mezzo-soprano Janis Taylor, the tenor Richard Leech, the baritone Robert Holl, and the hardworking New York Choral Artists. Holland wrote of how Masur's interpretations in general do not plumb metaphysical depths or evoke mystery. Rather, they are "expressions of honest hard work," resulting in this case in an exemplary performance.

What to program before the Beethoven Ninth has often been a vexing problem for conductors. (Lately some have avoided the problem entirely by presenting the Ninth all by itself, even though it is only about sixty-five minutes long.) Masur's choice was to open the program with *The Unanswered Question* by Charles Ives, which is, in fact, a metaphysical piece that ponders the very question of existence. The pianissimo piece had to contend with so much coughing and fidgeting from the audience that Holland wrote, "Perhaps [Masur's] next artistic task is to persuade his subscribers to sit still and listen."

Holland's words were prophetic, for at the Tuesday evening performance, the orchestra had played about a minute of the Ives piece when Masur signaled them to stop. He then turned to the audience and spoke: "We are all never coughing onstage, and do you know why? Because we concentrate so much to perform, we don't feel like coughing. Just concentrating makes us healthy, so if you are listening with the same concentration to our music making, you would enjoy it and will forget to cough." The six-minute piece was begun again, against a background of total silence.

Later he said the coughing had been so strong that he could not hear the strings' pianissimo. But he also had some kind words for New York concertgoers: "I have just praise for them. They are interested in whatever work we play, even if we take risks. Compared with every great city, New York is one of the best. But it is also one of the best coughing audiences."

CHAPTER 15

1993–95

REMEMBERING LENNY

A proclamation by Mayor David N. Dinkins honored Leonard Bernstein and the New York Philharmonic, as the orchestra devoted a week to concerts and other events under the title Remembering Lenny. The celebration featured symposia, films, exhibits, and other memorabilia, but its centerpiece was the series of concerts on June 16, 18, and 19, in which another Leonard (but not a Lenny), Leonard Slatkin, led the Philharmonic in an all-Bernstein program in Avery Fisher Hall. Programmed were the jazzy ballet score *Fancy Free*; "A Simple Song" from *Mass*, sung by Vernon Hartman; *Opening Prayer*, which Bernstein had written for Carnegie Hall's centennial concert; Prelude, Fugue and Riffs for Clarinet and Jazz Ensemble, with Stanley Drucker as the irrepressible soloist; and the Symphony No. 2 ("The Age of Anxiety"), in which the solo pianist was Philippe Entremont, who had recorded the score with Bernstein in 1965. Rothstein concluded that Bernstein had "found his freedom" in shows such as *West Side Story*, and that it was in his conducting and teaching that he would be remembered most.

On July 6 it was announced that Allison Vulgamore, the Philharmonic's general manager, would be leaving the Philharmonic to become executive director of the Atlanta Symphony Orchestra. She had been in charge of coordinating the Philharmonic's tours and overseeing the personnel, education, and artistic administration departments.

Having given a successful Tchaikovsky festival in Carnegie Hall the year before, the Philharmonic returned to its former home for a series devoted to Brahms and Schumann. For the opening program on July 14 Masur conducted one of the most basic and well-known of symphonies, the Brahms First, in a performance of such power and eloquence as to make one appreciate why it is so well-known while marveling anew at the greatness of Brahms and his creation. This was no mere Kapellmeister on the podium, but a truly probing musician. Schumann was represented by his Overture to *Genoveva*, in a performance that made one wonder why it is not better known, and his Piano Concerto, of which Richard Goode gave a scintillating performance.

On July 21 Garrick Ohlsson was the commanding soloist in the Brahms Piano Concerto No. 2, which Masur followed with Schumann's Symphony No. 1 ("Spring"). The July 28 program included the Brahms Violin Concerto, played by Shlomo Mintz, and Schumann's Fourth Symphony, which Masur led propulsively. A joyous Brahms *Academic Festival Overture* opened the program; a sprightly Hungarian Dance No. 1 was a concluding encore. Throughout the three weeks, the Philharmonic continued to demonstrate its growth under Masur's fastidious direction.

As part of the Philharmonic's and New York City's Remembering Lenny celebration, a special ceremony was held on August 28 at the corner of Broadway and Sixty-fifth Street. Mayor Dinkins, various Lincoln Center officials, musicians, members of Bernstein's family, and many of his friends were present. After some appropriate speeches, Bernstein's three children, Alexander, Nina, and Jamie, unveiled a street sign that renamed the area of West Sixty-fifth Street between Broadway and Amsterdam Avenue "Leonard Bernstein Place."

September 12, 1993, brought news of the death of Erich Leinsdorf the previous day, at the age of eighty-one. Since first appearing with the Philharmonic in 1973, he had been an annual visitor for several weeks each season, both in New York and on tour. His programs were often uncommonly interesting in that they included seldom-performed works that proved well worth hearing. Holland, in his *Times* obituary, referred to him as "a conscience for two generations of conductors." He concluded that Leinsdorf "brought to music a kind of rectitude that at its best provided an antidote for orchestra musicians and listeners used to flamboyant and often empty conductorial salesmanship." A memorial tribute to Leinsdorf was given later, on October 14, at the Society for Ethical Culture—a program of chamber music played by the pianist Emanuel Ax, the Boston Symphony Chamber Players (Leinsdorf had been music director of the Boston Symphony from 1962 to 1969), and members of the Philharmonic.

A gala pension-fund benefit concert again opened the orchestra's season, this one on September 22 juxtaposing music by Beethoven and Shostakovich, a pairing Masur intended to explore further in this and later seasons. Beethoven was represented by his Overture to *Fidelio* and his Violin Concerto (in which Itzhak Perlman was the soloist), Shostakovich by his First Symphony. The concert was televised nationally by PBS in its *Live from Lincoln Center* series. Although Rothstein found the Beethoven performances unexceptional, he was full of praise for the Shostakovich, a "vigorous performance" that was played "with commitment and refinement."

The New York Philharmonic has a history of presenting young artists in the formative years of their careers—think of Yehudi Menuhin's debut at the age of eleven in 1927 (with the New York Symphony before it merged with the Philharmonic),

André Watts's at sixteen in 1962, Anne-Sophie Mutter's at sixteen in 1980, and Midori's at ten in 1982. To these names can be added that of Sarah Chang, who on October 7, at the age of twelve, performed the Tchaikovsky Violin Concerto with Masur conducting. On October 12 Oestreich wrote of her "stunningly secure" technique, which produced "a satisfying, often stirring account of the concerto." Like the other prodigies mentioned, she has gone on to have a major career.

On the evening of October 22 Kurt Masur stepped onto the podium at Avery Fisher Hall to conduct not the New York Philharmonic, but the Leipzig Gewandhaus Orchestra, which was beginning an American tour. Naturally the audience was curious to hear how this ensemble would compare with the Philharmonic, especially given that Masur had conducted both orchestras. In a program of Mendelssohn and Beethoven, culminating with the "Eroica" Symphony, the Gewandhaus was certainly impressive, with the lower strings especially emphasized, acting in effect as a cushion for the upper strings and woodwinds. It did not impress listeners as a particularly brilliant orchestra, but rather as a community of musicians with a long history and tradition behind it (the orchestra was 250 years old). As with so many European orchestras, most of its members had studied with former members, who had studied with their forebears, creating and nurturing the tradition. Masur's interpretation of the "Eroica" was, according to Rothstein, "taut, confident...excitingly human rather than coldly monumental." The critics felt that the sonority of the Gewandhaus Orchestra was something Masur was striving to achieve with the more aggressive New York Philharmonic, even as the former was in danger of being compromised by the diminution of funds allotted to it after the collapse of the East German government. If the two organizations could meet sonically at some halfway point, there would be much to applaud in both cities.

There are some composers whose music does not travel well, or at all, beyond its national boundaries. The music of Arnold Bax, for example, seems destined to remain confined to England, that of Gabriel Pierné to France. Another such composer is the Austrian Franz Schmidt, whose works are performed quite frequently in Vienna and rarely elsewhere. When pieces by these composers are played in other countries, it is usually because a native conductor presents them. So it was when Schmidt's Fourth Symphony was given by the Philharmonic on November 24 with Franz Welser-Möst on the podium. Composed in 1933, the work harks back to the turn of the century, with no indication that such upstarts as Schoenberg, Berg, and Webern, to mention only Viennese composers, had already made their mark on the world of music. Welser-Möst led the symphony with commitment, and Holland noted that the Philharmonic "seemed happy to be playing for him."

On December 7 it was reported that two of the Philharmonic's violinists, Richard and Fiona Simon, appeared in the federal tax court in lower Manhattan's Foley Square not to perform a concert (though they did play the finale of Bach's Double Concerto for the judge), but because the Internal Revenue Service had challenged their 1989 federal tax return. On it, the couple had listed a depreciation of 21 percent of the value of two Tourte bows. (Tourte is to bows what Stradivari is to violins.) The IRS contended that such bows appreciate in value and should therefore be considered art objects, while the Simons countered that, as tools of their trade, they were subject to wear and tear. At stake was the $3,000 the IRS wished to collect, though each side said the principle was more important than the money. Judge David Laro promised to render his decision in three months.

To conclude the year's subscription series, Kurt Masur and the Philharmonic offered, on December 15 and subsequent evenings, a program entitled "Brecht, Weill and Berlin, 1929–1935." The principal work was Kurt Weill's 1933 ballet score *The Seven Deadly Sins*, subtitled *A Sung Ballet*. The text, by Bertolt Brecht, was sung by Angelina Réaux and the vocal quartet known as Hudson Shad. Opening the program were Alban Berg's Symphonic Pieces from *Lulu*, in which Réaux was heard in "Lulu's Song." Rothstein was at pains to point out that the Berg work had little or nothing to do with Weill or Brecht, and that Weill, having left Berlin to escape the Nazis, wrote his piece in Paris. But Masur led a "compelling" performance of the Weill, and Réaux, a Weill specialist, "was likable: vocally lithe and absorbing to listen to." The two works were recorded and make up one of the most intriguing and significant CDs of the Philharmonic/Teldec partnership.

The policy of giving solo opportunities to members of the orchestra, one especially fostered during Mehta's tenure, continued into Masur's. A beneficiary of this policy was Cynthia Phelps, the principal violist since 1992 (Paul Neubauer had left to join the Chamber Music Society of Lincoln Center). On January 12, 1994, with Charles Dutoit conducting, she was heard in a performance of Berlioz's symphony *Harold in Italy*. Not quite a concerto for viola, that instrument has a featured solo role known as an *obbligato* part. Although a few composers have written actual viola concertos (Walton, Bartók, Piston), Berlioz's great Byron-inspired symphony remains the supreme solo vehicle for that instrument. Phelps was rewarded with a fine review from Oestreich, who noted that she even upstaged the evening's official guest soloist, the French pianist Jean-Philippe Collard. Dutoit was also praised for his idiomatic interpretation.

An honor came the Philharmonic's way on January 21 when it was named Orchestra of the Year at the Classical Music Awards ceremony in London's Royal Albert Hall. It was the second year of these awards, which had been started by the rock musician Bob Geldof and the television producer Ultan Guilfoyle. A few days later, on January 25, it was announced that Beverly Sills had been unanimously elected chairwoman of Lincoln Center, an unsalaried but highly influential post, especially now that it was occupied by the charming and persuasive Sills. Fundraising is a major part of the job, and there was no one better at it than she.

Like the viola, the English horn does not have myriad concertos to exploit its agility and expressive qualities (though there are, of course, many prominent solo passages in symphonic works). In the twentieth century Stanisław Skrowaczewski and Vincent Persichetti have contributed major works for the instrument, both written for and premiered by Thomas Stacy, the Philharmonic's principal player (who was in the same post in Minneapolis when he played Skrowaczewski's concerto). On January 27, with Masur conducting, Stacy played brilliantly in the premiere of a new concerto by Ned Rorem, an attractive example of the composer's melodic and quasi-impressionistic style.

Masur continued his juxtaposition of works by Beethoven and Shostakovich, programming on February 5 the former's *Wellington's Victory* and the latter's formidable Seventh Symphony ("Leningrad"). Both of them are, in one way or another, battle pieces (in fact, Beethoven's is also known as the "Battle" Symphony), though Beethoven's score is famously, though enjoyably, from the composer's bottom drawer (in the so-bad-it's-good category). The Shostakovich Seventh, however, is one of the composer's major statements, though a controversial one, its first movement notorious for its seemingly endless repetitions of an inane tune over an insistent snare drum rhythm, à la Ravel's *Bolero*, meant to depict the Nazi invasion of Russia. Yet it is a fine work containing much beautiful music. Masur and the Philharmonic performed it most convincingly, as their Teldec recording attests.

The *Times* of February 9 reported the death of the Polish composer Witold Lutosławski at the age of eighty-one. His most-performed work is probably his *Concerto for Orchestra* from 1954. But his style advanced over the years, and he came to include improvisatory sections in many of his works. In that respect his First and Second Symphonies could have been written by two different composers. He became one of the most frequently played composers of his time, one of the few to have a New York Philharmonic program devoted entirely to his music (in 1982 with Mehta and the composer conducting).

Another world premiere took place on February 10 when Masur presented Alfred Schnittke's Seventh Symphony, which the composer had dedicated to him. The Soviet-born Schnittke was considered by many the natural successor to Shostakovich, at least from the standpoint of the prominence he attained. His music can be enigmatic, quirky, and unpredictable in terms of style, sometimes descending to a pastiche of the neoclassical, even neobaroque styles. The Seventh Symphony was described by Rothstein as "frail, relatively brief, [and] somewhat uneven," but with "an often elegiac lyricism." Surprisingly for a modern work, it and the composer, who was present, received a standing ovation from an audience normally hostile or indifferent to such music.

As has been mentioned, Masur prefers Sergei Gorchakov's orchestral transcription of Mussorgsky's *Pictures at an Exhibition* to Ravel's more familiar version, presumably for its more darkly Russian sonorities. But the Russian conductor Valery Gergiev, in his February 17 Philharmonic program, opted for the Ravel, in which his attention to detail and orchestral color, not to mention his innate feeling for the score, moved Rothstein to proclaim the performance "one of the finest of this war horse" he had ever heard.

On February 27 came news of the death of Avery Fisher at the age of eighty-seven. The *Times* obituary, by Allan Kozinn, featured a quote from 1973: "I like to be thought of as a musician who incidentally manufactured high-quality high-fidelity equipment for music lovers." He was also a musician who guaranteed that New Yorkers would continue to enjoy a spacious and comfortable environment in which to hear music.

Masur's involvement with New York's musical life away from the Philharmonic continued when, on the afternoon of March 15, he led a rehearsal at Avery Fisher Hall not of the orchestra of one of the city's conservatories, but of a string orchestra made up of students from the Third Street Music School Settlement, which offers after-school or Saturday lessons and rehearsals for children and financial aid for those who cannot afford lessons. As part of the school's centennial celebration, Masur had been invited to conduct a rehearsal of Grieg's *Holberg Suite*. One student said he never thought he would be conducted by the Philharmonic's music director: "I was sweaty the whole time." At one point in the rehearsal, Masur advised the young students, "Be in heaven. Close your eyes, play as beautifully as you can and don't watch the conductor" (probably not a suggestion he would have made to the Philharmonic).

"The Immortal Beloved" was the theme of the Philharmonic's program of March 23. The title was a reference to the unidentified married woman Beethoven loved (eventually identified as Antonie Brentano). Schoenberg's *Verklärte Nacht*, Berg's Violin Concerto (with the Russian-born Viktoria Mullova as the soloist), and Beethoven's Eighth Symphony made up the program. Idealized love was meant to characterize the program. The Schoenberg deals with a woman's telling her lover that the child within her is not his, the lover's acceptance of the fact, and the intensification of their love for each other. Berg's great concerto, dedicated "To the Memory of an Angel," is a memorial for the young daughter of Walter and Alma Mahler Gropius, and includes carefully hidden musical references to Berg's wife as well as his mistress. Beethoven's Eighth was composed at the same time Beethoven wrote the famous letter to his "Immortal Beloved" that ended their relationship. Tenuous though the connections linking the three pieces were, they made for an engrossing program.

On March 27 an announcement was made of the establishment of the Bruno Walter Gallery in Avery Fisher Hall. Located on the orchestra-level promenade, the space would serve as a display area for material normally found in the Philharmonic archives. The initial exhibit was, appropriately, devoted to Bruno Walter, who had played an important role in the orchestra's life for many years, including as musical adviser from 1947 to 1949. It was, therefore, fitting that Masur's performances of Mahler's Ninth Symphony, beginning on March 30, were dedicated to Walter, who had led the work's premiere in 1912 as well as its first recording in 1938. Masur performed Bruckner more often than he did Mahler, at least with the Philharmonic, but like Walter's, his Mahler renditions did not emphasize the supposedly neurotic aspects of the composer's personality, but rather presented the music plainly and simply, with great warmth.

Masur had always displayed a special affinity for large choral works, a connection he demonstrated with the performances beginning on April 6 of Arthur Honegger's masterful oratorio *Jeanne d'Arc au bûcher* (Joan of Arc at the Stake). Charles Munch had conducted the American premiere of this work with the Philharmonic on New Year's Day of 1948, and Bernstein had repeated it ten years later. Seiji Ozawa led it in the Philharmonic's summer Festival of French Music in 1965. It is not an easy work to present, calling for a large orchestra and chorus, children's chorus, and many soloists, plus several speaking roles, the most prominent of which are Joan and her confidant, Brother Dominic. These roles were taken by the Swiss actress Marthe Keller and the English baritone David Wilson-Johnson. The singers included Heidi Grant Murphy, D'Anna Fortunato, Wendy Hoffman, John Aler, and Nathaniel Watson, along with the Westminster Symphonic Choir and the American Boychoir. The work was performed in French, and Oestreich praised Masur's "stirring success" with this fascinating score.

The Latvian-born conductor Mariss Jansons made his Philharmonic debut on April 27, evoking much praise from Holland on May 2 for his performance of the Sibelius Second Symphony, in which "the brass playing was exquisitely tuned and organized" and the "mighty string themes soared." The same program included "some astonishing piano playing by Yefim Bronfman" in Rachmaninoff's Third Concerto. The following week, on May 4, André Previn conducted such a splendid performance of Elgar's *Enigma Variations* that Holland wrote, "In his self-effacing way, Mr. Previn is one of the best musicians now among us. Music is fortunate to have him."

These days an all-Beethoven program is not news, particularly one that includes the *Leonore* Overture No. 3 and the Fifth Symphony, but on May 11 Kurt Masur showed how such a program can still be satisfying and meaningful when it is given forthrightly, with integrity and dignity. At least, Holland thought so in his review of May 14, with kind words also for Emanuel Ax's playing of the First Piano Concerto. He thought the Philharmonic was now purveying the Central European "qualities of a Leipzig or a Dresden orchestra but with twice the technique."

The May 26 *Times* carried the announcement that Catherine Cahill would become the Philharmonic's general manager, effective July 1. Since 1991 she had been both general director and artistic director of Chicago's Grant Park Music Festival, after having held positions with the American Symphony Orchestra League, the Marlboro Music Festival, the Dallas Symphony Orchestra, and the Santa Fe Chamber Music Festival.

"American Eccentrics" was the title of the program beginning on May 26, with Masur conducting music by Ives, Carl Ruggles, Wallingford Riegger, and Henry Brant. Ives was represented by his most celebrated piece, *Three Places in New England*, which is in turn probably best known for its central movement, "Putnam's Camp, Redding, Connecticut." In it many popular and patriotic songs of the day, such as "Yankee Doodle," "The British Grenadiers," and others, are played simultaneously, resulting in a positive jumble of sounds. Yet the individual tunes are easily recognizable if one can pick them out. Ives also uses the sound of two marching bands heard together, but in slightly different tempos.

The Riegger piece was his *Study in Sonority*, for an orchestra of violins (ten of them or any multiple thereof—Masur stuck with ten), while the craggy *Sun Treader* was Ruggles's contribution, a great work, comparable to the big scores of Edgard Varèse, that deserves more frequent hearings (as do those of Varèse, for that matter). The only living member of this eccentric quadrumvirate was Henry Brant, then eighty-one, who was at the piano for his *Desert Forests*, wearing full concert dress and a visor of the type usually worn by poker dealers. Like most of his music, the piece abounds in spatial effects, with musicians onstage, in the balconies, in fact all over the place. Although Masur could not be said to be in his element with this program, he led it with his customary authority. He deserves great credit for his successful cracking of four very tough nuts.

In the *Times* of June 30 it was noted that, in spite of the efforts of Masur as music director and Borda as executive director, the Philharmonic was still operating at a deficit, which was expected to surpass the $1 million mark the following season. Although all orchestras were having budgetary problems, the Philharmonic's sum total of deficits for the past six years, $7.6 million, was expected to surpass the deficits the orchestras of Boston, Chicago, Cleveland, and Philadelphia had run for the previous ten years. But the Philharmonic's chairman, Stephen Stamas, was not worried about the deficits, which he said were "really investments, because we wanted Kurt Masur and the orchestra to start out in the best possible way."

No Summer Festival

One of the most frequent piano soloists with the Philharmonic had been the Czech-born Rudolf Firkušny, known for his elegant playing and courtly manner. It was therefore with much sadness that the news of his death, at the age of eighty-two, was received on July 20, 1994. Known for his performances of Mozart and Beethoven concertos, he also championed those of his compatriot Bohuslav Martinů and in his time was virtually the sole interpreter of the seldom-heard Dvořák Piano Concerto, with which he had made his Philharmonic debut in 1943. Perhaps his most unusual non-Philharmonic appearance occurred in 1990, when, at age seventy-eight, he was seen in a TV commercial for Nike sneakers, in concert dress on a basketball court, mixing it up with David Robinson of the San Antonio Spurs. "Music needs all kinds of encouragement," he said later. A memorial tribute was scheduled for later in the year.

Beethoven was the composer for what was now the Philharmonic's annual summertime visit to Carnegie Hall. On July 20 the bill of fare, with Masur conducting, was the *Leonore* Overture No. 3, the Fourth Piano Concerto (played in memory of Firkušny), and the Fifth Symphony, with Alicia de Larrocha as the soloist in the concerto. Again a rich sonority was achieved in Carnegie that could only be approximated in Avery Fisher. Larrocha did raise a few eyebrows by eschewing Beethoven's dynamic cadenzas, offering instead stylistically incompatible concoctions by the nineteenth-century German composer-conductor Carl Reinecke. The program a week later brought the Overture to *The Creatures of Prometheus*, the Triple Concerto, and the Seventh Symphony, the Beaux-Arts Trio holding forth in the concerto. A tremendous ovation after the symphony produced the *Egmont* Overture as an encore.

On July 29 the *Times* carried an article by Ralph Blumenthal delineating the many ways in which the FBI had surveilled Leonard Bernstein in his various activities. As a supporter of liberal causes, some of which were thought to be subversive or communist, he kept the FBI busy tracking virtually his every move. Something of a soft touch, he often lent his name to an organization without really checking into its background or purpose. His support of the civil rights movement and the anti–Vietnam War movement only added fuel to the FBI's fire. Even the Philharmonic's tours to the Soviet Union in 1959 and to Japan in 1961 were monitored, while the notorious Black Panther incident in 1970 was simply icing on the FBI's cake. Try as they might, however, the FBI was unable to find any evidence that Bernstein was a member of the Communist Party. Their findings were accurate; he was not.

Finally, on August 23, 1994, came good news for Richard and Fiona Simon. The federal tax court in Washington ruled ten to seven in favor of the violinists in their dispute with the IRS over deducting the depreciation of their valuable bows. It was good news not only for the Simons, but also for the thousands of other musicians who would be similarly affected.

Kurt Masur's fourth Philharmonic season began on September 21 with the annual opening-night gala, this time with Yo-Yo Ma as the guest soloist in the Luigi Boccherini Cello Concerto in B-flat Major and Tchaikovsky's *Rococo Variations*. On its own, the orchestra opened the evening with Weber's Overture to *Oberon* and closed it with Bartók's *Concerto for Orchestra*. As Rothstein pointed out, this concert demonstrated that the Philharmonic under Masur had become conservative in the very best sense, as a conservator of music's best traditions.

The concert was dedicated to Carlos Moseley, in honor of his eighty years of life and his forty years of devotion to the Philharmonic as managing director, president, and chairman. After intermission Stamas presented him with a commemorative scrapbook and Masur praised him. Moseley responded with thanks for the music itself, which he called "the ultimate tribute.... It touches me, heart and soul, and makes me immensely happy." The occasion was the first time the Philharmonic had ever dedicated a concert to a living person.

An unusual work was unveiled at the concerts beginning October 6: *Symphony for Two Worlds*, by the Japanese composer Minoru Miki. It is scored for a full symphony orchestra plus a sixteen-member ensemble playing Japanese instruments, in this case Miki's own group, Pro Musica Nipponia. The piece is, for all intents and purposes, an East-West concerto for orchestra, with every instrument from both groups prominently displayed at one time or another, though the effect of the colorful score was most striking when everyone played at once. The second half of the program, which Masur conducted, was devoted to that Asian-influenced de facto concerto for orchestra, Rimsky-Korsakov's *Scheherazade*.

The Philharmonic continued its encouragement of young artists with the concerts beginning October 13, when the violinist Midori, by now a seasoned veteran of twenty-two, was scheduled to play the Bruch Concerto No. 1. An indisposition caused her to withdraw, her place taken by the fourteen-year-old Hilary Hahn. Holland, who gave her performance a very good review, was relieved that her artistry was still in a formative stage: "I, for one," he said, "am tired of being frightened by children who play the violin like 50-year-olds. Ms. Hahn is still part accomplishment and part potential. Something of the child remains in her psyche, and I find that appealing." Hahn has since become one of the leading violinists of our time, with many distinguished recordings to her credit.

The conductor for her Philharmonic debut was the Finnish maestro Paavo Berglund, who on his own offered symphonies by two of his compatriots. Sibelius has for so long dominated the musical life of Finland, even fifty years after his death, that it was refreshing to be introduced to the First Symphony by Joonas Kokkonen, even though it was a rather bleak-sounding piece. But Sibelius had his day, for the concert ended with his wonderful First Symphony, not played so often these days. It is a reminder of more optimistic times in the composer's musical life before he, too, descended into darkness and depression.

On November 9 it was announced that Klaus Tennstedt, who had conducted so many dynamic performances with the Philharmonic and other orchestras, would retire from public concerts because of ill health. Throat cancer and two hip replacements had taken their toll on his energy. It was hoped he would continue to make recordings.

It is a rare occasion indeed when a contemporary composition receives a four-minute standing ovation, but such was the case on January 6, 1995, when Joseph Schwantner's Concerto for Percussion and Orchestra, which the Philharmonic had commissioned, received its world premiere. The orchestra's principal percussionist, Christopher Lamb, was the exceedingly nimble soloist, required to play a multitude of instruments including, among many others, glockenspiel, marimba, vibraphone, water gong, Japanese wind chimes, cowbells, and bass drum. It was no doubt not the music alone but also Lamb's brilliant performance that produced the ovation. Leonard Slatkin, a champion of Schwantner's music, also conducted a sensitive and exciting performance of Tchaikovsky's Fifth Symphony.

Another bow to youth occurred at the concerts beginning February 2. They were the formal debut (she had performed on a Young People's Concert at the age of nine) of the twelve-year-old pianist Helen Huang, whose vehicle was the Beethoven Concerto No. 1. She made a very fine impression and became a favorite of Kurt Masur, with whom she has made several recordings, including the Beethoven First.

The *Times* of February 19 included an article by Roberta Hershenson on Stephen and Elaine Stamas, he the Philharmonic's chairman of the board, she a board member of Westchester's Hoff-Barthelson Music School. (The family's involvement in music extended to her brother, who was the president of the board of the Boston Symphony.) A retired vice president of Exxon, Stephen Stamas was also, at the time, a vice chairman of Lincoln Center. Entitled "Two Who Cherish Symphony Orchestras," the article delineated the couple's multifarious involvements with the world of classical music. It was under Stephen's leadership that Exxon began its sponsorship of the *Live from Lincoln Center* and *Great Performances* series, as well as the Philharmonic's radio broadcasts, which it sponsored for eighteen years. Loyal attendees of the orchestra's Thursday night concerts and enthusiastic fund-raisers, the couple have long presented a most gracious face for the arts in New York City.

The Estonian-born conductor Neeme Järvi, lately of the Detroit and the New Jersey Symphony Orchestras, led two weeks of Philharmonic concerts beginning February 16, only the second of which had been scheduled for him. In the first week he substituted for the young Italian maestro Daniele Gatti, who was to have made his debut with the orchestra (in fact, his engagement was labeled Conductor Debut Week). A shoulder injury prevented his appearance, thus bringing in Järvi and causing Oestreich to wonder how he happened to have a free week in his schedule. The author shares Oestreich's puzzlement, since Järvi seemed at the time to be involved in recording the complete works of everybody.

An example of the more obscure repertoire championed by Järvi was programmed for his second week: the Fifth Symphony by the Estonian composer Eduard Tubin, whose music is little known outside his homeland. It is through the recording efforts of Järvi, and lately his son Paavo, that the rest of the world has begun to be aware of Tubin. That his music deserves to be heard is without question, and the Fifth Symphony (of a total of ten) made a profound effect in its first Philharmonic performance. Of the work's dramatic conclusion, a long crescendo rising from near silence to an overwhelming fortissimo with two pounding timpanists supported by exclamations from the brass and the full orchestra, Alex Ross wrote, "It is one of the most astonishing coups de théâtre ever devised by a symphonic composer."

Apart from Järvi, no conductor seems to be busier than Valery Gergiev. A typical example of his activities was the week of March 1, when he led four performances with his Kirov Opera of St. Petersburg at the Brooklyn Academy of Music and four concerts with the Philharmonic at Avery Fisher Hall. He is one of a breed of seemingly indefatigable maestros whom one encounters virtually everywhere. One wonders when they have time to relax, eat, or sleep. Gergiev's Philharmonic program included a seldom-heard (at least in concert) work: Rimsky-Korsakov's lovely and tuneful symphony *Antar* (or symphonic suite, as it is sometimes designated). Anyone who enjoys *Scheherazade* will surely respond to *Antar*, though it is not as dramatic a score. On March 9, Oestreich wrote that Gergiev, in a program of

Liadov, Berlioz, and Tchaikovsky, "drew the finest, loveliest threads of sound from this orchestra in recent memory." A passionate performance of the "Pathétique" Symphony concluded the program as it had begun (with Liadov's *Enchanted Lake*), with the quietest sounds imaginable.

Sir Colin Davis has made a specialty of the music of Berlioz and Sibelius, and it was to the latter composer that he devoted a Philharmonic program beginning with the concert of March 23. Sibelius's Sixth Symphony is the least played of his seven, a work even more elusive and enigmatic than the starkly brooding Fourth, though certainly more approachable. It was the Sixth that opened Davis's all-Sibelius program, which continued with the early tone poem *En Saga* and the lighthearted *Karelia* Suite and ended with the almost equally enigmatic one-movement Seventh Symphony. All of this Davis managed "handsomely," according to Holland, "and in the process [made] the Philharmonic speak in his own strong, calm voice. . . . Good conductors can have a profound effect on good orchestras and with only a few rehearsals."

Kurt Masur continued to demonstrate his affinity with large choral works, of which the latest example was the Brahms *German Requiem* on March 29. The work is so serious that it can easily be made dull, but Oestreich found the rendition "highly characterized and anything but soporific," with "a fine flow from beginning to end." Sylvia McNair was the soprano soloist and Hakån Hagegård the baritone, with the Westminster Symphonic Choir. The Requiem's little cousin, Brahms's *Song of Destiny*, opened the program.

The name John Williams is normally associated with film music, for he has to his credit such masterpieces as the scores for *Star Wars* and the *Indiana Jones* movies. But he is also a fine composer of concert music, as was proven on April 12 with the world premiere of his concerto for bassoon and orchestra, entitled *The Five Sacred Trees*. One of the Philharmonic's 150th anniversary commissions, it was written for the orchestra's principal bassoonist, Judith LeClair, who played the difficult work brilliantly and beautifully.

On the same program Masur conducted Schumann's rarely heard *Konzertstück* (Concert Piece) for four horns and orchestra. In what would, over the years, become a sort of rondo form of criticism, Kozinn found fault with the Philharmonic's horn section, "with its tenuous intonation and imprecise attacks" and wondered why, "if visiting orchestras can offer fabulous horn playing week after week, . . . are the Philharmonic's horns so accident prone?" Having to play such a demanding work twice in one day may have been the cause.

The *Sinfonia Domestica* by Richard Strauss used to be a Philharmonic specialty in the days of Dimitri Mitropoulos. It returned during Zubin Mehta's tenure, but it has definitely become a fringe repertoire piece. That is unfortunate, for, if one can overlook its program of a day in the life of the Strauss family, it really is a beautiful score, with some of Strauss's most beguiling themes. André Previn conducted the work on May 11 in what Holland described as "a splendid performance" in which the conductor "admirably controlled its complexities."

Kurt Masur continued the tradition he had established in his first season of a free Memorial Day concert in the Cathedral of St. John the Divine. Past performances there had been of Britten's *War Requiem* and of Beethoven's and Mahler's Ninth Symphonies. In 1995 he offered Richard Strauss's *Metamorphosen* for string instruments and Beethoven's "Eroica" Symphony. The two works make an apt combination, for the Strauss concludes with a quotation from the Funeral March of Beethoven's symphony. That theme is suggested throughout the *Metamorphosen*, which is a sort of requiem for the Munich destroyed in World War II, perhaps a requiem for Germany itself. The "Eroica," of course, was originally intended as a tribute to Napoleon, whom Beethoven had once admired, but the tribute was disavowed once Napoleon declared himself emperor of France. Both of these works held great meaning for Masur, who led inspired performances. The cathedral's extremely reverberant acoustics mitigate against aural clarity. Tim Page, in the May 31 edition of *New York Newsday*, wrote that the "Eroica" sounded "rather as a dream about the piece might sound." Yet it still managed to sound like the "Eroica," for which he was grateful.

From time to time a great concert work appears that originated as music for a film. Probably the prime example is Prokofieff's cantata *Alexander Nevsky* (with his *Lieutenant Kijé* Suite a close second). The music for *Nevsky* was the result of a collaboration with the great Russian director Sergei Eisenstein. Another Eisenstein film that Prokofieff scored was *Ivan the Terrible*. Although it has great music, unfortunately the composer did not arrange a concert piece from it. On June 1, with Yuri Temirkanov conducting, the Philharmonic presented a version of *Ivan the Terrible* as an accompaniment to Eisenstein's film. It was not a successful undertaking, according to Rothstein; though the performance and conducting were certainly fine in and of themselves, scenes were shown out of sequence, destroying Eisenstein's "meticulous use of visual rhythm," and the live orchestra often intruded and drowned out the screen dialogue.

Ever since the demise of the Lewisohn Stadium Concerts, the Philharmonic has been on the lookout for a suitable site for summer concerts. The Parks Concerts fill the bill to a certain extent, but they are presented only for two or three weeks and in several different venues. At one time a site on Long Island was considered, but nothing came of it. Now, in 1995, a location in Purchase, New York, just north of White Plains, was explored, the campus of the State University of New York (SUNY Purchase), thought to be an ideal site for a Tanglewood-like summer festival.

According to a May 17 *Times* article by Joseph Berger, the Philharmonic, SUNY Purchase, and the New York State Urban Development Corporation agreed to collaborate in a feasibility study. While proposals for a summer festival had been received from Lake Placid and the Catskills, the Purchase possibility seemed the most attractive, especially because of its proximity to New York City. There were drawbacks, however. For one, the residents of the area had not been polled on their receptivity to heavy summer traffic. Also, the campus was approachable only by two-lane roads, which presumably would not be able to accommodate thousands of cars. Furthermore—shades of Lewisohn Stadium!—the Westchester County Airport was nearby. In the end, everyone's wishful thinking came to naught, and the Philharmonic, alone among the Big Five orchestras, is still without a summer festival.

CHAPTER 16

1995–97

A New Contract and Its Aftermath

From June 7 to June 27, 1995, the Philharmonic was in Europe, with concerts in Paris, Cologne, Düsseldorf, Amsterdam, Birmingham, London, Vienna, Istanbul, and Athens. Only one American work, Barber's *Second Essay for Orchestra*, was in the tour repertoire, which otherwise included Beethoven's Symphonies Nos. 3 and 7, his *Egmont* and *Leonore* No. 3 Overtures, Mahler's First and Shostakovich's Fifth Symphonies, Strauss's *Metamorphosen*, Wagner's Prelude to *Die Meistersinger*, and Webern's *Im Sommerwind*. Time was when an American orchestra performing abroad would include more than one American work in its programs, and substantial ones at that. The program of the *Metamorphosen* and the "Eroica" Symphony was given in several locations, including London and Vienna, with the *Leonore* Overture No. 3 a quite substantial encore. Again, public and press reaction was most enthusiastic.

An unusual incident occurred in Amsterdam, where a group of the musicians were to leave for Luxembourg for a chamber music concert. On the way to the airport their bus was delayed because an empty car was blocking the road. With no help in sight, six of the burlier musicians got off the bus and lifted the car off the road. They made their flight.

On July 13 the *New York Times* announced that two of its music critics were to be given new assignments, effective with the beginning of the fall season: Edward Rothstein would take up the new position of cultural critic at large, and Bernard Holland would become the new chief music critic. Holland, who had been with the *Times* since 1981, was a graduate of the University of Virginia and had studied piano and composition in Paris, Vienna, and London.

The Philharmonic did not play a Carnegie Hall series in the summer of 1995. Instead, a two-week Mostly Vienna festival was scheduled in Avery Fisher Hall. Three programs were given July 13–22, opening with a concert presentation of Johann Strauss's operetta *Der Zigeunerbaron* (The Gypsy Baron). This was the composer's attempt to write a more serious piece, yet he could not help but revert to form, producing another frothy stage work, though it did have a few somewhat heavier moments.

New to the *Times*'s critical staff was Anthony Tommasini, who had come to the paper from the *Boston Globe*. His feeling was that Kurt Masur's treatment of the score was not idiomatic, that it was "foursquare and stolid," lacking in the proper Viennese lilt and inflections. He did praise the singing of Stanford Olsen, Julia Migenes, Jan Opalach, Dominique Labelle, Rosalind Elias, and others, as well as Amy Kaiser's Concert Chorale of New York. But according to the late, lamented Shirley Fleming in the *New York Post* of July 17, Masur had "the Viennese idiom in his fingertips," and his rhythmic finesse was "exhilarating." Peter G. Davis, in the July 31 *New York Magazine*, wrote of how "Kurt Masur clearly adores this piece, and the orchestra played gorgeously for him." The work was given in German, the spoken dialogue replaced by an English narration written by Andrew Porter and delivered in her inimitable manner by Beverly Sills.

The twelve-year-old pianist Helen Huang appeared again, this time on the concerts of July 18 and 19 playing Mozart's Concerto No. 23 in A Major, K. 488, with Masur conducting. Rothstein, while finding her gifted beyond her years, objected strongly to her performing in public at such a young age, when she should be studying (which presumably she was) and learning more about music than just the notes, which obviously she could play, but without projecting the depth of feeling required for Mozart. Soon afterward she recorded the concerto with Masur and the Philharmonic.

Masur's program also included Richard Strauss's *Alpine Symphony*, another work once programmed by Mitropoulos and seldom heard since. As with the *Sinfonia Domestica*, opinion is divided about this piece, some finding its description of an ascent and descent of an Alpine mountain (replete with thunderstorm embellished by a wind machine) pretentious and superficial, others finding it a great work of nature painting. Rothstein belonged to the first group: "How successful can a work of program music be when it has to rely on a wind machine for the impression of wind?" (Of course, an impression of wind is precisely what one gets from a wind machine.) He judged Masur too tasteful a musician to do the piece justice.

The German pianist Peter Roesel was the soloist in the third program, July 21 and 22, playing Liszt's arrangement for piano and orchestra of Schubert's *Wanderer* Fantasy, which the composer wrote for a solo piano. Liszt's arrangement does not turn up very often, and Oestreich noted that this version was heard at a disadvantage because, in a pre-concert recital, Roesel had performed Schubert's brilliant original. On the orchestral program Masur gave a distinguished reading of Schubert's "Unfinished" Symphony and two actual Liszt works, the once extremely popular Second Hungarian Rhapsody and the *Mephisto Waltz* No. 1. Johann Strauss Sr.'s

Radetzky March was an appropriate encore, the audience clapping along like true Viennese.

An unusual guest conductor appeared in the Parks Concerts beginning July 31. Bobby McFerrin was just beginning to carve out a conducting career. Already known as an astonishing jazz vocalist, this was his Philharmonic debut, for which his credentials included a thorough study of classical music before he moved into jazz. Another point in his favor was that his father, the baritone Robert McFerrin, had been the first African American man to be engaged by the Metropolitan Opera, so opera had been a part of the younger McFerrin's upbringing. An audience of about seventy thousand heard his straightforward renditions of such light classical fare as Bizet's *L'Arlésienne* Suite No. 1, Dukas's *Sorcerer's Apprentice* (not *that* light), and the Overture to Johann Strauss Jr.'s *Die Fledermaus*, the playing of which Tommasini found "buoyant and lilting." Many of the orchestra musicians stayed to listen to what Tommasini called "his stupefying vocal and body drumming improvisations."

As happens every few years with a major orchestra, it was contract negotiation time at the Philharmonic, with the old agreement scheduled to expire at the end of the season-opening gala concert on September 20. Negotiations had begun in the spring, and the situation was becoming tense on both sides as the deadline approached. When the previous contract was negotiated, the musicians took into account the fact that both Kurt Masur and Deborah Borda were new in their jobs. Thus they played without a contract for eighteen weeks before an agreement was reached. This time they were less inclined to do so and, in fact, during a meeting after the dress rehearsal for opening night, they authorized their negotiators to call for a strike if no agreement were reached.

Meanwhile, opening night proceeded as scheduled, Masur conducting a program of Richard Strauss and Wagner with Jessye Norman ("an orchestra in herself," according to Holland) the formidable soprano soloist in Strauss songs and the Immolation Scene from *Götterdämmerung*. Masur was praised for the remedial quality of his work with the Philharmonic, which still needed it, though critics felt the orchestra could do much more than what was asked of it.

Again there was the threat of a strike, this time before the season's first Saturday night concert. Negotiations continued the following week, with the possibility of a strike before the Thursday night concert on September 28. At issue were salaries, pensions, seniority pay, and health care. Thursday came and went, however, with no strike. But the musicians had held a meeting before that evening's concert, a meeting that went twenty minutes past the strike deadline, which meant that the scheduled 8:00 p.m. concert did not begin until 8:30, the audience patiently waiting.

That concert opened with Bach's Brandenburg Concerto No. 5 performed by an ensemble of twenty musicians, thus giving the impression of a job action, according to Oestreich. But the full orchestra assembled for the rest of the program, which concluded with an uplifting performance of Mendelssohn's "Reformation" Symphony, music that always finds Masur at his best.

But all was not settled. As negotiations continued, another strike deadline was set for 7:00 p.m. on Thursday, October 5, one hour before the scheduled concert. There would be no keeping the audience waiting this time, for there would be no concert. Again the deadline was postponed, this time for twenty-four hours, thus affecting the Friday evening concert. There was no strike called then either, and on October 7 came the announcement that an agreement had been reached by a vote of seventy-six to twenty-one.

The new contract called for a minimum salary of $81,120 in its third year, roughly $10,000 more than at the end of the expired contract, at which time the Philharmonic would be the country's highest-paid orchestra, higher than the Chicago Symphony, the Boston Symphony, the Metropolitan Opera Orchestra (the ensembles nearest in salary)—higher than anyone. The pension benefit would now be $43,500 a year ($48,000 had been sought), and musicians with twenty-five years service or more would receive a weekly seniority bonus of $108, which did not match Chicago's seniority pay of $145. It was agreed that if the organization's health insurance costs were to be more than $1.2 million, the players would pay weekly premiums of $10.

The agreement was ratified, but reluctantly so, for the musicians' negotiating team felt that a strike would not result in a better settlement. And when all was said and done, much resentment remained toward management on the part of the musicians, who were extremely critical of management's proposal and unhappy with the way the negotiations were handled. Before the final balloting the players passed a resolution in which they expressed their lack of confidence in their executive director, Borda, and the board's labor relations committee. It would be some time before the feelings of resentment would disappear. They did not even want to continue with the cooperative committee that had been established in the previous contract negotiations.

Meanwhile, the saga of Richard and Fiona Simon, their violin bows, and the IRS continued. The Simons had won their case in federal tax court in August 1994, but the IRS had appealed the decision to the United States Court of Appeals for the Second Circuit. On October 13, 1995, by a vote of two to one, that court ruled in favor of the Simons, deciding that their rare bows were not art objects, but tools of their trade, and thus subject to depreciation. For the IRS, an appeal to the Supreme Court would be the next step, but no decision had been made to pursue it.

Returning to musical matters, the concert of October 26 brought the Philharmonic debut of the young German conductor Christian Thielemann, who had made a successful Metropolitan Opera debut the year before. He did not make things easy for himself: he chose as his major work Schoenberg's *Pelleas und Melisande*. This early work does not play itself, and Thielemann was praised by Tommasini for bringing "clarity and definition to this ruminative score," the Philharmonic responding "with a luminous performance." Less successful was the rendition by Vladimir Feltsman of the Brahms Piano Concerto No. 2, in which he and the conductor had obvious differences of opinion about the piece that they failed to reconcile. After a performance of Schumann's Second Symphony the following week, Tommasini described Thielemann as "a masterly conductor and an important artist."

On November 3 came the news of the death of the Viennese-born violinist Erica Morini at the age of ninety-one. She had long been a frequent soloist with the Philharmonic, especially when Bruno Walter and George Szell were on the podium, and was especially known for her interpretations of the Beethoven and Brahms Concertos. It was during a 1953 broadcast performance of the Brahms with Walter conducting that the A string on her violin snapped. Exchanging instruments with the concertmaster, John Corigliano, she missed only a couple of notes and continued playing while Corigliano replaced the string and returned the instrument to her in time for the cadenza. A bizarre turn of events occurred as she lay on her deathbed, when her rare Stradivarius, valued at $3.5 million, was stolen from her New York apartment.

An article by Holland on November 5 discussed the issue of musicians' wages and orchestral life in general, mentioning that a recent study by Harvard University psychologists ranked orchestra musicians just below federal prison employees in terms of happiness and satisfaction with their jobs. This in spite of the fact that Philharmonic musicians were now earning a minimum of $76,000 a year, enjoying good job security, enjoying long vacations, and benefiting from good medical coverage and pension plans. Yet they were unhappy. "You think we're overpaid crybabies, don't you?" one musician had said to Holland. What rankled, apparently, was their perception that, even as artists, they were merely cogs in a wheel. They had no representation on the board, had no say in the selection of repertoire or conductors, and were obliged to abide by decisions made by people in the organization who were not artists and not even particularly knowledgeable about the art they were directing, at that. The cooperative committee, formed after the previous contract settlement, failed to make an impact in everyday decisions; the players complained they had been sidetracked onto long-term policy committees. Holland concluded that, considering the lessening impact of classical music on the public, this was not the time for labor unrest. Whether democracy in the musical workplace would be the answer or benign totalitarianism was an open question.

The concerts beginning November 9 were designated Composer Week. This time they celebrated the music of Lukas Foss, two of whose major works were performed with Masur conducting. Oestreich wondered on November 11 why it should take such a week to have Foss's music played by the Philharmonic. He had been "a New York institution" for many years as a composer, conductor, and pianist, and had written many fine works that were not likely to offend the audience, not to mention a few that might. The works programmed for this week were the *Renaissance Concerto* from 1986, with the Philharmonic's principal flutist, Jeanne Baxtresser, as the soloist; and the 1946 *Song of Songs*, in which Florence Quivar was the mezzo-soprano soloist. Both works are among the composer's loveliest, and both were eloquently performed.

The German composer Carl Orff is best known for his cantata *Carmina Burana*, which people either love or hate. It is rare for one of his other works to turn up in a concert, even rarer when it is part of an all-Orff program, which is precisely what Masur offered for the concerts beginning December 7. Opening the program was a charming piece, *The Christmas Story*, which the composer had specified should be adapted to the musical forces available and to the regional vernacular of the presenters. For the Philharmonic performance the instruments used were recorders, guitars, lutes, xylophones, and a large array of percussion instruments, with the Boys Choir of Harlem singing carols and the piece's choral passages. The other work on the program was, of course, *Carmina Burana*, in which the soloists were the soprano Harolyn Blackwell, the tenor John Aler, and the baritone William Stone in his Philharmonic debut, with the New York Choral Artists. Tommasini thought the combination of the two pieces a bit curious but felt "it was hard to resist this dynamic performance" of *Carmina Burana*.

On January 9, 1996, the public learned of the death, at age eighty-eight, of Howard Taubman, with whom this book began. He was music editor of the *New York Times* from 1935 to 1955, when he was appointed chief music critic following the death of Olin Downes. In 1960 he switched desks at the *Times* to become the paper's chief theater critic, a post he held until 1965, when he was appointed critic at large, enabling him to write on any cultural event of his choosing. Regardless of his various positions, he is perhaps best remembered for his attack on Mitropoulos and the Philharmonic in 1956.

Having led impressive performances of Bach's *St. Matthew Passion* three years earlier, Kurt Masur returned to Bach's sacred music on January 18 with the great

Mass in B Minor. Steeped in the music and the aura of Bach during his many years in Leipzig, Masur had developed a natural affinity for the master's large choral works, which he conducted with devotion. He was adept at combining a traditional approach with the more modern, scholarly view of how to perform baroque music. For this rendition an orchestra of forty-five was employed, with fifty members of the New York Choral Artists, augmented by the American Boychoir, with the soloists Edith Wiens, soprano; Janis Taylor, mezzo-soprano; John Aler, tenor; and William Stone, baritone. Oestreich wrote of Masur's "buoyant" and "brisk" performance that gave the impression it had been "tailored . . . specifically to the qualities and needs of Avery Fisher Hall, and the fit was invariably good." If that was indeed Masur's intention, it was a sensible approach, for the ambience, or lack of it, plays an important part in the success or failure of any performance. In *New York* magazine of February 5, Peter G. Davis wrote of "a fastidiously articulate and lovingly shaped performance, if seldom an overwhelming one."

On January 22 it was announced that Lorne Munroe, the Philharmonic's principal cellist since 1964, would be retiring after the concert of February 27. At age seventy-two, he wanted to spend more time with his family. As that family consisted of his wife, ten sons, a daughter, seventeen grandchildren, and one great-grandchild, undoubtedly he would be keeping busy.

Kurt Masur continued his policy of conducting the orchestras of New York's music conservatories by directing a concert of the orchestra of the Mannes College of Music on January 29 at Riverside Church. Commemorating the sixty-fifth anniversary of the church and the eightieth anniversary of Mannes College, the program included the Seventh Symphony of Beethoven and the First Symphony of Shostakovich, another pairing of the two composers.

On January 30 came the news of the death of Saul Goodman, the Philharmonic's great timpanist for forty-six years, at the age of eighty-nine. Having joined the orchestra in 1926 at the age of nineteen, he became noted for the expressivity of his playing on an instrument that had previously been considered tubby-sounding drums. As a faculty member at Juilliard he taught countless pupils, many of whom went on to play in the percussion sections of the great American orchestras. One of his students was his successor at the Philharmonic, Roland Kohloff.

The next day, January 31, it was announced that, beginning with the 1996–97 season, the Philharmonic would embark on a four-year survey of American music. Called American Classics, the series would focus on symphonies the first season, then in successive seasons on vocal works and shorter pieces, concertos, and music for the theater, dance, opera, and film. In the same announcement came the news that Sir Colin Davis would become the orchestra's principal guest conductor, beginning with the 1998–99 season. He would be the first conductor to hold that title with the Philharmonic since William Steinberg in the 1960s.

A mini-controversy erupted in the *Times* of February 18, though its cause dated back to the previous May. At that time Amsterdam's Concertgebouw presented a Mahler festival involving three great orchestras, the Vienna Philharmonic, the Berlin Philharmonic, and the Royal Concertgebouw Orchestra. The New York Philharmonic was not invited. The director of the Concertgebouw, Martijn Sanders, explained the apparent snub by claiming that the three invited orchestras had a tradition in this music established by Mahler himself, who had conducted them frequently, and that this tradition had been nurtured over the decades. And what of our Philharmonic, of which Mahler had been the conductor from 1909 to 1911? According to Oestreich in his article, Sanders maintained that "the orchestra has not adequately tended to its tradition."

This comment, of course, was rubbish. Think of the many Mahler performances the Philharmonic has given since the composer's death, led by such as Mengelberg, Walter, Mitropoulos, Bernstein, Mehta, Maazel, and many others (not to mention the Mahler survey of 1960 and the Mahler Festival of 1976). Oestreich's article quoted the orchestra's English horn player, Thomas Stacy: "Sitting on stage playing Mahler, we feel as if we have a laser beam going right back to 1911." Kurt Masur admitted he had come to Mahler relatively late in his career; he did not feel it necessary that he conduct all the symphonies—there are a great many fine Mahler conductors today, and guest conductors would certainly "keep the tradition alive."

The Mahler tradition was indeed kept alive during two weeks in February, beginning on the 15th when, according to Ross, Michael Tilson Thomas led "a bold, intelligent" performance of the Fifth Symphony, which he programmed with two works of Charles Ives, *From the Steeples and the Mountains* and *Decoration Day*. Then, on February 22, the young Italian maestro Daniele Gatti, in his Philharmonic debut, offered the formidable Sixth Symphony. The performance honored the one hundredth birthday of Dimitri Mitropoulos, who had conducted the American premiere of the work with the Philharmonic in 1947. (In one of the most incongruous bits of programming ever, the Mahler Sixth had begun that concert; after intermission came Gershwin's Piano Concerto in F with Oscar Levant as soloist.) Tommasini hailed Gatti's ability to draw "radiant, incisive playing from the orchestra," whose members "remained seated and applauded him" at the conclusion (as they had Mitropoulos almost fifty years before).

The composer Morton Gould died on February 21 at the age of eighty-two. During the Philharmonic tenure of Dimitri Mitropoulos, and even before, Gould was one of the most-performed American composers, even though critics did not take his attractive and vernacular-influenced music very seriously. Since Mitropoulos, the Philharmonic has played his music very infrequently. For many years the president of ASCAP, the engaging and witty Gould won the Pulitzer Prize for music in 1995 with his *Stringmusic.*

"What may well stand as the most thrilling moment of the New York Philharmonic season," according to Oestreich, took place on March 7: the Philharmonic debut of the Scottish percussionist Evelyn Glennie in her countryman James MacMillan's *Veni, Veni, Emmanuel.* A "riveting" percussion concerto in all but name, the work (based on the Advent hymn "O Come, O Come, Emmanuel") was given "a stunning performance" by Glennie, "quite simply a phenomenon as a performer, and the fact that she is profoundly deaf is the least of it."

It is a rare occurrence when an orchestra presents the five Beethoven piano concertos with a single pianist over a ten-day span. At the time of this writing the Austrian-born pianist Alfred Brendel has retired from the concert stage, but in 1996, at the age of sixty-five, he was a very active and inspired performer of those great works with Masur and the Philharmonic. Nos. 1 and 3 were played on March 20 and 23, with Nos. 2 and 4 to come on March 26 and 28 and No. 5 on March 30 and April 1. Reviewing the first program in the March 22 edition, Tommasini did not gloss over the pianist's idiosyncrasies and occasionally less-than-polished technical passages, but he noted how he managed to probe to the heart of these works, especially emphasizing their many humorous passages.

If Beethoven concerto cycles are rare, so are all-Shostakovich programs. On April 18 Valery Gergiev led one that included two of the composer's lesser-known works, the song cycle *From Jewish Folk Poetry* and the Fourth Symphony. The latter score, composed in 1935–36, had to wait until 1961 for its first performance: Stalin's denunciation of the opera *Lady Macbeth of the Mtsensk District* had prompted the composer to withdraw the symphony for fear of further recriminations. The work can be described as a massive compendium of everything Shostakovich had written up to that point—satirical, tragic, dissonant, and reflective, as well as a sort of thematic sketchbook, for many themes, once heard, disappear into the overall fabric, never to be distinguished again. Holland found the performance "first-rate" and thought the song cycle, with the beautiful singing of the soprano Marina Shaguch, the contralto Larissa Diadkova, and the tenor Constantin Pluzhnikov, perhaps a more successful work than the symphony.

Another seldom-heard symphony was given on April 25—the Sixth of Anton Bruckner. The guest conductor was the American-born Swedish maestro Herbert Blomstedt, who had recently completed a ten-year stint as music director of the

San Francisco Symphony. Probably the most difficult of the Bruckner symphonies to play convincingly, it was given a performance of great "authority and deep feeling," according to Tommasini, who also praised Blomstedt's projection of "the grand design of the music."

One does not normally associate Kurt Masur with American vernacular composers, but there he was on May 23 conducting music by Morton Gould and Duke Ellington, along with pieces by Ulysses Kay, Adolphus Hailstork, and a German interloper, Karl-Heinz Koper, whose *Popcorn Concerto* featured Philip Myers as the horn soloist. Additionally, the Boys Choir of Harlem was heard in some lively gospel singing. For Holland, it was the Gould and Ellington pieces that made the deepest impression. One of Gould's most popular pieces was the *Spirituals for Orchestra* (listed as *Spirituals in Five Movements* on Masur's program). Holland called the piece "razor-sharp," further stating that "Gould's orchestral writing represents everything good and important in the American urban sensibility." He praised Gould's "exceptional craftsmanship. Popular music does not drown in its symphonic setting; it is transformed." Masur obviously enjoyed conducting this piece, as he did the Ellington work, *The Three Black Kings*, which Holland felt "reorganizes symphony orchestra sound. . . . One was fascinated by the elegance of this music."

The Philharmonic community was saddened by the death on May 24 of the composer Jacob Druckman at the age of sixty-seven. Several of his works had been performed by the orchestra, one of which, *Windows*, won the Pulitzer Prize for music in 1972. He was appointed the Philharmonic's composer-in-residence in 1982, after which he was the director of its three Horizons festivals of contemporary music. His son, Daniel, is a member of the Philharmonic's percussion section. Kurt Masur and the orchestra dedicated the season's final concerts, beginning May 30, to Druckman's memory.

Another Philharmonic death was reported on June 7, that of cellist Martin Ormandy at the age of ninety-five. A member of the orchestra from 1929 to 1965, he continued playing as a freelance musician in New York City until his death, at which time he was the oldest active orchestral musician in the United States, if not the world. He was a familiar figure in many of New York's freelance ensembles, such as the Mostly Mozart Orchestra, the New York Chamber Symphony, and the New York Pops, with which he had performed on May 7, and had been contracted to play again with Mostly Mozart in its coming season. His brother was the conductor Eugene Ormandy, whom he closely resembled.

Two resignations from the Philharmonic's board were noted on June 14—those of Stephen Stamas, its chairman, and H. Frederick Krimendahl II, its president.

Though both had been affected by anger against the board as a result of the recent contract settlement, as had Deborah Borda, they said this was not a factor in their decision to resign. Borda praised the two as "a terrific team."

AMERICAN CLASSICS

In what was to become an annual event, the first Lincoln Center Festival was held in the summer of 1996, at which a lively assortment of concerts, opera, dance, and theater was presented. Three programs were given by Kurt Masur and the New York Philharmonic, the first of which followed directly on the heels of one by John Eliot Gardiner and his period-instrument ensemble, the Orchestre Revolutionnaire et Romantique. Essentially the two groups performed the same program, though with significant differences: Beethoven's *Fidelio* in both its versions, the earlier which is known as *Leonore*. Gardiner's *Leonore* was given in the relatively intimate confines of Alice Tully Hall, Masur's *Fidelio* in the much larger Avery Fisher Hall; Gardiner's in costume with a small amount of staging, Masur's as a concert performance.

Beethoven struggled for years over his only opera, and although the final version justifies his effort, it is instructive to hear his first thoughts and fascinating to observe his creative process. Writing on August 2, Holland asked the audience "to see [the concert *Fidelio*] with their ears," and, in truth, concert performances of operas can allow the listeners to concentrate on the music while avoiding the dramatic excrescences so often perpetrated by contemporary stage directors. Holland singled out Deborah Voigt's singing of Leonore's aria "Abscheulicher! Wo eilst du hin" as "the musical high point of the two days and the fuel for gripping moments to follow." Also in the cast of the Philharmonic's version were Gary Lakes, Dominique Labelle, Paul Plishka, Gordon Gietz, and Matthew Best, with the New York Choral Artists as prisoners and townspeople. *New York* magazine's Peter G. Davis found Masur's conducting "unusually demonic" and declared it was "a treat just to hear [him] lead an opera in New York."

The Czech maestro Rafael Kubelík had been a regular and popular guest conductor of the Philharmonic from 1973 to 1985, when he retired because of heart disease and severe arthritis. Audiences and musicians had long appreciated his warmhearted approach to music, which stressed the grand line of a composition rather than concentrating on every last detail. The music world was saddened to learn of his death on August 11, at the age of eighty-two.

As the beginning of the 1996–97 season approached it was announced that Carter Brey would be the Philharmonic's new principal cellist, succeeding Lorne Munroe, who had held the post for thirty years. Since winning the Rostropovich

International Competition in Paris fifteen years before, Brey had established himself as one of New York's leading chamber music players and had also embarked on a solo career. It was unusual for such a musician to take an orchestral position, but with the Philharmonic he would still have the opportunity for solo and chamber playing while enjoying the security afforded by a permanent post.

On September 16 it was announced that Paul B. Guenther, past president of the Paine Webber Group, would be the new chairman of the Philharmonic's board, succeeding Stephen Stamas. Having had both a president and a chairman, the organization decided to consolidate the two positions. Guenther stated that he hoped to be able to ameliorate what had become an antagonistic relationship between the orchestra members and the board as a result of the most recent contract negotiations.

The new season began on September 18 with the usual opening-night gala concert. This time a rather serious program was planned consisting of the Brahms Violin Concerto and the Tchaikovsky Fourth Symphony, with Masur conducting. The Brahms work was part of what would be a season-long commemoration of the hundredth anniversary of the composer's death. Its soloist was Anne-Sophie Mutter, who played the difficult piece with "poise and rectitude," according to Holland, who also wrote appreciatively of Masur's Tchaikovsky. However, repeating a comment he had made at least once before, Holland thought the Philharmonic could do much more than Masur asked of it, in spite of his laudable corrective efforts: "His programs are safe, solid, and played with relentless correctness."

Once a staple of the radio airwaves, the Philharmonic had been notably absent from them for eight years. Thus it was a pleasure to read on October 3 that the orchestra would be returning to the air in January, this time with live broadcasts instead of the taped programs that had become common to all broadcasting orchestras. However, one concert per month would be offered, and for only five months. Underwritten by a grant from Time Warner, which owned the German Teldec label that had been recording Masur and the Philharmonic, the broadcasts would be produced by New York's classical music station, WQXR, carrying them locally and in syndication to other cities.

The orchestra's survey of American music began on October 3 when Masur led the Second Symphony of Howard Hanson. It was perhaps understandable that Masur, given his background, would conduct only one of the nine American symphonies scheduled, and perhaps even predictable that he would choose this particular example. The longtime director of the Eastman School of Music in Rochester, Hanson was an extremely conservative composer, and this work, called the "Romantic," is probably his most conservative composition. It is not only his most often performed piece, but may well be the most often performed of all American symphonies, for it has long been a favorite of college and youth orchestras, though seldom given by major professional orchestras. Tommasini described it as a "hokey, bombastic symphony," but it has many touching moments, not to mention a recurring theme that most composers would die to have written (though they would never admit it).

Leonard Slatkin continued the American series on October 17 with the Sixth Symphony of Walter Piston, which had never been played by the Philharmonic. Like Hanson's Second, it had been commissioned by the Boston Symphony, the Hanson for its fiftieth anniversary, the Piston for its seventy-fifth. One of the most respected of American composers, Piston, also musically conservative, was basically a neoclassicist whose works are noted for their fastidious construction, superb orchestration, bracing rhythms, and harmonic piquancy, all laced with an occasional touch of humor. (It is no coincidence that he wrote important textbooks on harmony, counterpoint, and orchestration.) Slatkin is deeply committed to American music, and his conducting of this neglected work fully justified its revival.

Discord at the Philharmonic between Kurt Masur and Deborah Borda was reported in the *Times* of October 22. Shortly after the season opened, the conductor had told the orchestra committee, which represents the musicians, that the executive director "was trying to drive a wedge between him and the players." Many of the players were still angry at Borda for "insulting behavior" during the most recent contract negotiations—witness their vote of no confidence in her management. Meanwhile, after an initially rocky relationship, a close bond had been established between the musicians and Masur.

All Masur would say was, "Look, it is like a marriage, *ja*?" There were rumors that Borda had been approached by the Los Angeles Philharmonic, but she firmly stated that no departure was planned, and Paul Guenther, the new chairman, stressed that neither Masur nor Borda was going to leave: "We're firmly committed to both of them. He does his job. She does her job." Said Masur of their disagreements, "I learned to live with the Stasi [the East German secret police] . . . and this doesn't frighten me." (A letter to the *Times* from Ernest Fleischmann, the retiring executive director of the Los Angeles Philharmonic, was extremely critical of this last remark of Masur's.) For her part, Borda felt that perhaps "the spotlight has been turned on me because I'm a woman."

It should be mentioned that, at the Gewandhaus, Masur had free rein. He was not only the orchestra's music director, but its manager. Furthermore, he had full authority in virtually all aspects of running the auditorium, from the ushers to choosing the menu for the restaurant (although one assumes he was not in the box office selling tickets). It was therefore very difficult for him to adjust to the American way of doings things, where there were many other people in charge of these various duties. It was especially hard for him to separate the music director's authority from the general manager's.

The Brahms commemoration continued with the concerts beginning October 24, when the Polish pianist Krystian Zimerman was heard in the Piano Concerto No. 1, with Herbert Blomstedt conducting. In effect a symphony for piano and orchestra, the work was given "a performance that had blood coursing through its veins, not a waxwork model of a revered work," according to Allan Kozinn in the *Times* two days later. Additionally, Blomstedt conducted the string orchestra version of Bruckner's Adagio from his string quintet and a "thoughtful, characterized account of Hindemith's *Mathis der Maler*."

Having been tested in a series of summer Parks Concerts, Bobby McFerrin made his debut in the Philharmonic subscription series beginning October 31, bringing with him as soloist the jazz pianist Chick Corea, who played Mozart's D Minor Concerto, no less. Except for the Mozart concerto, the program did not exactly plumb music's depths; it included the Overture to Mozart's *Marriage of Figaro*, Fauré's *Pavane* (to which McFerrin added his own vocalise), and Bizet's delightful Symphony in C Major. The last score had been a staple of the Philharmonic's repertoire during the Rodzinski and Mitropoulos years and was later given by Bernstein and Thomas Schippers, but it had been rarely heard since.

Although Corea did not jazz up Mozart, he did improvise introductions to the first and second movements, and his rather extended cadenzas were a bit anachronistic. He and McFerrin concluded the program with some of their improvisations, prompting Oestreich to comment that "McFerrin is a phenomenon," while Corea is "'merely' a greatly gifted musician."

Premiered in 1939 by Serge Koussevitzky and the Boston Symphony, the Third Symphony of Roy Harris was long considered "the great American symphony," or at least the quintessential American symphony. Bold and vigorous in tone, it radiates optimism even though it ends tragically. Leonard Bernstein was a great champion of this work, programming it six times with the Philharmonic and recording it twice with them. Harris could be considered a member of the one-hit-wonder fraternity (whose membership includes such composers as Paul Dukas and César Franck), for even though he produced fourteen symphonies and many other compositions, it was always his Third Symphony that was most often played. It is strange, therefore, that such a once popular and worthy work has virtually disappeared from the repertoire. In any case, the Harris Third was the next installment in the Philharmonic's survey of American symphonies, given on November 9 with

Zdeněk Macál conducting. Tommasini found it to be music of "irrepressible character" given a "bold, involving performance."

Similar in form to the Harris Third, a one-movement work with several connected subsections, is the First Symphony by Samuel Barber, which Leonard Slatkin conducted on December 19. Bruno Walter, not a conductor normally associated with American music, had performed and recorded this work with the Philharmonic in 1944. A more lyrical work than the Harris Third, though with its share of dynamism, especially in the fugal scherzo section, it deserves to have been played at least as often as the Harris but somehow did not attract the same attention. Even today its status as a repertoire piece is rather tenuous. Slatkin was born to conduct this kind of music, of which, according to Tommasini, he gave a "cogent and exciting" rendition.

Also on his program of December 21 were Dukas's ingenious *Sorcerer's Apprentice* (his "one hit"), less frequently played on serious concerts than in earlier times (to the detriment of concert life), and an unusual presentation of William Walton's music for the Laurence Olivier film *Henry V*. Dubbed "A Shakespeare Scenario," the sequence was devised by Christopher Palmer for the actor Christopher Plummer, who delivered relevant speeches from the play with his customary aplomb.

Zubin Mehta returned, first for a New Year's Eve program of Mozart, Johann Strauss, Franz Lehár, and Fritz Kreisler, then in two subscription weeks. Since the critics were often less than kind to him during his tenure, it is interesting to note their reaction during this visit. For New Year's Eve Kozinn wrote of "a spirited reading" of the Overture to *The Marriage of Figaro*; Renée Fleming's "plangent" and passionate singing of two Mozart arias, the first with "focused wind playing"; and Midori's "gorgeously polished account" of Mozart's Violin Concerto No. 3, K. 216. Kozinn's review revealed him to be no fan of Johann Strauss, but the critic complimented Mehta on his bringing out "the music's fleeting elegance" and on the flexibility of his tempos, which "gave his readings an authentic lilt."

Paul Griffiths reviewed the program given on January 7, 1997, for which Midori returned to play the Bartók Violin Concerto No. 2 and Mehta conducted Tchaikovsky's Symphony No. 5. Griffiths felt that Midori's cautious approach to the Bartók may have been influenced by Mehta's accompaniment, which resembled "a sometimes enthusiastic but generally uncomprehending fog." Although he found Mehta "well disposed" to the Tchaikovsky, eventually "the performance had begun to irritate me as trivial and vulgar, and yet it never quite lost its charm." Reading this, one wonders how something can be trivial, vulgar, and charming at the same time.

For his second week, beginning January 9, Mehta addressed himself to Mahler's Third Symphony, with the assistance of the mezzo-soprano Florence Quivar, the

American Boychoir, and the women of the New York Choral Artists. Kozinn returned for this concert and wrote that Mehta, conducting from memory, "drew a vital, well-focused performance that did justice to Mahler's grand vision," and that Mehta "conducted the work with an energy and sweep" that met the work's conflicting demands. Additionally, "the Philharmonic was in superb form." One is reminded of the many negative reviews Leonard Bernstein received during his tenure and the many positive ones that came his way once he had given up the Philharmonic post. The same may be holding true for Mehta.

Kurt Masur had originally intended to leave his post as director of Leipzig's Gewandhaus Orchestra in 1994, after the ensemble celebrated its 250th anniversary. However, he continued a while longer as a gesture of support for the institution, from which the government had withdrawn its subsidy of $1.3 million. Now, with the New Year's Eve concert of 1996–97, the traditional performance of Beethoven's Ninth Symphony, he decided the time was right to step down. At the end of the concert he was given the title of honorary director, under which he led the repeat performance on New Year's Day. Although he would not be breaking his ties entirely with Leipzig and the Gewandhaus, he was now free to spend more time in New York.

Masur returned to his New York podium for the subscription week beginning January 15, a program televised on that date by PBS in its *Live from Lincoln Center* series. Works by Dvořák and Tchaikovsky that were off the beaten path made up the bill of fare: the Overture to Dvořák's opera *The Devil and Kate* and his Violin Concerto, and Tchaikovsky's Second Symphony ("Little Russian"). All the pieces make use of folk or folklike themes and rhythms. The young Russian violinist Maxim Vengerov, from Siberia, was the commanding soloist, and Masur "superbly conveyed the spirit of the Tchaikovsky," the orchestra playing "wonderfully," according to Oestreich on January 17.

The first live radio broadcast of the new series was on January 25, when Masur conducted Britten's *Simple Symphony*, Leon Kirchner's Music for Cello and Orchestra, and Richard Strauss's *Don Quixote*. Yo-Yo Ma was the soloist in the Kirchner and Strauss pieces, Cynthia Phelps the violist in *Don Quixote*.

The year 1997 marked the two hundredth anniversary of the birth of Franz Schubert, which Masur celebrated on January 30 with a performance of the Ninth Symphony. Although the work has been called the "Great C Major" to distinguish it from the Sixth Symphony in the same key, it also merits that appellation for its scope and depth of content, which place it on a par with Beethoven's "Eroica." Tommasini felt that Masur and the orchestra performed it "compellingly" and pointed out that Masur had a historic claim to this particular symphony, which had received its first performance eleven years after Schubert's death—by the Leipzig Gewandhaus Orchestra, conducted by Felix Mendelssohn.

A week later, on February 6, Masur conducted Benjamin Britten's *War Requiem*, which has been described earlier in these pages. In his review Tommasini wrote that "Kurt Masur had what must rank as one of his finest achievements with the orchestra." Carol Vaness, Jerry Hadley, and Thomas Hampson were the vocal soloists, with Joseph Flummerfelt's Westminster Symphonic Choir and James Litton's American Boychoir. Samuel Wong conducted the separate chamber orchestra that accompanies the male soloists who sing the Wilfred Owen poems. Teldec Records taped the performance, and Tommasini felt "the recording may take an important place next to the classic one conducted by the composer."

The American Classics series continued on February 21 when the indefatigable Neeme Järvi led two fairly neglected works, the First Symphony of Roger Sessions and the lovable Second by Randall Thompson. Also included was the premiere of one of the Philharmonic's 150th anniversary commissions, Olly Wilson's *Shango Memory*, named for the Yoruban god of thunder and lightning in Nigeria. Oestreich wrote that the attractive piece showed "how much inspiration can still be drawn from Stravinsky's *Rite of Spring*." The program climaxed with a "stunning performance" of Rachmaninoff's Third Piano Concerto by the young Norwegian pianist Leif Ove Andsnes.

It was apparently a season for requiems, for one month after the Britten work, Sir Colin Davis returned to conduct Verdi's great masterpiece. Though not necessarily associated with Verdi, certainly not as much as with Berlioz, he led the Requiem "with devastating effect," according to Holland. The soloists were all making their Philharmonic debuts: the soprano Kallen Esperian, the mezzo-soprano Markella Hatziano, the tenor Stuart Neill, and the baritone René Pape, with the New York Choral Artists. Holland wrote of Davis as "a conductor who goes beyond technique but not before wringing from it every possible advantage." Referring to his forthcoming tenure as the Philharmonic's principal guest conductor, Holland thought it better that he "come to New York periodically rather than permanently," for "orchestras tend to turn on conductors they see all the time. . . . so let him come, work this kind of magic and then leave. Just be sure he comes back."

The previous *Live from Lincoln Center* telecast had been devoted to relatively unhackneyed works, demonstrating that such offerings need not be limited to symphonic warhorses. But the pieces by Dvořák and Tchaikovsky heard on that occasion were chestnuts when compared with what viewers heard and saw on the April 3 telecast, when the major work was a substantial portion of the music Debussy wrote for Gabriele d'Annunzio's mystery play, *The Martyrdom of St. Sebastian.*

Scored for three solo women's voices, women's chorus, and orchestra, this is Debussy at his most austere and ascetic, definitely not something to provoke tremendous ovations. In fact, according to Holland, "subscribers on Thursday did not know quite what to make of it."

Composed in 1911 and premiered in Paris in that year, *St. Sebastian* was conceived as a piece of what today would be called performance art, with choreography by Michel Fokine, sets by Léon Bakst, and solo dancing by Ida Rubinstein in the title role. The Roman Catholic church opposed it, warning that it might be blasphemous—and then there was the matter of the star's nudity. There were no such concerns with Masur's version, a concert presentation with the soloists Elizabeth Norberg-Schulz, Nancy Maultsby, and Mary Ann McCormick and the Westminster Symphonic Choir. Maria Ewing recited in French d'Annunzio's excessively purple text.

Leonard Slatkin conducted the Composer Week of May 2, which honored the music of John Adams. Gidon Kremer was the brilliant soloist in the lively Violin Concerto, and the program also included the intriguingly titled *Slonimsky's Earbox*, named for the subtly humorous musicologist Nicolas Slonimsky. Oestreich again cited *The Rite of Spring* as "fertile...inspirational ground." Slatkin continued the American symphony survey with the gentle and folksy Ives Third and also offered Duke Ellington's *Harlem*.

Copland's Third Symphony concluded the survey, also led by Slatkin, on May 15. Commissioned by Serge Koussevitzky for the Boston Symphony and first performed by them in 1946, it is a combination of Copland in his several styles: folksy, introspective, gritty, and majestic. He knew that Koussevitzky liked big, impressive endings, and he certainly gave him one. The conclusions of *Pictures at an Exhibition* and *The Pines of Rome* pale before that of the Copland Third, which includes references to his earlier *Fanfare for the Common Man*. This is certainly one of the most effective of American symphonies, worthy of performance at least as often as some Shostakovich symphonies, though more difficult to play. According to Kozinn, Slatkin and the orchestra gave it "a shapely, well-paced and vividly played performance." (Two excellent recordings of the work were made by Bernstein and the Philharmonic.)

On May 22 Masur presented a program of Wagner and Bruckner, opening with the former's Prelude and "Liebestod" from *Tristan und Isolde*. Wagner himself made the concert version that links the two excerpts—the opening and closing portions of the opera—and managed to do so while eliminating Isolde's vocal line. Masur, however, restored it and engaged the English soprano Jane Eaglen to sing it. At the time Eaglen was hailed as the natural successor to Birgit Nilsson as a Wagnerian, an opinion that was justified by this performance, though one couldn't help but be disappointed that her contribution to the evening was limited to this one excerpt of about seven minutes' duration. But it was the Bruckner Symphony No. 3 that occupied most of the program. Masur's "affecting performance of this elusive score was a notable achievement," according to Tommasini.

Carter Brey made his first solo appearance as the Philharmonic's principal cellist on May 29, when he performed Tchaikovsky's *Variations on a Rococo Theme*. Although this charming and beautiful piece is often encountered, it is rarely given in its original version, which is what Brey and Masur performed. The cellist Wilhelm Fitzenhagen had worked closely with Tchaikovsky on its composition and after the composer's death rearranged the order of the variations and made the solo line more difficult in places, ending the piece with the most brilliant variation. This is the version usually heard today. Carter Brey went back to the original, less brilliant but more sensitive version, which had been given its American premiere in 1957 at Tanglewood by Samuel Mayes, then principal cellist of the Boston Symphony, with Charles Munch conducting. Tommasini found Brey's performance "elegant, lithe and supple." Masur ended the evening with "a fervent account" of Tchaikovsky's *Romeo and Juliet Overture-Fantasy*, once an extremely popular piece but one that is unfortunately heard less and less frequently on today's concert programs.

CHAPTER 17

1997–99

A Historic Labor Agreement

For the opening of the 1997 Lincoln Center Festival on July 8 the Philharmonic took an excursion into the world of jazz, at least jazz in a symphonic context. Many composers, from Milhaud and Gershwin onward, have incorporated jazz elements into symphonic and chamber compositions, while others, who shall be nameless, have attempted to combine jazz ensembles with symphony orchestras. (A rare successful example of the latter is Ned Rorem's *Lions*.) The work performed on this occasion, lasting almost the entire evening, was *Skies of America*, by the jazz saxophonist Ornette Coleman, who was the soloist along with his Prime Time septet, with Masur conducting the Philharmonic.

As often with such hybrid pieces, the orchestra did its bit, the jazz musicians theirs, with occasional clashes of the two. "The irreconcilable differences in cultures, styles, traditions, procedures, not to mention sound colors, meter and rhythm," according to Holland on July 10, "described the character of" the piece, though he then conceded that "benign disunity" may have been what the composer had in mind. In a later article Holland wondered, "Why does a man so distinguished in his field go to such trouble to write bad classical music? . . . Mr. Coleman has better things to do than *Skies of America*."

In a return to partially familiar territory, on July 12 the Philharmonic offered a mostly Wagner program. The words "partially" and "mostly" are used advisedly, for the principal work, at least in terms of length, was Hans Werner Henze's *Tristan*, written for orchestra, piano, and magnetic tape. This piece had been given its American premiere by the Philharmonic in its 1984 Horizons festival, at which time the composer conducted, with Emanuel Ax as the piano soloist. In 1997, with Masur on the podium, the soloist was the Uruguayan-born pianist Homero Francesch. Kozinn described the way the composer "deconstructs the chromaticism that makes Wagner's setting so emotionally irresistible, and transforms Wagner's passion into streams of question marks and nightmarish imagery."

Actual Wagner made up the rest of the program, with Deborah Voigt as the splendid soprano soloist in the five *Wesendonck-Lieder*, which are thought of as studies for *Tristan und Isolde*, and the Prelude and "Liebestod" from that opera. Voigt gave a "gorgeous account" of the songs and brought to the "Liebestod" "sheer power, tonal richness and clarity of phrasing" that "made it impossible not to be swept into Isolde's emotional world."

The Philharmonic concluded its portion of the festival on July 19, when Anne-Sophie Mutter repeated the Brahms Violin Concerto, which she had played on opening night of the 1996–97 season, and Kurt Masur presented a Mendelssohn rarity, the cantata *Die erste Walpurgisnacht,* a setting of a text by Goethe. Paul Griffiths wrote somewhat disparagingly of the composer's "primitive ritual," meant to depict scary doings on "the first Walpurgis night," sometimes referred to as "the other Halloween." If one can accept the romantic era's fascination with the supernatural and matters macabre, then Mendelssohn's piece is an effective example of its kind. Participating were the Royal Opera Chorus from London (imported to take part in that company's production of Hans Pfitzner's *Palestrina*), the mezzo-soprano Mary Ann McCormick, the tenor Carl Halvorson, and the baritone Nathan Gunn.

On August 11 came the news of the death of William Lincer, the orchestra's principal violist from 1943 to 1972, at the age of ninety. He had played the solos in Strauss's *Don Quixote* in Bernstein's Philharmonic debut and had made fifty-seven solo appearances with the orchestra, with which he had played in over four thousand concerts. Another death was reported on September 6, that of the conductor Sir Georg Solti. Although he had not been a frequent guest with the Philharmonic, he did appear with them from time to time. Of course, he was best known for his long tenure as music director of the Chicago Symphony.

To continue the Brahms centennial commemoration, Masur led the composer's First Symphony on the season-opening gala concert of September 17. All four of the symphonies, which Masur and the Philharmonic had already recorded, would be given during the next few weeks. Tommasini felt this performance was "a remarkable achievement," remarking that this much-heard score was made to sound "like an indisputedly great piece." The much-admired soprano Renée Fleming was the lustrous soloist in Mozart's *Exultate, jubilate* and three songs by Richard Strauss.

The concert also celebrated Kurt Masur's seventieth birthday, the actual date of which was July 18. That day there had been a special luncheon in Avery Fisher Hall and an evening concert of lighter works that, critics complained, did not belong in the august Lincoln Center Festival. On the September date a black-tie dinner was held after the concert, with surprise appearances by Wynton Marsalis, the Boys Choir of Harlem, and Renée Fleming, who sang popular songs accompanied at the piano by André Previn.

The Brahms Second and Third Symphonies were performed together, though in reverse order, on the concerts beginning September 25. Oestreich praised Masur's "compelling accounts," replete with "well-turned phrases and subtle touches" as well as "a remarkable transparency." He also reported that, at a pre-concert forum, Masur had spoken of the Brahms symphonies as a single "life symphony in four movements," and of how the quiet ending of the Third represented not resignation, but transfiguration. When asked why he programmed the Second and Third in reverse order, he replied, "I'm a very selfish man. I want to go home uplifted, not sad." The Fourth Symphony was given on October 2 and succeeding concerts of the week. Reviewing the performance of the 6th, Kozinn felt that in Masur's hands the work "did not suggest [the composer's] leave-taking so much as an assertion of mastery."

Of interest to the Philharmonic's musicians was the news, reported on October 5, that their colleagues in the Chicago Symphony had unanimously approved a new three-year contract. Under its terms the Chicago musicians now had the highest annual salary of any American orchestra, $81,900. The New York Philharmonic was second at $81,120.

Kurt Masur has always had a liking for works that include the spoken word. Sometimes, if that element is lacking, he will add it, as he did to César Franck's rarely performed symphonic poem *Psyché*. For the performances beginning October 8, an English-language narration was provided by the playwright John Guare and spoken by the actress Cherry Jones. The New York Choral Artists sang the interludes, which Holland found "drab and uninspired," in sharp contrast to the purely orchestral sections, which are quite musically sensuous and erotic in the manner of Wagner and Scriabin. He felt that the word "languid" was foreign to Masur's vocabulary but praised the conductor's pacing and sense of proportion, finally urging anyone unfamiliar with the piece to attend one of the remaining performances.

Composer Week came around again beginning October 30, this time featuring the music of the Pole Krzysztof Penderecki, who conducted two of his own works and Beethoven's Piano Concerto No. 3 with the American pianist Christopher O'Riley in his Philharmonic subscription debut. The program opened with Penderecki's most celebrated piece, *Threnody for the Victims of Hiroshima*. Written for fifty-two string instruments, it is an example of the composer's early style, containing massive chord clusters and using the instruments to create all manner of sound effects, including tapping the wood with the knuckles. The work vividly portrays its subject matter, even though it was composed as an abstract entity, the title having been added later.

Penderecki's Symphony No. 5, in its New York premiere, belongs to a later period, a neoromantic work that is not recognizably by the same composer. In it the composer seems to be striving to make a big statement, at times in the manner of Mahler. Tommasini felt that Penderecki "elicited an impassioned performance from the orchestra that was hard to resist," just as he found him an impressive conductor of the Beethoven concerto, of which O'Riley "gave a superb account."

Richard Westerfield, who in 1993 was a last-minute substitute for Erich Leinsdorf, appeared with the Philharmonic on November 20 as a full-fledged (and scheduled) guest conductor. Recently appointed associate conductor of the Boston Symphony, he programmed the difficult Shostakovich Symphony No. 8. Given its American premiere by the Philharmonic in 1944 and seldom played by them since, the hourlong work has been gradually gaining ground in the repertoire, and Westerfield gave it "a blazing, authoritative performance," according to Tommasini, "impassioned, yet impressively controlled."

Mendelssohn's *Elijah* appears once a decade or so on Philharmonic programs and is usually greeted patronizingly by critics, who tend to dismiss it as a bit stuffy. Yet to Oestreich it is a "great oratorio," as he wrote in his December 6 review of Masur's performance two days earlier, and Avery Fisher Hall is the best place to hear Mendelssohn's music, other than, perhaps, the Leipzig Gewandhaus. So steeped in this music is Masur, so convincingly does he conduct it, that, according to Oestreich, he "swept away the last remnants of the Victorian stodginess" that have long afflicted Mendelssohn's choral music. Making an important contribution to the success of the performance was the dynamic Welsh baritone Bryn Terfel in the title role. Other soloists were the American soprano Kelley Nassief and the English tenor John Mack Ainsley. Joseph Flummerfelt's Westminster Symphonic Choir was its usual superb self.

Contractual history was made on December 12, 1997, when the musicians of the New York Philharmonic ratified a new labor agreement lasting six years, the longest contract ever for a symphony orchestra. To add to its uniqueness, the agreement was reached a full year before the expiration of the existing contract. There had been so much unrest in the profession of late—the Philadelphia Orchestra and the San Francisco Symphony had been on strike for nine weeks, the Atlanta Symphony for ten, and the Oregon Symphony for fifteen days, while other orchestras had come close to striking—that Deborah Borda and the Philharmonic musicians wished to avoid any further unpleasantness. Under the terms of the new agreement, minimum yearly salaries would rise above $100,000 for the first time in the profession, with each player earning at least two thousand dollars a week. Pensions would increase to $53,000 a year, and health care payments would no longer require the musicians to pay a $10 weekly charge if the costs were over $1.2 million a year. The players' labor lawyer, I. Philip Sipser, remarked that in his thirty-year career he "had never seen an orchestra contract wrapped up so quickly." He felt it would set the standard for future negotiations for all orchestras, concluding that "Chicago will come into the next negotiations yelling bloody murder."

The Philharmonic gave all music lovers a Christmas present when on December 14 it announced the release of its ten-CD set *The Historic Broadcasts, 1923 to 1987.* Here was a treasure trove of live performances under such conductors as Toscanini, Klemperer, Mengelberg, Rodzinski, Stokowski, Barbirolli, Monteux, Mitropoulos, Munch, Szell, Bernstein, Reiner, Leinsdorf, Kubelík, and others, mostly in repertoire they had not recorded commercially, and with soloists that included Rubinstein, Schnabel, Heifetz, and Oistrakh. No other American orchestra has such a rich broadcasting history as the Philharmonic, and this set was the first of several that would be released in the next few years.

Once such a rarity that it did not receive its American premiere until 1947 and was not heard again in the United States until 1955, Mahler's great Sixth Symphony has gradually come into its own and now seems to be given by major orchestras every two or three years. Valery Gergiev was the latest to program it with the Philharmonic in concerts beginning January 2, 1998. The energetic Gergiev was "satisfying and revelatory" in his approach to the work, according to Oestreich, though he found the conductor's work curiously lethargic in the second movement. But the Philharmonic "played like the fine Mahler orchestra it is."

On January 13 the public read of the death from throat cancer of Klaus Tennstedt at the age of seventy-one. Between the time he arrived in the West in 1971 and his retirement from the concert stage in 1994 owing to illness, the East German maestro had established himself as a dynamic interpreter of the Austro-German repertoire and had been a frequent and welcome guest of the Philharmonic and many other orchestras.

The Israel Philharmonic came to New York for two concerts, January 19 and 21, each with a different conductor. The first, in Carnegie Hall, was led by their music director for life, Zubin Mehta, who concluded the program with one of his specialties, *The Rite of Spring.* Just as Masur had followed Mehta with the New York Philharmonic, so did he follow him in this instance, conducting Beethoven's Ninth Symphony in Avery Fisher Hall. Reviewing both concerts, Kozinn felt that Mehta "often seemed more interested in details than in the larger picture," while Masur "seemed concerned with the broader view." But "there was an irresistible vigor" in both performances, "something the players gave both conductors in equal measure."

The New York Philharmonic continued its survey of American music with its concerts beginning January 22. Leonard Slatkin, a fervent advocate of this repertoire, was on the podium this time, leading two classics of the genre, a recent work, and a new one in its premiere. The classics were William Schuman's *New England Triptych* and Aaron Copland's Suite from *Billy the Kid.* Joseph Schwantner's Percussion Concerto had received its extremely successful premiere in 1995, with the Philharmonic's Christopher Lamb as the spectacular soloist then and again on this occasion. The new piece was John Zorn's *Orchestra Variations.* According to Kozinn, Slatkin "conducted confidently" and the orchestra displayed what it "can do when the music engages it." The six-minute Zorn piece "seemed a deft parody of academic atonality."

Time was when Bruckner's monumental Eighth Symphony was not considered sufficient for an entire program. Among Philharmonic conductors alone, Bruno Walter prefaced it with Richard Strauss's *Metamorphosen* in 1948, George Szell with Casella's *Paganiniana* in 1950, and Josef Krips with Beethoven's *Coriolan* Overture and Webern's *Passacaglia* in 1961. Even allowing for the fact that programs tend to be shorter today than in earlier times, conductors today feel that at about eighty minutes long, the symphony can stand on its own. On January 29 Christoph Eschenbach devoted his entire Philharmonic program to Bruckner's Eighth, leading an expansive performance lasting eighty-six minutes. Kozinn, whom the *Times* was keeping busy covering the Philharmonic, felt that Eschenbach presented "Bruckner's introspection... tempered with a measure of earthiness and anxiety" and at times gave the work much visceral excitement.

Since first performing it in the Bach tricentennial year, Masur had become a distinguished interpreter of the *Passion According to Saint Matthew.* He had presented the work successfully with the Philharmonic in 1993, and now, in 1998, he gave it once more. Masur had a special reason to offer it again, beginning February 12, for these performances had the participation of the Thomanerchor, the boys' choir of St. Thomas Church in Leipzig, which Bach himself directed from 1723 to 1750. Masur, too, had had a close relationship with the group during his long tenure in Leipzig. Oestreich judged the Thomanerchor "wonderful to hear: unfailingly full of spirit, secure in pitch and beautifully balanced." He regretted that Masur appeared to have submitted to the dictates of the early-music movement in terms of pacing and dynamics; he missed the warmth and grandeur of the conductor's earlier performances. The soloists this time were the soprano Sylvia McNair, the mezzo-soprano Annette Markert, the tenors John Aler and Stanford Olsen, and the baritone William Stone. Oestreich concluded that if Masur "was thrilled with the outcome, he was entitled."

For his next week, beginning February 19, Masur conducted Lukas Foss's *Time Cycle* as part of the American Classics series. Premiered by Bernstein and the Philharmonic in 1960, this work, which sets texts by W. H. Auden, A. E. Housman, Franz Kafka, and Friedrich Nietzsche, is an early example of the composer's abandonment of tonality in favor of the twelve-tone system. It proved an excellent vehicle for the talents of the delightful soprano Dawn Upshaw, whose tone Tommasini described as "radiant." She also was the soloist in Joseph Canteloube's exquisite settings of *Songs of the Auvergne*. In keeping with the theme of *Time Cycle*, Masur opened the program with Haydn's Symphony No. 101 ("The Clock"). Prokofiev's barbaric *Scythian Suite* was a boisterous closer.

The recent friction between Masur and the Philharmonic's management continued to make news. In a *Times* article on February 27, Ralph Blumenthal wrote of "a bitter row" in which, according to Masur, he had been "pressured to resign." Left unmentioned was Masur's pleading with the orchestra musicians for their support. The article went on to state that Masur and the Philharmonic Society had agreed on an extension of his contract to 2002, but that plans would be made to find a successor.

Although some board members had nothing but praise for Masur, some of the more outspoken orchestra members, as well as critics, wondered why the conductor was being confronted at this time. For his part, Masur was said to be insulted at the manner in which the issue had been raised. It had initially been proposed that his contract be terminated with the 2000–2001 season, during which he would conduct a limited number of concerts while various guest conductors auditioned for the job. This idea infuriated Masur. "I would say that I was surprised," he said in an understatement. Many people questioned why the Philharmonic had to join the ranks of other orchestras seeking new music directors, such as Philadelphia, Cleveland, and perhaps Boston. One Philharmonic board member, William J. McDonough, said, "There's certainly no notion we wish to push him out the door. Quite the contrary." The chairman, Paul Guenther, maintained that the new agreement guaranteed Masur's leadership into the twenty-first century and "eliminates any uncertainty about who the music director is and also gives us plenty of time to deal with whatever strategic issues come after that." In a review in the *Times* of March 2, Kozinn reported that "Mr. Masur and the orchestra offered a brilliantly conceived and spectacularly played performance of the Tchaikovsky 'Pathetique' Symphony that argued forcibly that the board is out of its collective mind." In a March 8 column, Holland wrote that the Philharmonic was being "run more by bottom-liners than by musical visionaries," and that Masur, for all his musical conservatism, "has been good for this orchestra, administering strong, sometimes bitter medicine to a patient that needed a little calming down. He, on the other hand, was never a permanent solution. When Mr. Masur leaves, we should be grateful to him but not unhappy for ourselves."

David Zinman was the guest conductor for the concerts beginning March 25, on which he programmed a once-popular rarity from the nineteenth century, Carl Goldmark's engaging *Rustic Wedding Symphony*. The busy Kozinn, after commenting on Mitsuko Uchida's "alternately forceful and poetic reading" of Chopin's First Piano Concerto (which in fact is his second, though published first) before an almost full house in the first half of the program, wondered why there were so many empty seats for the Goldmark in the second half. It was not as though they feared subjection to a harsh modern score, for the Goldmark is a thoroughly charming and melodic work. "Can it be that the Philharmonic's audience doesn't want to hear what it doesn't already know?" queried Kozinn. "That's a scary thought." Many laypersons have commented to the author that they like certain pieces because they are familiar with them, because they have heard them before; they feel comfortable with them. Yet there must have been a time when they heard their favorite pieces for the first time. Did they dislike them then because they were unfamiliar? When did their lack of curiosity begin? In any event, Zinman and the Philharmonic "made the Goldmark sound spectacular."

In a departure from its customary format, the Philharmonic presented the Hungarian-born pianist András Schiff in a two-week residency, during which time he played concertos with the orchestra and took part in chamber music and lieder performances as well. On April 8 he offered the Brahms Concerto No. 2 with Masur conducting. In his review Holland described Schiff as "one of our important pianists, combining elegance, seriousness of purpose, musicianly rectitude, reliable technique and touching directness." The following week, beginning April 16, Schumann's Piano Concerto was Schiff's vehicle, in which Kozinn felt that he "produced a reading that seemed fresh and slightly provocative, but fully justifiable." On each of the programs Masur conducted a Schumann symphony, No. 4 the first week, No. 2 the second. Holland wrote that it was one of the best Philharmonic evenings he could remember.

Those who do enjoy hearing relatively unfamiliar works had their wish granted during four weeks in April and May 1998. On April 23 Sir Colin Davis conducted Elgar's Symphony No. 2, as part of a program of English music that also included the Ritual Dances from Sir Michael Tippett's opera *The Midsummer Marriage*, performed in memory of the composer, who had died earlier in the year at the age of ninety-three. The Elgar symphony had last been played by the Philharmonic in 1966, when William Steinberg programmed it. The following week, on April 30,

Leonard Slatkin offered a work never before played by the orchestra: the Symphony No. 2 ("Asrael") by the Czech composer Josef Suk, a pupil of Dvořák and later his son-in-law. Slatkin was a guest for two weeks, and in the second, beginning May 7, he revived the Symphony in C Major by Paul Dukas, last heard by Philharmonic audiences when Charles Munch conducted it in 1949. Finally, on May 14, James Conlon gave the first Philharmonic performance of the extended tone poem *Die Seejungfrau* (The Mermaid) by Alexander Zemlinsky, who had been Schoenberg's teacher and later became his brother-in-law.

After this series of esoterica, Shostakovich's Seventh Symphony ("Leningrad") must have seemed like an old friend to Philharmonic subscribers when Masur led it on May 21. Kozinn called the performance one that would cause doubters to revise their opinion: "Mr. Masur made it sound less like patriotic poster art and more like the wrenching human drama that Shostakovich intended."

The *Times* of May 23 reported the death of Francis Goelet at the age of seventy-two. A member of the Philharmonic-Symphony Society's board since 1959 and the chair of its music policy committee at the time of his death, he was known for his commissioning of new music, including works in celebration of the orchestra's 125th anniversary as well as an impressive series of concertos written for the Philharmonic's principal players.

David Del Tredici was the Philharmonic's composer in residence for the 1997–98 season. He was especially known for his series of pieces inspired by Lewis Carroll's *Alice's Adventures in Wonderland*, with which he had apparently had a thirty-year obsession. Of these, *Final Alice* is the best known, largely for its having been recorded by Sir Georg Solti and the Chicago Symphony, with Barbara Hendricks as the soprano soloist. Curiously, *Final Alice*, in spite of its title, was not the last of these pieces, which continued to appear regularly.

Now, in 1998, Del Tredici announced he was through with *Alice*. On May 28 Masur and the Philharmonic premiered a new, non-*Alice* work called *The Spider and the Fly*, a setting of the children's poem by Mary Howitt, calling for a soprano (Hila Plitmann as the Fly) and a baritone soloist (Nathan Gunn as the Spider). Referring to the orchestra part as "an extravagant jumble of pretty sounds," Holland went on to describe the many stylistic references in the piece, from *Das Rheingold* to Nelson Riddle to Richard Strauss to George Gershwin to jazz syncopations: "We are treated to the composer as disk jockey." The high-lying, shrieking soprano part contrasted markedly with the more comfortable baritone line. Both voices were amplified, "a ghastly mistake," according to Holland. In the end, he opined, "Mr. Del Tredici's music couldn't hurt a fly, even if Howitt's poem can."

The program also celebrated Stanley Drucker's fiftieth anniversary as a member of the Philharmonic, which he observed by giving another virtuoso performance of what had become his signature piece, Copland's Clarinet Concerto. And Drucker's Philharmonic tenure was far from over.

BEETHOVEN AGAIN?

Another Asian tour brought Masur and the Philharmonic for the first time to China, where they played a June 24 concert in Beijing in the Great Hall of the People, the night before the U.S.–China summit meeting attended by President Bill Clinton. The orchestra also visited Japan and, in honor of its centennial celebration, the Philippines.

Back home, the Philharmonic again participated in the Lincoln Center Festival, which had as one of its themes a series called Leonard Bernstein Remembered. The festival's main attraction was to have been performances of the sixteenth-century Chinese opera *The Peony Pavilion*, but at the eleventh hour the government of China refused to send the production abroad, so the Bernstein celebration took on greater prominence than originally planned. The Philharmonic's two concerts combined Bernstein with composers he championed, the first program on July 7 pairing Bernstein's Symphony No. 2 ("The Age of Anxiety") with Mahler's Symphony No. 1. The obvious common thread of those pieces is that the two composers were both music directors of the New York Philharmonic. Beyond that, Holland could find no reason for juxtaposing them, for the Mahler work is heard often enough and, in the reviewer's opinion, had no business in a festival. He did not have very kind words for Bernstein's piece but was surprised that the musicians played the Mahler better than they played the Bernstein, though even that was "not tidy." Lukas Foss played the important piano part in "The Age of Anxiety," which moved Holland to lament that the eminent composer-conductor was not heard more often in that capacity.

Between its two festival concerts, Masur and the orchestra took part in a special program on the Great Lawn in Central Park, one of many summer events celebrating New York City's centennial of the merging of the five boroughs into one city. The Philharmonic, playing Gershwin and Bernstein, shared the evening with Skitch Henderson and the New York Pops and with the Lincoln Center Jazz Orchestra.

Returning to Avery Fisher Hall and the festival, Masur conducted an all-American program on July 14 including Ives's *Three Places in New England*; Copland's Clarinet Concerto, with Stanley Drucker; Bernstein's Symphony No. 1 ("Jeremiah"), with the Israeli mezzo-soprano Susanna Poretsky as the soloist in the finale; and Gershwin's *Rhapsody in Blue*, in which the soloist was the young Turkish pianist Fazil Say.

On July 27 was noted the death of the Russian-born violinist Tossy Spivakovsky at the age of ninety-one. Known especially for his advocacy of contemporary music, he had given the American premiere of Bartók's Violin Concerto No. 2 in 1943 and was a frequent soloist with the Philharmonic during the 1950s and 1960s. It was with the Philharmonic that he gave the New York premiere of Roger Sessions's Violin Concerto in 1959, with Bernstein conducting. He was also known for his idiosyncratic style of bowing, which enabled him to play solid chords in Bach's works rather than arpeggiating them.

As a follow-up to its set of historic broadcast performances, the Philharmonic announced on September 10 a second set, this one of twelve CDs, entitled *The Mahler Broadcasts, 1948–1982*. Included were all the Mahler symphonies, the two movements of the unfinished Tenth, *Das Lied von der Erde*, and the *Songs of a Wayfarer*, led by Barbirolli, Boulez, Kubelík, Mehta, Mitropoulos, Solti, Steinberg, Stokowski, Tennstedt, and Walter, with vocal soloists Kathleen Battle, Kathleen Ferrier, Dietrich Fischer-Dieskau, Maureen Forrester, Yvonne Minton, Irmgard Seefried, and Set Svanholm. Also included were two hours of interviews of musicians who played under Mahler's direction. Conspicuously absent from the list of conductors was Bernstein, but because he had recorded nearly all the Mahler symphonies with the Philharmonic (though not part II of No. 8), the producers thought that other conductors' interpretations would be of historical interest.

If there is one thing to which the New York music critics do not look forward, it is a Beethoven cycle by the Philharmonic, no matter how much it may appeal to the public. When one was announced to begin the 1998–99 season, Holland wrote of having to "wade through another Beethoven cycle at the Philharmonic," and once it began, Tommasini found "no especially compelling reason" for Masur and the orchestra to present one at that time.

To complain of "another Beethoven cycle" is to ignore the fact that the most recent Beethoven cycle by the Philharmonic had been its spring festival in 1980, eighteen years before, and the last one before that was the cycle Bruno Walter conducted during the 1948–49 season. Masur would be performing the symphonies in numerical order, which had not been done since Toscanini's cycle at the end of the 1941–42 season.

Bernstein had conducted all the Beethoven symphonies during his tenure, but spread out over several seasons, and Masur himself had already given most of them up to that point. So, what with the omnipresence of Beethoven in New York seasons by the Philharmonic and by visiting orchestras, the idea that "another Beethoven cycle" was unnecessary or unwelcome might seem reasonable. As Tommasini himself pointed out, Masur "is a fine Beethoven conductor," one who "has a special claim [to this repertoire] through heritage." His renditions of the Second and Third Symphonies on September 22 were conducted "with insight, energy and an exceptional sense of structural cohesion." Still, Tommasini regretted that "something more adventurous was not happening instead." Kozinn felt the Beethoven cycle itself was not the issue, but rather the Philharmonic's general timidity of programming. The impact of the 150th anniversary commissions had been dissipated because they had been spread over several seasons. The American Classics series pointed up the fact that the Philharmonic should have been playing this repertoire anyway, without special pleading. The annual Composer Week was merely a marketing ploy, the featured composer represented by one or two works mixed in with standard repertoire pieces.

And yet, when one actually sits down to listen to a Beethoven symphony, all such reservations disappear, and one hears this great music for what it is. On September 28, 1998, the Sixth and Seventh Symphonies made their customary impact. For the Ninth Symphony on October 1, Masur and the orchestra had the assistance of the soprano Kelley Nassief, the mezzo-soprano Marietta Simpson, the tenor John Aler, the baritone Håkan Hagegård, the Westminster Symphonic Choir, and, unusually for this piece, the American Boychoir. Although Tommasini had some reservations about the preceding Eighth Symphony, he praised Masur's "comprehension of the scope and structure" of the Ninth, his "bringing a sense of shape and architecture to the finale."

Although Sir Edward Elgar is most often represented on concert programs by his *Enigma Variations*, opportunities to hear his expansive Violin Concerto are comparably rare. One was afforded, however, on the concerts beginning October 29 when the English violinist Nigel Kennedy gave an impressive performance with the Philharmonic, with Leonard Slatkin conducting. For Tommasini, "his intense involvement with the music was hard to resist," while the orchestra under Slatkin "played splendidly." The American Classics series continued with a rendition of Barber's *Capricorn Concerto*, which had been premiered by the Philharmonic in 1946. This is Barber in a rare (for him) neoclassical vein, redolent of Stravinsky. Neobaroque might be another term for the work, which is really a concerto grosso for three wind instruments, flute, oboe, and trumpet, and string orchestra. The respective soloists from the orchestra were Sandra Church, Joseph Robinson, and Philip Smith, all of whom "played beautifully," according to Tommasini.

An entire program of American music was given the following week beginning November 5, again with Slatkin in charge. Most music lovers know the name of

Peter Schickele as the creator of that undistinguished and needlessly prolific composer, P. D. Q. Bach. But Schickele is a highly inventive and engaging composer in his own right, as was evidenced by the Philharmonic's performance of his Symphony No. 1, a work that Paul Griffiths felt "sounded like a gifted musician having fun." Also heard that evening were Edward MacDowell's Piano Concerto No. 2, with André Watts as the commanding soloist, and the Concerto for String Quartet and Orchestra by Benjamin Lees, which featured four orchestra soloists: Glenn Dicterow, Marc Ginsberg, Cynthia Phelps, and Carter Brey. Griffiths found this energetic piece "an interesting venture" in combining the intimacy of a quartet with the extroversion of an orchestra.

Masur would apparently end his Philharmonic tenure just as he had begun it: in charge of two orchestras. On November 12 came the announcement that he had accepted the post of principal conductor of the London Philharmonic Orchestra, to take effect in 2000. London orchestras generally do not have music directors in the manner of American orchestras, but rather principal conductors, who direct more concerts than any other conductor, but not really the majority of the orchestra's concerts. In 1961, when the eighty-six-year-old Pierre Monteux accepted the post of principal conductor of the London Symphony Orchestra, with which he had first appeared as a guest conductor, he told his students, "That means I conduct five concerts instead of four." Masur reassured New Yorkers that his new appointment would not affect his commitment to their Philharmonic.

Sir Colin Davis made his first appearance in his new role as the Philharmonic's principal guest conductor on November 12 in a program on which the major work was songs from Mahler's *Des Knaben Wunderhorn* (The Youth's Magic Horn). The soloists were the Danish soprano Inger Dam-Jensen and the remarkable German baritone Thomas Quasthoff. Oestreich had great praise for Quasthoff, less than that for Dam-Jensen, and felt Davis had the orchestra showing "its Mahlerian stripes beautifully." Also on the program was the *Petite symphonie concertante* by the Swiss composer Frank Martin. Uniquely scored for double string orchestra, it is the only work the author can think of in which the solo instruments are a piano, a harpsichord, and a harp, which does make for balance problems. The Philharmonic's Harriet Wingreen, Lionel Party, and Nancy Allen were the respective soloists.

The year 1998 marked the centennial of the birth of George Gershwin, whose music rarely figures on serious symphonic concerts, though Rodzinski and Bernstein had no reservations about playing it on Philharmonic concerts. Masur was of the same mind. "I treat Gershwin as a serious composer," he said. "I don't want to use him as a ticket seller." Accordingly, the Philharmonic scheduled three programs of his music, the first, on December 10, offering the *Cuban Overture*, the Piano Concerto in F (with André Previn as the idiomatic soloist), *An American in Paris*, and Robert Russell Bennett's arrangement entitled *Symphonic Picture of "Porgy and Bess."* This last had been commissioned by Fritz Reiner in 1943 and premiered and recorded by him with the Pittsburgh Symphony. He later programmed it with the Philharmonic, which also played it under Rodzinski. Tommasini found it a "blaringly orchestrated medley of hit tunes," but the sequence of tunes was requested by Reiner, who also suggested details of the orchestration. As for the rest, Tommasini enjoyed Masur's treatment of the music, for Gershwin himself took these pieces seriously.

The second Gershwin program, given on December 12 and also conducted by Masur, had the Turkish pianist Fazil Say as soloist in the *Rhapsody in Blue* and the rarely heard Variations on *I Got Rhythm*. Sylvia McNair sang a group of songs, and the program opened with the Overture to *Let 'Em Eat Cake*, not something normally found in Masur territory. The Gershwin festivities concluded on December 17 with a concert performance of *Porgy and Bess* conducted not by Masur, but by Bobby McFerrin. It was apparently thought that McFerrin's experience as a jazz performer would bring just the right touch to Gershwin, but according to Griffiths the reverse was true, the performance sagging at times, even becoming dull. High marks, however, were given to the Morgan State University Choir, which "made the piece their own," and the soloists Kevin Deas, Marvis Martin, Harolyn Blackwell, Camellia Johnson, Michael Forest, and Lester Lynch.

On December 29 Masur was once again faced with a barrage of bronchial explosions, this time during the playing of the third movement of Shostakovich's Fifth Symphony. So obtrusive did the coughing become that he not only stopped the performance, but left the stage. Some members of the audience applauded as he did so, as they did when he returned about two minutes later. He then began the movement again and conducted the rest of the symphony in comparative silence. Quoted on December 31, Masur said, "It was unbearable. This is one of the deepest slow movements of any composer. . . . we tried our best, but with the kind of uncontrolled coughing in the audience, I felt more and more that nobody could concentrate. . . . I just wanted to make people aware that they were disturbing the process of listening."

In the fall of 1998 the Philharmonic acquired a new principal associate concertmaster in the person of Cheryl Staples. A Los Angeles native, she had been associate concertmaster of the Cleveland Orchestra. Now, on January 2, 1999, she was the soloist in Tchaikovsky's Violin Concerto with Masur conducting. Tommasini found her to be "a perceptive musician" who gave "a most rewarding performance."

Shortly thereafter the orchestra embarked on a seven-concert tour of the United States—strangely enough, its first domestic tour since 1990. Traveling from West to East, the Philharmonic stopped in cities it had not visited in more than ten years, such as Los Angeles, San Francisco, and Chicago, and finished the tour in Boston on January 15. Although audiences were enthusiastic and the critics laudatory, there were some complaints that the Philharmonic played no American music, one critic finding its absence "little short of disgraceful." Masur wondered why it was thought necessary to play American music in America, since the orchestra always did so when it played outside the country. He concluded by remarking that "you cannot very often hear Shostakovich the way the New York Philharmonic plays it."

The long-delayed Philharmonic debut of Riccardo Muti occurred on January 20. For the occasion he chose a characteristically unhackneyed program (most of it, anyway), the Brahms Serenade No. 1 in D major, excerpts from Busoni's *Turandot* Suite, and Ravel's *Bolero*. Holland praised Muti as "a sound musician who knows precisely how to make an orchestra do what he wants them to do." He also felt that, "like all good conductors, Mr. Muti knew when to let his players alone and when to keep their strict attention."

On January 26 was reported the death of the great choral conductor Robert Shaw at the age of eighty-two. Also known as an orchestral conductor, he had been for many years the music director of the Atlanta Symphony and had conducted choral works with the Philharmonic on several occasions, most notably Haydn's *Creation* and the Brahms *German Requiem*.

An unusual program of Prokofieff and Shostakovich was presented by Valery Gergiev on February 5 consisting of the former's Suite from *The Love for Three Oranges* and Piano Concerto No. 1, and the latter's Piano Concerto No. 1 and Symphony No. 6. The pianist was the impressive Yefim Bronfman. Shostakovich's concerto is scored for string orchestra and has an important obbligato solo trumpet part, which was played by the Philharmonic's principal, the equally impressive Philip Smith. Contributing to the unusualness of the program was the fact that all four works are examples of the composers' penchant for satire (with the exception of the long, slow first movement of the Shostakovich Symphony). For example, the Prokofieff suite is taken from an opera inspired by the literary satire of the Italian playwright Carlo Gozzi, while the symphony begins in a broodingly serious vein and ends up with music that would not be out of place in the Moscow Circus. Its closing measures bring to mind, in a rather perverse way, the final cadence of Mozart's "Jupiter" Symphony.

Although not exactly a Liszt specialist, Masur has recorded all thirteen of the composer's symphonic poems with the London Philharmonic. He further enhanced his Liszt credentials by offering, on February 26, the rarely heard *Symphony to*

Dante's "Divina Commedia," a performance that Oestreich found to be "one of the orchestra's finer efforts of the season." Preceding the Liszt work the French pianist Hélène Grimaud was heard in a "compelling" rendition of Beethoven's Concerto No. 4 in G major.

The Italian maestro Daniele Gatti had made a fine impression in his Philharmonic debut in 1996, when he conducted Mahler's Sixth Symphony, but had been less impressive in Mahler's Fifth in 1998. Now scheduled to lead the composer's Fourth Symphony on March 5, he canceled the engagement for medical reasons. His place was taken by the Hungarian conductor Iván Fischer, who also made a good impression in his Philharmonic debut, as did the British soprano Amanda Roocroft in hers. For reasons that are unclear, the final performance of the sequence, on March 9, was led without rehearsal by the Uruguayan-born Israeli conductor Gisele Ben-Dor. She had previously been an unpublicized substitute conductor for Masur in 1993, also without rehearsal. On the later occasion she succeeded in bringing something of her own interpretation to the work. As Oestreich said, "She has this trick down pat."

On March 13 came news of the death of the violinist Yehudi Menuhin, at the age of eighty-two. The *Times* obituary duly acknowledged as well his work as a conductor, founder of music festivals, educator, and humanitarian supporter of countless charities. Even accounting for a seven-year gap in his Philharmonic performances, brought about by his having dared to play an encore in 1957, he was a frequent soloist with the orchestra, with which he first performed in 1927 at the age of eleven in the Beethoven Violin Concerto, no less. Wrote the *Times*'s Olin Downes of that performance, "It may seem ridiculous to say that he showed a mature conception of Beethoven's concerto, but that is the fact." At the age of sixteen he recorded Elgar's Violin Concerto with the composer conducting, a legendary recording that is still in the catalog. A frequent performer of contemporary music, he made the first recording of Bartók's Concerto No. 2, still *the* Bartók Violin Concerto, despite the later discovery of the so-called Concerto No. 1. The violinist Gil Shaham dedicated his performance of the Concerto No. 2 with the Philharmonic on March 13 to Menuhin's memory.

The year 1999 marked another composer centennial—Francis Poulenc's, which Charles Dutoit celebrated on March 25 by programming the breezy ballet suite *Les biches* (usually given the English title, *The House Party*). This is one of the composer's most delectable scores, combining his sensuous lyricism with the atmosphere of a French music hall (which could actually be said about many of his works).

Sir Colin Davis returned on April 15 for an all-Mozart program consisting of the "Haffner" Symphony, K. 385; the Piano Concerto No. 25 in C Major, K. 503, with the English pianist Imogen Cooper in her Philharmonic debut; and the great "Posthorn" Serenade, K. 320. (All of this composer's works are great, but the adjective is used specifically for the "Posthorn" because it is a lesser-known piece of grand dimensions—seven movements—that deserves more frequent exposure.) Tommasini pointed out that Davis does not adhere to the strictures of the early-music movement, but follows more in the footsteps of Sir Thomas Beecham, who did not hesitate to offer "big band" Mozart and Haydn, often with relaxed tempos that emphasized the music's lyrical aspects. In the right hands, that approach can give the impression that the performers are actually enjoying the music.

Davis returned a week later to give the American premiere of a work by the Scottish composer James MacMillan. Entitled *The World's Ransoming*, it is partially inspired by the Roman Catholic liturgy for Maundy Thursday and thus is concerned with the Last Supper. It is also a concertante work for English horn, in which the Philharmonic's Thomas Stacy was the characterful protagonist. Kozinn wrote approvingly of the work and its performance, but less so of Davis's interpretation of Bruckner's Ninth Symphony, finding the tempos unusually expansive: "Bruckner in slow motion is a scary prospect."

One can count on the fingers of one hand the major works written for viola and orchestra. From the nineteenth century the great work is Berlioz's symphony *Harold in Italy*, in which the viola both plays an obbligato role and is often silent for pages at a time. From the twentieth century we have actual concertos by Walton, Bartók, and Walter Piston. It is safe to say, however, that until 1999 there was no piece for two violas and orchestra (though a thorough search through the four hundred or so concertos by Vivaldi might unearth one). This situation was remedied by the Philharmonic's commissioning just such a work from the Russian composer Sofia Gubaidulina. It was actually Masur's wife, Tomoko, herself a former violist, who commissioned it for the Philharmonic's first desk violists, Cynthia Phelps and Rebecca Young.

Born in 1931, Gubaidulina managed to pursue a compositional course that was not approved by the powers that were in the former Soviet Union, in much the same way as had her colleague Alfred Schnittke, with the result that she was rarely performed in her native land until the collapse of Communism, by which time she had moved to Paris. She is today regarded, along with Schnittke, as one of the most important Russian composers since Shostakovich. Her double viola concerto, enti-tled *Two Paths*, portrays musically the sisters Martha and Mary of the Gospel of St. John. On May 3 Holland wrote of the composer as "an absolute master of orches-tration," of the work itself as having "the dark, troubled rhetoric of modern

Europe," and of the two soloists as possessing "the high-powered techniques necessary to fill Avery Fisher Hall."

In an interview the day before, Kurt Masur spoke of how, in his first seven years at the Philharmonic, he was confronted with "a backlog of new works," most commissioned by his predecessor, Zubin Mehta, to celebrate the orchestra's 150th anniversary in 1992. He was impatient to be able to commission his own series of works. Now his wait was over, starting with *Two Paths* and continuing in the coming weeks with Christopher Rouse's *Seeing* for piano and orchestra and Tan Dun's Concerto for Water Percussion and Orchestra.

The Rouse piece was commissioned for Emanuel Ax, who, more than most of his pianistic colleagues, takes an active interest in performing new music. *Seeing* is a tribute to Robert Schumann and to the late rock composer Skip Spence, both of whom were institutionalized while suffering from mental illness. The title is taken from one of the latter's songs, fragments of which are heard in the work, as are themes from Schumann's Piano Concerto, but in a distorted manner. Kozinn described the piece on May 10 as "a colorful, thorny, eclectic imagining of psychosis" and Ax's performance as a "powerful rendering," ably partnered by Leonard Slatkin and the orchestra.

In the past the New York Philharmonic had given the American premieres of the Eighth and Tenth Symphonies of Shostakovich and the New York premiere of his Ninth, not to mention performing most of the earlier ones many times (excepting the Second and Third). Thus it was surprising to learn that on May 19, 1999, the Philharmonic gave its first performance of the composer's Symphony No. 11 ("The Year 1905"), written in 1957. The guest conductor, in his Philharmonic debut, was the Russian-born Yakov Kreizberg, who had made a specialty of this particular work. Opinions differ as to whether Shostakovich overtly intended the work to memorialize the failed revolution of 1905, or meant it as a private protest against his government's quashing of the 1956 Hungarian uprising. Whatever he had in mind, the work has been slow to gain acceptance in the West, only lately beginning to do so through the efforts of Kreizberg and Rostropovich. Kozinn wrote on May 22 of the "sense of tragedy that pervades the score" and felt that Kreizberg balanced the work's various elements in such a way as to support both interpretations of its meaning.

Beethoven's *Missa Solemnis* is one of the composer's greatest, and yet most problematic, works, difficult to perform, difficult to listen to (even difficult to anticipate listening to). As Sir Colin Davis once remarked to the author, "It's such a great work, it should never be performed." Of course, it is performed, even by Sir Colin, and on May 27 Kurt Masur presented it with the soloists Christine Brewer,

Florence Quivar, Anthony Rolfe Johnson, and Peter Rose, as well as the New York Choral Artists. Holland felt that, given Masur's tendency to bluntness, the performance of this craggy score was surprisingly smooth and beautiful, although none the worse for it, and "sufficient to send the early-music movement into a collective shudder." He concluded, "Swift tempos and a no-nonsense sincerity asked us to take this Missa Solemnis on his own specific terms, and we did."

What is a water percussion concerto? Obviously a concerto for percussion instruments, but with the difference that the performer, in this case the Philharmonic's stellar principal percussionist, Christopher Lamb, is asked to hold them underwater and splash around with them, as well as to manipulate the water with his hands by swirling it, patting it—whatever one might do with a body of water. The work of the Chinese-born composer Tan Dun, the piece was composed in memory of the composer Toru Takemitsu. As for the accompanying musicians, the strings were asked to play percussively and the winds had to play on reeds and mouthpieces without the benefit of actual instruments. Oestreich commented on June 5 that, although the piece would probably not make much of an impression when heard on a recording, heard and seen live it did provide enough spectacle to receive a "semi-standing ovation" from the "semi-jaded" audience.

It was now forty years since President Eisenhower had lifted the first shovelful of dirt symbolizing the start of construction on Lincoln Center. The intervening years had taken their toll on the arts complex, and a major renovation of the facilities was now in order. The renovation of just the Metropolitan Opera House and Avery Fisher Hall was estimated to cost over half a billion dollars. A major consideration for Lincoln Center was how to mount a major fund-raising drive that would not interfere with the normal fund-raising of the thirteen constituent organizations. Yet Paul B. Guenther, the chairman of the Philharmonic, was unequivocal: "The sooner work can begin the better."

Meanwhile, the announcements that in 2002 Sir Simon Rattle would become the new music director of the Berlin Philharmonic, that Seiji Ozawa would resign from the Boston Symphony in the same year to take over the Vienna State Opera, and that Franz Welser-Möst would become music director of the Cleveland Orchestra added some new configurations to the musical chessboard on which orchestras and conductors were moved around. Major orchestras in New York, Boston, Philadelphia, Atlanta, Houston, Indianapolis, and Cincinnati would be seeking music directors, while Rattle, on the short list for several of those positions but reputedly hard to get, was now unavailable.

In a June 24 *Times* article, Tommasini lauded Kurt Masur for restoring "excellence and confidence" to the Philharmonic and wondered whether the board would take a chance on a younger maestro to replace him when his contract expired, as it happened, also in 2002. After all, Bernstein had been thirty-nine when he was selected in 1957, and that appointment had proved felicitous. Would they be willing to go that route again? There was "a young conductor doing remarkable work with the Brooklyn Philharmonic, Robert Spano." With so many vacancies abounding, the Philharmonic and other orchestras might have to take some chances—"and that could be for the good."

CHAPTER 18

1999–2000

MUTI FOR THE PHILHARMONIC?

Having suffered through "another Beethoven cycle" the previous fall, the critics were none too happy to learn that the Philharmonic would, in a way, be offering more of the same for the 1999 Lincoln Center Festival. This time it was not the nine symphonies, but the five piano concertos, with Emanuel Ax as the soloist. Was it really necessary to present these oft-performed works as part of a festival, which should have been concentrating on something different, something out of the ordinary? Each concerto occupied one half of a program, the other half consisting of a non-Beethoven work that had been given its American or New York premiere by the Philharmonic (or by the New York Symphony before the 1928 merger). On July 7 the pairing was of Beethoven's Piano Concerto No. 1 with Tchaikovsky's Serenade for Strings. Though he gave the performances a good notice, Kozinn felt that for Masur and the orchestra, "it was business as usual."

Such combinations worked well enough during the series, but the final program, on July 15, coupled the Concerto No. 5 ("Emperor") with the American premiere of a work by the Israeli composer Dov Seltzer. A sixty-minute work entitled *Lament to Yitzhak* and scored for vocal soloists, chorus, boys' chorus, and a large orchestra, it memorializes the assassinated Israel Prime Minister Yitzhak Rabin. Tommasini acknowledged that it was a piece for a public occasion but otherwise found it "not musically distinguished," though he had praise for the soloists Wendy Nielsen, Hadar Halevi, and Marc Molomot, as well as for the folk singer Haya Samir, the Philadelphia Singers Chorale, Masur, and the Philharmonic. He was especially taken by the Boys Choir of Harlem singing in Hebrew. He had praise as well for Emanuel Ax's rendition of the "Emperor" Concerto but felt it was rather dwarfed by the magnitude of the program's second half.

The 1999–2000 season began with the usual pension-fund gala, this time with Mstislav Rostropovich performing his signature piece (and every other cellist's, it seems), the Dvořák Cello Concerto. Tchaikovsky's Fifth Symphony completed Masur's program. Holland wrote of Rostropovich's smothering the Dvořák concerto "under his oversized personality," but doing so with a bear hug of affection. Masur's

Tchaikovsky was on the stern side but lovely all the same, with splendid playing by the orchestra, especially the principal players who had important solos, such as Philip Myers and Stanley Drucker.

It was announced on September 30—having been earlier intimated but denied—that the orchestra's executive director, Deborah Borda, would be leaving the New York Philharmonic to take the position of executive vice president and managing director of the Los Angeles Philharmonic, a job that would also include managing the Hollywood Bowl and the construction of the new Walt Disney Hall. As Borda put it, "It's sort of like running the New York Philharmonic, Carnegie Hall and Tanglewood. . . . I think it's an extraordinary opportunity. The scope of the job is enormous." Although Borda's Philharmonic tenure included some difficult moments between her and the musicians and disagreements with Masur, it was also notable for the unprecedented six-year contract for the musicians, as well as for the establishment of two new series, the Rush Hour Concerts and Casual Saturdays, both of which brought in new audiences for the Philharmonic.

In 1957 the Philharmonic had given the first New York performance of Stravinsky's melodrama *Perséphone*, with the composer conducting. It was given again in the 1966 Stravinsky Festival, conducted by Ernest Ansermet. Now, over thirty years later, on September 30, 1999, Kurt Masur revived the work with the assistance of the New York Choral Artists, the American Boychoir, the tenor Stanford Olsen, and the actress Marthe Keller as narrator. Tommasini, who referred to the score as a neglected masterpiece, felt it would have been better served had it not been preceded on the program by the Tchaikovsky Violin Concerto, with the eighteen-year-old Sarah Chang as the brilliant soloist. He wondered whether Masur felt he had to pander to the audience to compensate for the unknown Stravinsky work that was to follow and said that either pieces by other composers from the same Paris period (1933) or other works inspired by mythology would have better complemented the Stravinsky. The fact that the audience received the Tchaikovsky rapturously and the Stravinsky rather lukewarmly only served to illustrate the unsuitability of the pairing.

On October 10 the Philharmonic's third release of archival performances was announced. Called *An American Celebration*, the ten-disc set was devoted to historic performances of American music: forty-nine works by thirty-nine composers, led by a panoply of conductors from Toscanini to Masur. Like the previous sets, it was produced by the editor and critic Sedgwick Clark, with audio editing by Seth B. Winner, Lawrence L. Rock, and Jon B. Samuels. Among its treasures are the broadcast premiere of Copland's *Appalachian Spring*, conducted by Rodzinski in 1945; the Symphony No. 2 by Paul Creston, conducted by Monteux in 1956; and

Bernstein's performances of the Roy Harris Symphony No. 3 in 1957, the William Schuman Symphony No. 6 in 1958, and the Ned Rorem Symphony No. 3 in 1959. Even though Bernstein had made two commercial recordings of the Harris Third with the Philharmonic, Clark found the live performance to be the most impressive of all. It is, in fact, one of only two performances in the set given by a conductor who had also recorded the work commercially (the other is Howard Hanson's direction of his Symphony No. 2 ["Romantic"]). Many shorter works are included, conducted by Leopold Stokowski, John Barbirolli, Guido Cantelli, Erich Leinsdorf, Zubin Mehta, George Szell, Paul Paray, Pierre Boulez, and Leonard Slatkin. The set offers dramatic proof that American music has not been neglected by the Philharmonic, even though its fortunes have risen and fallen over the years.

The approach of the millennium brought forth new compositions appropriate to the event. On October 7 Masur presented two of them by young American composers who had been commissioned by the Walt Disney Company to write "millennium symphonies." In the end, Aaron Jay Kernis and Michael Torke composed not symphonies, but large-scale works for vocal soloists, chorus, and orchestra. Kernis's *Garden of Light* exulted in harmonies, colors, and rhythms that Griffiths felt related to other composers' music from Scriabin to Bernstein, rather than having any millennial relevance. Torke's *Four Seasons* was judged the more successful piece, offering "vignettes of recent American life for each of the twelve months," laced with musical and verbal humor. Masur and the Philharmonic gave "resounding and remarkably assured performances of both works," assisted by the indefatigable New York Choral Artists and American Boychoir, with the soloists Margaret Lloyd, Mary Phillips, Anthony Dean Griffey, Dean Ely, Jubilant Sykes, and Lili Thomas.

On November 4 Sir Colin Davis conducted the Philharmonic's first performance of Sir Michael Tippett's oratorio *A Child of Our Time*. Tippett's music has not crossed the Atlantic as often as that of Benjamin Britten, and when it has, it has usually been programmed by English conductors, as was the case here. Composed between 1939 and 1941, *A Child of Our Time* is a response to tragic events that occurred in 1938. A young Polish Jew named Herschel Grynszpan shot and killed a minor Nazi official in Paris, after which the Germans retaliated with *Kristallnacht*, during which Jewish buildings and property were destroyed and Jewish people murdered. Tippett's oratorio recounts these happenings and is modeled to a degree on the Bach *Passions*, with the difference that, where Bach employed Lutheran chorales to comment on the action, Tippett has the chorus sing African American spirituals, concluding with "Deep River." Holland applauded the efforts of Davis, the Philharmonic, the New York Choral Artists, and the soloists Deborah Riedel,

Nora Gubisch, Jerry Hadley, and Robert Lloyd, as well as the sentiments expressed in the work, but not their realization, which he found awkward, even amateurish at times. He did concede the possibility that *"A Child of Our Time* possesses virtues to which I am blind."

Masur and the Philharmonic also contributed to the millennial celebrations by commissioning six composers, of as many nationalities, to write works that would be presented under the title *Messages for the Millennium.* The pieces were to be between ten and fifteen minutes long and to express a feeling of optimism for the coming century. Five of the works were performed on the concerts beginning November 11. First on the program was *America (A Prophecy)* by the young Englishman Thomas Adès, whom many regard as the successor to Benjamin Britten. The hopeful message, however, was absent from his composition, which instead suggested retribution for this country's treatment of its Native American population. (Should the Philharmonic have asked for its money back?) Despite its theme, Oestreich found it to be the strongest work of the five, with Beth Clayton as the sensitive mezzo-soprano soloist.

Next came the German Hans Werner Henze's *Fraternité.* Henze, the most senior (born 1926) and best known internationally of the group, did adhere to the requested theme, as did the Japanese composer Somei Satoh in his *Kisetsu,* which he dedicated "to the silence of mothers." He felt that "the new century should manifest a feminine spirit." The Finn Kaija Saariaho's *Oltra Mar* (Beyond the Sea) was described by Oestreich as "choral meditations on love, waves and death, separated by movements of water music." Finally, the American John Corigliano's *Vocalise,* with Sylvia McNair as its wordless soprano soloist, involved electronic sounds and, according to Oestreich, seemed to have "little concern for the project's underlying humanism."

It was quite a chunk of new music to prepare for one program, yet Masur, the orchestra, and the Westminster Symphonic Choir came through valiantly with "intense performances." Although Oestreich found the Adès piece somewhat impolite, he felt the final expression of that quality came from the audience. Once again, after beginning Satoh's delicate piece Masur had to stop the performance because of loud and incessant coughing. No leaving the stage this time, merely a loud cough from Masur himself, and the work was restarted. During the Adès some people were observed sleeping, "one snoring loudly."

The sixth millennial commission was too long to be included in the November 11 program, so it was presented the following week on the concerts beginning November 18. By the Georgian composer Giya Kancheli, the work is entitled *And Farewell Goes Out Sighing…* and is scored for a solo violin, played by Gidon

Kremer, and a countertenor, in this case Derek Lee Ragin, along with the orchestra. In the program notes Kancheli wrote, "For me, the change of millenniums is a concept that is arithmetic rather than something that brings hope for the improved world." He added, "I dare to ask you for one favor: please try to cough during the loud segments, and if possible restrain yourselves in the quiet ones." Evidently he was familiar with the Philharmonic's audiences or had heard about them from Masur.

As in many of Kancheli's works, the music is mostly quiet and mystical in its atmosphere, with occasional sonic eruptions that resolve into serenity. Kozinn felt that everyone involved made a good case for the piece and noted that, about midway through the piece, the audience was comparatively silent. Bruckner's Seventh Symphony completed the program in a performance that was not up to Masur's usual standard in this work, according to Kozinn, "uneven" with various "wind and brass imperfections" in the first movement, though improving as the work progressed. (Again, a final rehearsal on the day of the concert may have contributed to the imperfections.)

The year 2000 marked the centennial of the birth of Aaron Copland, the celebration of which the Philharmonic observed at the end of 1999 with a three-week Completely Copland festival. (The title was obviously inspired by that of Lincoln Center's Mostly Mozart festivals, which spawned similarly titled festivals throughout the country.) Heard on the opening program of November 24 were the 1929 *Symphonic Ode* (in its 1955 revision made for the Boston Symphony's seventy-fifth anniversary) conducted by Miguel Harth-Bedoya, the perennial Clarinet Concerto (played by Stanley Drucker), *Inscape*, and the Four Dance Episodes from *Rodeo*, the last three works conducted by Kurt Masur. The idea was not to present only Copland's most popular works, of which *Rodeo* is surely one, but the gamut of his compositional styles, including works that were only marginally successful.

Four conductors took over for the concert on November 30: Markand Thakar led the early ballet score *Hear Ye! Hear Ye!*, Leslie B. Dunner the late ballet *Dance Panels*, George Hanson the early *Dance Symphony*, and Harth-Bedoya *Appalachian Spring*, for which the designations "early," "late," and even "middle" are irrelevant. The composer John Adams was in charge of the program on December 3 and 4, leading performances of the Party Scene from *The Tender Land, Music for the Theater*, the jazzy Piano Concerto (with Garrick Ohlssohn as soloist), *Danzón Cubano, Three Latin-American Sketches*, and the Suite from *Billy the Kid*. Also included in the festival were concerts of chamber music, lectures, panel discussions, and exhibits. The critics generally wrote positively of the performances, though Holland felt that the festival had been devised principally as a response to "an unusually adventurous and substantial set of programs" scheduled by Carnegie Hall, and that it reflected "the lack of any real musical vision that has ruled this organization in recent years."

On Tuesday, December 7, Marin Alsop, in her Philharmonic subscription debut, led Copland's *El salón México*, the most popular work on a program that also included *Statements for Orchestra*, which the Philharmonic had premiered in 1942, *Connotations*, the Lincoln Center opening-night piece, *Quiet City*, with trumpeter Philip Smith and English horn player Thomas Stacy as soloists, and *Music for a Great City*, which the composer derived from the score for the film *Something Wild*. Alsop, who led "an impassioned performance" of *Great City*, according to Tommasini, has since become renowned as the music director of the Baltimore Symphony.

The Copland concert of December 11, conducted by Andrew Litton, then music director of the Dallas Symphony, in his Philharmonic debut had as its major work the Third Symphony. A concertgoer perusing the orchestra's personnel carefully for that performance might have noticed an additional musician in the oboe section. She was sixteen-year-old Johanna Johnson of Grass Valley, California, near Sacramento. After being diagnosed with Hodgkin's disease, which was now in remission, she had been asked by the Make-a-Wish Foundation to choose the one thing she would most want to do. As an aspiring oboist, her response was, "I want to sit in the middle of a great orchestra." After an Internet search the New York Philharmonic and its principal oboist, Joseph Robinson, were selected. Robinson invited Johanna to visit the orchestra, receive an oboe lesson, and sit next to him as acting assistant principal oboe for the rehearsal and performance of the Copland symphony. The Philharmonic's musicians have always been very welcoming to young musicians, making them feel at home. As a final fillip, after her oboe lesson Robinson presented her with a new Lorée oboe from Paris, the usual $5,000 price of which had been greatly reduced by the manufacturer. Robinson had raised the rest through contributions from himself and various players and friends. As for the actual performance, though, Oestreich felt that the orchestra reverted to "its blatant sound of a decade ago. . . . Fortissimos were earsplitting." Referring to Johnson, he pointed out, "No fledgling instrumentalist, doubling lines, could hope to be heard amid such a clatter."

From time to time the Philharmonic has performed a work combining so-called serious music with jazz, and in no case has the attempted fusion of the two idioms been deemed a success. Hopes were raised, however, for the new work premiered on December 29, a joint commission by the New York Philharmonic and Jazz at Lincoln Center. The composer was Wynton Marsalis, and the piece was entitled *All Rise*. Written to celebrate the millennium, the piece called for participation by the two commissioning organizations and the Morgan State University Choir, a total of two hundred performers, requiring that the stage be extended. It clocked in at a hundred minutes—about the duration of Mahler's Third Symphony. The *Times*'s jazz critic, Ben Ratliff, reviewed the performance and found the piece to be "odd music," with neither an identifiable character nor even any memorable themes. Even the jazz lacked the strengths of Marsalis's best jazz as heard with his small band. Masur evidently believed in the piece, however, for he conducted it again in New York and in London as well.

Masur and the Philharmonic closed out the twentieth century on the eve of the twenty-first, not with Viennese waltzes and the like, but with Beethoven's Ninth Symphony. According to Kozinn, the performance "rose to the occasion in every regard," the orchestra playing the work "with an unusual fervency, as if performing the Ninth was something special and rare." The New York Choral Artists and the American Boychoir took part, with the impressive soloists Sylvia McNair, Florence Quivar, Stuart Neill, and René Pape.

Masur preceded the Ninth with Bach's Violin Concerto No. 2 in E Major, in which the soloist was Anne-Sophie Mutter. She was beginning a three-week residency with the Philharmonic during which she would play major works of the twentieth century. Her first such appearance, on January 6, offered Lutosławski's Partita and *Chain 2*, the two pieces played as one, separated by an Interlude, and Bernstein's Serenade for Violin, Strings, and Percussion. This last has proven lately to be very popular with young violinists, and no wonder, for it is one of the composer's finest concert works. Calling her "a wonder of adaptability," Holland wrote of Mutter's glamorous image as portrayed in publicity for her concerts. He felt that "if such as this draws the wary into the concert hall, let her be as glamorous as she chooses."

Mutter's second program, on January 12 and televised by PBS, presented the violin concertos of Alban Berg and Sibelius. It was rare for *Live from Lincoln Center* to broadcast a program that included a twelve-tone work such as the Berg to a national audience, but it was Mutter who was the main attraction. Her series concluded on January 15 with two works composed especially for her, Wolfgang Rihm's *Gesungene Zeit* (Time Chant) and Penderecki's Concerto No. 2, which the composer conducted, Masur having led everything else in the series. Griffiths proclaimed Mutter's performance "a triumph."

On January 26 came news of the death of Amyas Ames at the age of ninety-three. Originally an investment banker, he had been a board member of the Philharmonic since 1955, becoming its president in 1963 and its chairman from 1970 to 1983. In 1970 he also became chairman of Lincoln Center, a post he held for ten years. A tireless fund-raiser and advocate for the arts, the patrician Ames said in a 1970 interview, "We're fighting the pollution of the inner city, and along with it we should be fighting the pollution of the inner mind." He was the instigator of the Philharmonic's Parks Concerts, helped to create the *Live From Lincoln Center* telecasts, and was responsible for gaining the support of Avery Fisher in the renovation of Philharmonic Hall.

Riccardo Muti returned to the Philharmonic on February 3 with a typical program of music largely off the beaten path: Rossini's Overture to *Il viaggio a Reims*, the Divertimento from Stravinsky's *The Fairy's Kiss* (loosely based on music by Tchaikovsky), and Richard Strauss's early and rarely played symphonic fantasy *Aus Italien* (From Italy). He must have made a good impression, for on April 24 the *Times* carried the announcement that Muti had been selected to succeed Kurt Masur as music director of the New York Philharmonic upon the expiration of Masur's contract in 2002.

Apparently negotiations with Muti had been ongoing for some time, but no offer had been made, for according to the article there was some question as to whether or not he would accept the position. At the time music director of La Scala in Milan, Muti had been music director of the Philadelphia Orchestra from 1980 to 1992 and upon leaving that position had said he did not wish to be involved with another American orchestra because of the time commitment involved and the travel back and forth to Europe, where he had steady relationships with both the Berlin and the Vienna Philharmonics. Still, he was said to be intrigued with the idea of directing the New York Philharmonic.

Meanwhile, in between conducting performances of Shostakovich's *Lady Macbeth of the Mtsensk District* at the Metropolitan Opera, Valery Gergiev managed to squeeze in two weeks with the Philharmonic, the second of which, on March 24, included a rare performance of Tchaikovsky's "Manfred" Symphony. The composer called it a symphonic poem, but because it is in four movements and is longer than any of Tchaikovsky's numbered symphonies, "Manfred"'s designation as a symphony has stuck. At one time Arturo Toscanini was the score's most ardent champion, and even he made a sizable cut in the finale. Most people consider it an inferior work (Leonard Bernstein described it to the author as "trash"), yet a few (the author among them) consider it—at least, most of it—one of Tchaikovsky's greatest scores. American critics generally disparage it, while English critics tend to treat it seriously. The *Times*'s Griffiths is English, so it was no surprise to read on March 30 that the work "is a passionate song of the self," and that "it was passionately sung by the orchestra, with full vigor. . . . The fierce ending of the first movement was thrilling."

Having twice programmed Bach's *Passion According to St. Matthew* with the Philharmonic, Kurt Masur now offered the more rarely given *St. John Passion* on the concerts beginning April 6. Some controversy has lately arisen over this work, for the text, from the Gospel of St. John, assigns most of the blame for Christ's crucifixion to the Jews. Yet a case can be made for Bach's treatment as fixing the blame on all sinners. Oestreich had high hopes for Masur's *St. John*, which involved the superb participation of the American Boychoir and the men of the Westminster Symphonic Choir, but felt the performance was let down by the male soloists, who were not in good form. The women, however, Heidi Grant Murphy and Marietta Simpson, fared much better. On the whole, Oestreich was left "imagining what might have been."

The Philharmonic, having presented a concert version of Stephen Sondheim's *Follies* a few years back. on May 5 offered the same composer's *Sweeney Todd*. Holland began his laudatory review by asking if the piece is an opera. He had three answers: "(1) I don't care. (2) It doesn't matter. (3) No." Conducted by Andrew Litton, the work was given in a semistaged version with a combined cast of Broadway (George Hearn, Patti LuPone, Audra McDonald, Davis Gaines, and Neil Patrick Harris) and opera and concert (Heidi Grant Murphy, Paul Plishka, John Aler, and Stanford Olsen) singers, plus the New York Choral Artists. In the end, Holland decided that, whatever it is, "Mr. Sondheim has created powerful and lasting theater."

Sir Colin Davis returned on May 11 for an all-Mozart program, one of several composers, including Berlioz and Sibelius, of whom he has made a specialty. Opening with the seldom-played Symphony No. 28 in C Major, K. 200, and closing with the well-known Symphony No. 38 in D Major ("Prague"), K. 504, he collaborated in between with Alfred Brendel in the Piano Concerto No. 22 in E-flat Major, K. 482. Kozinn felt this was a concert "that didn't go out of its way to pursue a theme. It mainly asked to be enjoyed." By the same token, Davis is not a conductor who goes out of his way to "interpret" a piece of music, but rather presents it in a healthily straightforward manner while still managing to reveal its depths.

On June 1 it was announced that Zarin Mehta, executive director of Chicago's Ravinia Festival, would become the Philharmonic's executive director in September, succeeding Deborah Borda, who had left for Los Angeles. No announcement was made concerning the successor to Kurt Masur, though Riccardo Muti was still the first choice, pending the working out of various details. Mehta, the brother of Zubin Mehta, said he was looking forward to working with Masur and, if everything worked out, with Muti. When asked if he could have worked with his brother, he replied, "We would have fought tooth and nail."

Masur closed the 1999–2000 season with two programs, the Bruckner Seventh Symphony, on what had become the annual free Memorial Day concert at the Cathedral of St. John the Divine, and Mahler's Ninth Symphony, for the final subscription series beginning June 1. Although Masur's Mahler lacks the overt emotionalism found in other conductors' readings, Kozinn felt some listeners might find his approach refreshing. He declared this performance "admirable in every quantifiable way" and thought the orchestra played superbly, giving Masur "everything he needed."

The *Times* of June 4, in an article by Oestreich entitled "Who Dares Call This Maestro a Lame Duck?," referred to the Philharmonic's ongoing negotiations with Riccardo Muti and to other possible candidates for the music director position. It concentrated, however, on the fact that there were still two seasons remaining for Masur, "surely no one's idea of a lame duck." Also mentioned were Masur's appointment as principal conductor of the London Philharmonic, to take effect in the fall, and a similar appointment with the Orchestre National de France in Paris, scheduled to begin in 2002. Said Masur, "The major point for me is still the New York Philharmonic. . . . The players are expecting that I will fight till the last day." He continued that he would like to leave behind a feeling of responsibility, of pride that would not be dependent on the identity of the music director or the board chairman or the organization's financial situation. He felt that a feeling of trust had been established between himself and the musicians, that they had grown together, and that it was the most wonderful thing he had achieved. Masur added that his disappointment was in no way directed at the orchestra, but at a change of politics by the Philharmonic board precipitated by the new chairman. He wanted, and was ready, to stay longer, but would have left even earlier if the right successor had been found; he thought there were some people on the board who were not honest, but were looking out for their own interests and power. Masur spoke enthusiastically about the pending arrival of Zarin Mehta as executive director: "He is an incredible man, so full of imagination. I will be lucky if I have two years with him."

Also quoted in the article was the Philharmonic's chairman, Paul B. Guenther, who stated that, in its long history, the Philharmonic had had very few music directors who stayed longer than ten years. (Zubin Mehta's thirteen years was the longest tenure in modern times.) The society's philosophy was that change is often necessary for an organization such as the Philharmonic, and that "Kurt Masur has done a spectacular job." (Guenther has cited his own resignation as chair in 2009 as an example of his belief that one should not remain too long in such a job.)

The *Times* of June 18 printed a response in the form of a letter to the editor from Stefan Westerhoff of Manhattan. Westerhoff complained that Kurt Masur's treatment by the Philharmonic's administration was "truly repulsive," and that Oestreich's article illustrated that not much had changed at the Philharmonic since the days of Gustav Mahler.

MUTI SAYS NO

Again the Philharmonic took part in the Lincoln Center Festival, this one, of course, designated 2000. One of the themes of the festival was a celebration of the music of Olivier Messiaen, with three of his major works scheduled. Of these, *Des canyons aux étoiles* (From the Canyons to the Stars), would be given by the Chamber Music Society of Lincoln Center, but the other two would be performed by the New York Philharmonic under the Dutch conductor Hans Vonk, then music director of the St. Louis Symphony. The first of these, on July 11, was Messiaen's last composition, *Éclairs sur l'au-delà...*, the world premiere of which the Philharmonic had given in 1992. Oestreich found the music "glorious" and the performance "excellent," even though the orchestra included a heavy sprinkling of substitute players (a fact of life with summer concerts).

No sooner had this performance been given than the announcement came that Riccardo Muti would not be coming to the Philharmonic as its music director. It had been widely assumed in the music world that his appointment was virtually a done deal, so the news brought surprise and disappointment. Apparently the negotiations ended amicably, for he would continue to be a guest conductor of the Philharmonic. But now another Great Conductor Search was about to begin, one made more difficult because of simultaneous music director openings in Boston and Philadelphia.

On July 21 the Lincoln Center Festival continued with the Philharmonic's performance of what is probably Messiaen's orchestral magnum opus, the ten-movement *Turangalîla Symphony*. Griffiths thought the rendition "underpowered," without the passion and conviction needed to project the score convincingly. There was still much to enjoy, such as the work of the percussionists and the performers of the two important solo parts, Andreas Haefliger on piano and Valérie Hartmann-Claverie on the ondes Martenot.

The opening of the Parks Concerts was delayed a day, not by inclement weather, but by the eradication of mosquitoes carrying the West Nile virus. Central Park had been thoroughly sprayed with insecticide the day before, and on July 25 the Great Lawn was deemed safe. In the end, an audience estimated at 35,000 attended (rather small by Central Park standards) to hear a program of music by Glinka, Corigliano, Copland, and Shostakovich led by André Raphel Smith, the assistant conductor of the Philadelphia Orchestra, in his Philharmonic debut. Allan Kozinn found him "an agile, demonstrative conductor," for whom the orchestra "played brilliantly." The second week of Parks Concerts was to have brought the Philharmonic debut of the young Finnish conductor Mikko Franck, who canceled the engagement, his place then taken by the young American Delta David Gier. His program included the 1945 version of Stravinsky's *Firebird* Suite and the Trumpet Concerto by Alexander Arutunian, with the Philharmonic's Philip Smith as soloist. While not a great piece of music, the Arutunian concerto, composed in 1949, is extremely brilliant and tuneful in an Armenian sort of way, reminiscent of Khachaturian.

In the *Times* of August 2, Tommasini wrote of the Philharmonic's conductor search that it was time for the organization to consider a young American, just as it had done with Leonard Bernstein over forty years before. Masur was all well and good and had certainly improved the orchestra, but his programming was becoming increasingly conventional. It was just as well that Riccardo Muti had dropped out of the running, for, despite his greatness as a conductor, he lacked identification with even one modern composer. As he would continue to do until the actual selection was made, Tommasini cited two young Americans he thought would do a splendid job at the Philharmonic. The first was Robert Spano, then thirty-eight, music director of the Brooklyn Philharmonic, who had carved out a niche for himself there with his imaginative programming. Unfortunately for the Philharmonic, he had very recently accepted the music directorship of the Atlanta Symphony, where his work has been similarly acclaimed.

The second was forty-one-year-old David Robertson, an associate of Pierre Boulez and music director of the Orchestre National de Lyon in France, who had conducted outstanding performances of Janáček's *Makropoulos Affair* at the Metropolitan Opera. In an article on November 19, Tommasini would write of the forty-nine-year-old American Kent Nagano, who had been achieving spectacular success all over Europe but had not been approached by a single American orchestra seeking a music director. Any one of the three would have been an inspired choice for the Philharmonic, said Tommasini. Instead, the front-runners now appeared to be the Latvian-born Mariss Jansons, fifty-seven, then with the Pittsburgh Symphony as well as associate principal conductor of the St. Petersburg Philharmonic in Russia, and the German Christoph Eschenbach, sixty-one, formerly of the Houston Symphony and then chief conductor of the NDR Symphony in Hamburg.

On August 20 Holland weighed in with his views on why Riccardo Muti was not the right man for the job. First of all, his "body language told us he did not want the job." His "demands were extravagant." (Muti had proposed spending eight weeks with the orchestra during his first season, ten in the second, twelve in the third. Holland had heard that he would have wanted a salary as high as $2 million.) His "manner is imperious if not downright arrogant." His repertoire is conservative, his forays into modern music limited to the great twentieth-century classics and "works by second-rate Italian composers." Holland felt the Philharmonic had been underutilized since the days of Bernstein and Boulez and repeated his belief that Masur, for all his fine work, had not realized the orchestra's full potential. Whatever Muti might have brought to the job, eight weeks was certainly not enough to transform the orchestra in the way that James Levine had done at the Met, where he spent months, not weeks, working with his musicians. In response to Holland's article, several letters to the editor appeared in defense of Muti.

The 2000–2001 season opened on September 20, again with the now traditional televised opening-night gala. Masur conducted, and Kiri Te Kanawa was the soprano soloist in arias by Mozart and Richard Strauss, the orchestra on its own performing Mendelssohn's "Italian" Symphony and Strauss's *Till Eulenspiegel*. Holland praised Te Kanawa's beautiful voice while criticizing her lack of interpretive depth. Of the Philharmonic, he thought it might be "the most urban of all the world's major orchestras." Where the Vienna Philharmonic's sound might cause one to think of "swaying chestnut trees and green fields," the New York Philharmonic brought to mind "the Chrysler Building—sharp edges and splendid engineering, and no less beautiful because of them."

On September 22 came the news that Kurt Masur would miss two weeks of his scheduled concerts, November 2–14, because he would "undergo an unspecified surgical procedure" and needed time to recover. His replacements for those weeks would be Mikko Franck and Christoph Eschenbach.

The performance of the "Italian" Symphony on opening night was a sort of appetizer for the first three weeks of the season, which had been designated a Mendelssohn Festival. Critics who complained of Masur's conservative programming might have had their feelings confirmed by this event, and yet it was a natural project for Masur to undertake. After all, he had come out of the Gewandhaus's Mendelssohn tradition. And New York had not had a Mendelssohn Festival in living memory. In the pantheon of the great composers, Mendelssohn has long been a seriously underrated composer who has never really been forgiven for having been born into a well-to-do family. He never had to suffer for his art, which has perforce not been considered profound enough to be taken seriously—as if beauty and grace counted for nothing in music.

In any case, the subscription season opened on September 21 with the *Hebrides Overture* (also known as *Fingal's Cave*), the Violin Concerto, the Overture to *Ruy*

Blas, and, again, the "Italian" Symphony. The soloist in the concerto was the Philharmonic's principal associate concertmaster, Cheryl Staples, who gave the popular work a "lovely, expert reading," according to Oestreich. The following week, beginning September 27, Masur presented the work with which he had made such a fine impression in the summer of 1991, just before assuming his duties: the complete incidental music to *A Midsummer Night's Dream*. For this performance he had the assistance of the actor John de Lancie (who recited relevant excerpts from the play between the musical numbers), the soprano Danielle De Niese, the mezzo-soprano Margaret Lattimore, and the American Boychoir, which had opened the program with four of the composer's choral pieces conducted by their director, James Litton, with Scott Dettra at the piano. Holland wrote of "a satisfying evening," the Philharmonic providing "the kind of delicacy and fineness that Mr. Masur associates with this music."

The high point of the festival, as far as Masur was concerned, was the Philharmonic's first performance ever, on October 5, of Mendelssohn's oratorio *St. Paul*. He had wanted to present this work ever since he came to the Philharmonic. Patterned after the Bach Passions and the Handel oratorios, it has never achieved the popularity of Mendelssohn's *Elijah*. But Masur believed in the work and, according to Tommasini, "was at his best" in conducting it: "This affecting performance was a milestone in Mr. Masur's tenure." The Westminster Symphonic Choir and the American Boychoir participated with their usual exemplary singing, along with the soloists Edith Wiens, Margaret Lattimore, Stuart Neill, and Christopher Maltman, the latter in the title role. As if to emphasize the Philharmonic subscribers' resistance to seldom-heard choral works, Masur and everyone else were rewarded for their efforts with many empty seats.

The *Times* of October 14 announced that Bernard Holland, its chief music critic for the past five years, had been named to a new position, that of national music critic, in which capacity he would review major musical events across the country. Anthony Tommasini, of the paper's music staff, would succeed Holland as chief music critic. Tommasini had already been reviewing extensively for the *Times*, as well as writing feature articles.

In October 2000 the Philharmonic issued the fourth of its historic broadcast compilations, a ten-CD set entitled *Bernstein Live* commemorating the tenth anniversary of Bernstein's death. Most of the contents were works he had not recorded commercially, at least not with the Philharmonic. An exception was the 1951 broadcast premiere of the Symphony No. 2 by Charles Ives, which had been given its world premiere only a few days before. Bernstein did later record the work twice with the Philharmonic. Yet, hearing the premiere was an exceptional experience. One difference between this and the 1958 and 1987 recordings is that Bernstein did not originally prolong the final dissonant chord. Prolonging it emphasizes the dissonance, while playing it as written, a short accented chord, causes the listener to wonder, as Ives might have said, whether his or her ears were on straight. The set includes the 1970 performance of scenes from *Götterdämmerung* with Eileen Farrell and Jess Thomas, excerpts from the controversial 1964 avant-garde series with Bernstein's spoken introductions, a 1976 Bruckner Sixth Symphony from Bernstein's only Philharmonic performances of that work (Bruckner did not interest him as much as Mahler, for he only played Nos. 6 and 9), collaborations with the piano soloists Vladimir Ashkenazy, Lazar Berman, Byron Janis, and Wilhelm Kempff (the latter's only Philharmonic appearance), and much, much more. The set was coproduced by Sedgwick Clark and the Philharmonic's archivist, Barbara Haws, with major funding from Rita E. and Gustave M. Hauser.

When Sir Colin Davis arrived on October 2 to direct a program of Schubert, Mozart, and Haydn, Holland lamented how much more elegant musical life might have been in New York had Davis not declined an invitation to become the Philharmonic's music director some twenty-five years before. Still, it was good to have him as the principal guest conductor, for his relaxed approach subdued the orchestra's aggressive style. His program included three works that are seldom performed, at least in New York: Schubert's youthful First Symphony, Mozart's almost equally youthful Bassoon Concerto (with the principal player, Judith LeClair, as the soloist), and Haydn's Symphony No. 98 in B-flat Major. Once a favorite of Toscanini, No. 98 is probably the least often performed of the twelve London symphonies, in spite of its being one of the greatest of the lot.

Mariss Jansons has been mentioned as a leading candidate for the Philharmonic's music directorship. He had last appeared with the orchestra in 1996, but because there were no subscription weeks available for him in the 2000–2001 season, a special nonsubscription single performance was arranged on October 31. Itzhak Perlman was his soloist in Bernstein's Serenade for Violin, Strings, and Percussion, one of several works the orchestra was playing for a Bernstein commemoration. Perhaps the fact that the concert was given on Halloween governed the choice of Berlioz's *Symphonie fantastique* for the second half, although one hardly needs an excuse to program this score. Tommasini wrote of Perlman's playing lacking "interpretive focus" and of Jansons leading "a brilliant account" of the Berlioz. While acknowledging that Jansons was "a gifted musician," he wondered what kind of artistic leader he would be. In reading his biographical note in the program, Tommasini did not see the name of a single living composer, and he commented that the programs of the Pittsburgh Symphony, of which Jansons was music director, were fairly conservative. He thought several American conductors known for their innovative programming should be considered. A conductor such as Jansons could always come to the Philharmonic as a guest.

Filling in for Kurt Masur in the first of the two weeks he was gone was to have been the young Finn Mikko Franck. He had already canceled his Parks Concerts engagement the previous summer. Now he canceled again, raising the question of just how badly he wanted to appear with the Philharmonic. Engaged as the substitute for the substitute was the young Israeli Ilan Volkov, assistant conductor of the Boston Symphony, in his Philharmonic debut. Emanuel Ax was the soloist on November 2 in the New York premiere of *Red Silk Dance*, a capriccio for piano and orchestra by Bright Sheng. Inspired by the Silk Road, the ancient trade route between Europe and East Asia, the piece was well received by Oestreich, who wrote of its "spiky and scintillating Bartokian effusion," its "gaudy colors and piquant flavors," and also praised Ax for playing it with "appropriate flair and drive." Ax was also lauded for his rendition of Liszt's Concerto No. 2 in A Major, "giving the work everything it was worth (and, to one listener's taste, more)." Unfortunately, Volkov did not fare so well with the Sibelius Second Symphony, where he seemed unable "to lead, follow, or get out of the way."

The following week's concerts, beginning November 9, were led by Christoph Eschenbach in what was probably his de facto audition for the music directorship. Soon to become principal conductor of the Orchestre de Paris, he conducted an excellent performance of the Brahms Double Concerto, in which the superb soloists were the Philharmonic's concertmaster, Glenn Dicterow, and principal cellist, Carter Brey. Masur had programmed Prokofiev's Fifth Symphony for the second half, but Eschenbach elected to play Dvořák's "New World" Symphony instead. Although the performance had its lovely moments, Tommasini felt that Eschenbach conducted as though he were trying to prove something. "Naturalness and spontaneity in the playing" were missing. Still, Eschenbach impressed as "an exceptional musician."

When it comes to the technique of conducting and the ability to control an orchestra in the most complex compositions, no one is more expert than Lorin Maazel. He had last appeared with the Philharmonic in 1977 after having been a fairly frequent guest since 1962. Now, to help him celebrate his seventieth birthday, he was invited for two weeks in November 2000. For the first, beginning on the 16th, his program was devoted to his own arrangement of highlights from Wagner's *Ring of the Nibelung*. Entitled *The Ring without Words*, the score travels without pause from the opening of *Das Rheingold* to the cataclysmic final pages of *Götterdämmerung*, with visits to *Die Walküre* and *Siegfried* along the way, all in one seventy-minute span. There was no questioning the Philharmonic's execution of this splendid music, but Griffiths felt Maazel's version was "a project in the process of collapse." The transitions from one scene to the next were often abrupt, he wrote, and some of the episodes were unconvincing when heard out of context. Maazel has recorded the score (though not with the Philharmonic), so listeners can judge it for themselves.

On November 22 Maazel began his second week, again with a single work, Bruckner's Eighth Symphony, which Oestreich said he conducted "from memory with typical flair and assurance." (Maazel conducts virtually everything from memory.) Although Oestreich felt that Maazel belonged to that school of conductors who make the work "seem disjointed and episodic and long" (it certainly is the last), he led the symphony with "remarkable flexibility." Not long after these appearances, the names of Mariss Jansons and Christoph Eschenbach were joined by that of Lorin Maazel as potential music directors of the Philharmonic, though on December 27 it was reported that the Philharmonic "is not close to naming Mr. Masur's successor."

CHAPTER 19

2001–2

IT'S MAAZEL

Kurt Masur and the Philharmonic again ended the old year and greeted the new with Beethoven's Ninth Symphony, following it in 2001's first subscription week with the Brahms *German Requiem*. As his tenure wound down, Masur revisited some of the highlights of his earlier years; he had recorded the Brahms in 1995. With the Westminster Symphonic Choir, the soloists were the soprano Heidi Grant Murphy and the baritone Thomas Quasthoff, the latter also singing in the opening work, Frank Martin's Six Monologues from *Jedermann* (Everyman), to texts from Hugo von Hofmannsthal's translation of the medieval English morality play.

The orchestra then embarked on a two-week tour of Spain, during which time there were interesting developments back home. On January 16 the *Washington Post* published an article by Tim Page, its music critic, stating that Lorin Maazel would be the next music director of the New York Philharmonic. The *New York Times* countered by insisting that the *Post* story was inaccurate and said that they planned to publish an article on January 17 reporting that no choice had been made by the Philharmonic, two officials of which had been contacted by telephone in Spain. The orchestra's new executive director, Zarin Mehta, firmly denied that any selection had been made, adding, "It's disturbing when things are inaccurate. It has an impact on our day-to-day lives. I'm here talking to the press instead of listening to a concert." The public relations director, Eric Latzky, termed the *Post* report "speculative and incorrect." Asked to retract his story, Page, a former *New York Times* music critic, stuck by it: "I'll run a retraction the moment another candidate is nominated by the Philharmonic." Meanwhile, Christoph Eschenbach, one of the Philharmonic's top candidates, had recently accepted the position of music director of the Philadelphia Orchestra and dropped out of the running.

On January 17, as promised, the *Times* published a piece by Ralph Blumenthal in which he claimed that Kurt Masur's successor had not been appointed, and that there would probably be no decision for weeks, if not months. Speaking from Barcelona, Latzky said, "No one is close to being selected." Zarin Mehta said that he was "still searching, still talking to other people," though the article noted that Maazel and Mariss Jansons continued to be the two best-known candidates.

On January 18 it was announced that Maazel and the Cuban-born philanthropist Alberto W. Vilar would be forming a $5 million competition and training program for young conductors. Called the Maazel/Vilar Conductors' Competition Foundation, the program was designed to help conductors make the transition from music school to professional opportunities. Said Maazel, "Young musicians are thrown to the lions before they are ready to deal with the problems of real-life conducting." Vilar had already made a name for himself as a major contributor to opera companies in the United States and Europe. On January 27 came the announcement that the Philharmonic would be one of his beneficiaries, for he had pledged $250,000 to subsidize three performances of Verdi's Requiem in 2002, with Riccardo Muti conducting.

In the *Times* of January 29 Tommasini continued his crusade for a young American to lead the Philharmonic. David Robertson and Kent Nagano were again named as conductors who would bring imaginative and innovative ideas on programming to the job, as would James Conlon and Marin Alsop. But the new music director did not have to be American. The Russian Valery Gergiev was mentioned as someone who would be "a brilliant music director." Tommasini's most intriguing idea was to bring back Pierre Boulez, even for a limited transitional period, for Boulez had evolved into "one of the most elegant and distinguished conductors ever."

As for Maazel, no one questioned his expertise, his brilliance, his ability to draw the best from an orchestra in terms of subtlety and color, but there were concerns over the lack of spontaneity and warmth in many of his interpretations, and of his micromanagement of details at the expense of the larger picture. All orchestras, not just the Philharmonic, were at a turning point: their core audiences were aging, and they needed to attract younger listeners. So an infusion of relative youth on the podium was considered important in keeping symphony orchestras relevant to prospective audiences. From that perspective, replacing the seventy-three-year-old Masur with the seventy-year-old Maazel didn't make sense. The Philharmonic had taken a chance on the young Leonard Bernstein in 1957. Were they willing to take a chance on another young American today?

No sooner had Tommasini's article appeared than the announcement came on January 30 that Lorin Maazel had indeed been selected as the Philharmonic's next music director, effective with the 2002–3 season. It was the most controversial appointment in the Philharmonic's history. Maazel did qualify as an American (born in Paris of American parents), though not, of course, a young American. The hubbub was perhaps best summed up by a comment by the critic Greg Sandow that appeared in the *Wall Street Journal* of January 17, the day after the premature *Post* story appeared. Sandow wrote of the conductor's ego, his habit of micromanagement, his "chilly distance from warmth and art," and his "virtuoso glitz," concluding that if the self-important Maazel was the best choice the Philharmonic could make, Sandow preferred that no one be chosen.

One interesting aspect of the turn of events was that Mariss Jansons, who had succeeded Maazel in Pittsburgh, would now be succeeding him in his European post with the Bavarian Radio Symphony Orchestra in Munich. When all is said and done, a case can be made that, of all the conductors available at the time, young, old, or in between, American or otherwise, Maazel was the most qualified for the Philharmonic job. Every conductor has, or should have, his or her own personality. Some music lovers remember or can hear from recordings how radically the interpretations of such conductors as Wilhelm Furtwängler and Leopold Stokowski differed from the norm. Whatever Maazel's personal stamp might be, his performances were perfectly acceptable.

There was then some question as to whether Maazel was, in fact, American or European. American, yes, by virtue of having been born to American parents (albeit in France); European because much of his career had been spent in Europe, as music director of the Deutsche Oper Berlin, the Berlin Radio Symphony, the Vienna State Opera, and the Bavarian Radio Symphony. He had also been associate principal conductor of London's Philharmonia Orchestra. On the other hand, ten years in Cleveland and almost as long in Pittsburgh did bring some balance to his appointments. It might be more accurate to say that he is more an international conductor, rather than either an American or a European one.

Also of concern to many critics and observers was whether Maazel, at the age of seventy, had the vision and the interest to steer the orchestra in a new direction for its audience and its community, something at which Bernstein was a master. It is important to remember, however, that, as much as Bernstein was lionized in his later career and his memory revered today, he was not immediately embraced by the critics or the musicians when he was starting out. As for Maazel, the composer Ned Rorem, quoted in the January 31 *Times*, spoke of the conductor's playing one of his pieces in Cleveland, concluding, "I am interested in him insofar as he is interested in me, or rather me and the other men and women who are writing music. We will be lying in wait to see how much contemporary music he will play."

In contrast to the way music directors were selected in days gone by, when a powerful manager or board of directors would make the decision with little or no input from the musicians, who had no choice but to accept the outcome, in this instance the Philharmonic's players were actually consulted and their opinions seriously considered. Maazel had a history of alienating his musicians with what was judged to be an imperious and arrogant manner. (In 1971, when his appointment to the Cleveland Orchestra was announced, it was revealed that an informal poll taken by the musicians beforehand had resulted in a vote of seventy-seven to two against him, which the management and board did not take into consideration.)

Whatever the contentious issues at the time, it was evident that the passage of thirty years had brought about a mellowing of Maazel's approach to his musicians. He was so pleased with the Philharmonic's playing during the preparation of the Bruckner Eighth Symphony the previous fall that he canceled one of the rehearsals. In a *Times* article of February 25 Tommasini referred to Maazel's having "won the hearts" of the musicians by canceling the rehearsal, implying that this was a factor in the players' support of his candidacy. He also wrote of the orchestra's having treated Jansons and Eschenbach poorly in their recent guest engagements. These comments brought forth a rebuke from the Philharmonic violinist Hanna Lachert in the form of a letter to the editor that was printed on March 11. In it she questioned Tommasini's apparent lack of knowledge of the selection process, asking if he really believed the musicians would choose a conductor because he had canceled a rehearsal. She also disputed that the orchestra had treated "two of today's greatest conductors" poorly, conductors with whom they wished to work for many years in the future.

A death in the Philharmonic family occurred on February 14: that of violinist Richard Simon, at the age of sixty-five. He had retired in 1998 well after his and his wife's victory over the IRS in the matter of their Tourte bows.

Despite the controversy over the Maazel appointment, the season had to go on. On February 23 Masur conducted the American premiere of the Symphony No. 9 by Hans Werner Henze in honor of the composer's seventy-fifth birthday. Shostakovich aside, from Beethoven onward the writing of a ninth symphony has tended to produce a work of major proportions, as witness the Ninths of Schubert, Bruckner, Mahler—and now Henze. Whereas Beethoven's Ninth employs Schiller's *Ode to Joy* in an appeal for universal brotherhood, Henze's setting of a text by the German poet Hans-Ulrich Treichel makes the point that brotherhood can only be achieved by condemning the Nazi regime and honoring those who opposed it. Tommasini praised the work and also Masur, for his "committed and involving account of an important work that clearly speaks to him." The audience received the score and its composer with "a tremendous ovation." The Berlin Radio Choir, which participated, was also heard in the opening work, Beethoven's Fantasia in C Minor for Piano, Chorus, and Orchestra (also known as the Choral Fantasy), in which the twenty-year-old American pianist Jonathan Biss made an impressive Philharmonic debut.

After the intermission of an all-Mozart program on March 1, conducted by Sir Colin Davis, honorary membership in the New York Philharmonic-Symphony Society was conferred on Carlos Moseley, the orchestra's chairman emeritus (and before that its press director, managing director, president, and chairman). Moseley, the sixty-third person to be so honored, became one of only four living honorary members, joining Isaac Stern, Pierre Boulez, and Zubin Mehta, the first two of whom were present for the occasion. Stanley Drucker was the evening's ingratiating and enlivening soloist in Mozart's Clarinet Concerto.

On March 8 Davis gave New Yorkers a rare opportunity to experience Elgar's great oratorio *The Dream of Gerontius*, last presented by the Philharmonic in January 1959 when Sir John Barbirolli conducted it. The Westminster Symphonic Choir and the soloists Anthony Dean Griffey, tenor, in the title role; John Relyea, baritone; and Michelle DeYoung, mezzo-soprano, were effective collaborators in Elgar's setting of a poem by Cardinal Newman (1801–1890). Both composer and poet were Roman Catholics at a time when that religion was not regarded highly by members of the Church of England. That tension is reflected in Elgar's oratorio, which, like Richard Strauss's *Death and Transfiguration*, follows a dying man from his deathbed to his final destination—in the Strauss heaven, but in the Elgar, purgatory (and he takes much longer to get there).

In a move that would involve him with the Philharmonic fairly soon, the forty-four-year-old Robert J. Harth was announced on March 29 as the new executive and artistic director of Carnegie Hall, effective in September. For twelve years the executive director of Colorado's Aspen Music Festival and School, Harth would succeed the German Franz Xaver Ohnesorg, whose less-than-two-year tenure at Carnegie had been marked by controversy and discord.

On March 29 Christoph Eschenbach presented Mahler's now rather frequently performed Sixth Symphony. New to the *Times*'s critical staff was Anne Midgette (now with the *Washington Post*), who felt the "uneven performance" was not necessarily the conductor's fault, the orchestra having been by turns wonderful and sloppy. The problem with doing a huge work like the Mahler Sixth more and more frequently is that it ceases to be a special event. To turn this piece into an everyday occurrence and give it just another routine performance is to defeat the composer's vision—witness what has happened to Beethoven's Ninth in recent years, when it has ceased, owing to overexposure, to be a special event.

The year 2001 marked the seventy-fifth anniversary of the Westminster Choir, which had performed frequently with the Philharmonic over the years, and its thirtieth year under the direction of Joseph Flummerfelt. To honor both occasions, a specially commissioned work received its world premiere on the concert of April 12, *Voices of Light* by the American composer Stephen Paulus. Masur, who led the bulk of the program, generously turned the conducting of the new piece over to Flummerfelt, who rarely, if ever, had the chance to actually direct a performance of a work for which he had prepared the chorus. Kozinn wrote of Paulus's "attractively eclectic style" and of how the work showed off "the considerable strengths" of the choir.

Preceding the Paulus on the program was the Shostakovich Piano Concerto No. 2, played by Helen Huang. It is interesting to note how critics of different eras react to the same piece. The concerto had its American premiere on January 2, 1958, with Bernstein as both soloist and conductor on his first concert after having been named music director of the Philharmonic. At the time, Howard Taubman found the work "saddening" when compared with the composer's youthful First Piano Concerto. He found the new work "machine-made.... It is as if fresh ideas, let alone progress, had stopped." Other critics thought the piece trivial. More than forty years later, however, we have Kozinn writing of "a tightly focused, biting work written in a sharply defined, personal style." Of course, how Taubman would have perceived the piece in 2001, or Kozinn in 1958, is anyone's guess. (The author sides with Kozinn.)

News of the death of the conductor Giuseppe Sinopoli, at the age of fifty-four, appeared on April 22. He had suffered a heart attack while conducting a performance of *Aida* at the Deutsche Oper in Berlin and died in the hospital. He had appeared as a guest conductor with the Philharmonic from 1985 to 1991, during which time he made several recordings with the orchestra. Of extramusical interest is the fact that he was also a trained psychiatrist.

One of the young American conductors Tommasini had hoped might be considered for the Philharmonic's music directorship, David Robertson, made his debut with the orchestra at the concerts beginning April 26. Tommasini had written about Robertson's imaginative programming, and he did not disappoint, offering a mix of difficult early twentieth-century music surrounded by familiar standard repertoire: Wagner's Prelude to *Tristan und Isolde*, Schoenberg's monodrama *Erwartung* for soprano and orchestra, and Beethoven's Fifth Symphony. As Tommasini noted, it was a courageous move for a young conductor to make a debut in a complex modernist score such as *Erwartung*, which the orchestra had not played in a while, and equally so in such a familiar work as Beethoven's Fifth. But in opening with the chromatic harmony of the *Tristan* Prelude, Robertson set the stage for the atonal Schoenberg work, especially because he went from one to the other without pause. The Beethoven was presented not with an interpretive agenda, but as "a pathbreaking Viennese Classical symphony." In her Philharmonic debut, the French soprano Françoise Pollet was "a cool, radiant and powerful" protagonist in the Schoenberg. Tommasini concluded his laudatory review by musing on "what might have been" for the Philharmonic.

Kurt Masur returned to his beloved Bruckner on May 24 with the composer's Fourth Symphony ("Romantic"). The performance was dedicated to the memory of Bruno Walter, a great Bruckner interpreter and an important figure in the Philharmonic's mid-twentieth-century history. Tommasini felt that the "breadth and spaciousness" of the performance showed Masur "at his best." Opening the program was Schumann's rarely heard *Konzertstück* for Four Horns and Orchestra, a veritable minefield for a horn section but one negotiated successfully by the Philharmonic's Philip Myers, R. Allen Spanjer, Erik Ralske, and Howard Wall. After the intermission the orchestra honored the violinist Michael Gilbert, who was retiring after thirty-one years of service, as well as the violists Irene Breslaw and Dorian Rence and the double bassist Randall Butler, who were celebrating twenty-five years with the Philharmonic.

On May 31 Masur conducted the American premiere of the Concerto for Flute, Harp, and Orchestra by the German composer Siegfried Matthus. Robert Langevin, in his first season as the Philharmonic's principal flutist, "played with the understated virtuosity" the work demands, according to Kozinn, with Nancy Allen's harp playing "as fluid and nimble as ever." Masur continued to treat Gershwin as a serious composer by offering his *Rhapsody in Blue* in a rare subscription performance (it is usually relegated to pops and festival concerts and was last played in a Philharmonic subscription concert by Leonard Bernstein in 1958). Kozinn felt that Masur's persistence paid off—he finally made the piece swing. Fazil Say, who had been the soloist in a 1998 Lincoln Center Festival performance, played in a more idiomatic Gershwin style on this occasion, which also included an excellent rendition of the Shostakovich First Symphony.

SEPTEMBER 11

Before the Philharmonic's concert in Central Park on July 10, 2001, the United States Postal Service officially unveiled its stamp honoring Leonard Bernstein. The first half of the program was devoted to his music, albeit in "questionable arrangements," as Kozinn described them. In his Philharmonic debut, William Eddins conducted. He was the resident conductor of the Chicago Symphony (as opposed to the peripatetic music director), and the winner of the Seaver-N.E.A.

Conducting Award. He also served as master of ceremonies, since the program was videotaped by PBS.

Apart from the Overture to *Candide*, the "Mambo" from *West Side Story*, and "Glitter and Be Gay" from *Candide*, sung by Kristin Chenoweth, the "questionable arrangements" predominated. Prime among these was a *West Side Story Suite* for violin and orchestra, arranged by William David Brohn for Joshua Bell, who performed it with his customary flair. According to Kozinn, "themes from the show are turned into a 19th-century concerto pastiche.... the themes were beaten to a treacly pulp. What could the Bernstein estate have been thinking when it authorized this?" Bell also played "equally saccharin arrangements" of other Bernstein tunes, and then John Corigliano's arrangement of "Make Our Garden Grow" from *Candide* as a duet with Chenoweth. The concert's second half was devoted to Prokofieff's Fifth Symphony, of which Eddins led "a solid if only fleetingly compelling account."

In early September 2001 the Philharmonic was on tour in Germany, safely away from New York City on the terrible day of September 11. Concerns regarding the safety of the airlines delayed them in Europe for four days; they finally returned on September 15 in three separate planes. The opening-night gala now seemed unthinkable and was canceled. Instead, a special performance of the Brahms *German Requiem* was scheduled for September 20. Writing soon after losing his mother and his close friend Robert Schumann, Brahms chose for his text not the traditional Latin liturgy, but verses from the Bible intended to console survivors. This profoundly human work was given as a memorial to the victims of the terrorist attack on the World Trade Center and as a benefit concert to aid the families of firefighters, police officers, and rescue workers who died in the aftermath.

It was just what New Yorkers needed. Avery Fisher Hall was packed, and many more listeners gathered together outside the hall, in a drizzling rain, to watch and hear the performance on a large screen that had been set up on Lincoln Center Plaza. Tommasini pointed out on September 22 that memorial events do not require critical comments, but felt he could not hold back in this instance, "for the music making was inspired." Heidi Grant Murphy and Thomas Hampson were the soloists, with the New York Choral Artists and the American Boychoir. The work was, of course, part of Kurt Masur's cultural upbringing, having received its world premiere in 1869 by the Leipzig Gewandhaus Orchestra. It had been requested that there be no applause at its conclusion, and the ensuing silence was described by Tommasini as "both a comfort to us all and the highest possible tribute to Mr. Masur and the dedicated performers." Although Tommasini did feel "a sense of letdown" after the first subscription concert on September 22, which ended with the César Franck Symphony in D Minor in a "weighty and Germanic" rendition rather than one of French refinement, he concluded by saying that "just having the Philharmonic back is a small triumph, and a reassuring sign that New York is moving on."

On September 23 came news of the death of Isaac Stern at age eighty-one. He was renowned as one of the world's greatest violinists, having made almost annual appearances with the Philharmonic since his debut with the orchestra in 1944, and many recordings as well; as a teacher and mentor to many young musicians; as the leader of the campaign to save Carnegie Hall, of which he became president; and as a staunch supporter of Israel and many other causes. The main hall of Carnegie is now the Isaac Stern Auditorium.

The next day, September 24, it was announced that Kurt Masur would miss two subscription weeks in December, as well as Beethoven's Ninth on New Year's Eve, because he had to undergo a kidney transplant in Europe in November. In the meantime, Masur's all-Russian program for the concerts beginning September 28 was notable not for its inclusion of Alfred Schnittke's amusing *(K)ein Sommer-nachtsraum* ((Not) a Midsummer Night's Dream), nor for the hearty rendition of Tchaikovsky's Fourth Symphony, but for the Philharmonic's first performance of a work written more than sixty years before, the attractive and tuneful Violin Concerto by Aram Khachaturian. Famous (or infamous) for the once-popular "Sabre Dance" from his ballet *Gayne*, this composer is usually maligned in intellectual circles for his frankly populist music, inspired by his Armenian and Georgian heritage. Sylvia Marcovici was the Philharmonic's passionate soloist in a work that had boasted David Oistrakh and Leonid Kogan among its prime performers.

A Philharmonic debut of more than usual significance occurred on October 18: that of the young American conductor Alan Gilbert. Then chief conductor of the Royal Stockholm Philharmonic, his program opened with Sibelius's *Swan of Tuonela*, in which Thomas Stacy was the sensitive English horn soloist; continued with the Serenade in F Major by the Swedish composer Wilhelm Stenhammar; and closed with Beethoven's Sixth Symphony. Although Stenhammar has never achieved the status in Sweden (at least to the non-Swedish world) as Sibelius in Finland, Grieg in Norway, or Nielsen in Denmark, he nevertheless wrote attractive and appealing music that has, in recent years, been making some headway in terms of recordings, if not of plentiful performances. As for Gilbert, Anne Midgette wrote of some restraint in his work but proclaimed him "the real thing" and "someone to watch."

On October 24 it was announced that members of the Philharmonic, in the form of chamber groups, had begun to give free lunchtime concerts near the site of the World Trade Center. The first of these, on October 13, had been played at 120 Broadway by four of the orchestra's horn players, and on October 20 the flutist

Mindy Kaufman, the violinists Fiona Simon and Hanna Lachert, the violist Judith Nelson, and the cellist Eileen Moon played works by Mozart and Beethoven in the auditorium of the Federal Reserve Bank of New York, located on Liberty Street. The series was to continue through the Monday before Thanksgiving.

On November 1 Masur offered an unusual mixture of works, opening with the world premiere of a work by Susan Botti entitled *Echo Tempo*. A trained singer as well as a composer, Botti was the soprano soloist in her own work, a setting of American Indian texts that includes an important part for a solo percussionist, expertly played by the Philharmonic's Christopher Lamb. The Finnish pianist Olli Mustonen was the soloist in Rachmaninoff's *Rhapsody on a Theme of Paganini*, and the program also included Liszt's once-popular symphonic poem *Les préludes* and Prokofieff's propulsive *Scythian Suite*. Mélange or not, it was a program the author would have been pleased to attend.

For the past several years the Philharmonic had been issuing CD sets of historic performances from its archives. Now, during his last season as music director, a set devoted to Kurt Masur was issued. Entitled *Kurt Masur at the New York Philharmonic*, the ten-CD set includes such large-scale works as Bach's *Saint Matthew Passion*, Beethoven's Ninth Symphony and *Missa solemnis*, Honegger's *Jeanne d'Arc au bûcher*, and Stravinsky's *Perséphone*, as well as Henze's Ninth Symphony, Gubaidulina's *Two Paths*, Tan Dun's Concerto for Water Percussion, Shostakovich's First Symphony, and shorter pieces such as Strauss's *Till Eulenspiegel* and Dukas's *Sorcerer's Apprentice*. Strangely enough, although Masur selected the repertoire himself there is nothing by Mendelssohn.

In commenting most favorably about the set on November 6, Oestreich, who had shown himself a strong supporter of Masur, wrote that "the city and the orchestra have never summoned more than a fraction of what this imposing figure has to offer. We have scarcely taken the measure of the man." The set, he said, "is a worthy tribute: an essential memento of an impassioned, disciplined and committed artist who will surely leave his mark on the orchestra and the city."

On November 15 Masur revisited Shostakovich's Symphony No. 13 ("Babi Yar"), a performance that, according to Paul Griffiths, "was a triumph for the Philharmonic, all the way down to the poetic tuba." The men of the New York Choral Artists took part, along with the Russian baritone Sergei Leiferkus. "Another magnificent protagonist" was heard in the concert's first half: the Russian Yuri Bashmet, who played the Viola Concerto by Sofia Gubaidulina.

Joshua Bell was the soloist in Samuel Barber's ingratiating Violin Concerto on November 21, with Leonard Slatkin conducting. Also on the program was the complete music of Stravinsky's *Firebird*. Unlike *Petrushka* and *The Rite of Spring*, the complete *Firebird*, when heard divorced from the stage action, demonstrates the composer's wisdom in fashioning concert suites of excerpts from it, which contain the best music. But, as Holland put it, "The Philharmonic was created to play music like this [complete version], and no one does it better."

An unusual program was given on December 13, with Slatkin conducting one of the programs originally scheduled for Masur. These days Tchaikovsky's *Nutcracker* Suite is normally offered on pops and special holiday concerts, and arrangements by Duke Ellington and Billy Strayhorn in the same context. But here was the Philharmonic, in a regular subscription concert, joined by the Lincoln Center Jazz Orchestra directed by Wynton Marsalis, in a hybrid performance of Tchaikovsky's suite. Performed in alternation, movement by movement, the Philharmonic played the original version and the Jazz Orchestra played the Ellington/Strayhorn arrangement. On the first half, the two groups performed four sections from Marsalis's *All Rise*, the work that had its premiere in 1999. The *Times*'s Ben Ratliff was kinder to the piece this time, stating that "the segues between orchestra and jazz band were tight and occasionally breathtaking."

Masur may have missed the New Year's Eve concert, but Beethoven's Ninth was performed on schedule, conducted this time by Sir John Eliot Gardiner in his Philharmonic debut. As a prime mover and shaker in the period-instrument and historically informed performance-practice movements, Gardiner brought his own ideas to the performance, which could easily have been Beethoven's ideas as well. That meant considerably faster tempos than had become the norm, adhering as much as possible to Beethoven's controversial metronome markings. Preceding the Ninth were a chorale and recitative from J. S. Bach's Cantata No. 27 ("Who Knows How Near My End Approaches"), which led seamlessly into the Beethoven; the entire performance lasted little more than an hour. Participating were the New York Choral Artists, the soprano Madeline Bender, the mezzo-soprano Marietta Simpson, the tenor Stuart Neill, and the bass-baritone John Relyea. Kozinn characterized the performance as "an exhilarating reading."

On January 27 Tommasini wrote of the Philharmonic's forthcoming first season under Lorin Maazel, details of which had recently been announced. Even considering that much of the season had been planned before Maazel's engagement as music director, Tommasini conceded that he had "exceeded expectations" in terms of programming contemporary and unusual repertoire, even though the Philharmonic was basically continuing its conservative ways. The guest engagements of the young American conductors David Robertson and Robert Spano, either of whom, Tommasini still believed, "might have been a dynamic choice" as music director, meant that new and intriguing works would be presented.

Nine weeks after undergoing surgery, Kurt Masur returned on February 7 to conduct excerpts from Wagner's *Tristan und Isolde*: the Prelude to Act I, Act II complete, the Prelude to Act III, and Isolde's "Liebestod." Deborah Voigt and Stig Andersen sang the title roles, with Violeta Urmana as Brangäne, the seventy-five-year-old Theo Adam as King Mark, and Thomas Studebaker as Melot. Masur was praised by Tommasini for a "distinguished, affecting and impressive" performance, as was Voigt for singing "so beautifully and intelligently." He concluded, "The big news of the evening was that Ms. Voigt may be the Isolde of the future. The good news was that Mr. Masur is back."

Each year Masur conducted a concert with one of New York City's conservatory orchestras and gave master classes for young conductors at those institutions. The last of these programs was with the Juilliard Orchestra at Avery Fisher Hall on February 18 and included excerpts from Prokofieff's *Romeo and Juliet*, Bartók's Viola Concerto (with Kyle Armbrust as the student soloist), and Beethoven's Second Symphony. After accepting a certificate of merit from Juilliard's president, Joseph W. Polisi, before the Beethoven performance, Masur admitted, "I treated the orchestra very badly during rehearsals," but he felt the hard work justified the results. Praising the entire concert, Tommasini wrote of a "charged, incisive performance" of the Beethoven symphony and observed that the orchestra musicians joined the audience in applauding Masur at the end.

The German conductor Ingo Metzmacher made his Philharmonic debut on February 21 in a program that began with a work by his late countryman Karl Amadeus Hartmann, *Miserae: Symphonic Poem for Orchestra*, dedicated to the Nazis' first concentration camp victims at Dachau. The program continued with Richard Goode as the soloist in Mozart's last piano concerto, No. 27 in B-flat Major, K. 595, and concluded with Richard Strauss's autobiographical *Ein Heldenleben*, with the concertmaster, Glenn Dicterow, effective in the lengthy violin solo. Overall, Griffiths felt that Metzmacher gave "a vital performance."

The *Times* on March 25 reported the death of the great American soprano Eileen Farrell, at age eighty-two. The possessor of an extremely powerful voice, ideally suited for Wagner, she had been a frequent soloist with the Philharmonic, especially in the Bernstein era, when she performed excerpts from *Götterdämmerung* and *Tristan und Isolde*, as well as the *Wesendonck-Lieder*. In 1951 she sang the role of Marie in Dimitri Mitropoulos's concert performances of Berg's *Wozzeck*. Equally at home with pop and jazz, she was one of the first of the so-called crossover artists.

On April 4 Masur conducted an unusual juxtaposition of two great choral works, Mozart's Requiem and Prokofieff's *Alexander Nevsky*. With the soloists Edith Wiens, Nancy Maultsby, Stanford Olsen, and Nathan Berg in the Mozart,

Maultsby in the Prokofieff, and the New York Choral Artists in both, Holland wrote of "a happy evening," a fairly unusual description for a requiem. He devoted no space to the issue of which version of Mozart's unfinished masterpiece was performed. He did, however, mention that the Philharmonic tends to honor its music directors only when they leave, and that on this occasion there was "a love fest from both sides of the footlights."

Riccardo Muti, the one that got away, led a "magnificent performance of the Verdi Requiem," according to Tommasini, on April 17, the beginning of the second week of his two-week engagement. (In the first he had programmed the rarely heard First Symphony of Scriabin, whose music is one of Muti's specialties.) For the Requiem his soloists were Barbara Frittoli, Violeta Urmana, Giuseppe Sabbatini, and Samuel Ramey. Together with Joseph Flummerfelt's Westminster Symphonic Choir, they all produced "a great night for the Philharmonic."

Sir Colin Davis returned on April 25 for a program devoted to one of his specialties, the music of Sibelius. He led the first Philharmonic performance of the Six Humoresques for Violin and Orchestra, essentially Sibelius in a (for him) lighter mood. Glenn Dicterow "brought radiant sound and wistful elegance to all six," wrote Tommasini in his April 27 review. In his accounts of *Pohjola's Daughter* and the Fifth Symphony, Davis was praised for the "dramatic urgency and flow" of the former, the "clarity and breadth" of the latter, and the orchestra was with him every step of the way.

Of all the New York critics, none wrote more warmly and appreciatively of Kurt Masur than Oestreich. In a May 12 article, he reiterated his sentiments from an earlier piece: "In a sense, New York hardly knew the man, and it may be the poorer for it." The article was in the form of an interview with the conductor before the beginning of his final three weeks as music director, to which the Philharmonic had given the heading "Thank you, Kurt Masur."

In the interview Masur expressed some unhappiness that he had not been able to fulfill all his ideas for the orchestra. He was happy, however, about one aspect of his departure: that he was doing so at a time when people said, "I'm sorry he's leaving," rather than being glad he was at last gone. He regretted his failure to institute a summer program for the orchestra comparable to the Boston Symphony's Tanglewood or the Proms in London. (The Philharmonic actually played the first concerts at Tanglewood in 1936 but did not pursue a permanent arrangement there, thus allowing the Boston Symphony to step in.). The lack of a pipe organ in Avery Fisher Hall was still one of his disappointments, even though a German woman had contributed $1 million for such a purpose. "There are more than 200 pieces we cannot play because of the lack of an organ," said Masur. He would have liked to play a part in choosing his successor, preferably a young American, with a few more years to be able to do so.

Masur further stated that he had several enemies on the board who felt the managing director should be the top person, the music director second—not a good way to succeed, he felt. As for the friction between himself and Deborah Borda, he said, "We should work together instead of fighting each other, because a divided leadership for an orchestra is deadly." To this, Borda countered, "Kurt Masur did a magnificent job, and I have tremendous admiration for his accomplishments at the New York Philharmonic. He was the right man at the right time, and our partnership in so many ways was deeply successful for the institution." The differences in the way European and American orchestras are run must have made some conflict inevitable. Yet Borda later invited Kurt Masur to be a guest conductor with the Los Angeles Philharmonic during the 2009–10 season, an engagement he accepted.

Masur concluded by stating that he now actually felt more American than German: "If you have been a New Yorker, Germany is not so easy for you. . . . The collaboration with the New York Philharmonic is the crowning point of my life. I had a longer time at the Gewandhaus, but this was like being at home."

"Thank You, Kurt Masur"

Lincoln Center concertgoers of 2009, and other New Yorkers as well, probably breathed a sigh of relief when the construction work and rubble at Broadway and Sixty-sixth Street finally disappeared. In its place now stands the newly reconstituted and gleaming Alice Tully Hall. But in 2002 the plans for an overhauling of the Lincoln Center campus did not concentrate on Alice Tully Hall, but on Avery Fisher Hall, which was in need of cosmetic repairs and, in spite of all the previous renovations, still more acoustic improvement. The question facing the Lincoln Center board was: should Avery Fisher Hall be renovated or razed and replaced? If the latter, should it continue to carry the name of Avery Fisher or should it be named in recognition of a major contributor to the reconstruction? Each possibility had its proponents.

As for changing the name, the family of Avery Fisher informed Lincoln Center that they might take legal action if, after a reconstruction, a new name were appended, and furthermore they would be prepared to seek the return of the remainder of the endowment—more than $17 million. In response, Lincoln Center gave no assurance that the Fisher name would be retained. It was thought it would be easier to attract new donors if naming rights were an inducement. As of this writing in 2009, the point is moot, for Avery Fisher Hall still stands, but stay tuned. Also at the time of this writing, the Lincoln Center campus is a mess, with much construction taking place. And none of it involves Avery Fisher Hall, whose renovation could come as late as 2020.

In early 2002 Beverly Sills resigned her post as president of Lincoln Center. She was succeeded on May 1 by Reynold Levy, who actually began work a bit sooner. Additionally, Sills remained for a while after May 1 in order to effect a smooth transition. Levy had been executive director of the Ninety-second Street Y as well as president of the AT&T Foundation. At the time he assumed the Lincoln Center position he was president of the International Rescue Committee.

Meanwhile, Kurt Masur's final weeks as music director of the New York Philharmonic—a period publicly designated "Thank You, Kurt Masur"—were at hand. There were still a few orchestra members who did not appreciate Masur's tough rehearsal methods and preferred the designation "Thank You for Leaving." But they were in the minority. In fact, one member told the author that, of all the music directors under whom he had played, starting with Bernstein, Masur was the only one who knew what the job was all about. He had been brought in to improve the orchestra and restore its standing in the community, and he had succeeded. Whatever his rehearsal methods—and they were far from the intimidation tactics of Toscanini, Reiner, or Szell—the musicians respected him for the results he achieved.

On May 12 a warm tribute to Masur by Rockwell appeared in the *Times*. Rockwell wrote of his time as director of the Lincoln Center Festival, when he and Masur collaborated on the programming of the Philharmonic's appearances in the festival; of getting Masur to conduct Ornette Coleman's *Skies of America*; of his pairing of Henze's *Tristan* with Wagner's; of his performing the final version of Beethoven's *Fidelio* in juxtaposition with John Eliot Gardiner's performance of the original *Leonore*; and of his conducting challenging works by Morton Feldman and Krzysztof Penderecki. He said of Masur, "I admire him, I think he's a noble conductor, and I will regret his departure. . . . Not that he is disappearing from the planet. But I shall miss him at the Philharmonic and as a part of New York's cultural life."

The first of Masur's programs, on May 16, featured works by two former Philharmonic music directors: Bernstein's Serenade for Violin, Strings, and Percussion and Mahler's First Symphony. Holland contrasted the two compositions, Bernstein's an urban work, Mahler's a country one. Of Glenn Dicterow's solo playing in the Bernstein, he wrote: "What a marvelous player. His presence as concertmaster is for the Philharmonic a weekly luxury." He further commented that "the orchestra played beautifully for Mr. Masur. . . . The Masur regime was not a transcendent one, but a tough orchestra in need of discipline got it. Mr. Masur deserves thanks from everyone."

The following week, on May 23, Masur conducted Alfred Schnittke's Cello Concerto No. 1 and Bruckner's Third Symphony, a program that, according to Tommasini, showcased "his greatness as a musician." Natalia Gutman was the cello soloist in the work she and Masur had performed in its American premiere in 1991. Now they played it with "such conviction and mystery" as to minimize the work's potential long-windedness and ponderousness. The Bruckner was conducted by Masur "with unflagging energy and calm authority." Following the intermission several orchestra members were honored: the double bassist Walter Botti, retiring after fifty years of service; the violinist Jacques Margolies, retiring after thirty-eight years; and the cellists Nancy Donaruma and Valentin Hirsu, for their twenty-fifth anniversaries as orchestra members.

Masur's final concert as music director took place on Saturday, June 1, an all-Beethoven program consisting of the Violin Concerto, with Anne-Sophie Mutter, and the "Eroica" Symphony. Before the performance of the symphony, Zarin Mehta came forth with Masur and announced that the board of directors had awarded Masur the title of music director emeritus—making him only the second Philharmonic conductor to be given an honorary title upon retirement (the first being Bernstein, whose title was laureate conductor). With much applause from a standing, shouting audience, everyone naturally expected a speech from Masur, but none was forthcoming. He merely acknowledged the applause.

As reported by Tommasini, Zarin Mehta then spoke of "a historic night," the "culmination of eleven glorious seasons" for Kurt Masur. There was then a loud shout of "Why?" from a man in the audience, followed by extended applause. Mehta apparently thought the applause was a supportive response to his remarks, rather than an endorsement of the question of why Masur was being let go when he clearly wanted to stay.

Concerning the concert itself, Mutter was criticized for her mostly slow and inconsistent tempos, though Masur followed her completely throughout. The "Eroica" had Masur's usual structural integrity and fervor, but also a more relaxed freedom and spontaneity. The standing ovation lasted at least five minutes, and it was only after Masur grasped Glenn Dicterow's hand and led him and the orchestra offstage that it came to an end.

But Masur's work with the Philharmonic was not quite over, for on June 3 he and the orchestra left for a week of concerts in Germany, four in Cologne and two in Baden-Baden (the Philharmonic's first appearance in that city), followed immediately by a tour of Asia from June 16 to July 2, with concerts in Japan (Yokohama, Tokyo, Nagoya, Fukuoka, Kyoto, and Hamamatsu), Taiwan (Taipei), and South Korea (Seoul).

Holland, whose writing had been generally favorable to Kurt Masur while constantly reminding readers how much more the Philharmonic was capable of than

Masur asked of it, delivered himself of a few more words on the subject on June 30. Recalling his performances of the standard Central European repertoire with which Masur felt most at home, Holland spoke of the bluntness of his Beethoven and Brahms, "unassailable but less often heartwarming," his renditions of the classical and romantic repertoire like those of "a passionately meticulous keeper of records." His toughness in rehearsals, while producing an "absence of superficiality," was noted for its "boot camp rigors." It was only in the final weeks of his tenure, when everyone knew he was leaving, that the orchestra's sound "broadened, deepened, floated, shone." Masur's musical rectitude and the orchestra's great potential finally "seemed to coalesce." The irony was that "had he remained as music director, it might never have happened."

Be that as it may, Masur's actual final concerts as music director took place on July 18, 20, and 21. The first date was at Avery Fisher Hall; as part of the Lincoln Center Festival, there was a televised concert celebrating Masur's seventy-fifth birthday. The program was almost all pops, uncharacteristically (for Masur) consisting of movements from larger compositions as well as short works of a popular nature that were mostly designed to show off the orchestra's principal players in solo passages. There were three encores, the third of which (unfortunately not televised) was the famous Air from Bach's Third Orchestral Suite. As described by Kozinn, "during its final moments, [Masur] slowly walked off the stage, letting the players finish on their own." Before the encores Masur spoke briefly of his admiration for the orchestra, and told the audience, "I'm still with you, and we don't forget the time here." Kozinn concluded, "The Philharmonic is a tough bunch, but at the end of the Bach, some of the players were in tears."

On the weekend of July 20 and 21 the orchestra played at Tanglewood, normally the province of the Boston Symphony. Oestreich covered these concerts, writing of "superb accounts" of the Brahms Double Concerto and the Mahler Symphony No. 1 on the Saturday, when Glenn Dicterow and Carter Brey were the elegant and eloquent soloists in the Brahms. Oestreich thought the Mahler one of Masur's "finest performances with the Philharmonic," with stunning sonorities and an ending that was "positively cataclysmic."

Sunday afternoon brought Beethoven's "Emperor" Concerto and "Eroica" Symphony, with Yefim Bronfman a "predictably strong pianist in the concerto." Although the "Eroica" was something of an anticlimax after its New York performance in June, it was still "a wrenching experience," and the audience sent him off "with clamorous warmth." As Oestreich put it, "So a wild 11-year ride with a seemingly staid maestro, exhilarating and frustrating in varying proportions for all concerned, is finally over."

CHAPTER 20

2002–4

ENTER MAAZEL

When Lorin Maazel began his tenure as music director of the New York Philharmonic, he was seventy-two years old. But he made his first podium appearance when he conducted the orchestra of the Interlochen Music Camp at the New York World's Fair in 1939—when he was nine. At the more advanced age of eleven he conducted a nationwide radio broadcast with the NBC Symphony Orchestra, and in 1942, at the age of twelve, he made his debut with the New York Philharmonic at Lewisohn Stadium. After appearances with other major American orchestras, he enrolled at the University of Pittsburgh at sixteen, received a Fulbright Fellowship in 1951 to study baroque music in Italy, and made his adult conducting debut in Catania, Sicily, in 1953. Engagements with European orchestras followed, and in 1960 he became the first American and the youngest conductor to appear at Germany's prestigious Bayreuth Festival. (The word "appear" is perhaps misleading, for the orchestra and conductor are hidden from view.)

His contract was for four years, and there were some in the profession who regarded it as something of a stopgap for the Philharmonic. Already there was talk of a search for Maazel's successor. Maazel, however, spoke of his appointment as possibly "the fruition of my experience as a conductor, to work with an orchestra I really love . . . I'm more enthusiastic about my future with this orchestra than I have ever been about anything I have ever done anyplace."

A conductor naturally wants to make a big statement on his first program with a new orchestra. Zubin Mehta had selected Mahler's First Symphony, Kurt Masur Bruckner's Seventh Symphony. For his first subscription week, beginning with the concert of September 19, Maazel chose Beethoven's Ninth Symphony. The real attention was focused, however, on the program's opening work. To mark the occasion, the New York Philharmonic and Lincoln Center's Great Performers series commissioned a score from John Adams that received its world premiere that night. He met the Philharmonic's and Lincoln Center's request for a memorial to the tragedy of September 11 with *On the Transmigration of Souls*. The composer did not refer to his work as a musical composition. Rather, as he said in the program notes, he wished to create a "memory space" where "you can go and be alone with your thoughts and emotions." Thus the piece, calling for chorus, children's chorus, and a large orchestra, is not the cantata one might have expected. Rather, live music is combined with electronic elements, taped street sounds, the names of victims read by family and friends, and phrases from missing-persons posters in the neighborhood of Ground Zero. Like Brahms's Requiem, Adams's piece is for the survivors.

The critics applauded Maazel and the Philharmonic for including the Adams piece on the opening week's concerts, but lambasted them for their failure to program it on the opening-night gala the night before, when Beethoven's *Leonore* Overture No. 3 was substituted as the prelude to the Ninth Symphony. The reason given was that there was insufficient rehearsal time to prepare the complex work for the gala concert. Critics (Tommasini included) suspected, however, that the Philharmonic's board did not want to dampen spirits on a gala occasion, which included a formal dinner following the concert.

Tommasini was also critical of Maazel's choice of the Beethoven Ninth for his first program. After all, the Beethoven symphonies had been a staple of Kurt Masur's repertoire, and the Ninth in particular had become his message for greeting the New Year. Was Maazel trying to one-up Masur? Although Tommasini had nothing but praise for the Adams work and its significance, he found Maazel's Beethoven performances wanting: the overture lacked spontaneity and passion, and the symphony had no dramatic tension, in spite of the great technical expertise of both performances. Joseph Flummerfelt's New York Choral Artists and Dianne Berkun's Brooklyn Youth Chorus sang in the Adams piece, the Choral Artists and the soloists Marina Mescheriakova, Jill Grove, Michael Schade, and René Pape in the Ninth Symphony.

Greg Sandow, who had written disparagingly about the mere possibility of Maazel's appointment, decided to attend the two opening concerts. Of the gala opening night he wrote that the orchestra played "better than it used to. Spectacularly better, in fact." It sounded "richer, warmer and far more unanimous." Though marveling at the technical brilliance heard in the overture and the symphony, he found the overall results cold and heartless. The symphony's fourth movement was particularly joyless—a dispiriting performance for an "Ode to Joy." But the second performance "came alive," especially toward the end of the first movement. The Scherzo was played with "unexpected bite," and the third movement was at least not dull, as it had been the night before. The finale, however, was uneven, with moments of "light and heat," others of "blankness." Concluding with the observation that Maazel was impulsive and unpredictable, he nonetheless kept an open mind as to what the future would bring: "We just might be surprised."

On September 23 was reported the death of the violinist Rafael Druian at the age of eighty. He had been the Philharmonic's concertmaster from 1971 to 1974, during the tenure of Pierre Boulez. Earlier he had served as concertmaster of the Dallas Symphony, Minneapolis Symphony, and the Cleveland Orchestra, the last under George Szell's direction.

The finals of the Maazel/Vilar Conductors' Competition were drawing near at the end of September. Now it was revealed that Vilar had failed to make good on his pledges to at least two major arts groups because of losses he had sustained in high-tech stocks—and the Conductors' Competition was one of those groups. Maazel was placed in the position of providing money himself and soliciting other sources to come up with the $700,000 needed for the finals.

Having begun one year before, with regional auditions on five continents, submitted video and audio tapes, and 362 candidates, it all boiled down to the evening of September 28, 2002, in Carnegie Hall, when six finalists conducted New York's Orchestra of St. Luke's before a large audience and a prestigious international jury. The winner would receive a cash prize of $45,000, a conducting fellowship, and symphonic engagements under Maazel's supervision. In the end there was not one winner, but two, and not with a divided prize, but with duplicate awards totaling $90,000. Emerging victorious were Xian Zhang, twenty-eight, of China, and Bundit Ungrangsee, thirty-one, of Thailand. At the time, Zhang was the conductor of the orchestra at the University of Cincinnati College Conservatory of Music, and Ungrangsee was the assistant conductor of the Charleston Symphony Orchestra in South Carolina. Maazel said he was not searching for a finished conductor, but "for the musician in the conductor."

After a successful guest appearance by André Previn, Maazel returned for a program on October 3 including Rimsky-Korsakov's orchestration of Mussorgsky's *Night on Bald Mountain*, Rachmaninoff's Piano Concerto No. 2, with the twenty-year-old Lang Lang as soloist, and Sibelius's Second Symphony. In what would become a litany throughout Maazel's tenure, Tommasini wrote of "technically brilliant and eerily controlled performances that lacked breadth and spontaneity." Lang Lang was praised for his technical brilliance, but not for his mannered physical movements or his musical distortions (another litany in the making), which Maazel apparently went along with.

Kurt Masur returned to New York, this time as principal conductor of the London Philharmonic Orchestra, which played two concerts at Carnegie Hall on October 7 and 8. This time Holland did not write that Masur was not asking enough from the orchestra, or that the orchestra was not living up to its potential. In fact, he praised the orchestra as one that cared, especially in its performance of

that Masur specialty, the Bruckner Seventh Symphony. He did find the programming generally unimaginative and the playing of Beethoven's First and Prokofiev's
Fifth Symphonies less than persuasive. But he wrote sympathetically of the
orchestra's self-governance (true of all the London orchestras except the BBC
Symphony), its virtual hand-to-mouth existence, its hectic schedule, and its lack of
cynicism under the circumstances. (London orchestras have a remarkable esprit de
corps.)

On October 16 the *Times* published an article by Robin Pogrebin about the fact
that symphony orchestra audiences are buying fewer and fewer season subscriptions,
preferring instead to purchase single tickets for concerts or, at most, subscriptions
to short series. There was a time, for example, when subscribers to the Boston
Symphony thought nothing of buying a subscription to twelve or twenty-four
concerts, and the season would be largely sold out. For the New York Philharmonic
it was the same, except that their concerts would be divided into two series of
fourteen concerts each. Today's concertgoers did not wish to commit themselves to
an extensive series, said Pogrebin, or perhaps they did not want to plan that far ahead.
The change in ticket-buying habits could be attributed to uncertain economic
conditions, the increasingly varied attractions available for the entertainment dollar,
and consumers' desire for greater flexibility in choosing an event to attend. People
did continue to attend symphony concerts in goodly numbers, but their ticket-buying
decisions were less organized, less predictable.

In an October 20 article, Tommasini wrote of the great impact Maazel had
already made on the Philharmonic, and in less than a month's time. Masur had left
the orchestra in fine shape, and Maazel had increased the level of precision with
which it played. But again, he found Maazel's interpretations willful and calculated,
not at all spontaneous. It was as though the conductor wished to make his performances novel and different at all costs. Yet with the Adams piece he demonstrated
that he could be a convincing advocate of contemporary scores. Tommasini hoped
the Philharmonic management and board would encourage Maazel to play as
much new and recent music as possible, for that appeared to be the only way he
could ensure his artistic legacy in New York.

Sir Colin Davis, in his fifth season as the Philharmonic's principal guest
conductor, after a program of Stravinsky, Mozart, and Haydn, led an all-English
one on November 14. In his Philharmonic debut the English tenor Ian Bostridge
was the committed soloist in Benjamin Britten's cycle on Rimbaud poems, *Les
Illuminations* (once mentioned in a London newspaper as "Lazy Luminations"),
and Davis offered one of his specialties, the First Symphony of Elgar. Midgette felt
that Davis was "passionately convincing" in a work she finds stodgy, although one

might say that stodginess is in the ear of the beholder, and there is nothing like passion to sweep it away.

On December 7 the New York Philharmonic celebrated its 160th anniversary, important enough for a special concert on the date of the orchestra's very first concert. As has been customary on such events, Beethoven's Fifth Symphony was performed, for it had been included on that earlier program. Lorin Maazel conducted, and Deborah Voigt was the soprano soloist in the aria "Ocean, thou Mighty Monster" from Weber's *Oberon* (also included on the first concert) and two arias by Beethoven, one from *Fidelio*, the other the concert aria "Ah! Perfido." The Overtures to *Fidelio* and *Oberon* were also heard (the latter having been played on the original program). Holland did not review the performances per se but in a related article referred to the Philharmonic as "a Rolls-Royce of an orchestra" and Maazel as "an extraordinary executant just a little too aware of how extraordinary he is."

After eighteen years as music director of the Cleveland Orchestra, Christoph von Dohnányi stepped down. He was thus free to accept guest engagements with other orchestras, including the Philharmonic. The second week, beginning December 4, of a two-week engagement opened with Charles Ives's delicate *Unanswered Question*. Apparently Dohnányi was unaware of the problem Masur had with this piece a few years before, when a noisily coughing audience drove him to stop the performance and begin again. Yet here were the coughers again, and the uncomfortable rustlers. Dohnányi did not stop, but, according to Holland, the noise made the thoughtful playing of the piece "useless."

The poor audience behavior continued through the quiet opening of Bartók's *Music for Strings, Percussion and Celesta*, although, as the music got louder, attention to it stabilized. Holland stated that he had never heard the piece played better. The German Christian Tetzlaff was the soloist in Beethoven's Violin Concerto in a straightforward performance that Holland said gave "orthodoxy a good name." It was a reading in which the composer was prominent, not the interpreter, for which Holland was thankful.

Another guest was subjected to audience rudeness. No coughing to speak of this time, merely the sound of a cell phone. In his debut appearance with the Philharmonic, on December 12, the Finnish conductor Sakari Oramo was leading a performance of Carl Nielsen's Fourth Symphony ("The Inextinguishable") when the dreaded apparatus made its presence known, naturally in a quiet expressive passage. Oramo stopped conducting, and then it was he who apologized to the audience for the interruption, not the offender, after which the performance continued. The young Finn was well received by Midgette, who found his work promising enough to warrant further exposure.

Occasionally, usually at holiday time, the Philharmonic schedule includes what are termed "split weeks," that is, a division of the orchestra into two separate units playing simultaneously in different venues. For the concerts beginning December 19, a little less than half the orchestra was performing Handel's *Messiah*, with Sir Neville Marriner conducting, at Riverside Church on the Upper West Side. Marriner, an adept practitioner of early-music performance style, was not able to avoid a feeling of heaviness, according to Midgette, his efforts toward clarity blurred by the church's echoing acoustics. The Westminster Symphonic Choir participated, along with the soprano Elizabeth Futral, the mezzo-soprano Anna Larsson, the countertenor David Daniels, the tenor Richard Croft, and the bass-baritone Nathan Berg.

At the same time at Avery Fisher Hall, Lorin Maazel conducted the world pre-miere of a concert opera by the Russian composer Rodion Shchedrin. Entitled *The Enchanted Wanderer*, the work was commissioned by the New York Philharmonic and dedicated to Maazel. Shchedrin, seventy years old at the time, was never in the fore-front of cutting-edge Russian composers, such as Schnittke and Gubaidulina, never mind Prokofieff and Shostakovich. His music lacks a signature style because the composer chose to write differently according to the needs of each composition.

The Enchanted Wanderer, a ninety-minute full-evening piece, is based on a story by the nineteenth-century Russian author Nikolai Leskov. The opera mingles the sounds of the Russian Orthodox church with folkloric elements, punctuated by lots of percussion. Three soloists depicted the principal characters as well as all the minor ones: the mezzo-soprano Lilli Paasikivi, the tenor Evgeny Akimov, and the bass Ain Anger, all in their Philharmonic debuts. Tommasini found them excellent, as he did the New York Choral Artists and Maazel's conducting. As for the work itself, it was "unchallenging...contemporary music for those who don't like con-temporary music."

After ringing in the New Year with an all-Gershwin program, Maazel offered, on January 2, two of the most basic pieces in the standard repertoire of fifty or sixty years before, the Grieg Piano Concerto and Beethoven's Fifth Symphony. Beethoven's Fifth has always been with us, of course, but Grieg's concerto rarely turns up today on "serious" symphonic concerts (though it continues to be recorded quite often). This is unfortunate, for it is a lovely piece that once attracted the talents of such giants as Arthur Rubinstein, Walter Gieseking, Dinu Lipatti, and Clifford Curzon, among others. On this occasion the exemplary Norwegian pianist Leif Ove Andsnes was the soloist in a performance that demonstrated why the work was once so popular and why it should be heard more often today. An enter-taining piece by William Bolcom, called *Ragomania*, opened the program

On January 9 the nineteen-year-old German Julia Fischer made an impressive debut in the Sibelius Violin Concerto, deftly accompanied by Maazel. Fischer has since returned several times to the Philharmonic and has developed into one of the outstanding violinists of our time.

On January 21 the Israel Philharmonic came to town with Zubin Mehta for one of Mehta's spectacular two-orchestra extravaganzas. This time it was Maazel's turn to take the helm, leading the two Philharmonics in Mahler's First Symphony. It was the first time the two groups had performed together in over twenty years. Griffiths wrote of the performance as "a triumph," though any suspicion of kindness toward Mehta evaporated when he dismissed the conductor's program-opening Tchaikovsky Fourth Symphony as "a coarse account."

Mehta redeemed himself in Griffiths's eyes the next night by devoting the first half of his New York Philharmonic program to the music of Anton Webern, something he had done during his tenure as music director. On this occasion he proceeded from early to late Webern: the Idyll *Im Sommerwind* (In the Summer Wind); the *Passacaglia*, Op. 1; the *Six Pieces for Orchestra*, Op. 6; and the *Concerto for Nine Instruments*, Op. 24. The four pieces in total take less than thirty minutes to perform, but they can still be a tough nut for audiences to crack. Yet there was no description of people streaming to the exits, probably because it was the first part of the program, and Midori's account of the Elgar Violin Concerto awaited.

On January 28 the death of the pianist John Browning, at the age of sixty-nine, was reported. A pupil of the legendary Rosina Lhévinne at Juilliard, Browning was noted for the elegance of his playing. He performed frequently with the Philharmonic and in 1962 gave the world premiere of Samuel Barber's Piano Concerto, written for him, with Erich Leinsdorf and the Boston Symphony during the opening week of Philharmonic Hall.

The year 2003 marked the bicentennial of the birth of Hector Berlioz. The Philharmonic would be programming several of his works throughout the year, starting with the great *Grande Messe des Morts* (Requiem) on February 17, with Charles Dutoit conducting. Joseph Flummerfelt's Westminster Symphonic Choir participated, with Paul Groves as the tenor soloist in the Sanctus. Griffiths wrote of "glorious singing" by the choir, "superbly delivered" sounds from the orchestra, and "exquisite command" of the tenor lines. Mitigating against frequent performances of this work are its extravagant demands: an exceptionally large chorus, multiple sets of timpani, and four additional brass groups placed at the north, east, south, and west regions of the hall. Although the work is noted for the tremendous and thrilling sonority of the Dies irae, much of the score is actually quite sensitive and contemplative.

A program of new and recent works was given on March 5 that prompted Kozinn to remark, "The New York Philharmonic could take what ought to be its rightful place as a vital contributor to the growth of this country's musical culture if it regularly presented programs like the one it played on Wednesday evening." The works in question were *Song and Dance of Tears* by Bright Sheng (in its world premiere), Music for Cello and Orchestra by Leon Kirchner, and *Seeing* by Christopher Rouse. David Zinman, a strong advocate for contemporary American music, conducted, with Yo-Yo Ma as the soloist in the Kirchner, Emanuel Ax in the Rouse, and both together in the Sheng. They were joined by two Chinese performers on traditional native instruments, Wu Man playing the *pipa*, a lutelike instrument, and Wu Tong playing the *shō*, a Japanese organ in which the wind for the pipes is supplied by the mouth. Like Zinman, Ax and Ma are noted for their performances of new music. In fact, Kirchner's piece was written for and first played by Ma, just as the Rouse work was for Ax. Both distinguished themselves on this occasion, as did Zinman and the orchestra.

Mstislav Rostropovich had celebrated his seventh-fifth birthday in 2002, conducting and playing the cello around the world. The festivities continued in 2003, with the Philharmonic presenting a three-week festival entitled Slava and Friends in which he performed works by composers with whom he had been closely associated either personally or musically. March 20 saw him conducting pieces by Bernstein, Prokofieff, Dutilleux, and Lutoslawski, with the young Ukrainian pianist Konstantin Lifschitz substituting for Martha Argerich in the Prokofieff Concerto No. 3. It was his seventy-sixth birthday that Rostropovich celebrated on March 27 and 28, with Shostakovich, Britten, and more Prokofieff. Yevgeny Kissin was the powerful soloist in the latter's Piano Concerto No. 2, Maxim Vengerov the persuasive one in Britten's Violin Concerto.

The Berlioz anniversary observance continued with the concerts beginning April 9, when Sir Colin Davis led a semistaged concert performance of the composer's last opera, *Beatrice and Benedict*, which is adapted from Shakespeare's *Much Ado about Nothing*. One of Berlioz's most delightful works, it is a comic opera with much spoken dialogue, double cast for these performances. The singers—Suzanne Mentzer, Susan Gritton, Nancy Maultsby, Gordon Gietz, and Keith Phares—performed in French (with English supertitles), and their thespian counterparts—Harriet Harris, Linda Powell, David Hyde Pierce, and Joel de la Fuente—spoke in English. The sole non-singing speaking role was taken by the inimitable Philip Bosco. Tommasini praised Davis's conducting, the orchestra, the Westminster Symphonic Choir, the singers, and the actors, and had especially good words for "the innovative work" of the stage director, Edward Berkeley, in his handling of the two casts.

André Previn returned on April 24 to conduct the New York premiere of his Violin Concerto, written for his wife, Anne-Sophie Mutter, who was the soloist. Holland wrote most favorably of Previn's fondness for Ravel and Strauss, and of how these influences showed up in the work, as well as of what a splendid violinist Mutter is. Kurt Masur conducted the rest of the program, opening with a delicate performance of Brahms's *Variations on a Theme of Haydn* and closing with a brilliant and touching account of Dvořák's Eighth Symphony, a score for which he has always shown a special affinity.

Previn had the program to himself on May 15, when he led a rare performance of the Symphony No. 2 ("Le Double") by Henri Dutilleux, a piece dating from 1959. Born in 1916 and still alive at the time of writing, Dutilleux, with a relatively small body of works considering his longevity, is one of the most sensitive and fastidious of contemporary composers, each composition a unique gem. Previn was in total command of the piece, which Kozinn thought remained fresh after more than forty years and would most likely continue so even if it became as well-known as it deserved to be.

One of the young American conductors who Tommasini hoped would be considered for the music directorship of the Philharmonic, Robert Spano, finally appeared for the first time with the orchestra on May 22. Spano was already known in New York, having been the adventuresome music director of the Brooklyn Philharmonic since 1996. Recently he had become music director of the Atlanta Symphony. For his Philharmonic debut he selected a work by the contemporary Finnish composer Kaija Saariaho, *Château de l'âme*, for soprano, women's chorus, and orchestra, which received its New York premiere. Taking its texts from ancient Hindu and Egyptian writings, the work is mystical in nature but also striking in its orchestral and choral effects. The Canadian soprano Valdine Anderson was the soloist in her Philharmonic debut, with women of the New York Choral Artists.

Tommasini did not review this concert, but Kozinn praised Spano's leadership of the new piece, as well as of the surrounding works, the rarely heard Sibelius tone poem *The Oceanides* and Rachmaninoff's last composition and arguably his greatest orchestral work, the *Symphonic Dances*, still not played as often as it should be. (Mitropoulos was a great champion of the score.)

On May 28 came the news of the death of the composer Luciano Berio at the age of seventy-seven. In the forefront of the European avant-garde, he first came to international prominence in 1968 with his *Sinfonia*, a pioneering work that set the stage for the practice of extensively quoting other composers' works in one's own composition. The *Sinfonia* was given its American premiere and was recorded by the Philharmonic with the composer conducting. In 1973 Pierre Boulez conducted the American premiere of Berio's Concerto for Two Pianos.

The next day, May 28, Lorin Maazel conducted the first Philharmonic perfor-mance of Krzysztof Penderecki's Symphony No. 4, a work composed in 1989 and commissioned in honor of the bicentennial of the Declaration of the Rights of Man. Maazel had led its world premiere in Paris with the Orchestre National de France and gave it "a finely polished, vigorous reading," according to Kozinn. Like most of Penderecki's recent work, it is a far cry from the avant-garde writing with which the composer made his name in the 1950s and 1960s. Dissonance is largely absent from his later pieces. The program concluded with the Fifth Symphony of Shostakovich. Between Maazel's manipulation of the score and his antics on the podium, Kozinn felt the performance was more about him than about Shostakovich.

RETURN TO CARNEGIE?

The big news of the year, and a surprise to almost everyone, was the announcement on June 2, 2003, that the New York Philharmonic would be moving to Carnegie Hall, perhaps as early as 2006. It would not be simply a case of the orchestra's moving there, but was actually a merger of the two institutions. Said Sanford I. Weill, chairman of Carnegie Hall, "There's no reason why it shouldn't be a done deal. I've worked on a lot of mergers, and I've never seen a fit as perfect as this." According to Zarin Mehta, "We've got two major institutions—one is the greatest hall in the world, the other is the greatest orchestra in the world. This merger is to strengthen our respective positions."

The one party that reacted to this development with displeasure was, of course, Lincoln Center, which was blindsided by it, having had virtually no advance notice, and which was now to lose its very first and most constant tenant. The center's chairman, Bruce Crawford, and its president, Reynold Levy, said they were taken aback by the news, and Martin E. Segal, the chairman emeritus, referred to the merger as "a form of cultural cannibalism," while the Philharmonic's chairman, Paul B. Guenther, claimed that "it was not a question of luring the Philharmonic to Carnegie Hall, but of the Philharmonic doing what is best for its long-term interests." The announcement was a particularly hard blow for Lincoln Center, coming as it did on the heels of the New York City Opera's decision to leave the New York State Theater as soon as a downtown location could be established, most likely one near the site of the destroyed World Trade Center.

An advantage to the Philharmonic in moving to Carnegie was that it would not be involved in paying the cost for the proposed reconstruction of Avery Fisher

Hall, estimated at the time at approximately $260 million. And, of course, it would have the advantage of the wonderful acoustics of Carnegie rather than . . . well, the acoustics of Avery Fisher have been discussed enough. However, from Carnegie's standpoint, the departure of the Philharmonic in 1962 had allowed the hall to develop and present its own various concert series, involving many visiting orchestras, both domestic and international, as well as chamber music and solo performers, workshops and master classes. With the Philharmonic in residence, what would become of them all?

In days gone by when the Philharmonic held sway in Carnegie Hall, the Philadelphia Orchestra and the Boston Symphony each played ten concerts a season there, the Cleveland Orchestra had its series, and the Berlin and Vienna Philharmonics and many other orchestras appeared, as did a multitude of recitalists. Of course, the variety of Carnegie's presentations did increase significantly after Lincoln Center opened, but it was thought that Carnegie would be able to accommodate the Philharmonic along with other attractions. An adjunct to the main hall had always been the former Carnegie Recital Hall, now known as Weill Recital Hall, and in the fall of 2003 the subterranean Judy and Arthur Zankel Hall was scheduled to open. Carnegie's executive director, Robert J. Harth, stated that, with the three halls, "a tremendous variety of music" would soon be available. When it was suggested that, in acquiring the Philharmonic, Carnegie was taking a step backward, Harth responded, "What we have here is an opportunity to develop a highly inventive new kind of musical organization that's going to reflect forward thinking and not a return to the past."

Lincoln Center, too, had developed its own series apart from the Philharmonic, and the opportunity now arose for an even greater variety of presentations. In the words of Bruce Crawford, "Times have changed, a half century has passed and we have to do business somewhat differently. But we still can be and should be the world's greatest performing arts center."

Not to be overlooked were the feelings of the Philharmonic's musicians. The *Times* of June 7 printed a letter from Fiona Simon, chair of the orchestra committee, which she wrote on behalf of all the musicians. She stated that her colleagues were "ecstatic about going 'home' to the greatest hall in the world." On the same page, however, a letter from an audience member, one David Breger, contrasted the comfort and spacious surroundings of Avery Fisher Hall with the "sardine-can lobby" of Carnegie, the "aerobically challenged staircase," and the closeness of the seats, which caused his knees to "develop indentations from the back of the chair in front."

Meanwhile, the Philharmonic had to finish its season. On June 5 Maazel presented an almost-all-twentieth-century program. The exception was Debussy's

Prelude to the Afternoon of a Faun—an almost-twentieth-century piece, composed in 1894. The program was to have opened with the world premiere of the Symphony No. 4 by the English composer Oliver Knussen, but the work was not ready in time. Instead Maazel substituted an American classic, the Third Symphony of Roy Harris, giving it, in Tommasini's words, a "gripping performance." Gershwin's Concerto in F was played by the Viennese pianist Rudolf Buchbinder, he and Maazel treating the score seriously, as the composer intended (the work may be jazzy, but it is not jazz). To conclude, there was Edgard Varèse's immensely scored *Amériques*, which Maazel made sound "more radical than ever." In fact, said Tommasini, the entire concert contained the most impressive work he had heard from Maazel all season.

For the season's final subscription program, beginning June 19, Maazel led Mahler's "Resurrection" Symphony. Usually this eighty-to-ninety-minute work is thought sufficient for an entire program. In earlier times, though, when programs were longer, it was often preceded by another work, and Maazel reverted to those times by opening the program with a piece by the American composer Aaron Jay Kernis, a song cycle for soprano and orchestra entitled *Simple Songs*. The work was a homage to Leonard Bernstein, but Tommasini found the music, though beautiful, "wanly derivative." Jessica Jones was the soprano soloist, as she also was in the Mahler symphony, where Cornelia Kallisch was the mezzo-soprano and the New York Choral Artists held forth as well. Tommasini wrote of Maazel's "commandingly conducted account" of that formidable score, even though the performance was, at times, "cool and calculated." Still, it was an impressive conclusion to the season, producing a great ovation from the audience.

On June 17 the *Times* reported that the executives of Lincoln Center had told their board of directors that the Philharmonic's announced move to Carnegie Hall was a breach of contract. The possibility of legal action arose, for the Philharmonic's lease ran through 2011, and the orchestra planned to move in 2006. Reynold Levy insisted that "Lincoln Center intends to be firm and clear about its rights." The Philharmonic's chairman, Paul B. Guenther, maintained that he did not know of any breach of the lease, which was called a constituency agreement, yet Levy continued to argue otherwise.

Tommasini on June 26 wrote of perceived "early signs of strain" between the Philharmonic and Carnegie Hall. He said that Zarin Mehta and Robert J. Harth had expressed different views on how details would be worked out concerning the Philharmonic's schedule of about 130 concerts a season with rehearsals and how those events would impact Carnegie's weekly schedule. Said Harth, "The opportunity here is to create a merged institution that is forward-thinking. We are looking at new ways of presentation and new types of scheduling." The problem with that, Tommasini felt, was that the Philharmonic had not been a forward-thinking organization since the departure of Pierre Boulez in 1977. Zarin Mehta said there was no thought of changing the Philharmonic's subscription format: "I don't want to change just for the sake of change if something is already working."

By July 17 it became known that the Philharmonic was having second thoughts about the Carnegie merger, for Guenther had asked the trustees to consider the possibility of the Philharmonic's becoming a tenant at Carnegie Hall rather than an equal partner, as it would be if there were a merger. Since moving to Lincoln Center in 1962, the orchestra had been a tenant there. This was at variance with the plan as originally announced, that the merger was a fait accompli. Guenther then stated that he was asking the board not to approve a merger, but merely "to approve the beginning of discussions toward a merger."

From the beginning, some on the Philharmonic's board had been against the idea of a merger. For one thing, they felt the Philharmonic would lose its identity. Should the merger take place, there were questions concerning a combined board of directors—who would serve on it and how many, who would be in charge as executive director and music director. There were also concerns about expenses, for expanded backstage space would be needed to accommodate the Philharmonic (though in pre–Lincoln Center days that space appeared to be adequate). In addition, any merger plans had to be submitted to the New York state attorney general, Elliott Spitzer, who would in turn submit them to a state supreme court justice for final approval. This step in the process had yet to be taken. In a meeting on July 17 the board approved the idea of the merger, though not the merger itself, with 85 percent voting in favor. Yet there was still resentment on the part of some board members, who felt they had not been consulted properly in the original decision to merge.

On July 27 came news of the death of Harold C. Schonberg at the age of eighty-seven. For twenty years, from 1960 to 1980, he had been the senior music critic of the *New York Times*, and he had been a member of the paper's staff both before and after his tenure in that post. Although initially a thorn in Leonard Bernstein's side, he gradually came to appreciate his work once Bernstein had retired from the Philharmonic. Unlike some of his colleagues, he had also written approvingly of Zubin Mehta at the beginning of the latter's music directorship. A great pianophile, he was an admirer of the generation of pianists that included Rachmaninoff and Josef Hofmann and campaigned vigorously for the study of performance practice in the romantic era.

Another death was reported on August 8: that of the flutist Julius Baker, also at the age of eighty-seven. Baker had been principal flute of the Philharmonic from

1965 to 1983 and was also widely recognized as one of the finest teachers of that instrument. His recording of Carl Nielsen's Flute Concerto with Bernstein and the Philharmonic is highly regarded.

Negotiations between the Philharmonic and Carnegie Hall continued. Carnegie said that it would not agree to a merger until the Philharmonic had settled its financial obligations to Lincoln Center, which reiterated through Reynold Levy that the Philharmonic had breached the constituency agreement. A Lincoln Center official insisted that, if the Philharmonic left, it had to contribute to the expense of creating a new orchestra for the center—which would come to over $100 million. That assertion was denied by the Philharmonic's executives. The resignation of one of the Philharmonic's most philanthropic directors, Rita Hauser, from the committee working on the merger had a great impact on the orchestra. She was opposed to the merger, fearing the orchestra would lose its independence as a result.

The Philharmonic began its 2003–4 season on September 17 with the annual opening-night gala concert. Verdi overtures and arias occupied the program's first half, with the great bass Samuel Ramey as the soloist; Tchaikovsky's Fifth Symphony made up the second half. Besides finding the symphony "hard-driven and contorted," Tommasini was also critical of Maazel's "beefed-up, slowed-down, exacting and deliberate performance" of the season-opening "Star Spangled Banner" and concluded by wondering how any number of younger conductors would lead it.

Maazel redeemed himself the very next night, however, by opening the subscription season with the world premiere performance of the American composer Stephen Hartke's Symphony No. 3. Like the Adams work the year before, which went on to win the Pulitzer Prize for music, Hartke's piece was commissioned by the Philharmonic to commemorate the anniversary of September 11. Tommasini described Hartke as "one of the most accomplished and interesting composers working today" and the Philharmonic's account of the new work as "luminous and involving." Hartke used as his text words from a poem, *The Ruin*, by an anonymous eighth- or ninth-century Anglo-Saxon poet, which he set for four voices, countertenor, two tenors, and baritone, sung by members of the Hilliard Ensemble, an all-male vocal group. "A challenging new work," wrote Tommasini, an admirer of the composer. Mahler's Fifth Symphony, heard after intermission, was "brilliant and incisive," but also "at times hard-hearted" in Maazel's performance.

The Berlioz bicentennial observances were still going on, and on October 2 Maazel offered a rare opportunity to hear the composer's complete dramatic symphony *Roméo et Juliette*, of which the orchestral excerpts are the most well-known portions. The work is not a retelling of the famous story, but rather the composer's thoughts and musings on it. The mezzo-soprano Suzanne Mentzer, the tenor Matthew Polenzani, and the bass-baritone José van Dam were the soloists, each in a single aria, and the chorus was the New York Choral Artists. Kozinn praised the soloists and the chorus and felt there were noticeable orchestral thrills and beautiful string playing, but "not much depth or dimension beyond these pleasing surfaces."

On October 7 the seemingly inevitable happened. The Philharmonic and Carnegie Hall announced that their plans to merge were off. The Philharmonic would remain at Lincoln Center, and Carnegie Hall would continue on its way without what would have been its most prestigious partner. Failure to agree on which organization would be the dominant one was cited as the principal reason for the collapse of the negotiations. Guenther was quoted in a *Times* article as saying, "In the end we realized that, due to a variety of reasons, trying to get the two organizations together became insurmountable. We decided to call it a day. To try to force them together wouldn't have made any sense."

Weill said that he usually did not become involved in public negotiations: "When something is disclosed prematurely, it's usually a bad sign." As for Lincoln Center, Levy remarked, "If you were to capture our feelings about this, they could be succinctly stated, 'Welcome home. All is forgiven. We have a lot to discuss.'" To this, Crawford added, "What we need to have is a partnership based on trust." Hauser said she thought the independence and the integrity of the Philharmonic should not be jeopardized and hoped for "a healthy, fruitful relationship with Lincoln Center."

Regardless of the pros and cons of the proposed merger, the prospect of again hearing the Philharmonic regularly in Carnegie Hall was extremely enticing and exciting, especially for anyone who grew up hearing them there. But the important and independent niche that Carnegie has carved out for itself since Lincoln Center opened must be recognized, and so we have to content ourselves with Avery Fisher Hall. As Tommasini wrote on October 8, "On a good night during an exciting program few audience members sit through a Philharmonic concert thinking about acoustics."

Another article by Pogrebin on October 14 told of the bitterness still harbored by some Lincoln Center officials over the planned merger, particularly in the way it was presented to them. There was talk of resisting further negotiations with Guenther, even of urging his resignation. In fact, Pogrebin reported, the Philharmonic's board itself might request it. Guenther responded that he had no plans to resign—he was "still very happy as chairman of the Philharmonic." Voicing his support of Guenther, Zarin Mehta said, "He's totally devoted to us. He's done a great job raising money for us. He's terrific."

The death of the pianist Eugene Istomin, at the age of seventy-seven, was reported on October 11. He had first appeared with the Philharmonic in 1943 after winning the prestigious Leventritt Competition at the age of eighteen. He played again with the orchestra the following season and frequently in the ensuing years. Always a serious artist, he was especially noted for his playing of Beethoven, Brahms, Schubert, and Schumann. Atypically for an artist who concentrated on the Germanic repertoire, he also performed concertos by Rachmaninoff and Tchaikovsky.

The pianist Alicia de Larrocha, then eighty years old, had been a frequent and favorite soloist with the Philharmonic since her debut with the orchestra in the 1965–66 season and had been generally a New York favorite thanks to her many appearances in the Mostly Mozart Festival and her solo recitals. With the concerts beginning October 15 she bade her farewell to the Philharmonic with performances of Manuel de Falla's *Nights in the Gardens of Spain* and Haydn's Concerto in D Major, in both of which she displayed "her accustomed grace," according to Oestreich. On the podium in his Philharmonic debut was the impressive Finnish maestro Osmo Vänskä, who was in his first season as music director of the Minnesota Orchestra. Oestreich felt his rendition of Nielsen's Fifth Symphony "was gripping from beginning to end."

When plans for a European tour in the fall foundered, the Philharmonic found itself with a three-week gap in its schedule. To the consternation of the local critics, this gap was filled by a Beethoven festival featuring all the symphonies and piano concertos. As Kozinn mentioned, in reviewing the October 21 first concert, "There is nothing wrong with Beethoven of course." But the Philharmonic normally played much Beethoven anyway, and had played a cycle of his music under Kurt Masur only a few years before. Plus, Maazel's Beethoven performances the previous season did not make the listener look forward to more.

But review the program Kozinn did, the First and Second Symphonies and the Piano Concerto No. 2 with Rudolf Buchbinder as soloist. Noting that Maazel was adhering to musicological emphasis on the validity of Beethoven's controversial metronome markings, once thought to be too fast, Kozinn wrote of the conductor's speeding through the symphonies at breakneck tempos, with only occasional moments of relaxation. The trouble was that those tempos were effective with the smaller ensembles of Beethoven's day, and the full Philharmonic, no matter how superbly they were playing at the time, was just too large to make them work. Buchbinder's rendition of the concerto had "much to admire." Yet, perhaps as a protest against another Beethoven cycle, Kozinn's was the only review of a Beethoven festival concert to appear in the *New York Times*, although the series was almost completely sold out. (Rockwell, on November 7, did write negatively about a specific pianist in the series, Gianluca Cascioli, but not about the concert per se.)

On November 4 the *Times* reported that Rita Hauser had resigned from the board after twenty-five years, stating that it was time to move on, that "the board must engage in a serious rethinking of the orchestra's future directions," and that "bold and imaginative leadership is required if the New York Philharmonic is to fulfill its mission in the years ahead." Later, on December 9, the paper announced that she had joined the board of Lincoln Center.

More Berlioz appeared on November 13, when Sir Colin Davis led a program of the composer's shorter and less well-known works, three of which, *Sara la baigneuse*, *Tristia*, and *Herminie*, were performed that night for the first time by the Philharmonic. The third section of *Tristia*, the "Funeral March for the Last Scene of *Hamlet*," is one of Berlioz's most striking short pieces. Midgette considered it a high point of the program, with Davis and the orchestra giving it "a stirring performance." The cantata *Herminie* was one of several failed attempts by Berlioz to win the Prix de Rome. This seems to be one of those tests that prove the rule, for the Prix de Rome jury of the day was noted for its extreme conservatism. The mezzo-soprano Monica Groop made her Philharmonic debut as the soloist in this work, and the Westminster Symphonic Choir participated elsewhere on the program.

For five years Sir Colin Davis had held the title of the Philharmonic's principal guest conductor. But, beginning with the 2003–4 season, that title was no longer listed on the orchestra's masthead. No explanation was given for the change, and Davis continued to appear regularly with the orchestra.

For the 2003–4 season Maazel appointed Roberto Minczuk to the position of associate conductor, making the Brazilian the first person to hold that title since Franco Autori in the 1950s. Although he had led the orchestra in some Parks Concerts, he made his subscription concert debut on November 22, 2003, in a program consisting of Wagner's Prelude to *Parsifal*, Ligeti's *Lontano*, Mozart's Horn Concerto No. 4 in E-flat Major, K. 494 (with Philip Myers as soloist), and the Third Symphony of Brahms. Co–artistic director of Brazil's São Paulo State Symphony, Minczuk was well received by the *Times*'s new staff member Jeremy Eichler, who dubbed his Brahms "satisfying if unspectacular" (and the Third is the most unspectacular of the Brahms symphonies, and possibly the most satisfying).

One of Tommasini's favorite younger conductors, David Robertson, returned for the concerts beginning November 26. He managed to make clear the structure of Richard Strauss's tone poem *Thus Spake Zarathustra*, a feat that eludes many conductors, in "a lucid and impassioned performance." The brilliant French pianist Pierre-Laurent Aimard was heard in two seldom-performed works, Debussy's *Fantaisie* for Piano and Orchestra and Prokofieff's Concerto No. 1.

On December 10 Robin Pogrebin reported in the *Times* that several of the Philharmonic's musicians had been invited to speak at a board meeting. They told of how much they enjoyed working with Lorin Maazel and urged the board to extend his contract beyond 2006, when it was due to expire. It was no secret that the board was already planning to begin a search for Maazel's successor, but the musicians felt there were no clear candidates for the position. One of them was quoted as saying, "If we have no one to replace Maazel, we just can't let him go. I just don't think we're in a rush to replace someone as brilliant as Mr. Maazel."

MTV AT THE PHILHARMONIC?

Kurt Masur returned to the Philharmonic as its music director emeritus for a three-week engagement beginning January 8, 2004. A month earlier several orchestra musicians had expressed relief that they no longer had to be subjected to his authoritarian, even abusive rehearsal manner. But it must be remembered that the orchestra stood behind him when the board and management attempted to terminate his contract in 2000, leading them to extend it for two more years. If there was any tension between orchestra and conductor upon his return, it was not evident at the first program, which included Haydn's Symphony No. 88, Szymanowski's Violin Concerto No. 1 (with the concertmaster, Glenn Dicterow, as the soloist), and Max Reger's *Variations and Fugue on a Theme of Mozart*. It was not a surefire "box-office" program, to be sure, which may have accounted for quite a few empty seats in the hall, but Masur became a popular figure with audiences as his tenure progressed, so one would have thought more people would have greeted him on his return.

In earlier times Haydn's Symphony No. 88 in G Major was one of a handful of the master's 104 symphonies that were played frequently, to the detriment of about 98 others. As conductors began belatedly to "discover" many of the others, it appeared less and less often, to the point that by the time Masur programmed it, it was something of a rarity, at least on Philharmonic programs. The other items on the program were, in fact, rarities, both from the early twentieth century. The concerto by Szymanowski appears to have been solely the property of Philharmonic concertmasters, for John Corigliano had played it in 1946 (the orchestra's first performance of the work) and again in 1951. Rodney Friend offered it in 1977, and now Glenn Dicterow, in a beautifully sensitive performance of an exotically tinged piece that does not sell itself.

The Reger *Variations*, the theme of which comes from Mozart's Piano Sonata in A Major, K. 331, was a specialty of Masur, who recorded it with the Philharmonic early in his tenure. Although it is rarely given in the United States, Masur's great love for the work permeated every measure of his performance, which he led from memory.

New York's musical world was shocked to learn on February 1 of the death at age forty-seven, apparently of a heart attack, of Robert J. Harth, executive director of Carnegie Hall. He had been in the job only since September 2001 but had already made his mark as a strong and visionary leader. His mild-mannered disposition contrasted strongly with that of his immediate predecessor, Franz Xaver Ohnesorg, whose brief but autocratic tenure had driven out a number of senior staff members. It was Harth who picked up the pieces, assuaged hurt feelings, and then oversaw the opening of Carnegie's third stage, Zankel Hall. Unwilling to compromise or jeopardize Carnegie Hall's independence as a presenter of concerts and related events, he also held firm in the negotiations with the Philharmonic concerning the orchestra's moving there. Said Reynold Levy "He was a true impresario. He did more in a shorter time to diversify what audiences experience at Carnegie Hall than anyone I can remember."

On February 2 it was learned that Lincoln Center had relaxed its stance toward the Philharmonic and would no longer claim the orchestra had breached its constituency agreement with the center. Thus, it would drop its legal action against the Philharmonic. Lincoln Center had also included, in a new agreement, a statement that the Philharmonic's share of any deficit incurred by Avery Fisher Hall would be increased; that stipulation was now rescinded, and the Philharmonic would continue to pay one-third of the deficit and Lincoln Center the rest. Because there had been some resistance to negotiating with Paul Guenther, who was still the Philharmonic's chairman, Lincoln Center's Bruce Crawford considered it important to reestablish a good working relationship.

In recent years symphony orchestras have been experimenting with new ways to lure listeners, especially younger ones, into the concert hall, where they normally fear to tread. The Philharmonic's Rush Hour Concerts and Casual Saturdays have been successful examples of this trend that have been adopted by other orchestras. Now electronic technology has entered the picture. As reported by Robin Pogrebin in the *Times* of February 23, when audience members arrived for a Philharmonic open rehearsal, they were greeted by a huge fifteen-by-twenty-foot screen hanging over the orchestra on which could be seen close-ups of the musicians and of Lorin Maazel. It was the musical equivalent of attending a TV show or watching a huge MTV video.

But it was only an experiment to see if this kind of technology could enhance the concertgoing experience, especially since potential younger listeners are more attuned to visuals than their more sedate elders. The idea originated with a Philharmonic trustee, Benjamin M. Rosen, who also financed it—at a cost of "tens of thousands of dollars." The musicians did not take kindly to the idea. Observed the violinist Newton Mansfield: "We're not movie stars. You don't need to blow people up to that degree. I wouldn't be able to come in if I had a wart on my nose." Said Glenn Dicterow, "I found it very distracting. It was extremely difficult for me to keep my place in the music." The problem for the musicians seated at the rear of the stage was especially vexing. According to the public relations director, Eric Latzky, "The half of the orchestra behind the screen was looking up at a giant projection of Lorin, and half of the orchestra was seeing him conduct backwards." Obviously, more work needed to be done if this arrangement were to become viable. As Dicterow put it, "If you want to see better, take binoculars."

Over the years, many pianists have become proficient in the art of conducting while maintaining their skills at the keyboard. One thinks immediately of Daniel Barenboim, Vladimir Ashkenazy, and Christoph Eschenbach (Ashkenazy has recently retired from piano playing). Occasionally violinists play and conduct baroque and classical concertos, but Itzhak Perlman appears to be the first in modern times to branch out and conduct purely orchestral compositions. (In more "ancient" times, Eugène Ysaÿe conducted the Cincinnati Symphony from 1918 to 1922.) On March 18 Perlman made his Philharmonic conducting debut in a program consisting of Bach's Violin Concerto No. 1 in A Minor (in which he played the solo part), Mozart's Symphony No. 29 in A Major, and Dvořák's Symphony No. 8 in G Major. Although Kozinn wrote of Perlman's "inherent musicality" and his ability to achieve what he wanted from the orchestra, with gestures that "often had a sweep and clarity of purpose," he found the Mozart and Dvořák performances bland, with little to complain about, but with not much memorable either. (The author has heard Perlman conduct the Berlioz *Roman Carnival Overture*—not with the Philharmonic—in a performance that was full of character.)

From the first, New York critics had expressed serious reservations concerning Maazel—his micromanaging of details, his frequent distortion of the musical lines in romantic repertoire. An alternative view appeared in the April 9 *Times* in an article by Rockwell. He had decided to attend as many Maazel concerts as he could, without any preconceptions based on what others had written. In the end, he heard six programs, and he began his retrospective with the declaration that the Philharmonic was playing better than he had ever heard it. His first concert had been in September: Richard Strauss's *Don Quixote*, featuring the principals Carter Brey and Cynthia Phelps, and Stravinsky's *Rite of Spring*. The beautifully played Strauss was exhilarating, Maazel seemingly "a born Straussian." The Stravinsky, however, was "pulled and twisted out of shape," nothing like the composer's own straightforward recorded account of the work. (It is a mystery why, if a composer has left a recording of a given work, conductors do not attempt to approximate it to some degree, at least in the matter of tempo.)

Later concerts Rockwell attended included Penderecki's Violin Concerto No. 2 ("Metamorphosen") played by Julian Rachlin ("done well"); John Corigliano's *Pied Piper Fantasy* with the flutist James Galway ("nicely done"); Holst's *Planets* ("the orchestra making all the right, lush noises"); and three Wagner selections followed by that composer's Prelude to *Die Meistersinger* ("impassioned") and Prelude to Act III of *Lohengrin* ("glittering"—the Philharmonic was now often playing encores!). Rockwell had high praise for Maazel's account of Bruckner's Symphony No. 7 ("about as good as Bruckner conducting gets"). Schubert's Ninth was almost as good, with only the second movement falling victim to Maazel's sectional approach. Rockwell concluded by characterizing Maazel as "a thought-provoking, intellectual and sometimes even emotionally compelling conductor."

The concerts beginning April 22 brought Sir Colin Davis in a pairing of two of his special composers, Berlioz and Sibelius. Midgette characterized the composers as mavericks, Davis as "a kind of Eagle Scout of the classical music world." The Berlioz portion of the program consisted of the rarely heard overture *Les francs-juges* (The Judges of the Secret Court) and three vocal numbers sung by the Swedish mezzo-soprano Anne Sofie von Otter: arias from *The Damnation of Faust* and *Les Troyens* and the "Villanelle" from the song cycle *Les nuits d'été*. Mostly rarities by Sibelius were heard after intermission: the suite for strings and timpani called *Rakastava* (The Lover), four songs in which von Otter "truly shone," and, less rare and an undisputed masterpiece, the single-movement Seventh Symphony, which set the example for many similarly formatted symphonies by later composers, and of which Davis and the orchestra gave a poetic account.

The exciting and mercurial pianist Martha Argerich was scheduled to give four performances of Schumann's Piano Concerto beginning April 28 but canceled the engagement because of illness. On fairly short notice, the Canadian pianist Louis Lortie agreed to step in. There was nothing unusual about his doing so, especially because he had substituted for Argerich in the same concerto in San Francisco a short time before. What *was* unusual is that Lortie already had a scheduled recital at the Metropolitan Museum of Art on the second night of the Philharmonic sequence. But the Thursday Philharmonic concert began at 7:30. To accommodate Lortie's predicament, the Philharmonic changed the order of the program so that the Schumann Concerto could be played first, and the Metropolitan Museum delayed the start of the recital. Upon finishing the concerto, Lortie was whisked to the museum in a rented car, arriving only twenty minutes late. Later, the Met's concert manager Hilde Limondjian, marveled, "In my lifetime, I haven't known a pianist who's played a concerto and a recital in different halls on the same night, let alone on both sides of Central Park."

The Overture to Bernstein's *Candide* has been a well-loved staple of orchestral concerts ever since the composer first led it with the Philharmonic in 1957, and since Bernstein's death the Philharmonic has made a specialty of playing it without a conductor. But the orchestra had never before performed the entire score of *Candide* until May 7, 2004, when it gave the first of three semistaged performances conducted by Marin Alsop.

Candide has always been a problematic work. The score was revised several times by Bernstein as well as others since its premiere in 1956. Lonny Price was the director for this hybrid version, which received much praise from Tommasini, except for the insertion of lame, even dumb, topical jokes that often distracted attention from the superb musical performance. Kristen Chenoweth triumphed in the coloratura role of Cunegonde, Paul Groves was endearing in the title role, Patti LuPone was comically impressive as the Old Lady, and Sir Thomas Allen was "an inspired choice" as Dr. Pangloss, the Narrator, and Voltaire himself. The Westminster Symphonic Choir sang resplendently in the final chorus, "Make Our Garden Grow." Alsop's conducting brought out the charm of the score by respecting the music, which the Philharmonic played beautifully.

A festival commemorating the fiftieth anniversary of the death of Charles Ives was played by the Philharmonic from May 11 to May 29. Entitled An American Original in Context, it was not devoted to Ives's music, but presented representative works of his together with works of other composers, not only of Ives's time, but before and after. Thus were heard works by Ives's friends Henry Cowell and Carl Ruggles, as well as by Aaron Copland, John Cage, and John Adams, on whom Ives exerted some influence. But Ives was also programmed alongside works by Debussy, Ravel, and Varèse, composers he "cordially despised," according to the musicologist Richard Taruskin in a May 16 *Times* article. Taruskin said that Ives's "special favorite composer" was César Franck, of all people, perhaps because of their similar backgrounds as organists.

Nevertheless, Debussy and Varèse were Ives's programmatic companions on the first festival concert of May 11, conducted by David Robertson. The Ives works were the *Variations on America* (an organ piece orchestrated by William Schuman) and two movements from *Symphony: New England Holidays*, "Washington's Birthday" and "Decoration Day." The first two of Debussy's *Nocturnes* and Varèse's wild *Arcana* provided the context, as did Copland's jazzy Piano Concerto, with Garrick

Ohlsson as the brilliant soloist. Tommasini described the various works and praised the performances, writing that the concert "was a good start to what looks to be a worthwhile festival."

Alan Gilbert was in charge of the May 15 program, on which the Ives works were the song "General William Booth Enters into Heaven," sung by the baritone Nathan Gunn, and the formidable Fourth Symphony, in which the Dessoff Symphonic Choir participated. So complex are some sections of the symphony that often a second conductor is employed to help keep everything together. In this case Roberto Minczuk had that unenviable task (Stokowski, for the work's posthumous premiere in 1965, used two assistants). As for the brief choral parts, which are confined to the first and last of the four movements, Ives, in a preface to the score, noted that they were optional and even indicated a preference for their omission. On the same program Nathan Gunn sang songs from Mahler's *Des Knaben Wunderhorn* (The Youth's Magic Horn) and two of Copland's *Old American Songs*. Alban Berg's *Three Pieces for Orchestra* completed the program.

On May 22 John Adams conducted a program that could have been entitled "Scarcely Ives," for that composer's music made up barely fifteen minutes of the concert: three short orchestral pieces and three songs, the latter performed by the superb vocalist Audra McDonald, who was also heard in an excerpt from Adams's opera *Doctor Atomic*, a recent work that had not yet been performed. One of the composer's best-known works, *Harmonium*, with the Choral Arts Society of Washington, concluded the evening on an exuberant note.

An article by Robin Pogrebin in the *Times* of May 20 reported that the New York Philharmonic had decided to rebuild the interior of Avery Fisher Hall. The plan was to make it a more intimate space with, of course, improved acoustics. Also to be redesigned were the lobby and other public areas. The problem was: where would the orchestra perform for the approximately two years the construction would take? As of this writing, the hall and the orchestra are still there. As for a temporary home for the orchestra, no announcement has been made. Although one keeps hearing and reading about the Seventh Regiment Armory on the East Side as a possibility, this venue has been mentioned so many times over so many, many years in one context or another for the Philharmonic that one cannot help but think, "Not that again," every time it is mentioned.

The following day Midgette reported that many musicians feel the acoustics of Avery Fisher Hall are not so bad. The only Philharmonic musician quoted was the concertmaster, Glenn Dicterow, who felt he got "good feedback" when playing there. In some halls the sound is wonderful out front, but he does not feel it coming back to him. Like a violin, the hall had improved with age. Two members of the London Symphony, which had recently performed in Avery Fisher, were quoted, one saying that playing there was "a breath of fresh air" compared to London's Barbican Hall, where they normally play. The other said he had always enjoyed playing in Avery Fisher, because from where he sits he can hear the rest of the orchestra (something Philharmonic players have repeatedly said they cannot). In Pogrebin's article Zarin Mehta had said that the problem with Avery Fisher Hall's acoustics was that they were always being compared to those of Carnegie Hall.

Another idea to make the concerts more user-friendly was tried out on May 27, when seventy-five audience members tested a hand-held device called the Concert Companion. Somewhat resembling a Palm Pilot, the CoCo, as its creators dubbed it, had a small screen on which a running commentary on the music would appear as it was being performed. At times Lorin Maazel's face was the point of interest. The program was fairly challenging for those who might have been unfamiliar with the pieces: Ives's *Three Places in New England*, Ravel's Piano Concerto for the Left Hand (with Leon Fleisher as the soloist), and Stravinsky's *Petrushka*. The Ravel concerto was not subject to this scrutiny because Fleisher did not like the idea and would not allow his performance to be videotaped. Reaction from the audience members tested was mixed. One found it stressful to switch his attention back and forth from the screen to the Philharmonic before him; he felt as though he were multitasking, though he did find the commentary on *Petrushka* helpful. Another found the experience phenomenal. Yet another, who did not have a CoCo, was distracted by the glowing light next to her and was glad when it was turned off: Her comment: "What a terrible idea."

On June 3 Lorin Maazel led an all-Russian program consisting of one certifiable warhorse and two less frequently encountered works. Tchaikovsky's "Pathétique" Symphony opened the program in what Kozinn described as a "fiery but oddly chilling rendering." In fact, he suggested that prospective attendees of the last two performances might wish to linger over dinner and arrive after intermission to avoid "being pummeled" by it. In his view, the program's second half provided the real thrills of the evening: a supple, "finely nuanced" account by Yefim Bronfman of Rachmaninoff's underrated Piano Concerto No. 4 and "a passionate, explosive performance" of Scriabin's *Poem of Ecstasy*. As if that were not enough, there was an encore: the final two sections of Mussorgsky's *Pictures at an Exhibition*. As we know, encores were once severely frowned on at the Philharmonic. Now they seem to be a common occurrence, at least when Maazel conducts.

It was announced on June 16 that Maazel's contract as music director would be extended to 2009. In addition, a triumvirate of conductors would share the season with him: Riccardo Muti for four weeks, Alan Gilbert and David Robertson each for two, an arrangement that the *Times*'s Robin Pogrebin described as "a bake-off": one of the three could conceivably be Maazel's successor. The idea that Muti might be considered for the job was not taken seriously, for he had already turned it down. The other two were definite prospects, however, though Zarin Mehta stated that there were no obvious candidates and that others would be considered as well.

Lately it has become customary for the Philharmonic to close its season with a Mahler symphony. For the concerts beginning June 16, Maazel chose the Third Symphony, at around one hundred minutes the longest in the repertory. In six movements, the work is Mahler's paean to nature. The first movement alone, originally titled "Pan Awakes. Summer Marches In," is longer than at least five of the Beethoven symphonies. And yet, a true Mahler lover would not think of eliminating one note of it (even though Dimitri Mitropoulos was forced to cut the work in 1956 so it would fit into a ninety-minute Sunday broadcast). Anna Larsson was the mezzo-soprano soloist in the fourth movement, and the American Boychoir and women of the Westminster Choir were heard in the delightful fifth movement. Although he had reservations about Maazel's treatment of portions of the score, Tommasini had nothing but praise for the "great elegance" with which he shaped the long final movement. The principal trumpet, Philip Smith, and principal trombone, Joseph Alessi, were singled out for their "magnificent playing" of important solo passages.

Maazel began his Philharmonic tenure with the premiere of John Adams's commemoration of the September 11 attacks, *On the Transmigration of Souls*, which in 2003 won the Pulitzer Prize for music. So there was consternation in Philharmonic circles when it was learned that Nonesuch Records planned to release a performance given at the London Proms by the BBC Symphony Orchestra. But the composer was American, and so was the prestigious award the work had garnered. And it was, above all, a New York piece, inextricably linked to and having profound emotional significance for the city in which it had been premiered. The Philharmonic had allocated $40,000 to subsidize a recording, but the orchestra's artistic administrator, Jeremy Geffen, reported that the BBC performance would cost Nonesuch 20 percent less than the Philharmonic's. Later, however, it was learned that the difference was $95,000, not $40,000. When Barbara Haws, the Philharmonic's archivist, informed her husband, the attorney William Josephson, of the situation, he made up the difference with his own money, with the result that Nonesuch released the Philharmonic version after all. Thus, this important New York score, commissioned and played by New York's orchestra, achieved its rightful recording, which, incidentally, went on to win a Grammy.

CHAPTER 21

2004–6

MAAZEL AT SEVENTY-FIVE

Where once were the post-season Promenade Concerts, with lighter musical fare and tables and chairs, Boston Pops style, the Philharmonic now began a new series called Summertime Classics. Under the direction of the British conductor Bramwell Tovey, music director of the Vancouver Symphony, the first program, on June 24, 2004, was entitled "Eviva España" and was devoted to Spanish-flavored music. Some of the best of this kind of music is by French and Russian composers, hence the programmatic appearance of such stalwarts as Émmanuel Chabrier, Ravel, Jules Massenet, and Rimsky-Korsakov. But Spain was not denied a place, with works by Falla and Joaquín Rodrigo; the latter's popular *Concierto de Aranjuez* was performed by the guitarist Sharon Isbin in her Philharmonic debut. Guitarists are rarely encountered on "serious" symphonic concerts, even though there is a fairly substantial repertoire for their instrument. As Midgette mentioned, "It takes a pops concert to bring a serious guitarist to the Philharmonic stage." Bramwell Tovey, often described as an avuncular figure, continues to conduct these concerts and has become noted for his often witty comments to the audience.

In July of 2004 the Philharmonic began what has become an annual residency of a week to ten days in Vail, Colorado. Vail has long been a rival of its state-mate Aspen as a prime skiing locale, and it was now prepared to go head to head with that city as a summer music haven as well. Of course, Aspen has its music school and attendant orchestras, but Vail now had the New York Philharmonic in its Bravo! Vail Valley Music Festival. The orchestra would perform at least six concerts under Maazel and other conductors.

Another festival, this one actually in Spain, was scheduled for the Philharmonic, which was to appear in five concerts at the first Seville International Music Festival in early September, followed by concerts in Italy in Turin and Verona. Sir Colin Davis was to have conducted, but the Philharmonic was forced to cancel. It was the third tour in a year that had to be canceled because of insufficient financial guarantees by the presenters, beginning with the European tour in the fall of 2003 (which was replaced by the Beethoven Festival at home) and followed by a West Coast tour in February.

On July 28 it was reported that the Philharmonic and Lincoln Center were experimenting with a stage in Avery Fisher Hall that would place the orchestra in the center of the hall, with seats surrounding the stage, in another stab at improving the acoustics. This was similar to the arrangement used for the Boulez Rug Concerts, with the orchestra thrust forward into the hall, though in the earlier instance not exactly to the center. That configuration was a good one from the standpoint of acoustics, but it was not used for the regular subscription concerts. Many European concert halls, and some in the United States as well, do have surround seating, but as Henry Fogel, then president and chief executive officer of the American Symphony Orchestra League, pointed out, those halls were specifically designed and built that way, not adapted to it later. It was hoped that any reconstruction work that might be done on Fisher Hall could be accomplished during the summer months, when the Philharmonic was not in residence.

The 2004–5 season opened on September 21 with the traditional gala concert, televised by PBS. Two absolute staples of the repertoire made up the program, Beethoven's Violin Concerto and Dvořák's "New World" Symphony. Maxim Vengerov, the impressive Russian violinist, was the soloist in the concerto, playing his own cadenzas. According to Tommasini, Maazel led an "exciting and brilliantly played" account of the symphony, such interpretive mannerisms as it possessed deemed not excessive. At the start of the concert, following the national anthem, the first cell phone of the season rang out, after which Paul B. Guenther spoke in tribute to the Philharmonic's chairman emeritus, Carlos Moseley, whose ninetieth birthday it was. Moseley, who was present, rose and was greeted by resounding applause.

The program for September 29, with Maazel conducting, included the premiere of a work commissioned by the Philharmonic, *Gathering Paradise* by Augusta Read Thomas. Thomas, for several years composer-in-residence with the Chicago Symphony, where she had had major works performed by Daniel Barenboim and Pierre Boulez, selected seven poems by Emily Dickinson as the texts for her cycle, a continuous piece lasting almost thirty minutes. Tommasini praised the "alluring colors" the work evoked and also its orchestral effects, though he did not care for the manner in which the Dickinson texts were set. Heidi Grant Murphy was the "luminous" soprano soloist in a challenging part.

The program actually had two soloists. The other was the charismatic young pianist Lang Lang, whose vehicle was the Tchaikovsky Concerto No. 1. As has become customary with his performances, there were virtuosity and bravura galore, combined with the milking and distorting of melodic lines and effects that seemed calculated to attract attention. Still, as Tommasini said, he made playing the Tchaikovsky Concerto "a joyous romp" rather than an "arduous battle," which it can sometimes seem in other hands. Bartók's Suite from *The Miraculous Mandarin* closed the program brilliantly.

On October 3 Jim Oestreich wrote of the release on DVD of twenty-five of Leonard Bernstein's Young People's Concerts with the Philharmonic. He began by asking, "Where is a new Leonard Bernstein . . . when we really need one?" In general, he said, music education today is in such a sorry state that the waning of interest in classical music on the part of young people can be laid directly at its virtual absence from public school curricula. A month later, on November 18, Anthony Tommasini wrote in a similar vein about the release of the Bernstein concerts. Amazingly, these programs were not aired on public television, but on the CBS network, a gesture unimaginable today. Tommasini mentioned that they were presented without commercials, which brought a "correction" in the *Times* stating that the programs "did in fact have commercials." The author, who was present for several of them and participated in one, disputes this correction. The programs were sponsored, to be sure, but the sponsor was mentioned only briefly at the beginning and the end. There were no commercial interruptions.

Through a strange confluence of events, the contracts of four major symphony orchestras were scheduled to expire at roughly the same time—those of New York, Philadelphia, Chicago, and Cleveland. These were four of the so-called Big Five (a somewhat outmoded term in any case, as several other orchestras now deserve to be counted as part of a Big Eight or Big Ten). Only Boston's contract was not up for renewal. After playing for three weeks without a contract, the Philharmonic's musicians agreed on a new one on October 10. This one was for the usual three years (the previous six-year contract having been most unusual), at the end of which the minimum wage was to increase from $103,000 to $113,360. However, the Philharmonic would no longer be the country's highest-paid orchestra; rather, it would now be second, by a slight margin, to the Boston Symphony. The matter of increasing pensions was postponed for a year because of the uncertain state of the economy. At the time, the Philharmonic's pensions were $53,000, while in Chicago they were $63,000 and in Boston, $65,000. The Philharmonic negotiations were quite amicable compared to those going on in some of the other three orchestras. The New York musicians were also pleased that the Philharmonic management did not seek to make personnel and pension cutbacks, as was the case elsewhere.

November 11 saw the Finnish conductor Sakari Oramo returning to the Philharmonic, and in a completely unhackneyed program: Sibelius's seldom-heard tone poem *The Bard*, the American premiere of the orchestral version of the song cycle *Quatre instants* (Four Moments) by Kaija Saariaho, and Tchaikovsky's "Manfred" Symphony. The soloist in the new piece was the charismatic Finnish soprano Karita Mattila in her Philharmonic debut. Tommasini wrote a generally favorable review of the entire program and the performers, concluding with the suggestion that Oramo should be on the Philharmonic's short list of candidates to succeed Maazel.

The composer Peter Lieberson has long been a follower of Buddhism and maintained an interest in other religions of the Far East. On November 18, with James Conlon conducting, the Philharmonic gave the New York premiere of Lieberson's piece for piano and orchestra, *Red Garuda*, with Peter Serkin as soloist. In Hinduism, Garuda is the king of the birds, and Holland described the woodwinds as chirping "subtly like birds." In fact, for him "Mr. Lieberson's orchestra is an instrument of pleasure." His response carried over to Conlon's "beautifully conceived and executed performance" of Mahler's First Symphony.

Tommasini has long been an admirer of the conductor David Robertson, who appeared with the Philharmonic on the concerts beginning November 24. A former associate of Boulez, Robertson follows his mentor's example of performing new music as though it were classic, and classical music as though it were new. In this way Robertson "makes everything seem fresh and startling." So it was with this program, which included three familiar compositions: Prokofieff's *Classical Symphony*, Chopin's Piano Concerto No. 2 (with Emanuel Ax as soloist), and Mendelssohn's "Italian" Symphony. The one unfamiliar piece was György Ligeti's *Concert Românesc*, an early work in the composer's output. Tommasini pointed out that Robertson would become the music director of the Saint Louis Symphony the following fall and concluded with the words "Lucky St. Louis."

The following week Midgette seemed less taken with Robertson's work, finding his direction of the orchestral part of Bartók's Violin Concerto No. 2 "curiously muted" in spite of the "easy, incisive virtuosity" of the soloist, Christian Tetzlaff. In the rest of the program, which featured the New York premiere of the orchestral version of Steve Reich's Triple Quartet and Beethoven's Eighth Symphony, Robertson seemed to be "concentrating on the trees but not the forest." When it came to the Beethoven, this concentration "produced a kind of sameness that dulled the impact of the music."

On December 9 Sir Colin Davis returned to demonstrate that he, too, could assemble an interesting program of non-mainstream works: the Sibelius tone poem *En Saga*, the Janáček *Rhapsody for Orchestra: Taras Bulba*, and the Elgar Violin Concerto, in which the soloist was Hilary Hahn. Holland characterized Hahn as "a splendid young player" who performed with "the kind of taste and purity that rescue Elgar from himself." As for Davis, it was evident that the orchestra likes to play for him.

In recent years the Philharmonic had begun to establish its own tradition of presenting Handel's *Messiah* in the Christmas season. The performances in River-side Church beginning December 15 were conducted this time by Alan Gilbert, who, according to Kozinn, "transformed what could have been a lumbering *Messiah* into a magical one" through "decisive phrasing, generally brisk pacing," and "crys-talline textures." The well-matched soloists were Celena Schafer, Nancy Maultsby, Kurt Streit, and Jonathan Lemalu, with the Westminster Symphonic Choir.

During the same split week, Sir Colin Davis led the non-*Messiah* half of the orchestra in a mostly classical program: Mozart's Symphony No. 31 ("Paris") and an aria from his *La clemenza di Tito*, Benjamin Britten's cantata *Phaedra*, and Haydn's Symphony No. 103 ("Drum Roll"), the penultimate of his London symphonies. Singing the Mozart aria and the Britten cantata was the remarkable mezzo-soprano Lorraine Hunt Lieberson, the "starkness and concentration" of whose voice "attacks our nerve endings," according to Holland. As for the Haydn symphony, he felt he had never heard it played better.

Kurt Masur returned to close out 2004, first with a subscription series beginning December 28. The Russian program consisted of Rachmaninoff's lugubrious symphonic poem *The Isle of the Dead*, Prokofieff's Piano Concerto No. 3 with the Finnish pianist Olli Mustonen, and Masur's favored transcription of Mussorgsky's *Pictures at an Exhibition*, that of Sergei Gorchakov, which presents a darker, less brilliant treatment of the work than the more familiar Ravel transcription. Holland wrote positively of Masur's treatment of the purely orchestral works, but found Mustonen's brilliant playing offset by the theatrical visual aspect of his performance, finding it "a little distasteful—just one more public victory of performer over music."

An interview with Masur by Jeremy Eichler appeared on December 31. Said Masur, "I've felt immediately back at home here. The orchestra is still remembering our collaboration, so the work goes very quickly.... I'm not ashamed of the time I was here. I gave something to them which they kept, and this makes me happy." That evening he was to conduct the Philharmonic in its New Year's Eve performance of Beethoven's Ninth Symphony. When asked whether this work, which he had conducted hundreds of times, could remain fresh for him, his reply was that of one who had survived both Nazism and Communism: "The message of Beethoven brings us back to what we should do. Fear can never unite people. Pain cannot unite people. Joy unites people. Beethoven is always fresh. It is like a Bible for a priest."

When Lorin Maazel returned on January 12, he led only the first half of the program, ceding the podium in the second half to Xian Zhang, who had been a co-winner of the Maazel/Vilar Conductors' Competition in 2002. In 2004 Maazel had appointed Zhang assistant conductor of the Philharmonic, and on this occasion she conducted two British works, *Scherzoid* by Mark-Anthony Turnage, which received its American premiere, and the Four Sea Interludes from Benjamin Britten's *Peter Grimes*. Turnage's energetic piece, with its rhythmic syncopations and occasional jazzy passages, was a good test for a young conductor, and one that Zhang passed with no difficulty. She also did well in the Britten pieces. Allan Kozinn described her gestures as "grand and sweeping," as well as "kinetic," but never for the sake of showmanship.

Kozinn also gave high marks to Maazel's "fully transparent" account of Mozart's Symphony No. 29 in A Major, K. 201, as well as to the orchestra's vivid contribution of Richard Strauss's Horn Concerto No. 1 in E-flat Major, Op. 11. Often critical of the Philharmonic's horn section, he pronounced the principal player, Philip Myers, "in exceptionally good form," playing "with power, assurance and at times a lovely poetic lilt."

On January 13 was announced Bruce Crawford's resignation, to take effect in June. Two months shy of his seventy-sixth birthday, he stated, "I think the time is right, for Lincoln Center and for me." A former president and general manager of the Metropolitan Opera, he had been appointed chairman of Lincoln Center three years before as a stabilizing influence in the midst of turmoil among the center's various constituents.

Maazel scored a hit for Tommasini with his January 26 performance of Ravel's complete score of the ballet *Daphnis et Chloé*. Normally heard in excerpted form (usually the Suite No. 2), the entire score has much music worth hearing in concert, and Maazel was in his element drawing "lovely shadings and Impressionistic colors" from his players. The full score had been given impressive performances in the past by Bernstein and Boulez, and now Maazel added to that tradition by bringing out the work's many subtleties as well as its exciting climaxes, all within a coherent structure (the composer described the piece as a "Choreographic Symphony in Three Parts"). The Westminster Symphonic Choir sang its wordless passages beautifully, well integrated into the overall sound picture (for the chorus functions in this work not as an isolated choral group, but as another orchestral sonority).

The music of Mahler has continued to be a regular feature of Philharmonic concerts, and on February 10 the Italian conductor Riccardo Chailly brought the Seventh Symphony, one of the least played and perhaps least understood. It had been twenty years since Chailly had conducted the Philharmonic. During the interim he had a sixteen-year tenure as music director of Amsterdam's Royal Concertgebouw Orchestra, and he was now about to be in charge of Kurt Masur's former "other" ensemble, the Leipzig Gewandhaus Orchestra. Holland liked what he heard from Chailly and hoped the Philharmonic players liked him as well: "He makes a nice fit, and they have to think about their future." The following week Tommasini echoed his colleague's sentiments after Chailly's rendition of Stravinsky's complete *Firebird* ballet music on February 17. "May he come back often," he concluded. Yet as of this writing, Chailly has not been back.

A *Times* article on February 12 by Daniel J. Wakin dealt with the fact that six major orchestras were in the market for a principal oboist. Among these was the New York Philharmonic, whose principal for the past twenty-eight years, Joseph Robinson, had announced his retirement, effective at the end of the season. He told Wakin that, at age sixty-four, he did not wish to be in a position where people were thinking it was time for him to leave, and that "some things were easier 20 years ago."

Rimsky-Korsakov's *Scheherazade* has long been a staple of the orchestral repertoire, though there was a period of many years when it was absent from Philharmonic subscription programs. When it did turn up it was usually in a Kostelanetz special concert. Bernstein performed the work in 1959 and William Steinberg in 1968, and Mehta and Masur also gave it during their tenures. Now, on February 26, Tommasini wrote of two performances that occurred at the same time on the evening of February 24, Maazel's in Avery Fisher Hall, Masur's in Carnegie Hall with the Orchestre National de France. He was able to hear both by attending the Philharmonic's Rush Hour Concert on Wednesday, the 23rd, and the Orchestre National's on the 24th. Having been so impressed with Maazel's *Daphnis et Chloé* a few weeks before, he was disappointed by the conductor's return to his micro-managing self in *Scheherazade*, where Tommasini found the performance "blaring, blatant, and lacking in spontaneity." The best part was Glenn Dicterow's "radiant tone" in the violin solos. Masur's orchestra, while not technically on the level of the Philharmonic, produced a "vibrant account" of the work, with Sarah Nemtanu's violin solos played with "melancholic poignancy."

It is interesting that Tommasini wrote of Rimsky's masterpiece seriously as "a rigorous and formidable composition," and not patronizingly, like many of his colleagues. One cannot think of too many critics who would seize the opportunity to hear it twice on successive days. He returned to the Philharmonic for the Friday program to hear an oboe concerto by the Australian composer Ross Edwards, which had received its American premiere the night before. The Australian oboist Diana Doherty was the soloist, and she had to do more than play the oboe, for the work is in fact a choreographic concerto, requiring the soloist to dance about the stage while playing. Tommasini wrote positively of the piece, of Doherty, and of Maazel's leading "a beautifully shaded and beguiling performance."

On March 1, 2005, Lorin Maazel celebrated his seventy-fifth birthday with the Philharmonic (though his real birthday was a few days later, on the 6th) when he conducted a program devoted to his own music. Over the years, many conductors have composed to one degree or another, and many composers have conducted. In fact, the very first recognized great conductor was also a great composer: Felix Mendelssohn. In more recent times, the most celebrated musicians to successfully combine the two careers have been Leonard Bernstein and Pierre Boulez, with Esa-Pekka Salonen representing a younger generation. Maazel is part of this tradition, though his works did not really come to the fore until 1998, when three of them were released in recordings made with the composer conducting the Bavarian Radio Symphony Orchestra.

The program on March 1 was made up of five compositions: *Monaco Fanfares*; Music for Cello and Orchestra, written for Rostropovich but played here by Han-Na Chang; *Irish Vapors and Capers*, with James Galway as the flute soloist; and two works for narrator and orchestra—*The Giving Tree*, with a text by Shel Silverstein narrated by Maazel's wife, the actress Dietlinde Turban; and *The Empty Pot*, taken from a Chinese story and narrated by Jeremy Irons. Tommasini wrote a generally positive review of the program, except for the Irish piece, which he thought Maazel should drop from his catalog, and especially liked the two narrated pieces, both of which tell stories involving children. Turban's narration was "compelling," Irons's "mesmerizing." There was also "a remarkable boy treble," James Danner, in *The Empty Pot*, and the Brooklyn Youth Chorus sang "ardently." *The Giving Tree* has an extensive solo cello part, played "vibrantly" by Chang. On the whole, the critic's impressions of the music seemed to have been colored by the superb performances of the guest artists.

Two days later, on March 3, Maazel conducted an all–Richard Strauss program, one that could not help but demonstrate the brilliance and virtuosity of the Philharmonic: the tone poems *Ein Heldenleben* and *Don Juan* and the Suite from *Der Rosenkavalier*. Again Glenn Dicterow showed his mastery in the extended solo violin part in *Heldenleben* and the incidental solos in the other works. Although Kozinn noted that the orchestra had been playing at the top of its game since early in Kurt Masur's tenure, he also wrote that the brass section "has improved enormously" since Maazel's arrival, and that the opening horn flourish in the *Rosenkavalier* Suite "was as good as it gets."

One often hears selections from Mendelssohn's Incidental Music to *A Midsummer Night's Dream*. The Wedding March is its most familiar item played out of context— or rather, in context. Occasionally orchestras perform excerpts with the assistance of an actor or actress reciting appropriate lines from Shakespeare's play. On March 17 the Philharmonic went several steps further by presenting the complete incidental music together with a substantial portion of the play. The conductor Sir Neville Marriner, the soprano Susan Gritton, the mezzo-soprano Patricia Risley, and the women of the New York Choral Artists took care of the musical side of things, and a team of actors headed by Campbell Scott, Linda Edmond, and Marcia Gay Harden performed the play as adapted and directed by Edward Berkeley. Tommasini pronounced the event "an utterly delightful program."

The highly regarded American conductor Kent Nagano had made his Philharmonic debut in 1987, when he was thirty-six years old. Now, eighteen years later, he was invited to return, which he did with a most unorthodox program of works by Bach and Messiaen. The first half was devoted to the first and last sections of the unfinished *Art of Fugue*, separated by the Concerto in D Minor for Violin, Oboe, and Strings, played splendidly, according to Tommasini, by the associate concertmaster, Cheryl Staples, and the associate principal oboist, Sherry Sylar. The second half was given over to Messiaen's final composition, the Philharmonic-commissioned *Éclairs sur l'au-delà…*, of which Nagano led "a transfixing account." Tommasini noted that there was a gradual exodus of audience members during the Messiaen and concluded, "If this amazing music turns off some Philharmonic subscribers, then the orchestra should give up on them and entice new listeners to take their place." He also hoped Nagano would be back often.

The concerts beginning March 31 brought Charles Dutoit to conduct Berlioz's complete dramatic legend *The Damnation of Faust*, with Paul Groves as Faust, Sir Willard White as Mephistophélès, Suzanne Mentzer as Marguerite, and Christopher Feigum as the student, Brander. The Westminster Symphonic Choir and the Brooklyn Youth Chorus also took part in what Jeremy Eichler described as "a robust and satisfying performance."

On April 19 was reported the death of the conductor Kenneth Schermerhorn at the age of seventy-five. The music director of the Nashville Symphony at the time of his death, he did not appear often with the Philharmonic but is notable for his having been one of Leonard Bernstein's original three assistant conductors with the orchestra.

A new chairman for Lincoln Center was announced on May 5. Frank A. Bennack Jr. was named to replace Bruce Crawford, who in turn had succeeded Beverly Sills. The seventy-two-year old Bennack was already a member of Lincoln Center's board and in fact had been its vice chairman since 1999, and was also a member of the board of the Metropolitan Opera. When it was suggested that in his new position he would be in the nature of a father to the center's twelve constituents, often described as a dysfunctional family, he quipped, "I'm the father of five and, in light of my recent marriage, I've added three—so I'm not an inexperienced parent."

Most conductors, when programming a Haydn symphony, choose to place it at the beginning of the program, or at least in the first half of the concert. Few opt to close a program with it (although Stokowski had done so with the "Clock" Symphony way back in 1949), but such was the choice of Alan Gilbert on June 2 when he conducted Haydn's seldom-played Symphony No. 90 in C Major. Works in this key from the classical period are usually festive in nature, and the finale of this symphony contains several examples of Haydn's wit, making it an effective closing number.

Gilbert's entire program consisted of works from off the beaten path, beginning with Dvořák's symphonic poem *The Noon Witch*, a work that, strangely enough, the Philharmonic had never played before. (But then, most orchestras do not have the Dvořák symphonic poems, based on grisly Czech folk tales, in their repertoire.) Next came Samuel Barber's unabashedly neoromantic Cello Concerto, in which the principal cellist, Carter Brey, was an alternately impassioned and elegant soloist. A work by Henri Dutilleux, Messiaen's successor as the leading French composer of the day, called *Mystère de l'instant* (Mystery of the Moment), was found by Tommasini to contain "ravishing music," an apt description of many of that fine composer's scores.

Two deaths were reported on successive days. The first, on June 15, was that of the composer David Diamond at the age of eighty-nine. Early in his career his works were frequently performed by major American orchestras, including the Philharmonic, where he found a particular champion in Bernstein. In the 1950s and 1960s, as the twelve-tone composers gained ascendancy, Diamond's music faded from view, but the 1980s brought about a comeback for him, thanks largely to the conductor Gerard Schwarz. At the time of his death, Diamond was a highly respected composer.

The next day brought news of the second death, that of the conductor Carlo Maria Giulini, at the age of ninety-one. He did not have a long relationship with the Philharmonic, having appeared as a guest only in the 1968–69 and 1974–75 seasons, but he was universally recognized and admired as one of the great conductors of the second half of the twentieth century.

In June it was announced that the new executive and artistic director of Carnegie Hall would be Clive Gillinson, effective July 1. He would be coming from England, where he had been a cellist in the London Symphony Orchestra and, since 1984, its managing director. As such, he had been able to revive that orchestra's prestige, which had sunk considerably prior to his taking over. Meanwhile, at Lincoln Center, the Philharmonic's board voted to go ahead with the redesign of Avery Fisher Hall by the British architect Lord Norman Foster. Where the Philharmonic would play during the renovation, or for how long, no one knew.

Again, Mahler closed the Philharmonic's season, this time the Sixth Symphony, which Maazel conducted on the concerts beginning June 22. (The subscription season continues to grow in length; it used to close in mid-April.) Tommasini wrote of the first performance as being "deeply impressive and continuously exciting." He felt that Maazel's habitual coolness, coupled with his attention to detail, kept his Mahler from becoming melodramatic, and that "he should keep the Mahler coming."

MORE MOZART

Having been appointed the Philharmonic's assistant conductor in 2004, Xian Zhang was promoted to the post of associate conductor on July 8. She would be in charge of six of the orchestra's seven Parks Concerts, sponsored by Time Warner. The seventh would be led by Lorin Maazel on July 19. Zhang's first concert, on July 13, was on Central Park's Great Lawn, attended by 40,000 on an extremely humid night, and consisting of Wagner's Overture to *The Flying Dutchman*, Lalo's *Symphonie Espagnole* (with the violinist Karen Gomyo, making her Philharmonic debut), and Tchaikovsky's Fifth Symphony. Although he had some reservations about the first half of the program, Kozinn wrote enthusiastically about "a magnificent, passionate performance" of the Tchaikovsky.

Maazel's concert, also in Central Park, and also on a terribly humid night, drew an attendance estimated at 47,000 for an all-Dvořák program. It was Maazel's first Parks Concert since becoming music director (he had conducted there in 1967 and 1968). Lynn Harrell was the soloist in the Cello Concerto; the program also included the *Carnival Overture* and the "New World" Symphony.

Maazel's fourth season as music director began with the opening-night gala on September 21, on which an unprecedented $3.1 million was raised between the concert and the post-performance dinner. Moreover, according to a Philharmonic spokesman, subscription sales had increased by 32 percent for the season. Beethoven's Piano Concerto No. 5 ("Emperor") opened the program, with the highly regarded Russian Evgeny Kissin as soloist, while the second half included two Richard Strauss holdovers from the previous season, *Don Juan* and the Suite from *Der Rosenkavalier*. Tommasini was again unhappy with Maazel's treatment of "The Star-Spangled Banner," calling it "pompous" and "ponderously slow"; nor did he care for Kissin's overly romantic treatment of the concerto, in which he was abetted by Maazel. But the second half was another story, treating the audience to "vibrant and stylish Strauss playing. The orchestra sounded like a million dollars. Make that $3.1 million."

The subscription season opened the next night, with Lang Lang playing the Chopin Piano Concerto No. 1 in E Minor. Holland wrote approvingly of his tone, technique, and elegant phrasing, but disapprovingly of the visual aspect of his playing, for which Lang has consistently been criticized—"the wriggles of ecstasy, the stunned gazes into space, the smiles of complicity." When he had a free hand, he conducted to himself (shades of Glenn Gould). Maazel's conducting of Mahler's First Symphony, in comparison, "was a model of rectitude."

On September 24 it was reported that William Vacchiano had died at the age of ninety-three. In 1935 he had auditioned on trumpet for the Metropolitan Opera Orchestra and the Philharmonic and was selected for both on the same day. He chose the Philharmonic and in 1942 became the principal, a post he held until his retirement in 1973. As a teacher at Juilliard for sixty-seven years (1935–2002), the Manhattan School of Music (1937–1999), and the Mannes College of Music (1937–1983), he had over two thousand students, many of whom over the years have occupied chairs in major orchestras throughout the United States.

Another former Philharmonic musician's death was announced on October 14, that of the oboist Jerome Roth at the age of eighty-seven. A member from 1961 to 1992, he played second chair to the principal players Harold Gomberg and Joseph Robinson, having been oboist of the New York Woodwind Quintet prior to joining the Philharmonic. At a time when oboists had the reputation, rightly or wrongly, of having quirky, aggressive, even combative personalities toward conductors and colleagues, Roth was an exception, a mild-mannered and gracious man.

Although the general effects of Hurricane Katrina on New Orleans are well-known, there was less general awareness of the plight of the Louisiana Philharmonic Orchestra (formerly the New Orleans Philharmonic-Symphony), whose members were dispersed to temporary homes across the United States, with an attendant loss of income. The Louisiana Philharmonic is not an orchestra whose members command high salaries. A self-governing ensemble, its minimum salary at the time was $18,000 a year, while that of the New York Philharmonic was $106,000. But orchestra musicians throughout the country, of whatever economic and artistic bracket, invariably think of each other as colleagues, and are ready and willing to offer help and support when needed. Thus it came as no surprise that, with just a few weeks of organizational time, the musicians of the New York Philharmonic volunteered to play a benefit concert on October 28 for their beleaguered colleagues, with whom they shared the stage of Avery Fisher Hall. Accommodations and airline tickets for the Louisiana musicians were donated by generous sponsors. Also donating their fees were the several conductors and guest artists participating. Entitled "Bringing Back the Music," an all-American program was presented, not all of it symphonic, for the guests included the New Orleans native Wynton Marsalis and his quartet, Randy Newman, and Audra McDonald. Lorin Maazel, James Conlon, Leonard Slatkin, and Carlos Miguel Prieto (Louisiana's music director–designate) conducted, as did the Broadway conductor Ted Sperling. Beverly Sills was the host for a program featuring pieces by Gershwin, Copland, Barber (Itzhak Perlman playing a movement of the Violin Concerto), Adams, and Bernstein, with the combined orchestras taking part in the traditional conductorless rendition of the Overture to *Candide*. The sold-out event brought in over $300,000 for the cause. The concert made for a very tight schedule for the New Yorkers, who had played a Thursday night concert, one on Friday morning, then two rehearsals with the Louisianans, and the combined concert on Friday night. New York's personnel manager, Carl Schiebler, who was responsible for making the seating arrangements for the two orchestras, said at the beginning of the week, "It's going to be a hard couple of days for our people. But everybody felt this was something we needed to do. It was the right thing to do."

Having twice canceled scheduled Philharmonic appearances, the young Finnish conductor Mikko Franck finally made his debut with the orchestra on November 3. At the time he was chief conductor of the National Orchestra of Belgium and was about to become general music director of the Finnish National Opera. The novelty on his Philharmonic program was Alfred Schnittke's Concerto Grosso No. 5 for Violin, Invisible Piano, and Orchestra. The "invisible piano" was just that, a piano played offstage but amplified stereophonically. Gidon Kremer, a champion of the composer, was the authoritative violin soloist, with Andrius Zlabys the invisible pianist in what Kozinn described as a "quirky and often chaotic" work. Franck's program also included Beethoven's *Leonore* Overture No. 3 and Shostakovich's Symphony No. 5, the latter in what Kozinn felt was a "surprisingly understated" and "strangely inert" reading, such "hot spots" as it possessed having been written into the score by the composer.

Jeremy Eichler made much of the Philharmonic's pairing of music by Bartók and Rachmaninoff, led on December 2 by the highly regarded Hungarian conductor Ivan Fischer. Both were composers of the twentieth century, yet Bartók wrote in a modern idiom, Rachmaninoff in the late nineteenth-century romantic style (though one hears something of the twentieth century in his music as well). But the works performed that evening were poor representatives of the significant contrast between the two, for Bartók was represented by his extremely accessible (and brief) *Romanian Folk Dances*, Rachmaninoff by his popular and almost hour-long Second Symphony. Fischer was praised for his treatment of both works, as well as that of Henri Dutilleux's colorful violin concerto *L'arbre des songes*

(The Tree of Dreams), in which the Greek violinist Leonidas Kavakos was an effective soloist.

After an absence of thirty-five years, the Spanish conductor Rafael Frühbeck de Burgos returned on December 7 to direct a program of Wagner excerpts in the first half, followed in the second by the Piano Concerto No. 2 by Saint-Saëns, with André Watts a scintillating soloist, and the two suites from Manuel de Falla's *The Three-Cornered Hat*. Although the Saint-Saëns concerto is anything but profound, in the right hands, such as Watts's, it is a thoroughly delightful and delicious work. As for the brilliant Falla suites, Frühbeck truly lives this music when he conducts it, the Spanish equivalent of hearing Charles Munch conduct *Daphnis et Chloé*.

The Philharmonic's recently established *Messiah* tradition continued with four performances of that masterwork in Riverside Church, beginning December 14, this time under the direction of the English conductor Richard Hickox, who was making his debut with the orchestra. In what Eichler described as "a solid, even stately, performance" that successfully combined "delicacy and grandeur," the Westminster Symphonic Choir took part handsomely, along with the soloists Christine Brandes, Sarah Mingardo, Mark Tucker, and John Relyea, the last-named especially effective in "The Trumpet Shall Sound."

Meanwhile, in Avery Fisher Hall, the other half (or perhaps three-fifths) of the orchestra performed Haydn and Mozart with the German pianist and conductor Christian Zacharias: Mozart's Piano Concerto No. 18 in B-flat Major, K. 456, sandwiched between Haydn's Symphonies No. 83 in G Minor ("The Hen") and No. 86 in D Major. Holland characterized Zacharias as "an ideal Haydn-Mozart man: meticulous yet natural," and praised his ability to find just the right tempo, one at which details are clear but not at the expense of the music's character and energy. He concluded, "It was a satisfying evening."

The young English conductor Jonathan Nott, music director of the Bamberg Symphony in Germany, made his Philharmonic debut in the concerts beginning January 12, 2006, with a program that included the formerly seldom-played *Alpine Symphony* by Richard Strauss. This once-maligned work (now somewhat better accepted) represents the composer's musical trek up and down a mountain—perhaps the Zugspitze, which he could see from his Bavarian villa. Extravagantly scored, it never fails to captivate audiences, if not critics. Kozinn, who felt the work had not aged well, nevertheless wrote that "the orchestra sounded fantastic." Preceding it on the program was John Corigliano's Violin Concerto, derived from his score for the film *The Red Violin*. Corigliano had grown up with the Philharmonic, and the musicians think of him as one of their own. Joshua Bell, who played on the

The orchestra on tour in the Soviet Union, 1988. (Photo by Bert Bial. Courtesy of Philharmonic Archives)

Zubin Mehta enters the stage in Moscow's Tchaikovsky Hall, 1988. (Photo by Bert Bial. Courtesy of Philharmonic Archives)

Rehearsal in the Odeon of Herod Atticus, Athens, 1988. (Photo by Bert Bial. Courtesy of Philharmonic Archives)

Principal oboist Harold Gomberg (*right*) with his successor, Joseph Robinson, 1985. (Courtesy of Philharmonic Archives)

Zubin Mehta, *left*, and Olivier Messiaen, 1988. (Courtesy of Philharmonic Archives)

Rafael Kubelík in concert, Avery Fisher Hall, c. 1982. (Photo by Bill Jones. Courtesy of Philharmonic Archives)

Zubin Mehta rehearses the strings, 1989. (Photo by Bert Bial. Courtesy of Philharmonic Archives)

Left: Timpanist Saul Goodman, c. 1960. (Courtesy of Philharmonic Archives)

Below: Zubin Mehta rehearses with Luciano Pavarotti, c. 1980. (Courtesy of Philharmonic Archives)

Principal trumpet William Vacchiano, c. 1960. (Photo by Sedge LeBlang. Courtesy of Philharmonic Archives)

Concertmaster Glenn Dicterow, 1988. (Photo by Chris Lee. Courtesy of Philharmonic Archives)

Kurt Masur in concert, Avery Fisher Hall, c. 1992. (Photo by Chris Lee. Courtesy of Philharmonic Archives)

Kurt Masur conducts in Central Park, 1993. (Photo by Chris Lee. Courtesy of
Philharmonic Archives)

Left: Managing director Deborah Borda, c. 1994. (Courtesy of Philharmonic Archives)

Below: *Left to right*: Philharmonic chairman Stephen Stamas with Zubin Mehta, Kurt Masur, and Pierre Boulez in Salzburg, 1996. (Courtesy of Philharmonic Archives)

Above: Kurt Masur with young admirers at a Children's Promenade, c. 1994. (Photo by Chris Lee. Courtesy of Philharmonic Archives)

Right: Timpanist Roland Kohloff, c. 1994. (Photo by Chris Lee. Courtesy of Philharmonic Archives)

Sir Colin Davis in concert, 1996. (Photo by Chris Lee. Courtesy of Philharmonic Archives)

Riccardo Muti in concert, 2000. (Photo by Chris Lee. Courtesy of Philharmonic Archives)

Lorin Maazel conducts John Adams's *On the Transmigration of Souls*, 1992. (Photo by Chris Lee. Courtesy of Philharmonic Public Relations)

Lorin Maazel in concert, Avery Fisher Hall, 2003. (Photo by Chris Lee. Courtesy of Philharmonic Public Relations)

Lorin Maazel after his seventy-fifth-birthday concert. *Left to right*: flutist Sir James Galway, Maazel, actor Jeremy Irons, and Maazel's wife, actress Dietlinde Turban. (Photo by Chris Lee. Courtesy of Philharmonic Public Relations)

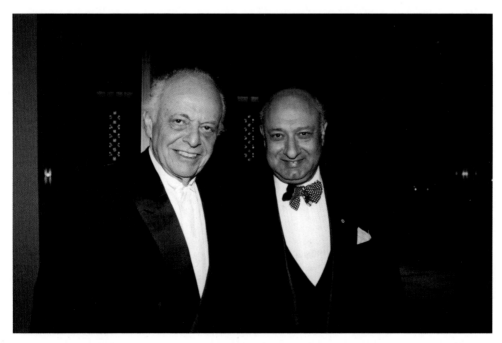

Lorin Maazel, *left*, and managing director Zarin Mehta at Maazel's seventy-fifth-birthday party. (Photo by Linsley Lindekens. Courtesy of Philharmonic Archives)

Above: The Philharmonic after landing in Pyongyang, North Korea, 2008. (Photo by Chris Lee. Courtesy of Philharmonic Public Relations)

Left: Principal clarinetist Stanley Drucker, 2004. (Photo by Chris Lee. Courtesy of Philharmonic Public Relations)

Opposite page: Lorin Maazel and the orchestra in Dresden's Frauenkirche, 2005. (Photo by Chris Lee. Courtesy of Philharmonic Public Relations)

Right: Alan Gilbert conducts in Central Park, 2008. (Photo by Chris Lee. Courtesy of Philharmonic Public Relations)

Below: Alan Gilbert in concert, 2009. (Photo by Chris Lee. Courtesy of Philharmonic Public Relations)

movie soundtrack and was thus involved with the music from its inception, was the soloist in a brilliant piece that "suits him perfectly," according to Kozinn.

Kurt Masur returned for his annual reappearance on January 20, bringing with him two of his favorites, Beethoven's "Pastoral" Symphony to open and Prokofieff's *Scythian* Suite to close, the latter one of the musical descendants of Stravinsky's *Rite of Spring.* In between came two works for piano and orchestra by Liszt, the Fantasy on Themes from Beethoven's *Ruins of Athens* and the demonic *Totentanz* (Dance of Death). The Canadian Louis Lortie, whom we remember for crossing Central Park for two performances on the same evening, was, according to Eichler, "a nimble and imaginative soloist." Masur, who was greeted warmly by the audience on his entrance, did not disappoint in his straightforward rendition of the Beethoven, which let the music speak for itself, and his controlled exposition of the Prokofieff, which let the music shout for itself.

The year 2006 was the 250th anniversary of the birth of Mozart. Knowing how the world of music loves to celebrate composers' anniversaries, one would justifiably expect all the stops to be pulled out for this one, just as they were in 1991, the 200th anniversary of his death. And so they were. The Philharmonic programmed a three-week festival entitled The Magic of Mozart. Lorin Maazel began it on January 26, the day before the birthday, with a program largely of works the orchestra had not played often and, in one instance, had never played. Opening the festivities was the elegant Symphony No. 28 in C Major, K. 200, which the Philharmonic had last played in 2000. The Violin Concerto No. 4 in D Major, K. 218, followed, with the associate concertmaster, Sheryl Staples, as the energetic soloist in a piece last heard on a Philharmonic program in 1972. One work frequently heard over the years was the great "Haffner" Symphony, which preceded the Philharmonic premiere of the "Coronation" Mass, K. 317, in which the vocal soloists were Celena Shafer, Joyce DiDonato, John Tessier, and Nathan Berg, with the Westminster Symphonic Choir. Kozinn wrote of "a passionate, rich-hued rendering" of the Mass.

Two of Mozart's great piano concertos, No. 17 in G Major, K. 453, and No. 20 in D Minor, K. 466, were conducted on February 2 from the keyboard by the pianist Jeffrey Kahane, who subsequently stood on the podium to lead the sublime Sinfonia Concertante in E-flat Major, K. 364, with the assistant concertmaster, Michelle Kim, and the associate principal violist, Rebecca Young, as soloists. Kahane succeeded in bringing out the operatic quality inherent in the concertos, as did Kim and Young in their collaboration, where Kozinn felt they "proved sensitive partners." Their playing was imbued with a "chamber music quality."

Maazel closed the festival on February 9 with the ultimate all-Mozart program, the last three symphonies: No. 39 in E-flat Major, K. 543; No. 40 in G Minor, K.

550; and No. 41 in C Major, K. 551 ("Jupiter"). These great works make such a natural grouping that it is surprising that they are not performed together more often. Holland referred to the three as "Mozart's mystery symphonies," in that they were composed in about six weeks' time in 1788, apparently without any commission or other impetus for setting them down on paper, and probably were never heard by their composer. Holland praised the elegance of the playing, describing Maazel and the Philharmonic as "sophistication and attentiveness themselves."

With the decline in the classical recording industry, a number of orchestras, including the London Symphony, the San Francisco Symphony, the Boston Symphony, and the Royal Concertgebouw Orchestra, have taken matters into their own hands by forming their own labels, on which they release live recordings of concert performances. On February 9 it was announced that the New York Philharmonic had signed a three-year contract with Deutsche Grammophon Gesellschaft (DGG) that would involve not only the issuing of CDs of concert performances, but digital downloading as well. Under this agreement DGG would issue four of the orchestra's concerts a year through iTunes and possibly other Web sites and would also make the recordings available as CDs. The first such release would be the aforementioned concert of the last three Mozart symphonies. Additionally, an agreement was signed with New World Records, which would release two CDs a year devoted to new works commissioned by the Philharmonic. The recordings would be of the world premiere performances and would also be available through downloading.

The New York Philharmonic has a great recording history that has not been covered by this book, except incidentally. For more information on this important aspect of the orchestra's history, the reader is referred to *New York Philharmonic: The Authorized Recordings, 1917–2005: A Discography*, by James H. North (Scarecrow Press, 2006). This volume lists every recording made by the Philharmonic during that time, many with appropriate and pertinent comments by North.

Robert Spano, music director of the Atlanta Symphony, was the guest conductor for the concerts beginning February 23, on which he offered an interesting program of twentieth- and twenty-first-century works. The present century was represented by the world premiere of a Philharmonic-commissioned song cycle by John Harbison, *Milosz Songs*, a setting of ten poems by the Nobel Prize–winning Polish author Czesław Miłosz sung radiantly by Dawn Upshaw, for whom they were written. Tommasini described the shimmering score as "lucid and precisely wrought music" that "complements Milosz's gripping words."

To open the program, Spano led Bartók's great *Music for Strings, Percussion and Celesta* and closed it with the equally great Symphonic Dances from Bernstein's

West Side Story. While he seemed "curiously tentative" in the latter score, Tommasini felt Spano "excelled in what mattered most," the *Milosz Songs*, "which already seems a significant new work."

On March 3 came the news that Roland Kohloff, the Philharmonic's "Master of the Timpani," as the *Times* headline described him, had died on February 24 at the age of seventy-one. He had been the orchestra's timpanist from 1972, when he succeeded his teacher, Saul Goodman, until his retirement in 2004. He played the American premieres of Franco Donatoni's Concertino for Strings, Brass, and Solo Timpani and of the timpani concerto *Der Wald* ("The Forest") by Siegfried Matthus. As a faculty member of the Juilliard School, Kohloff taught many timpanists and percussionists who went on to play in major orchestras. His playing was marked by great character, depth, and musicality.

Every so often, a young conductor is asked to step in on short notice to substitute for an older colleague, often with great success. The prime example of such circumstances is, of course, the unscheduled debut of Leonard Bernstein in 1943. Another instance that could be cited is the New York debut of Michael Tilson Thomas in 1969. As assistant conductor of the Boston Symphony, he was called upon to take over from William Steinberg during the intermission of a New York concert, conducting the second half of the program and the rest of that week's performances.

The Philharmonic concerts beginning March 2 were to have been directed by Christoph von Dohnányi, but his illness brought about the Philharmonic debut of the young French conductor Ludovic Morlot, whose studies included attendance at the Pierre Monteux School in Hancock, Maine. At the time an assistant conductor with the Boston Symphony, Morlot took over Dohnányi's program, which included a recent work by Elliott Carter, *Allegro scorrevole*. Carter's music is never easy to perform, but Morlot had had experience with it in Boston (though not with this piece), where James Levine has been a champion of the composer's works.

Tommasini wrote appreciatively of Morlot's conducting, with its "fluid yet unostentatious technique, palpable confidence and appealing energy," and of his performance of the difficult Carter score. He also praised his direction of the Schumann Fourth Symphony and the Brahms Violin Concerto, the latter with "the brilliant German violinist" Frank Peter Zimmermann as an expressive soloist. It was evident from this very first appearance that Ludovic Morlot had embarked on an important career—a conclusion supported by subsequent performances.

The bronchitis that had sidelined Dohnányi was one of several indispositions that befell conductors at roughly the same time. An injured shoulder resulting from a fall caused James Levine to miss performances with the Boston Symphony and at the Metropolitan Opera, while Kurt Masur's heart palpitations in Dublin affected his ability to lead concerts in the United States by the London Philharmonic. But Dohnányi recovered in time for his second scheduled Philharmonic week, beginning March 9, when the program was Schubert's "Unfinished" Symphony and a concert performance of Bartók's one-act opera *Bluebeard's Castle*, in which Anne Sofie von Otter and Matthias Goerne were the protagonists. Holland felt they sang beautifully and coped valiantly with the Hungarian text. As for the Schubert, it was played with the clarity of chamber music.

The Philharmonic's associate conductor, Xian Zhang, was given a scheduled program of her own beginning on March 16. Tchaikovsky's Fifth Symphony was her major offering, a work so familiar that it is difficult to say anything new about it, but she succeeded in making it fresh with "an assured and exhilarating account" of the work, according to Tommasini. The German violinist Ingolf Turban made his Philharmonic debut in Paganini's virtuosic First Concerto, which he performed with no apparent effort whatsoever.

Lorin Maazel showed two sides of his conductorial self on March 22, as noted by Tommasini: an "exasperatingly restrained," even ponderous rendition of Schubert's delightfully innocent Fifth Symphony, followed by "an electrifying account" of Schoenberg's formidable *Variations for Orchestra*, Op. 31. By playing this twelve-tone composition expressively and bringing out its inherent emotionalism, he succeeded in making the score palatable to those who might ordinarily resist it. Also of note was the "auspicious" Philharmonic debut of a young Venezuelan-born pianist, Gabriela Montero, who offered everything one could wish for in Rachmaninoff's *Rhapsody on a Theme of Paganini*.

One often speaks of Bernstein's identification with the music of Mahler, an affinity based on temperament and empathy. The same can be said of Rafael Frühbeck de Burgos and the music of Falla. Frühbeck was only thirteen years old when Falla died in 1946 in Argentina, but they were of the same nationality. A more recent example of conductor-composer identification is surely that of Mstislav Rostropovich and Dmitri Shostakovich. Their association goes even deeper: not only did they know each other, but Rostropovich studied orchestration with the composer, who later dedicated his two cello concertos to him. So closely identified with Shostakovich did the exuberant Rostropovich become, so intently did he "live" his mentor's music and throw himself into the conducting of it that, technical limitations aside, all he had to do was show up on April 19 to have "the Philharmonic playing for all it was worth (which is quite a bit)," in the words of Holland.

The Shostakovich works performed that night were the Violin Concerto No. 1, powerfully played by Maxim Vengerov, and the Symphony No. 10. Both works had received their American premieres by the Philharmonic under Dimitri Mitropoulos, the concerto at the end of 1955 with David Oistrakh as the soloist, the symphony in the fall of 1954. Many consider the Tenth the greatest of the Shostakovich symphonies, an opinion bolstered by Rostropovich's inspired interpretation.

When Roland Kohloff retired as timpanist of the Philharmonic in 2004, there was, of course, a search for his successor. But this process, like the Philharmonic's conductor searches, takes time. A lengthy article by Anthony Tommasini in the *Times* of April 21 profiled Joseph Pereira, the acting principal timpanist since Kohloff's retirement. Pereira had joined the Philharmonic as a percussionist and assistant timpanist in 1998 at the age of twenty-three. At the time he was still a student at Juilliard, in the second year of the master's program, with Kohloff as his teacher. The demands of the Philharmonic job forced him to attend Juilliard part-time, so that he earned his degree in four years instead of two.

Tommasini's article described Pereira's continuing search in junkyards for unusual objects that could be used as percussion instruments, such as automobile and truck brake drums that proved useful for certain effects in John Adams's *On the Transmigration of Souls*. Like many timpanists, he makes his own sticks; he told Tommasini of fashioning six sticks from bamboo he acquired in New York's gardening district, the insides of the mallets constructed from plastic corks found in wine bottles. Those particular sticks, he said, "are perfect for the third movement of Bartók's Music for Strings, Percussion and Celesta."

As a spinoff of its Young People's Concerts, the Philharmonic has begun a series of Very Young People's Concerts for children from ages three to five, for which Pereira has served as the master of ceremonies and principal educator. As might be expected, he auditioned for the Philharmonic's principal timpani opening, advancing to the finals while enjoying the support of many of his colleagues. In the end, the job went to another, the German timpanist Markus Rhoten, with Pereira returning to his assistant position. He was quoted as saying, "I'm not disappointed. I'm really happy with how I played. The rest is not up to me." A composer of works for various ensembles and solo instruments, he has since brought his artistry to the Los Angeles Philharmonic, where he was engaged as principal timpanist in 2009.

Some distinguished composers of concert and operatic music have also written significant music for films—Prokofieff, Shostakovich, Copland, and Virgil Thomson, among others. Conversely, there are composers best known for their film music who have also written distinctive scores for the concert hall, such as Bernard Herrmann and John Williams. For two special concerts, on April 24 and 25, the Philharmonic engaged Williams to conduct a program of film scores by Herrmann and Williams himself. Williams, who succeeded Arthur Fiedler as conductor of the Boston Pops from 1980 to 1993, led to great effect excerpts from Herrmann's scores to *Psycho*, *Vertigo*, *North by Northwest*, *Taxi Driver*, *Citizen Kane*, and *The Devil and Daniel Webster*. Williams's own music included selections from *Jaws*, *Close Encounters of the Third Kind*, *Schindler's List* (with Glenn Dicterow a sensitive violin soloist), *Indiana Jones and the Last Crusade*, *E.T.: The Extra-Terrestrial*, and, of course, *Star Wars*. Martin Scorsese and Steven Spielberg served as hosts for this event, which included a demonstration of how music can enhance a film. A chase scene from the *Indiana Jones* film was shown without the music, then with it, to show how much the score added to the tension of the visual image. There are those who look down on movie music as inferior to the great concert music, but in the hands of a master composer (Erich Korngold also comes to mind), it can not only complement a film, but, as this evening demonstrated, can be heard effectively in its own right. A capacity audience roared its approval.

Sir Colin Davis arrived for a two-week stay, with his first concert scheduled for April 27. The Mozart celebrations were continuing, so what better than to include the composer's longest concert work, the eight-movement, hour-long "Haffner" Serenade (No. 7 in D Major, K. 250). Not to be confused with the much shorter "Haffner" Symphony, it was nevertheless written for the same Haffner family, in this case for a wedding celebration. Of interest is the fact that three of its middle movements are a de facto violin concerto, the solo part stylishly rendered in this instance by Glenn Dicterow. Holland wrote of how Davis "is always a welcome presence" at the Philharmonic, his relaxed brand of music making tempering the orchestra's normal urban tensions. But Davis did not neglect his beloved Berlioz; he brought with him his countryman Ian Bostridge, whose "fine, pure tenor voice" was heard in the great song cycle *Les nuits d'été*.

More Mozart turned up in Davis's second week, beginning May 3, which opened with the Overture to *La clemenza di Tito*, played, according to Holland, "with a warmth not every conductor can get out of this orchestra." Two highly regarded soloists performed, the Finnish soprano Soile Isokoski and the Japanese pianist Mitsuko Uchida. Together they collaborated on the concert scena *Ch'io mi scordi di te?*, after which Uchida was heard in the often underrated Concerto No. 26 in D Major ("Coronation"), K. 537. Sibelius occupied the program's second half. Isokoski was heard in the rarely performed tone poem *Luonnatar*, the orchestra then concluding the program with yet another underrated work, the Third Symphony. Less imposing than some of the composer's other symphonies (and less often heard), it makes a refreshing change of pace from more formidable repertoire.

The Philharmonic continued its tradition of free Memorial Day concerts at the Cathedral of St. John the Divine on May 29. Reconstruction work on portions of the cathedral limited the seating capacity to about 900 rather than the usual 2,700.

As she had the previous year, Xian Zhang officiated, leading a dynamic performance of Tchaikovsky's Fifth Symphony, which she had conducted earlier in the season at Avery Fisher Hall. The cathedral's lengthy reverberation time compelled her to make some adjustments in the tempos from her previous performances, lest the whole piece turn into acoustical mush. Verdi's Overture to *La forza del destino* opened the program, played before as much of a capacity audience as could be accommodated, with the overflow watching and listening to a video and audio relay in the cathedral campus's Synod Hall while others listened in the cathedral garden.

For once, a Mahler symphony did not end the subscription season on June 1–3. Rather, the concluding work was Berlioz's *Symphonie fantastique*, of which Maazel led "a bang-up account," according to Tommasini. While impressed with the performance, he was especially enthusiastic about the two contemporary works on the first half of the program, Elliott Carter's *Dialogues* for Piano and Chamber Orchestra and Stravinsky's Concerto for Piano and Wind Orchestra, both of which featured "the astounding French pianist" Pierre-Laurent Aimard as soloist, his playing "by turns scintillating, incisive and tender." Following the intermission several Philharmonic musicians were honored: the principal bassoonist Judith LeClair for her twenty-five years in the orchestra, and, on their retirements, the violinists Emanuel Boder after twenty-seven years and Matitiahu Braun after thirty-six years, and the double bassist Lew Norton after thirty-nine years.

On June 22 was reported the death of Howard Shanet at the age of eighty-seven. A conductor, composer, and professor at Columbia University, whose music department he chaired from 1972 to 1978, he was known for his unorthodox choices of repertoire for orchestras he conducted. For example, who had ever heard, or even heard of, William Henry Fry's *Santa Claus: Christmas Symphony* (1853) before Shanet played it at Columbia? A conducting student of Serge Koussevitzky at Tanglewood, he ultimately became known as a writer, first as the author of the Philharmonic's program notes during 1959–60, then for his impressive *Philharmonic: A History of New York's Orchestra*, (1975), the predecessor of this book.

CHAPTER 22

2006–7

BRAHMS THIS TIME

The New York Philharmonic has for decades been in search of a summer home. True, they once played a six- to eight-week season of summer concerts at Lewisohn Stadium in upper Manhattan, but that series was not administered by the Philharmonic Society, and during its later years the ensemble was called the Stadium Symphony Orchestra, though it was still composed largely of Philharmonic musicians. In any case, those concerts ended for the Philharmonic in 1964.

Although Tanglewood has long been the summer home of the Boston Symphony Orchestra, it should be noted that the first concerts played there, in 1934 and 1935, were by the New York Philharmonic. The Saratoga Performing Arts Center in upstate New York was originally planned with the Philharmonic in mind, but in the end it was occupied by the Philadelphia Orchestra. The proposed summer home on the campus of SUNY in Purchase, New York, did not pan out; nor has the talk, every few years, of a London Proms–style series at the Seventh Regiment Armory on New York City's East Side. To be sure, the Philharmonic has its Parks Concerts, its Summertime Classics, and its residency in Vail, Colorado, but none of these can really be described as a summer festival.

In 2006 another possibility for summer concerts appeared: the Bethel Woods Center for the Arts. It was the brainchild of the cable television magnate Alan Gerry, whose family foundation was largely responsible for its construction. Located in Sullivan County, New York, the center stands on the site of the original Woodstock music festival. The Philharmonic played the inaugural concert on Saturday, July 1, Bramwell Tovey conducting a mostly light program taken more or less from the Summertime Classics series. The young Russian pianist Alexander Kobrin, winner of the 2005 Van Cliburn International Piano Competition, played Rachmaninoff's *Rhapsody on a Theme of Paganini* (substituting for the indisposed Lang Lang); Audra McDonald sang Gershwin and Broadway classics; and Tchaikovsky's *1812 Overture* provided fireworks, figuratively and actually. The stage was deemed to have good acoustics, and a sell-out crowd of approximately 16,800 attended, with 4,800 in the pavilion and another 12,000 or so on the lawn.

The Philharmonic was followed on other nights by Wynton Marsalis, Ashlee Simpson, the Goo-Goo Dolls, Counting Crows, and Crosby, Stills, Nash, and Young. When the Philharmonic's chairman, Paul B. Guenther, who has a home in Sullivan County, was asked whether he foresaw a future for the orchestra at Bethel Woods, he replied, "Step No. 1, let's get through Saturday. The next step might be, let's play two concerts instead of one." As of the time of this writing, the Philharmonic does not have a festival at Bethel Woods.

The July 5 papers carried news of the death of the greatly admired mezzo-soprano Lorraine Hunt Lieberson at the age of fifty-two. She was especially known for her riveting performances of baroque and contemporary music, including works by her husband Peter Lieberson, which he wrote especially for her. On its program of American music the same day, the Philharmonic played Barber's Adagio for Strings in her memory.

The 2006 Parks Concerts were unusual in that they were led entirely by female conductors; furthermore, each program boasted a female violin soloist. One can recall a time when Erica Morini was the sole woman violinist to appear regularly with the Philharmonic and other orchestras (with the exception of Ruth Posselt in Boston). Recent years have seen a profusion of female violinists, starting with Kyung-wha Chung, Anne-Sophie Mutter, and Viktoria Mullova, continuing on to Midori, Sarah Chang, Hilary Hahn, and Julia Fischer, and the two in this instance, Jennifer Koh and Leila Josefowitz.

Similarly, female conductors have been extremely rare until now. When Nadia Boulanger conducted the Philharmonic in 1962, she was the first woman to do so for an entire concert (the pianist Rosalyn Tureck had directed two Bach concertos from the keyboard in 1958). Later, Sarah Caldwell led a series of Parks Concerts and a special program devoted to women composers. As with violinists, the ranks of female conductors have burgeoned in recent years and now include Eve Queler, Victoria Bond, JoAnn Falletta, Simone Young, Ann Manson, Marin Alsop, and, of course, Xian Zhang.

Zhang led off her series with a concert in Cunningham Park, Queens, on July 13, the Central Park performance having been rained out the night before (it was not made up). Both she and Koh made excellent impressions in the Tchaikovsky Violin Concerto. The *Times*'s Vivien Schweitzer, who was new to the paper's staff, contrasted Koh's flamboyance with Zhang's precise gestures. A "decisive" rendition of Dvořák's Eighth Symphony elicited much applause.

The weather was barely kinder to Alsop's Central Park concert on July 18. Steve Smith, also new to the *Times*, began his review by noting that, according to the Philharmonic's program notes, Beethoven's Fifth Symphony was last played in its entirety by the orchestra on October 30, 2003. He then stated that the record remained intact, for the threat of rain obliged Alsop to announce that only the first and fourth movements would be played, much to the audience's disapproval. In the end, the third movement was also given, and then, following the usual fireworks, the rains came. Leila Josefowitz, like Koh a recent graduate of the Curtis Institute of Music, was praised for "a memorable performance" of Prokofieff's Violin Concerto No. 1, which preceded the Beethoven.

On August 4 it was announced that orchestra managers and musicians throughout the profession had reached an agreement that would facilitate the release of live recordings made from concerts. Under its terms, the players would receive greatly reduced up-front payments for their services but would share in future revenues from a recording. The cost of producing recordings would thus be substantially reduced, and the orchestras would own their recordings, which could then be licensed for distribution. Zarin Mehta, who chaired the orchestra committee, characterized the revenue-sharing decision as a breakthrough.

Oestreich began his review of the orchestra's September 13 season-opening gala by noting that the Philharmonic "had observed the fifth anniversary of the Sept. 11 attacks" and had revived for the occasion John Adams's *On the Transmigration of Souls*, which had been commissioned to commemorate the attacks. Oestreich then exclaimed, "In your dreams!" The Philharmonic had done no such thing. Instead, it had offered, with Maazel conducting, a conventional program of Beethoven's *Egmont* Overture and "Eroica" Symphony, with Mozart's Concerto for Two Pianos sandwiched between them. Emanuel Ax and Yefim Bronfman were the excellent soloists, but Oestreich termed the observance "toothless," though he did acknowledge that PBS, with its national telecast, may have had something to say about the program.

Maazel saved a new piece for the first subscription program on September 14, *Dream of Sebastian* by Hans Werner Henze, which Holland said was "one of the most impressive Henze pieces" he had ever heard. It was the work's American premiere, and "no orchestra could play it better" than the Philharmonic. The rest of the program was quite standard, consisting as it did of Bruch's Violin Concerto No. 1, with Itzhak Perlman as the tonally beautiful soloist; Ravel's *Rapsodie espagnole*; and Stravinsky's *Firebird* Suite. The last two items have been released by DGG under its agreement with the Philharmonic.

The Shostakovich centennial celebrations continued with the concerts beginning September 28, when Maazel conducted the Cello Concerto No. 1, which Lynn Harrell played energetically and sympathetically, and the Fifth Symphony, when all is said and done still the most popular of the composer's symphonies. Holland commented that, although Maazel's programming can be criticized, his interpretations may occasionally be labeled perverse, and his relationship to New York's musical life was aloof, the Philharmonic nevertheless sounded "terrific." Further, he felt that the orchestra might be too well paid and comfortable to come to grips with "the naked sensibilities" of Shostakovich's music, but one could hardly call the playing "cold and removed," and we were fortunate to have its treatment of the composer's works in company with the many other points of view it engenders.

Operas in concert form have long been an occasional feature of Philharmonic seasons—Dimitri Mitropoulos's presentations of Alban Berg's *Wozzeck* and Richard Strauss's *Elektra* (not to mention William Steinberg's performance of the latter) and Pierre Boulez's of Stravinsky's *The Nightingale*. On October 5 Maazel offered one of the most magical of all operas, Ravel's *L'enfant et les sortilèges*. The title is difficult to translate. *The Oxford Dictionary of Music* gives it as "The Child and the Spells," which is not very descriptive; other sources have it as "The Bewitched Child." In any case, this one-act *fantaisie lyrique* with libretto by Colette, the tale of a naughty child on whom various household objects (furniture, wallpaper, teacups, etc.) exact their revenge for the abuse they have suffered at his hands, is pure enchantment.

Tommasini praised Maazel's treatment of the score in that he took the story seriously, even though the libretto is laced with much humor. (Opera Quiz question: In what opera is the name of the Japanese actor Sessue Hayakawa mentioned? Answer: *L'enfant et les sortilèges*, sung by the Chinese teacup.) Suzanne Mentzer sang the role of the boy, with a large cast and the New York Choral artists impersonating inanimate objects. Saint-Saëns's Symphony No. 3 ("Organ") concluded the program, the choice of work emphasizing the fact that Avery Fisher Hall still lacked a pipe organ. The substitute on this occasion was a digital organ using the sampled sounds of Aeolian-Skinner organs and a customized loudspeaker system. Tommasini felt it was "close enough to the real thing" for Maazel "to lead a swashbuckling account of this exuberantly Romantic work." Let us hope that this expedient does not persuade the powers that be to forgo the installation of a real organ in the newly renovated hall, whenever that appears.

One of the most famous of all film scores is Prokofieff's music for Sergei Eisenstein's *Alexander Nevsky*, which deals with the defeat in 1242 of the German Knights of the Teutonic Order by the Russian Prince Alexander and his forces. From the complete score Prokofieff extracted a concert cantata of the same name, for chorus, solo mezzo-soprano (in one section), and large orchestra. The work has been performed several times by the Philharmonic and has been recorded under the baton of Thomas Schippers. But on the concerts beginning October 19, the orchestra took the logical next step: the complete score for the film, accompanied by the film itself. Xian Zhang's conducting of this presentation prompted Tommasini to remark that she "seems a bigger talent with every appearance." Meredith Arwady was the affecting soloist in the section called "The Field of the Dead," and the New York Choral Artists sang with tremendous impact.

October 26 brought the news of the death of the pianist Leonid Hambro at the age of eighty-six. Known during the 1960s as the not-so-straight man to the pianist and comedian Victor Borge, he was in fact a brilliant musician who served as the pianist of the New York Philharmonic throughout the 1950s, and for seventeen years before that he was the staff pianist at radio station WQXR in New York. Following his stint with Borge, he was head of the piano faculty at the California Institute of the Arts.

Lorin Maazel surprised the musical world on November 28 by announcing his preference for a conductor to succeed him at the Philharmonic: Daniel Barenboim. Maazel said that Barenboim, who had in June stepped down as music director of the Chicago Symphony Orchestra, had all the right qualifications for the job. Not mentioned was the fact that Barenboim had already said that he did not want another music-director position, although he was close to the Philharmonic's Zarin Mehta, who had been in charge of the Chicago Symphony's summer home at the Ravinia Festival. The Philharmonic's management was taken aback by Maazel's announcement, though the public relations director, Eric Latzky, stated that the selection process for a new music director was "proceeding in an orderly and a timely way."

Equally taken aback, though flattered, was Barenboim himself, who had not been consulted by Maazel prior to the announcement. According to him, the possibility of another permanent position with an American orchestra was the furthest thing from his mind, and it would be inappropriate for him to accept or reject the proposal: "Nobody has offered me the job, so why should I say yes or no?"

An extremely interesting program involving two soloists was offered by Maazel on the concerts beginning November 30. The first half presented the great pianist Leon Fleisher, who had recovered the use of his right hand after forty years of being incapacitated by focal dystonia, a condition forcing him to concentrate on works for the left hand. After beginning the program with an exquisite rendition of Mozart's Concerto No. 12 in A Major, K. 414, he continued with a virtually unknown piece by Paul Hindemith: the Piano Music with Orchestra, Op. 29, the score of which was lost until 2004. This was one of many works commissioned by the pianist Paul Wittgenstein, who had lost his right arm in World War I. Wittgenstein, who disliked and did not perform most of the works he commissioned, rather selfishly kept Hindemith's score under wraps, thus preventing anyone else from playing it. "A fantastic work," Kozinn called it, and one that Fleisher dispatched with ease. Roussel's *Bacchus et Ariane* Suite No. 2 opened the second half, the only work on the program the orchestra had to itself. It was followed by "a searing performance" of the final scene from Richard Strauss's *Salome*. Nancy Gustafson was the dramatic soprano soloist, with brilliant and powerful support from the orchestra.

Bramwell Tovey, of the Summertime Classics, did winter duty by conducting the concerts beginning December 6, offering in the second half excerpts from Tchaikovsky's *Nutcracker* both in the original version and in the arrangement by Duke Ellington and Billy Strayhorn that Kurt Masur had programmed a few seasons back. Wynton Marsalis and the Lincoln Center Jazz Orchestra took part, though Kozinn felt it would have been more effective to play each version straight through, rather than alternating movements. Of interest on the first half was the Symphony No. 2 by Christopher Rouse, an energetic and tuneful piece given "an eloquent performance" by the Philharmonic. Copland's *El salón México* was given a surprisingly tepid performance.

In 2006 the Philharmonic instituted a new series called Hear and Now, hosted by the composer Steven Stucky, in which a work, frequently a new one, is discussed and analyzed, usually with the composer present. Questions from the audience are taken, and then the piece is played, in a kind of preview performance, before its official premiere on a subscription concert. On December 13 the Finnish composer Kaija Saariaho's *Adriana Songs* was given the Hear and Now treatment the night before its official American premiere. Adapted from Saariaho's opera *Adriana Mater*, with a libretto by Amin Maalouf, the dark-hued but haunting work was conducted expertly by David Robertson and sung passionately by the mezzo-soprano Patricia Bardon in her Philharmonic debut. The official premiere on December 14 shared the program with Sibelius's seldom-heard tone poem *Night Ride and Sunrise* and two works of Debussy, the Symphonic Fragments from *The Martyrdom of St. Sebastian* and *La mer*, the latter in "a knockout performance," according to Tommasini.

Zubin Mehta arrived for two weeks of concerts beginning January 4, 2007. Only two works made up his first program, Beethoven's Violin Concerto, with Pinchas Zukerman, and *The Rite of Spring*. Having received so much critical abuse during his tenure as music director, he must have felt vindicated by the response to this program. *The Rite*, according to Kozinn, was given "a virtuosic performance," the kind of rendition one hoped for in vain in earlier times. There was a suppleness to the playing not only in the work's climactic sections, but in the quieter moments as well. For all the score's familiarity, Mehta succeeded in making it "all the more dramatic and shocking." Mehta and the orchestra were also lauded for their support in the concerto, though Kozinn found Zukerman's playing of the solo line to be "often generic."

Praise for Mehta was not limited to his first week, but carried over into the second, when Tommasini wrote of a "distinguished account" of Bruckner's Seventh Symphony, conducted "from memory with unfailing attentiveness and stamina." (Stamina is needed for this seventy-minute score.) The several movements, with their different moods, "emerged as parts of an overall architectonic conception of the work," everything in proper balance. The Bruckner was the second of two pieces on this program, which opened with Elgar's haunting Cello Concerto, superlatively played by the young American cellist Alisa Weilerstein, with whom Mehta and the orchestra collaborated elegantly.

The year 2007 marked the fiftieth anniversary of the death of Arturo Toscanini. A year earlier an orchestra of young musicians, the Symphonica Toscanini, had been founded in Rome, and it was now making an American tour with Lorin Maazel, who had been selected as its music director. On January 16, the date of Toscanini's death, the group performed a joint concert with the New York Philharmonic in Avery Fisher Hall, the program of which ostensibly included works associated with the maestro. The Philharmonic opened with Richard Strauss's *Don Juan*, followed by the Symphonica Toscanini in Respighi's *Pines of Rome*. So far, so good. After a group of operatic arias sung by the bass René Pape, the two orchestras combined for what Midgette described as "a powerhouse reading" of Tchaikovsky's *Francesca da Rimini*. But Toscanini never played that particular score. *Romeo and Juliet*, yes; *Francesca*, no.

One contemporary Italian conductor in the Toscanini tradition is Riccardo Muti, who returned to the Philharmonic for two weeks beginning January 18. Called "one of the towering musicians of our time" by Tommasini, Muti, at least in New York, likes to program works that are slightly off the beaten path, or perhaps even more than slightly. The major such work of his first week was Scriabin's Symphony No. 3 ("The Divine Poem"), a piece influenced by the composer's great involvement with theosophy. Its three connected movements bear the titles "Struggles," "Sensual Pleasure," and "Divine Play"; the entire sequence lasts more than fifty minutes. Somehow, Muti was able to make the score sound "almost lucid." Earlier in the program the Russian violinist Vadim Repin had given a stunning account of Tchaikovsky's Violin Concerto.

For his second week Muti unearthed a work that is played even less often than the Scriabin: the Piano Concerto No. 2 in B-flat Minor by Giuseppe Martucci, one of the few Italian composers of his time (1856–1909) to concentrate on instrumental music rather than opera. This concerto had last appeared on a Philharmonic program in 1911, but Americans became fairly well acquainted with Martucci's music during the life of the NBC Symphony Orchestra, for Toscanini championed the composer with performances of his two symphonies, the Piano Concerto No. 2, and several other works. The German pianist Gerhard Oppitz was Muti's effective soloist in a brilliant display piece worthy of greater exposure.

Muti concluded his program with the seldom-heard ballet music from Verdi's *Macbeth* and the third symphonic poem of Respighi's Roman trilogy, *Feste Romane* (Roman Festivals). The composer pulls out all the stops in this piece, and the Philharmonic played it "at full throttle," according to Kozinn. A point in favor of Kozinn's writing in general is that, when discussing a piece such as *Feste Romane*, he does not write condescendingly about it or the composer, as so many critics do. Rather, he takes the piece seriously, at face value, describing it and the performance in such a way as to imply that he actually enjoys it.

The Finnish conductor Esa-Pekka Salonen, who recently completed an eighteen-year tenure as music director of the Los Angeles Philharmonic, has developed into a significant composer. On February 1 he led the New York Philharmonic in the world premiere of his Piano Concerto, featuring the work's dedicatee, Yefim Bronfman, as the soloist. With this piece Salonen demonstrated that he could absorb the techniques and styles of composers whose music he had conducted in his career and produce something uniquely his own. Bronfman played it with full command of its many difficulties, the performance and the work itself eliciting a great ovation from the audience.

Having provoked critical disdain for daring to present a Beethoven festival a few years before, the Philharmonic now embarked on a Brahms series. There was a difference, however, in that the Beethoven concerts were given in a concentrated time period; the Brahms programs, on the other hand, would be spread out from February through the end of the season. Some of the critics questioned whether such a schedule could legitimately be called a festival, as the Philharmonic had dubbed it. (In 1951 Bruno Walter conducted a Brahms cycle of all the symphonies, concertos, overtures, as well as the *Haydn Variations* and a few Hungarian Dances, in a four-week period.) Maazel and the orchestra began the series with two programs in the week beginning February 14, the first consisting of the seldom-played Serenade No. 1 in D Major and the much-played Piano Concerto No. 1 in D Minor, with the superb Emanuel Ax as soloist.

Holland complained of "so-called festivals celebrating composers already so celebrated that they don't need festivals in the first place." Brahms's two serenades and the First Piano Concerto alike were his early attempts at writing a symphony.

Holland astutely noted that, although we could use more Furtwänglers and Toscaninis in our lives, and that the spirits of neither were seen or heard at this concert, "there is also room for the graceful, literate music making that did appear."

The concerts of February 16 and 19 brought the natural sequel to the first program, the Serenade No. 2 in A Major and the Piano Concerto No. 2 in B-flat Major, with Ax again the indefatigable soloist. The A Major Serenade is notable for the absence of violins, trumpets, and timpani from its instrumentation, lending it a relatively warmer, mellower tone. Kozinn mentioned the stamina required for a pianist to play the two Brahms Concertos, the longest in the standard repertoire, in a single week, but in 1964 Arthur Rubinstein, who was close to eighty at the time, played both of them in one concert. Ax, Maazel, and the orchestra were praised by both critics for the opening salvo of the "festival."

Trombone concertos do not appear frequently on symphonic concerts, principally because there are so few of them. One was added to the meager list on February 22 with the world premiere of a concerto by the Pulitzer Prize–winning American composer Melinda Wagner. Midgette wrote of a "vital and fresh" piece "strikingly" well written for the orchestra. The Philharmonic's principal trombonist, Joseph Alessi, was the rich-toned soloist. Gershwin's *An American in Paris* followed ingratiatingly, just as it did in 1993 when it followed Christopher Rouse's Trombone Concerto.

In 2007 Kurt Masur turned eighty, and the orchestra celebrated with a party for him following his concert on February 28 (though his actual birthday was not until July), a party that doubled as a fund-raiser for the International Mendelssohn Foundation in Leipzig. Masur is president of the foundation, which plans to publish the first complete edition of the composer's works. The sole representation of Mendelssohn on the program was the opening *Hebrides Overture*. The Sibelius Violin Concerto followed in a sensitive and assured performance by the twenty-two-year-old Armenian violinist Sergey Khachatryan, who had won the Sibelius Competition in Helsinki in 2000. Masur concluded with Tchaikovsky's "Pathétique" Symphony, of which he has long been a distinguished interpreter. Kozinn described his performance as "gripping."

The Philharmonic took another excursion to the world of Broadway with four staged performances of *My Fair Lady* on March 7–10. Actors from television and the stage played the leading roles: Kelsey Grammer (star of TV's *Frasier*) as Henry Higgins, Charles Kimbrough (from *Murphy Brown*) as Colonel Pickering, and Brian Dennehy (memorably seen on Broadway as Willy Loman) as Alfred P. Doolittle. The *Times*'s theater critic, Charles Isherwood, was very enthusiastic about the presentation, reserving special praise for the performer of Eliza Doolittle, Kelli

O'Hara, who had been seen on Broadway in *The Light in the Piazza* and *The Pajama Game*. This was her first Eliza, and Isherwood ventured to hope it would not be her last. To have the Lerner and Loewe score played by the Philharmonic, with Rob Fisher conducting, was a special treat. Also in the cast were the tenor Philippe Castagner as Freddy Eynsford-Hill and, in an ironic bit of casting, Marni Nixon as Mrs. Higgins. Nixon was the voice of many actresses in Hollywood movie musicals, including that of Audrey Hepburn in *My Fair Lady*. Yet, as Mrs. Higgins, she had not one note to sing.

On March 14 it was announced that the Philharmonic would tour Europe May 3–18, playing in Warsaw, Budapest, Vienna, Frankfurt, Cologne, Paris, and Luxembourg. Maazel would conduct, and the repertoire would concentrate on Brahms. Gone are the days when an American orchestra traveling abroad would take along at least one American composition.

Alan Gilbert conducted an unusual program beginning with the March 15 concert. At least two generations ago it was common to hear orchestral transcriptions of Bach organ works, particularly those of Leopold Stokowski, on symphonic concerts. Even at that time, Stokowski's transcriptions were denounced by many critics as not in the spirit of Bach, garish, even vulgar. But Stokowski had been an organist, and it was his expressed desire to bring Bach's music to audiences that would not normally hear it, for those who attended symphony concerts were rarely found at organ recitals. The same holds true today. However, since Stokowski's time his transcriptions (and those of others, such as Eugene Ormandy) have gone out of fashion and are rarely encountered today. And yet, here was Alan Gilbert opening his Philharmonic program with the most famous of all Stokowski's transcriptions, that of the great Toccata and Fugue in D Minor. Yet the roof of Avery Fisher Hall did not cave in, the orchestra seemed to enjoy playing it, and the audience seemed to enjoy listening to it. And here was the critic, Kozinn, not objecting to it, finding it "colorful . . . Bach to splash around in."

Gilbert opened the second half of the program with another Bach transcription, the Ricercar from *The Musical Offering* as orchestrated by Anton Webern. Critics have never objected to this version. Webern was a respected twelve-tone composer of the Second Viennese School, so of course it is acceptable for him to arrange Bach—but not the glamorous and controversial Stokowski. Webern's orchestration is ascetic, even skeletal, while Stokowski's is pure Technicolor (and was used, after all, in Walt Disney's *Fantasia*).

In between the two Bach pieces came the 1992 Violin Concerto by György Ligeti, with Christian Tetzlaff as the accomplished soloist. As Kozinn aptly described it, Ligeti's music "is couched in a language just beyond the bounds of the

Western musical vocabulary." (At the conclusion of a Philharmonic performance of his Cello Concerto in 1971, the cellist, Siegfried Palm, fingered the cello and moved his bow above the strings, producing no sound at all.) The final work on the program was the most infrequently performed of the Schumann symphonies, No. 3 in E-flat Major ("Rhenish"), somewhat heavy in concept, but played passionately nonetheless.

When Sir Colin Davis appears with the Philharmonic, the repertoire is often purely classical, as it was on March 22: Haydn's Symphony No. 85 in B-flat Major ("La Reine"); Mozart's Piano Concerto No. 19 in F Major, K. 459, played winningly by Mitsuko Uchida; and Schubert's Symphony No. 4 in C Minor ("Tragic"). No adherence to modern ideas of period performance practice for Sir Colin, but rather cleaving to the venerable style that has come down through great interpreters of the past, namely sensible tempos and warm, eloquent phrasing. The following week Radu Lupu was heard elegantly in Mozart's last piano concerto, No. 27 in B-flat Major, K. 595, and Davis, getting away from the classical style, led a bracing account of Sibelius's *Four Legends of Lemminkainen* (also known as the *Lemminkainen Suite*), the Philharmonic's first performance of the complete work.

On April 4 the *Times* ran an article by Daniel J. Wakin about the increasing number of musicians from China who were making their way to Western conservatories and then orchestras. This was followed on April 8 by an article by the same author profiling the Philharmonic's new principal oboist, the twenty-six-year-old Liang Wang. It detailed Wang's studies at the Curtis Institute of Music, where his teacher was Richard Woodhams, principal oboe of the Philadelphia Orchestra; his winning the principal position with the Richmond Symphony in 2003 but not showing up because he had won the equivalent position with the San Francisco Ballet; and his subsequent move to the San Francisco Symphony as associate principal, where he remained for all of two weeks before joining the Cincinnati Symphony as principal oboe. After one year in Cincinnati he was offered the Philharmonic position, which he began in the 2006–7 season.

On April 9 it was announced that the next music director of the Los Angeles Philharmonic, the successor of the highly regarded Esa-Pekka Salonen, would be the twenty-six-year-old Venezuelan dynamo Gustavo Dudamel. The selection of Dudamel was considered daring in the classical music world, not least because of his youth. (Of course, his tenure was not due to begin until 2009, when he would be a veteran of twenty-eight.) But Salonen was only thirty-one when he began, and Zubin Mehta was just twenty-six.

Another Finnish conductor, Sakari Oramo, was in charge of the Philharmonic's concerts beginning April 12, on which the Russian violinist Lisa Batiashvili was heard in an assertive account of Shostakovich's First Violin Concerto. As if to demonstrate that Sir Colin Davis does not have a monopoly on Sibelius, and on seldom-heard Sibelius at that, Oramo programmed the enigmatic Sixth Symphony and the coldly austere *Tapiola*. In Finnish mythology Tapio is the god of the forests, and this tone poem includes a graphic depiction of a freezing winter storm, with its howling wind (but without the use of a wind machine). Oramo conducted the two works as if to the manner born, which, of course, he was.

On April 15 Tommasini, citing the hiring of Dudamel in Los Angeles, as well as of David Robertson in St. Louis, Marin Alsop in Baltimore, and the Dutchman Jaap van Zweden in Dallas, practically pleaded with the Philharmonic to hire a young, innovative conductor as its next music director. He noted that the orchestra's musicians had recently been impressed with Riccardo Chailly and Ludovic Morlot and felt that Alan Gilbert would be "a refreshing choice." Once again Riccardo Muti's name cropped up, but although he admired the conductor, Tommasini felt the Philharmonic did not need yet another elder statesman in charge.

The death of the conductor Walter Hendl, at the age of ninety, was noted on April 16. Hendl had been the Philharmonic's assistant conductor from 1945 to 1949, when he became music director of the Dallas Symphony, after which he was associate conductor of the Chicago Symphony during Fritz Reiner's tenure as well as artistic director of the Ravinia Festival. From 1964 to 1972 he was director of the Eastman School of Music in Rochester, and then music director of the Erie Philharmonic in Pennsylvania until 1990.

An announcement on April 25 told of the Philharmonic's plans to add a position at the top of its masthead, that of principal conductor. The idea was that the music director would lead twelve to fourteen weeks of concerts, the principal conductor another eight to ten weeks. The latter would exercise more control than a principal guest conductor, but the music director would still have the final say on musical matters. The arrangement is reminiscent of the final years of Bernstein's tenure, when William Steinberg held the title of principal guest conductor and led twelve weeks of the season, which, in 1967–68, was one week more than Bernstein led.

Another death was announced on April 28, that of Mstislav Rostropovich at the age of eighty. Arguably the greatest cellist of the second half of the twentieth century and an intensely emotional conductor, particularly of works by Russian composers, he had appeared often with the Philharmonic in both capacities. The repertoire for the cello was greatly enriched by works that had been written for him by such composers as Prokofieff, Shostakovich, and Britten, among many others. As a conductor he was best known, at least in the United States, as music director of Washington's National Symphony Orchestra, which he led from 1977 to 1994.

He was also well known for his political stance against the Soviet government, which revoked his citizenship in 1978. It was restored in 1990 after the collapse of Communism.

The Brahms Festival concluded with the concerts beginning May 31, following May's European tour. On that date Maazel led the Third and Fourth Symphonies, and Kozinn was not happy with the performances, to put it mildly. First of all, he again questioned the validity of a festival spread out over such a long period of time. He then wondered how neglected those two symphonies would have been had they not been scheduled at that time. The Third had last been played by the Philharmonic in 2003, the Fourth in 2005. Coming up were the *Haydn Variations* and *A German Requiem*, last heard in 2006 and 2001. The performances of the symphonies were "coldly unemotional," replete with "magnified dynamics" and "vulgar overstatement." Technically, the renditions were admirable, save for "a few braying horn notes" in the Third and some brief imprecision in the Fourth.

Anne Midgette reviewed the final program of the series, given on June 5. The *German Requiem* "smacked of routine," which was ironic when remembering Kurt Masur's 2001 performance in the wake of the September 11 attacks. The soloists were the soprano Celena Shafer and the baritone Matthias Goerne, with the New York Choral Artists. In Maazel's hands, Brahms the Romantic, as the festival was called, emerged as Brahms the Lugubrious: "heavy, ponderous, and dark, like the furniture of the period."

Riccardo Muti returned on June 7, joined by Lang Lang for Beethoven's "Emperor" Concerto—a peculiar combination, according to Kozinn, that resulted in the dullest possible "Emperor." At times the conductor and orchestra seemed to be playing a different piece than the soloist. As is his wont, Muti provided a rarity on the second half, a concert performance of the one-act opera *Sancta Susanna* by Paul Hindemith. This 1921 score about a novice whose discovery of her sexuality throws her convent into turmoil was played by the Philharmonic "with an appealing ferocity," according to Kozinn. Tatiana Serjan and Brigitte Pinter were the principal singers, with the hard-working New York Choral Artists.

Mahler again concluded a Philharmonic season, this time the Seventh Symphony on June 20. Holland wrote of Maazel's holding "late Romantic effusiveness at arm's length," but also of Deborah Voigt's "commanding voice" in a group of Richard Strauss songs that opened the concerts. Five retirees were honored: the violinist Kenneth Gordon, the cellist Nancy Donaruma, the trombonist Donald Harwood, the horn player L. William Kuyper, and the orchestra librarian Thad Marciniak. Each spoke a few words, and Holland wrote of how normal these people sounded, as opposed to those who expound on "the mysteries of art" and "do much less."

There was sadness within and beyond the world of classical music at the news on July 3, 2007, of the death of Beverly Sills, at the age of seventy-eight. One of the world's great coloratura sopranos, with her ebullient personality she did much to popularize classical music, and opera in particular, through her many television appearances with Johnny Carson, Carol Burnett, and others. She was also the charming host of *Live from Lincoln Center*. A mainstay of the New York City Opera from 1955 to 1979, where she became known for her performances in the bel canto repertoire and Handel, she became director of the company in 1979, holding that post for ten years. She had made her belated Metropolitan Opera debut in 1975. Sills retired as chairwoman of the board of Lincoln Center in 2002, after serving for eight years. But no sooner did she "retire" than the Metropolitan Opera lured her to become its chairwoman. Not least among her many attributes, both musical and personal, was her ability as a fund-raiser par excellence. The flags at Lincoln Center flew at half-mast in honor of Sills, and several of the halls dimmed their lights in tribute. For its Summertime Classics program on July 3, the Philharmonic considered playing Barber's Adagio for Strings in her memory, but because Sills exuded such happiness and good cheer, the Overture to *Candide* was selected instead, the orchestra holding with tradition in a conductorless performance.

CHAPTER 23

2007–8

THE DECISION MADE

The big news for the Philharmonic, eagerly awaited in New York and elsewhere, was the announcement in the *Times* on July 18, 2007, that Alan Gilbert had been appointed the orchestra's next music director, to succeed Lorin Maazel in 2009. Much was made of the fact, and rightly so, that he would be the first native New Yorker to hold the post, and that he was the son of two Philharmonic violinists, Michael Gilbert, who had retired in 2001, and Yoko Takebe, still a member of the orchestra. Thus he had grown up around the Philharmonic, attending rehearsals and concerts, and had been known by many of the musicians since he was a young boy. Forty years old at the time of the announcement, he had been chief conductor of Sweden's Royal Stockholm Philharmonic Orchestra since 2000, as well as music director of the Santa Fe Opera for three summer seasons. He began appearing as a guest conductor of the New York Philharmonic in 2001 and by the time of his appointment had conducted the orchestra in thirty-one concerts. The orchestra's chairman, Paul B. Guenther, said that the choice was "the right thing for the orchestra at this time in this city." Orchestra members quoted in the article were without exception enthusiastic about the news.

An article on July 19 by Tommasini began with what he said would be "some sober critical comments" on Gilbert's appointment. Those comments were "Hooray! At last!" He found the unpretentious Gilbert "a refreshing choice" and noted that he would be the first music director since Bernstein and Boulez "to have an infectious enthusiasm" for new music.

Also announced at the same time was that Riccardo Muti would have, at his request, an untitled position with the Philharmonic, serving as an unofficial principal guest conductor leading six to eight weeks a season. Apparently the administration had reconsidered the plan to appoint a principal conductor as well as a music director. The only reservation expressed in the press was that Gilbert, though a superb musician and conductor, was not yet a "household name." Would he be able to attract audiences to the Philharmonic? His supporters, and there were many, felt that this was not an issue, that his relatively young age would help to draw in younger listeners, and that he would indeed become a household name very quickly.

The other big news of the summer, though mentioned only briefly in the *Times* on August 14, was that the Philharmonic had received an invitation from the Republic of North Korea to perform in the capital city of Pyongyang. The orchestra's spokesman, Eric Latzky, said this possibility would be given the same consideration as any other invitation.

Maazel's sixth season as music director, that of 2007–8, began on September 18 with the usual opening night gala, an all-Dvořák program with Yo-Yo Ma as the soloist in the Cello Concerto. So great was the interest in this concert that the Philharmonic opened the Tuesday morning dress rehearsal to the public free of charge. Even then, several hundred people were turned away, but everyone, both inside and outside the hall, was given a discount coupon for a future concert. Yo-Yo Ma, playing "with more maturity, breadth and insight than ever," according to Tommasini, gave a magnificent account of a work he had played hundreds of times. Maazel bracketed the concerto with the rambunctious *Carnival Overture* and the heartfelt and buoyant Symphony No. 7 in D Minor. The orchestra was in marvelous form throughout the nationally televised concert, the symphony authoritatively and elegantly conducted by Maazel. Tommasini did wonder if a new work, perhaps by an American, could have been played instead of the symphony, but noted that such scores would be coming during the season.

Having presented a Brahms Festival the previous season, Maazel now programmed a series entitled The Tchaikovsky Experience for the first three weeks of the season. His thesis was that Tchaikovsky is a "very well-known but not completely understood composer." He also objected to the prevailing tendency to perform the composer in an overly emotional manner. The first subscription program, on September 19, was technically not part of the festival, for it included only one Tchaikovsky work, the Symphony No. 2 in C Minor ("Little Russian"), probably the least emotional of the composer's symphonies, which makes its point best in a straightforward performance. And that is how it was given here, in a brilliant rendition. On the same program the Russian violinist Lisa Batiashvili gave a romantically oriented account of the Beethoven Concerto, a work that can certainly withstand that approach.

The Tchaikovsky Festival began in earnest the following week, on September 26, in which one of the composer's most popular and one of his least-played works were juxtaposed: the Piano Concerto No. 1, with the twenty-eight-year-old Macedonian pianist Simon Trpčeski , and the Symphony No. 1 in G Minor ("Winter Dreams"), which, according to Tommasini, was given a "vibrant and brilliant" performance. (It used to be said that Tchaikovsky had composed three symphonies, Nos. 4, 5, and 6.)

On September 27 it was reported that a new labor agreement had been reached between the Philharmonic and Local 802. There does not appear to have been any tension or suspense in the negotiations, and the announcement was fairly perfunctory in tone. The new contract was for five years, during which time the annual salary would rise from $113,360 to $140,400, with pensions rising to $70,000. No mention was made of how these figures compared with those of other orchestras.

By October 5 it was clear that Philharmonic officials were seriously considering the possibility of a concert in North Korea in February, at the end of an already-planned tour of China. The state department was encouraging the North Korea visit, and Zarin Mehta, Eric Latzky, and Fiona Simon, chair of the players' committee, had already left for Beijing and would be in Pyongyang on October 6 to ascertain the appropriateness of several concert halls, check out the hotels, discuss travel arrangements, and, of course, meet with North Korean officials. At the time it was hoped that the Philharmonic's visit would further a lessening of tensions between the United States and North Korea that had already begun with an agreement limiting North Korea's nuclear capability.

Meanwhile, the Tchaikovsky Festival continued. Kozinn did not care for Maazel's performance of the popular Fifth Symphony, which he felt was poorly balanced in the outer movements, with the brass allowed, even encouraged, to overpower the string sections. Some excerpts from *Swan Lake* demonstrated how fine the strings and woodwinds are when they are allowed to be heard properly. The *Variations on a Rococo Theme* employed the talents of the German cellist Johannes Moser, whose playing was praised for its warmth and elegance.

Upon returning from North Korea, the Philharmonic's delegation reported favorably on the possibility of the orchestra's playing there. First, though, they had to convince the musicians. A group of players was opposed to the trip, which they felt would legitimize a regime that had been accused of human rights violations, including starving hundreds of thousands of its citizens. Experts on Korea said that such a concert would be a major publicity coup for North Korea.

The conductor James Conlon, music director of the Los Angeles Opera and the Ravinia Festival, has undertaken a project of performing music by composers who had been suppressed by the Nazi regime, among them Viktor Ullmann, Erwin Schulhoff, and Alexander Zemlinsky, the teacher and brother-in-law of Arnold Schoenberg. On October 18 Conlon presented the Philharmonic's first performance of Zemlinsky's one-act opera *A Florentine Tragedy*, based on a play by Oscar Wilde. Zemlinsky, who ended his days in Larchmont, New York, in 1942, wrote in a late-romantic style influenced by Richard Strauss and Mahler. Vivien Schweitzer wrote of "a terrific performance" of the work, with the singers Anthony Dean Griffey, James Johnson, and Tatiana Pavlovskaya, the latter two in their Philharmonic debut. Preceding Zemlinsky on the program was Beethoven's Piano Concerto No. 2 in B-flat Major, played gracefully and with humor by Jonathan Biss.

While still considering the North Korean proposal, the Philharmonic announced the itinerary for its Asian tour, which would take place February 11–24: Taipei and Kaohsiung in Taiwan, and Hong Kong, Beijing, and Shanghai in the People's Republic of China. Lorin Maazel would conduct, with Xian Zhang sharing the podium with him in Hong Kong on February 18.

On November 1 the Russian-born conductor Semyon Bychkov, music director of the Cologne Radio Symphony Orchestra, appeared as guest with the Philharmonic. (Remember when there were radio symphony orchestras in the United States? Think NBC, CBS.). Although his program included pieces by Dutilleux (*Métaboles*) and Martinů (Concerto for Two Pianos, with Katia and Marielle Labèque as the irrepressible soloists), the major work was Rachmaninoff's Symphony No. 2 in E Minor. Holland considered Bychkov "just what the doctor ordered" to cure the orchestra's recently acquired "repressed-emotion syndrome." Of interest is the fact that, in his only previous Philharmonic appearance in 1984, Bychkov conducted the same Rachmaninoff symphony. Had he not learned any other pieces since then? Recorded evidence proves otherwise.

Having given several Broadway musicals in recent years, the Philharmonic honored the eightieth birthday of one of Broadway's great performers, the lyric soprano Barbara Cook, in two special sold-out concerts on November 19 and 20 (a third date was added in January). With her aptly named musical director, Lee Musiker, conducting, she offered a gamut of Broadway show tunes, from happy to sad and back again, according to the *Times*'s Stephen Holden, "with a tenderness and honesty that could break your heart and mend it all at once."

The Philharmonic debut of the year, if not of several years, was that of Gustavo Dudamel as guest conductor on November 29. At age twenty-six already slated to become music director of the Los Angeles Philharmonic in 2009, he was the most hyped conductor in classical music. He had made his New York debut to great effect two weeks before with the Simón Bolívar Youth Orchestra of Venezuela. But that was his own orchestra, the one he had grown up with, the one he had taught and had taught him. How would he fare with the tough New York Philharmonic?

Very well indeed, as it turned out. In a program consisting of the *Sinfonia India* by Carlos Chávez, Dvořák's Violin Concerto with Gil Shaham an inspired soloist, and Prokofieff's Fifth Symphony, Dudamel clearly inspired the players through "the boundless joy and intensity of his music-making," according to Tommasini. The critic contrasted Dudamel's episodic interpretation of the Prokofieff symphony to that of Bernstein, who approached every score with the mind of a composer, thus making clear a work's architecture.

In a rare gesture, Dudamel was allowed to use one of Bernstein's batons, three of which reside safely in the Philharmonic's archives. These treasures are almost never lent to guest conductors. It was later revealed that the baton had broken just before the end of the final performance. The orchestra's archivist, Barbara Haws, assured the public that the broken tip had been retrieved and the two pieces returned. She would reattach them, she said, adding, "It's now taken on a new dimension, this little baton has."

The *Times* of December 3 told of the death of the classical-music record and television producer David Oppenheim at the age of eighty-five. Trained as a clarinetist, from 1950 to 1959 he was the director of the Masterworks division of Columbia Records, working with Bernstein, Walter, and Szell, among others. In television he helped to produce the series *Leonard Bernstein and the New York Philharmonic*. From 1969 to 1991 he was dean of New York University's School of the Arts, which eventually became the Tisch School of the Arts after Oppenheim secured a major donation from Laurence A. Tisch and Preston Robert Tisch.

On December 10 it became official: the New York Philharmonic had agreed to play in North Korea in February, the first visit by any American cultural group to that country. But controversy still dogged the planned trip. There were still orchestra members who opposed it. The arts critic Terry Teachout wrote on the *Wall Street Journal*'s online opinion page that the trip would "lend legitimacy to a despicable regime." Richard V. Allen and Chuck Downs, both of whom were board members of the United States Committee for Human Rights in North Korea (Allen had also served as President Reagan's national security adviser), wrote in the *New York Times* of October 28 that "it would be a mistake to hand Kim Jong-il a propaganda coup."

On the other hand, Ambassador Christopher R. Hill, who was also the assistant secretary of state for East Asian and Pacific affairs, while acknowledging that theoretically any kind of opening would appear to legitimize the North Korean government, said that, as far as "bringing North Korea out of its shell" was concerned, no positive effect had been achieved by not opening up. He further stated that the visit would bring about a shift in how the North Koreans view us, which could be helpful as we continued negotiations over nuclear weapons. Letters both pro and con appeared in the *Times* of December 14, one of them from the conductor Bernard Rubenstein congratulating the Philharmonic on its forthcoming trip, but despairing that our government had not achieved an open cultural policy with Cuba.

In negotiations between the Philharmonic and North Korean officials, the orchestra put forward several conditions: foreign journalists would be present, there would be a nationwide broadcast of the concert, acoustical adjustments would be made to the auditorium (the East Pyongyang National Theater), the eight Philharmonic musicians of Korean origin would not be subjected to difficulties, and the orchestra would play "The Star-Spangled Banner." This would not be the first time the Philharmonic had played in a totalitarian country: after the orchestra toured the Soviet Union in 1959, it made later visits there as well.

The Philharmonic began its first concert of 2008 on January 3, with a tribute to its associate principal horn player, Jerome A. Ashby, who had died of prostate cancer on December 26 at the age of fifty-one. One of the few African American musicians to be found in American symphony orchestras, Ashby had been a member of the Philharmonic since 1979 and had taught at Juilliard, the Manhattan School, the Curtis Institute, and the Aspen Music Festival. Zarin Mehta spoke of how Ashby had become particularly fond of a recording of the Evening Prayer from Humperdinck's *Hansel and Gretel*. Ashby's portrait was then projected over the stage while the orchestra's brass players expressively intoned the prayer.

Two soloists occupied center stage that evening, first the youthful violinist Viviane Hagner in the Mendelssohn Concerto. Kozinn had good things to say about her, finding her playing spirited and flexible, with a full and well-projected tone. Appropriately for a program that had honored Jerome Ashby, the second soloist was the principal horn player, Philip Myers, who offered Mozart's Concerto No. 2 in E-flat Major, K. 417. Kozinn, often critical of the horns, stated that Myers was "at his best" in a "rich, virtually flawless rendering" of the concerto. His only complaint—and here it must be remembered that Mozart's accompanying orchestra is very slight—was that Myers "overpowered the orchestra." Maazel, who had begun the program with an appropriately mercurial account of the seventeen-year-old Mendelssohn's *Midsummer Night's Dream* Overture, concluded it with a thrilling if at times exaggerated account of Elgar's *Enigma Variations*.

From time to time a Philharmonic music director can be found in the orchestra pit of the Metropolitan Opera. Mitropoulos conducted Richard Strauss's *Salome* and Verdi's *Un ballo in maschera* during the 1954–55 season and returned to the Met each season until his death in 1960, even after he had ceased to be the Philharmonic's music director. In 1964 Bernstein made his Met debut conducting Verdi's *Falstaff* but did not appear there at any other time during his Philharmonic tenure. (He led Mascagni's *Cavalleria rusticana* and Bizet's *Carmen* in later seasons.) Although Zubin Mehta frequently conducted at the Met, his engagements there preceded his time at the Philharmonic. When Maazel led five performances of Wagner's *Die Walküre* in January and February 2008, it had been forty-five years since his last appearances in the house. He received tremendous ovations from the audience and much praise from Tommasini for the performance on January 7.

A typical day for a conductor doing such double duty was Thursday, January 3, which began with a Philharmonic rehearsal from 10:00 a.m. to 12:15 p.m. After barely time for lunch, there was a rehearsal at the Met from 1:00 to 3:25, followed by a meeting with the singers and the musical staff. Following a short rest at home, Maazel was back at Avery Fisher Hall for a Philharmonic concert at 7:30. At the time he was seventy-seven years old.

Riccardo Muti returned on January 17, when he and the highly regarded Norwegian pianist Leif Ove Andsnes collaborated in what Tommasini termed "a vibrant, brilliant performance" of the Brahms Piano Concerto No. 2 in B-flat Major. Muti, long a champion of the music of Scriabin, also directed an appropriately "ecstatic performance" of the *Poem of Ecstasy*. The chemistry that had been established between Muti and the Philharmonic continued.

The 2007–8 season included several works by the Italian composer Luciano Berio, who had died in 2003. His most celebrated work, the *Sinfonia*, had been commissioned by the Philharmonic, and was given its world premiere, in its original four-movement form, by the orchestra on October 10, 1968, with the composer conducting on a program otherwise led by Bernstein. Maazel revived the score on January 30, its first performance by the orchestra in twenty years. Also taking part was the group Synergy Vocals. Commentary by the composer Steven Stucky was heard first, a shortened version of the presentation normally given in the Philharmonic's Hear and Now series. The commentary was interspersed with musical examples by the singers and the orchestra. Tommasini found the actual performance so "mesmerizing" that, untypically, the Brahms Fourth Symphony that closed the program seemed "an afterthought."

As the Philharmonic prepared for its visit to North Korea, it was reported on February 7 that the Pyongyang concert on February 26 would be shown in New York on WNET, Channel 13, and two days later on PBS, the result of an unusual collaboration between ABC News and WNET. ABC's Bob Woodruff would provide commentary. It was also announced that the orchestra's program would be Wagner's Prelude to Act III of *Lohengrin*, Dvořák's Symphony No. 9 in E Minor ("From the New World"), and Gershwin's *An American in Paris*. On February 19 came the news that the concert would be shown live on North Korean television.

PYONGYANG

Although the Philharmonic had visited China in 2002, its schedule did not include an appearance in Shanghai, an omission that was rectified in 2008. It was a much-anticipated visit, and the musicians were kept busy during their stay. Several of the orchestra's Chinese members coached players from a student orchestra, which then played a concert conducted by Lorin Maazel; he also appeared in a television interview. Orchestra members participated in an educational program involving local schools and also worked with students, helping them to compose their own pieces using both traditional Chinese and Western instruments.

On February 22 Daniel J. Wakin reported that some concern had been voiced by the Philharmonic's two most prominent Chinese members—the principal oboist, Liang Wang, and the associate conductor, Xian Zhang—that they would not be featured in any of the concerts in Shanghai or Beijing (though Wang did play the Richard Strauss Concerto in Hong Kong with Zhang conducting). They felt it would be logical for them to have prominent roles in concerts in their homeland. But Chinese audiences naturally wished to hear the Philharmonic conducted by the legendary Maazel, and they preferred to hear Western soloists as well.

Western concert presenters who are disturbed by applause between movements might wish to adopt the solution employed in Shanghai. During the concluding measures of a movement, a large sign lights up on either side of the hall, asking (or perhaps ordering) the audience not to applaud, an injunction that is invariably obeyed. On one occasion, failure to light the sign as the final lugubrious notes of the "Pathétique" Symphony were dying away caused the audience to begin applauding prematurely.

Meanwhile, the North Korean government agreed to televise the Philharmonic's concert there live throughout the country. Yet, there was some question as to how many North Koreans actually had television sets. Some did not even have electricity. According to Evans Rovere, president of the Korea Society, however, a live telecast was unprecedented. Major events were usually taped and shown later.

The New York Philharmonic arrived in Pyonyang on Monday, February 25, 2008. That included not only the musicians, but also staff members, television production crews, journalists, and patrons—about four hundred people in all, the largest group of Americans to visit the country since the Korean War ended in 1953. That evening everyone was treated to a gala concert of traditional music and dance, with beautiful costumes, followed by a spectacular banquet. The Philharmonic's assistant concertmaster, Michelle Kim, herself a native of South Korea, found the concert "mesmerizing." The bass clarinetist, Stephen Freeman, was "captivated by it."

The Philharmonic's concert on the 26th was given in the East Pyongyang Grand Theater before a rather serious audience. To judge from the broadcast, it was made up mostly of dignitaries and upper-echelon bureaucrats. Kim Jong-il was nowhere to be seen, although some of his high-level officials did attend. The North Korean and American national anthems opened the program, the audience standing for both. Maazel introduced the program in English, with an occasional Korean phrase interpolated. When he got to Gershwin's *An American in Paris*, he said that perhaps one day someone will write a piece called *Americans in Pyongyang*.

On February 27 Tommasini wrote of watching the streamed-in concert on his desktop computer at 4:00 a.m. Eastern time on the PBS-WNET Web site. Later it would be shown at a more conventional time on WNET and other PBS stations. He commented favorably on the performances of the "New World" Symphony and the Gershwin but felt that an opportunity had been missed when the orchestra chose not to play at least a short piece by a living American composer, perhaps an Asian American. He nevertheless termed the concert "historic," which it certainly was. For encores the Philharmonic played its conductorless Overture to *Candide* and then a Korean folk song, "Arirang," known to both North and South. This last greatly touched those present, at the end producing tears both in the hall and onstage as audience and orchestra waved good-bye to each other.

The following morning four Philharmonic string players—the concertmaster, Glenn Dicterow; the violinist Lisa Kim; the principal violist, Cynthia Phelps; and the principal cellist, Carter Brey—were joined by four North Korean string players to play Mendelssohn's Octet in the Moranbong Theater. The New York musicians had expected to work on the first movement with the North Koreans, but the latter were so well prepared that the entire octet was played before an intent audience. Maazel then led a short rehearsal and renditions of Wagner's Prelude to *Die Meistersinger* and Tchaikovsky's *Romeo and Juliet* with the State Symphony Orchestra of the Democratic People's Republic of Korea. Afterwards he commented on how very professional, how precise and well trained they were. He was very impressed.

The tour ended with a concert in Seoul, South Korea, on February 28. Again "Arirang" was played as an encore, this time producing a more vociferous response than in the North, with many cries of "Bravo!" Afterward Maazel and the orchestra members were told by Park Sam-koo, chairman of the Kumho-Asian Culture Foundation, "Seventy million Koreans love you," this statement referring to the combined population of both Koreas.

Returning to New York, the series begun on March 5 brought Alan Gilbert to lead his first concerts since being named the Philharmonic's next music director. According to Kozinn, Gilbert got quite an earful at the outset with the faulty horn playing in Haydn's Symphony No. 48 in C Major ("Maria Theresia"). This work abounds in treacherously high horn passages that are extremely difficult to play on modern instruments. Kozinn wrote of "uncommonly ruinous playing" and then received quite a bit of negative comment on his blog. (Once again, having to play the difficult score twice in one day may have contributed to the mishaps.) Gilbert's program also included Luciano Berio's *Folk Songs*, beautifully sung by soprano Dawn Upshaw, and Beethoven's Fourth Symphony, a rendition Kozinn found "superbly polished and full of fire."

Tommasini praised Gilbert the following week for his inclusion on the March 13 concert of a work by a living composer, *Quintessence*: Symphony No. 2 by Marc Neikrug, which received its world premiere. At least, it was its world premiere in that form, for the piece began life as a piano quintet; it was Gilbert who encouraged the composer to orchestrate it. The critic found the work to have "directness and emotional clarity" that caused the music to seem "utterly honest." Richard Strauss's *Ein Heldenleben* closed the program in a "brilliant yet never flashy performance." Said Tommasini, "The future of the Philharmonic looks good so far."

During Holy Week, Kurt Masur returned for four performances of the *Saint Matthew Passion*, for several years in the 1940s an annual event under Bruno Walter's direction. Steeped as he is in the Bach tradition, Masur adhered to it in his warmly expansive presentation, yet bowed to some of the conventions of the early-music movement, such as the inclusion of the recorder, viola da gamba, oboe d'amore, and baroque organ. Tommasini singled out two soloists for special praise, the tenor James Taylor as the Evangelist and the baritone Matthias Goerne as Jesus. The "impeccable singing" of the Westminster Choir and the American Boychoir was "the glory of this performance."

The Fourth Symphony of Vaughan Williams sounds like a wartime piece, angry, bleak, despairing, and grim. It certainly disrupts the popular notion of the composer as a writer of pastoral music. The conductor Sir Adrian Boult referred to it as "the bad-tempered one" among Vaughan Williams's nine symphonies (though much of the Sixth can be characterized in the same way). Yet the Fourth was composed between 1931 and 1934, when there was no war in Europe, "merely" one on the horizon. After conducting the work, the composer is reputed to have said, "I don't know if I like it, but it is what I meant." Sir Colin Davis brought the work to his concerts beginning April 3, and, as Holland pointed out, he "does this orchestra a lot of good." On the same program, Richard Goode was the dedicated soloist in Beethoven's Fourth Piano Concerto.

The Chinese-born composer Tan Dun was heard on April 9 when Lang Lang played the premiere of his Piano Concerto under Slatkin. The orchestration includes both Western and Asian instruments, particularly in the percussion section. According to the composer, the work was inspired by his love for the martial arts, on stunning display in the film *Crouching Tiger, Hidden Dragon*, for which he wrote the Academy Award–winning score. Tommasini wrote of his "treating Mr. Lang as a martial artist of the keyboard," and of the concerto's combining the percussive elements of Bartók's concertos with the lyricism of Rachmaninoff. If nothing else, the concerto was described as "a crowd pleaser."

On April 23 Charles Dutoit demonstrated how an interesting program can be assembled from works of the fairly standard repertoire. Opening with a breathless rendition of Mozart's Overture to *The Marriage of Figaro*, it proceeded to Beethoven's First Piano Concerto, with André Watts at the keyboard. Watts, normally associated with more virtuosic and romantic concertos, proved singularly adept in this sprightly work, giving it "a playful, rambunctious account," according to Kozinn. Two brilliant orchestral works completed the program, Rachmaninoff's *Symphonic Dances* and Ravel's *La valse*, both performed with "fluidity, and sumptuousness."

Muti had declined the Philharmonic's offer to make him its music director on the grounds that he did not wish to assume the responsibilities of a position with an American orchestra, which include nonmusical as well as musical duties; that his base of operations was in Europe; and that he did not wish to have long separations from his family. Imagine everyone's surprise, then, when it was announced on May 6 that he had accepted the music directorship of the Chicago Symphony Orchestra, effective with the 2010–11 season. There was disappointment at the Philharmonic, some members of which spoke anonymously about Muti's having been their top choice for the job. He would continue as a guest in New York, perhaps not to the extent hoped for, but he would not appear with the Philharmonic once he took over in Chicago, for, according to Zarin Mehta, the Philharmonic does not engage guests who are music directors of other American orchestras. He then reiterated that Alan Gilbert was the right person for the Philharmonic.

Another trip to Broadway occurred on May 7, when the Philharmonic presented Lerner and Loewe's *Camelot*. Again, it was a pleasure to hear a great orchestra perform familiar tunes, this time led by the musical theater conductor Paul Gemignani, with Gabriel Byrne as King Arthur and Marin Mazzie as Guinevere. The baritone Nathan Gunn, normally heard at the Met, was "triumphant" as Sir Lancelot, and Tommasini gave the whole production a rave review.

The Austrian-born composer Erich Wolfgang Korngold is best known today for his many scores for Hollywood films of the 1930s and 1940s, among them *The Adventures of Robin Hood*, *The Prince and the Pauper*, and *The Sea Hawk*. His concert music is rarely heard today, but in 1947 Jascha Heifetz gave the New York premiere of his Violin Concerto with the Philharmonic. ("More corn than gold" was how the critic Irving Kolodin unfairly described it.) Therefore, Glenn Dicterow's decision to perform the work on May 22, 2008, with David Robertson conducting, was an enterprising one, for it is a highly melodious work in the romantic tradition, with much bravura writing for the solo instrument and enough harmonic piquancy to enable one to identify the century in which it was written. Kozinn felt that Dicterow "made a powerful case" for the concerto. He also wrote approvingly of Robertson's interpretations of Schubert's "Unfinished" Symphony and Sibelius's Symphony No. 1.

In a sense, more Schubert was heard the following week, beginning May 29, when Robertson programmed Luciano Berio's *Rendering*, a work inspired by the sketches Schubert left behind for a Tenth Symphony. Berio does not merely "render" the sketches, but composes his own ideas based on the sketches and provides links between them, sometimes bringing Schubert into the twentieth century and placing himself in the nineteenth. Tommasini praised Robertson's performance of the piece, as well as his spoken introduction to it, which was replete with musical examples. The Swiss composer Michael Jarrell's orchestration of three Debussy etudes opened the program, and Emanuel Ax's buoyant rendition of Beethoven's "Emperor" Concerto closed it.

Mahler's Ninth Symphony was conducted by Maazel on the concerts beginning June 4. There was no micromanaging here, according to Tommasini, merely a performance of great precision, expressivity, and integrity. A return to Carnegie Hall on June 11 was devoted to Maazel's arrangement of excerpts from Wagner, *The Ring without Words*. This score was one of two led by Maazel (the other was Bruckner's Eighth Symphony) on Philharmonic concerts in 2000 that eventually resulted in his being offered the music directorship. While some people object to synopses, the fact is that not everyone has the time or the inclination to devote seventeen hours to experiencing the complete *Ring*, and works such as Maazel's arrangement give less committed (or fanatical—take your pick) audiences a chance to hear at least some of Wagner's great *Gesamtkunstwerk* (total artwork). Kozinn especially praised the brass section, citing Philip Myers's offstage horn solo in "Siegfried's Rhine Journey" as one of the performance's high points.

When conductors program operas in concert form, the subject is usually something such as Strauss's *Elektra*, Berg's *Wozzeck*, or Ravel's *L'enfant et les sortilèges*. It was unusual, therefore, for Maazel and the Philharmonic to present one of the quintessential operatic staples, a work offered regularly by most opera companies, the Met included. Yet there was Puccini's *Tosca* on June 14. The Chinese soprano Hui He sang the title role, the Italian tenor Walter Fraccaro was Cavaradossi, and the Georgian baritone George Gagnidze was Scarpia. All received high marks from Tommasini, but Maazel's manipulation of the tempos made life difficult for the singers at times. What the critic objected to was the plethora of microphones and loudspeakers on the stage, which were apparently being used to record the performance and amplify the organ and the electronic cannon shots. But even though the cannons were not amplified and the front speakers were not used, the volume of the performance was unpleasantly loud, even blaring at times. This may have been the result of the stage area's having been extended into the hall and the first seven rows of seats removed. (What happens to the subscribers who normally sit in those seats?)

Just as there had been *The Ring without Words*, so was there again the Bruckner Eighth, this time to close the season on June 20 and 21. The reviewer, Oestreich, had reacted less than favorably to the 2000 performance. This one was different, however—one of the finest performances Maazel had given during his tenure, not idiosyncratic at all, but with "more real heart and soul" than one would have come to expect from him. The audience roared its approval, and there was much to look forward to in Maazel's forthcoming and final season.

A Controversial "Resurrection"

Still seeking a suitable site for a summer festival, the Philharmonic journeyed to Governors Island in New York Harbor for a free concert on July 5, 2008. The island was a U.S. Army post from 1783 to 1966, after which the Coast Guard occupied it until 1996. Since 2003 the combined fortifications have constituted the Governors Island National Monument. Situated between Lower Manhattan and the Statue of Liberty, the site, accessible only by a seven-minute ferry trip, presents spectacular views. Bramwell Tovey conducted the concert, a program of the type normally played in the Summertime Classics series, with music by Rossini, Copland, Rimsky-Korsakov, and Tchaikovsky, whose *1812 Overture* made its customary effect.

On June 25 Tovey had led the orchestra in a concert on the Great Lawn of Central Park. Thanks to technology, the concert was a display of democracy in action, for the audience of 61,000 was given the opportunity to choose the program's encore. After the opening Shostakovich *Festive Overture*, Tovey instructed everyone, contrary to normal concert policy, to take out their cell phones and turn them on. He then explained that by entering a numerical code and text messaging, they could vote for Jimi Hendrix's *Purple Haze* or Rimsky-Korsakov's *Flight of the Bumblebee*. The program continued with Mendelssohn's "Italian" Symphony, the *1812 Overture*, and some Sousa marches, after which the dramatic result was announced: Jimi Hendrix by a landslide. It is interesting to note that Tommasini reviewed this concert, and the Summertime Classics opening program the night before, as he had done in previous years. Normally these lighter programs (not that the "Italian" Symphony is all that light) are assigned to someone other than the chief critic. It is to Tommasini's credit that he takes this repertoire seriously.

The Summertime Classics program included excerpts from Prokofieff's *Romeo and Juliet*, not exactly summer fare. Nor is Rachmaninoff's Piano Concerto No. 2, though it does fit into the popular category. In the latter work Joyce Yang, silver medal winner of the 2005 Van Cliburn Competition, was a supple soloist, if lacking in the power needed to be heard over the orchestra at climactic moments (though she would not be the first pianist to have that particular problem in that particular concerto). In both these programs, according to Tommasini, Tovey demonstrated that he is an accomplished conductor, as well as a witty commentator on the music.

Gilbert led the Central Park concert on July 15, on which Lang Lang was heard—and seen—in the Tchaikovsky Piano Concerto No. 1. Of visual interest was the fact that Lang Lang played on a red piano. In speaking to the audience of 63,000, he said that it was one of only two red Steinways in the world, and that it was to be auctioned off to raise funds for the relief of earthquake victims in China. Again Tommasini was there, writing of Lang Lang's brilliant performance of the Tchaikovsky, apparently unmarred by the musical distortions for which he had often been criticized. Whether one warms to his playing or not, it cannot be denied that he is a popular and charismatic performer who is making friends for classical music. Beethoven's Fourth Symphony and Sibelius's *Finlandia* completed an unusually satisfying Parks Concert, except that there was then an encore, again selected by audience vote. The candidates were an orchestral arrangement of the "Toreador Song" from *Carmen* and the Overture to Rossini's *William Tell*. Rossini was declared the winner, followed by the customary fireworks.

A fleeting presence on the depleted New York newspaper scene was the *New York Sun*, which made its first appearance on April 16, 2002, its last on September 30, 2008. (The paper is not to be confused with the former tabloid the *Sun*, which was absorbed by the *World-Telegram* in 1950.) During its six-year existence, the *New York Sun's* chief music critic was Jay Nordlinger, who is a senior editor of the *National Review* and also the music critic for the magazine *New Criterion*. In contrast to his New York colleagues, his opinion of Maazel has been generally positive. For example, in the issue of June 13, 2008, reviewing Maazel's Carnegie Hall performance of his *Ring without Words*, which Nordlinger did not like, he concluded that whether one likes him or not on a given night, Maazel "is a big musical brain who always has something to teach."

Nordlinger even praised Maazel's rendition of "The Star Spangled Banner" on the opening-night gala of September 17, stating that he "conducted the anthem nobly, elegantly, and purposefully." That opening night began Maazel's final season as the Philharmonic's music director. Sir James Galway was the soloist in the mildly insouciant Flute Concerto by Jacques Ibert, who could deservedly have been a seventh in the group of French composers known as Les Six. The next night brought the American premiere of *Rhapsodies* by Steven Stucky, the host of the Philharmonic's Hear and Now series. In the November *New Criterion*, Nordlinger thought *Rhapsodies* "a good and worthwhile piece" reminiscent of such mid-century American composers as Piston, Schuman, and Persichetti. Of Yefim Bronfman's rendition of the Rachmaninoff Piano Concerto No. 3, he stated that "no one now living plays this work better than he." In Ravel's *Mother Goose Suite* Maazel was "suave and urbane, but also child-like"; in Bartók's *Miraculous Mandarin* Suite, "stylish, daring, exotic—like the music itself."

An unusual program was given on the concerts beginning September 25, one consisting of music by all the Philharmonic music directors who were (or are) composers: the Adagio from Mahler's Tenth Symphony; Maazel's own Music for Flute and Orchestra, with the orchestra's principal flutist, Robert Langevin, as the soloist; Boulez's Improvisation on Mallarmé No. 2, with the soprano Kiera Duffy; and Bernstein's Symphony No. 2, in which the piano soloist was Joyce Yang.

One aspect of the season was Maazel's daring, and the word is not used lightly here, to program all of Bach's Brandenburg Concertos, not all at once, but at discrete intervals. The sequence began with the Concerto No. 5, given on October 1 and 2, in which the solo parts were taken by the orchestra members Anna Rabinova on violin, Sandra Church on flute, and Lionel Party on harpsichord. These and other baroque works, such as Handel and Vivaldi concerti grossi, rarely appear today on symphony concerts, having been co-opted by the original-instruments movement. Conductors are reluctant to program them for fear of scorn from critics and members of the movement. Maazel was not scorned, but the *Times*'s Steve Smith did find his approach to the work no better than dutiful, in spite of fine playing by the soloists.

The same program included the world premiere of *Chains like the Sea* by the English-born composer Bernard Rands, which was commissioned by the Philharmonic. Inspired by Dylan Thomas's *Fern Hill*, it was well received by Smith and by the audience, as was the closing work, Tchaikovsky's rarely played Suite No. 3 in G Major, which the Philharmonic last presented in 1973. In days gone by, the final movement, the brilliant Theme and Variations, was often heard on its own, but the entire work is definitely worth hearing, especially as an alternative to one of the ubiquitous last three symphonies. Those who enjoy the composer's ballet music will certainly respond to this charming and exciting score, which was received with great enthusiasm.

As for those earlier times, so well-known was Dvořák's "New World" Symphony that it was rarely given by the Philharmonic. Recent years have seen it appearing more frequently, most notably in North Korea. Now here it was again, conducted by Marin Alsop on the concerts of October 7 and 11, as well as on October 10 as part of a new series called Inside the Music. On this and similar programs the actor Alec Baldwin narrated a multimedia presentation devised by the writer and critic Joseph Horowitz, giving background on the composer and his times as well as on the work itself, all with musical examples. After an intermission, the work was played complete, as in a normal concert. Baldwin has now assumed the role of host and commentator for the Philharmonic's new series of weekly broadcasts.

The "New World" Symphony, of course, has a special place in Philharmonic history, for the orchestra played the world premiere in 1893 in Carnegie Hall. Tommasini thought Alsop's performance more spontaneous than Maazel's somewhat calculated way with the piece, and also praised her conducting of Bartók's suite from his ballet *The Wooden Prince*. The young Polish pianist Rafał Blechacz, in his Philharmonic debut, gave an elegant account of Chopin's Concerto No. 2 in F Minor.

Another concert opera was given during the week of October 16, the seldom-heard one-act *La vida breve* by Manuel de Falla. Rafael Frühbeck de Burgos conducted a large cast of Spanish singers and dancers in an evocative presentation of the composer's first major work, an example of Spanish verismo. Frühbeck's colorful orchestration of five pieces from the *Suite Española* by Isaac Albéniz completed the unusual program.

A highlight of the fall season was another celebration of Leonard Bernstein, this one a two-month triple observance of the ninetieth anniversary of his birth, the sixty-fifth of his debut with the Philharmonic, and the fiftieth of his assuming its music directorship. Entitled "Bernstein: The Best of All Possible Worlds" (a line from *Candide*), the event was a joint presentation by the Philharmonic and Carnegie Hall. (Oestreich wondered what remained to be done for the Bernstein centennial in 2018.) Having played "The Age of Anxiety" under Maazel in September, the Philharmonic later performed several Bernstein selections on a Young People's Concert on October 18, Delta David Gier conducting, and the Symphony No. 1 ("Jeremiah") under David Robertson on October 30–November 1, with Michelle DeYoung as the mezzo-soprano soloist. The main event for the Philharmonic, however, took place on the anniversary date of the debut, November 14, in

Carnegie Hall, when Gilbert led an all-Bernstein program: the Symphonic Suite from *On the Waterfront*; the Serenade for Violin, Strings, and Percussion, with Glenn Dicterow as the soloist; and excerpts from *West Side Story*, in the form of two suites. The tenor Paul Groves and the soprano Ana María Martínez were the principal singers among many, along with the New York Choral Artists. According to Oestreich, the best performance was, once again, the conductorless Overture to *Candide*, played as an encore.

When the Philharmonic has given concert performances of Richard Strauss's *Elektra*, they have usually been given, for some reason, in December—in the Christmas season. Dimitri Mitropoulos's 1949 Sunday broadcast performance was actually given on Christmas Day, while William Steinberg's in 1964 was heard two weeks before Christmas. One wonders what there is about this harrowing and lurid, albeit great, opera that makes it appropriate for that time of year. In 2008 Lorin Maazel conducted it on the concerts beginning December 4 with a stellar cast headed by the soprano Deborah Polaski in the title role, the sopranos Anne Schwanewilms and Jane Henschel, the tenor Richard Margison, and the baritone Julian Tovey, again with the New York Choral Artists. According to Tommasini, Maazel conducted with a combination of coolness and fiery intensity that led the critic to wonder why the conductor had not offered more concert operas at the Philharmonic, for this one was absolutely riveting and gripping. The orchestra was astounding, Polaski superb.

A somewhat controversial performance took place a few days later. A bit of background: In 1965 a young economist named Gilbert E. Kaplan, then working at the American Stock Exchange, heard for the first time Mahler's "Resurrection" Symphony, conducted by Leopold Stokowski. So captivated, so enthralled, in fact so obsessed with the work did he become that, some years later, he felt he must conduct it, even though he was not a trained musician (three years of boyhood piano lessons did not count). He was then forty years old and had made a fortune when much younger as the founder of a magazine called *Institutional Investor*. After spending seven months studying conducting privately with Charles Z. Bornstein, a Juilliard graduate (and frequent Philharmonic pre-concert lecturer), obtaining advice from a number of Mahler experts, and immersing himself thoroughly in the Mahler Second (including attending every performance of it he could get to around the world), Kaplan felt confident enough to indulge his singular conducting ambition.

In 1982 he hired the American Symphony Orchestra (which Stokowski had founded and which played the performance Kaplan heard in 1965) and the Westminster Choir, engaged the soprano Carole Farley and the contralto Birgit Finnilä, and booked Avery Fisher Hall, all for a private concert for members of the International Monetary Fund, which was having a conference in New York City. With that performance under his belt, Kaplan began an odyssey, conducting the Mahler Second at least a hundred times with fifty-seven orchestras. In 1987 he recorded it with the London Symphony Orchestra, producing the best-selling Mahler recording of all time, with over 180,000 copies sold. He recorded it again in 2002 with the Vienna Philharmonic, no less—a version that has sold close to 40,000 copies. Meanwhile, he has acquired Mahler's original manuscript score and is co-editor of the new critical edition, now the official score of the International Gustav Mahler Society in Vienna. He would appear to be the world's foremost authority on the Mahler Second, the only work he conducts (except for the Adagietto from Mahler's Fifth Symphony).

On December 8, 2008, the New York Philharmonic became the fifty-eighth orchestra to perform Mahler's "Resurrection" Symphony under Gilbert Kaplan's direction. The date was significant, for it was the one hundredth anniversary to the day of the work's American premiere by the New York Symphony (later to merge with the Philharmonic), conducted by Mahler himself. In later years the Philharmonic played it under the direction of Willem Mengelberg, Otto Klemperer, Bruno Walter, Artur Rodzinski, Leonard Bernstein, Zubin Mehta, James Levine, and Lorin Maazel. How would Kaplan compare with this august lineup?

The concert was a benefit for the Philharmonic's Pension Fund and involved the participation of the Westminster Symphonic Choir, the soprano Esther Heideman, and the mezzo-soprano Janina Baechle. Steve Smith, in his review of the performance for the *Times*, acknowledged that Kaplan was not a professional conductor, though he did conduct the eighty-minute score from memory, with straightforward gestures and appropriate cues as needed. But, Smith continued, Kaplan led a shatteringly powerful performance in which every detail emerged with great clarity and in proper balance, the orchestra playing beautifully and with astounding control. Smith concluded it would be wrong to think that Kaplan revealed all there is to know about the work, but that most likely he is best equipped to reveal what Mahler actually wrote.

All well and good. Except that in a December 18 *Times* article, Daniel J. Wakin revealed that Philharmonic musicians were not happy, to say the least, with Kaplan's amateurish conducting of a magnificent piece, or with the fact that their management had engaged him in the first place, apparently at Maazel's suggestion. On the day of the concert, players had met for an hour with Zarin Mehta, complaining about Kaplan's unsuitability to conduct the Philharmonic. Prime among the disgruntled members was the trombonist David Finlayson, who vented his spleen at great length on his blog. Musicians from other orchestras Kaplan had conducted described his work as being without passion, saying that he was little more than a traffic cop. His performances were always well received by audiences, they said, including the sold-out house at Avery Fisher, because Mahler's great finale invariably produces a standing ovation. Kaplan himself was philosophical, saying it was natural for musicians to have strong opinions, that no one would confuse him with Maazel, and that he did get the results he wanted.

Three days after Mahler conducted the American premiere of his Second Symphony, the composer Elliott Carter was born on December 11, 1908. Thus this was the year of his centennial. But unlike all other composers the Philharmonic had honored in this way, Carter was very much alive and still composing prolifically. On the concerts beginning October 30, the Philharmonic presented his 2002 vocal work, *Of Rewaking*, set to texts by William Carlos Williams. Conducted by David Robertson and sung by the mezzo-soprano Michelle DeYoung, the work was most sympathetically reviewed by Steve Smith, who also praised DeYoung's performance, not only of the Carter score, but of her contribution to the finale of Bernstein's "Jeremiah" Symphony, also on the program.

On December 12 Carter was feted at a program of his solo and chamber music given at Zankel Hall, the newest addition to the Carnegie Hall complex. During an interview with Jeremy Geffen, Carnegie's director of artistic planning, Carter commented on the attention he had been receiving during his special year: "It's a little bit frightening, because I'm not used to being appreciated."

CHAPTER 24

2009

FAREWELLS

Plans were announced on January 13 for an Asian tour in October 2009, the first tour the orchestra would undertake with its new music director, Alan Gilbert. Besides visiting Japan, where they had played several times before, the Philharmonic would appear for the first time in Vietnam, as well as in Abu Dhabi, the capital of the United Arab Emirates. So much attention did the concert in North Korea receive internationally that Vietnam was thought to be the next logical place for such a visit.

Gustavo Dudamel returned for a Rush Hour concert on January 14, then a subscription sequence beginning the next day. He had impressed everyone in his debut in 2007 and now offered Mahler's Fifth Symphony as his major work. In fact, it was the only work on the Rush Hour program. For the subscription audiences it was preceded by the Violin Concerto by the English composer Oliver Knussen, with Pinchas Zukerman as the soloist. Tommasini reviewed the first performance of the Mahler, in which he found Dudamel to display depth and maturity in an impassioned, coherent, and brilliant performance, which he led from memory. Vivien Schweitzer the next day thought the Knussen concerto a striking piece, well played by Zukerman, who brought a sense of enjoyment to the work.

A two-week visit by Riccardo Muti followed, his first since being named music director of the Chicago Symphony. In his first week, beginning January 22, he honored the bicentennial of the death of Joseph Haydn by programming the seldom-played Symphony No. 89 in F Major and arias from two operas sung by the compelling baritone Thomas Quasthoff. His second week, starting January 29, brought a further demonstration of the maestro's enthusiasm for the music of Scriabin. This time it was the Symphony No. 2 in C Minor, which the Philharmonic had first, and last, played in 1969. The score lacks the extravagance and mysticism of the later, better-known works; it strikes the listener as a more or less normal and colorful romantic symphony. Schweitzer felt Muti demonstrated his great affinity for the composer, as he did for Beethoven in the Piano Concerto No. 3, also in C minor, of which the great Romanian pianist Radu Lupu delivered a superb account.

The death of the respected composer, conductor, and pianist Lukas Foss, at the age of eighty-six, was reported on February 2. Over the years he had appeared with the Philharmonic in all three capacities. He was the artistic director of the summer festivals in 1965 and 1966, which featured French music and Stravinsky, respectively.

Another bicentennial was observed in 2009: that of the birth of Felix Mendelssohn. And what better conductor to engage for an all-Mendelssohn program than Kurt Masur? On February 4 and the three ensuing days he offered the dramatic Overture to *Ruy Blas*; the popular Violin Concerto in E Minor, in which the soloist was Anne-Sophie Mutter; and the little-known cantata *Die erste Walpurgisnacht*, with the Westminster Symphonic Choir. A setting of a poem by Goethe, this work has been described earlier in these pages, when it was reviewed somewhat patronizingly by a *Times* critic. This time, Allan Kozinn was a more sympathetic listener.

On February 21 Maazel and the orchestra began a tour that started in Atlanta and proceeded south to several cities on Florida's west coast, then to Miami and San Juan, Puerto Rico, with two concerts in the latter city. Two concerts in Chapel Hill, North Carolina, followed; one in Danville, Kentucky; two in Ann Arbor, Michigan; and finally one in Chicago on March 9. The weather in the northeast was cold and miserable, so the orchestra was glad for a reason to make a trip to southern climes.

The death of Myor Rosen at the age of ninety-one occurred on March 13. For twenty-seven years, from 1960 until his retirement in 1987, he was the Philharmonic's principal harpist, and his artistry can be heard on many of the orchestra's recordings made during that time ("many" only because there are no harp parts in Beethoven or Brahms symphonies).

Zubin Mehta returned for concerts beginning March 18, bringing with him a work by the Israeli composer Avner Dorman in its American premiere. Entitled *Spices, Perfumes, Toxins!*, it is a concerto for percussion instruments. The soloists were the two Israeli musicians, Tomer Yariv and Adi Morag (known collectively as PercaDu), who had played the world premiere in Tel Aviv in 2006. The work is an amalgam of Western and Middle Eastern influences, both sensual and boisterous, with the percussion often dominating the orchestra. The brilliant performance by the two soloists produced a tremendous ovation, and Bartók's *Concerto for Orchestra* appropriately complemented the Dorman piece in Mehta's incisive performance.

Two weeks with Gilbert began on April 30, the first program including two seldom-played works by Czech composers: the tone poem *The Golden Spinning Wheel* by Dvořák and the Symphony No. 4 by Bohuslav Martinů The Dvořák tone (or symphonic) poems deserve greater exposure, though *Spinning Wheel* was notably recorded by Sir Thomas Beecham at a time when no one else played these pieces. Martinůs symphonies are interesting and fastidiously crafted works also deserving of wider hearing, especially Nos. 5 and 6.

For his second week, starting May 9, Gilbert presented the world premiere of a Philharmonic commission, a cantata by Peter Lieberson entitled *The World in Flower*. Like the composer's earlier *Neruda Songs*, it was written for his wife, the mezzo-soprano Lorraine Hunt Lieberson. She died in 2006, so for the premiere the much-praised mezzo Joyce DiDonato was the soloist, with the baritone Russell Braun and the New York Choral Artists. Using texts from a wide variety of poets, the work is an expression of spirituality from many points of view, including those of medieval mystics and North American shamans. Tommasini found much to praise in the piece, save its possibly excessive length. Mahler's First Symphony was a formidable and exciting conclusion to the program, before which Gilbert offered the delicate *Blumine*, which Mahler had originally included in the symphony and later removed, allowing it to stand as an independent work.

The final four weeks of the 2008–9 season were the last for Lorin Maazel as music director. They were also the last for several musicians who would be retiring. Of these, one stands out: Stanley Drucker, whose sixty years with the Philharmonic constitute the longest tenure of anyone in the orchestra's history. In fact, it may be the longest tenure of anyone in any orchestra. (The Chicago Symphony's principal trumpet, Adolph Herseth, retired in 2001 after a fleeting fifty-three years.) When Drucker joined the Philharmonic in 1948 at the age of nineteen, it was not even his first job, for he had already played with the Indianapolis Symphony and the Buffalo Philharmonic. His first New York Philharmonic position was as assistant principal and E-flat clarinetist; he became principal clarinetist in 1960. Since then he has been heard on all the orchestra's recordings and has performed as a soloist many times in a wide variety of concertos, frequently that of Aaron Copland, which has become his signature piece and which he recorded with Bernstein conducting. It was with the Copland Concerto that he made his final solo appearances, Maazel conducting, on the concerts beginning June 4, described by Vivien Schweitzer as "a memorable performance." At the concert it was announced that Drucker, who had played in 10,200 concerts with the Philharmonic, had set a Guinness World Record for the "longest career as a clarinetist": as of June 4, sixty-two years, seven months, and one day. Also announced was the naming of Drucker as an honorary member of the Philharmonic-Symphony Society of New York, the first orchestra musician to be so honored.

One does not have to look very hard to find a reason for Drucker's longevity, apart from his good health. He has a very positive and enthusiastic attitude and, after more than sixty years in the profession, still loves music. Many orchestra musicians, in much less time, become very cynical in their outlook. During an interview for this book, Drucker spoke not one harsh word about conductors (even some of the tyrants of yesteryear), colleagues, or anyone else in music. Often in a concerto accompaniment, one sees an assistant or associate player in the principal chair. Not in the Philharmonic's clarinet section, where Drucker, nine times out of ten, has been a constant presence.

The second of Maazel's final weeks, beginning June 11, was devoted to performances of Britten's *War Requiem*, with Nancy Gustafson, Vale Rideout, and Ian Greenlaw as the soloists, along with the New York Choral Artists, the Dessoff Symphonic Choir, and the Brooklyn Youth Chorus. Lionel Bringuier conducted the work's chamber orchestra element. Although Oestreich wrote of the "sheer musical beauty" of many passages, the final hushed choral phrases shaped "exquisitely," he found the performance generally lacking the tension and atmosphere it demonstrated in the hands of such humanist conductors as Robert Shaw and Kurt Masur. He felt Maazel did not realize the work's potential, and that "the concert was an apt symbol of Mr. Maazel's tenure."

On June 12 it was announced that the investment banker Gary W. Parr, a deputy chairman of Lazard, would succeed Paul B. Guenther as chairman of the New York Philharmonic, effective in September. Parr was quoted in the *Times* as saying, "I think of this as the best job someone would pay to have." Orchestra members were impressed, on meeting him, when he said his favorite piece of music is the Mozart Requiem.

Maazel rarely programmed his own music with the Philharmonic. Exceptions were his seventy-fifth birthday concert on March 1, 2005, and the program of music by Philharmonic music directors on September 25, 2008. For the penultimate week of his tenure, beginning June 17, Maazel offered two of his works, the slight but attractive *Monaco Fanfares* and the more imposing and less attractive *Farewells*—less attractive only because of its subject matter (according to the composer's own program note, "the obtuseness of human nature and the inhuman crunching of the machines of our invention"). The title, *Farewells*, while suitable for Maazel's Philharmonic leave-taking, was not related to that event; the piece was premiered in 2000 by the Vienna Philharmonic, which commissioned it.

Following the intermission, five musicians were recognized on their retirement: Stanley Drucker, already honored, the clarinetist Stephen Freeman, the cellist Valentin Hirsu, and the double bassists Jon Deak and Michele Saxon. The Second Symphony of Sibelius provided a grandly expansive and blazingly majestic conclusion to the concert.

Philharmonic music directors tend to conclude their tenures with extremely large-scale works, the more performers the better. Although Mitropoulos ended with a rather unassuming program, Bernstein chose Mahler's Third Symphony. For Boulez it was Berlioz's *Damnation of Faust*, for Mehta Schoenberg's *Gurre-Lieder*. Masur opted more modestly for Beethoven's "Eroica" Symphony. For his final concerts, beginning June 24, Maazel's choice was Mahler's Eighth Symphony, the "Symphony of a Thousand," last given by the Philharmonic in the Mahler Festival of 1976. The cast included the same choral ensembles as for the *War Requiem*, plus the soloists Christine Brewer, Nancy Gustafson, and Jeanine De Bique, sopranos; Mary Phillips and Nancy Maultsby, mezzo-sopranos; Anthony Dean Griffey, tenor; Jason Grant, bass-baritone; and Wolfgang Schöne, bass.

One might have assumed that Tommasini would review this performance, because of the occasion and because the Mahler Eighth is not performed that often. However, the assignment went to Kozinn, who wrote that New York's mayor, Michael Bloomberg, had proclaimed that day "Maestro Lorin Maazel Day," and that Maazel self-usurped the honor by calling it "Gustav Mahler Day" instead. Kozinn noted that Maazel let the score "flow naturally, shaping it subtly," and that he did "a fine job balancing the sizable forces at hand," after noting that the work's "size, scope and sheer structural oddity" precluded the kind of excessive interpretive manipulation so characteristic of this conductor's work. Much praise was given to the soloists and choruses, with the orchestra delivering "a polished performance" and Maazel directing "a focused, dignified reading." A certain "workaday tepidness" did intrude from time to time, and only at the end did Maazel strike one of his characteristic "conductorial poses."

And so the Maazel era came to an end. That the orchestra consistently played brilliantly for him is undeniable, as is the fact that in rehearsals he was extremely efficient and respectful of his musicians. On July 5 Tommasini summed up Maazel's tenure, contrasting it with that of his predecessor, Masur, and the prospective tenure of his successor, Gilbert. In the matter of the Parks Concerts, it was mentioned that Maazel, in a seven-year span, had conducted only one of these events, in 2005. Gilbert, appearing as a guest, had already led two of them in 2008. As music director–designate, he would conduct all of them in 2009. Having grown up with the Philharmonic, he had stated publicly how much he loves the orchestra, New York, Central Park, and the concerts in the park. In short, he was already extending himself to the people of New York in a way that the more aloof Maazel had never done. Even Masur had conducted Parks Concerts. Masur had also made himself available to the city's music conservatories, conducting their orchestras and giving master classes.

Maazel was praised for his brilliance in conducting such complex and large-scale works as Mahler's Third Symphony, Strauss's *Elektra*, and Schoenberg's *Variations for Orchestra* (though he did not officially review it, Tommasini found Maazel's Mahler Eighth to be "rather blunt"). Again he was faulted for his often idiosyncratic interpretations of the more standard repertoire, works he had been conducting for so many years that he probably found it necessary to "do something" with them to maintain his interest. (As a young student, Maazel had played violin in the Pittsburgh Symphony, whose music director was then Fritz Reiner. The Hungarian maestro was himself often guilty of interpretive idiosyncrasies. Perhaps he influenced Maazel in that respect. In any case, that was an era when such conductors as Reiner, Stokowski, and Koussevitzky held sway with their own personalized interpretations, as can be heard on recordings. Such liberties as they took are frowned upon today.)

By the time this book appears in print, Gilbert will have embarked on his second season as music director of the New York Philharmonic. His first season included the orchestra's first visit to Vietnam. The Philharmonic's first composer-in-residence in twenty years, the Finn Magnus Lindberg, had a new work premiered on the gala televised opening night. György Ligeti's modernist opera *Le grand macabre* had its New York premiere in a semistaged production. A three-week Stravinsky festival was led by Valery Gergiev. All of this, of course, was combined with a generous assortment of standard repertoire, often presented in provocative combinations with lesser-known works.

It is hoped that Gilbert's tenure will be a long and successful one, that he will develop into a household name, and that a future *New York Times* article will sport the headline "The Philharmonic—What's Right with It and Why." In the meantime, perhaps the last word should come from Bernstein, first noted in chapter 3: "I give the Philharmonic forever."

MEMBERS OF THE
NEW YORK PHILHARMONIC
1956–2009

(C)	= concertmaster
*	= principal or co-principal player
(ext)	= contracted extra musician
(sub)	= contracted substitute musician
(pm)	= personnel manager
(OF)	= orchestral fellow

CONCERTMASTER

John Corigliano	1943–66	Frank Gullino	1975–76
David Nadien	1966–71	Rodney Friend	1976–80
Frank Gullino	1970–71	Sidney Harth	1979–80
Rafael Druian	1971–74	Glenn Dicterow	1980–
Eliot Chapo	1973–76		

VIOLIN

W. Sanford Allen	1962–77	Morris Borodkin	1928–69
Bjoern Andreasson	1949–87	Matitiahu Braun	1969–2006
Denise Ayres	1982–85	Alfred Breuning	1958–62
Duoming Ba	2006–	Leopold Busch	1928–64
Gabriel Banat	1970–93	Luigi Carlini	1955–80
William Barbini	1970–84	Jesse Ceci	1959–62
Socrate Barozzi	1934–59	Minyoung Chang	2006–
Eugene Bergen	1962–86	Eliot Chapo (C)	1973–76
Joseph Bernstein	1953–71	Mary Corbett-Laven	1985–87
Emanuel Boder	1978–2006	(OF)	

Violin *(cont'd.)*

John Corigliano (C)	1935–66	Gary Levinson	1987–2002
Mordecai Dayan	1928–69	Alfred Lora	1928–61
William Dembinsky	1934–74	Kuan-Cheng Lu	2004–
Robert de Pasquale	1957–64	Newton Mansfield	1961–
Michael de Stefano	1928–70	Jacques Margolies	1942–2002
Enrico Di Cecco	1961–	Kerry McDermott	1982–
Glenn Dicterow (C)	1980–	Robert Menga	1962–67
Rafael Druian (C)	1971–74	Alfio Micci	1949–80
Marilyn Dubow	1971–	David Nadien (C)	1966–71
Martin Eshelman	1956–	Armand Neveux (pm)	1928–65
Barry Finclair	1972–77	William Nowinski	1943–83
Joachim Fishberg	1928–69	Sarah O'Boyle	2003–08
Louis Fishzohn	1930–70	Sandra Park (sub)	2000–
Rodney Friend (C)	1976–80	Carlos Piantini	1956–72
Quan Ge	2008–	Theodor Podnos	1965–84
Antonio Gerardi	1931–57	Imre Pogany	1929–58*
Michael Gilbert	1970–2001	Anton Polezhayev	2002–2005
Judith Ginsberg	1984–	George Rabin	1928–64
Marc Ginsberg	1969–*	Anna Rabinova	1993–
Nathan Goldstein	1964–2002	Oscar Ravina	1965–2004
Kenneth Gordon	1961–2007	Daniel Reed	1983–
Frank Gullino (C)	1942–79	Joseph Reilich	1932–64
Hae-Young Ham	1986–	Carlo Renzulli	1957–82
Sidney Harth (C)	1979–80	Charles Rex	1979–
Stanley Hoffman	1961–64	Bernard Robbins	1955–83
Mei Ching Huang	2005–08	Michael Rosenker	1943–62*
Joseph Kim (sub)	1979–81	David Rosensweig	1928–62
Lisa Kim	1994–	Leon Rudin	1946–79
Michelle Kim	2000–	Leopold Rybb	1950–71*
Myung-Hi Kim	1977–	Gino Sambuco	1967–2003
Morris H. Kreiselman	1928–65	Allan Schiller	1964–99
Marina Kruglikov	1979–87	Mark Schmoockler	1974–
Soohyn Kwon	2001–	Arthur Schuller (keybd)	1928–65
Hanna Lachert	1971–	Louis Sherman	1928–61
Renato Ladetto	1953–56	Fiona Simon	1985–
Hyunju Lee	2008–	Richard Simon	1965–98

VIOLIN *(cont'd.)*

Sheryl Staples	1998–*	Carol Webb	1977–
Isidor Strassner	1928–61	Max Weiner	1946–94
Na Sun	2005–	Oscar Weizner	1962–2003*
Yoko Takebe	1978–	Donald Whyte	1971–2000
Leon Temerson	1946–70	Sharon Yamada	1987–
Vladimir Tsypin	1982–	Elizabeth Zeltzer	2003–
Frederick Vogelgesang	1953–56	Yulia Ziskel	2001–

VIOLA

Eugene Becker	1957–89	Bernard Linden (sub)	1957–58
William Berman	1954–57	Ralph Mendelson	1953–79
Irene Breslaw	1975–*	Kenneth Mirkin	1981–
Ronald Carbone (sub)	1989–90	Judith Nelson	1983–
		Paul Neubauer	1984–90*
William Carboni	1955–84	Larry Newland	1960–80
Leonard Davis	1949–91*	Henry Nigrine (sub)	1957–89 1989–91
Mary Helen Ewing (sub)	1990–92	Cynthia Phelps	1992–*
Mary Gigliotti (sub)	1991–92	Selig Posner	1956–76
		Dorian Rence	1975–
Katherine Greene	1990–	Robert Rinehart	1992–
Sol Greitzer	1953–84*	Raymond Sabinsky	1943–83
Dawn Hannay	1979–	Max Serbin (sub)	1957–58
Aaron Juvelier (sub)	1957–58	Erich Silberstein (sub)	1967–68
Vivek Kamath	1997–		
Gilad Karni	1992–97	Richard Spencer (OF)	1983–85
David Kates	1933–76		
Peter Kenote	1982–	Basil Vendryes	1983–85
Godfrey Layefsky	1952–57	Joseph Vieland	1931–60
Barry Lehr	1972–	Robert Weinrebe	1948–83
Elias Lifschey	1954–59	Rebecca Young	1985–*
William Lincer	1943–72*		

CELLO

Bernardo Altmann	1952–96	Avram A. Lavin	1962–2004
Gerald K. Appleman	1966–98	Thomas Liberti	1966–96
Eric Bartlett	1996–	Dimitry Markevitch	1958–63
Evangeline Benedetti	1967–	Prudence McDaniel	1990–91
Lorin Bernsohn	1957–2000	(OF)	
Carter Brey	1996–*	Eileen Moon	1998–
Mario Caiati	1929–58	Lorne Munroe	1964–96*
Albert Catelli (sub)	1958–59	Hai-Ye Ni	1999–2007
Paul Clement	1962–95	Martin Ormandy	1929–66
Avron Coleman	1958–66	Asher Richman	1957–93
(sub)	1989–97	Toby Saks	1970–76
Jurgen de Lemos	1964–68	Rudolph Sims	1939–66
Naoum J. Dinger	1928–64	Brinton Smith	2002–06
Nancy Donaruma	1976–2007	Anthony Sophos	1949–57
Elizabeth Dyson	1996–	Alan Stepansky	1988–99*
George Feher	1949–74	Carl Stern	1944–64*
Eileen Folson (OF)	1981–83	Nathan Stutch	1946–89
Milton Forstat	1938–58	Zela Terry (OF)	1979–81
Igor Gefter (sub)	1998–	Qiang Tu	1995–
Jerry Grossman	1974–76	Laszlo Varga	1951–62*
Valentin Hirsu	1976–2009	Ru-Pei Yeh	2006–
Henrich Joachim	1949–58	Wei Yu	2007–
Maria Kitsopoulos	1995–	Frederick Zlotkin (ext)	2006–
Sumire Kudo	2005–		

BASS

William Blossom	1974–	Jon C. Deak	1968–2009*
Walter Botti	1952–2002	Robert Gladstone	1956–66
James Brennand (sub)	1960–61	David J. Grossman	1999–
Robert Brennand	1933–75*	Eugene Levinson	1984–*
Randall Butler	1975–	Homer R. Mensch	1938–75
James V. Candido	1966–99	Lew Norton	1967–2006
William Chartoff	1943–61	Orin O'Brien	1966–

Bass *(cont'd.)*

Satashi Okamoto	2003–	Michele Saxon	1970–2009
Mario Polisi	1944–69	John Schaeffer (pm)	1951–96*
Carlo Raviola	1938–67	Benjamin Schlossberg	1936–69
William Rhein	1961–66	George Wellington (OF)	1987–89
Daniel Rybb	1928–56	Frederick Zimmermann	1930–66

Harp

Nancy Allen	1997–*	Marjorie Tyre McGinnis	1958–60
Sarah Bullen	1986–89*	(ext)	
Theodore Cella	1928–57*	Ruth Negri (ext)	1969–97
Edward Druzinsky	1955–58	Myor Rosen	1960–87*
(ext) (sub)	1959–60*	Sonya Simenauer (ext)	1962–63
Sonya Kahn (ext)	1960–61	(see also Kahn)	
(see also Simenauer)		Christine Stavrache	1957–60*
		Phyllis Wright (ext)	1967–68

Flute

Julius Baker	1965–83*	F. William Heim (picc)	1944–79
Jeanne Baxtresser	1983–98*	Mindy Kaufman (picc)	1978–
Paige Brook	1952–88*	Robert Langevin	2000–*
Sandra Church	1988–*	Robert Morris	1955–74
Julie Duncan (sub)	1998–99	Renée Siebert	1974–
Mary Kay Fink (sub)	1989–90	John Wummer	1942–65*
(picc)			

Piccolo

Mary Kay Fink (sub)	1989–90*
F. William Heim	1952–79*
Mindy Kaufman	1979–*

Oboe

Robert Botti	1992–	Joseph Robinson	1977–2005*
Engelbert Brenner	1931–61	Ronald Roseman	1973–78*
(Eng hrn)		Jerome Roth	1960–92*
Albert Goltzer	1938–84*	Sherry Sylar	1983–*
Harold Gomberg	1943–77*	Liang Wang	2006–*
Michel Nazzi	1928–56		
(Eng hrn, 2nd ob)			

English Horn

Engelbert Brenner	1960–72*
Michel Nazzi (2nd ob)	1928–61*
Thomas Stacy	1972–*

Clarinet

Michael Burgio	1959–2000	Robert McGinnis	1948–60*
Napoleon Cerminara	1948–60	Mark Nuccio	1999–
Stanley Drucker	1948–2009*	(E-flat clar)	
(E-flat clar)		Leonard Schaller	1945–66
Mitchell Estrin (sub)	1998–99	(bass clar)	
Pascual Martinez Forteza	2000–	Peter Simenauer	1959–98
Stephen Freeman	1966–2009	(E-flat clar)	
(bass clar)			

Bass Clarinet

Stephen Freeman	1966–2009*
Leonard Schaller	1945–66*

E-flat Clarinet

Stanley Drucker	1948–60*
Mark Nuccio	1999–*
Peter Simenauer	1959–98*

SAXOPHONE

Albert Regni (ext)   1969–70*

BASSOON

Bert Bial (contrabsn)	1957–95	Judith LeClair	1980–*
David Carroll	1983–2000	Roger Nye	2005–
Arlen Fast (contrabsn)	1995–	William Polisi	1943–58*
Marc Goldberg	2000–2002	Frank Ruggieri	1949–72
Harold Goltzer	1958–83*	Roberto Sensale	1937–57
Leonard Hindell	1972–2005	(contrabsn)	
Kim Laskowski	2006–	Manuel Zegler	1945–81*

CONTRABASSOON

Bert Bial	1957–95*
Arlen Fast	1995–*
Roberto Sensale	1937–57*

HORN

Jerome Ashby	1978–2008*	L. William Kuyper	1968–2007
John Carabella	1959–94	Philip Myers	1979–*
John Cerminaro	1969–79*	William Namen	1945–70
James Chambers (pm)	1946–69*	Erik Ralske	1993–
Ranier De Intinis	1950–93	Luigi Ricci	1928–62
Aubrey Facenda	1970–93	Joseph Singer	1943–74*
Marcus Fischer	1946–62	William Slocum (ext)	1960–61
Joseph Golden	1959–60	Martin Smith	1974–80*
A. Robert Johnson	1962–69*	R. Allen Spanjer	1992–
Thomas Jöstlein	2007–	Howard Wall	1993–
Fred Klein (ext)	1967–68		

TRUMPET

Ethan Bensdorf	2007–	Gerard Schwarz	1973–77*
George F. Coble	1990–93	Zachary Shnek (sub)	1979–80
Carmine Fornarotto	1962–93	James Smith	1942–77
Albert Ligotti (ext)	1967–68	Philip Smith	1978–*
Matthew Muckey	2005–	Thomas V. Smith	1998–
Vincent Penzarella	1977–2005	Robert Sullivan	1993–
Nathan Prager	1929–63	William Vacchiano	1935–73*
Louis Ranger	1976–78*	John R. Ware	1948–88*
James Ross	2005–07	James Wilt	1993–95

BASS TRUMPET

Gordon Pulis (trbn, bar)   1949–56

TROMBONE

Joseph Alessi	1984–*	Earle Leavitt (sub)	1958–59
Gilbert Cohen	1963–85	James Markey	1997–
Edward Erwin	1958–93*	Gordon Pulis	1946–56*
David Finlayson	1985–	(bass trpt, bar)	
Edward Herman, Jr.	1952–85*	Lewis Van Haney	1946–63
Nitzan Hroz	1993–96		

BASS TROMBONE

Donald Harwood	1974–2007*
Allen Ostrander	1946–75*

TUBA

Alan Baer	2003–*
William Bell	1943–61*
Warren Deck	1979–2003*
Joseph Novotny	1961–79*

TIMPANI

Saul Goodman	1928–72*
Roland Kohloff	1972–2004*
Morris Lang (perc)	1971–96
Joseph Pereira (perc)	1997–2008
Markus Rhoten	2006–*

PERCUSSION

Elden C. Bailey	1949–91	Morris Lang (timp)	1955–96
Daniel Druckman	1991–	Joseph Pereira (timp)	1997–2008
Herbert Harris (ext)	1960–63	Walter Rosenberger	1946–85*
Christopher Lamb	1985–*		

KEYBOARD

Jonathan Feldman (ext)	1983–	Bruce Prince-Joseph (ext)	1957–74
		Leonard Raver (ext)	1976–92
Paul Jacobs (ext)	1960–83	Kent Tritle (ext)	2000–
Lionel Party (ext)	1987–	Harriet Wingreen (ext)	1987–

LIBRARIAN

Robert De Celle	1968–88*	John Perkel	1988–99
Howard W. Keresey	1944–71*	Louis Robbins	1970–85*
Thad Marciniack	1985–2007	Lawrence Tarlow	1984–*
Sandra Pearson	1998–	Joseph Zizza	1953–69

PERSONNEL MANAGER

James Chambers	1968–86*
Joseph De Angelis	1952–69*
John Schaeffer (bass)	1965–96*
Carl R. Schiebler	1985–*

Notes

Chapter 1

3   "*The Philharmonic—What's Wrong*": Howard Taubman, *New York Times*, April 29, 1956.

4   "*The men who do the playing*": ibid.

4   "*a powerful, if not*": ibid.

4   "*unenterprising choice*": ibid.

5   "*a valued guest conductor*": ibid.

5   "*a strong note of brilliance*": Louis Biancolli, "Philharmonic Season Exciting," *World-Telegram and the Sun*, May 5, 1956.

5   "*Both New York and the Philharmonic*": Louis Biancolli, "Mitropoulos Is Dedicated Artist," *World-Telegram and the Sun*, September 29, 1956.

8   "*I simply cannot understand*": Paul Henry Lang, review, *New York Herald Tribune*, December 28, 1956.

8   "*There was neither self-seeking*": Irving Kolodin, "Music to My Ears," *Saturday Review*, January 12, 1957.

7   "*be responsible for orchestral discipline*" et seq.: Howard Taubman, "Long Way to Go," *New York Times*, May 12, 1957.

9   "*Surely something is radically wrong*" et seq.: Paul Henry Lang, "Crisis at the Philharmonic," *New York Herald Tribune*, October 13, 1957.

10 "*abdicating with joy*": Dimitri Mitropoulos, quoted in Ross Parmenter, "Leonard Bernstein Heads Philharmonic," *New York Times*, November 20, 1957.

10 "*Mr. Mitropoulos is a great genius*": Leonard Bernstein, quoted in ibid.

10 "*wise to take it*" et seq.: Howard Taubman, "Bear by the Tail," *New York Times*, November 24, 1957.

11 "*worst of all*": Howard Taubman, review, *New York Times*, December 13, 1957.

11 "*I am not allowed*" et seq.: Yehudi Menuhin, quoted in Edward Downes, review, *New York Times*, December 15, 1957.

10 "*that would have been a wrong reason*" et seq.: Lester Trimble, "Music," *Nation*, December 21, 1957.

15 "*If one man no stand*": John Ware, associate principal trumpet, to the author.

17 *A backstage confrontation*: Saul Goodman, timpanist, to the author.

18 "*overwhelming*": Osgood Carruthers, *New York Times*, August 26, 1959.

18 *"The Russians are a race apart"* et seq.: Leonard Bernstein, quoted in "Philharmonic Ends Tour in Washington," *New York Times*, October 13, 1959.

21 *"was of an order"*: Irving Kolodin, "Music to My Ears," *Saturday Review*, March 19, 1960.

22 *"had another good season"* et seq.: Howard Taubman, "Good on Paper," *New York Times*, May 15, 1960.

23 *"There is no excuse"*: Robert E. Simon Jr., quoted in Ross Parmenter, "Concert Season Shifts to Hunter," *New York Times*, January 6, 1960.

23 *"full cooperation"* et seq.: "New Unit Formed to Save Carnegie," *New York Times*, March 31, 1960.

24 *"a fine opportunity"*: Henry Ford II, quoted in Ross Parmenter, "Philharmonic Set For German Date," *New York Times*, June 27, 1960.

CHAPTER 2

26 *"While a man can learn"*: Harold C. Schonberg, review, *New York Times*, October 1, 1960.

26 *"a great conductor, a gentleman"*: Walter Botti to the author, October 17, 2009.

27 *"Enjoy this while you can"* et seq.: John Carabella to the author, October 25, 2006.

28 *"the equal of any living conductor"* et seq.: Harold C. Schonberg, "Spreading Thin," *New York Times*, April 16, 1961.

29 *"What next?"*: Harold C. Schonberg, review, *New York Times*, March 17, 1961.

30 *"smell a conductor"*: Leonard Bernstein to the author and other prospective assistant conductors, March 3, 1961.

30 *"last and best offer"*: Philharmonic management, quoted in "City Issues Plea to Philharmonic," *New York Times*, September 30, 1961.

30 *"Why weren't we invited?"* et seq.: Harold C. Schonberg, "Back to Work," *New York Times*, October 15, 1961.

31 *"Beethoven's imagined nightingale"*: Alan Rich, review, *New York Times*, November 13, 1961.

32 *"I've played hundreds"*: Harold Gomberg to the author, November 24, 1961.

32 *"You know, there were two"*: Armand Neveux to the author, November 25, 1961.

33 *"I never conduct"*: Josef Krips to the author and other Philharmonic assistants, December 5, 1961.

35 *"A few million people"*: Harold C. Schonberg, review, *New York Times*, March 12, 1962.

37 *"Such goings-on"* et seq.: Harold C. Schonberg, review, *New York Times*, April 7, 1962.

37 *"not exactly a big deal"* et seq.: Harold C. Schonberg, "6,456th Concert Spells Finis," *New York Times*, May 20, 1962.

38 *"I wasn't called"*: Leopold Stokowski, heard by those present, May 29, 1962.

39 *"all sweaty"*: Leonard Bernstein, in "Opening Night at Lincoln Center," CBS television, September 23, 1962.

42 *"constantly diminishing"*: Arthur Hull Hayes, president of CBS radio, quoted in Val Adams, "C.B.S. Radio Drops the Philharmonic," *New York Times*, May 27, 1963.

43 *"the entire season"*: Harold C. Schonberg, "An Old Orchestra, a New Hall," *New York Times*, May 26, 1963.

43 *"the genius that makes Bernstein Bernstein"*: ibid.

CHAPTER 3

47 *"bad: bad psychology"*: Harold C. Schonberg, review, *New York Times*, January 3, 1964.

47 *"one of the best"*: Harold C. Schonberg, review, *New York Times*, January 17, 1964.

48 *"intensity of the experience"* et seq.: Howard Klein, review, *New York Times*, January 26, 1964.

48 *"It takes about three weeks"*: George Szell, quoted in Raymond Ericson, "Catching Up with His 'Image,'" *New York Times*, April 5, 1964.

48 *"came down with one of those"* et seq.: Harold C. Schonberg, review, *New York Times*, April 8, 1964.

48 *"the listener is not quite sure"*: Winthrop Sargeant, "Kaddish," *New Yorker*, April 18, 1964.

49 *"I am sure"*: Al Manuti, quoted in Theodore Strongin, "Philharmonic and Musicians Agree on Year-Round Contract," *New York Times*, May 1, 1964.

50 *"smoother and mellower"* et seq.: Harold C. Schonberg, review, *New York Times*, September 30, 1964.

51 *"a blob of molasses"*: Harold C. Schonberg, review, *New York Times*, February 26, 1965.

52 *"It's hard enough"*: Sir Colin Davis to the author, April 8, 1969.

56 *"The symphony is not really"*: Leonard Bernstein, quoted in "Bernstein Lists Season's Music," *New York Times*, April 28, 1965.

56 *"better to expose"* et seq.: ibid.

57 *"the new acoustic setup"* et seq.: Harold C. Schonberg, review, *New York Times*, October 1, 1965.

57 *"almost a legend"*: Theodore Strongin, "Philharmonic Gets a Concertmaster," *New York Times*, February 11, 1966.

57 *"an extraordinary musician"*: Leonard Bernstein, quoted in ibid.

58 *"one of the greatest"* et seq.: Harold C. Schonberg, "Transformation from 'Lenny' to 'Maestro,'" *New York Times*, May 22, 1966.

58 *"too old to be bothered"*: Ernest Ansermet, quoted in Raymond Ericson, "At Odds in Their Eighties," *New York Times*, July 3, 1966.

59 *"A time is arriving"*: Leonard Bernstein, quoted in Theodore Strongin, "Bernstein to Leave Philharmonic in '69," *New York Times*, November 3, 1966.

59 *"threatening to turn into"* et seq.: Harold C. Schonberg, "Bernstein: Wrong Time to Leave," *New York Times*, November 13, 1966.

60 *"one of the most brilliant"*: Harold C. Schonberg, review, *New York Times*, March 27, 1967.

CHAPTER 4

63 *"A lot of us think"*: Zubin Mehta, quoted in Donal Henahan, "Mehta Tells Union He Respects the Philharmonic," *New York Times*, January 4, 1968.

64 *"strict and stern"* et seq.: Max Arons, quoted in "Philharmonic Drops Mehta's Visit in 1968–69," *New York Times*, April 27, 1968.

64 *"I am here to prove"* et seq.: Leonard Bernstein, quoted in "Rumors on Health Irritate Bernstein," *New York Times*, September 24, 1968.

65 *"not merely beautiful"*: Irving Kolodin, "Music to My Ears," *Saturday Review*, March 1, 1969.

65 *"What should sound noble"* et seq.: Harold C. Schonberg, review, *New York Times*, January 31, 1969.

66 *"a great performance"* et seq.: Winthrop Sargeant, "Musical Events," *New Yorker*, February 1, 1969.

67 *"I just couldn't find a word"*: Leonard Bernstein, quoted in Donal Henahan, "Bernstein Given a Hero's Farewell," *New York Times*, May 19, 1969.

67 *"What Bernstein did"*: Harold C. Schonberg, "At Last, the Patina of an Old Master," *New York Times*, May 11, 1969.

68 *"conducting the orchestra"* et seq.: Irving Kolodin, "Music to My Ears," *Saturday Review*, February 15, 1969.

69 *"Doesn't he know any other"* et seq.: Harold C. Schonberg, "What's New? Too Little at the Philharmonic," *New York Times*, September 7, 1969.

69 *"one of the criteria"*: Harold C. Schonberg, review, *New York Times*, November 14, 1969.

69 *"gleaming performance"*: Donal Henahan, review, *New York Times*, November 21, 1969.

69 *"it was unfair"* et seq.: Harold C. Schonberg, review, *New York Times*, January 16, 1970.

70 *"a meeting, a very serious meeting"*: Leonard Bernstein, quoted in Charlotte Curtis, "The Bernsteins' Party," *New York Times*, January 24, 1970.

70 *"silent about Jewish civil rights"*: Jewish Defense League, quoted in Albin Krebs, "Bernstein Incurs J.D.L.'s Wrath," *New York Times*, May 27, 1971.

70 *"essentially uncommunicative"* et seq.: Harold C. Schonberg, review, *New York Times*, February 6, 1970.

70 *"What kind of snobbery"*: ibid.

71 *"Radical Chic: That Party at Lenny's"*: Tom Wolfe, *New York*, June 8, 1970.

71 *"it is safe to say"*: Harold C. Schonberg, review, *New York Times*, May 23, 1970.

72 *"one does not have to like"*: Harold C. Schonberg, review, *New York Times*, September 25, 1970.

72 *"It is a precedent"*: Harold C. Schonberg, review, *New York Times*, October 2, 1970.

73 *"well before this decision"*: Carlos Moseley, quoted in "Rights Unit Clears Philharmonic," *New York Times*, November 17, 1970.

73 *"We have everything to lose"*: Earl Madison, quoted in ibid.

73 *"a shot across the bow"*: Alan Rich, "Classical Music," *New York*, April 26, 1971.

73   *"Nevertheless, a good part of the audience"* et seq.: Harold C. Schonberg, review, *New York Times*, April 17, 1971.

73   *"in a surgically minded way"* et seq.: Harold C. Schonberg, review, *New York Times*, May 1, 1971.

74   *"magnificently re-created"* et seq.: Irving Kolodin, "Music to My Ears," *Saturday Review*, May 15, 1971.

75   *"in the future, Mr. Boulez"*: Harold C. Schonberg, review, *New York Times*, October 3, 1971.

75   *"obvious attributes"*: Irving Kolodin, "Music to My Ears," *Saturday Review*, October 16, 1971.

75   *"absolutely gorgeous"*: Harold C. Schonberg, review, *New York Times*, February 10, 1972.

75   *"a first-rate conductor"* et seq.: Raymond Ericson, review, *New York Times*, October 9, 1971.

76   *"a masterpiece"* et seq.: Harold C. Schonberg, review, *New York Times*, October 23, 1971.

76   *"one of the most nourishing"* et seq.: Harold C. Schonberg, review, *New York Times*, October 30, 1971.

77   *"every bit of applause"*: Harold C. Schonberg, review, *New York Times*, December 16, 1971.

77   *"some of the complaints"* et seq.: Harold C. Schonberg, "The Philharmonic: From Rut to Ruckus," *New York Times*, December 12, 1971.

77   *"been in a rut"*: ibid.

78   *"after playing the life out of "* et seq.: Harold C. Schonberg, review, *New York Times*, March 11, 1972.

78   *"titan among pianists"*: Amyas Ames, quoted in ibid.

78   *"frankly sensuous"* et seq.: Harold C. Schonberg, review, *New York Times*, May 10, 1972.

CHAPTER 5

81   *"Ha! That's better"*: Pierre Boulez, quoted in Raymond Ericson, review, *New York Times*, July 26, 1972.

82   *"has arrived at the stage"* et seq.: Harold C. Schonberg, review, *New York Times*, February 17, 1973.

82   *"rather aseptic ideas"*: Harold C. Schonberg, review, *New York Times*, February 10, 1973.

82   *"I'm going crazy"*: quoted in Stephen E. Rubin, "The Iceberg Conducteth," *New York Times*, March 25, 1973.

82   *"He's one of the finest"*: Roland Kohloff, quoted in ibid.

82   *"he has everything"*: Bert Bial, quoted in ibid.

83   *"He is not a star conductor"*: Christa Ludwig, quoted in ibid.

83   *"make the music overblown and fat"* et seq.: Pierre Boulez, quoted in ibid.

84 *"the audience Mr. Boulez"* et seq.: Donal Henahan, review, *New York Times*, June 16, 1973.

84 *"major gift"*: Donal Henahan, "Philharmonic Hall Gets $8-Million Gift," *New York Times*, September 21, 1973.

85 *"We intend to scour"*: Avery Fisher, quoted in ibid.

85 *"Someday it will be"*: Avery Fisher, quoted in Lawrence Van Gelder, "Low-Key, High-Fidelity Donor," *New York Times*, September 21, 1973.

85 *"I'll be honest with you"*: Avery Fisher, quoted in *New York Post*, October 6, 1973.

85 *"ridiculous"*: Max Arons, quoted in Glenn Fowler, "Strike Is Begun by Philharmonic," *New York Times*, September 26, 1973.

86 *"contracted in blood"*: I. Philip Sipser, quoted in Donal Henahan, "Why Philharmonic Strike Drags On," *New York Times*, October 24, 1973.

86 *"We're absolutely convinced"*: Ralph Mendelson, quoted in ibid.

86 *"was right to accept"*: Amyas Ames, quoted in ibid.

87 *"It was electrifying"*: Eugene Becker to the author, September 1981.

88 *"Agreement Reached in Orchestra Strike"*: Emanuel Perlmutter, *New York Times*, November 29, 1973.

88 *"It was important to end"*: Amyas Ames, quoted in ibid.

88 *"a bit too lovely"*: Michael Gielen to the author, July 1979.

89 *"If I am asked"*: Erich Leinsdorf, *Cadenza: A Musical Career*, 298.

89 *"agreed lightheartedly"*: ibid, p. 298.

89 *"No, I have not closed the door"*: Pierre Boulez, quoted in "Boulez Says Story on Quitting Errs," *New York Times*, January 31, 1974.

90 *"lightened the string texture"*: Raymond Ericson, review, *New York Times*, February 22, 1974.

91 *"articulation was among the cleanest"*: Raymond Ericson, review, *New York Times*, April 27, 1974.

92 *"how the same kind"*: Donal Henahan, "For Good Listening Why Not Try the Philharmonic's Floor?," *New York Times*, June 30, 1974.

93 *"eloquent performance"*: Allen Hughes, review, *New York Times*, October 13, 1974.

93 *"sublime...with an angelic glow"* et seq.: Raymond Ericson, review, *New York Times*, March 8, 1975.

94 *"We have great confidence"*: Amyas Ames, quoted in Harold C. Schonberg, "Lincoln Center to Gut Fisher Hall," *New York Times*, March 26, 1975.

94 *"I've just made a decision"*: Leonard Bernstein, quoted in "Bernstein Discloses Decision to Return," *New York Times*, April 26, 1975.

94 *"an impulsive thing"* et seq.: Harold Lawrence, quoted in ibid.

94 *"delighted that Mr. Bernstein"*: Carlos Moseley, quoted in ibid.

94 *"It was like the resumption"*: ibid.

94 *"All I meant"*: Leonard Bernstein, quoted in Harold C. Schonberg, "Boulez to Leave Philharmonic in '77," *New York Times*, May 15, 1975.

Chapter 6

97 *"a greater warmth"*: David Hamilton, "Why Boulez Likes the Rugs," *New York Times*, July 20, 1975.

97 *"with clarity and elegance"* et seq.: Raymond Ericson, review, *New York Times*, June 19, 1975.

98 *"Welcome to our friends in the Colonies"* et seq.: quoted in Andreas Freund, "Boulez Conquers Europe in 23 Days," *New York Times*, September 21, 1975.

98 *"the Philharmonic was one of the finest"* et seq.: Jacques Lonchampt, quoted in ibid.

99 *"in an honest performance"* et seq.: Donal Henahan, review, *New York Times*, September 27, 1975.

99 *"brittle, swift, high-strung"* et seq.: Irving Kolodin, "Music to My Ears," *Saturday Review*, November 15, 1975.

99 *"interminable"* et seq.: Donal Henahan, review, *New York Times*, October 11, 1975.

100 *"there was no move"*: Harold C. Schonberg, review, *New York Times*, November 27, 1975.

100 *"a rather tedious preview"*: Donal Henahan, review, *New York Times*, January 30, 1976.

100 *"an electrifying finale"*: Raymond Ericson, review, *New York Times*, February 5, 1976.

100 *"cool, austere and rigorous"* et seq.: "Imperious on Podium," *New York Times*, February 26, 1976.

101 *"the young man from Bombay"*: editorial, "Into the Lion's Den," *New York Times*, February 28, 1976.

101 *"impressive"* et seq.: Harold C. Schonberg, review, *New York Times*, March 5, 1976.

101 *"an eloquent and rich work"*: Raymond Ericson, review, *New York Times*, March 7, 1976.

101 *"superb performance"*: Harold C. Schonberg, review, *New York Times*, March 26, 1976.

102 *"It went differently"* et seq.: Leonard Bernstein, quoted in Flora Lewis, "An American in Paris," *New York Times*, June 19, 1976.

102 *"We are in the business"*: Albert K. Webster, quoted in ibid.

102 *"a conductor with great knowledge"*: Tass, quoted in "Philharmonic Praised in Soviet," *New York Times*, September 8, 1976.

103 *"the combination of ravishing lyricism"* et seq.: Harold C. Schonberg, review, *New York Times*, September 27, 1976.

103 *"I wasn't asked"*: a Philharmonic musician to the author, February 25, 2009.

104 *"tenuous financial condition"*: "Musicians Ratify a 3-Year Contract," *New York Times*, October 20, 1976.

104 *"infinitely superior to the old"* et seq.: Harold C. Schonberg, review, *New York Times*, October 20, 1976.

104 *"very clean, precise"*: Pierre Boulez, quoted in Donal Henahan, "Boulez and His Orchestra Express Pleasure," *New York Times*, October 20, 1976.

104 *"a tremendous response"*: James V. Candido, quoted in ibid.

104 *"even more impressive"* et seq.: Harold C. Schonberg, review, *New York Philharmonic*, October 22, 1976.

105 *"with well paced tempos"* et seq.: ibid.

105 *"Hundreds Walk Out"* et seq.: Allen Hughes, review, *New York Times*, November 5, 1976.

105 *"from a work in progress"*: Allen Hughes, review, *New York Times*, November 26, 1976.

105 *"admirable vocal writing"*: ibid.

105 *"towering masterpiece"*: Leonard Bernstein, quoted in Raymond Ericson, review, *New York Times*, December 5, 1976.

106 *"very striking and special"* et seq.: ibid.

106 *"The Philharmonic—A Troubled Giant Facing Change"*: Helen Epstein, *New York Times*, December 19, 1976.

106 *"Between now and next May"* et seq.: ibid.

106 *"suck the blood"*: ibid.

106 *"We are the lifeblood"*: quoted in ibid.

106 *"We perform a conductor's concert"*: Gerard Schwarz, quoted in ibid.

106 *"schizophrenic"* et seq.: ibid.

106 *"We're reserving judgment"*: quoted in ibid.

107 *"a formidable score"* et seq.: Harold C. Schonberg, review, *New York Times*, January 14, 1977.

107 *"lively and attractive"* et seq.: Raymond Ericson, review, *New York Times*, January 30, 1977.

107 *"One of Mr. Boulez's great evenings"* et seq.: Harold C. Schonberg, review, *New York Times*, February 5, 1977.

107 *"a work of stunning authority"*: Irving Kolodin, "Music to My Ears," *Saturday Review*, April 2, 1977.

108 *"temperamental fire"*: Donal Henahan, review, *New York Times*, March 12, 1977.

108 *"sensitive, powerful"* et seq.: Harold C. Schonberg, review, *New York Times*, May 7, 1977.

108 *"a special debt of gratitude"*: Aaron Copland, quoted in Harold C. Schonberg, review, *New York Times*, May 13, 1977.

108 *"did not give the feeling"* et seq.: Harold C. Schonberg, ibid.

109 *"Going to one of his concerts"*: Harold C. Schonberg, "Summing Up the Boulez Era," *New York Times*, May 15, 1977.

109 *"simply tired of being a symbol"* et seq.: Sanford Allen, quoted in Donal Henahan, "One Black in Philharmonic Is Resigning," *New York Times*, August 29, 1977.

110 *"played the difficult concerto"* et seq.: Harold C. Schonberg, review, *New York Times*, September 3, 1977.

111 *"the proportion and the moods"*: Donal Henahan, review, *New York Times*, September 24, 1977.

113 *"sensitive and often powerful"*: Harold C. Schonberg, review, *New York Times*, January 6, 1978.

113 *"glaringly early entry"* et seq.: Donal Henahan, review, *New York Times*, March 31, 1978.

114 *"I intend to give"*: Carlos Moseley, quoted in Allen Hughes, "For Carlos Moseley, a Coda," *New York Times*, June 1, 1978.

114 *"They are like our nonsubscription audiences"*: Erich Leinsdorf, quoted in "Japan Opens Heart to Leinsdorf," *New York Times*, June 30, 1978.

114 *"You should all go to your teachers"* et seq.: Erich Leinsdorf via Henry Fogel to the author, October 2006.

CHAPTER 7

119 *"a faceless work"* et seq.: Donal Henahan, review, *New York Times*, December 1, 1978.

119 *"musical showman and playboy"*: Harold C. Schonberg, "Mehta, Sills and Other Musical Chairs," *New York Times*, December 31, 1978.

119 *"that could serve as a model"* et seq.: Donal Henahan, review, *New York Times*, February 2, 1979.

119 *"If the Philharmonic has not"*: Donal Henahan, review, *New York Times*, February 21, 1979.

120 *"cotton candy"* et seq.: Donal Henahan, review, *New York Times*, March 2, 1979.

120 *"If you put mustard and pepper"*: Jean Morel in rehearsal of the Juilliard Orchestra, heard by the author and the rest of the orchestra, April 1954.

120 *"a performance that will set"*: Harold C. Schonberg, review, *New York Times*, May 3, 1979.

120 *"Four rehearsals and four concerts"*: Zubin Mehta, quoted in "Philharmonic Extends Mehta's Contract," *New York Times*, May 3, 1979.

121 *"Mr. Kubelík leaves flamboyance"*: Harold C. Schonberg, review, *New York Times*, September 14, 1979.

122 *"there was never a dull moment"* et seq.: Harold C. Schonberg, review, *New York Times*, October 19, 1979.

122 *"to help Zubin out"*: Sidney Harth, quoted in John Rockwell, "Philharmonic Gets Help," *New York Times*, November 29, 1979.

123 *"emotionally empty stuff"* et seq.: Donal Henahan, review, *New York Times*, November 30, 1979.

123 *"with love and affection"* et seq.: Harold C. Schonberg, review, *New York Times*, December 14, 1979.

123 *"delicate shadings and sweet tone"*: Donal Henahan, review, *New York Times*, January 4, 1980.

124 *"Only in television"*: John J. O'Connor, "TV: 8-H Salutes Toscanini," *New York Times*, January 11, 1980.

124 *"energetic, eloquent"* et seq.: Harold C. Schonberg, review, *New York Times*, January 12, 1980.

124 *"a sudden inability"*: Donal Henahan, review, *New York Times*, February 7, 1980.

125 *"When I heard"*: Zubin Mehta, quoted in John Rockwell, "Philharmonic Performs in Harlem," *New York Times*, April 22, 1980.

125 *"There's no way"*: Leontyne Price, quoted in ibid.

125 *"We haven't seen anything like this"* et seq.: Samuel DeWitt Proctor, quoted in ibid.

127 *"represented both Mr. Mehta and the orchestra"*: Donal Henahan, review, *New York Times*, October 3, 1980.

127 *"It was just as much fun"*: Raymond Ericson, review, *New York Times*, October 13, 1980.

127 *"addressed this score"*: John Rockwell, review, *New York Times*, November 21, 1980.

128 *"cleansed Bruckner without scrubbing"*: John Rockwell, review, *New York Times*, November 28, 1980.

128 *"Has any American orchestral piece"*: Donal Henahan, review, *New York Times*, February 6, 1981.

128 *"To be invited back"* et seq.: Zubin Mehta, quoted in Peter G. Davis, review, *New York Times*, February 17, 1981.

128 *"Hearing Verdi's mighty 'Libera me'"*: Peter G. Davis, ibid.

129 *"managed to find"*: Donal Henahan, review, *New York Times*, March 26, 1981.

129 *"held the attention"*: Donal Henahan, review, *New York Times*, April 3, 1981.

130 *"made a splendid impression"*: Donal Henahan, review, *New York Times*, May 28, 1981.

130 *"a superior example"* et seq.: Donal Henahan, review, *New York Times*, June 17, 1981.

130 *"a passionate, personal and altogether convincing"*: John Rockwell, review, *New York Times*, June 20, 1981.

130 *"just didn't sound at home"*: John Rockwell, review, *New York Times*, September 10, 1981.

130 *"Mr. Mehta's Brahms Third"*: John Rockwell, review, *New York Times*, September 28, 1981.

131 *"a somewhat meandering"*: Donal Henahan, review, *New York Times*, October 6, 1981.

131 *"an absent-minded quality"* et seq.: Donal Henahan, review, *New York Times*, January 8, 1982.

131 *"a rough and inelegant"*: Donal Henahan, review, *New York Times*, January 15, 1982.

131 *"dared the orchestra"* et seq.: Donal Henahan, review, *New York Times*, February 13, 1982.

131 *"direct, intense and passionate"* et seq.: Donal Henahan, review, *New York Times*, February 21, 1982.

132 *"has a way"* et seq.: Bernard Holland, review, *New York Times*, March 7, 1982.

132 *"a marvelous atmospheric performance"* et seq.: Donal Henahan, review, *New York Times*, April 30, 1982.

132 *"expertise served him"*: John Rockwell, review, *New York Times*, May 27, 1982.

132 *"baton technique in Petrushka"* et seq.: John Rockwell, review, *New York Times*, June 3, 1982.

Chapter 8

135 *"among the top orchestras"* et seq.: John Rockwell, "Philharmonic," *New York Times Magazine*, September 19, 1982.

136 *"The Philharmonic is the only orchestra"*: ibid.

136 *"may have come along too late"*: ibid.

138 *"was shaped as it only can be"*: John Rockwell, review, *New York Times*, October 8, 1982.

138 *"He has nearly everything"*: Bernard Holland, review, *New York Times*, January 9, 1983.

138 *"urgently communicates"*: Peter G. Davis, "Music," *New York*, January 24, 1983.

139 *"a timely and timeless work"*: Donal Henahan, review, *New York Times*, March 15, 1983.

139 *"did the orchestra and its conductor honor"*: Donal Henahan, review, *New York Times*, April 1, 1983.

139 *"I will be 77 years old"* et seq.: Amyas Ames, quoted in Edward Rothstein, "Ames to Leave Philharmonic," *New York Times*, April 13, 1983.

140 *"showed what intelligent artists can do"*: Donal Henahan, review, *New York Times*, April 22, 1983.

140 *"Mehta's finest achievement"* et seq.: Peter G. Davis, "Music," *New York*, May 9, 1983.

142 *"a Romantic look backward"*: Edward Rothstein, review, *New York Times*, June 9, 1983.

142 *"freedom of action"*: Sampson R. Field, quoted in Edward Rothstein, "Philharmonic Musicians Complain," *New York Times*, June 30, 1983.

143 *"seems to happen"*: Constance Hoguet, quoted in ibid.

143 *"mediocre playing"* et seq.: Donal Henahan, "Will the Philharmonic Live Up to Its Advertising?," *New York Times*, September 11, 1983.

143 *"conductor and orchestra seemed"*: Bernard Holland, review, *New York Times*, September 16, 1983.

144 *"a muscular, frequently gripping"* et seq.: Donal Henahan, review, *New York Times*, October 12, 1983.

144 *"the Philharmonic was a virtuoso ensemble"* et seq.: Allen Hughes, review, *New York Times*, October 20, 1983.

144 *"It was certainly a vote"*: Albert K. Webster, quoted in John Rockwell, "Mehta's Contract Extended to 1990," *New York Times*, November 4, 1983.

144 *"Zubin Mehta's commitment to us"*: Carlos Moseley, quoted in ibid.

145 *"the Philharmonic can sound"*: Donal Henahan, "Mehta Has a Mandate," *New York Times*, November 13, 1983.

145 *"straightforward and often pedestrian"*: Donal Henahan, review, *New York Times*, January 6, 1984.

145 *"This was easily"*: Donal Henahan, review, *New York Times*, January 13, 1984.

146 *"I have never seen"*: Donal Henahan, review, *New York Times*, January 27, 1984.

146 *"When Veronica Plays the Harmonica"* et seq.: Leopold Stokowski, heard on New York Philharmonic WQXR 1982 Radiothon Special Edition.

147 *"to correct a severe chronic inflammation"*: John Rockwell, "Zubin Mehta Out for Season," *New York Times*, March 28, 1984.

148 *"Every guest conductor"*: Donal Henahan, "Acoustical Problems Still Plague Philharmonic," *New York Times*, May 20, 1984.

148 *"The old-time conductors"*: quoted in ibid.

148 *"a real modern masterpiece"*: John Rockwell, review, *New York Times*, June 1, 1984.

149 *"both proved to be works"* et seq.: Donal Henahan, review, *New York Times*, June 8, 1984.

149 *"still a foreigner"* et seq.: Zubin Mehta, quoted in Harold C. Schonberg, "Mehta and Orchestra Tune Up for Foreign Tour," *New York Times*, August 7, 1984.

149 *"screening, portrayal, or musical representation"*: John Rockwell, "No Malaysia Visit for Philharmonic," *New York Times*, August 11, 1984.

149 *"if the Malaysians seek to tell"*: Rabbi Alexander M. Schindler, quoted in John Rockwell, "Philharmonic Replaces Work by Bloch," *New York Times*, August 10, 1984.

150 *"won't hurt anybody"*: quoted in "Malaysian Dismisses Loss of Philharmonic," *New York Times*, August 14, 1984.

150 *"This is unprecedented"*: Albert K. Webster, quoted in Barbara Crossette, "Philharmonic Visit Gets Enthusiastic Thai Effort," *New York Times*, September 4, 1984.

150 *"more meaty"*: quoted in ibid.

150 *"I've never seen him this excited"* et seq.: quoted in William K. Stevens, "Cheers for Mehta," *New York Times*, September 17, 1984.

150 *"But if I get too excited"* et seq.: Zubin Mehta, quoted in ibid.

CHAPTER 9

151 *"a sure, practiced"*: John Rockwell, review, *New York Times*, October 11, 1984.

152 *"the best thing"*: Donal Henahan, review, *New York Times*, November 22, 1984.

151 *"Praise for a pianist"* et seq.: Donal Henahan, review, *New York Times*, November 27, 1984.

152 *"heartfelt but oddly vaporous and diffuse"*: Donal Henahan, review, *New York Times*, December 14, 1984.

153 *"an open, accessible"* et seq.: John Rockwell, review, *New York Times*, January 4, 1985.

153 *"not insignificant"* et seq.: John Rockwell, review, *New York Times*, January 11, 1985.

153 *"sounded nothing like"* et seq.: Bernard Holland, review, *New York Times*, January 19, 1985.

153 *"kept the action flowing"*: Donal Henahan, review, *New York Times*, February 2, 1985.

154 *"for vocal purity"* et seq.: Donal Henahan, review, *New York Times*, February 23, 1985.

155 *"I know that, whatever I do"*: James Dixon to the author, January 1985.

155 *"One never had any doubt"* et seq.: Donal Henahan, review, *New York Times*, April 5, 1985.

155 *"In spite of his abilities"*: Donal Henahan, "Competence Was the Rule at the Philharmonic," *New York Times*, May 19, 1985.

156 *"like carrying coals"*: Francis Little, quoted in E. J. Dionne Jr., "On Tour, Philharmonic Warms to the Ovations," *New York Times*, June 22, 1985.

156 *"unfriendly act"*: Melina Mercouri, quoted in Edward Schumacher, "Philharmonic Cancels Stop in Greece," *New York Times*, June 23, 1985.

156 *"There's no program rustling"* et seq.: Thomas Stacy, quoted in Moshe Brilliant, "Mehta Combines New York and Israeli Orchestras," *New York Times*, August 1, 1985.

156 *"Our subscribers judge us"*: Joseph Robinson, quoted in ibid.

157 *"thrilling—and possibly historic"* et seq.: Frank Rich, review, *New York Times*, September 7, 1985.

157 *"hodge-podge"* et seq.: Donal Henahan, review, *New York Times*, September 13, 1985.

158 *"disjointed, diffuse"* et seq.: Donal Henahan, review, *New York Times*, September 20, 1985.

159 *"a piece worth hearing again"*: Donal Henahan, review, *New York Times*, September 27, 1985.

159 *"a shorter interval"*: ibid.

159 *"the man who may have been"*: John Rockwell, "Carlos Moseley Reflects on Philharmonic Years," *New York Times*, November 7, 1985.

159 *"it's a terrible strain"* et seq.: Carlos Moseley, quoted in ibid.

160 *"A birthday party disguised"*: Donal Henahan, review, *New York Times*, November 15, 1985.

160 *"an hour and twenty minutes of emotional extravagance"*: Donal Henahan, review, *New York Times*, November 28, 1985.

161 *"was another of those Bernstein concerts"*: ibid.

161 *"Why Today's Orchestras Are Adrift"*: Will Crutchfield, *New York Times*, December 22, 1985.

161 *"to achieve an apocalyptic level"*: Michael Tilson Thomas, quoted in ibid.

162 *"one of the best in the business"*: Donal Henahan, review, *New York Times*, January 17, 1986.

163 *"a remarkable performance"*: Donal Henahan, review, *New York Times*, February 21, 1986.

163 *"a static, shimmering piece"* et seq.: Donal Henahan, review, *New York Times*, March 7, 1986.

163 *"if they're still in the hall"* et seq.: John Rockwell, review, *New York Times*, March 14, 1986.

164 *"the music snapped like a whip"*: Will Crutchfield, review, *New York Times*, March 18, 1986.

164 *"provided Mr. Drucker"*: Donal Henahan, review, *New York Times*, March 28, 1986.

164 *"a wider freedom of interests"*: Erich Leinsdorf, quoted in Bernard Holland, "Youth Revitalizes the Symphony Orchestra," *New York Times*, April 13, 1986.

164 *"If, as it is said,"*: Martin Eshelman, letter to the editor, *New York Times*, May 18, 1986.

CHAPTER 10

167 *"a pair of phantasmagorical"* et seq.: Donal Henahan, review, *New York Times*, May 22, 1986.

168 *"common grave"*: George Szell, quoted in Donal Henahan, "Pondering the New Music Dilemma," *New York Times*, June 15, 1986.

168 *"That is what the great conductors"*: Donal Henahan, ibid.

168 *"seems one of the few"*: Bernard Holland, review, *New York Times*, October 18, 1986.

169 *"all in all"*: Donal Henahan, review, *New York Times*, October 24, 1986.

169 *"more noble"*: John Rockwell, review, *New York Times*, November 2, 1986.

169 *"established the archives"* et seq.: Barbara Haws, quoted in Tim Page, "The Philharmonic Archivist at Work," *New York Times*, November 23, 1986.

170 *"derivative and second-rate stuff"* et seq.: Donal Henahan, review, *New York Times*, November 27, 1986.

170 *"had nothing but respect"* et seq.: Stephen Stamas, quoted in Ari L. Goldman, "Musicians in Philharmonic Boycott Harlem Church," *New York Times*, December 19, 1986.

170 *"This may not have been"*: Donal Henahan, review, *New York Times*, December 12, 1986.

171 *"rewarded with what will surely rank"* et seq.: Donal Henahan, review, *New York Times*, January 23, 1987.

172 *"a splendid conductor"*: Donal Henahan, review, *New York Times*, January 30, 1987.

172 *"the complete musician"*: Donal Henahan, review, *New York Times*, February 20, 1987.

172 *"his great economy"*: Donal Henahan, review, *New York Times*, March 6, 1987.

173 *"Perhaps it takes"*: Donal Henahan, review, *New York Times*, April 10, 1987.

173 *"a singular but heart-piercing performance"*: Donal Henahan, review, *New York Times*, April 17, 1987.

173 *"I am Gustav Mahler"*: Leonard Bernstein to the author.

173 *"polished off this Adagio"*: Donal Henahan, review, *New York Times*, May 29, 1987.

174 *"You know, we cannot do two"*: Dimitri Mitropoulos, heard by the author, April 12, 1956.

176 *"one of the grandest works"* et seq.: Donal Henahan, review, *New York Times*, September 19, 1987.

176 *"duplication is only dull"*: Will Crutchfield, review, *New York Times*, September 25, 1987.

177 *"no plans to take another position"*: Zubin Mehta, quoted in John Rockwell, "Mehta, with Buts, Talks of Leaving the Philharmonic in 1991," *New York Times*, December 16, 1987.

177 *"Lila literally means 'play'"*: Olivier Messiaen, liner notes for *Messiaen, Turangalila Symphony*, cond. Seiji Ozawa (RCA Victor LSC-7051, 1967).

178 *"a pleasure to hear the piano"*: Donal Henahan, review, *New York Times*, January 14, 1988.

178 *"Mr. Leinsdorf conducted"* et seq.: Bernard Holland, review, *New York Times*, January 23, 1988.

178 *"of irresistible momentum"*: Donal Henahan, review, *New York Times*, February 13, 1988.

179 *"solid and musicianly performance"* et seq.: Donal Henahan, review, *New York Times*, February 17, 1988.

179 *"on the whole fashioned"* et seq.: Donal Henahan, review, *New York Times*, May 21, 1988.

CHAPTER 11

181 *"This is the most wonderful performance"*: Zubin Mehta, quoted in Esther B. Fein, "An Exultant Zubin Mehta Offers Mahler in Moscow," *New York Times*, June 6, 1988.

182 *"a forceful, listenable piece"* et seq.: Donal Henahan, review, *New York Times*, June 15, 1988.

182 *"What an exceptional—almost unique"*: Bernard Holland, review, *New York Times*, June 20, 1988.

183 *"the perennial wonder boy"* et seq.: Donal Henahan, "America's Musician at 70," *New York Times*, August 21, 1988.

183 *"It is a career with more heads"*: ibid.

183 *"businesslike"*: Will Crutchfield, review, *New York Times*, September 18, 1988.

184 *"a work that invariably seizes"* et seq.: Donal Henahan, review, *New York Times*, September 25, 1988.

184 *"ponderous and hard driven"* et seq.: Donal Henahan, review, *New York Times*, October 8, 1988.

184 *"this virtuoso orchestra"* et seq.: Bernard Holland, review, *New York Times*, October 15, 1988.

185 *"the greatest orchestra in the world"*: Zubin Mehta, quoted in John Rockwell, "Mehta to Step Down as Music Director of the Philharmonic," *New York Times*, November 3, 1988.

185 *"has provided outstanding artistic leadership"*: Stephen Stamas, quoted in ibid.

185 *"At Mr. Mehta's pace"*: Donal Henahan, review, *New York Times*, November 5, 1988.

185 *"Please do not say 'the cemetery'"* et seq.: Donal Henahan, "Lincoln Center Sends Out Search Parties," *New York Times*, November 13, 1988.

186 *"You'll hate this one"*: Leonard Bernstein, quoted in John Rockwell, review, *New York Times*, November 20, 1988.

186 *"everyone chuckled"* et seq.: John Rockwell, ibid.

187 *"transform clumps"* et seq.: Donal Henahan, review, *New York Times*, November 25, 1988.

187 *"the sound and feel of music"*: Donal Henahan, review, *New York Times*, December 3, 1988.

187 *"the formally ingenious"*: ibid.

187   *"very impressive"*: John Rockwell, review, *New York Times*, December 11, 1988.

187   *"rich and brilliant sonic onslaught"* et seq.: John Rockwell, review, *New York Times*, December 18, 1988.

188   *"I can't believe my Jimmy is gone"*: Leonard Bernstein, quoted in Glenn Collins, "James Chambers, 68, Former Orchestra Hornist," *New York Times*, January 2, 1989.

188   *"Working with him on a daily basis"*: Zubin Mehta, quoted in ibid.

188   *"downright satisfying"* et seq.: John Rockwell, review, *New York Times*, January 7, 1989.

188   *"a taut, well-played"* et seq.: John Rockwell, review, *New York Times*, January 14, 1989.

188   *"not at all like neglected masterpieces"* et seq.: Donal Henahan, review, *New York Times*, January 21, 1989.

189   *"a natural conductor"*: Donal Henahan, review, *New York Times*, February 3, 1989.

189   *"a masterly score"* et seq.: Donal Henahan, review, *New York Times*, February 11, 1989.

189   *"took a prize"*: Donal Henahan, review, *New York Times*, March 12, 1989.

190   *"confident, technically well-knit"*: Donal Henahan, review, *New York Times*, March 25, 1989.

190   *"this 'Resurrection' seemed"*: Donal Henahan, review, *New York Times*, April 1, 1989.

190   *"a reflective, melancholy tinge"*: Donal Henahan, review, *New York Times*, April 8, 1989.

190   *"Tea Leaves at the Philharmonic"*: Donal Henahan, *New York Times*, April 9, 1989.

191   *"Mr. Leinsdorf, an impeccable technician"*: ibid.

191   *"has access to the same music libraries"* et seq.: Donal Henahan, review, *New York Times*, May 6, 1989.

192   *"For those of you who haven't been there"*: Erich Leinsdorf, heard by the author and 119,999 others, July 24, 1989.

193   *"I think it was the biggest discovery"*: Stephen Stamas, quoted in David E. Sanger, "In Japan, Midori Is a New Yorker," *New York Times*, September 16, 1989.

193   *"view of the mass"*: Donal Henahan, review, *New York Times*, October 7, 1989.

193   *"The American Premiere of an 1869 Musical Camel"*: Donal Henahan, *New York Times*, October 14, 1989.

195   *"this was the most enjoyable performance"*: John Rockwell, review, *New York Times*, November 4, 1989.

195   *"very deftly played"*: John Rockwell, review, *New York Times*, December 16, 1989.

195   *"a bullied account"*: James R. Oestreich, review, *New York Times*, December 23, 1989.

195   *"gave an exquisite solo performance"*: ibid.

195   *"It was one of those dangerously personal"*: Donal Henahan, "The Year's Best: Music View," *New York Times*, December 24, 1989.

CHAPTER 12

197   *"they're not the bunch of wild men"*: Sir Colin Davis, quoted in John Rockwell, "Philharmonic May Name 3 Conductors to Share its Directorship," *New York Times*, February 15, 1990.

198   *"The music director today"*: Erich Leinsdorf, quoted in ibid.

198   *"referring to currently active conductors"*: Ronald Wilford, quoted in Donal Henahan, "It's Troika Time at the Philharmonic," *New York Times*, February 25, 1990.

198   *"it is a fact of life"* et seq.: ibid.

199   *"I believe that most musicians"*: Kurt Masur, quoted in Allan Kozinn, "Kurt Masur to Head New York Philharmonic," *New York Times*, April 12, 1990.

199   *"I came into politics unwillingly"*: ibid.

199   *"to provide a steadier musical life"* et seq.: ibid.

199   *"unless he has a few surprising ideas"* et seq.: Donal Henahan, "Mehtaville Awaits Masur's Leadership," *New York Times*, April 22, 1990.

200   *"gave Mr. Mehta the chance"*: Bernard Holland, review, *New York Times*, May 19, 1990.

200   *"Chest Pains Send Masur to Hospital"*: *New York Times*, May 21, 1990.

200   *"He did not strike me"*: Albert K. Webster, quoted in "Masur, Out of Clinic, Returns to Conducting," *New York Times*, June 5, 1990.

201   *"Concert music can be greater"*: Erich Leinsdorf, New York Philharmonic program note, May 24, 1990.

201   *"is an honorable conductor"*: John Rockwell, review, *New York Times*, June 2, 1990.

202   *"solid German musicians"* et seq.: John Rockwell, "The Future of the Philadelphia and Germanism on the Rise," *New York Times*, August 28, 1990.

203   *"made an incendiary combination"*: Donal Henahan, review, *New York Times*, September 14, 1990.

203   *"The New York Philharmonic has grown"*: Stephen Stamas, quoted in John Rockwell, "Administrator Quits Philharmonic," *New York Times*, October 6, 1990.

204   *"Music's Monarch"*: Donal Henahan, *New York Times*, October 15, 1990.

204   *"The Last Days of Leonard Bernstein"*: John Rockwell, *New York Times*, October 16, 1990.

204   *"We love you—stop smoking"*: quoted in ibid.

204   *"Lenny is the only conductor"*: quoted in ibid.

204   *"The great thing about conducting"*: Leonard Bernstein, quoted in ibid.

204   *"Remembering a Musician's Musician"*: Bernard Holland, *New York Times*, October 16, 1990.

204   *"He might get a little faster"* et seq.: Newton Mansfield, quoted in ibid.

205   *"We were surprised"*: Leonard Davis, quoted in ibid.

205   *"I want to keep on trying"*: Leonard Bernstein, quoted in "The Musician" [editorial], *New York Times*, October 16, 1990.

205   *"Leonard Bernstein was an important part"*: ibid.

206   *"What fun we all had"*: Jamie Bernstein Thomas, quoted in John Rockwell, "Leonard Bernstein Is Remembered with Music, Words and Laughter," *New York Times*, November 15, 1990.

206   *"He's the best we have"*: Leonard Bernstein to the author.

206   *"laying down of the law"*: Philip Ramey, liner notes for *Copland Conducts Copland* (Columbia M-31714, 1972).

207 *"When Mr. Masur agreed"*: Stephen Stamas, quoted in Allan Kozinn, "Kurt Masur to Join the Philharmonic in 1991, a Year Early," *New York Times*, December 18, 1990.

207 *"a tirelessly demanding impression"* et seq.: John Rockwell, review, *New York Times*, December 20, 1990.

208 *"I know my place is in Israel"*: Zubin Mehta, New York Philharmonic program insert, January 17, 1991.

208 *"Now, when I hear the personnel manager"*: Samuel Wong, quoted in Allan Kozinn, "An Emergency Call from the Philharmonic," *New York Times*, January 17, 1991.

208 *"emphasized the graceful, feminine side"*: Donal Henahan, review, *New York Times*, January 26, 1991.

209 *"brisk, sprightly performances"* et seq.: John Rockwell, review, *New York Times*, February 2, 1991.

209 *"about the best Mozart conducting"* et seq.: John Rockwell, review, *New York Times*, February 10, 1991.

211 *"went off exactly as scheduled"*: Donal Henahan, review, *New York Times*, April 13, 1991.

211 *"Rest easy, Toscanini"*: Donal Henahan, review, *New York Times*, April 27, 1991.

212 *"This is a consecrated house"*: Isaac Stern, quoted in John Rockwell, "Carnegie Celebrates 100 Years and Itself," *New York Times*, May 6, 1991.

213 *"as spirited and attentively accented"*: Allan Kozinn, review, *New York Times*, May 18, 1991.

213 *"who lifted the evening"*: Donal Henahan, review, *New York Times*, May 25, 1991.

213 *"I speak for eight million New Yorkers"*: David Dinkins, quoted in John Rockwell, "Mehta Bids Farewell to the Philharmonic," *New York Times*, May 29, 1991.

213 *"a man of the people"* et seq.: George H. W. Bush, quoted in ibid.

214 *"I cannot tell you what this means to me"*: Zubin Mehta, quoted in ibid.

214 *"malicious attacks in the New York press"* et seq.: Zubin Mehta, *Zubin Mehta: The Score of My Life*, p. 139.

214 *"If he has a fault in rehearsal"*: Charles Rex, quoted in James R. Oestreich, "For Mehta, the Final Melody Is Bittersweet," *New York Times*, May 26, 1991.

214 *"Most of the time, orchestras"*: Werner Klemperer, quoted in ibid.

CHAPTER 13

216 *"This was a fine, invigorating way"*: James R. Oestreich, review, *New York Times*, July 16, 1991.

216 *"himself thoroughly comfortable"* et seq.: Edward Rothstein, review, *New York Times*, September 12, 1991.

217 *"exhibited refined ideas"*: Edward Rothstein, review, *New York Times*, September 21, 1991.

218 *"sweet"*: Edward Rothstein, review, *New York Times*, September 28, 1991.

218 *"moments of pleasure taken"*: ibid.

218 *"did their work"*: Bernard Holland, review, *New York Times*, October 1, 1991.

218 *"great"* et seq.: Edward Rothstein, review, *New York Times*, October 22, 1991.

218 *"Mr. Masur is making it clear"*: Edward Rothstein, review, *New York Times*, October 21, 1991.

218 *"to have a series of open discussions"* et seq.: Allan Kozinn, "Kurt Masur to Answer the Public," *New York Times*, October 19, 1991.

219 *"very interested in the thoughts and wishes"*: Kurt Masur, quoted in ibid.

219 *"I am a dreamer"*: Kurt Masur, quoted in Allan Kozinn, "More Tinkering with Acoustics at Avery Fisher," *New York Times*, November 16, 1991.

220 *"by gradually varying"*: Edward Rothstein, review, *New York Times*, November 17, 1991.

220 *"When I conduct Beethoven"* et seq.: Kurt Masur, quoted in Allan Kozinn, "Masur, as Just Plain Kurt, Gives His Audience Some Answers," *New York Times*, November 20, 1991.

221 *"made the Requiem seem to be"* et seq.: Edward Rothstein, review, *New York Times*, December 9, 1991.

224 *"extremely entertaining"* et seq.: Edward Rothstein, review, *New York Times*, March 1, 1992.

224 *"it was beautifully tailored"* et seq.: Bernard Holland, review, *New York Times*, March 8, 1992.

225 *"Is Bernstein Passé on Television? Only in America"*: Joseph Horowitz, *New York Times*, April 5, 1992.

225 *"With his coonskin-cap haircut"* et seq.: Bernard Holland, review, *New York Times*, April 18, 1992.

226 *"not so much performed as stalked"* et seq.: Bernard Holland, review, *New York Times*, May 4, 1992.

227 *"a fallacy at the heart of this work"*: Edward Rothstein, review, *New York Times*, May 23, 1992.

227 *"impressive"* et seq.: Edward Rothstein, "Sweetness? At the Philharmonic?," *New York Times*, May 24, 1992.

CHAPTER 14

231 *"Mr. Masur calls us"*: Deborah Borda, quoted in Allan Kozinn, "Philharmonic Past Meets Future," *New York Times*, September 20, 1992.

231 *"the most thrilling sound"* et seq.: James R. Oestreich, review, *New York Times*, September 26, 1992.

232 *"These 'Pictures' glowed"*: Alex Ross, review, *New York Times*, October 4, 1992.

232 *"invite us to listen"* et seq.: Bernard Holland, review, *New York Times*, October 10, 1992.

233 *"a hard, glassy quality"*: Edward Rothstein, review, *New York Times*, November 7, 1992.

233 *"should stand as a highlight"*: Alex Ross, review, *New York Times*, December 5, 1992.

234 *"impressively accomplished soloist"* et seq.: Edward Rothstein, review, *New York Times*, December 15, 1992.

235 *"the complete violinist"*: Glenn Dicterow, quoted in Harold C. Schonberg, "Nathan Milstein Dies at 88: An Exalted Violin Virtuoso," *New York Times*, December 22, 1992.

236 *"One did not have the sense"*: Allan Kozinn, review, *New York Times*, January 30, 1993.

236 *"splendid debut"* et seq.: Bernard Holland, review, *New York Times*, February 6, 1993.

237 *"that spoke of a deep love"*: Edward Rothstein, review, *New York Times*, February 20, 1992.

237 *"big post-Mahlerian statement"* et seq.: Bernard Holland, review, *New York Times*, February 17, 1993.

238 *"the composer's voice was precise"*: Edward Rothstein, review, *New York Times*, March 6, 1993.

238 *"no trace of the Kapellmeister"*: Vienna Kurrier, quoted in John Rockwell, "Masur Takes the Philharmonic on the Road," *New York Times*, April 5, 1993.

239 *"partly a soap opera of its era"*: Edward Rothstein, review, *New York Times*, May 15, 1993.

239 *"Speak Loudly, Carry No Stick"*: James R. Oestreich, *New York Times*, May 23, 1993.

239 *"volatile temperament"*: ibid.

239 *"there is still talk of a honeymoon"* et seq.: ibid.

239 *"up to the last second"* et seq.: Newton Mansfield, quoted in ibid.

240 *"expressions of honest hard work"*: Bernard Holland, review, *New York Times*, May 24, 1993.

240 *"Perhaps Masur's next artistic task"*: ibid.

240 *"We are all never coughing"*: Kurt Masur, quoted in Nadie Brozan, "Chronicle," *New York Times*, May 27, 1993.

240 *"I have just praise for them"*: Kurt Masur, quoted in ibid.

CHAPTER 15

241 *"found his freedom"*: Edward Rothstein, review, *New York Times*, June 18, 1993.

242 *"a conscience for two generations"* et seq.: Bernard Holland, "Erich Leinsdorf, 81, a Conductor of Intelligence and Utility, Is Dead," *New York Times*, September 12, 1993.

242 *"vigorous performance"* et seq.: Edward Rothstein, review, *New York Times*, September 23, 1993.

243 *"stunningly secure"* et seq.: James R. Oestreich, review, *New York Times*, October 12, 1993.

243 *"taut, confident"*: Edward Rothstein, review, *New York Times*, October 24, 1993.

243 *"seemed happy"*: Bernard Holland, review, *New York Times*, November 26, 1993.

244 *"compelling"* et seq.: Edward Rothstein, review, *New York Times*, December 17, 1993.

246 *"frail, relatively brief"* et seq.: Edward Rothstein, review, *New York Times*, February 12, 1994.

246 *"one of the finest"*: Edward Rothstein, review, *New York Times*, February 19, 1994.

246 *"I like to be thought of"*: Avery Fisher, quoted in Allan Kozinn, "Avery Fisher, Philanthropist, Dies at 87," *New York Times*, February 27, 1994.

246 *"I was sweaty the whole time"*: John Sykes, quoted in James Barron, "For Settlement Orchestra, a Big-Time Downbeat," *New York Times*, March 17, 1994.

246 *"Be in heaven"*: Kurt Masur, quoted in ibid.

247 *"stirring success"*: James R. Oestreich, review, *New York Times*, April 8, 1994.

247 *"the brass playing was exquisitely tuned"* et seq.: Bernard Holland, review, *New York Times*, May 2, 1994.

248 *"In his self-effacing way"*: Bernard Holland, review, *New York Times*, May 6, 1994.

248 *"qualities of a Leipzig"*: Bernard Holland, review, *New York Times*, May 14, 1994.

249 *"really investments"*: Stephen Stamas, quoted in Diana Jean Schemo, "Philharmonic's Deficit Persists Despite New Regime's Gains," *New York Times*, June 30, 1994.

249 *"Music needs all kinds"*: Rudolf Firkušny, quoted in James R. Oestreich, "Rudolf Firkusny, an Elegant and Patrician Pianist, Is Dead at 82," *New York Times*, July 20, 1994.

250 *"the ultimate tribute"*: Carlos Moseley, quoted in Edward Rothstein, "Masur and the Philharmonic: A Comfortable Partnership," *New York Times*, September 23, 1994.

251 *"I, for one, am tired"*: Bernard Holland, review, *New York Times*, October 15, 1994.

252 *"Two Who Cherish Symphony Orchestras"*: Roberta Hershenson, *New York Times*, February 19, 1995.

252 *"It is one of the most astonishing"*: Alex Ross, review, *New York Times*, February 25, 1995.

253 *"drew the finest, loveliest threads"*: James R. Oestreich, review, *New York Times*, March 11, 1995.

253 *"handsomely"* et seq.: Bernard Holland, review, *New York Times*, March 25, 1995.

253 *"highly characterized"* et seq.: James R. Oestreich, review, *New York Times*, March 31, 1995.

253 *"with its tenuous intonation"* et seq.: Allan Kozinn, review, *New York Times*, April 14, 1995.

254 *"a splendid performance"* et seq.: Bernard Holland, review, *New York Times*, May 13, 1995.

254 *"rather like a dream"*: Tim Page, "Remembering on Memorial Day," *New York Newsday*, May 31, 1995.

254 *"meticulous use of visual rhythm"*: Edward Rothstein, review, *New York Times*, June 3, 1995.

CHAPTER 16

258 *"foursquare and stolid"*: Anthony Tommasini, review, *New York Times*, July 15, 1995.

258 *"the Viennese idiom in his fingertips"*: Shirley Fleming, review, *New York Post*, July 17, 1995.

258 *"Kurt Masur clearly adores this piece"*: Peter G. Davis, review, *New York*, July 31, 1995.

258 *"How successful can a work"*: Edward Rothstein, review, *New York Times*, July 20, 1995.

259 *"buoyant and lilting"* et seq.: Anthony Tommasini, review, *New York Times*, August 2, 1995.

259 *"an orchestra in herself"*: Bernard Holland, review, *New York Times*, September 22, 1995.

261 *"clarity and definition"* et seq.: Anthony Tommasini, review, *New York Times*, October 28, 1995.

261 *"a masterly conductor"*: Anthony Tommasini, review, *New York Times*, November 4, 1995.

261 *"You think we're overpaid"*: quoted in Bernard Holland, "A Pathetic Living at the Symphony?," *New York Times*, November 5, 1995.

262 *"a New York institution"*: James R. Oestreich, review, *New York Times*, November 11, 1995.

262 *"it was hard to resist"*: Anthony Tommasini, review, *New York Times*, December 9, 1995.

263 *"buoyant"* et seq.: James R. Oestreich, review, *New York Times*, January 20, 1996.

263 *"a fastidiously articulate"*: Peter G. Davis, "Classical Music," *New York*, February 5, 1996.

264 *"the orchestra has not adequately tended"*: Martijn Sanders, quoted in James R. Oestreich, "A Flagging Tradition? Says Who?," *New York Times*, February 18, 1996.

264 *"Sitting on stage playing Mahler"*: Thomas Stacy, quoted in ibid.

264 *"keep the tradition alive"*: Kurt Masur, quoted in ibid.

264 *"a bold, intelligent"*: Alex Ross, review, *New York Times*, February 17, 1996.

264 *"radiant, incisive playing"* et seq.: Anthony Tommasini, review, *New York Times*, February 24, 1996.

265 *"What may well stand"* et seq.: James R. Oestreich, review, *New York Times*, March 9, 1996.

265 *"first-rate"* et seq.: Bernard Holland, review, *New York Times*, April 20, 1996.

266 *"authority and deep feeling"* et seq.: Anthony Tommasini, review, *New York Times*, April 27, 1996.

266 *"razor-sharp"* et seq.: Bernard Holland, review, *New York Times*, March 25, 1996.

267 *"a terrific team"*: Deborah Borda, quoted in Ralph Blumenthal, "Two Top Directors Are Resigning," *New York Times*, June 14, 1996.

267 *"to see...with their ears"* et seq.: Bernard Holland, review, *New York Times*, August 2, 1996.

267 *"unusually demonic"* et seq.: Peter G. Davis, "Classical Music," *New York*, August 19, 1996.

268 *"poise and rectitude"* et seq.: Bernard Holland, review, *New York Times*, September 20, 1996.

269 *"hokey, bombastic symphony"*: Anthony Tommasini, review, *New York Times*, October 5, 1996.

269 *"was trying to drive a wedge"*: Kurt Masur, quoted in Ralph Blumenthal, "For the Philharmonic, It's Harmony On Stage and Sour Notes Off," *New York Times*, October 22, 1996.

269   *"Look, it is like a marriage"*: Kurt Masur, quoted in ibid.

269   *"We're firmly committed to both of them"*: Paul B. Guenther, quoted in ibid.

269   *"I learned to live with the Stasi"*: Kurt Masur, quoted in ibid.

269   *"the spotlight has been turned on me"*: Deborah Borda, quoted in ibid.

270   *"a performance that had blood"* et seq.: Allan Kozinn, review, *New York Times*, October 26, 1996.

270   *"McFerrin is a phenomenon"* et seq.: James R. Oestreich, review, *New York Times*, November 2, 1996.

271   *"irrepressible character"* et seq.: Anthony Tommasini, review, *New York Times*, November 11, 1996.

271   *"cogent and exciting"*: ibid.

271   *"spirited reading"* et seq.: Allan Kozinn, review, *New York Times*, January 2, 1996.

271   *"a sometimes enthusiastic"* et seq.: Paul Griffiths, review, *New York Times*, January 9, 1997.

272   *"drew a vital, well-focused performance"* et seq.: Allan Kozinn, review, *New York Times*, January 11, 1997.

272   *"superbly conveyed the spirit"* et seq.: James R. Oestreich, review, *New York Times*, January 17, 1997.

272   *"compellingly"*: Anthony Tommasini, review, *New York Times*, February 1, 1997.

273   *"Kurt Masur had what must rank"* et seq.: Anthony Tommasini, review, *New York Times*, February 8, 1997.

273   *"how much inspiration can still be drawn"* et seq.: James R. Oestreich, review, *New York Times*, February 23, 1997.

273   *"with devastating effect"* et seq.: Bernard Holland, review, *New York Times*, March 8, 1997.

274   *"subscribers on Thursday"*: Bernard Holland, review, *New York Times*, April 5, 1997.

274   *"fertile… inspirational ground"*: James R. Oestreich, review, *New York Times*, May 4, 1997.

274   *"a shapely, well-paced"*: Allan Kozinn, review, *New York Times*, May 17, 1997.

275   *"affecting performance"*: Anthony Tommasini, review, *New York Times*, May 24, 1997.

275   *"elegant, lithe and supple"* et seq.: Anthony Tommasini, review, *New York Times*, May 31, 1997.

Chapter 17

277   *"The irreconcilable differences in cultures"* et seq.: Bernard Holland, review, *New York Times*, July 10, 1997.

277   *"Why does a man so distinguished"*: Bernard Holland, "Jazz Musicians with Nothing Better to Do," *New York Times*, July 27, 1997.

277   *"deconstructs the chromaticism"*: Allan Kozinn, review, *New York Times*, July 14, 1997.

278   *"gorgeous account"* et seq.: ibid.

278 *"primitive ritual"*: Paul Griffiths, review, *New York Times*, July 21, 1997.

278 *"a remarkable achievement"* et seq.: Anthony Tommasini, review, *New York Times*, September 19, 1997.

279 *"compelling accounts"* et seq.: James R. Oestreich, review, *New York Times*, September 29, 1997.

279 *"I'm a very selfish man"*: Kurt Masur, quoted in ibid.

279 *"did not suggest"*: Allan Kozinn, review, *New York Times*, October 8, 1997.

279 *"drab and uninspired"* et seq.: Bernard Holland, review, *New York Times*, October 10, 1997.

280 *"elicited an impassioned performance"* et seq.: Anthony Tommasini, review, *New York Times*, November 1, 1997.

280 *"a blazing, authoritative performance"* et seq.: Anthony Tommasini, review, *New York Times*, November 22, 1997.

280 *"great oratorio"* et seq.: James R. Oestreich, review, *New York Times*, December 6, 1997.

281 *"had never seen an orchestra contract"* et seq.: I. Philip Sipser, quoted in Ralph Blumenthal, "Philharmonic's Musicians Negotiate a 6-Year Contract," *New York Times*, December 13, 1997.

281 *"satisfying and revelatory"* et seq.: James R. Oestreich, review, *New York Times*, January 4, 1998.

281 *"often seemed more interested"* et seq.: Allan Kozinn, review, *New York Times*, January 23, 1998.

282 *"conducted confidently"* et seq.: Allan Kozinn, review, *New York Times*, January 27, 1998.

282 *"Bruckner's introspection"*: Allan Kozinn, review, *New York Times*, January 31, 1998.

282 *"wonderful to hear"* et seq.: James R. Oestreich, review, *New York Times*, February 14, 1998.

283 *"radiant"*: Anthony Tommasini, review, *New York Times*, February 21, 1998.

283 *"a bitter row"* et seq.: Ralph Blumenthal, "Philharmonic Retains Masur, but Will Seek a Successor," *New York Times*, February 27, 1998.

283 *"I would say that I was surprised"*: Kurt Masur, quoted in ibid.

283 *"There's certainly no notion"*: William J. McDonough, quoted in ibid.

283 *"eliminates any uncertainty"*: Paul B. Guenther, quoted in ibid.

283 *"Mr. Masur and the orchestra"*: Allan Kozinn, review, *New York Times*, March 2, 1998.

283 *"run more by bottom-liners"* et seq.: Bernard Holland, "Classical View: Which Conductors Will End Up Where?," *New York Times*, March 8, 1998.

284 *"alternately forceful and poetic"* et seq.: Allan Kozinn, review, *New York Times*, March 27, 1998.

284 *"one of our important pianists"*: Bernard Holland, review, *New York Times*, April 10, 1998.

284 *"produced a reading"*: Allan Kozinn, review, *New York Times*, April 18, 1998.

285 *"Mr. Masur made it sound"*: Allan Kozinn, review, *New York Times*, May 23, 1998.

285 *"an extravagant jumble"* et seq.: Bernard Holland, review, *New York Times*, May 30, 1998.

286 *"not tidy"* et seq.: Bernard Holland, review, *New York Times*, July 9, 1998.

287 *"wade through another Beethoven cycle"*: Bernard Holland, "The New Season/Classical Music," *New York Times*, September 13, 1998.

287 *"no especially compelling reason"*: Anthony Tommasini, review, *New York Times*, September 24, 1998.

288 *"is a fine Beethoven conductor"* et seq.: ibid.

288 *"comprehension of the scope"*: Anthony Tommasini, review, *New York Times*, October 3, 1998.

288 *"his intense involvement"* et seq.: Anthony Tommasini, review, *New York Times*, October 31, 1998.

289 *"sounded like a gifted musician"*: Paul Griffiths, review, *New York Times*, November 7, 1998.

289 *"That means I conduct five"*: Pierre Monteux to his students, August 1961.

289 *"its Mahlerian stripes"*: James R. Oestreich, review, *New York Times*, November 14, 1998.

289 *"I treat Gershwin"* et seq.: Kurt Masur, quoted in Anthony Tommasini, review, *New York Times*, December 12, 1998.

290 *"blaringly orchestrated medley"*: ibid.

290 *"made the piece their own"*: Paul Griffiths, review, *New York Times*, December 19, 1998.

290 *"It was unbearable"*: Kurt Masur, quoted in Allan Kozinn, "A Reprimand for Concert Coughers," *New York Times*, December 31, 1998.

290 *"a perceptive musician"* et seq.: Anthony Tommasini, review, *New York Times*, January 4, 1999.

291 *"little short of disgraceful"*: David Mermelstein, "For Californians, Musical Visitors Are Worth the Wait," *New York Times*, January 14, 1999.

291 *"you cannot very often hear Shostakovich"*: Kurt Masur, quoted in ibid.

291 *"a sound musician"*: Bernard Holland, review, *New York Times*, January 22, 1999.

292 *"one of the orchestra's finer efforts"* et seq.: James R. Oestreich, review, *New York Times*, February 28, 1999.

292 *"She has this trick down pat"*: James R. Oestreich, review, *New York Times*, March 11, 1999.

292 *"It may seem ridiculous"*: Olin Downes, quoted in Allan Kozinn, "Sir Yehudi Menuhin, Violinist, Conductor and Supporter of Charities, Is Dead at 82," *New York Times*, March 13, 1999.

293 *"Bruckner in slow motion"*: Allan Kozinn, review, *New York Times*, April 24, 1999.

293 *"an absolute master"* et seq.: Bernard Holland, review, *New York Times*, May 3, 1999.

294 *"a backlog of new works"*: Kurt Masur, quoted in David Wright, "Finally, Masur Gets to Call the Tune in New Music, Too," *New York Times*, May 2, 1999.

294 *"a colorful, thorny, eclectic imagining"* et seq.: Allan Kozinn, review, *New York Times*, May 10, 1999.

294 *"sense of tragedy"*: Allan Kozinn, review, *New York Times*, May 22, 1999.

294 *"It's such a great work"*: Sir Colin Davis to the author, June 1968.

295 *"sufficient to send the early-music movement"* et seq.: Bernard Holland, review, *New York Times*, May 29, 1999.

295 *"semi-standing ovation"* et seq.: James R. Oestreich, review, *New York Times*, June 5, 1999.

295 *"The sooner work can begin"*: Paul B. Guenther, quoted in Ralph Blumenthal, "Midlife Hits Lincoln Center with Calls for Rich Face Lift," *New York Times*, June 1, 1999.

295 *"excellence and confidence"* et seq.: Anthony Tommasini, review, *New York Times*, June 24, 1999.

CHAPTER 18

297 *"it was business as usual"*: Allan Kozinn, review, *New York Times*, July 9, 1999.

297 *"not musically distinguished"*: Anthony Tommasini, review, *New York Times*, July 17, 1999.

297 *"under his oversized personality"*: Bernard Holland, review, *New York Times*, September 24, 1999.

298 *"It's sort of like running"*: Deborah Borda, quoted in Ralph Blumenthal, "Top Executive to Leave Philharmonic Post," *New York Times*, September 30, 1999.

299 *"vignettes of recent American life"* et seq.: Paul Griffiths, review, *New York Times*, October 9, 1999.

300 *"A Child of Our Time possesses virtues"*: Bernard Holland, review, *New York Times*, November 6, 1999.

300 *"to the silence of mothers"*: James R. Oestreich, review, *New York Times*, November 13, 1999.

300 *"the new century should manifest"*: Somei Satoh, quoted in ibid.

300 *"choral meditations on love"* et seq.: Oestreich, ibid.

300 *"intense performances"* et seq.: ibid.

301 *"For me the change of millenniums"*: Giya Kancheli, quoted in Allan Kozinn, review, *New York Times*, November 20, 1999.

301 *"uneven"*: ibid.

301 *"an unusually adventurous"* et seq.: Bernard Holland, review, *New York Times*, December 2, 1999.

302 *"an impassioned performance"*: Anthony Tommasini, review, *New York Times*, December 9, 1999.

302 *"I want to sit"*: Johanna Johnson, quoted in Ralph Blumenthal, "Ailing Teenager Makes a Wish, to Play with the Philharmonic," *New York Times*, December 11, 1991.

302 *"its blatant sound"* et seq.: James R. Oestreich, review, *New York Philharmonic*, December 13, 1999.

303 *"odd music"*: Ben Ratliff, review, *New York Times*, December 31, 1999.

303 *"rose to the occasion"* et seq.: Allan Kozinn, review, *New York Times*, January 2, 2000.

303 *"a wonder of adaptability"* et seq.: Bernard Holland, review, *New York Times*, January 8, 2000.

303 *"a triumph"*: Paul Griffiths, review, *New York Times*, January 17, 2000.

304 *"We're fighting the pollution"*: Amyas Ames, quoted in Anthony Tommasini, "Amyas Ames Is Dead at 93; A Champion of Lincoln Center," *New York Times*, January 26, 2000.

304 *"is a passionate song"* et seq.: Paul Griffiths, review, *New York Times*, March 30, 2000.

305 *"imagining what might have been"*: James R. Oestreich, review, *New York Times*, April 6, 2000.

305 *"(1) I don't care"* et seq.: Bernard Holland, review, *New York Times*, May 7, 2000.

305 *"that didn't go out of its way"*: Allan Kozinn, review, *New York Times*, May 13, 2000.

305 *"We would have fought"*: Zarin Mehta, quoted in Ralph Blumenthal, "Philharmonic Appointing Zarin Mehta as Executive," *New York Times*, June 1, 2000.

306 *"admirable in every quantifiable way"* et seq.: Allan Kozinn, review, *New York Times*, June 3, 2000.

306 *"surely no one's idea"*: James R. Oestreich, "Who Dares Call This Maestro a Lame Duck?," *New York Times*, June 4, 2000.

306 *"The major point for me"* et seq.: Kurt Masur, quoted in ibid.

306 *"Kurt Masur has done"*: Paul B. Guenther, quoted in ibid.

307 *"truly repulsive"*: Stefan Westerhoff, letter to the editor, *New York Times*, June 18, 2000.

307 *"glorious"* et seq.: James R. Oestreich, review, *New York Times*, July 13, 2000.

307 *"underpowered"*: Paul Griffiths, review, *New York Times*, July 24, 2000.

308 *"an agile, demonstrative conductor"* et seq.: Allan Kozinn, review, *New York Times*, July 27, 2000.

308 *"body language told us"* et seq.: Bernard Holland, "Muti Was the Wrong Man for the Philharmonic," *New York Times*, August 20, 2000.

309 *"the most urban of all"* et seq.: Bernard Holland, review, *New York Times*, September 22, 2000.

309 *"undergo an unspecified surgical procedure"*: James R. Oestreich, "Masur Withdraws from Concerts," *New York Times*, September 22, 2000.

310 *"lovely, expert reading"*: James R. Oestreich, review, *New York Times*, September 23, 2000.

310 *"a satisfying evening"* et seq.: Bernard Holland, review, *New York Times*, September 29, 2000.

310 *"was at his best"* et seq.: Anthony Tommasini, review, *New York Times*, October 7, 2000.

311 *"interpretive focus"* et seq.: Anthony Tommasini, review, *New York Times*, November 2, 2000.

120 *"spiky and scintillating"* et seq.: James R. Oestreich, review, *New York Times*, November 4, 2000.

312 *"Naturalness and spontaneity"* et seq.: Anthony Tommasini, review, *New York Times*, November 11, 2000.

313 *"a project in the process"*: Paul Griffiths, review, *New York Times*, November 18, 2000.

313 *"from memory"* et seq.: James R. Oestreich, review, *New York Times*, November 24, 2000.

313 *"is not close"*: Allan Kozinn, "Philharmonic Broadens Search for a Conductor," *New York Times*, December 27, 2000.

CHAPTER 19

315 *"It's disturbing"*: Zarin Mehta, quoted in Elisabeth Franck, *New York Observer*, January 17, 2001.

315 *"speculative and incorrect"*: Eric Latzky, quoted in ibid.

315 *"I'll run a retraction"*: Tim Page, quoted in ibid.

315 *"No one is close"*: Eric Latzky, quoted in Ralph Blumenthal, "No Choice on Conductor, the Philharmonic Says," *New York Times*, January 17, 2001.

316 *"still searching, still talking"*: Zarin Mehta, quoted in ibid.

316 "Young musicians are thrown": Lorin Maazel, quoted in Doreen Carvajal, "New Foundation to Aid Aspiring Conductors," *New York Times*, January 18, 2001.

316 *"a brilliant music director"* et seq.: Anthony Tommasini, "Seeking Young Conductors (Bernstein Flair a Must)," *New York Times*, January 29, 2001.

317 *"chilly distance"*: Greg Sandow, "Music," *Wall Street Journal*, January 17, 2001.

317 *"I am interested in him"*: Ned Rorem, quoted in Celestine Bohlen, "Debating Maazel's Musical Identity: Is It American or European?," *New York Times*, January 31, 2001.

318 *"won the hearts"*: Anthony Tommasini, "Why to Expect the Best of an Unexpected Maestro," *New York Times*, February 25, 2001.

318 *"two of today's greatest conductors"*: Hanna Lachert, letter to the editor, *New York Times*, March 11, 2001.

318 *"committed and involving account"* et seq.: Anthony Tommasini, review, *New York Times*, February 25, 2001.

319 *"uneven performance"*: Anne Midgette, review, *New York Times*, March 31, 2001.

320 *"attractively eclectic style"*: Allan Kozinn, review, *New York Times*, April 14, 2001.

320 *"saddening"* et seq.: Howard Taubman, review, *New York Times*, January 3, 1958.

320 *"a tightly focused, biting work"*: Allan Kozinn, review, *New York Times*, April 14, 2001.

320 *"a pathbreaking Viennese Classical symphony"*: Anthony Tommasini, review, *New York Times*, April 28, 2001.

321 *"breadth and spaciousness"* et seq.: Anthony Tommasini, review, *New York Times*, May 26, 2001.

321 *"played with the understated virtuosity"* et seq.: Allan Kozinn, review, *New York Times*, June 2, 2001.

321 *"questionable arrangements"*: Allan Kozinn, review, *New York Times*, July 12, 2001.

322 *"themes from the show"* et seq.: ibid.

322 *"for the music making"* et seq.: Anthony Tommasini, review, *New York Times*, September 22, 2001.

322 *"a sense of letdown"* et seq.: Anthony Tommasini, review, *New York Times*, September 24, 2001.

323   *"just having the Philharmonic back"*: ibid.

323   *"the real thing"* et seq.: Anne Midgette, review, *New York Times*, October 20, 2001.

324   *"the city and the orchestra"* et seq.: James R. Oestreich, "Measuring the Stride of a Giant," *New York Times*, November 4, 2001.

324   *"was a triumph"*: Paul Griffiths, review, *New York Times*, November 17, 2001.

325   *"The Philharmonic was created"*: Bernard Holland, review, *New York Times*, November 23, 2001.

325   *"the segues between orchestra and jazz band"*: Ben Ratliff, review, *New York Times*, December 15, 2001.

325   *"an exhilarating reading"*: Allan Kozinn, review, *New York Times*, January 2, 2002.

325   *"exceeded expectations"*: Anthony Tommasini, "On the Docket Next Season, Transitions," *New York Times*, January 27, 2002.

325   *"might have been a dynamic choice"*: ibid.

326   *"distinguished, affecting and impressive"* et seq.: Anthony Tommasini, review, *New York Times*, February 9, 2002.

326   *"I treated the orchestra very badly"*: Kurt Masur, quoted in Anthony Tommasini, "From the Young, Nothing Less than Full Commitment," *New York Times*, February 20, 2002.

326   *"charged, incisive performance"*: ibid.

326   *"a vital performance"*: Paul Griffiths, review, *New York Times*, February 23, 2002.

327   *"a happy evening"* et seq.: Bernard Holland, review, *New York Times*, April 6, 2002.

327   *"magnificent performance"* et seq.: Anthony Tommasini, review, *New York Times*, April 19, 2002.

327   *"brought radiant sound"* et seq.: Anthony Tommasini, review, *New York Times*, April 27, 2002.

327   *"In a sense, New York hardly knew"*: James R. Oestreich, "A Bittersweet Goodbye with Might Have Beens," *New York Times*, May 12, 2002.

327   *"There are more than 200 pieces"*: Kurt Masur, quoted in ibid.

328   *"We should work together"*: Kurt Masur, quoted in ibid.

328   *"Kurt Masur did a magnificent job"*: Deborah Borda, quoted in ibid.

328   *"If you have been a New Yorker"*: Kurt Masur, quoted in ibid.

329   *"I admire him"*: John Rockwell, "A Conductor of Authority and Warmth," *New York Times*, May 12, 2002.

329   *"What a marvelous player"* et seq.: Bernard Holland, review, *New York Times*, May 18, 2002.

330   *"his greatness as a musician"* et seq.: Anthony Tommasini, review, *New York Times*, May 25, 2002.

330   *"a historic night"* et seq.: Zarin Mehta, quoted in Anthony Tommasini, "Honored as Emeritus, Masur Is Speechless," *New York Times*, June 3, 2002.

331   *"unassailable but less often heartwarming"* et seq.: Bernard Holland, "Departures Make Hearts Grow Fonder," *New York Times*, June 30, 2002.

331 *"during its final moments"*: Allan Kozinn, review, *New York Times*, July 20, 2002.

331 *"I'm still with you"*: Kurt Masur, quoted in ibid.

331 *"The Philharmonic is a tough bunch"*: ibid.

331 *"superb accounts"* et seq.: James R. Oestreich, review, *New York Times*, July 23, 2002.

331 *"predictably strong pianist in the concerto"* et seq.: ibid.

CHAPTER 20

333 *"the fruition of my experience"*: Lorin Maazel, quoted in Joseph Horowitz, "Anybody Listening? A Hapless History," *New York Times*, September 15, 2002.

334 *"memory space"* et seq.: John Adams, New York Philharmonic program book, September 19, 2002.

334 *"better than it used to"* et seq.: Greg Sandow, "Enigmatic Debut," *Wall Street Journal*, September 24, 2002.

335 *"for the musician in the conductor"*: Lorin Maazel, quoted in Ralph Blumenthal, "And Then There Were Two; Prize Is Shared in Conductors' Competition," *New York Times*, September 29, 2002.

335 *"technically brilliant and eerily controlled"*: Anthony Tommasini, review, *New York Times*, October 5, 2002.

336 *"passionately convincing"*: Anne Midgette, review, *New York Times*, November 21, 2002.

337 *"a Rolls-Royce of an orchestra"* et seq.: Bernard Holland, "Beethoven and Weber in a Return to 1842," *New York Times*, December 9, 2002.

337 *"useless"*: ibid.

337 *"orthodoxy a good name"*: ibid.

338 *"unchallenging . . . contemporary music"*: Anthony Tommasini, review, *New York Times*, December 21, 2002.

339 *"a triumph"* et seq.: Paul Griffiths, review, *New York Times*, January 23, 2003.

339 *"glorious singing"* et seq.: Paul Griffiths, review, *New York Times*, February 17, 2003.

340 *"The New York Philharmonic could take"*: Allan Kozinn, review, *New York Times*, March 8, 2003.

340 *"the innovative work"*: Anthony Tommasini, review, *New York Times*, April 14, 2003.

342 *"a finely polished, vigorous reading"*: Allan Kozinn, review, *New York Times*, May 30, 2003.

342 *"There's no reason"*: Sanford I. Weill, quoted in Ralph Blumenthal and Robin Pogrebin, "The Philharmonic Agrees to Move to Carnegie Hall," *New York Times*, June 2, 2003.

342 *"We've got two major institutions"*: Zarin Mehta, quoted in ibid.

342 *"a form of cultural cannibalism"*: Martin E. Segal, quoted in ibid.

342 *"it was not a question"*: Paul B. Guenther, quoted in ibid.

343 *"a tremendous variety of music"* et seq.: Robert J. Harth, quoted in Robin Pogrebin, "Orchestra Maneuver," *New York Times*, June 2, 2003.

343 *"Times have changed"*: Bruce Crawford, quoted in ibid.

343 *"ecstatic about going 'home'"*: Fiona Simon, letter to the editor, *New York Times*, June 7, 2003.

343 *"sardine-can lobby"* et seq.: David Breger, letter to the editor, *New York Times*, June 7, 2003.

344 *"gripping performances"* et seq.: Anthony Tommasini, review, *New York Times*, June 7, 2003.

344 *"wanly derivative"* et seq.: Anthony Tommasini, review, *New York Times*, June 21, 2003.

344 *"Lincoln Center intends to be firm"*: Reynold Levy, quoted in Robin Pogrebin, "Lincoln Center Says Orchestra Is Breaking Lease," *New York Times*, June 17, 2003.

344 *"early signs of strain"*: Anthony Tommasini, "A Prickly Courtship for Orchestra and Hall," *New York Times*, June 26, 2003.

344 *"The opportunity here"*: Robert J. Harth, quoted in ibid.

345 *"I don't want to change"*: Zarin Mehta, quoted in ibid.

345 *"to approve the beginning of discussions"*: Paul B. Guenther, quoted in Robin Pogrebin, "Philharmonic Is Rethinking Carnegie Plan," *New York Times*, June 16, 2003.

346 *"hard-driven and contorted"* et seq.: Anthony Tommasini, review, *New York Times*, September 19, 2003.

346 *"one of the most accomplished"* et seq.: Anthony Tommasini, review, *New York Times*, September 20, 2003.

347 *"not much depth or dimension"*: Allan Kozinn, review, *New York Times*, October 4, 2003.

347 *"In the end we realized"*: Paul B. Guenther, quoted in Robin Pogrebin, "Carnegie Abandons Merger Discussions with Philharmonic," *New York Times*, October 8, 2003.

347 *"When something is disclosed prematurely"*: Sanford I. Weill, quoted in ibid.

347 *"If you were to capture our feelings"*: Reynold Levy, quoted in ibid.

347 *"a healthy, fruitful relationship"*: Rita E. Hauser, quoted in ibid.

347 *"On a good night"*: Anthony Tommasini, quoted in ibid.

347 *"still very happy"*: Paul B. Guenther, quoted in Robin Pogrebin, "No Easy Homecoming for the Philharmonic," *New York Times*, October 14, 2003.

347 *"He's totally devoted"*: Zarin Mehta, quoted in ibid.

348 *"her accustomed grace"* et seq.: James R. Oestreich, review, *New York Times*, October 17, 2003.

348 *"There is nothing wrong"*: Allan Kozinn, review, *New York Times*, October 23, 2003.

348 *"much to admire"*: ibid.

349 *"The board must engage"*: Rita E. Hauser, quoted in Robin Pogrebin, "A Major Donor Leaves the Philharmonic," *New York Times*, November 4, 2003.

349 *"a stirring performance"*: Anne Midgette, review, *New York Times*, November 15, 2003.

349 *"satisfying if unspectacular"*: Jeremy Eichler, review, *New York Times*, November 24, 2003.

349 *"a lucid and impassioned performance"*: Anthony Tommasini, review, *New York Times*, November 28, 2003.

350 *"If we have no one to replace Maazel"*: Glenn Dicterow, quoted in Robin Pogrebin, "Musicians Urge to Keep Maazel," *New York Times*, December 10, 2003.

351 *"He was a true impresario"*: Reynold Levy, quoted in Robin Pogrebin, "Robert Harth, 47, Dies; Ran Carnegie Hall," *New York Times*, February 1, 2004.

352 *"tens of thousands of dollars"*: Benjamin M. Rosen, quoted in Robin Pogrebin, "For Symphony Fans, the Touch of MTV," *New York Times*, February 23, 2004.

352 *"We're not movie stars"*: Newton Mansfield, quoted in ibid.

352 *"I found it very distracting"*: Glenn Dicterow, quoted in ibid.

352 *"The half of the orchestra behind the screen"*: Eric Latzky, quoted in ibid.

352 *"If you want to see better"*: Glenn Dicterow, quoted in ibid.

352 *"inherent musicality"* et seq.: Allan Kozinn, review, *New York Times*, March 20, 2004.

352 *"a born Straussian"* et seq.: John Rockwell, "A Maazel Balance Sheet: Resounding Ideas, Some Unconventional," *New York Times*, April 9, 2004.

353 *"done well"* et seq.: ibid.

353 *"a kind of Eagle Scout"* et seq.: Anne Midgette, review, *New York Times*, April 24, 2004.

354 *"In my lifetime, I haven't known"*: Hilde Limondjian, quoted in James Barron, "A Pianist's Hands Encompass Two Sides of Central Park," *New York Times*, April 30, 2004.

354 *"cordially despised"* et seq.: Richard Taruskin, "Underneath the Dissonance Beat a Brahmsian Heart," *New York Times*, May 16, 2004.

355 *"was a good start"*: Anthony Tommasini, review, *New York Times*, May 13, 2004.

355 *"good feedback"*: Glenn Dicterow, quoted in Anne Midgette, "Musicians Say Fisher Hall Isn't as Bad as All That," *New York Times*, May 21, 2004.

356 *"a breath of fresh air"*: David Pyatt, quoted in ibid.

356 *"What a terrible idea"*: unidentified concertgoer, quoted in Lola Ogunnaike, "Concert-goers Multitasking to Stravinsky," *New York Times*, May 29, 2004.

356 *"fiery but oddly chilling reading"* et seq.: Allan Kozinn, review, *New York Times*, June 5, 2004.

357 *"bake-off"*: Robin Pogrebin, "A Bake-Off at the Philharmonic? Guest Leaders Picked; Maazel Post Extended," *New York Times*, June 16, 2004.

357 *"great elegance"*: Anthony Tommasini, review, *New York Times*, June 18, 2004.

CHAPTER 21

359 *"It takes a pops concert"*: Anne Midgette, review, *New York Times*, June 29, 2004.

360 *"exciting and brilliantly played"*: Anthony Tommasini, review, *New York Times*, September 23, 2004.

360 *"alluring colors"* et seq.: Anthony Tommasini, review, *New York Times*, October 1, 2004.

361 *"a joyous romp"* et seq.: ibid.

361 *"Where is a new Leonard Bernstein"*: James R. Oestreich, "Mahler and Me, Both Close to My Heart," *New York Times*, October 3, 2004.

361 *"did in fact have commercials"*: correction, *New York Times*, December 8, 2004.

362 *"subtly like birds"* et seq.: Bernard Holland, review, *New York Times*, November 20, 2004.

362 *"makes everything seem fresh"* et seq.: Anthony Tommasini, review, *New York Times*, November 26, 2004.

362 *"curiously muted"* et seq.: Anne Midgette, review, *New York Times*, December 3, 2004.

362 *"a splendid young player"* et seq.: Bernard Holland, review, *New York Times*, December 11, 2004.

363 *"transformed what could have been"* et seq.: Allan Kozinn, review, *New York Times*, December 17, 2004.

363 *"starkness and concentration"* et seq.: Bernard Holland, review, *New York Times*, December 18, 2004.

363 *"a little distasteful"*: Bernard Holland, review, *New York Times*, December 30, 2004.

363 *"I've felt immediately back at home"*: Kurt Masur, quoted in Jeremy Eichler, "Masur Visits, Message and Integrity Intact," *New York Times*, December 31, 2004.

363 *"The message of Beethoven"*: ibid.

364 *"grand and sweeping"* et seq.: Allan Kozinn, review, *New York Times*, January 14, 2005.

364 *"in exceptionally good form"* et seq.: ibid.

364 *"I think the time is right"*: Bruce Crawford, quoted in Robin Pogrebin, "Lincoln Center Chairman Is to Resign," *New York Times*, January 13, 2005.

364 *"lovely shadings and Impressionistic colors"*: Anthony Tommasini, review, *New York Times*, January 28, 2005.

365 *"He makes a nice fit"*: Bernard Holland, review, *New York Times*, February 12, 2005.

365 *"May he come back often"*: Anthony Tommasini, review, *New York Times*, February 19, 2005.

365 *"some things were easier"*: Joseph Robinson, quoted in Daniel J. Wakin, "Suddenly, 'Oboist Wanted' Signs Are Everywhere," *New York Times*, February 12, 2005.

365 *"blaring, blatant and lacking"* et seq.: Anthony Tommasini, review, *New York Times*, February 26, 2005.

365 *"a rigorous and formidable composition"*: ibid.

366 *"compelling"* et seq.: Anthony Tommasini, review, *New York Times*, March 3, 2005.

366 *"has improved enormously"* et seq.: Allan Kozinn, review, *New York Times*, March 5, 2005.

367 *"an utterly delightful program"*: Anthony Tommasini, review, *New York Times*, March 19, 2005.

367 *"a transfixing account"* et seq.: Anthony Tommasini, review, *New York Times*, March 26, 2005.

367 *"a robust and satisfying performance"*: Jeremy Eichler, review, *New York Times*, April 2, 2005.

367 *"I'm the father of five"*: Frank A. Bennack Jr., quoted in Robin Pogrebin, "Lincoln Center Picks New Leader," *New York Times*, May 5, 2005.

368 *"ravishing music"*: Anthony Tommasini, review, *New York Times*, June 4, 2005.

369 *"deeply impressive and continuously exciting"* et seq.: Anthony Tommasini, review, *New York Times*, June 24, 2005.

369 *"a magnificent, passionate performance"*: Allan Kozinn, review, *New York Times*, July 15, 2005.

369 *"pompous"* et seq.: Anthony Tommasini, review, *New York Times*, September 23, 2005.

370 *"the wriggles of ecstasy"* et seq.: Bernard Holland, review, *New York Times*, September 24, 2005.

371 *"It's going to be a hard couple of days"*: Carl Schiebler, quoted in Daniel J. Wakin, "From the Philharmonic, Relief for Louisiana Colleagues," *New York Times*, October 28, 2005.

371 *"quirky and often chaotic"* et seq.: Allan Kozinn, review, *New York Times*, November 5, 2005.

372 *"a solid, even stately performance"* et seq.: Jeremy Eichler, review, *New York Times*, December 16, 2005.

372 *"an ideal Haydn-Mozart man"* et seq.: Bernard Holland, review, *New York Times*, December 16, 2005.

372 *"The orchestra sounded fantastic"* et seq.: Allan Kozinn, review, *New York Times*, January 14, 2006.

373 *"a nimble and imaginative soloist"*: Jeremy Eichler, review, *New York Times*, January 21, 2006.

373 *"a passionate, rich-hued rendering"*: Allan Kozinn, review, *New York Times*, January 28, 2006.

373 *"proved sensitive partners"*: Allan Kozinn, review, *New York Times*, February 2, 2006.

374 *"Mozart's mystery symphonies"* et seq.: Bernard Holland, review, *New York Times*, February 10, 2006.

374 *"lucid and precisely wrought music"* et seq.: Anthony Tommasini, review, *New York Times*, February 25, 2006.

375 *"curiously tentative"* et seq.: ibid.

375 *"fluid yet unostentatious technique"* et seq.: Anthony Tommasini, review, *New York Times*, March 2, 2006.

376 *"an assured and exhilarating account"*: Anthony Tommasini, review, *New York Times*, March 18, 2006.

376 *"exasperatingly restrained"* et seq.: Anthony Tommasini, review, *New York Times*, March 24, 2006.

376 *"the Philharmonic playing for all it was worth"*: Bernard Holland, review, *New York Times*, April 21, 2006.

377 *"are perfect for the third movement"*: Joseph Pereira, quoted in Anthony Tommasini, "Philharmonic Musician Seeks the Perfect Boom, Bang or Ping," *New York Times*, April 21, 2006.

377 *"I'm not disappointed"*: ibid.

378 *"is always a welcome presence"* et seq.: Bernard Holland, review, *New York Times*, April 29, 2006.

378   *"with a warmth not every conductor can get"*: Bernard Holland, review, *New York Times*, May 5, 2006.

379   *"a bang-up account"* et seq.: Anthony Tommasini, review, *New York Times*, June 3, 2006.

Chapter 22

382   *"Step No. 1, let's get through Saturday"*: Paul B. Guenther, quoted in Anne Midgette, "New York Philharmonic Plays Summer Guest at Bethel Woods Art Center," *New York Times*, July 1, 2006.

382   *"decisive"*: Vivien Schweitzer, review, *New York Times*, July 15, 2006.

383   *"a memorable performance"*: Steve Smith, review, *New York Times*, July 20, 2006.

383   *"had observed the fifth anniversary"* et seq.: James R. Oestreich, review, *New York Times*, September 15, 2006.

383   *"one of the most impressive Henze pieces"* et seq.: Bernard Holland, review, *New York Times*, September 16, 2006.

384   *"terrific"* et seq.: Bernard Holland, review, *New York Times*, September 30, 2006.

384   *"close enough to the real thing"* et seq.: Anthony Tommasini, review, *New York Times*.

385   *"seems a bigger talent"*: Anthony Tommasini, review, *New York Times*, October 21, 2006.

385   *"proceeding in an orderly and timely way"*: Eric Latzky, quoted in Daniel J. Wakin, "Unprompted, Lorin Maazel Nominates His Successor," *New York Times*, November 28, 2006.

385   *"Nobody has offered me the job"*: Daniel Barenboim, quoted in Mark Landler, "Proposed Philharmonic Candidate Is Flattered, if Coy," *New York Times*, November 30, 2006.

386   *"a fantastic work"* et seq.: Allan Kozinn, review, *New York Times*, December 2, 2006.

386   *"an eloquent performance"*: Allan Kozinn, review, *New York Times*, December 8, 2006.

386   *"a knockout performance"*: Anthony Tommasini, review, *New York Times*, December 16, 2006.

386   *"a virtuosic performance"* et seq.: Allan Kozinn, review, *New York Times*, January 6, 2007.

387   *"distinguished account"* et seq.: Anthony Tommasini, review, *New York Times*, January 13, 2007.

387   *"a powerhouse reading"*: Anne Midgette, review, *New York Times*, January 18, 2006.

387   *"one of the towering musicians"* et seq.: Anthony Tommasini, review, *New York Times*, January 20, 2007.

388   *"at full throttle"*: Allan Kozinn, review, *New York Times*, January 27, 2007.

388   *"so-called festivals"* et seq.: Bernard Holland, review, *New York Times*, February 16, 2007.

389   *"vital and fresh"* et seq.: Anne Midgette, review, *New York Times*, February 24, 2007.

389   *"gripping"*: Allan Kozinn, review, *New York Times*, March 2, 2007.

390   *"colorful . . . Bach to splash around in"*: Allan Kozinn, review, *New York Times*, March 17, 2007.

390   *"is couched in a language"*: ibid.

392 *"a refreshing choice"*: Anthony Tommasini, "Passing the Baton: Be Bold, New York," *New York Times*, April 15, 2007.

393 *"coldly unemotional"* et seq.: Allan Kozinn, review, *New York Times*, June 2, 2007.

393 *"smacked of routine"* et seq.: Anne Midgette, review, *New York Times*, June 7, 2007.

393 *"with an appealing ferocity"*: Allan Kozinn, review, *New York Times*, June 9, 2007.

393 *"late Romantic effusiveness"* et seq.: Bernard Holland, review, *New York Times*, June 22, 2007.

CHAPTER 23

395 *"the right thing"*: Paul B. Guenther, quoted in Daniel J. Wakin, "For Its Next Music Director, the Philharmonic Turns to Family," *New York Times*, July 18, 2007.

395 *"some sober critical comments"* et seq.: Anthony Tommasini, "Philharmonic Opts For Generation Next," *New York Times*, July 19, 2007.

395 *"household name"*: ibid.

396 *"with more maturity"*: Anthony Tommasini, review, *New York Times*, September 20, 2007.

396 *"very well-known"*: Lorin Maazel, quoted in Anthony Tommasini, "A No-Nonsense Approach to the Work of a Master," *New York Times*, September 28, 2007.

396 *"vibrant and brilliant"*: ibid.

398 *"a terrific performance"*: Vivien Schweitzer, review, *New York Times*, October 20, 2007.

398 *"just what the doctor ordered"* et seq.: Bernard Holland, review, *New York Times*, November 3, 2007.

398 *"with a tenderness and honesty"*: Stephen Holden, review, *New York Times*, November 21, 2007.

399 *"the boundless joy and intensity"*: Anthony Tommasini, review, *New York Times*, December 1, 2007.

399 *"It's now taken on a new dimension"*: Barbara Haws, quoted in Daniel J. Wakin, "A Tough Night for a Bernstein Baton," *New York Times*, December 6, 2007.

399 *"lend legitimacy to a despicable regime"*: Terry Teachout, "Serenading a Tyrant," *Wall Street Journal* online ed., October 27, 2007.

399 *"it would be a mistake to hand"*: Richard V. Allen and Chuck Downs, "Concert without Strings," *New York Times*, October 28, 2007.

399 *"bringing North Korea out of its shell"*: Christopher R. Hill, quoted in Daniel J. Wakin, "Philharmonic Agrees to Play in North Korea," *New York Times*, December 10, 2007.

400 *"at his best"* et seq.: Allan Kozinn, review, *New York Times*, January 5, 2008.

401 *"a vibrant, brilliant performance"* et seq.: Anthony Tommasini, review, *New York Times*, January 19, 2008.

401 *"mesmerizing"* et seq.: Anthony Tommasini, review, *New York Times*, February 1, 2008.

402 *"mesmerizing"*: Michelle Kim, quoted in Daniel J. Wakin, "North Korea Welcomes New York Philharmonic," *New York Times*, February 26, 2008.

402 *"captivated by it"*: Stephen Freeman, quoted in ibid.

403 *"historic"*: Anthony Tommasini, "Catching a Streamed-In Philharmonic Live from North Korea," *New York Philharmonic*, February 27, 2008.

403 *"Seventy million Koreans love you"*: Park Sam-koo, quoted in Lawrence Van Gelder, "Asian Tour Ends on a High Note," *New York Times*, February 29, 2008.

404 *"uncommonly ruinous playing"* et seq.: Allan Kozinn, review, *New York Times*, March 7, 2008.

404 *"directness and emotional clarity"* et seq.: Anthony Tommasini, review, *New York Times*, March 15, 2008.

404 *"impeccable singing"* et seq.: Anthony Tommasini, review, *New York Times*, March 21, 2008.

404 *"The bad-tempered one"*: Sir Adrian Boult to the author, June 1972.

404 *"I don't know if I like it"*: Ralph Vaughan Williams, booklet notes, *Vaughan Williams Conducts Vaughan Williams* (Dutton CDBP 9731, 1937).

404 *"does this orchestra a lot of good"*: Bernard Holland, review, *New York Times*, April 5, 2008.

405 *"treating Mr. Lang as a martial artist"* et seq.: Anthony Tommasini, review, *New York Times*, April 11, 2008.

405 *"a playful, rambunctious account"* et seq.: Allan Kozinn, review, *New York Times*, April 25, 2008.

405 *"triumphant"*: Anthony Tommasini, review, *New York Times*, May 9, 2008.

406 *"made a powerful case"*: Allan Kozinn, review, *New York Times*, May 24, 2008.

407 *"more real heart and soul"*: James R. Oestreich, review, *New York Times*, June 22, 2008.

408 *"is a big musical brain"*: Jay Nordlinger, review, *New York Sun*, June 13, 2008.

409 *"conducted the anthem nobly"*: Jay Nordlinger, review, *New York Sun*, September 19, 2008.

409 *"a good and worthwhile piece"* et seq.: Jay Nordlinger, review, *New York Sun*, September 20, 2008.

413 *"It's a little bit frightening"*: Elliott Carter, quoted in Steve Smith, "A Lifetime of Music, a Weekend with Old Friends," *New York Times*, December 16, 2008.

Chapter 24

417 *"a memorable performance"* et seq.: Vivien Schweitzer, review, *New York Times*, June 6, 2009.

418 *"sheer musical beauty"* et seq.: James R. Oestreich, review, *New York Times*, June 13, 2009.

418 *"I think of this as the best job"*: Gary W. Parr, quoted in Daniel J. Wakin, "New York Philharmonic Names Gary Parr Chairman," *New York Times*, June 11, 2009.

419 *"flow naturally, shaping it subtly"* et seq.: Allan Kozinn, review, *New York Times*, June 26, 2009.

420 *"rather blunt"*: Anthony Tommasini, "For Philharmonic, Music and Change Are In the Summer Air," *New York Times*, July 5, 2009.

SELECTED BIBLIOGRAPHY

For a discography, the reader is referred to James H. North's *New York Philharmonic: The Authorized Recordings, 1917–2005; A Discography* (2006). For the complete programs of the New York Philharmonic from 1842 to the present, the reader is referred to the Web site assembled by the orchestra's archives, http://nyphil.org/CARLOS.

Bernstein, Burton, and Barbara B. Haws. *Leonard Bernstein: American Original*. New York: HarperCollins, 2008.

Burton, Humphrey. *Leonard Bernstein*. New York: Doubleday, 1994.

Inverne, James, ed. *The Best of All Possible Worlds: Leonard Bernstein*. Teddington, England: Gramophone, 2008.

Kurt Masur at the New York Philharmonic. New York: Random House. 2001.

Leinsdorf, Erich. *Cadenza: A Musical Career*. Boston: Houghton Mifflin, 1976.

Mehta, Zubin, and Renate Gräfin Matuschka. *Zubin Mehta: The Score of My Life*. New York: Amadeus Press, 2009.

New York Philharmonic: The Mehta Years. New York: Philharmonic-Symphony Society of New York, 1990.

North, James H. *New York Philharmonic: The Authorized Recordings, 1917–2005: A Discography*. Lanham, MD: Scarecrow Press, 2006.

Shanet, Howard. *Philharmonic: A History of New York's Orchestra*. Garden City, NY: Doubleday, 1975.

Stamas, Stephen, and Sharon Zane. *Lincoln Center: A Promise Realized, 1979–2006*. Hoboken, NJ: John Wiley & Sons, 2007.

Trotter, William R. *Priest of Music: The Life of Dimitri Mitropoulos*. New York: Amadeus Press, 1995.

INDEX

ABOUT THE AUTHOR

John Canarina is professor emeritus of Drake University, Des Moines, Iowa, where he was director of orchestral studies from 1973 to 2008. A Juilliard graduate, he has been conductor of the Seventh Army Symphony Orchestra, assistant conductor of the New York Philharmonic under Leonard Bernstein's direction, and music director of the Jacksonville Symphony Orchestra. Also active as a writer and critic, he is the author of *Uncle Sam's Orchestra: Memories of the Seventh Army Symphony* (1998) and *Pierre Monteux, Maître* (2003), the latter also published by Amadeus Press. He now lives in Savannah, Georgia, with his wife, Audrey.